HANDBOOK OF QUALITATIVE RESEARCH IN EDUCATION

Handbook of Qualitative Research in Education

Edited by

Sara Delamont

School of Social Sciences, Cardiff University, UK

With assistance from

Angela Jones

School of Social Sciences, Cardiff University, UK

Edward Elgar
Cheltenham, UK • Northampton, MA, USA

Published by
Edward Elgar Publishing Limited
The Lypiatts
15 Lansdown Road
Cheltenham
Glos GL50 2JA
UK

Edward Elgar Publishing, Inc.
William Pratt House
9 Dewey Court
Northampton
Massachusetts 01060
USA

A catalogue record for this book
is available from the British Library

Library of Congress Control Number: 2011932896

ISBN 978 1 84980 509 4 (cased)

Typeset by Servis Filmsetting Ltd, Stockport, Cheshire
Printed and bound by MPG Books Group, UK

Contents

Figures

Tables

Contributors

Alexandra Allan is a lecturer in the Graduate School of Education, University of Exeter. Her research interests reside in the fields of Research Methodology and the Sociology of Education. Alexandra's research has largely focused on issues relating to educational inequalities. She has a particular interest in young femininities, sexualities and social class. This research has been published in a number of journals, including: *Gender and Education* and *Discourse: Cultural Studies in the Politics of Education.*

Louisa Allen is an Associate Professor in the Faculty of Education, University of Auckland. Her research interests lie in the areas of youth, sexualities and schooling and innovative research methodologies which seek to engage hard to reach research populations. She examines these areas through the lenses of queer, feminist post-structural and critical masculinities and critical youth studies theoretical frameworks. Louisa has written three books in these fields, the latest of which is entitled *Young People and Sexuality Education: Rethinking Key Debates* (2011).

Paul Atkinson is Distinguished Research Professor of Sociology at Cardiff University. He is an Academician of the Academy of Social Sciences. He and Sara Delamont are the founding editors of the journal *Qualitative Research.* His latest publications include Katie Featherstone and Paul Atkinson, *Creating Conditions: The Making and Remaking of a Genetic Syndrome* (2011).

Carl Bagley is Professor of Educational Sociology and Director of Postgraduate Research in the School of Education, Durham University. His research interests reside in the fields of education policy and research methodology. He co-edited the book *Dancing the Data* and its enclosed CD-ROM 'Dancing the Data Too' (with Mary Beth Cancienne), the first arts-based educational research text to incorporate print and audio-visual material. His latest book – which includes the use of arts-based performance for critical praxis – written with Ricardo Castro-Salazar is entitled *Navigating Borders: Critical Race Theory Research and Counter History of Undocumented Americans.*

Ghazala Bhatti is Senior Lecturer and Deputy Director of Postgraduate Research in the Education School at the University of Southampton.

She is a member of the Social Justice and Inclusive Education Research Group. She is a founder member of the Social Justice and Intercultural Education network at the European Conference on Educational Research. Her research interests include ethnicity, gender and social class and how they affect educational experiences.

Russell Bishop is foundation Professor for Maori Education in the School of Education at the University of Waikato, Hamilton. His research experience is in the area of collaborative storying as Kaupapa Maori research, having written a book *Collaborative Research Stories: Whakawhanaungatanga* (1996) and published nationally and internationally on this topic. His other research interests include collaborative storying as pedagogy and culturally responsive pedagogies. His more recent books include *Culture Speaks: Cultural Relationships and Classroom Learning* (2006), with Mere Berryman, *Scaling Up Education Reform* (2010) and *Freeing Ourselves* (2011).

Ruth Boyask is Lecturer in Education Studies at Plymouth University. She has led projects and published in areas such as alternative conceptualizations of schooling, learner diversity and educational policy reform. The use of social theory to address issues of equity in educational policy and practice is a continual feature of her work.

Hugh Busher is Senior Lecturer and a member of the Social Justice SIG in the School of Education, University of Leicester. He is currently researching students' and teachers' perspectives on education, and teaches courses on research methods and on leadership, inclusive schooling and learning communities.

Ricardo Castro-Salazar is Associate Researcher at the University of Arizona Center for Latin American Studies and a faculty member in History and Political Sciences at Pima Community College in Tucson, Arizona. His research interests include immigration and Latino issues in the United States.

Randall F. Clemens is Dean's Fellow in Urban Education Policy and Research Assistant at the Center for Higher Education Policy Analysis, University of Southern California. His research focuses on educational reform, policy design, school and community partnerships, and qualitative research methods.

Martin Cortazzi is Visiting Professor in the Centre for Applied Linguistics, University of Warwick, and at a number of key universities in China. He has published books and articles on narrative analysis, the application of metaphor analysis, primary education and issues in language and education such as vocabulary learning and cultures of learning. With Lixian Jin, he has co-edited *Researching Chinese Learners, Skills, Perceptions and Intercultural Adaptations* (2011).

Zoë B. Corwin is a qualitative researcher at the Center for Higher Education Policy Analysis, University of Southern California. She held Haynes and Spencer Foundation dissertation fellowships while working on a study examining college access and persistence for students from foster care. She is currently working on a series of hard copy and online game-based college access interventions.

Dawn H. Currie is Professor of Sociology at the University of British Columbia. Her research interests include girl cultures and feminist media education. She is author of *Girl Talk: Adolescent Magazines and Their Readers* (1999) and co-author of *'Girl Power': Girls Reinventing Girlhood* (2009).

Peter de Vries is Senior Lecturer in the Faculty of Education, Monash University, Melbourne. Peter's research revolves around early childhood learning and engagement in music, music teaching in the primary school and active engagement with music in older age.

Sara Delamont is Reader in Sociology at Cardiff University. She was the first woman President of the British Educational Research Association in 1984. Her books include *Interaction in the Classroom* (1983) and *Fighting Familiarity* (with P. Atkinson, 1995). Currently she edits the journal *Qualitative Research* and she has edited *Teaching and Teacher Education*.

Mark Dressman is Professor of Curriculum and Instruction specializing in English education at the University of Illinois at Urbana-Champaign. He is co-editor of *Research in the Teaching of English* and the author of *Using Social Theory in Educational Research* (2008) and *Let's Poem: The Essential Guide to Teaching Poetry in a High-Stakes, Multimodal World* (2010). His research interests include transcultural teacher education, the rhetoric of educational research and semiotic analysis of multimodal texts.

Jane Elliott is Professor of Social Research at the Institute of Education, London, and is the Director of the Centre for Longitudinal Studies (an ESRC Resource Centre). She has been Principal Investigator of the 1958 British Birth Cohort, known as the National Child Development Study (NCDS), since July 2004. Jane's main research interests include gender and employment, women's careers, healthy ageing, longitudinal research methodology, combining qualitative and quantitative research, and narrative. Her book *Using Narrative in Social Research: Qualitative and Quantitative Approaches* was published by Sage in 2005. She has also published on women's employment and fertility histories, occupational segregation in Britain and the US, gender and children's essays from the NCDS.

Martin Forsey is Lecturer in Anthropology and Sociology at the University of Western Australia. His publications include *Challenging the System? A Dramatic Tale of Neoliberal Reform in an Australian High School* (2007). His research interests are neoliberalism and education, school choice among students, parents and teachers and, more recently, qualitative research methods, writing about interviews and questioning the mythic positioning of participant observation at the centre of anthropological/ ethnographic research.

Blye Frank is Dean of the Faculty of Education, University of British Columbia. He has worked with Faculties of Medicine across Canada towards the promotion of diversity and cultural competency within the medical education environment and contributed to the development of a programme for Association of Faculties of Medicine of Canada (AFMC), a cultural diversity training programme for teachers of internationally educated health care professionals. His particular module, Education for Cultural Awareness, is being used extensively throughout Medical Schools in Canada. He is a recognized expert in the field of gender studies and has been called upon to provide advice on issues of equity in schools and health care environments. He is one of five national researchers developing the Health, Illness, Men and Masculinities (HIMM) theoretical framework, which is intended to inform methodology and analysis of how the social construction of masculinity intersects with men's health and well-being.

Andrew Gitlin is Professor at the University of Georgia. His recent research is on the possibilities of using experimental art as the basis for an innovative epistemology that can open up unknown worlds.

Judith Green is Professor of Education and Director of the Center of Literacy and Inquiry in Networking Communities (LINC), Gevirtz Graduate School of Education, University of California. Her recent research examines the unexpected impact of policy on opportunities for learning in classrooms and on the construction of identities for both the collective and the individual in complex educational settings in and out of schools. She was co-editor of the *Handbook of Complementary Methods in Education in Education Research* (2006) and editor of the *Review of Research in Education* (2006, 2008, 2010).

Martyn Hammersley is Professor of Educational and Social Research at the Open University. His research interests are in the sociology of education, the sociology of the media and the methodological issues surrounding social inquiry. His books include *Questioning Qualitative Inquiry* (2008) and *Methodology, Who Needs It?* (2011).

Janet Holland is Professor of Social Research in the Weeks Centre, London South Bank University and Co-Director of Timescapes. She has published in youth, education, gender, sexualities, family life and methodological development.

Rachel Holmes is Reader in Cultural Studies of Childhood within the Centre for Early Years and Childhood Studies at the Educational and Social Research Institute, Manchester Metropolitan University. Her research interests include the interstices of applied educational research, social science research and arts-based research within the field of childhood.

William Housley is Reader in Sociology at the Cardiff School of Social Sciences, Cardiff University. He is author of *Interaction in Multidisciplinary Teams* (2003) co-author (with Paul Atkinson) of *Interactionism: An Essay in Sociological Amnesia* (2003) and (with Paul Atkinson and Sara Delamont) *Contours of Culture: Complex Ethnography and the Ethnography of Complexity* (2008).

Nalita James is Lecturer in Employment Studies at the Centre for Labour Market Studies, University of Leicester. Her research interests lie in the broad field of young adults' and teachers' work, identity and learning in informal and formal educational settings, as well as the methodological capacities of the Internet.

Lixian Jin is Professor of Linguistics and Intercultural Learning at De Montfort University, where she is Director of the Centre for Intercultural Research in Communication and Learning (CIRCL). Her research interests are in cultures of learning, bilingual language assessments, narrative and metaphor analysis, academic intercultural communication and Chinese learners of English. Together with Martin Cortazzi, she has authored and edited over 30 textbooks for learners and teachers of English in China.

Angela Jones holds an honours degree in English Literature, and has worked at Cardiff University School of Social Sciences since 2004 as Editorial Assistant and Managing Editor. She has worked for international editorial teams based in the UK, Australia and the USA, for various publishers including Sage and Elsevier. She has worked on journals in the fields of criminology, education, gender and qualitative research; and assisted in the compilation of academic research handbooks. She is also a freelance copy editor.

Wayne Journell is Assistant Professor and Secondary Social Studies Program Coordinator at the University of North Carolina at Greensboro. His research interests include the civic development of adolescents, especially the teaching of politics and political processes in secondary education, and online learning in K-12 education. Recent publications include articles in *Theory and Research in Social Education, Educational Leadership, Educational Studies, Phi Delta Kappan* and the *Journal of Social Studies Research.*

Deirdre M. Kelly is Professor of Sociology of Education in the Department of Educational Studies, University of British Columbia. Her research interests include teaching for social justice and democracy, gender and youth studies, and critical media education. She is the author of *Last Chance High: How Girls and Boys Drop In and Out of Alternative Schools* (1993) and *Pregnant with Meaning: Teen Mothers and the Politics of Inclusive Schooling* (2000) and co-author of '*Girl Power': Girls Reinventing Girlhood* (2009).

Sean Kelly is Visiting Assistant Professor in the Department of Educational Administration, Michigan State University and a leading expert on the social organization of schools, student engagement and teacher effectiveness. He is the author of over 25 scholarly articles and book chapters, as well as *Assessing Teacher Quality* (2011).

Margarethe Kusenbach is Associate Professor and incoming Graduate Program Director in the Department of Sociology, University of South Florida. Her research interests include cities and communities, disasters, emotions and qualitative research methods. She has published papers in *City & Community, Ethnography, Qualitative Sociology, Forum Qualitative Social Research (FQS), Natural Hazards, Symbolic Interaction* and *Studies in Symbolic Interaction.*

Lisa Lucas is a Senior Lecturer in Education at the Graduate School of Education, University of Bristol. Her research interests include the organization, funding and development of higher education in a global context, including international comparative work on the funding and evaluation of research within universities and research on academic work and academic identities. She has published a number of journal articles and books, including, *The Research Game in Academic Life* (2006) and *Academic Research and Researchers* (edited with Professor Angela Brew) (2009), both published by McGraw-Hill/Open University Press.

Anna MacLeod is Assistant Professor and the Education Specialist in the Division of Medical Education, Faculty of Medicine, Dalhousie University in Halifax, Canada. A qualitative education researcher, her research interests are on social issues and undergraduate medical education.

Richard Majerus is Assistant Dean of Admissions at Carleton College, Northfield, Minnesota. His current research focuses on the admission processes at highly selective colleges and universities with an emphasis on new applications of predictive analytics in higher education.

Jay Mann is Director of the Office of Clinical Experiences for the College of Education and is a doctoral student in the Department of Curriculum and Instruction, University of Illinois at Urbana-Champaign. His areas of interest include secondary social studies education and service learning projects within secondary classrooms.

Sue Middleton's research focuses on local and global connections between theoretical, political, institutional and everyday lived dimensions of educational ideas in New Zealand. Completed life-history projects include studies of feminist teachers, teaching practices, a PhD in education, and a study of the impact of research assessment on subject(s) of education. Her archive-based studies include projects on letters of 1840s immigrants to Wellington, Sylvia Ashton-Warner as progressive educator and, currently, New Zealand-related British correspondence concerning the New Education Fellowship. Sue is interested in the interface between historical research and geographical theories.

David Mills is Director of Graduate Studies in the Department of Education at the University of Oxford. His recent publications include: *Difficult Folk: A Political History of Social Anthropology* (2008) and articles on anthropological careers, ethnographic methods and the future of disciplinarity. He is currently completing a textbook entitled *Ethnography in Education*.

Lindsay Pérez Huber is Visiting Scholar at the University of California, Los Angeles (UCLA) Chicano Studies Research Center and Visiting Faculty at California State University, Long Beach. Her research areas are in race, immigration and education, critical race theory and critical race methodology in education, and the Latina/o educational pipeline. She has published academic articles, reports and book chapters on Latina/o students generally, and undocumented immigrant students in particular. Her work can be found in the journals *Harvard Educational Review* and *International Journal of Qualitative Studies in Education*, and in academic law reviews such as the *Journal of Gender, Social Policy and the Law* and the *Nevada Law Journal.*

Lindsay Prior is Professor of Sociology in the School of Sociology, Social Policy and Social Work, and a Principal Investigator and member of the management committee of the Centre of Excellence for Public Health, Queen's University Belfast. His latest publication is *Using Documents and Records in Social Research* (2011). As well as research in the role of documents, he is also interested in developing novel methods for analysing and displaying interview and other forms of qualitative data.

Lesley Pugsley is a Sociologist and Senior Lecturer in Medical Education in the School of Postgraduate Medical and Dental Education, Cardiff University. She has undertaken a number of qualitative studies in a variety of different educational settings and has published on a number of topics relating to ethnographic studies.

Paul Reader is Adjunct Senior Lecturer, in the School of Humanities, University of New England, Australia. His research interests are in the visual arts, adult education and transformative learning. 'Painterly methodology: painting and digital inquiry in adult learning', his doctoral thesis (2007), explored visual methods in education research, with a strong emphasis on the relationship between consciousness, theory and inquiry through visual practice.

Jude Robinson is Reader in the Anthropology of Health and Illness Department of Sociology, Social Policy and Criminology, School of Law and Social Justice at the University of Liverpool. Dr Robinson is a social anthropologist researching choice in constrained circumstances, specifically the complex issues that people experience when attempting to make 'positive' changes to their lifestyles to improve health and wellbeing. Her research centres on developing understanding of the opportunities and barriers experienced by people living in poverty and disadvantage, and she has a particular interest in the development and use of (feminist) research methodologies, gendered inequalities, issues around social justice, alternative moralities and 'othering' and the health of women and children living in the UK. Recent research includes collaborative projects exploring smoking and second-hand smoke; working with young people and smoking and alcohol; and researching reading and health, particular the links between reading aloud and mental health and wellbeing.

Wolff-Michael Roth is Research Professor at Griffith University. His research focuses on the learning of mathematics and science across the life span. His recent books include *Passibility: At the Limits of the Constructivist Metaphor* (2011), *Geometry as Objective Science in Elementary Classrooms: Mathematics in the Flesh* (2011) and *Language, Learning, Context: Talking the Talk* (2010).

Jane Salisbury is Senior Lecturer at Cardiff University's School of Social Sciences where she teaches sociology of education, education policy and qualitative research methods. Research interests include post-compulsory education and training, VET, gender and attainment, occupational socialization and educational ethnography. She is the current Director of the PGCE (PCET) Teacher Education programme at Cardiff University.

Pat Sikes is Professor of Qualitative Inquiry in the School of Education, University of Sheffield. Her research focuses on four inter-related concerns: educators' lives and careers; life history research; qualitative methodologies; and social justice issues. Her publications include, with Heather Piper, *Researching Sex and Lies in the Classroom: Allegations of Sexual Misconduct in Schools* (2010).

Margaret J. Somerville is Professor of Education and Senior Researcher at the University of Western Sydney, Australia. She is a pioneer of place studies in Australia and is interested in innovative methodologies and modes of representation in qualitative research. She is author, with Tony Perkins, of *Singing the Coast* (2010) and, with Bronwyn Davies, Kerith Power, Susanne Gannon and Phoenix de Carteret, of *Place Pedagogy Change* (2011). Her forthcoming book, *Water in a Dry Land: An Ethnography of Country* will be published in Routledge's new Innovative Ethnography series.

Anissa Stewart received her PhD in Education from the Gevirtz Graduate School of Education at the University of California. She is interested in how teachers integrate various types of technology into the instructional design and execution of higher education courses and how students engage in learning and interaction in the classroom through those various technologies.

Kate Stewart is Lecturer in Social Aspects of Medicine and Health Care at the School of Graduate Entry Medicine and Health, University of Nottingham. Her interests are in the fields of medical sociology and social science research methods, and she has been providing training in CAQDAS packages to students and research staff since 1994.

Maria Tamboukou is Professor of Feminist Studies and Co-director of the Centre of Narrative Research, University of East London. Her research interests are in auto/biographical narratives, feminist theories, Foucauldian and Deleuzian analytics, the sociology of gender and education, gender and space and the sociology of art. She is the author of *Women, Education and the Self: A Foucauldian Perspective* and co-editor, with Stephen Ball, of *Dangerous Encounters: Genealogy and Ethnography*.

Rachel Thomson is Chair of Childhood and Youth Studies at Sussex University. She has research interests in childhood, youth, motherhood and the life course as well as methodological strategies for capturing personal and social change.

William G. Tierney is University Professor, Wilbur-Kieffer Professor of Higher Education and Director of the Center for Higher Education Policy Analysis at the University of Southern California. His research focuses on increasing access to higher education, improving the performance of post-secondary institutions and analysing the quality of for-profit institutions. His most recent books are a set of cultural biographies, *Urban High School Students and the Challenge of Access* and a study of privatization, *For-profit Colleges and Universities: Their Markets, Regulation, Performance and Place in Higher Education* (with G. Hentschke and V. Lechuga).

Cate Watson is Senior Lecturer in the School of Education, University of Stirling. Her research interests are in institutional/professional identities and professional knowledge/learning. She is also interested in narrative as a research methodology and has published widely in this area, including on the uses of fiction in the social sciences. She is the author of *Reflexive Research and the (Re)turn to the Baroque. (Or, How I Learned to Stop Worrying and Love the University)* (2008), and has co-edited (with Joan Forbes) *Service Integration in Schools. Research and Policy Discourses, Practices and Future Prospects* (2009) and *The Transformation of Children's Services. Examining and Debating the Complexities of Inter/professional Working* (2012).

Cassandra Wells is pursuing a PhD in the Faculty of Education at the University of British Columbia.

ML White is Senior Lecturer in Education at the Central School of Speech and Drama, University of London. She was awarded a PhD in 2009 for research looking at how young people engage with new digital video technologies and the use of digital technology in ethnographic educational research. ML manages an Initial Teacher Education programme. She is interested in how visual images can be used to construct teacher identities and in developing collaborative research methodologies.

1.   Introduction: leaving Damascus
Sara Delamont

In James Elroy Flecker's poem 'The Gates of Damascus' (1947), the poet imagines four exits from the safe comfortable city to the outside world. Each gate takes the traveller into a different set of temptations and dangers. The Aleppo Gate leads to trade and commerce, the Mecca Gate is for faith and pilgrimage, the Lebanon Gate for exploration and the search for enlightenment, and the Baghdad Gate leads to danger and even death. When we educational researchers leave our safe city, our ivory tower, our Damascus, we can choose which gate we take: that is, our destination, our goal, our dream. This introduction will explore the choices that face educational researchers, and the consequences of those choices. Issues of funding, faith, exploration and danger will be discussed with examples from controversies about educational research.

There are multiple dangers when a metaphor such as the gates of Damascus is taken to write about educational research in the post-industrial, or postmodern, globalized world. Flecker lived and wrote in a very different era: Constantinople and Smyrna have vanished. The most obvious danger is orientalism (Said, 1978): that is, authors in the west will always prefer their idealized orient to any corrective or corrected realities, because accepting the latter would force the westerner to abandon the unthinking superiority embodied in the 'othering' of the orient and the oriental (Marcus, 2001). Despite the dangers, I like the poem's extended metaphor, and am going to behave like the caravan passing out of Damascus, and press on, ignoring the perils, and use my four gates metaphor as ways to think about educational research. The Damascus, Aleppo, Baghdad and Lebanon of the poem are long gone. If there were a poem with rich imagery about the four great gates of Vancouver, or Brasilia, or Dunedin, that would have served just as well.

There are six sections. First, the routes leading out of each gate in Flecker's poem are distinguished. It has splendidly 'purple' passages where the metaphors and similes are heaped up like piles of oranges and lemons, and the images shimmer like silks in the bazaar. Each gate leads in a different direction geographically, philosophically, emotionally and socially, and those who leave by each gate are setting forth on very different journeys. The type of educational research each gate and route symbolize is explained. Then the introduction explores the familiarity problem in educational research. This is followed by a mapping of 'two traditions' in qualitative educational research, where a gulf of mutual incomprehension has existed between sociological and anthropological scholars for 40 years. The introduction then points out three ways in which qualitative researchers in education have not drawn on major changes in their parent disciplines, returns to the familiarity problem offering five strategies to fight familiarity and perhaps, do Lebanon Gate research.

THE FOUR GATES

The Aleppo Gate – the North Gate – is chosen by traders. They have only a short journey ahead of them: two days and two nights, and there are no dangers. 'Fleas' are 'the only foes'. In Aleppo trade goods sell for three times the price they would fetch in Damascus, so the journey is amply rewarded. In the poem a merchant tells the reader that men (*sic*) have different ways of gaining status in the world: noble birth, warfare and the sword, science, the arts or trade. He exclaims:

> *Some praise a science or an Art,*
> *But I like honourable Trade!*

By contemporary standards this is too sexist, and few people have gained status in educational research by being born into the nobility, but the potential to advance in research by warfare, science, art or trade certainly exists. The Mecca Gate – the South Gate – leads to Saudi Arabia. This is a longer and more perilous journey than the route from Damascus to Aleppo. Pilgrims take that route, and God watches over them, providing 'shade from well to well'. These travellers have their bodies purified, gain stoic endurance, and can hope to achieve eternal life in the paradise gardens. For educational researchers, eternal life is to be read as academic immortality. The Baghdad Gate – the East Gate – is the 'Postern of Fate, the Desert Gate, Disaster's Cavern, Fort of Fear, the Doorway of Diabekir.' The route to Baghdad is across the desert, which sensible people approach with justifiable apprehension. It is not a route to take light-heartedly. The gatekeeper warns:

> *'Pass not beneath, O Caravan, or pass not singing'*

The heat, the thirst, the pitiless sun and the fierce Bedouin are bad enough, but worse still the desert route is the way madness lies.

Finally, the Lebanon Gate – the West Gate – leads to the sea:

The dragon-green, the luminous, the dark serpent-haunted sea,
The snow-besprinkled wine of earth, the white-and-blue-flower
foaming sea.

However the sea is not the destination. Travellers who take the West Gate cross the sea to find, beyond it, strange lands full of giants, screaming rocks that spout waterfalls of blood, ancient vessels full of 'metal mariners' and eventually in the farthest west, Solomon himself. This is the exit taken by explorers and seekers for enlightenment.

In the next section, the type of research which is beyond each of the four gates is described.

GATES AND EDUCATIONAL RESEARCH

Damascus is our safe ivory tower, our university or college where we can read, and think, and teach, and reflect. There we are paid to be intellectuals, to be creative, to be iconoclasts, to be gadflies. Of course our ivory towers are full of disputes and feuds, best reflected in all those campus novels Ian Carter (1990) has written so entertainingly about, but we are privileged to work in them. However as educational researchers we cannot stay in our safe Damascus – we have to leave by one of the four gates, to raise funds, enter research settings, gather data, meet face to face, or via our research instruments, teachers, pupils, students, employers, parents, managers, and other dangers. Because educational researchers have to keep leaving Damascus to mix with the outside world its status is low, and it can even be stigmatized. As Basil Bernstein put it, education is, in universities 'a pariah discourse', and educational researchers 'are not kosher and live in profane places' (Bernstein, 2000). So educational researchers have no choice but to leave the ivory tower but do have a choice between four gates. We can choose the Aleppo Gate and engage in Honourable Trade, the Mecca Gate and be pilgrims, or the Lebanon Gate for exploration. It is not clear that anyone would or should choose the Baghdad Gate but sometimes we realize that in retrospect that was our exit. We discover that we left that way when we find ourselves alone and mad in the desert.

The Aleppo Gate is for trade and commerce. If we take this route we can sell our products for a good price. In educational research this is the route we choose when we undertake customer-contractor research, to answer relatively straightforward, practical, policy-related questions. The funders, the customers, the policy makers do not want intellectual curiosity and epistemological challenge: they want answers. The funders, the customers, the policy makers do not want methodological speculation, risky new methods, open-ended theorizing, unending searches for obscure literatures or poetry: the demand is for findings, facts, clear expositions and straightforward policy recommendations. Flecker's merchant said he liked 'Honourable Trade' rather than science, art or warfare: and much educational research is exactly that: academic goods equivalent to

> *filigrane, apricot paste, coffee tables botched with pearl, and little*
> *beaten brassware pots.*

Educational researchers sell their skills in research design, in data collection, in analysis and in report writing.

The Mecca Gate is for pilgrims. When we take that gate we are motivated not by money but by faith and hope. We set out in faith and seek a destination where our beliefs are reinforced and revitalized. In educational research this is the gate we leave by when we are secure in our epistemology, in our methodology, and in our understandings of what education is, what its purposes are and why it matters. It is the Mecca Gate we choose when our research is guided by what we believe to be morally right, true and good. Because we are sure of our epistemology, we have faith in our methods, in our methodology, in the data we will generate, the analytic techniques we will use and the style in which we will write them up. We take the Mecca Gate when we are snug inside a paradigm, want our faith renewed by the pilgrimage. The aim is to have our intellectual self revitalized by the fountains in the paradise gardens.

The fourth and final gate to consider is the Lebanon Gate – the West Gate – the exit to the sea. This is a high risk choice: it could lead us to danger – we could drown. However it is also the most exciting route to take. The explorer crosses the sea to find not only the giants and screaming rocks gushing blood, but also if she reaches the isles of the utmost west, where Solomon is brooding for all eternity, wisdom and enlightenment. The Lebanon Gate is the high risk and high reward alternative. Many educational researchers never choose the Lebanon Gate because it exposes us to risk. We could lose our epistemological certainties, our standpoints, our methodological foundations, and we could be forced to find new literatures, new theories, new perspectives on education itself.

FOUR GATES AND THE FAMILIARITY PROBLEM

Leaving our ivory tower by three of the four gates produces no solution to the biggest problem facing educational ethnography: the need to fight familiarity. By definition Mecca Gate research is firmly inside the researchers' faith, their secure comfort zone. Baghdad Gate projects are so awful that no solutions to core problems are reached. Neither of these directions fight familiarity. Nor does 'contract' research. The Aleppo Gate – the route for trade and commerce – is always being urged upon us. There are pressures to undertake funded projects which are of immediate practical value to teachers and higher education staff, school managers, and higher education governors, local government, policy makers or central government. Aleppo Gate research is designed to answer questions posed by, and to gain information for, those with power and position. We are rarely urged to undertake research of immediate use to pupils, or students, to school and university cleaners, to clerical staff, to canteen workers, to the members of the trade unions. It is also designed to improve the status quo: the value of education is not challenged. Research is never commissioned to help those who reject or resist the dominant value system escape from the education system or resist it more effectively. Policy makers do not commission research to help truants escape the gaze of the truancy inspector or help non-reflexive teachers escape the rhetoric of reflexivity or self-satisfied ones avoid any staff development activities.

The Aleppo Gate is an honourable route, and one which it is perfectly sensible to take sometimes. Whenever we are contracted to solve a specific puzzle, do applied research, investigate a specific issue: whenever we are funded by a ministry, or its equivalent, we take the Aleppo Gate. So the Aleppo Gate is respectable, but educational research is not advanced by taking it, because there are no challenges to familiarity. The biggest problem facing educational research, as Blanche Geer (1964), Howard Becker (1971), M.F.D. Young (1971) and Harry Wolcott (1981) pointed out, is that it is 'all too familiar', it 'takes educators' problems', it is dominated by the educator subculture.

Geer (1964, p. 384) pointed out that familiarity was the enemy of decent research:

> Untrained observers . . . can spend a day in a hospital and come back with one page of notes and no hypotheses. 'It was a hospital', they say, 'everyone knows what hospitals are like'.

She demonstrated how she 'fought' the familiarity of American college life, at the start of the research project that became Becker, Geer and Hughes (1968). It was simultaneously an account of how the researcher's initial encounters with a field setting can be disproportionately valuable, as long as the researcher works hard to construct and abandon working hypotheses (or foreshadowed problems as they are often termed), and a plea for treating the familiar (be it hospital, college or classroom) as anthropologically strange.

Geer's second point was subsequently taken up and reiterated by her collaborator, Howard Becker (1971, p. 10) in a famous statement, tucked away as a footnote added to a paper by the educational anthropologists Murray and Rosalie Wax (1971).

> It is not just the survey method of educational testing, or any of those things, that keeps people from seeing what goes on. It is first and foremost a matter of it all being so familiar . . . It takes a tremendous effort of will and imagination to stop seeing the things that are conventionally 'there' to be seen . . . It is like 'pulling teeth' to get researchers to see or write anything beyond what 'everyone' knows.

The same year that Becker published his classic statement of the familiarity problem – interestingly not in a paper of his own, but added as a footnote to an editorial in an edited collection by others – a parallel argument was published in the UK. Young (1971) was the editor of the manifesto of the Young Turks who were arguing for a radical shift in the sociology of education: a shift from a focus on structures and outcomes to a concern with curriculum and pedagogy. Young argued that educational researchers too frequently studied research questions that had been formulated by 'insiders' (teachers, school principals, local government, central government) to the educator subculture, rather than setting their own agenda of research questions from their outsider vantage point. Too often, Young said, researchers 'take' problems instead of 'making' them.

  A decade later Harry Wolcott (1981) made a parallel point; arguing that educational researchers are too submerged in the 'educator subculture', and rarely try to get outside it. A specific example, central to research at the time, was the investigation of pupils' 'time on task' (Denham and Lieberman, 1980), which Wolcott suggested, was fundamentally a confusion of 'busyness' with learning. The American graduate schools of Education, Wolcott suggested, compounded the problems by despatching graduate students to do their projects in educational settings, rather than forcing them to learn their trade in unfamiliar settings.

> We have not systematically encouraged our students . . . to go and look at something else for a while. We keep sending them back to the classroom. The only doctoral student I have sent off to do fieldwork in a hospital was a nurse-educator who returned to her faculty position in a school of nursing! (p. 253)

Aleppo Gate research is always grounded in that educator subculture, always 'takes' problems, and does not struggle enough to pull many teeth.

  While Young was formulating his ideas, Becker and Geer were following up their own manifesto, by studying learning in a range of non-educational settings. The papers in Geer (1972) are all examples of learning and teaching for non-academic occupations such as hairdressing. Young's impassioned call for a shift from taking problems to making them launched a short-lived, but highly controversial, flourishing of sociological research on the curriculum, called the 'new' sociology of education in the UK (Bernbaum, 1977). The wider issues implicit in Young's manifesto were not, however, taken up by Anglophone ethnographers. During the 1970s ethnographic methods began to be more widely accepted in educational research than they had been when Geer, Becker, and Wax and Wax were writing (Jacob, 1987; Spindler and Spindler, 1987; Atkinson, Delamont and Hammersley, 1988). While that growth took different forms in the USA and in the UK, in both countries the problems outlined by Geer and Becker were not tackled.

In 1980 Paul Atkinson and I drew attention to the gulf between the two predominant types of ethnographic research: by anthropologists of education in the USA and sociologists of education in the UK (Atkinson and Delamont, 1980). Despite the differences between these two ethnographic traditions, they shared a failure to make their own education systems problematic. The anthropological ethnographies of education done in the USA (Spindler, 1955, 1982) took many aspects of American schooling for granted, while the British sociological ethnographers took many aspects of UK schooling for granted. The scholarly purpose of that paper was not only to map the two terrains and reveal their differences, although as Metz (1984) was later to point out, as her novel discovery, that gap had not been previously documented, nor its implications explored. More important was fighting familiarity. We argued that if American ethnographers read British sociological ethnographies, they would develop a better standpoint from which to fight familiarity, and vice versa. The latter argument was elaborated in Delamont (1981): a critique of British sociological ethnographic research on the grounds that it focused on a very narrow range of educational settings and signally failed to make those settings anthropologically strange. In that paper six strategies for fighting familiarity were proposed with examples of how well they had worked, could work and should work.

The pattern of isolated voices raising the familiarity problem was perpetuated when George and Louise Spindler (1982) rehearsed similar ideas reflecting on their 30 years of fieldwork, in a paper subtitled 'From familiar to strange and back again'. As summarized by Parman (1998) the Spindlers compared 'the experience of doing ethnography in familiar and "exotic" settings'.

> Each setting imposes its own anthropological dilemma: first how to observe situations so familiar that it is almost impossible to extract oneself from one's own

cultural assumptions and be objective; the second, how to observe situations so different from what one is used to that one responds only to differentness. (p. 395)

Parman continues that 'making the familiar strange' is 'the ultimate goal of every anthropologist' (p. 395). What is striking about the Spindlers's formulation is that they, unlike Becker or Young, do mention some strategies to fight it, such as the use of film.

Ethnographic research on schools and classrooms continued to flourish during the 1980s, conducted by anthropologists and sociologists. Most repeated the pattern of failure: they did not start with robust foreshadowed problems designed to make schooling anthropologically strange; nor did they achieve strangeness in their eventual portraits of teachers and pupils.

During the 1980s the textual conventions and rhetorical genres used to publish qualitative research came under increased scrutiny (Clifford and Marcus, 1986; Atkinson, 1990, 1992, 1996; Spencer, 2001; Atkinson and Delamont, 2008). Educational ethnographies were one suitable set of texts for genre analysis. Atkinson and Delamont (1990; Delamont and Atkinson, 1995) showed, by close textual analysis of six monographs – three British and three American – that the rhetoric tropes, the unanalysed features of schooling and the citations were systematically different between the American anthropological ethnographies of education and the British sociological ethnographies.

The anthropologists of education had not addressed the familiarity problem for nearly two decades until in 1999 *Anthropology of Education Quarterly* (*AEQ*) celebrated its thirtieth birthday and key figures returned to the topic. Hess (1999, p. 401) recapitulated the ideas of Wax and Wax (1971), and raised the issue of whether anthropologists of education 'are still asking good rather than trivial questions, whether we are asking the right questions?' (p. 400). John Singleton (1999) argued that the anthropology of education needed to be better connected to anthropological work outside schools. He wrote: 'The critical confusion of education with schooling continues to bedevil us' (p. 457). He cites Lave and Wenger (1991), and draws his readers' attention to his research on apprentices learning Japanese folk pottery and to studies of occupational training and socialization in Japan in a range of other, non-school, settings (Singleton, 1998).

In 2007 Hervé Varenne edited a special issue of *Teachers' College Record* on educational anthropology. In his editorial essay (2007a, 2007b) he approvingly quotes Bourgois's (1996) dictum that 'the streets are almost always more powerful than the schools' (p. 1562) and remarks:

> The great paradox of work on education by social scientists is that it is mostly about schools . . . work on education is, paradoxically, rarely about education. (p. 1539)

Thus leading figures in the anthropology of education have raised the familiarity problem in their field for 50 years. In contrast sociologists of education after Young (1971) did not face up to the familiarity problem at all, and never engaged with the issues raised by Geer and Becker. A state of mutual ignorances between the anthropology of education and the sociology of education; and a strong ethnocentricism among researchers in the USA and in the UK have compounded the separation of the disciplines. Qualitative educational research could have been much better – taken the Lebanon Gate more often – if these failures to engage outside academic and national borders had not weakened it.

FOUR SIGNS OF DISCONNECTION

The sociology and the anthropology of education both show 'disconnects' between the subspecialisms and the mainstream disciplines, largely because of the failure to fight familiarity and 'make' problems. The more qualitative educational researchers 'take' problems, the less they draw strength from the mainstream discipline. This can be illustrated by four specific points: methods, analytic concepts, theoretical frameworks and rhetorical, textual strategies.

1. Methods and Methodology

Sociologists of education who use qualitative methods have been self-consciously reflexive about them, and consistently ground their work in methodological ways. However qualitative sociological educational research has relied heavily on semi-structured interviews, rather than deploying all the possible qualitative methods which are explored in this volume, and there has been relatively little attention paid to the methodological implications of the rhetorical or literary turn.

Although the past 30 years has seen an enormous increase in the number of methods books, especially handbooks, the anthropology of education is characterized by very brief, unreferenced, factual accounts of the data collection methods; no methodology; and noticeably very little reflection on methods of data collection, analysis, writing and representation or reading of the types that have become widespread since 1986 and are common in sociology (for example, Coffey, 1999). The papers in *AEQ* do not cite the methods texts that exist, even those by anthropologists. Noticeable too is the lack of attention paid by most anthropological educational ethnographers to the work of sociologists who do highly relevant ethnographies which do analyse their methods, reflect on methodology and experiment with new textual forms. This work is neither utilized, cited, nor criticized. There are collections of papers by anthropologists which contain some reflections on methods, and autobiographical accounts of projects such as Lareau and Shultz (1990), Eisner and Peshkin (1990), De Marrais (1998), Generett and Jeffries (2003) and McLean and Leiberg (2007). However these focus much more on the personal, confessional narratives and autobiographies of the authors and their projects, rather than raising methodological issues.

2. Analytic Concepts

There are two points to be made here. First, the sociology of education and anthropology of education are not, generally, deploying the analytic concepts at the frontiers of, respectively, sociology and social and cultural anthropology; and second, the emphasis on student failure in both sociology and anthropology has produced a series of familiar 'stories'. These are both serious criticisms. Sociology of education has been focused on failure rather than success. There has been a lack of engagement with powerful analytic concepts from the mainstream of sociology: a disconnect between sociology of education and the frontiers of sociology itself.

The first point can be illustrated by three works from mainstream sociology and mainstream anthropology that produced clear analytic advance, relevant to ethnographies in educational settings, that were not seized upon and deployed in the sociology and anthropology of education. In mainstream sociology Lash and Urry (1994) developed the idea of new, post-industrial economies of signs and space. They contrasted the identities of the educated, affluent and computer literate which are geographically dispersed but emotionally and intellectually close with the traditional, industrial working-class identity, grounded in a locality and an occupation. Their book did not address the educational causes or consequences of their analysis (which it should have done) but qualitative sociologists of education have not engaged with its implications either.

Qualitative sociologists of education have failed to draw on key concepts from the vibrant sociology of science and technology. Susan Leigh Star (1989, 2010) and Lucy Suchman (1994) have developed a sophisticated discourse around the ideas of boundary objects and boundary crossing which has rich potential for the sociological study of teaching and learning. Those powerful concepts have not crossed into educational research. A more controversial example is Beck and Beck-Gersheim's (1995) exploration of the concept of a risk society's implications for interpersonal emotional relations. Their application of Beck's analysis of postmodernity is potentially valuable for rethinking any educational setting and any pedagogical relationship, but that potential has not been realized.

Parallel examples abound in the anthropology of education. Herzfeld (1985), for example, used the analytic concept of poetics to advance the anthropological understanding of manhood and masculinities. Subsequent mainstream anthropology builds on that concept, but educational anthropology does not cite Herzfeld or utilize his analytic insights. Connerton's (1989) discussions of memory and forgetting initiated a vibrant research strand in mainstream anthropology (for example, Littlewood, 2009) which has not produced analytic work on memory in educational settings, although it would provide an anthropological 'take' on school 'reform'. Similarly it is 20 years since Lutz (1988) drew attention to the analytic power of a focus on emotion and sentiment, launching a rich vein of anthropological work. This is an approach of enormous potential for the anthropology of education, yet is largely unexploited.

These are just three examples of 20-year-old analytic traditions in mainstream anthropology that are not readily apparent in the anthropology of education, which rarely deploys the same conceptual repertoire as the wider discipline. Anthropology of education routinely deploys the concept of culture clash. Anthropologists have focused most on clashes of ethnicity or language, sociologists on class inequalities. Both fields have included gender, but primarily focused on failure.

An outsider reading the anthropology of education could become seriously pessimistic about schooling. Study after study focuses on culture clashes between state schooling and ethnic or linguistic minorities, which produce drop out, low achievement, alienation and resistance in the pupils. An outsider reading the sociology of education could become seriously pessimistic about schooling. Study after study focuses on the failure of children from working-class families in the education system. The sociology and the anthropology of education are overwhelmingly the close observation of failure.

3.   Theoretical Frameworks

Anthropology of education papers do not normally embed the research in anthropological theory. If one takes papers from each decade since 1970 and compares *AEQ* papers with those in other anthropological journals, such as the *Journal of the Royal Anthropological Institute* (*JRAI*) or *Current Anthropology* the theoretical disputes in mainstream anthropology are not apparent. The rise and fall of big theoretical concepts in the parent discipline is not mirrored in *AEQ* or the chapters in the edited collections. Structuralism, Marxism, semiotics, post-structuralism, postmodernism, feminist theory and the rhetorical turn are very rarely apparent. Reed-Danahay's (1996) use of Bourdieu is a striking exception in an under-theorized field. Spindler (2000) does not list Bourdieu, Douglas, Geertz, Herzfeld, Levi Strauss or Sperber in the author index, nor are there any index entries on structuralism, semiotics, poststructuralism, postmodernism, rhetoric, Marxism or feminist theory in the subject index. Anthropologists of the next generation are no more likely to embed their work in anthropological theory, so, for example, Peshkin's 1972, 1982, 1986, 1991, 1994, 1997, 2001 series of insightful ethnographies on Nigerians, rural Americans, school amalgamations, separatist born again Christians and on the schooling of Native Americans are largely devoid of anthropological theory.

The majority of sociologists of education have been active users of Bourdieu and, in the UK, Bernstein, and there are scholars who deploy Foucault and Butler. However, central figures in mainstream sociology, such as, in the UK Urry, Scott, Savage, Crossley, Bradley, Walby or Stanley, are not central in the sociology of education. In the USA a similar disconnect is apparent: major theorists are not central to qualitative sociology of education. No American sociologist of education today deploys Goffman in the way he deserves, for instance.

4.   Rhetorical Textual Strategies

Although there were scholarly analyses of the rhetoric of social science long before Clifford and Marcus (1986), as Atkinson and Delamont (2008) demonstrate, the publication of *Writing Culture* was the paradigm changing volume in anthropology. Three new research areas opened up. Papers were published in anthropological journals and edited collections which analysed the rhetoric of the canonical texts; which reflected on the writing of both fieldnotes and publications; and which attempted to change the rhetorical canon. This last trend involved putting the authorial voice into texts in much less detached and authoritative styles, experimenting with new textual forms and trying to preserve the voices of the informants. Brown's (1991) study of a vodou priestess, for example, has traditional ethnographic text, fictional episodes, autoethnography and autobiography blended in one text. While these trends are seen in many anthropological journals and collections, they are not noticeable in *AEQ*.

Anthropology of education has not internalized the paradigm shift that Clifford and Marcus (1986) crystallized.

A parallel judgement can be made about the lack of attention paid by qualitative sociologists of education to the rhetoric of 'canonical' texts (even Willis); to reflexivity around writing fieldnotes or publications, and few experiments with textual forms.

Both anthropologists and sociologists of education feel marginal to their mainstream disciplines, yet themselves fail to engage with core elements of that mainstream. The focus on schools and schooling, and failure to fight familiarity are compounded by the four disconnects I have just outlined. Fighting familiarity is essential.

STRATEGIES TO FIGHT FAMILIARITY

This section sets out five strategies which will help scholars – especially ethnographers – fight familiarity particularly by providing the raw materials from which to construct robust working hypotheses or foreshadowed problems. Self-conscious strategies to create such hypotheses that enable, even require the researcher to fight familiarity are essential. The five strategies to fight familiarity proposed here are:

1. Revisiting 'insightful' educational ethnographies of the past.
2. Studying learning and teaching in formal education in other cultures.
3. Taking the standpoint of the researcher who is 'other' to view the educational process. (For example, by doing ethnography from the standpoint of participants from a different social class, race or ethnicity, gender or sexual orientation.)
4. Taking the viewpoint of actors other than the commonest types of 'teachers' and 'students' in ordinary state schools. (This can mean focusing on unusual settings in the school system, such as schools for learning disabled pupils, or the deaf or blind, or in the UK Welsh or Gaelic medium schools, or 'other' actors in ordinary schools such as secretaries, laboratory technicians, campus police, cooks.)
5. Studying learning and teaching outside formal education settings.

Examples of how each strategy can serve to strengthen qualitative research on education follow, addressing two agendas; first, fighting familiarity, and second, fighting fashion. The educational sciences 'forget' research very quickly and consistently reinvent the same wheels. It urgently needs to cultivate the *longue durée*.

1.   Revisit the Insightful Educational Ethnographies of the Past

Educational researchers in general, and educational ethnographers are no exception, operate with very short timescapes or time horizons. Fashions come and go, terminology changes so that previous research seems obsolete, and work is quickly forgotten. It is salutary to revisit apparently obsolete, neglected, out of print ethnographies, using them as a lens through which contemporary educational settings can be re-envisioned.

2.   Formal Education in Other Cultures

It may seem paradoxical that educational ethnographers are frequently parochial, and fail to read, cite and use ethnographies of schooling and higher education in other cultures. Exemplary scholarship that would be sovereign in the fight against familiarity is ghettoized and neglected. Such research done by fellow countrymen and countrywomen is ghettoized into 'the anthropology of education' or 'comparative education', equivalent research done by scholars from other countries is not registered at all.

3.   Take the Standpoint of the 'Other'

Taking the standpoint of the 'other' is a valuable research strategy. All educational researchers should try to understand how the setting is perceived by, and experienced by, people who come to it, and live in it, from standpoints other than their own. This is partly an ethical and political point, drawing upon Becker's (1967, 1970) classic question 'Whose side are we on?' That paper is not routinely cited, although it addresses concerns fundamental to educational researchers. Its core concerns are still highly relevant, although a contemporary scholar may find its unproblematic treatment of the researcher a little perplexing. Atkinson, Coffey and Delamont (2003) explore how that paper should be read in a new century. For our purposes here, the word to be emphasized is 'we'. Too often the ethnographer has been a straight, highly educated middle-class white or Jewish man from the USA. With few exceptions the research has been done from that standpoint. Work by gay and lesbian authors, by women and by non-whites has been less common, and, once done, less widely known. The work from other countries that does get known in the USA also tends to be by straight white men. For example, the two books by British ethnographers regularly cited in America are Lacey (1970) and Willis (1977), when, for example, Cecile Wright's (1986) work, from the standpoint of an African-Caribbean woman, provides a far more useful comparator for American writers. The handbook edited by Denzin,

Lincoln and Smith (2008) focused on critical and indigenous methods and could provide fresh approaches for future ethnographers.

4. Study Unusual Schools, or 'Other' Actors

The vast majority of educational ethnographies focus on pupils aged between 6 and 18 in state schools. Researchers rarely focus on schools for those with physical or mental disabilities; on the expensive schools that educate the children of the elite; on rural schools rather than urban and suburban ones. The few studies in religious schools, for Jews, Catholics, evangelicals or Muslims are not used for contrastive purposes as they should be. In the UK there are Welsh and Gaelic medium schools yet the very existence of these is not known by most ethnographers and there are no ethnographic monographs on them, nor are there scholarly evidence-based comparisons of everyday life inside them and in English medium schools. Educational ethnography would be far better if the research on the unusual, exceptional studies were systematically drawn upon to provide contrasts that force the research in the normal school to think about it in novel ways. An alternative way to achieve that critical distance is to focus on non-teacher actors in the setting. Ursula Casanova's (1991) ethnography focused on secretaries in Arizona elementary schools is a (rare) example of such a study.

5. Education Outside 'Education'

Many settings outside formal schooling and universities are the location for teaching and learning. The research on that teaching and learning rarely crosses into the mainstream of educational research, and many settings have hardly been studied at all.

ABOUT THE VOLUME

Both traditions and the five strategies to fight familiarity have been deliberately showcased in this handbook. The authors have been chosen to demonstrate why qualitative educational research needs to make the familiar strange. A range of disciplines, data collection methods, analytic techniques, and a set of reflections on the ways in which representations can be made. Additionally there are chapters on the ways in which qualitative methods have been used in different spheres and sections of formal and informal education. Overall the volume showcases the best that qualitative educational researchers have produced by leaving Damascus.

The volume opens with chapters focused on disciplinary traditions in qualitative educational research, not only sociology and anthropology but also sociolinguistics, social psychology and history. Then there are chapters on three more recent approaches to qualitative research, which are more like standpoints than traditional disciplines (7–9). I had intended to include a chapter on Critical Race Theory, but although I commissioned it twice, neither the original author, nor the replacement team, were able to deliver it. Part 2 contains overviews of the qualitative educational research done outwith schools (10–16) from cyberspace to medical school, from student dorms to apprenticeship. Part 3 focuses on data collection methods, and Part 4 on analysis and representational strategies. There is no section on schools, because so much educational research is de facto about schools, and all the chapters provide ample citations to studies of schooling. The other omission is discussion of ethics, because ethical concerns are present in different ways in all the chapters. The alert reader will notice I have written two chapters: this was due to the original author of one of them withdrawing too late to get it recommissioned.

REFERENCES

Atkinson, P.A. (1990), *The Ethnographic Imagination*, London: Routledge.
Atkinson, P.A. (1992), *Understanding Ethnographic Texts*, Walnut Creek, CA: Sage.
Atkinson, P.A. (1996), *Sociological Readings and (Re)readings*, Aldershot: Ashgate.
Atkinson, P. and Delamont, S. (eds) (1980), 'The two traditions in educational ethnography', *British Journal of Sociology of Education*, **1** (2), 139–54.
Atkinson, P. and Delamont, S. (1990), 'Writing about teachers', *Teaching and Teacher Education*, **6** (2), 111–25.
Atkinson, P.A. and Delamont, S. (2008), *Representing Ethnography*, four vols, London: Sage.
Atkinson, P.A., Coffey, A. and Delamont, S. (2003), *Key Themes in Qualitative Research*, Walnut Creek, CA: Alta Mira Press.
Atkinson, P.A., Delamont, S. and Hammersley, M. (1988), 'Qualitative research traditions: a British response', *Review of Educational Research*, **58** (2), 231–50.
Beck, U. and Beck-Gernsheim, E. (1995), *The Normal Chaos of Love*, Cambridge: Polity Press.
Becker, H.S. (1967), 'Whose side are we on?', *Social Problems*, **14** (3), 239–47.
Becker, H.S. (1970), *Sociological Work*, Chicago, IL: Aldine.
Becker, H.S. (1971), 'Footnote added to the paper by M. Wax and R. Wax "Great tradition, little tradition and formal education"', in M. Wax, S. Diamond and F. Gearing (eds), *Anthropological Perspectives on Education*, New York: Basic Books, pp. 3–27.
Becker, H.S., Geer, B. and Hughes, E.C. (1968), *Making the Grade*, New York: Wiley.
Bernbaum, G. (1977), *Knowledge and Ideology in the Sociology of Education*, London: Macmillan.
Bernstein, B. (2000), Unpublished letter to the author.
Bourgois, P. (1996), *In Search of Respect*, Cambridge: Cambridge University Press.
Brown, K.M. (1991), *Mama Lola*, Berkeley, CA: University of California Press.
Carter, I. (1990), *Ancient Cultures of Conceit*, London: Routledge and Kegan Paul.

Casanova, U. (1991), *Elementary School Secretaries*, Newbury Park, CA: Corwin Press.
Clifford, J. and Marcus, G.E. (eds) (1986), *Writing Culture*, Berkeley, CA: University of California Press.
Coffey, A. (1999), *The Ethnographic Self*, London: Sage.
Connerton, P. (1989), *How Societies Remember*, Cambridge: Cambridge University Press.
Delamont, S. (1981), 'All too familiar?', *Educational Analysis*, **3** (1), 69–84.
Delamont, S. and Atkinson, P. (1995), *Fighting Familiarity*, Cresskill, NJ: Hampton Press.
De Marrais, K.B. (ed.) (1998), *Inside Stories*, Mahwah, NJ: Erlbaum.
Denham, C. and Lieberman, A. (1980), *Time to Learn*, Washington, DC: NIE.
Denzin, N., Lincoln, Y. and Smith, L.T. (eds) (2008), *Handbook of Critical and Indigenous Methodologies*, London: Sage.
Eisner, E.W. and Peshkin, A. (eds) (1990), *Qualitative Inquiry in Education*, New York: Teachers College Press.
Flecker, J.E. (1947), *Collected Poems*, London: Secker and Warburg.
Geer, B. (1964), 'First days in the field', in P. Hammond (ed.), *Sociologists at Work*, New York: Basic Books, pp. 372–98.
Geer, B. (ed.) (1972), *Learning to Work*, Beverley Hills, CA: Sage.
Generett, G.G. and Jeffries, R.B. (eds) (2003), *Black Women in the Field*, Creskill, NJ: Hampton Press.
Herzfeld, M. (1985), *The Poetics of Manhood*, Princeton, NJ: Princeton University Press.
Hess, G.A.(1999), 'Keeping educational anthropology relevant: asking good questions rather than trivial ones', *Anthropology and Education Quarterly*, **30** (4), 404–12.
Jacob, E. (1987), 'Qualitative research traditions', *Review of Educational Research*, **57** (1), 1–50.
Lacey, C. (1970), *Hightown Grammar*, Manchester: Manchester University Press.
Lareau, A. and Shultz, J. (eds) (1990), *Journeys through Fieldwork*, Boulder, CO: Westview.
Lash, S. and Urry, J. (1994), *Economies of Signs and Space*, London: Sage.
Lave, J. and Wenger, E. (1991), *Situated Learning*, Cambridge: Cambridge University Press.
Littlewood, R. (2009), 'Neglect as project', *Journal of the Royal Anthropological Institute*, **15** (1), 113–30.
Lutz, C. (1988), *Unnatural Emotions*, Chicago, IL: University of Chicago Press.
Marcus, J. (2001), 'Orientalism', in P. Atkinson, A. Coffey, K.S. Delamont, L. Lofland and J. Lofland (eds), *Handbook of Ethnography*, London: Sage, pp. 109–17.
McLean, A. and Leiberg, A. (eds) (2007), *The Shadow Side of Fieldwork*, Oxford: Blackwell.
Metz, M.H. (1984), 'Editor's foreword', *Sociology of Education*, **57** (2), 199.
Parman, S. (1998), 'Making the familier strange: the anthropological dialogue of George and Louise Spindler', in G. Spindler and L. Spindler (eds), *Fifty Years of Anthropology and Education 1950–2000*, Mahwah, NJ: Lawrence Erlbaum, pp. 393–416.
Peshkin, A. (1972), *Kanuri Schoolchildren*, New York: Holt, Rinehart and Winston.
Peshkin, A. (1982), *The Imperfect Union*, Chicago, IL: University of Chicago Press.
Peshkin, A. (1986), *God's Choice*, Chicago, IL: University of Chicago Press.
Peshkin, A. (1991), *The Color of Strangers, The Color of Friends*, Chicago, IL: University of Chicago Press.
Peshkin, A. (1994), *Growing Up American*, Prospect Heights, IL: Waveland Press.
Peshkin, A. (1997), *Places of Memory*, Mahwah, NJ: Erlbaum.
Peshkin, A. (2001), *Permissable Advantage*? New York: Routledge.
Reed-Danahay, D. (1996), *Education and Identity in Rural France*, Cambridge: Cambridge University Press.
Said, E. (1978), *Orientalism*, London: Routledge and Kegan Paul.
Singleton, J. (ed.) (1998), *Learning in Likely Places: Varieties of Apprenticeship in Japan*, Cambridge: Cambridge University Press.
Singleton, J. (1999), 'Reflecting on the reflections', *Anthropology and Education Quarterly*, **30** (4), 455–9.
Spencer, J. (2001), 'Ethnography after postmodernism', in P. Atkinson, A. Coffey, S. Delamont, J. Lofland and L. Lofland (eds), *Handbook of Ethnography*, London: Sage, pp. 443–52.

Spindler, G. (1955), *Education and Anthropology*, Stanford, CA: Stanford University Press.

Spindler, G. (ed.) (1982), *Doing the Ethnography of Schooling*, New York: Holt, Rinehart and Winston.

Spindler, G. (ed.) (2000), *Fifty Years of Anthropology and education*, Mahwah, NJ: Erlbaum.

Spindler, G. and Spindler, L. (1982), 'Roger Harker and Schoenhausen: from familiar to strange and back again', in G. Spindler (ed.), *Doing the Ethnography of Schooling*, New York: Holt, Rinehart and Winston, pp. 20–46.

Spindler, G. and Spindler, L. (eds) (1987), *Interpretive Ethnography of Education*, Hillside, NJ: Erlbaum.

Star, S.L. (1989), 'The structure of all-structured solutions: boundary objects and heterogeneous distributed problem-solving', in L. Gaiser and M. Huhns (eds), *Distributed Artifical Intelligence*, San Mateo, CA: Morgan Kaufman, pp. 37–54.

Star, S.L. (2010), 'This is not a boundary object: reflections on the origin of a concept', *Science, Technology and Human Values*, **35** (6), 600–617.

Suchman, L. (1994), 'Working relations of technology production and use', *Computer Supported Cooperative Work*, **2** (1), 21–39.

Varenne, H. (2007a), 'Alternative anthropological perspectives on education', *Teachers College Record*, **109** (7), 1539–58.

Varenne, H. (2007b), 'Difficult collective deliberations: anthropological notes towards a theory of education', *Teachers College Record*, **109** (7), 1559–88.

Wax, M. and Wax, R. (1971), 'Great tradition, little tradition and formal education', in M. Wax, S. Diamond and F. Gearing (eds), *Anthropological Perspectives on Education*, New York: Basic Books, pp. 3–27.

Willis, P. (1977), *Learning to Labour*, Farnborough: Gower.

Wolcott, H.F. (1981), 'Confessions of a trained observer', in T.S. Popkewitz and B.R. Tabachnick (eds), *The Study of Schooling*, New York: Praeger, pp. 247–63.

Wright, C. (1986), 'School processes: an ethnographic study', in S.J. Eggleston, D. Dunn, M. Anjoli and C. Wright (eds), *Education for Some*, Stoke on Trent, UK: Trentham Books, pp. 127–79.

Young, M.F.D. (1971), 'Introduction', in M.F.D. Young (ed.), *Knowledge and Control*, London: Collier-Macmillan, pp. 1–17.

PART 1

THEORETICAL AND DISCIPLINARY PERSPECTIVES

2. Sociology of education: advancing relations between qualitative methodology and social theory
Ruth Boyask

Perhaps the most fruitful distinction with which the sociological imagination works is between the 'personal troubles of milieu' and 'the public issues of social structure'. This distinction is an essential tool of the sociological imagination and a feature of all classic work in social science. (C. Wright Mills, 1970, p. 14)

To view education with a sociological imagination, using Wright Mills's term, is to identify and attend to its relationships with both the personal and public. Sociology in intellectual and political work sheds light on the personal troubles and public issues of the times as well as the inter-relationships between the two. In respect of the sociology of education, sociological theories and methodologies have been employed foremost to highlight and address inconsistencies in educational opportunity that are determined both at the level of the individual and in terms of social inequalities (Weis et al., 2009). With equivalent potential, but to a lesser extent in practice, the sociology of education contributes to the understanding and progression of the wider social world and how social equity in general terms might be achieved. Classical social science has made heavy use of abstract thought and theoretical speculation to construct knowledge of the social world and resolve its concerns, but evidence from observable reality also contributes to sociological understanding. As the discipline of sociology has developed there has been an accompanying and proliferating development in empirical methodologies. The methodological developments are informed by developments in other disciplines (most notably anthropology and psychology) and fields of study (for example, health and business). In the main, such methodologies are identified as either qualitative (like the methodological approaches described in this book), quantitative (largely measurable survey research) or mixed method approaches. All three are used in the sociology of education, and while the methods themselves are not necessarily sociological, different strands of sociological thought have greater affinity with some methodologies more than others (see Hammersley, 1984).

Whilst in this chapter I am concerned with relations between qualitative research methods and the sociology of education, much broader

contestations in educational knowledge impact crucially upon this relationship. Taking a broad view of the current modes of inquiry in the
field of education, empirical research is on the ascendance whereas the
discipline of sociology is in decline (Metz, 2000; Shain and Ozga, 2001).
Academics, policy-makers and practitioners are tending to look for solutions to educational concerns through empirical and methodological
approaches without necessarily working from a clear disciplinary stance.
Whilst sociology has historically played a prominent role in the study
of education, this has lessened alongside a progressive division between
explicit social theorizing and educational research (Boocock, 1980) or
educational methodologies and those practised in sociology departments
(Delamont, 1997). In 1997 Delamont concluded that the sociology of education was not 'well integrated with the sociology practised in sociology
departments' and that 'educational research is suffering from being ghet-
toised in schools of education' (p. 604). However, some have suggested
that focusing educational research upon education and professional
practice, and starting from this point rather than from the demands of a
discipline does not necessarily negate the contribution of the disciplines
to educational issues (Stenhouse, 1983; Riehl, 2001). Understanding of
these relationships is further enhanced by recognizing the political dimensions of the debates. The significance of the division between theory and
methodology to relations between sociology of education and qualitative research is intensified by the political nature of knowledge. Writing
on the relationship between qualitative research and the sociology of
education, Mary Haywood Metz (2000) argued that qualitative research
methodologies are largely marginalized and held only briefly a significant
position within the discipline of sociology in the United States through
the work of the Chicago School in the early twentieth century (consisting of sociologists George Herbert Mead, W.I. Thomas, Ellsworth Faris
and others). Whilst empirical research currently assumes importance
in the development and evaluation of education writ large, qualitative
research methodologies are largely considered secondary to quantitative
approaches in producing robust forms of evidence. Metz's concerns about
the state of the sociology of education and qualitative research expressed
at the beginning of 2000–10 remain issues for the current decade, but this
chapter also points out some differences and important developments in
approaches to theory and methodology that provide some hope for the
further enrichment of education through sociological understandings. It
is the goal of this chapter to outline these broad issues and debates on
the relations between qualitative methodology, social theory and future
directions for the sociology of education rather than review qualitative
research studies. Where this chapter does not provide significant detail

about particular sociological perspectives or individual qualitative studies, it cites significant review papers and other publications which can lead readers to specific studies.

Unprecedented global development in compulsory education throughout the twentieth century firmly planted education as a public issue. Through the early and mid twentieth century interest in the sociology of education was assurgent, and in many places sociologists of education had significant influence upon educational policy and practice. Development in compulsory education continues and educational research is currently a robust and productive area of investigation. However, the sociology of education as a discrete field of study appears to be in decline. In the United Kingdom its conferences have fewer delegates, contributions to its journals are in decline and it is a diminishing area of study in university programmes. There are numerous explanations for this change. Shain and Ozga (2001) suggested that in England the relationship between sociologists of education and policy-makers changed in the latter part of the twentieth century due to the predominance of Marxist sociology, which contrary to its intentions to address social inequalities merely served to perpetuate them. Writing from an American perspective, Riehl (2001) suggested that diminishment of the sociology of education has been a natural outcome of a trend towards interdisciplinarity and the inevitable contingency of knowledge; permeation of the boundaries of the sociology of education has produced hybrid forms of knowledge and altered the discipline.

Some have suggested that developments in the sociology of education have been hampered by a distinction in classical sociology between the different processes and effects of the macro and micro levels within a society, comparable to Wright Mills's distinction between the personal and the public (see Boocock, 1980; Hammersley, 1984; Metz, 2000). Boocock (1980) expressed concern that research in the sociology of education was divided into two methodological camps, principally affiliated with either macro- or micro-sociology. The first of these methodological camps stressed the importance of conducting research from which you could make robust generalizations and comparisons, and the 'other stresses sensitivity to the details and nuances of life in schools' (p. 35). Critics of the first camp suggested that 'such research tends to measure what is easily measurable and amenable to powerful statistical techniques rather than what is theoretically or substantively interesting' (p. 35). Whereas the other camp was criticized for producing research that is interesting and insightful, but lacks general application. Hammersley (1984) claimed that the distinction is further entrenched on the grounds of differences in substantive sociological understandings, and is underpinned by those who adhere intractably to different foundational social theories. Broadly speaking, macro-level interests such as the effects of social structures upon educational opportunity have tended to be associated with large-scale quantitative studies. Alternatively, investigations into the micro contexts of individuals and their immediate milieu have been more closely associated with qualitative methods of inquiry. Quantitative studies were the methods of Marxist sociology, whereas in-depth qualitative studies tended to be associated with interactionism. While Hammersley claimed that arguing for either side of the dichotomy was 'fruitless polemic' and that effort would be better directed towards testing sociological theories, the legacy of the macro/micro distinction is its ongoing permeation of many of the major debates within the field of education. Since the 1980s, quantitative researchers continue to challenge the generalizability of qualitative research (for example, Tooley, 1997) and qualitative researchers continue to defend their methodology (for example, Clegg, 2005).

Boocock's (1980) position, which today appears idealistic in light of the ongoing polemic, was that the sociology of education was enriched by drawing upon both methodological traditions, and that compiling evidence from a variety of high quality empirical research enables educationists to overcome the limitations of individual studies and methodologies. However, he also noted that others suggested that it is not a methodological distinction that determines the quality of educational research, but its relationship with substantive, theoretical knowledge about education (Boocock, 1980). It is on this basis that Clegg (2005) argues that whilst there is nothing to preclude the use of quantitative data to address significant questions of sociology, her qualitative research methods are the inevitable methods for answering her particular sociological questions. Clegg (2005) argues from a critical realist perspective and claims that it is necessary to study the lived reality of individuals, and the ways that they make meaning and act within that reality, in order to understand the extent of social structures, the nature of structural change and intervene in the production of social meanings. She suggests that qualitative research is a necessary means for investigating the 'everyday' or 'mundane', which will enrich understanding on the nature of human agency and practice. The profundity of such empirical methods is dependent upon having an underpinning 'adequate theorisation of the self' (p. 160). Thus, she stakes a claim for her work to contribute to general understandings of agency, practice and social structure.

Research such as Clegg's exemplifies what Wright Mills (1970) was 'getting at' when he claimed that the sociological imagination, 'our most needed quality of mind' (p. 20), fruitfully worked with 'personal troubles' and 'public issues'. His distinction was not made on the basis that the personal and public were distinct domains that addressed separate issues and demanded different methodologies, but because he perceived that the most pressing personal troubles of his time were produced through social structure *and were public issues*. Employing a sociological imagi-nation enabled one to probe and make connections between macro and micro contexts, making clear the uneasiness and indifference that he perceived were endemic in his society, and giving shape to the problems within the immediate social world of individuals that were a result of this general social malaise. Wright Mills was also critical of the detachment of theory and methodology from the practical concerns of the times. He critiqued the inflation of one or the other through what he called 'preten-tious over-elaboration of "method" and "theory"' (p. 86). However, a sociological imagination does not preclude weighting sociological work towards a theoretical orientation or a methodological one, either at a particular time or within the body of a single sociologist's work. For example, Edwards (2002) claimed that Basil Bernstein was very success-ful in meeting Wright Mills's criterion for a sociological imagination, even though Bernstein was resistant to practicality and self-consciously highly theoretical in his work. He pointed out that Bernstein's sociol-ogy has proved to be highly useful in application to practical problems and issues. Bernstein combined the sociology of education's traditional interests in structural inequalities with its new interest in 'the content and transmission of educational knowledge' (Edwards 2002, p. 530). 'They were his response both to sociologists' tendency to treat education merely as an unexamined "relay" for power relations external to itself, and to classroom researchers' habit of detaching teacher-pupil interactions from structures of power and control in which they were embedded' (Edwards, 2002, p. 530). Morais (2002) explained how sociological studies that she coordinated on the micro world of the classroom drew upon this aspect of Bernstein's sociology. The studies utilized a methodology that rejects both an atheoretical analysis of the empirical and the use of theory in a reified form, and alternatively proposes a dialectical relationship between theory and method. However, in doing this she claimed to step outside of the debate between the quantitative and qualitative research camps, suggesting that identification with either is problematic. She suggested that orthodox qualitative research methods have had a strong classifica-tion with practice and the empirical, and a much weaker association with theory, and thus are insufficient on their own to do the full work of edu-cational research, which she suggested is to 'diagnose, describe, explain, transfer and predict' (p. 565).

This dialectical approach to research in the sociology of education bears some resemblance to other tendencies in contemporary sociology.

Clear distinctions between binary groupings such as theory and methodology, personal and public, and qualitative and quantitative are challenged through the departure from classical social science and developments in contemporary social theory. The substance of the sociology of education has changed blurring these distinctions, and emphasizing relational, dialectic and discursive forms of knowledge. There is an increase of theories which attempt to describe the intricacies of twenty-first-century society (for example, multi-linear evolution, neo-Marxisms and postmodern theories) and the complex relationships between an individual and society (for example, structuration, figurational or process sociology). While there is a concomitant turn towards complex and well-theorized methodologies within some pockets of educational research, a significant amount of empirical research within education continues to lack a rigorous theoretical base. The United Kingdom has regular Research Assessment Exercises (RAEs) when universities submit a sample of publications to be graded by peer panels. In 2008 the Education Sub-Panel (45) concluded that there was significant under-theorization in commissioned research in the United Kingdom (HEFCE, 2008). (See the report from Sub-Panel 45 Education, 2008, p. 3 for the extent of under-theorization in commissioned research in the United Kingdom.)

There are structural changes that occurred throughout the last century and continued into this one that have had a profound effect on both the sociology of education and educational research. One of the most significant is that state-funded education is more prolific. While throughout the world there is continued development in compulsory education, governments also invested heavily in the post-compulsory sector with many countries widening access to further and higher education (Paterson, 2001; Postle and Sturman, 2003; Eckel and King, 2004). With a greater number of institutions brought into the university sector, more people receiving higher education and changed expectations about the qualifications and research activity for professional educators (such as in teacher education), there is consequently more educational research. The two main drivers for these changes are contradictory in nature. On the one hand, the increase in public spending on education has been driven by a globalized economic system and the desire to gain a competitive edge in a knowledge economy. On the other, there are democratic drivers with the aim of furthering social participation and equity. The paradoxical relations between these two drivers are intensified for those committed to the second, thus proving especially problematic for sociologists of education for whom social equity is the fundamental concern. This has been a preoccupation in my own work, finding that when educational research is divorced from social theory and enacted as an instrumental practice it meshes more readily with a logic of economics than humanistic beliefs about social inclusion (see Kaur et al., 2008). Whilst increasing the amount of educational research undertaken has the potential to further aims of social equity, there is a concerning tendency for empirical research to be used to further economic ends irrespective of its intended function. This has affected both the production of educational research, limiting its scope to what is expected to be economically useful, and the use of research, with empirical evidence employed instrumentally as a measure of accountability particularly in the work of professionals (see Quinlivan et al., 2008). If engagement with research is enforced and structured by economic expediency, it becomes far easier to engage with research that produces definitive conclusions on the effects of particular interventions (cause and effect) than grapple with complex educational relationships where direct cause and effect is not discernible (non-causal correlations), complex situational influences (context) or the impact of individuals and their paradigms on research findings (reflexivity). However, advocates for qualitative approaches do so because they recognize that educational research that emphasizes direct causality has limited application because of the complexities involved in the task of education.

For those concerned with the fairer distribution of education, it is therefore important to consider how empirical research might operate as a "'subject to work on" rather than as an "object of uncritical consumption and compliance"' (Kaur et al., 2008, p. 246). Social theory and methodologies that are sensitive to subjectivity provide conceptual frameworks to negotiate problems that arise in the objectification of research and the subjects of research. Sociologist Michael Burowoy (1998), writing on his extended case method, claimed that from a positivistic perspective reflexivity (or researchers' awareness of their own influence upon the research) and reactivity (the impact of participants' awareness of the research upon the findings) that are common in contemporary social science are generally precluded from 'good' science. Burowoy sets out an argument in support of two models of science: positivistic and reflexive. Both of these are flawed in some respects, but both have virtue also. Burowoy's (1998) extended case method is an enactment of reflexive science that embraces intersubjective knowledge arrived at through dialogue between researchers and the subjects of their research, whereas 'the premise that distinguishes positive from reflexive science is that there is an "external" world that can be construed as separate from and incommensurable with those who study it' (p. 10). While Burowoy's specific extended case method is significant in sociological but not educational research (which may illustrate Delamont's (1997) concern about the ghettoization of educational research) there are concepts underpinning the method and its reflexive science that are profoundly connected to the development of qualitative research in the sociology of education. Burowoy's method stems from the ethnographic tradition, which originating in anthropology, has developed along its own trajectory in sociology.

Traditionally the ethnographic methods of the sociology of education were closely associated with symbolic interactionism, ethnomethodology and the sociology of the Chicago School. Metz (2000) claimed that 'four critical elements in the methodology of qualitative research stem from the founding Chicago School' (p. 62). First, qualitative researchers in sociology attempt to understand a group from the group's own standpoint or worldview. Second, these insider perspectives are developed through participating in the lives of the groups. Third, the subjectivity of the sociologist and their association with the disciplinary understandings of sociology impacts upon their analysis. And fourth, sociologists study groups within complex settings made up of multiple and overlapping groups. She claims such insights are crucial for investigating the social phenomenon of education, which is made up of groups that can be studied as entities of their own but also related to other entities. Social interactionist ethnography emerged in education during the late 1960s/1970s when it largely focused upon the immediate life worlds of classroom and school (Gordon et al., 2007). The emphasis of interactionist ethnography upon relational and contextual meaning-making fed into the political and intellectual ferment of the times, as the personal became political. New social movements challenged the previously taken-for-granted authority of institutions and critical theorists turned essential truths into socially generated stories of power and control (see also Mills, Chapter 3, this volume).

The critical theory of the 1970s offered education compelling and rich theorization of the self, certainly fulfilling Clegg's (2005) criterion, and in response critical ethnography took root in educational research (Anderson, 1989, pp. 251–2). Willis's (1977) influential sociological ethnography of young, working-class 'lads' demonstrated that rather than passive recipients of oppression, his research participants were actively engaged in practices of resistance. However, the prevailing social conditions meant that these acts of resistance only served to cement their social location and limit their opportunities to unrewarding and poorly paid employment. Neo-Marxist ethnographic work like Willis's study and similar later studies emerging from critical feminism (for example, Weiler, 1988; Fine, 1991) highlighted problems of social structure and its distribution of power through depicting personal troubles. However, there were limits to critical ethnographic approaches in that while they described personal troubles they had limited resources to intervene in them. Other forms of educational research emerging from radical politics, such as participatory and action research methodologies, offered more potential for social transformation. Yet even these research methods are at risk of co-option when disconnected from their theoretical rationales. Jordan (2009) argued that the neoliberal culture in which we are now immersed has assimilated research methodologies associated with social and radical education movements. In this culture, subjectivity is a force for consumption rather than a force of cultural production (see also Willis, 2003).

In discussing educational ethnography Delamont et al. (2000) expressed concern that 'research methods have become remarkably divorced from empirical research in many ways' (p. 235). They suggested that whilst there are rich developments in methodological writing, methods run the risk of becoming self-referential and lacking utility for addressing the research questions they are intended to answer. I also add that they risk lacking utility in solving practical educational problems. Stenhouse (1983, p. 190) argued for placing education and professional practice at the centre of educational inquiry, rather than a discipline. Education as the subject of research 'is not characterised by a neglect of disciplines, upon which it draws eclectically, but rather by the fact that what is drawn from the disciplines and applied to education is not results or even theories which give shape to each discipline, but methods of inquiry and analysis together with such concepts as have utility for a theory of education' (p. 190). Since then there has been growth in research that starts with problems of educational practice, particularly evident in the growth of teaching and learning as a field of study (for example, the large government investments in teaching and learning research such as the Teaching and Learning Research Programme (TLRP) in the United Kingdom and Teaching and Learning Research Initiative in New Zealand). However, how much of this research fulfils Wright Mill's criteria for the sociological imagination? Whilst the socio-political context of twenty-first-century globalism is well theorized (for example, see Olssen et al., 2004; Apple et al., 2005), there are a limited number of empirical studies that come to grips with the full complexities and paradoxes of this age. From the 1980s qualitative research in education made a shift away from making explicit the public issues of the day, and this was even the case in the sociology of education. In 2001 Riehl (2001) claimed that mainstream researchers in the United States had made little connection between studies of schooling and 'broader social, political and economic issues, including the connections between education and the social implications of capitalism and modernity' (p. 127). This is a significant lack considering that, as I have suggested throughout this chapter, social structures and public issues implicitly shape contemporary knowledge even when such connections are not made explicit. However, there is some educational research that traverses this terrain and provides models for more socially conscious educational research (for examples, see Moje, 2007; Anyon, 2009). Also of relevance to this discussion is a very recent concern within the education academic community for building capacity in theorizing for educational research. For example, at the time of writing the British Educational Research Association and TLRP are jointly holding a series of research training workshops on 'The Role of Theory in Educational Research' aimed at doctoral and early career educational researchers.

The current challenge for sociologists of education is to strengthen approaches to educational research and assist in reconnecting social theorizing with research method. This may require working on a number of fronts to overcome the challenges of the numerous contestations in the field of education. Whilst critics of disciplinary approaches to education claim that the impetus for educational research should come from the field of practice, it is important to consider that their demand is not significantly at odds with conventional understanding of sociological inquiry. The problems faced by teachers, learners, educational leaders and others in their immediate milieu of educational institutions, organizations and communities correspond with Wright Mills's personal troubles. However, the profound insight offered by sociology to the field of education is that many of these problems are socially significant and integrally connected with the 'public issues of social structure'. Resolution therefore requires sensitivity to the political contestations and social dynamics of the macro context. While traditionally sociological inquiry at the macro level has been associated with large-scale, quantitative methods there are important opportunities for qualitative research. Burowoy's (1998) extended case method is an example of in-depth research where the analysis of the micro situation is 'extended out' through principles of dialogic method; for example, structuration whereby the micro is understood as both shaping and being shaped by macro-level influences. Other sociological perspectives, such as process sociology or postmodernism, also offer rich foundations for relating and negotiating between personal troubles and public issues. Such theorizing can help to resist the co-option of the individual to the role of consumer. Fundamentally, the assumption that qualitative research only describes particular cases of social reality and cannot contribute general understandings must be challenged. Significant developments have occurred in both the sociology of education and qualitative research that provide a basis for this work; qualitative research methods may yet realize the full potential of social theory's significance for education.

REFERENCES

Anderson, G.L. (1989), 'Critical ethnography in education: origins, current status, and new directions', *Review of Educational Research*, **59** (3), 249–70.

Anyon, J. (2009), *Theory and Educational Research: Toward Critical Social Explanation*, New York: Routledge.

Apple, M.W., Kenway, J. and Singh, M. (2005), *Globalizing Education: Policies, Pedagogies, & Politics*, New York: Peter Lang.

Boocock, S.S. (1980), *Sociology of Education: An Introduction*, Boston, MA: Houghton Mifflin.

Burawoy, M. (1998), 'The extended case method', *Sociological Theory*, **16** (1), 4–33.

Clegg, S. (2005), 'Theorising the mundane: the significance of agency', *International Studies in Sociology of Education*, **15** (2), 149–63.

Delamont, S. (1997), 'Fuzzy borders and the fifth moment: methodological issues facing the sociology of education', *British Journal of Sociology of Education*, **18** (4), 601–6.

Delamont, S., Coffey, A. and Atkinson, P. (2000), 'The twilight years? Educational ethnography and the five moments model', *International Journal of Qualitative Studies in Education*, **13** (3), 223–38.

Eckel, P.D. and King, J.E. (2004), *An Overview of Higher Education in the United States: Diversity, Access and the Role of the Marketplace*, Washington, DC: American Council on Education.

Edwards, T. (2002), 'A remarkable sociological imagination', *British Journal of Sociology of Education*, **23** (4), 527–35.

Fine, M. (1991), *Framing Dropouts: Notes on the Politics of an Urban High School*, Albany, NY: SUNY Press.

Gordon, T., Holland, J. and Lahelma, E. (2007), 'Ethnographic research in educational settings', in P. Atkinson, A. Coffey, S. Delamont, J. Lofland and L. Lofland (eds), *Handbook of Ethnography*, London: Sage, pp. 188–203.

Hammersley, M. (1984), 'Some reflections upon the macro-micro problem in the sociology of education', *Sociological Review*, **32**, 316–24.

HEFCE (2008), 'Subject overview report', available at http://www.rae.ac.uk/pubs/2009/ov/MainPanelK.zip (accessed 3 October 2010).

Jordan, S. (2009), 'From a methodology of the margins to neoliberal appropriation and beyond: the lineages of PAR', in D. Kapoor and S. Jordan (eds), *Education, Participatory Action Research, and Social Change: International Perspectives*, New York: Palgrave Macmillan, pp. 15–28.

Kaur, B., Boyask R., Quinlivan, K. and McPhail, J.C. (2008), 'Searching for equity and social justice: diverse learners in Aotearoa, New Zealand', in G. Wan (ed.), *The Education of Diverse Populations: A Global Perspective*, The Netherlands: Springer Science and Business Media, pp. 227–51.

Metz, M.H. (2000), 'Sociology and qualitative methodologies in educational research', *Harvard Educational Review*, **70** (1), 60–74.

Mills, C.W. (1970), *The Sociological Imagination* (first published 1959), Harmondsworth, Middlesex: Penguin Books.

Moje, E.B. (2007), 'Developing socially just subject-matter instruction: a review of the literature on disciplinary literacy teaching', *Review of Research in Education*, **31**, 1–44.

Morais, A.M. (2002), 'Basil Bernstein at the micro level of the classroom', *British Journal of Sociology of Education*, **23** (4), 559–69.

Olssen, M., Codd, J. and O'Neill, A.M. (2004), 'Education policy: globalization, citizenship and democracy', London: Sage.

Paterson, L. (2001), 'Education and inequality in Britain', paper prepared for the social policy section at the annual meeting of the British Association for the Advancement of Science, Glasgow, 4 September 2001, available at http://www.institute-of-governance.org/publications/working_papers/education_and_inequality_in_britain (accessed 5 April 2010).

Postle, G. and Sturman, A. (2003), Widening access to higher education – an Australian case study', *Journal of Adult and Continuing Education*, **8** (2), 195–212.

Quinlivan, K., Boyask, R. and Carswell, S. (2008), 'Dynamics of power and participation in school/university partnerships', *New Zealand Journal of Education Studies*, **43** (1), 65–84.

Riehl, C. (2001), 'Bridges to the future: the contributions of qualitative research to the sociology of education', *Sociology of Education*, **74**, 115–34.

Shain, F. and Ozga, J. (2001), 'Identity crisis? Problems and issues in the sociology of education', *British Journal of Sociology of Education*, **22** (1), 109–20.

Stenhouse, L. (1983), *Authority, Education and Emancipation*, London: Heinemann Educational Books.

Tooley, J. (1997), 'On school choice and social class: a response to Ball, Bowe and Gewirtz', *British Journal of Sociology of Education*, **18** (2), 217–30.

Weiler, K. (1988), *Women Teaching for Change*, New York: Bergin and Garvey.

Weis, L., Jenkins, H. and Stich, A. (2009), 'Diminishing the divisions among us: reading and writing across difference in theory and method in the sociology of education', *Review of Educational Research*, **79** (2), 912–45.

Willis, P. (1977), *Learning to Labour: How Working Class Kids get Working Class Jobs*, Farnborough: Saxon House.

Willis, P. (2003), 'Foot soldiers of modernity: the dialectics of cultural consumption and the 21st-century school', *Harvard Educational Review*, **73** (3), 390–415.

3. Anthropology and education
David Mills

Next up facing the students is the headmaster, flanked by the deputy and chaplain. Greeting them politely, and asking after their health, his approach is rather more subtle. *'I'd like to welcome the new students'*, he continues, *'to the University of Kiboga, as everyone calls Kikomera Secondary School, being the oldest and best secondary school in the district'* . . . But this warm rosy feeling does not last long . . . *'Now, about this late-coming. I'm seeing too many late-comers – it must stop'* comes as a sudden jolt. *'You are all due here before 8am to work at cleaning the grounds. And the standard of dress is too bad – I have seen pupils coming to school without shoes, and this is not acceptable. We cannot have bare feet in the University of Kiboga.'*

(Mills, 1999, p. 16)

I start with a vignette of one of the many weekly assemblies I witnessed whilst doing doctoral research in a rural Ugandan secondary school. Taken from my own fieldnotes, it captures something of the powerful imagery that surrounds education in many African countries. Studying social anthropology as an undergraduate, I decided that the best way to get at such imagery was to conduct participant observation in a Ugandan secondary school, and the best way to do that was to become a teacher. My aim was to see how broader discourses about gender, modernity, progress and nationhood circulated within Kikomera Secondary. I was less interested in what was being learnt in the classroom than in everything else happening in the school, and what that might reveal about the social worlds beyond the school gates.

I am the first to admit that my thesis ignored scholarship in education and the sociology of education. I never considered my work a 'school ethnography'. Influenced by debates about 'multi-sited ethnography' (Marcus, 1995), I was more intent on following flows of people and ideas than in understanding the social dynamics within the classroom. Kikomera was just one of a number of research sites. But as with any methodological choice, foregrounding one viewpoint means that others are less visible: a theme I return to throughout this chapter.

I begin by reviewing 80 years of Anglophone anthropological work on education, highlighting dominant trends and revealing hidden histories. In a key review of the field, Delamont and Atkinson (1980) argue that, compared to a vibrant US community of anthropologists studying education, there has been no identifiable intellectual tradition within 'British' social anthropology. I show how the story is both more complicated and more interesting: an adequate explanation of the differences needs to take into account the size of the respective academies, funding interests and contrasting attitudes towards specialization. In the second part of this chapter I discuss the challenge that anthropology faces in defending its methodological principles to educational researchers. I end by highlighting the lively diversity of recent anthropological scholarship on education, and possible futures for the field.

HISTORIES OF ANTHROPOLOGY AND EDUCATION

Mapping and understanding the American-dominated sub-field of the anthropology of education seems to be a straightforward task. Its existence seems indisputable, made real by its institutional trappings: a professional organization (Council of Anthropology and Education, founded in 1968), a journal (*Anthropology and Education Quarterly*), first published in 1974, and numerous reviews of the field. Two major new Readers (Anderson-Levitt, 2011; Levinson 2011) mark a further moment of consolidation in the field. The field's pre-history is admirably surveyed by Eddy (1985), whilst inclusive and theoretically engaged reviews include those by Yon (2003), Foley (1991) and Levinson, et al. (1996). An even broader review of the anthropology of teaching and learning by Pelissier (1991) ranges over the gamut of twentieth-century anthropological scholarship on modes of thought, communication, and work on apprenticeship and informal learning. But these readers, reviews and histories also highlight the different stories one can tell about the nature of the field in the USA, its theoretical and applied traditions, and its boundaries. Is the field's focus schooling, formal education or all forms of learning? Can one even talk of a 'field' if it is made up of very different methodological approaches and theoretical concerns? The map gets increasingly complex.

One common theme in this work is its practical and pragmatic outlook. The determination of Franz Boas to address the 'problems of modern life' resonated with the reformist attitudes of many early American anthropologists. After first working on childrearing in Samoa (Mead, 1928), Margaret Mead's subsequent writing on the challenges facing the American educational system (such as *The School in American Culture*, 1951) made her the public face of the discipline (di Leonardo, 1998). Mead and others benefited from the US Government's patronage of applied anthropology during the Second World War: many scholars were employed on war-related tasks (Price, 2008). In 1941, the US Department of the Interior and Commissioner of Indian Affairs funded

Margaret Mead to lead a programme of research on the Native American Personality (Pettitt, 1946). Anthropologists of education also benefited from federal grants to explore issues of acculturation amongst America's many 'minority' communities. Ideas from cultural psychology, such as Ruth Benedict's work on the 'Japanese personality' (Benedict, 1934) could be applied and tested in Japanese internment camps in California (Starn, 1986). 'Culture and personality' studies became fashionable, a theoretical approach that avoided questions of power and difference.

This question of how culture (the term was rarely unpacked) shaped individual identity preoccupied many in the field for the next 30 years. The vision and energy of George and Louise Spindler, a husband and wife team of cultural psychologists, was central to this focus. After a conventional psychological training, the Spindlers became interested in ethnographic methods whilst carrying out fieldwork amongst the Menominee Indians over six summers. Together they pioneered an innovative methodological brew that used psychological instruments (such as the Rorschach inkblot test) and theories of personality type to understand processes of what they called 'acculturation' (Spindler and Spindler, 1971). Interested in understanding the cultural and psychological resources individuals use to adapt to situations of social change, the Spindlers continued their work over a long and productive career, carrying out fieldwork amongst several different American Indian groups, as well as leading research teams studying Californian teachers, German villagers and rural Wisconsin schools, all groups Spindler described as 'hinterland populations' (Spindler, 2008).

Working with a range of collaborators over time, they championed a focus on cultural transmission and socialization (Spindler and Spindler, 2000). Whilst Louise died in 1997, George continued to write about projective methods (Spindler and Hammond, 2007) and inter-cultural studies (Spindler and Stockard, 2007), Proud of their involvement in teaching, they also edited a series of accessible and richly descriptive ethnographic 'case studies in education and culture' that sought to bring different educational cultures alive for the non-specialist and to enable comparative research (Spindler, 1982), as well as producing handbooks promoting the field (Spindler, 1963, 1974, 1982). Encouraging a range of scholars to write books with a strong narrative and sense of the researcher's values, the volumes ranged from socialization amongst the Amish (Hostetler and Huntington, 1971) to studies of the Kwakiutl Eskimos (Wolcott, 1967) and the Ngoni in Malawi (Read, 1959). Of these authors, Wolcott went on to write a number of methods texts (Wolcott, 1994, 2008), as well as his influential *The Man in the Principal's Office* (1973 [2003]), an intimate account of a primary school principal and his life.

Despite their role in nurturing the new field – they hosted a major

'Educational Anthropology' conference at Stanford in 1954 (Spindler, 1955) – not everyone was sympathetic to their use of psychological texts or their understanding of culture as a functioning and consensual system. The Spindlers's work was increasingly challenged by anthropologists seeking to draw on more critical sociological and materialist traditions. Examples include the conference and edited volume – also entitled *Anthropology and Education* – convened by Murray Wax, Fred Gearing and Stanley Diamond (1971), about which Spindler was rather disparaging (Spindler, 1973), and the international congress session led by Calhoun and Ianni (1976). Scholars such as John Ogbu questioned the narrow 'microethnographic' focus and the lack of attention to history, power and social structure in the culture-and-personality tradition (see also Levinson, 1992). His own research with African-American students, and their feelings of being a 'caste-like minority' (Ogbu, 1978) also led to work with Signithia Fordham on black students' fears about 'acting white' (Fordham and Ogbu, 1986). Others, such as Enrique Trueba, worked with the Spindlers (for example, Spindler et al., 1989) and found ways of linking their ideas on cultural therapy with more Frierian and critical approaches (Trueba and Zou, 1994).

Thus the field gradually broadened, making links with feminist work on social reproduction (for example, Holland and Eisenhart, 1990), with work on critical pedagogy and with debates in Marxism, for example, Heath's *Ways With Words* (1983) and Gilmore and Glatthorn's work (1982) on language and educational failure in school. The contributions to Levinson et al. (1996) and, more recently, to Levinson and Pollock (2011) capture this diversity, as do the case studies of educational globalization in Anderson-Levitt (2003). Despite these scholarly riches, the American field perceived itself to be somewhat marginal and self-contained, and established graduate programmes are found only in education departments.

Beyond the discipline, there is a great deal of qualitative ethnographic research carried out by educational researchers who feel no need to label themselves as anthropologists (Bogdan and Biklen, 1992). An example would be the work of Alan 'Buddy' Peshkin (1931–2000). Trained in Chicago, his first fieldwork was with schoolchildren in Nigeria (Peshkin, 1972), but he went on to conduct a series of lengthy fieldwork projects in American schools, including an evangelical academy and an elite private school (Peshkin, 1978, 1982, 1986, 1991, 2001). Each was highly readable, nuanced and full of attention to telling details, if less driven by theoretical questions. Unusual in his sustained commitment to fieldwork, his influence as a teacher and a commentator on methodological issues was reflected in a special issue of *Qualitative Research Journal* (Henne and Davison, 2007).

The story of British social anthropology's engagement with education starts during British colonial rule. The debate was initiated by the 1925 Phelps-Stokes commission, a well-meaning Carnegie initiative to transplant ideas about vocational schooling from the American South to Africa. Always on the lookout for funding, Bronislaw Malinowski, who perhaps did more than anyone to secure social anthropology's place within Britain's elite universities (Stocking, 1996; Mills, 2008), took up questions of adaptation and context in his popular writing about the risks of 'culture contact'. Aware of the importance of appealing to missionary philanthropists, Malinowski wrote influentially about education 'being bigger than schools' (Malinowski, 1936, 1943), laying out the challenges of what he called 'transculturation', and the importance of Western educators taking into consideration 'native' systems of informal education.

Whilst by the late 1930s, Malinowski's brand of functionalism was increasingly viewed as past its explanatory best, he continued to have a significant audience amongst colonial educators, and a loyal following amongst his students. Margaret Read, who wrote her doctorate on childhood in Malawi (later published as Read, 1959), began lecturing at the London Institute of Education, and in 1940 was asked to become Head of its Colonial Department. Despite having no training as an educationalist, she went on to become a Professor of Education at the Institute of Education, disseminating ideas about mass education and community development as a member of the Colonial Office's Advisory Committee on Education in the Colonies (Whitehead, 2003) for more than a decade.

Whilst never a theorist, she criticized both anthropologists and educationalists for not working together, arguing that anthropologists felt they had 'more interesting and more urgent problems in cultural change to investigate', whilst educationists were 'impatient with their [anthropologists'] outspoken criticisms and unwilling to revise their aims and methods in the light of these criticisms' (Read, 1955b, p. 74). Her *Education and Social Change in Tropical Areas* (Read, 1955a) was taught in the USA, but she always felt her work was neglected in the UK (Whitehead, 2003). This was hardly surprising. As Malinowski's influence was eclipsed by his rival Radcliffe-Brown's call for a 'natural science of society' (Radcliffe-Brown, 1952), the very colonial contexts that shaped the emergence of 'British social anthropology' were largely effaced in mid-century anthropological monographs. Modernist classics such as Evans-Pritchard's *The Nuer* (1940) relegated issues of missionary influence or formal schooling to footnotes.

Read was not the only mid-century anthropologist to reflect on matters of education and socialization. A 1970 edited volume of anthropological work on education (Middleton, 1970) amounts to a role-call of disciplinary grandees, from Raymond Firth to Melville Herskovits. That none described themselves as anthropologists *of* education reflects the disciplinary pursuit of holism (Thornton, 1988) rather than a disdain for educational concerns.

It was only with the appointment of Max Gluckman, a South African social anthropologist, to a Chair at Manchester University in 1949, that new theoretical debates and ethnographic approaches to education began to emerge. Having led an innovative multidisciplinary research institute in Northern Rhodesia called the Rhodes Livingstone Institute (RLI), Gluckman had an expansive vision for what he called the 'new RLI' at Manchester, developing the social anthropology of contemporary British society. Inspired by Lloyd Warner's work, the appointment of the Harvard sociologist George Homans and Chicago's Edward Shils as visiting research professors added intellectual legitimacy to this vision. Cultivating a strong *espirit de corps* amongst a group of leftist students and researchers, partly through enforced outings to support Manchester United, Gluckman's 'Manchester seminar' developed a fearsome reputation. His students and colleagues developed an innovative corpus of anthropological research 'at home', with notable publications on rural communities (Frankenberg, 1957), factories and coal-mining (Dennis et al., 1956).

The work of the department was linked together by a methodological commitment to the 'extended case-study' (Mills, 2005), a theoretical commitment to combining functionalism and conflict theory, and an epistemological commitment to describe the wider 'social system' in which particular social situations need to be understood. This vision was first laid out in Gluckman's influential account of the opening of a bridge in Zululand, later mythologized by generations of admiring students as simply '*The Bridge*' (Gluckman, 1940 [1958]).

Championing his vision of social anthropology as a 'general teaching subject', Gluckman was particularly keen on promoting anthropology within schools, and he organized a number of conferences with teachers in the mid 1950s. Growing interest in sociology led to the creation of a joint department, and together with the newly appointed Professor of Sociology Peter Worsley, he developed a research proposal to study schools as 'social systems'. In 1962 they obtained a Ministry of Education grant to do a comparative sociological study of two grammar schools in Manchester, with a focus on participant observation. Two of Gluckman's ex-students – Valdo Pons and Ronnie Frankenberg – coordinated the project, and assembled a research team of doctoral students around them. The aim was to use the techniques honed in the study of small-scale societies to study modern institutions, and to address extant policy debates.

Colin Lacey was appointed to the team in 1962, and his doctoral research on a Manchester grammar school was published as *Hightown Grammar* in 1970. David Hargreaves joined in 1963, and later published *Social Relations in a Secondary School* in 1967. A third member of the team – Audrey Lambert – studied social relations amongst girls in an urban grammar school and a secondary modern (Lambart, 1976). Together their work addressed issues that continue to concern many sociologists of education, such as the under-performance of working-class pupils, and the informal social dynamics shaping attitudes to learning and authority. Lacey was interested in the failure of the grammar schools to live up to their founding ideals, whilst Hargreaves focused on the consequences of streaming within a secondary school. Both Lacey's and Hargreaves's ethnographies were highly influential amongst educational ethnographers, if overshadowed by Willis's theoretically ambitious *Learning to Labour* (Willis, 1977) ten years later.

Whilst carrying out participant observation, all three were attracted to sociological ideas as a way of making sense of the implicit class dynamics within the classroom. Their work drew extensively on both Goffman's sociological ideas and the new field of symbolic interactionism, using tools such as sociometry (mapping relationships) to analyse group dynamics within and outside the classroom. As sociology boomed in popularity, many of Gluckman's students went on to posts in new sociology departments. Audrey Lambert worked within the Open University as a staff tutor, whilst Colin Lacey took up a lectureship in sociology at Sussex. After holding posts in education at Manchester and then at Oxford, Hargreaves went on to a career within educational policy. What of Gluckman himself? He found the eclipse of anthropology by the growing popularity of sociology difficult to handle, putting paid to his original research ambitions the denigration of anthropology for its colonial associations. With increasingly divergent research interests, the department acrimoniously split into two.

The generation of ethnographers trained within this raft of new sociology departments owed little allegiance to anthropology. Perhaps the most direct link between what Lacey called the 'third generation' and Manchester anthropology was his supervision of Stephen Ball at Sussex, leading to the publication of *Beachside Comprehensive* (Ball, 1981). Maintaining a commitment to critically addressing policy questions through empirical research, a new community of educational ethnographers increasingly saw the classroom as a site for observation rather than participation (Stubbs and Delamont, 1976). The journal *Ethnography and Education* best represents this work, but rarely engages with theoretical debates in anthropology. Some of this work is reviewed in Chapter 1.

So have social anthropologists in Britain neglected education? Certainly there has been an epistemological reluctance about restricting one's attention to institutional sites. Even the work carried out within the Manchester department sought to situate its cases within larger 'social systems'. But there are other more pragmatic factors to consider. Partly because of the popularity of sociology in the 1950s and 1960s, very few new anthropology departments were created. Even today there are only about 300 anthropologists employed in British university anthropology departments (Mills et al., 2006). Secure within the old universities, anthropologists remained more concerned with disciplinary solidarity and legitimacy than with addressing policy questions (Mills, 2008) or pursuing anthropological research 'at home'. Its small size also made the 'fractal divisions' (Abbott, 2001) and identity politics that characterize other fields less important. The focused thematic conferences of the Association of Social Anthropologists (ASA) of the UK and Commonwealth also resist moves towards over-specialization.

In conclusion, I would suggest that there have been many social anthropologists interested in educative processes. It is just that their theoretical interests overflow any single box or category. Some, such as Maurice Bloch and his students (for example, Rival, 1996), were influenced by Jean Lave's brand of cognitive anthropology, with its attention to cognition in practice, apprenticeship and craft knowledge (Lave and Wenger, 1991). Others focused on the politics of schooling in relation to social identity and nation-building (for example, McDonald, 1989; Reed-Danahay, 1996), or audit culture and its effects on universities (Strathern, 2000); others still looked at issues of childhood literacy and social literacy (James, 1993; Street, 1993). To this day, anthropological journals such as *American Ethnologist, American Anthropology, Cultural Anthropology* and the *Journal of the Royal Anthropological Institute* regularly publish anthropological work that links in some way to educational processes, even if this is not always foregrounded as 'educational ethnography'.

BEING EXPLICIT?

Does anthropology have particular approaches and insights to offer researchers in education? In this section I discuss the embodied nature of ethnographic expertise, the value accorded extended fieldwork and a reluctance to engage in collaborative work.

How do anthropologists learn their ethnographic skills? Marcus (2009, p. 3) has argued that it is 'less a matter of training in method' than of participating in a 'culture of craftsmanship'. Many British social anthropologists, gaining their spurs in a purist disciplinary culture focused on reading (Gay y Blasco and Wardle, 2007), departmental seminars (Spencer, 2000) and extended fieldwork (Marcus and Okely, 2007) would agree. Confident about their intellectual genealogy, they might argue that methods courses and textbooks are unnecessary, as they encourage a one-size-fits-all approach, downplaying the contingencies, uncertainties and anxieties that stimulate the ethnographic imagination. Instead they might advocate learning anthropology by example, through reading, listening and writing. As Neve and Unnithan-Kumar (2006, p. 19) note, 'there is never just one answer to an ethnographic exploration, never only one way of interpreting ethnographic data, and never just one way of being an anthropologist'. Perhaps it is only through helping students imaginatively inhabit and construct a sense of the ethnographic 'field' that one can begin to understand the ethnographic experience and its generative serendipity.

This work demonstrates the intense investment anthropologists have in their ethnographic embodiment. Many would claim that ethnography was not simply another research tool, but rather an ontological commitment to an open-ended, iterative approach to social research, fully acknowledging the complexity and unpredictability of the research encounter. Others would be more purist still, insisting that one only learns fieldwork through fieldwork. Yet not every apprentice anthropologist can access the unstructured methodological ambience of departments grounded in this intellectual tradition. Those anthropologists working outside the discipline may have to negotiate rather more formal expectations about the research process – expectations that foreground rigour, process and accountability. This rather different culture is reflected in the extensive writing and advice on methodological issues amongst sociological ethnographers of education (for example, Hammersley and Atkinson, 1983, 2007); Hammersley, 1995; Walford, 2008), a theme taken up in Chapter 2.

Connected to this embodied knowledge is the commitment to an extended period of 'ethnographic' fieldwork. It is both a disciplinary rite of passage, and a shibboleth of anthropological rigour. The emphasis has been on the quality of the social 'immersion' made possible through linguistic competency and the social relationships that develop over time (Marcus and Okely, 2007). Yet some US anthropological theorists have challenged the 'spatial metaphysics' of the British fieldwork tradition and its fetishization of the 'local'. Gupta and Ferguson (1997) sought to decentre and rethink the field, as the best way of capturing the multiple and multi-stranded networks of contemporary social life. George Marcus labelled this trend 'mobile ethnography': the shift from 'a conventional single-site location . . . to multiple sites of observation and participation', allowing the researcher to follow the 'circulation of cultural meanings, objects, and identities in diffuse time-space' (Marcus, 1995, p. 96). A collection entitled *Fieldwork is Not What it Used to Be* (Faubion and Marcus, 2009) shows how new generations of fieldworkers are rethinking the ethnographic project.

And what of collaboration? Multidisciplinary teams are increasingly common in the social sciences, but the history of anthropology is one of individuals pursuing field research. There is a growing literature on the complexities of working across different analytical frameworks (Strathern, 2004). They pose new ethical and professional challenges for the representation and use of ethnographic knowledge. Some welcome these new possibilities. Attentive to contemporary shifts in academic practice, Marcus has argued for work that 'blurs the boundaries between the professional community of observers and those observed'. The work of Holmes (2006) on the banking industry focuses on 'the key cultural practices of expert subjects' and how they 'converge with our own analytical endeavours' (p. 41). Rabinow and Marcus (2008) argue for a 'design anthropology' that brings together researchers with common interests. There are no easy answers. Collaboration underscores the end of a positivist research paradigm, blurs the us/them distinction and makes participatory knowledge creation more than just a normative vision. As fieldwork engagements become less defined by time and space, they become more intense and complex.

ANTHROPOLOGY AND EDUCATION TODAY

In concluding, a few recent personal favourites. Having worked in Uganda, I find Amy Stambach's work on schooling in East Africa (2000, 2010) helpful for questioning the analytical boundaries erected around both schools and the study of schooling, along with her insistence that 'schools are often pivotal social institutions around which the configuration of society as a whole is imagined, contested and transformed' (2000, p. 3). Kirsten Cheney (2009), also working in Uganda, brings together debates around nation-building, child-centred research and education, as does Kaplan's research on the Turkish 'pedagogical state' (2006). Closer to home, Gillian Evans's work on working-class attitudes to education returns anthropology into the sociological fray (2007). There are many other works that demonstrate anthropologists' ability at making unexpected connections across the social sciences, and at pursuing scholarship that unsettles easy categorization.

This work demonstrates anthropologists' commitment to self-questioning and reflection (see Rabinow and Marcus, 2008). The contributions to Anderson-Levitt (2011) 'parochialize' American and European debates, highlighting how different national traditions have reinterpreted the anthropology of education.

Beyond the anthropology of education, what does the discipline offer to qualitative research in education? At one level, methodological and epistemological 'trading' (Galison, 1997) between fields is always revealing. But I would go further. Anthropologists argue that their combination of theory and method works to challenge preconceived perspectives. This is not just disciplinary identity politics. The experiences of alienation and epistemological rupture that accompany fieldwork provide an antidote to certainty. Haraway's vision of ethnography as a 'method of being at risk in the face of the practices and discourses into which one inquires' (1999, p. 190) is one that many could learn from.

REFERENCES

Abbott, A. (2001), *Chaos of Disciplines*, Chicago, IL: University of Chicago Press.

Acker, S. (1984), *Women and Education* (World year book of education), London: Kogan Page.

Anderson-Levitt, K. (ed.) (2003), *Local Meanings, Global Schooling: Anthropology and World Culture Theory*, New York and Basingstoke: Palgrave Macmillan.

Anderson-Levitt, K.M. (ed.) (2011), *Anthropologies of Education: A Global Guide to Ethnographic Studies of Learning and Schooling*, Oxford: Berghahn.

Ball, S.J. (1981), *Beachside Comprehensive: A Case Study of Secondary Schooling*, Cambridge: Cambridge University Press.

Benedict, R. (1934), *Patterns of Culture*, New York: Houghton Miffin.

Bogdan, R. and Biklen, S.K. (1992), *Qualitative Research for Education: An Introduction to Theory and Methods*, Boston, MA: Allyn and Bacon.

Calhoun, C.J. and Ianni, F.A.J. (1976), *The Anthropological Study of Education* (World anthropology), The Hague: Mouton.

Cheney, K. (2009), *Children, Youth and National Development in Uganda*, Chicago, IL: University of Chicago Press.

Delamont, S. and Atkinson, P. (1980), 'The two traditions in educational ethnography: sociology and anthropology compared', *British Journal of Sociology of Education*, **1** (2), 139–52.

Dennis, N., Henriques, F. and Slaughter, C. (1956), *Coal is Our Life: An Analysis of a Yorkshire Mining Community*, London: Eyre and Spottiswoode.

di Leonardo, M. (1998), *Exotics at Home: Anthropologies, Others, American Modernity*, Chicago, IL: University of Chicago Press.

Eddy, E. (1985), 'Theory, research, and application in educational anthropology', *Anthropology & Education Quarterly*, **16** (2), 92–105.

Evans, G. (2007), *Educational Failure and Working Class White Children in Britain*, London: Palgrave Macmillan.

Evans-Pritchard, E.E. (1940), *The Nuer*, Oxford: Oxford University Press.

Faubion, J.D. and Marcus, G.E. (2009), *Fieldwork is Not What it Used to Be: Learning Anthropology's Method in a Time of Transition*, Ithaca, NY: Cornell University Press.

Foley, D. (1991), 'Rethinking ethnographies of colonial settings: perspectives of reproduction', *Comparative Education Review*, **35** (3), 32–57.

Fordham, S. and Ogbu, J.U. (1986), 'Black students' school success: coping with the "burden of 'acting white'", *The Urban Review*, **18** (3), 176–206

Frankenberg, R. (1957), *The Village on the Border*, London: Cohen and West.

Galison, P. (1997), *Image and Logic: A Material Culture of Microphysics*, Chicago, IL: University of Chicago Press.

Gay y Blasco, P. and Wardle, H. (2007), *How to Read Ethnography*, London: Routledge.

Gilmore, P. and Glatthorn, A. (1982), *Children In and Out of School: Ethnography and Education*, New York: Ablex Press.

Gluckman, M. ([1940] 1958), 'Analysis of a social situation in modern Zululand', *Rhodes Livingstone Papers*, No. 28.

Gupta, A. and Ferguson, J. (1997), *Culture, Power, Place: Explorations in Critical Anthropology*, Durham, NC: Duke University Press.

Hammersley, M. (1995), *The Politics of Social Research*, London: Sage.

Hammersley, M. and Atkinson, P. (1983), *Ethnography: Principles in Practice*, London: Tavistock.

Hammersley, M. and Atkinson, P. (2007), *Ethnography: Principles in Practice*, 3rd edn, London: Routledge.

Haraway, D. (1999), *Modest Witness@Second Millenium: FemaleMan Meets Oncomouse*, London: Routledge.

Hargreaves, D. (1967), *Social Relations in a Secondary School*, London: Routledge.

Henne, R.B. and Davison, J. (2007), 'Introduction: Alan (Buddy) Peshkin (1931–2000) – researcher, methodologist, teacher: a critical analysis of his contributions to qualitative research', *Qualitative Research Journal*, **6** (2), 95–8.

Holland, D. and Eisenhart, M. (1990), *Educated in Romance: Women, Achievement, and College Culture*, Chicago, IL: University of Chicago Press.

Holmes, D.R. (2006), 'Fast capitalism: para-ethnography and the rise of the symbolic analyst', in M. Fisher and G. Downey (eds), *Frontiers of Capital: Ethnographic Reflections on the New Economy*, Durham NC: Duke University Press.

Hostetler, J.A. and Huntington, G.E. (1971), *Children in Amish Society: Socialization and Community Education* (Case studies in education and culture), New York: Holt, Rinehart and Winston, p. xiv.

James, A. (1993), *Childhood Identities: Self and Social Relationships in the Experience of the Child*, Edinburgh: Edinburgh University Press.

Kaplan, S. (2006), *The Pedagogical State: Education and the Politics of National Culture in Post-1980 Turkey*, Palo Alto, CA: Stanford University Press.

Lacey, C. (1970), *Hightown Grammar*, Manchester: Manchester University Press.

Lambart, A. (1976), 'The sisterhood', in M. Hammersley and P. Woods (eds), *The Process of Schooling*, London: Routledge, pp. 152–9.

Lave, J. and Wenger, E. (1991), *Situated Learning: Legitimate Peripheral Participation*, Cambridge: Cambridge University Press.

Levinson, B. (1992), 'Ogbu's anthropology and the critical ethnography of education: a reciprocal interrogation', *International Journal of Qualitative Studies in Education*, **5** (3), 205–25.

Levinson, B.A. and Pollock, M. (2011), *A Companion to the Anthropology of Education*, New York: Blackwells.

Levinson, B. Foley, B.A. and Holland, D. (eds) (1996), *The Cultural Production of the Educated Person: Critical Ethnographies of Schooling and Local Practice*, Albany, NC: SUNY Press.

Malinowski, B. (1936), 'Native education and culture contact', *International Review of Missions*, **25**, 480–515.

Malinowski, B. (1943), 'The Pan-African problem of culture contact', *American Journal of Sociology*, **48** (6), 649–65.

Marcus, G. (1995), 'Ethnography in/of the world system: the emergence of multi-sited ethnography', *Annual Review of Anthropology*, **24**, 95–117.

Marcus, G. (2009), 'Notes towards an ethnographic memoir of supervising graduate research through Anthropology's decades of transformation', in J. Faubion and G. Marcus (eds), *Fieldwork is Not What it Used to Be: Learning Anthropology's Method in a Time of Transition*, Cornell: Cornell University Press, pp. 1–32.

Marcus, G. and Okely, J. (2007), 'How short can fieldwork be?', *Social Anthropology*, **15** (3), 261–4.

McDonald, M. (1989), *'We are Not French!' Language, Culture and Identity in Brittany*, London: Routledge.

Mead, M. (1928), *Coming of Age in Samoa*, New York: W. Montow and Company.

Mead, M. (1951), *The School in American Culture*, Cambridge, MA: Harvard University Press.

Middleton, J. (1970), *From Child to Adult: Studies in the Anthropology of Education* (American Museum sourcebooks in anthropology), Garden City, NY: Natural History Press (published for the American Museum of Natural History).

Mills, D. (1999), '"The nation's valiant fighters against illiteracy": locations of learning and progress', *Social Analysis*, **43** (1), 3–17.

Mills, D. (2005), 'Made in Manchester? Methods and myths in disciplinary history', *Social Analysis*, **49** (3), 129–43.

Mills, D. (2008), *Difficult Folk: A Political History of Social Anthropology*, Oxford: Berghahn.

Mills, D., Anne, J., Coxon, T., Easterby-Smith, M., Hawkins, P. and Spencer, J. (2006), *Demographic Review of the Social Sciences*, Swindon: Economic and Social Research Council.

Neve, G. and Unnithan-Kumar, M. (2006), *Critical Journeys: The Making of Anthropologists*, Maidenhead: Ashgate.

Ogbu, J. (1978), *Minority Education and Caste: The American System in Cross-Cultural Perspective*, New York: Academic Press.

Pelissier, C. (1991), 'The anthropology of teaching and learning', *Annual Review of Anthropology*, **20**, 75–95.

Peshkin, A. (1972), *Kanuri Schoolchildren; Education and Social Mobilization in Nigeria* (Case studies in education and cultures), New York and London: Holt, Rinehart and Winston.

Peshkin, A. (1978), *Growing up American: Schooling and the Survival of Community*, Chicago, IL: University of Chicago Press.

Peshkin, A. (1982), *The Imperfect Union: School Consolidation & Community Conflict*, Chicago, IL: University of Chicago Press.

Peshkin, A. (1986), *God's Choice: The Total World of a Fundamentalist Christian School*, Chicago, IL: University of Chicago Press.

Peshkin, A. (1991), *The Color of Strangers, the Color of Friends: The Play of Ethnicity in School and Community*, Chicago, IL and London: University of Chicago Press.

Peshkin, A. (2001), *Permissible Advantage?: The Moral Consequences of Elite Schooling*, Mahwah, NJ: Lawrence Erlbaum.

Pettitt, G.A. (1946), *Primitive Education in North America*, Berkeley, CA: University of California Press.

Price, D. (2008), *Anthropological Intelligence: The Deployment and Neglect of American Anthropology in the Second World War*, Durham, NC: Duke University Press.

Rabinow, P. and Marcus, E. (2008), *Designs for an Anthropology of the Contemporary*, Durham, NC and London: Duke University Press.

Radcliffe-Brown, A.R. (1952), *Structure and Function in Primitive Society*, London: Cohen and West.

Read, M. (1955a), *Education and Social Change in Tropical Areas*, London and New York: Thomas Nelson.

Read, M. (1955b), 'The contribution of social anthropologists to educational problems in underdeveloped territories', *Fundamental and Adult Education*, **7**, 98–103.

Read, M. (1959), *Children of their Fathers: Growing Up Among the Ngoni of Nyasaland*, London: Methuen.

Reed-Danahay, D. (1996), *Education and Identity in Rural France: The Politics of Schooling* (Cambridge studies in social and cultural anthropology), Cambridge: Cambridge University Press.

Rival, L. (1996), 'Formal schooling and the production of modern citizens in the Ecuadorian Amazon', in B.A. Levinson, B.A. Foley and D.C. Holland (eds), *The Cultural Production of the Educated Person: Critical Ethnographies of Schooling and Local Practice*, Albany, NY: SUNY Press, pp. 153–68.

Spencer, J. (2000), 'British social anthropology: a retrospective', *Annual Review of Anthropology*, **29**, 1–24.

Spindler, G. (1955), *Education and Anthropology*, New York: Russell Sage Foundation.

Spindler, G. (1963), *Education and Culture: Anthropological Approaches*, New York and London: Holt, Rinehart and Winston.

Spindler, G. (1973), 'An anthropology of education?', *Council on Anthropology and Education Newsletter*, **4** (1).

Spindler, G. (1974), *Education and Cultural Process; Toward an Anthropology of Education*, New York: Holt, Rinehart and Winston.

Spindler, G. (1982), *Doing the Ethnography of Schooling: Educational Anthropology in Action*, New York: Holt, Rinehart and Winston.

Spindler, G. (2008), 'Using visual stimuli in ethnography', *Anthropology and Education Quarterly*, **39** (2), 127–40.

Spindler, G.D. and Hammond, L.A. (2006), *Innovations in Educational Ethnography: Theory, Methods and Results*, Mahwah, NJ: L. Erlbaum Associates.

Spindler, G. and Spindler, L. (1971), *Dreamers with Power: The Menominee*, New York: Holt, Rinehart and Winston.

Spindler, G. and Spindler, L. (2000), *Fifty Years of Anthropology and Education, 1950–2000: A Spindler Anthology*, Mahwah, NJ and London: Lawrence Erlbaum.

Spindler, G. and Stockard, J.E. (eds) (2007), *Globalization and Change in Fifteen Cultures: Born in One World, Living in Another*, Belmont, CA: Thomson.

Spindler, G., Spindler, L. and Trueba, H. (eds) (1989), *What Do Anthropologists Have to Say About Dropouts?*, New York: Falmer Press.

Stambach, A. (2000), *Lessons from Mount Kilimanjaro: Schooling, Community, and Gender in East Africa*, New York: Routledge.

Stambach, A. (2010), *Faith in Schools*, Palo Alto, CA: Stanford University Press.

Starn, O. (1986), 'Engineering internment: anthropologists and the War Relocation Authority', *American Ethnologist*, **13** (4), 700–721.

Stocking, G. (1996), *After Tylor: British Social Anthropology 1881–1951*, Wisconsin, WI: University of Wisconsin Press.

Strathern, M. (ed.) (2000), *Audit Cultures: Anthropological Studies in Accountability, Ethics and the Academy*, European Association of Social Anthropology, London: Routledge.

Strathern, M. (2004), *Commons and Borderlands: Working Papers on Interdisciplinarity, Accountability and the Flow of Knowledge*, Wantage: Sean Kingston Publishing.

Street, B. (ed.) (1993), *Cross-cultural Approaches to Literacy*, Cambridge Studies in Oral and Literate Culture, Cambridge: Cambridge University Press.

Stubbs, M. and Delamont, S. (eds) (1976), *Explorations in Classroom Observation*, Chichester: John Wiley and Sons.

Thornton, R. (1988), 'The rhetoric of ethnographic holism', *Cultural Anthropology*, **3** (3), 285–303.

Trueba, H. and Zou, Y. (1994), *Power in Education: The Case of Miao University Students and its Significance for American Culture*, Washington, DC and London: Falmer Press.

Walford, G. (ed.) (2008), *How to do Educational Ethnography*, London: Tufnell Press.

Wax, M. Gearing, F. and Diamond, S. (eds) (1971), *Anthropological Perspectives on Education*, New York: Basic Books.

Whitehead, C. (2003), *Colonial Educators: The British Indian and Colonial Education Service 1858–1983*, London: I.B. Tauris.

Willis, P. (1977), *Learning to Labour: Why Working Class Kids get Working Class Jobs*, Farnborough: Saxon House.

Wolcott, H.F. (1967), *A Kwakiutl Village and School* (Case studies in education and culture), New York and London: Holt, Rinehart and Winston.

Wolcott, H.F. (1994), *Transforming Qualitative Data: Description, Analysis and Interpretation*, London: Sage.

Wolcott, H.F. ([1973] 2003), *The Man in the Principal's Office: An Ethnography*, Updated edn, Walnut Creek, CA and Oxford: AltaMira.

Wolcott, H.F. (2008), *Ethnography: A Way of Seeing*, 2nd edn, Lanham, MD: Altamira Press.

Yon, D. (2003), 'Highlights and overview of the history of educational ethnography', *Annual Review of Anthropology*, **32**, 411–29.

4. Social identities and schooling: ethnographic studies
Sean Kelly and Richard Majerus

Ever since the classic studies of comprehensive schooling in England by Hargreaves (1967), Lacey (1966), Ball (1981), Willis (1977 [1981]) and others, ethnographic research has played a crucial role in understanding how social identities impact the school experience as well as levels of educational inequality. Among the many educational disciplines as a whole, ethnographic methods have made perhaps their most indelible mark by identifying key conceptual dimensions of teaching and learning, which have been articulated as compelling ideal types that have come to define our understanding of how schools work. For example, Metz's (1978) classic study of teacher perspectives on authority in the classroom provided us with the organizing contrast between 'developmental' versus 'incorporative' approaches to instruction. In research on the effects of students' social identities, the peer groups themselves – the 'Lads,' 'Burnouts,' or 'Hallway Hangers' – have become prime examples of oppositional alignments to school. Although such memorable labels tend to obscure the heterogeneity of individuals' alignments to school among the student population as a whole, these compelling portraits of disengagement have made a significant contribution to the educational sciences by uncovering the logic underlying the iterative social negotiations occurring between students, social groups, and schools.

Using the social-psychological framework of Tajfel and Turner (1986), in this chapter we provide a review of four seminal studies of social identity and schooling. On the basis of this review we reach two important conclusions. First, ethnographic studies of social identity confirm Tajfel and Turner's complex framework for understanding how individuals respond to social identities. How low-status student groups respond to educational challenges cannot be neatly predicted. For example, if there is occasionally a 'burden of acting white' among minority students, there are also countervailing processes of collective action that support success in school. Second, even when students exhibit anti-school attitudes, the studies we review demonstrate the powerful social forces acting on low-status students; disengagement with school is not as self-defeating as it may seem at first, and it can rarely be understood as primarily a 'student' problem, detached from the larger institutional context of schools.

SOCIAL IDENTITY THEORY

Traditionally, ethnographies of schooling have demonstrated that a student's social category, whether it be race (Fordham and Ogbu, 1986; Fordham, 1996) or class (Willis, 1977 [1981]; McLaren, 1986 [1999]; Eckert, 1989), is associated with both that student's social status and views of traditional academic success. Students of low academic status, and in particular those from socially disadvantaged origins, may come to reject traditional norms of success in school. Rather than competing with their higher-status schoolmates for high marks and access to higher education, some student groups disengage from school. As a result, low-performing students often engage in behaviors that put them at an even greater disadvantage. How can we understand this type of student disengagement? In this chapter, we review some of the most compelling educational studies of this phenomenon. First though, we introduce social identity theory (Tajfel and Turner, 1979, 1986), which provides a unifying framework for understanding the social processes described in the school-based ethnographies we review here.

A core premise of social identity theory is that individuals aim to maintain a positive self-worth (Goffman, 1963; Covington and Berry, 1976). Tajfel and Turner (1986) extend this reasoning to include social groups, concluding that 'if social groups or categories are differentiated along a status dimension, then low status group members will be driven to correct their low status, either individually or collectively.' Accordingly, Tajfel and Turner's presentation of social identity theory posits three potential avenues for low-status individuals to improve their social positioning, the first of which is individual, while the latter two are based on collective action. These means of garnering social status are referred to as (a) individual mobility, (b) social creativity, and (c) direct competition.

One option for the low-status student is to engage in 'individual mobility', putting forth effort in school and establishing a new identity as a high-performing student. However, for many low-performing students with a history of failure and strained relations with teachers, improving their status in school represents a daunting challenge; the individual mobility option appears to hold little promise. Although individual mobility would appear to be the most 'rational' approach to take, as the studies reviewed here show so well, it is not always pursued.

The most important insight of social identity theory is that it is also possible for an individual to improve their social identity outside of the dominant normative framework in which they are evaluated. A low-status student may seek out other students, who like him have been relegated to low-status positions within their shared schooling environment, and work collectively to redefine their social situation.

Tajfel and Turner's (1986) framework puts forth three 'socially creative processes', which low-status groups may employ in an effort to maintain a positive social identity. First, the low-status peer group may (1) change the social dimension that they, as the in-group, use to compare themselves to the high-status group (that is, the out-group). For example, if the low-status group members are not academically successful students, rather than attempting to individually increase their academic performances, they may collectively establish new norms of pride and accomplishment based on a non-academic dimension of social life, such as 'hooking-up' with members of the opposite sex. In this way, the low-status peer group collectively redefines the social rules governing the within-group distribution of rewards. It is this first form of social creativity which figures most prominently in ethnographic studies of students' social identities. Traditionally, adolescent societies maintain their own well-established, internal system of rewards and sanctions, which are to some extent independent of school-based sources of identity (Coleman, 1961). This process of social creativity, when employed by low-status peer groups in an effort to maintain a positive social identity, leads to disengagement and increasing educational inequality.

Alternatively, the low-status group may (2) change the out-group to which they are compared. For example, the scholastic achievement of immigrant students may look quite favorable when compared to their parents' generation. Yet, in many cases, low-status youth lack alternative frames of reference which would allow them to maintain a positive alignment to school.

Lastly, the low-status group may (3) attempt to change the social value that is assigned to the characteristics and capacities which they already possess. In this case, low-status students attempt to make poor academic performance synonymous with 'being cool.' In school settings this third form of social creativity is rarely effective unless paired with other approaches as the countervailing norm of achievement is too strong.

Finally, a low-status student may again band together with his low status peers in a collective effort to 'directly compete' for social status with the high-status group. However, it is rare in adolescent societies for low-status peer groups to directly compete with high-status groups for social standing; social competition generally takes place on an individual level and within peer groups rather than between them. Efforts to garner status through direct competition, as defined by Tajfel and Turner (1986), are rare in schools because students simply do not have the necessary power (or do not believe they have the power) to take on the social system that has relegated them to a low-status position.

Using the social-psychological framework of Tajfel and Turner (1986), we review Paul Willis's *Learning to Labor* (1977), Penelope Eckert's *Jocks and Burnouts* (1989), Jay MacLeod's *Ain't No Makin' It* (1987 [2009]), and Prudence Carter's *Keepin' It Real* (2005). Low-status students do indeed engage in the forms of social creativity that Tajfel and Turner posited. Importantly, these studies show that when low-status peer groups engage in the most harmful form of social creativity, changing the basis of comparison to a new dimension, the effects on students' attachment to school, engagement in their academic work, and ultimate success are profoundly negative. Yet, low-status students' responses to their social situations vary considerably across and within these four seminal ethnographies of schooling; negative forms of social creativity are not an inevitable reaction to difficulties in school.

WHY THE LADS LEARNED TO LABOR

In the early 1970s, Paul Willis undertook an extensive ethnographic study of social identities and academic engagement at a West Midlands high school, which he called 'Hammertown Boys' (recently revisited in Dolby and Dimitriadis, 2004). At the center of his research was a focal group of 12 working-class white teenage boys, who dubbed themselves 'the Lads.' The Lads reject the notion that education provides opportunities, or is worthwhile. Instead, they intentionally cultivate a counter-school subculture based on having a 'laff,' which describes a plethora of mischievous activities ranging from the covert destruction of school property to overtly mocking the academic efforts of other students. The laffs of the Lads frequently come at the expense of students with pro-school attitudes, who the Lads refer to as 'the Ear'oles.'

Willis's portrait of the Lads is a classic example of social creativity in action. As students from working-class origins that do not do well in school, the Lads are able to maintain a positive social identity by focusing their efforts on hell-raising. While doing well in school would have certainly been an option for some of the Lads, any interest in schoolwork was quickly sanctioned by the others; social creativity is only effective if the attitudes and behaviors of the group reinforce anti-school norms. Central to this successful effort at social creativity is the Lads' projection of manual labor as masculine, and schoolwork as feminine. According to the Lads, academic work is for 'cissies,' while manual labor is men's work. Rejection of schooling among the Lads thus sits at the intersection of both their social class identity and gender identity, and is highly successful. In the Lads' case, that they end up as shop-workers, as their fathers before them, seems on the surface to be a willing (and masculinity-affirming) choice. Willis's study has been critiqued for its singular focus on working-class white males (see Griffin, 2005). Yet, although the Lads' rejection of schooling is notably extreme and their monitoring and sanctioning of pro-school behavior particularly effective, other authors find similar forms of social creativity among mixed-gender and female student groups (Eckert, 1989).

WHY IT MAKES SENSE TO BE A BURNOUT

Like the Lads in *Learning to Labor*, Penelope Eckert's portrait of the Burnouts in *Jocks and Burnouts: Social Categories and Identity in the High School* (1989) is a classic example of how socially creative processes can be used by an adolescent peer group to cultivate a positive social identity. From 1980 to 1982 Eckert conducted ethnographic fieldwork at 'Belten High' in suburban Detroit. Eckert's research at Belten involved a careful sampling of peer group interactions throughout the school (Eckert, 1989, p. 32); her observations capture students' daily routines in both informal and formal activities. Occasionally, her research spilled outside of school walls as she accompanied students to various hangouts. In addition, Eckert conducted in-depth interviews (including information on students' family background) with 118 male and female students, as well as less formal group interviews. As in other studies, group interviews often proceeded as unstructured discussions (Currie, Chapter 29, this volume); yielding insight into how peer groups oriented themselves to the social world of Belten. Her fieldwork at Belten High was supplemented by four separate one to two month ethnographic research experiences at four additional suburban high schools. In each of these schools, she found a certain class-based social opposition, which unlike the Willis's gender-based social creativity affected the social experiences of all students.

At Belten High the Jocks, who are primarily from middle-class backgrounds, embrace traditional norms of academic achievement and participate fully in school-sponsored extracurricular activities, while the Burnouts, who are primarily from working-class backgrounds, reject the social world of the school. If the Burnouts themselves seem somewhat less intensely anti-school than the Lads, their perspective is more widespread, and thus has a profound impact on educational inequality at Belten. The difference between the Jocks and Burnouts in their alignments to school is part of the reason why middle-class students are so much more successful at Belten than the working-class students.

The Jocks are Eckert's Ear'oles, or the cultural category she uses to label students who buy into the 'corporate life' of the school. The 'Jock' label is not meant to pertain solely to athletes and cheerleaders, but rather, it applies to all students who participate eagerly in the status hierarchy of officially sponsored school activities, from sports to yearbook, and includes both the schools' social elite and those who merely strive to be popular. The hub of a Jock's life is their participation in the school 'team': they attend class, participate in extracurricular activities, study diligently, and conceal any actions that may be perceived as rebellious from teachers. In return, they receive deference from teachers and administrators.

Similarly, while Eckert's use of the 'Burnout' label carries a certain connotation of drug use, drug use was in no way a prerequisite to group membership, nor is it the defining characteristic of the Burnouts. Rather, the dress, language, and behavior of the Burnouts are designed to signal their rejection of the ethos of the school. As in other instances of disengagement, many of the Burnouts at Belten have a history of failure and frustration at school, either in the academic or social realms. The Burnouts' opposition to school is exacerbated by the fact that they are largely relegated to low-track and vocational classes, which gives them little incentive to achieve.

As with any effort at social creativity, the Burnouts' rejection of school is accompanied by an elaborated set of anti-school norms and peer group enforcement of these norms; there is a certain inertia to the social categories at Belten High that perpetuates educational inequality as entering students are recruited into the disparate cultures of the Jocks and Burnouts. But why would a student find participation in the Burnout life attractive when the Jocks clearly experience a much greater degree of academic success? Eckert's detailed analysis shows that (1) the academic school experience at Belten High is a poor fit for many students' family backgrounds, occupational expectations, and lives outside of school; and (2) the Burnouts' social network meets low-status students' personal and social needs. Although the Burnouts' alignment to school will likely damage their chance to attain professional and managerial jobs, it provides much needed social support.

The Burnouts justify their rebellious attitudes and behaviors in part as a response to what they perceive as the school's imposition of a hegemonic formal curriculum (Connell et al., 1982), which in addition to being perceived as substantively irrelevant, emphasizes individual competition rather than cooperation. The formal curriculum at Belten, as at most comprehensive high schools, emphasizes traditional academic knowledge, and individual competition for grades and teacher praise. Academically, in the Burnouts' eyes, most of Belten High's curriculum is culturally irrelevant; it doesn't provide concrete skills that will enable them to be successful in the working-class labor market. While many of the Burnouts do take full advantage of the schools' vocational curriculum, those course offerings are underdeveloped, and it is clear that such courses are not taken as seriously by the school as the core academic curriculum. Moreover, the hegemonic curriculum fails to teach the soft skills that students need to succeed in the working-class labor market. Belten's working-class students view their classmates not as competitors in the race to acquire the best grade point average, but as future friends and co-workers; their goal is to cultivate the social networks that will enable them to gain autonomy from their parents and help them negotiate the transition to an independent, adult lifestyle.

In addition to their perception of the school curriculum as irrelevant and overly competitive, the Burnouts are bound together by shared experiences of social and academic struggle, and have developed supportive social norms. In contrast, the Jocks are focused on moving up the school's social status hierarchy and participate in activities that will make them the most popular and help distinguish themselves on college applications. The Jocks compete fiercely for social status, often tearing each other down in the process. In contrast, the Burnouts build each other up. In establishing their independence from the schooling environment, the Burnouts cultivate a self-sufficient, egalitarian peer group with a high degree of social solidarity. Compared to the Jocks, the Burnouts' peer groups may be characterized by two distinctive features – (1) a higher degree of independence; and (2) a more open and welcoming social dynamic – which make group membership attractive for students who have struggled to compete with the more successful Jocks in the corporate life of the school.

First, the Burnouts have much greater independence from traditional forms of authority than do the Jocks. In the pursuit of this independence, the Burnouts cultivate a lifestyle that is more adult-like; many of the Burnouts work while attending school and hope to start full-time jobs upon graduating, in addition to maintaining more serious romantic relationships, and some even live in their own apartments. Whereas the Jocks rely on school-sponsored activities to meet their social needs, the Burnouts fulfill their social needs internally and without adult support. The school and teachers act as gatekeepers of a college education for the Jocks, while it is the Burnout social network itself that they will likely draw on throughout their lives for social support as well as for economic assistance, namely, employment.

Second, the Burnout peer group is simply more welcoming than the Jocks. The Jocks must earn social power and prestige by coming of age within the school system and accordingly have to wait their turn to be a member of the Jock 'in-group.' Conversely, the Burnouts have a high degree of age-integration and welcome group members from all grades. Rather than requiring prospective group members to earn their group affiliation, like the Jocks, the Burnouts tend to make 'new recruits' feel wanted and good about themselves. Many Jocks feel that in order to succeed socially and run with the 'in-crowd' they must remain socially guarded, maintaining a pristine image. In contrast, the Burnouts, many of whom come from troubled backgrounds at home, display the exact opposite social outlook; they explicitly declare that it is 'ok to have problems' and view people who pretend to have idyllic family lives and to always be in a good mood as 'phonies.' For many students it makes a great deal of sense to affiliate with the Burnouts. Burnout membership provides students with what they are denied at Belten High, namely, working-class social skills and an open and supportive social network.

WHY THE BROTHERS BELIEVE

MacLeod's (1987 [2009]) *Ain't No Makin' It* presents another portrait of opposing peer groups, the 'Hallway Hangers' and the 'Brothers,' with an interesting twist: the students who are expected to fail don't. MacLeod's ethnographic study is similar to the work of Willis in that both focus exclusively on male peer groups. The Hallway Hangers, a lower-class white peer group comprised of eight young men, and the Brothers, a lower-class black peer group comprised of seven to ten young men, inhabit the same geographic, educational, and economic spheres and yet, it is the Brothers who develop and maintain pro-school attitudes, while the Hallway Hangers cultivate a counter culture based on anti-institutional norms. MacLeod's Hallway Hangers are as self-destructive as any of the Lads or Burnouts; they too develop an anti-institutional peer culture that hinges on hanging out, using drugs, and committing crimes (although it also includes positive experiences such as working). Conversely, the Brothers, who encounter the same bleak socioeconomic environment as the Hallway Hangers, fully embrace the institutional norms of Lincoln High. The Brothers attend class, study diligently, and participate in extracurricular activities. In MacLeod's words, 'the Brothers . . . accept the dominant culture's definitions of success and judge themselves by these criteria' (p. 45). Or as one of the Brothers puts it: 'I know I want a good job when I get out. I know that I have to work hard in school' (p. 98).

For MacLeod a distinctive feature of the Hallway Hangers is their inability to embrace the system of delayed gratification that undergirds the American educational institution. Although the Hangers would have liked to escape the tattered and torn neighborhoods their families had lived in for generations, school was seen as an obstacle to meeting their immediate economic and social needs. Furthermore, from the Hallway Hangers' perspective recent and current social policies and movements, especially the civil rights movement and affirmative action policies, favored African-Americans, not poor whites. The Hangers see their social position as worse than that of their parents and believe there is no viable route to social mobility for them. As low-achieving students, their day-to-day lives at school are not particularly rewarding, nor do they view the ultimate returns to education very favorably. Accordingly, the Hangers choose to rebel against the schooling institution, and develop – borrowing the description from Cohen's (1955) early work on delinquency – 'new criteria of status which define as meritorious the characteristics they *do* possess, the kinds of conduct of which they *are* capable' (p. 66, emphasis in original).

The Brothers, who also face difficulties in school, practice a different form of social creativity. Rather than comparing themselves to other students, as the Lads did with the Ear'oles, the Brothers derive their social status from comparisons with their parents' generation. On a micro-level, the Brothers view their situation positively because their families had recently been forced to relocate from a condemned housing development into what – at least to the Brothers – was a significantly better housing development. On a macro-level, the Brothers believe that their socioeconomic outlook was significantly improved, relative to that of their parents, because of the civil rights movement and affirmative action policies. Moreover, the Brothers know that those of their parents' generation were victims of racial injustice, and so they see their individual efforts in school as part of a collective effort to improve the social circumstances of African-Americans.

The different responses of the Brothers and Hallway Hangers to similar social circumstances clearly illustrates that students' collective response to low status is not always negative. The Brothers, largely as a result of viewing their social position relative to that of their parents, are dedicated to making good on the sacrifices of their parents' generation and firmly believe that hard work will pay off for them. In the Brothers' eyes their parents' sacrifices have opened social and economic doors for them. Race, the Brothers believe, is becoming less of a structural barrier in American society. The Brothers' alternative frame of reference not only allows them to maintain a positive social identity, but also helps them to cultivate pro-school attitudes and to achieve at a significantly higher academic level than the Hallway Hangers.

WHY THE STRADDLERS SUCCEED

In her 2005 work *Keepin' It Real: School Success Beyond Black and White,* Carter, like her predecessors, examines disadvantaged high school students who are collectively at risk of developing anti-school norms. In her ethnographic study, which makes use of surveys, interviews, and general observational techniques, Carter focuses on a large, mixed-gendered group of students: 68 African-American and second-generation Latino high school students in Yonkers, New York, the majority of whom are from disadvantaged family backgrounds. Like Eckert, Carter conducted both one-on-one and group interviews. Although Carter's interviews were somewhat more structured, the goal was the same, to illicit shared meanings and understandings, in this case concerning identity, culture, and achievement. As in the other studies we've reviewed, Carter found many students whose low performance in school was exacerbated by their race/ethnic identity. Yet, their rejection of school is less complete than in other studies, and it entails disillusionment with the cultural markers and practices of school, rather than norms of academic achievement. Carter labels such students 'noncompliant believers,' because while they maintain an underlying perspective which values academic achievement, they actively seek to distance themselves from the culture of the school in favor of styles of dress, language, and cultural preferences which create a sense of solidarity and distinctiveness among their race/ethnic peer group. As theorized by Mickelson (1990), in the abstract, the non-compliant believers hold an academic achievement ideology, but when it comes to concrete attitudes about school, teachers, and some specific aspects of school work, they are not so sanguine. Thus, certain elements of their youth culture, such as physical mannerism, style of dress, and linguistic codes, which the students used to cultivate group solidarity, are often perceived as a rejection of academic material by teachers and other school personnel, and the net effect, although unfair to the students, is lower performance in school. Although boys were somewhat more likely to be non-compliant believers than girls in Carter's study, at least half of the girls underperformed in school and felt pressure to maintain a 'tough' image (p. 94).

Then there are students who chose to act individually. A certain proportion of the students Carter studied came close to abandoning the observable cultural markers of their race/ethnic peer groups in favor of dominant cultural practices. Carter calls this second category of students 'cultural mainstreamers.'

The primary contribution of *Keepin' It Real* to the ethnographic literature on students' social identities is Carter's in-depth treatment of a third category of students she terms 'cultural straddlers.' Like the cultural mainstreamers, the cultural straddlers successfully negotiate the cultural norms of the school, but they are equally at ease with non-dominant ways of being. Rather than creating an entirely new set of social norms, the cultural straddlers switch back and forth between the cultural practices that are prevalent in (1) their racial peer community and (2) the traditional academic setting. They are thus regarded as competent, respected, and worthy within both the traditional schooling environment and their ethnically based peer group. The cultural straddlers literally move back and forth between 'white' and 'black' patterns of speech and behavior as dictated by the social situation. To talk one way at home and with friends, and another way at work or school, is a way for the cultural straddlers to avoid negative institutional judgments or being labeled as 'acting white' by less culturally adept peers. The cultural straddlers accomplish both the utilitarian goal of succeeding in school and the expressive goal of 'just being yourself' around friends.

The cultural straddlers reject the peer group sanctioning of mainstream approaches to academic striving which are central to negative forms of social creativity, but importantly, they do not reject their peers underlying source of a positive social identity – their cultural distinctiveness and pride. This strategy has allowed the cultural straddlers to be successful within the dominant schooling culture without completely assimilating and losing the 'sense of belonging, distinction, and support for how to critique and cope with inequality' that come from being a member of the minority peer culture (Carter, 2005, p. 6). For Carter, these students are the key to improving the academic achievement of the non-compliant believers. Cultural straddlers can concretely demonstrate to their fellow students how to coexist in what are traditionally viewed as mutually exclusive social spheres, and help disrupt the sanctioning of pro-school behaviors which accompany negative forms of social creativity.

CONCLUSION

Much educational inequality can ultimately be traced to the accumulating effect of disparities in engagement over the course of students' school careers. Thus, understanding the underlying sources of student disengagement and developing ways to foster widespread engagement and achievement motivation are central to providing equality of educational opportunity. In the social comparative world of schools, it is never easy to be on the bottom rung of the ladder, to struggle with math, literacy skills, or to be placed in a low-track ability group or classroom. When low academic status overlaps with students' social identities, educators are rightly concerned that the norms and behaviors of student peer groups will exacerbate problems of student disengagement, as students look for ways to maintain a positive social identity and sense of self-worth.

A rich body of ethnographic research on social identities and schooling details how this process occurs; from the development of an alternative system of norms to the monitoring and sanctioning of pro-school behavior, negative forms of social creativity can have powerful effects on patterns of student engagement. Yet, consistent with the broader framework of social identity theory, ethnographic research shows that disengagement is not the inevitable result of initial difficulties in school. Indeed, MacLeod's Brothers and Carter's cultural straddlers, as well as other examples that might have been discussed, show that social identities can serve as resources for a collective reinforcement of pro-achievement behavior.

Even when negative forms of social creativity do exist, this body of research shows that we must resist the temptation to treat disengagement as primarily a 'student' problem; attributable to an irrational and unprovoked dislike of school that is cultural in nature. As disruptive as the behavior of the Lads, Hallway Hangers, or Burnouts might be, it is at its most essential, an effort to maintain a positive sense of self-worth. This is an intrinsic human motive. As Eckert so carefully details, there is much that is positive about the Burnout peer culture. It is worth asking if today's schools, which operate in the era of test-based accountability, might do much more to meet students' social and personal needs. Moreover, these studies often reveal an institutional context, in terms of a curriculum that is highly stratified, predicated on individual competition, and which is disconnected from the lives of many disadvantaged and minority students, that makes problems of student engagement likely to occur.

REFERENCES

Ball, S.J. (1981), *Beachside Comprehensive: A Case Study of Secondary Schooling*, London: Cambridge University Press.

Carter, P.L. (2005), *Keepin' It Real: School Success Beyond Black and White*, New York: Oxford University Press.

Cohen, A.K. (1955), *Delinquent Boys*, Glencoe, IL: Free Press.

Coleman, J. (1961), *The Adolescent Society*, New York: Free Press of Glencoe.

Connell, R.W., Ashenden, D.J., Kessler, S. and Dowsett, G.W. (1982), *Making the Difference: Schools, Families, and Social Division*, St Leonards, Australia: Allen & Unwin.

Covington, M. and Berry, R. (1976), *Self-worth and School Learning*, New York: Holt, Rinehart and Winston.

Dolby, N. and Dimitriadis, G. with Willis, P. (2004), *Learning to Labor in New Times*, New York: Routledge Falmer.

Eckert, P. (1989), *Jocks and Burnouts: Social Categories and Identity in the High School*, New York: Teachers College Press.

Fordham, S. (1996), *Blacked Out: Dilemmas of Race, Identity, and Success at Capital High*, Chicago, IL: University of Chicago Press.

Fordham, S. and Ogbu, J.U. (1986), 'Black students' school success: coping with the "burden of acting white"', *The Urban Review*, **18**, 176–206.

Goffman, E. (1963), *Stigma: Notes on the Management of Spoiled Identity*, Englewood Cliffs, NJ: Prentice Hall.

Griffin, C. (2005), 'Whatever happened to the (likely) Lads? "Learning to Labour" 25 Years on Christine Griffin', *British Journal of Sociology of Education*, **26** (2), 291–7.

Hargreaves, D.H. (1967), *Social Relations in a Secondary School*, London and Henley: Routledge and Kegan Paul.

Lacey, C. (1966), 'Some sociological concomitants of academic streaming in a grammar school', *British Journal of Sociology*, **17**, 245–62.

MacLeod, J.C ([1987] 2009), *Ain't No Makin' It: Leveled Aspirations in a Low-income Neighborhood*, 3rd edn, Boulder, CO: Westview Press.

McLaren, P. ([1986] 1999), *Schooling as a Ritual Performance*, 3rd edn, Lanham, MD: Rowman & Littlefield Publishers.

Metz, M.H. (1978), *Classrooms and Corridors: The Crisis of Authority in Desegregated Secondary Schools*, Berkeley CA: University of California Press.

Mickelson, R.A. (1990), 'The attitude-achievement paradox among black adolescents', *Sociology of Education*, **63**, 44–61.

Tajfel, H. and Turner, J.C. (1979), 'An integrative theory of intergroup conflict', in S. Worchel and W.G. Austin (eds), The *Social Psychology of Intergroup Relations*, Chicago, IL: Nelson-Hall, pp. 33–47.

Tajfel, H. and Turner, J.C. (1986), 'The social identity theory of intergroup behavior', in S. Worchel and W.G. Austin (eds), *The Social Psychology of Intergroup Relations*, 2nd edn, Chicago, IL: Nelson-Hall, pp. 7–24.

Willis, P. ([1977] 1981), *Learning to Labor: How Working Class Kids Get Working Class Jobs*, New York: Columbia University Press.

5. Linguistic perspectives in qualitative research in education: a brief history
Judith Green and Anissa Stewart

Over the past six decades qualitative researchers in education, grounded in developments in linguistics, have contributed to systematic empirical qualitative approaches to studying what is accomplished in and through language in use in educational settings. These developments are intertwined with developments in anthropology, education, linguistics, and sociology, among other fields, in which a linguistic perspective is used to address areas of interest to the discipline. In this chapter, we examine developments across programs of research that today constitute a field called 'language and education' – (Corson, 1997; Hornberger, 2008) for example, anthropological linguistics, conversation analysis, critical discourse analysis, discourse analysis, ethnomethodology, ethnography of communication, microethnography, narrative analysis, sociolinguistics, and sociology of language.[1]

Two interdependent goals guide our approach. The first goal is to describe the roots of social, cultural, and linguistic challenges in education that the programs of research were developed to address, and how the conceptual focus on 'language in use' provides an empirical, grounded approach to understanding how language is constitutive of educational processes as well as an outcome of the work of people in formal and informal educational settings. The second goal is to make visible a developing set of conceptual principles (Heath, 1982; Green et al., in press), 'logic of inquiry' (orienting theory/theories), underlying the conceptualization of language in use 'as epistemology', as a way of knowing, not a method (Agar, 2006). By focusing on epistemological decisions, we make visible conceptual principles guiding qualitative researchers and through these principles make 'transparent' what counts as a linguistically grounded 'logic in use' (for example, Kaplan, 1964 [1998]; Birdwhistell, 1977; Green and Bloome, 1997; Gee and Green, 1998) and kinds of phenomena studied.

HISTORICAL ROOTS: CONCEPTUALIZING LANGUAGE IN USE AS EPISTEMOLOGY

Underlying developments in studying 'language in use' in educational contexts is a philosophical turn toward natural language in social and human sciences. Central to this turn are two interdependent conceptual arguments: the social construction of reality (Berger and Luckmann, 1966); and everyday life as socially constructed in and through everyday language in use of participants in social events (for example, Malinowski, 1922, 1967; Wittgenstein, 1958, cited in Sheridan et al., 2000; Gumperz and Hymes, 1964, 1972; Hymes, 1977; Kelly et al., 2000). The turn to 'language in use/linguistics' constitutes a reformulation of language as serving social and referential functions within and across social groups; that is, as a means of communicating, achieving personal and collective goals, and of constructing the events, meanings, processes, and practices of life.

The impact of this turn for studies in education across national borders will become visible as we trace the roots of qualitative research from a linguistic perspective. To illustrate this turn, we provide a sketch map of work in the UK and the USA from the 1960s to make visible how these epistemological directions led to (re)formulations of the relationship of language and education from one of 'linguistic deficits' to 'linguistic differences' to 'language in use' as constitutive of educational processes, practices, and knowledge constructions. Throughout the chapter, we add to this sketch map by including citations to work from a broad range of researchers in different national contexts.

THE UK: (RE-)EXAMINING ROOTS OF EDUCATIONAL FAILURE

The US and UK roots are diverse, and a complete explication is beyond the goals of this chapter. Therefore, we provide a sketch map of the roots in the UK and the USA. The UK programs of research have two roots, one grounded in linguistics and one in sociology. Doughty and Thornton (1973), in their general introduction to early work by linguist M.A.K. Halliday (1973), state that

> Many teachers . . . see themselves that 'Educational failure is primarily *linguistic* failure', and have turned to Linguistic Science for some kind of exploration and practical guidance. Many of those now exploring the problems of relationships, community or society, from a sociological or psychological point of view wish to make use of a linguistic approach to the language in so far as it is relevant to these problems. (p. 3, emphasis added)

This exploration led Halliday and other linguists to develop conceptual approaches to examining systematically the relationships between spoken and written language in use (for example, Stubbs, 1976, 1980, 1983; Wilkinson, 1982; Halliday, 2003). Building on the interplay between spoken and written language in use, researchers have developed new interdisciplinary fields that explore the often dynamic relationship among oral, written and graphic texts. These fields are referred to as 'New literacy studies' (for example, Gee, 1996; Lea and Street, 2006; Coiro, et al., 2008) and as semiotic studies of multimodal literacies (for example, Kress and Van Leeuwen, 2001).

The interdisciplinary nature of the UK dialogues is visible in a seminal volume at the intersection of sociology, sociolinguistics, and education, by sociologist Basil Bernstein (Bernstein, 1971) and his colleagues. This edited collection, the first of a series of published volumes, explored social phenomena at the intersection of language and lore of school children, linguistic codes, hesitation phenomena, intelligence, social class, grammatical elements, and a sociolinguistic approach to social learning, among others (see Atkinson et al., 1995 and Bernstein, 1996 for a history of this work). Together, these linguistic and sociological traditions provided a basis for understanding the complex nature of language in use. For examples of the international impact of these bodies of work see Christie and Misson (1998).

US ROOTS: FROM LINGUISTIC DEFICIT TO THE LINGUISTIC DIFFERENCE THESIS

US scholars from anthropology, education, linguistics, psychology, and sociology met in 1965–66 to propose a research agenda focusing on children's language and its relationships to school success (Cazden et al., 1972; Gage, 1974). An initial outcome of these meetings was a volume designed to 'illuminate the communicative demands of the school and the sociolinguistic discontinuities between a child's home community and his school culture' (Cazden, 1972b, p. viii). This interdisciplinary volume examined perspectives from nonverbal communication, varieties of language and verbal repertoire, and varieties of communicative strategies. These areas brought to the fore ways of communicating by different social, cultural, and linguistic groups.

This work, combined with work in the UK, made visible reasons for, and roots of, 'minority group school failure' (Gumperz and Cook-Gumperz, 2005). These studies were a response to dominant cognitive and behavioral approaches that viewed minority students as linguistically deprived, a perspective known as the 'linguistic deficit thesis' (for example, Bereiter and Engleman, 1966; Hess and Shipman, 1966). According to Gumperz and Cook-Gumperz (2006), this perspective 'suggested that the cultural environment in which low-performing children grew up did not provide adequate exposure to adult talk, resulting in lack of verbal stimulation that in turn impeded cognitive development' (p. 51). The deficit language thesis constituted a form of biological and environmental determinism, which led educators to develop programs designed to 'compensate' for perceived deficiency in what was called 'standard language' or schooled language. Hymes (1972) argued that research on linguistic deficit was based on anecdotal evidence of language, not on systematic empirical analysis of language in use within and across social groups in classrooms and communities. Therefore, the deficit model became the center of challenges based on studies of language in use (for example, Bernstein, 1971; Labov, 1972; Cook-Gumperz, 1986 [2006]; Rampton, 2000; Rampton et al., 2008).

The turn in the USA, therefore, was a turn 'away from' the linguistic deficit thesis, which in turn led to a (re)formulation of what counted as language. That is, 'away from' views of language as opaque – as a surrogate for a behavior or process that was context free 'to' language as communication in and across particular contexts of use. Thus, researchers guided by a language in use epistemology focused on studying how and in what ways, for what purpose(s), with whom, under what conditions, when and where, and with what outcomes or consequences language was used to accomplish social or academic life in classrooms and other contexts (Hymes, 1972; Green, 1983; Castanheira et al., 2007). This turn enabled researchers to examine how the different ways of using language in different contexts led to differences in social, cultural, and linguistic backgrounds of students, and how such differences supported and constrained access to academic work in classrooms. This thesis became known as the 'linguistic "difference" thesis' (Gumperz and Cook-Gumperz, 2005).

Hymes (1972) captured the conceptual basis of the language difference thesis succinctly in his argument that language 'may be said to constitute the *ways of speaking of a person, a group, or a community*' (p. xxiv, emphasis added):

> Means of speech may be differentiated from one another in many ways . . . indeed, by any and all of the elements that go to make up language and discourse. There is no way to decide except by discovering empirically just what features have been so used . . . Everything depends, not on the presence of variation in speech . . . but on whether, and to what extent difference is invested with social meaning . . . It is a principle fundamental to linguistics, namely, that the

meaningfulness of language is interwoven of two kinds of meaning, 'referential' and 'social.' (p. xxv)

Hymes (1972) further characterized the conceptual arguments as follows:

> The source of difficulty is that knowledge of a common language has been taken as equivalent to common understanding, or as linguists say, mutual intelligibility. It has become clear that mutual understanding depends not only on common linguistic means, in the narrow sense, but also on common ways of using and interpreting speech. People who know the same sounds, words, and syntax may not know the same rules for interpreting utterances as requests or commands; the same rules for the topics that can be introduced among people not intimate with each other; for taking turns and getting the floor; for making allusions, avoiding insults, showing respect and self-respect in choice of words, etc. In sum, mutual intelligibility is a function of shared means of speech, but the requisite means of speech include not only some variety of language but also its mode of use. (p. xx)

From this perspective, to study and understand the functions of language in the classroom, researchers need to consider more than language.

Over the next four decades, US qualitative researchers built on these understandings to generate a broad range of research examining what counts as language in classrooms, how language in use is consequential for what is possible to know, who people can be seen to be, and what is accomplished in and through verbal and written communication, among other social, cultural, and linguistic processes, modes, and outcomes (for example, Frederiksen, 1975, 1986; Green, 1979; Frederiksen et al., 1981; Green & Wallat, 1981; Gilmore and Glatthorn, 1982; Wilkinson, 1982; Bloome, 1985, 1987; Cazden, 1988; Golden, 1988; Green and Harker, 1988; Wells, 2000; Erickson, 2004; Bazerman, 2006; Duff, 2008). Summaries of this work can be found in Bloome and Clark (2006), Bloome and Green (1991), Gee (1990), Gee and Green (1998), and Hicks (1995).

TRACING CONTRIBUTIONS TO A DEVELOPING LOGIC OF INQUIRY

In this section, we describe conceptual and methodological contributions to qualitative research in education across programs of research. The contributions are presented as a set of conceptual principles: (1) members socially construct situated and contextualized perspectives on what counts as ways of knowing, being, and doing life in educational settings; (2) what counts as disciplinary knowledge is socially constructed; (3) multiple analyses of common records/data make visible differences in what can be

known through a particular program of research or theoretical perspective; and (4) video or audio recording are records and not the phenomena.

Conceptual Principle 1: Members socially construct local, situated and con-
textualized perspectives on what counts as ways of knowing, being, and doing
in educational settings.

At the center of the work on language in use is a converging set of ontological arguments about how knowledge and everyday life in classrooms,
as a form of reality, is socially constructed. The conceptual arguments
that follow constitute a sketch map of complementary perspectives that,
when brought together, provide a conceptual 'logic of inquiry' or what
Gumperz (cited in Gumperz and Levinson, 1996; Evertson and Green,
1986; Gumperz, 1986) calls a 'mental grid' or what we call an 'orienting
theory' (Green and Dixon, 1993) guiding qualitative studies of language
in use in education.
    Table 5.1 provides a sketch map of conceptual views of language in
use and its relationship to social life. The works cited represent interdisciplinary and international programs of research on language in use.
Collectively, the work cited constitutes a 'telling case' (Mitchell, 1984) of
how complementary arguments about the relationship of language in use
to social life are necessary to understand the orienting frameworks guiding
qualitative research on language in use in education. That is, these quotations and statements constitute the 'logic of inquiry' that makes theoretically transparent conceptual arguments guiding epistemological decisions
that constitute the researcher's 'logic in use' (Kaplan, 1964 [1998]) within
a particular project. Therefore, these conceptual arguments make visible
why we conceptualized language in use as 'epistemology'; that is, as a way
of knowing.

Conceptual Principle 2: What counts as disciplinary and social knowledge is
socially constructed.

Qualitative researchers in education have used particular dimensions presented in Conceptual Principle 1 to examine how disciplinary knowledge
is socially constructed, and thus how curriculum is talked into being (for
example, Bernstein, 1975; Barnes, 1976 [1992]; Barnes and Todd, 1977,
1995; Weade, 1987; Green and Dixon, 1993; Mercer and Hodgkinson,
2008). Discipline areas studied include: literacy, mathematics, the arts,
and science, among others.[2] This body of research argues that what students are afforded as science, mathematics, or arts in classrooms is not
what is planned prior to interactions but rather what is constructed in and

Table 5.1   *Conceptual views of language in use and its relationship to social life*

Conceptual Principle	Illustrative Work
A sociological approach to understanding action/discourse-as-action can illuminate what might otherwise be considered hidden dimensions and relationships, if we accept that:	Heap, 1980, 1991 Castanheira et al., 2001

- The individual is defined as an actor in a social system.
- It is imperative to define the situation as formulated by the actors.
- An actor defines his/her situation through interactions with others.
- An actor acts consciously.
- An actor has preferences.
- Each actor aligns his/her actions to the actions of others by ascertaining what they are doing or intend to do – in other words, by 'getting at' the meaning of their acts.
- Social structures are stable and governed by rules (norms, values), which may, or may not, be complete and are observable through the actions of others.

From an anthropological perspective, an interdependent relationship exists between '*language*' and '*culture*'. Agar (1994) argues that 'Language, in all its varieties, in all the ways it appears in everyday life, builds a world of meanings. When you run into different meanings, when you become aware of your own work to build a bridge to the others, "culture" is what you're up to. Language fills the spaces between us with sound; culture forges the human connection through them. Culture is in language, and language is loaded with culture' (p. 28). This interdependence Agar calls '*languaculture*'.	Bronson and Watson-Gegeo, 2008; Vine, 2003
From a linguist's perspective, language is viewed as a 'social semiotic' (Halliday, 1978). Cook-Gumperz (1981) characterizes the theory in this way: 'language is seen as existing within a complex pattern of social behavior to be used to achieve socially defined goals' (p. 27).	Vine, 2003
From a sociolinguistic perspective, Cook-Gumperz (1981, p.27) argues that 'Children [and others] interpret what other people mean when they speak, by drawing on their growing linguistic knowledge, as well *accumulated situational knowledge* developed through their social experiences'.	Cook-Gumperz, 1981 Gumperz, 1986

Table 5.1   (continued)

Conceptual Principle	Illustrative Work
From an interactional sociolinguistic perspective, Gumperz (1986) argues that people bring linguistic, cultural, and social presuppositions to new social situations that they use to interpret what is happening, how, in what ways, for what purposes, with what outcomes or consequences of their participation in developing events.	Green et al., 2011
From an ethnography of communication perspective, Hymes (1977) argues 'The fundamental point here is that when we reach consideration of style, we inevitably reach consideration of styles. Even when a speaker of a language can be thought of as having a single grammar, he or she cannot be thought of as having a single style. When we reach consideration of styles, we must consider speakers as having, not a grammar, but a verbal repertoire. In some cases that repertoire may comprise more than one language. In every case the consistent continuation of the principle of functional relevance leads to the questions – What are the differences by which the styles in a speaker's repertoire can be described as contrasting? What are the dimensions underlying those differences? (What are the relations between the styles and their occasions of use?)' (p. 169).	Hymes, 1977 Gee and Green, 1998
From a communicative perspective, Bakhtin (1986) argues that 'any understanding of live speech, a live utterance, is inherently responsive, although the degree of this activity varies extremely. Any understanding is embued with response and necessarily elicits it in one form or another: the listener becomes the speaker . . . An actively responsive understanding of what is heard . . . can be directly realized in action . . ., or it can remain for the time being, a silent responsive understanding (certain speech genres are intended for this kind of responsive understanding . . .), but this is, so to speak, responsive understanding with a delayed reaction' (pp. 59–60).	Green et al., 2011 Tuyay et al., 1995 Bloome et al., 2005
From a symbolic interaction perspective (Blumer, 1969, 1986), in classrooms members engage with academic content and particular social practices that are • constructed • established • negotiated	Hamido and César, 2009 Brilliant-Mills, 1994

Table 5.1 (continued)

Conceptual Principle	Illustrative Work
• modified • suspended • re-established.	
Building across traditions on intertextuality and sociolinguistics, Bloome and colleagues (Bloome and Egan-Robertson, 1993), argue that 'Whenever people engage in a language event, whether it is a conversation, the reading of a book, or diary writing, they are engaged in intertextual juxtapositions of various conversational and written texts . . . Intertextuality is a social construction in that these juxtapositions must be interactionally recognized by the participants in an event, acknowledged by those participants, and have social significance within the event' . . . (p. 198).	Bloome and Egan-Robertson, 1993 Bloome and Clark, 2006 Floriani, 1993 Green and Heras, 2011 Heras and Green, 2011
From a critical discourse perspective, Fairclough (1995) argues that 'Each discursive event [has] three dimensions or facets: it is a spoken or written language text, it is an instance of discourse practice involving the production and interpretation of text, and it is a piece of social practice . . .The connection between text and social practice is seen as being mediated by discourse practice: on the one hand, processes of text production and interpretation are shaped by (and help shape) the nature of the social practice, and on the other hand the production shapes (and leaves "traces" in) the text, and the interpretive process operates upon "cues" in the text' (p. 136).	Putney et al., 2000 Ivanic, 1994, 1998 van Dijk, 2001

through the interactions in developing events and cycles of activity (Green and Meyer, 1991).

The focus on language in use also intersects conceptual arguments grounded in sociocultural theories of learning and development (for example, John-Steiner et al., 1994; Lee and Smagorinsky, 2000; Moll, 1990). This work also has made visible how 'common knowledge' (for example, Edwards and Mercer, 1987), 'identity/identities' (for example, Ivanic, 1998; Castanheira et al., 2007; López Bonilla and Englander, 2001; Duff, 2002; Moita Lopes, 2003, 2006; Bloome et al., 2005; López Bonilla and Fragoso, 2011; Ligorio and César, in press), and 'communities' are socially constructed in and through discourse in use (Barton and Tusting, 2005; Bloome and Clark, 2006). These studies are illustrative of work on disciplinary and social knowledge construction and make visible how qualitative researchers in education are uncovering the situated, contextual, relational, and organizational nature of language, learning, knowledge, curriculum development, and social life in classrooms.

Conceptual Principle 3: Multiple analyses of common records/data make visible differences in what can be known through a particular program of research or theoretical perspective.

One area in which qualitative researchers in education have contributed to a conceptual understanding of the differences in focus and claims across theoretical perspectives is work on multiple analyses of common or the same data/records. In the past two decades, theorists, who share a qualitative orientation to the study of language in use, have come together to examine what each theoretical language makes visible and how each has a particular 'expressive potential' (cf. Strike, 1974, 1989). What this body of work demonstrates is that each study of the same records was guided by a particular theoretical orientation, conceptualized the phenomena of study in particular ways, involved the collection of a particular set of records (for example, video, documents, textbooks, written records), and provided a particular form of grounded or analytic approach to construct warranted accounts.

For example, Green et al. (1987) examined the same reading comprehension event from three theoretical traditions: sociolinguistic, semantic/ propositional analysis, and literary analysis/episodic text analysis. In contrasting what was possible to know across the three studies of the same data, the authors showed that in the two classrooms, students did not construct the same literacy event (Green et al., 1988), did not have the same cognitive demands (Harker, 1988), and did not hear the same story talked into being (Golden, 1988). This work provides evidence for arguing for the use of complementary perspectives to construct a more nuanced and conceptual understanding of the complexity of language in use in classrooms and the social construction of knowledge in classrooms.

An emerging body of work from different theoretical traditions supports this approach and demonstrates why contrastive analyses of research programs are needed if we are to construct grounded and theoretically driven understandings of teaching and learning in schools and other educational settings. This work makes visible that rather than competing perspectives, the different theoretical programs of research contribute complementary understandings of common phenomena when the types of records/data are held constant (for example, Grimshaw et al., 1994; Guzzetti and Hynd, 1998; Koschmann, 1999; Wyatt-Smith and Cummings, 2001). Additionally, over time studies are demonstrating how multiple theoretical traditions are necessary to trace the history of particular events marked in language (oral or written) in a particular setting (for example, Heath, 1982; Green and Heras, 2011). This work also focuses on analysis at multiple levels of analytic scale (for example, Dixon and Green, 2005), and on tracing the same student across multiple classes (for example, Rex, 2000, 2006; Castanheira et al., 2001; Yeager et al., 2009).

These studies also make visible how the analysis of a particular interaction can become a 'rich point' (Agar, 1994, 2006), or anchor, for a process of mapping backward in time across events or forward to identify the roots of the event or meanings under construction. By following the routes constructed by participants across time and events, these studies make transparent how qualitative researchers have examined the historical nature of a particular moment in time (for example, Bakhtin, 1986; Bloome and Egan-Robertson, 1993; Dixon and Green, 2005). By anchoring the overtime analysis in moments of communication, these researchers make visible the intersection between linguistic/language in use (in time) and ethnographic (over time) empirical research necessary to build warranted claims about the meaning of a particular event or the consequences of decisions at other levels of analytical scale on local and situated actions.

Conceptual Principle 4: Video and audio recording are records and not the phenomena.

At the center of studies of language and social life as social constructions are developments in technology. With the development of technologies that permit real time recording (audio and video) of language in use in educational and other social settings, anthropologists, linguists and sociologists, psychologists, and those interested in text as spoken, read or written in real time, have been able to record, revisit multiple times (for example, Barnes et al., 1969), transcribe, and (re)present the language and contextual surroundings of human activity. These recordings have led to archives of video and audio records that in some instances can be shared with others (for example, Child Language Data Exchange System (Childes) (MacWhinney and Snow, 1985), and in other instances serve as an archive within a particular research community or project (for example, Wyatt-Smith & Cummings, 2001; Baker et al., 2009).

The development of both the technologies and archives of technologically collected records (for example, video, audio, photographs, and written documents) of life in and out of schools has raised epistemological issues about what is recorded on videos and audio records, and how archived materials can be used to construct data sets. The challenge facing qualitative researchers, seeking to use such archives and records, is to make transparent 'what counts' (Heap, 1980) in their work as the event being studied; that is, how the events or phenomena on the video or audio record are conceptualized – whether the researcher views the record as the event/phenomena, or if not the event/phenomena, how what is recorded on the video is conceptualized. These two different ways of viewing a video or audio record are consequential for the claims that will be made from the record as well as the process of analysis (for example, Evertson and Green, 1986; Erickson, 2006; Goldman et al., 2007; Baker et al., 2009). An additional challenge is how to search an archive to construct a data set for analysis of a particular phenomena or how to trace the boundaries of units of analysis across times and events. These decisions reflect the constructed nature of research data and foreground the need for transparency in the decision-making process of who or what to record, how, in what ways, for what purposes, and what related materials are to be included in the archive (for example, Green et al., 2007).

These challenges raise questions about how studies of language in use are conceptualized. Such studies draw on video and other artifacts to systematically examine how, in the moment-by-moment interactions among members of a social group, language is constitutive of what members are jointly constructing. From this perspective, making visible the logic in use means making transparent epistemological decisions about the researchers' perspectives on the nature of language as social action as well as how such language is recorded, how particular bits of social life are selected for analysis, how talk and context are conceptualized, what counts as context (Duranti and Goodwin, 1992), how talk or social accomplishments through language are (re)presented, how the language user is represented through the process of transcribing (for example, Heap, 1991, 1992; Edwards and Lampert, 1993; Green et al., 1997; Roberts, 1997; Bucholtz, 2000; Mondada, 2007; Patai, 1988;), how accounts of social activity are constructed (Heap, 1991, 1992) and how warrants for claims are tied to data constructed and analysed (Heap, 1995). For a comprehensive discussion of related issues see Hammersley (Chapter 32, this volume) on transcribing.

SOME CLOSING COMMENTS

In tracing the roots of language in use, we uncovered how the turn to studies of language in use has created a foundation for linguistically oriented, empirical studies currently being undertaken by qualitative researchers in education and other disciplines. By tracing the roots of current directions, we made visible shifts on the relationship between language and education, and how a conceptual argument on the social construction of reality is central to these shifts. The conceptual principles presented represent complementary arguments that make transparent the theoretical logic of inquiry guiding research on language in use. As described, these principles also lay a foundation for ongoing epistemological decisions about what to collect, how to analyse records/data collected, and how to construct accounts of the local, situated, contextualized, and organizational phenomena under study.

NOTES

1. A full description of these traditions is beyond the scope of this chapter. The following are illustrative publications by qualitative researchers in education that are part of the field of language and education: anthropological linguistics (Duranti, 1997; Wortham and Rymes, 2003); applied linguistics (for example, Duff, 2002; Zuengler and Mori, 2002; Lee et al., 2008); conversation analysis (for example, Garfinkel, 1967; Atkinson et al., 1984; Baker, 1992); classroom discourse/communication (for example, Barnes et al., 1969, 1976, 1992; Cazden, 1972a, 1988; Wilkinson, 1982; Magalhães and Rojo, 1994) critical discourse analysis (Fairclough, 1995; van Dijk, 2001); discourse analysis (for example, Green and Dixon, 1993, 2008; Cameron, 2001; Schiffrin et al., 2003; Bloome and Clark, 2006; Martin-Jones and de Meija, 2008); educational linguistics (for example, Stubbs, 1976; Rampton, 2000; Spolsky and Hult, 2008); ethnomethodology (for example, Mehan and Woods, 1983; Heap, 1991, 1995); ethnography (for example, Green and Wallat, 1981; Atkinson et al., 2003); microethnography (for example, Corsaro, 1985; Bloome et al., 2005); narrative analysis (for example, Hymes, 2003); literacy studies (for example, Cook-Gumperz, [1986] 2006; Bloome and Green, 1991 Gee, 1996, Green and Bloome, 1997; Lea and Street, 2006; Coiro et al., 2008); sociolinguistics (for example, Gumperz, 1971, 1986; Gumperz and Hymes, 1972; Halliday, 1972; Hymes, 1974; Gumperz and Levinson, 1996; Halliday, 2003, 2006); and sociology (Bernstein, 1971; Fishman, 1972; Collins, 1988, 2009; Atkinson et al., 1995; Rampton et al., 2008). Today, comprehensive syntheses of work focusing on language and education can be found in the first (Corson, 1997) and second (Hornberger, 2008) editions of the *Encyclopedia of Language and Education* and the *Encyclopedia of Applied Linguistics* (Chapelle, 2011). The latter two volumes provide an international profile.
2. Construction of disciplinary knowledge: literacy (for example, Davies, 1989, 1993; Dixon et al., 2005; Baker and Luke, 1991; Beach et al., 1991, 2005; Heap, 1991; Magalhães and Rojo, 1994; Wells, 2000; Bloome et al., 2005; Carter, 2007); Mathematics (for example, Brilliant-Mills, 1994; Sfard, 2008; Moschkovich, 2009, 2010); The arts (for example, Gadsden, 2008; Baker et al., 2009); and Science (for example, Lemke, 1990; Kelly and Chen, 1999; Halliday, 2006; Lemke et al., 2006; Freitas and Castanheira, 2007).

REFERENCES

Agar, M. (1994), *Language Shock: Understanding the Culture of Conversation*, New York: William Morrow.

Agar, M. (2006), 'Culture: can you take it anywhere?', *International Journal of Qualitative Methods*, **5** (2), 1–12.

Atkinson, J., Maxwell, J. and Heritage, J. (eds) (1984), *Structures of Social Action: Studies in Conversation Analysis*, Cambridge: Cambridge University Press.

Atkinson, P., Davies, B. and Delamont, S. (1995), *Discourse and Reproduction: Essays in Honor of Basil Bernstein*, Cresskill, NJ: Hampton.

Atkinson, P., Coffey, A., Delamont, S. and Lofland, J. and Lofland, L. (2003), *Handbook of Ethnography*, London: Sage.

Baker, C.D. (1992), 'Description and analysis in classroom talk and interaction', *Journal of Classroom Interaction*, **27** (2), 9–14.

Baker, C. and Luke, A. (1991), *Toward a Critical Sociology of Reading Pedagogy*, Philadelphia, PA: John Benjamins.

Baker, W.D., Green, J. and Skukauskaite, A. (2009), 'Video-enabled ethnographic research: a microethnographic perspective', in G. Walford (ed.), *How to do Educational Ethnography*, London: Tufnell Press, pp. 77–114.

Bakhtin, M. (1986), *Speech Genres and Other Late Essays*, Austin, TX: University of Texas Press.

Barnes, D. ([1976] 1992), *From Communication to Curriculum*, Harmondsworth: Penguin.

Barnes, D. and Todd, F. (1977), *Communication and Learning: Creating Meaning through Talk*, London: Routledge and Kegan Paul.

Barnes, D. and Todd, F. (1995), *Communication and Learning Revisited: Creating Meaning through Talk*, Portsmouth, NH: Boynton/Cook, Heinemann.

Barnes, D., Britton, J. and Rosen, H. (1969), *Language, the Learner and the School*, London: Penguin.

Barton, D. and Tusting, K. (eds) (2005), *Beyond Communities of Practice: Language, Power and Social Context*, Cambridge: Cambridge University Press.

Bazerman, C. (2006), 'Analyzing the multidimensionality of texts in education', in J. Green, G. Camilli and P. Elmore (eds), *Complementary Methods in Research in Education*, Mahwah, NJ: Erlbaum, pp. 77–94.

Beach, R., Green, J., Kamil, M. and Shanahan, T. (eds) (1991), *Multiple Disciplinary Perspectives on Literacy Research*, Urbana, IL: NCRE and NCTE.

Beach, R., Green, J., Kamil, M. and Shanahan, T. (eds) (2005), *Multidisciplinary Perspectives on Literacy Research*, Cresskill, NJ: Hampton Press.

Bereiter, C. and Engleman, S. (1996), *Teaching Disadvantaged Children in the Preschool*, Englewood Cliffs, NJ: Prentice-Hall.

Berger, P. and Luckmann, T. (1966), *The Social Construction of Reality*, Garden City, NY: Doubleday.

Bernstein, B. (1971), *Class, Codes and Control: Theoretical Studies Towards a Sociology of Language*, Vol. 1, London: Routledge and Kegan Paul.

Bernstein, B. (1975), *Class, Codes and Control: Towards a Theory of Educational Transmission*, Vol. 3, London: Routledge and Kegan Paul.

Bernstein, B. (1996), *Pedagogy, Symbolic Control and Identity: Theory, Research, and Critique*, London: Taylor & Francis.

Birdwhistell, R. (1977), 'Some discussion of ethnography, theory, and method', in J. Brockman (ed.), *About Bateson: Essays on Gregory Bateson*, New York: Dutton, pp. 103–44.

Bloome, D. (ed.) (1985), *Classrooms and Literacy*, Norwood, NJ: Ablex.

Bloome, D. (ed.) (1987), *Literacy and Schooling*, Norwood, NJ: Ablex.

Bloome, D. and Clark, C. (2006), 'Discourse-in-use', in J. Green, G. Camilli and P. Elmore (eds), *Complementary Methods in Research in Education*, Mahwah, NJ: Erlbaum, pp. 227–41.

Bloome, D. and Egan-Roberston, A. (1993), 'The social construction of intertextuality in classroom reading and writing lessons', *Reading Research Quarterly*, **28** (4), 304–33.

Bloome, D. and Green, J. (1991), 'Educational contexts of literacy', in W. Grabe (ed.), *Annual Review of Applied Linguistics*, New York: Cambridge University Press, pp. 49–70.

Bloome, D., Carter, S.P., Otto, S. and Shuart-Faris, N. (2005), *Discourse Analysis and the Study of Language and Literacy Events: A Microethnographic Perspective*, Mahwah, NJ: Lawrence Erlbaum.

Blumer, H. (1969), *Symbolic Interactionism*, Englewood Cliffs, NJ: Prentice Hall.

Blumer, H. (1986), *Symbolic Interactionism: Perspective and Method*, Los Angeles, CA: University of California Press.

Brilliant-Mills, H. (1994), 'Becoming a mathematician: building a situated definition of mathematics', *Linguistics and Education*, **5** (3–4), 301–34.

Bronson, M. and Watson-Gegeo, K. (2008), 'The critical moment: language socialization and the (re)visioning of first and second language learning', in P.A. Duff and N.H. Hornberger (eds), *Encyclopedia of Language and Education, Volume 8: Language Socialization*, 2nd edn, New York: Springer, pp. 43–55.

Bucholtz, M. (2000), 'The politics of transcription', *Journal of Pragmatics*, **32**, 1439–65.

Cameron, D. (2001), *Working with Spoken Discourse*, London: Sage Publications.

Carter, S. (2007), '"Reading all that white crazy stuff": black young women unpacking whiteness in a high school British literature classroom', *Journal of Classroom Interaction*, **41** (2), 42–54.

Castanheira, M.L., Crawford, T., Dixon, C. and Green, J. (2001), 'Interactional ethnography: an approach to studying the social construction of literate practices', in J.J. Cumming and C.M. Wyatt-Smith (eds), *Special Issue of Linguistics and Education: Analyzing the Discourse Demands of the Curriculum*, **11** (4), 353–400.

Castanheira, M.L., Green, J.L., Dixon, C.N. and Yeager, B. (2007), '(Re)Formulating identities in the face of fluid modernity: an interactional ethnographic approach', *International Journal of Educational Research*, **46** (3–4), 172–89.

Cazden, C.B. (1972a), *Child Language and Education*, New York: Holt, Rinehart and Winston.

Cazden, C. (1972b), 'Preface', in C. Cazden, V. John and D. Hymes, *Functions of Language in the Classroom*, New York: Teachers College Press, pp. vii–ix.

Cazden, C. (1988), *Classroom Discourse: The Language of Teaching and Learning*, Portsmouth, NH: Heineman.

Cazden, C., John, V. and Hymes, D. (eds) (1972), *Functions of Language in the Classroom*, New York: Teachers College Press.

Chapelle, C.A. (2011), *Encyclopedia of Applied Linguistics*, Oxford: Wiley-Blackwell.

Christie, F. and Misson, R. (1998), *Literacy and Schooling*, London: Routledge.

Coiro, J., Knobel, M., Lankshear, C., Leu, J. and Donald, J. (eds) (2008), *Handbook of Research on New Literacies*, New York: Lawrence Erlbaum.

Collins, J. (1988), 'Language and class in minority education', *Anthropology & Education Quarterly*, **19** (4), 299–326.

Collins, J. (2009), 'Social reproduction in classrooms and schools', *Annual Review of Anthropology*, **38**, 33–48.

Cook-Gumperz, J. (1981), 'Persuasive talk – the social organization of children's talk', in J.L. Green and C. Wallat (eds), *Ethnography and Language in Educational Settings*, Norwood, NJ: Ablex, pp. 25–50.

Cook-Gumperz, J. ([1986] 2006), *The Social Construction of Literacy*, New York: Cambridge University Press.

Corsaro, W. (1984), *Peer Culture and Friendship of the Young Child*, Norwood, NJ: Ablex.

Corsaro, W. (1985), *Friendship and Peer Culture in the Early Years*, Norwood, NJ: Ablex.

Corson, D. (ed.) (1997), *Encyclopedia of Language and Education*, Dordrecht, the Netherlands: Kluwer Academic Publishers.

Davies, B. (1989), *Frogs and Snails and Feminist Tales. Preschool Children and Gender*, Sydney: Allen and Unwin, pp. 1–152.

Davies, B. (1993), *Shards of Glass. Children Reading and Writing Beyond Gendered Identities*, Sydney: Allen and Unwin, pp. 1–205.

Dixon, C. and Green, J. (2005), 'Studying the discursive construction of texts in classrooms through interactional ethnography', in R. Beach, J. Green, M. Kamil and T. Shanahan (eds), *Multidisciplinary Perspectives on Literacy Research*, Cresskill, NJ: Hampton Press/ National Conference for Research in Language and Literacy, pp. 349–90.

Dixon, C., Green, J. and Biandts, L. (2005), 'Studying the discursive construction of texts in classrooms through interactional ethnography', in R. Beach, J. Green, M. Kamil and T. Shanahan (eds), *Multidisciplinary Perspectives on Literacy Research*, Cresskill, NJ: Hampton Press/National Conference for Research in Language and Literacy, pp. 349–90.

Doughty, P. and Thornton, G. (1973), 'General introduction', in M.A.K. Halliday, *Explorations in the Functions of Language*, London: Edward Arnold Publishers, pp. 3–4.

Duff, P.A. (2002), 'The discursive co-construction of knowledge, identity, and difference', *Applied Linguistics*, **23** (3), 289–322.

Duff, P.A. (2008), 'Language socialization, higher education, and work', in P.A. Duff and N.H. Hornberger (eds), *Encyclopedia of Language and Education, Volume 8: Language Socialization*, 2nd edn, New York: Springer, pp. 257–70.

Duranti, A. (1997), *Linguistic Anthropology*, Cambridge: Cambridge University Press.

Duranti, A. and Goodwin, C. (1992), *Rethinking Context: Language as an Interactive Phenomenon*, New York: Cambridge University Press.

Edwards, D. and Mercer, B. (1987), *Common Knowledge*, London: Methuen.

Edwards, J.A. and Lampert, M.D. (eds) (1993), *Talking Data*, Hillsdale, NJ: Erlbaum.

Edwards, J.A. and Lampert, M.D. (eds) (1993), *Talking Data: Transcription and Cooling in Discourse Research*, New Jersey: Lawrence Erlbaum Associates.

Erickson, F. (2004), *Talk and Social Theory*, Cambridge: Polity.

Erickson, F. (2006), 'Definition and analysis of data from videotape', in J. Green, G. Camilli, P. Elmore, A. Skukauskaite and E. Grace (eds), *Handbook of Complementary Methods in Education Research*, New York: Taylor & Francis.

Evertson, C.M., and Green, J.L. (1986), 'Observation as inquiry and method', in M. Wittrock (ed.), *Handbook of Research on Teaching*, 3rd edn, Washington, DC: AERA, pp. 162–213.

Fairclough, N. (1995), *Critical Discourse Analysis*, New York: Longman.

Fishman, J. (1972), *The Sociology of Language: An Interdisciplinary Social Science Approach to Language in Society*, Rowley, MA: Newbury House.

Floriani, A. (1993), 'Negotiating what counts: roles and relationships, content and meaning, texts and context', *Linguistics and Education*, **5** (3–4), 241–74.

Frederiksen, C.H. (1975), 'Representing logical and semantic structure of knowledge acquired from discourse', *Cognitive Psychology*, **7** (3), 371–458.

Frederiksen, C.H. (1986), 'Cognitive models and discourse analysis', in C.R. Cooper and S. Greenbaum (eds) *Written Communication Annual. Volume 1: Linguistic Approaches to the Study of Written Discourse*, Beverly Hills, CA, Sage, pp. 227–67.

Fredericksen, C., Whiteman, M. and Dominic, J. (eds) (1981), *Writing: Process, Development, and Communication*, Hillsdale, NJ: Erlbaum.

Freitas, C.A. and Castanheira, M.L. (2007), 'Talked images: examining the contextualised nature of image use', *Pedagogies*, **2** (3), 151–64.

Gadsden, V.L. (2008), 'The arts and education: knowledge generation, pedagogy, and the discourse of learning', *Review of Research in Education*, **32** (1), 29–61.

Gage, N.L. (1974), *Teaching as a Linguistic Process in a Cultural Setting*, Panel 5, National Institute of Education (ERIC 111 806).

Garfinkel, H. (1967), *Studies in Ethnomethodology*, Englewood Cliffs, NJ: Prentice-Hall.

Gee, J.P. (1990), *Social Linguistics and Literacies: Ideology in Discourses*, New York: Falmer.

Gee, J. (1996), *Social Linguistics and Literacies: Ideology in Discourses*, 2nd edn, Philadelphia, PA: Falmer Press.

Gee, J.P. and Green, J.L. (1998), 'Chapter 4: Discourse analysis, learning, and social practice: a methodological study', *Review of Research in Education*, **23**, 119–69.

Gilmore, P. and Glatthorn, A. (eds) (1982), *Children In and Out of School: Ethnography and Education*, Norwood, NJ: Ablex.

Golden, J. (1988), 'The construction of a literary text in a story reading lesson', in J. Green, J. Harker and J. Golden (eds), *Multiple Perspective Analysis of Classroom Discourse*, Norwood, NJ: Ablex, pp. 79–106.

Goldman, R., Pea, R., Barron, B. and Derry, S. (eds) (2007), *Video Research in the Learning Sciences*, New York: Routledge.

Green, J.L. (ed.) (1979), 'Communicating with young children', *Special Issue: Theory Into Practice*, **18** (4).

Green, J.L. (1983), 'Teaching as a linguistic process: a state of the art', in E. Gordon (ed.), *Review of Research in Education*, Washington, DC: AERA, pp. 151–254.

Green, J. and Bloome, D. (1997), 'Ethnography and ethnographers of and in education: a situated perspective', in J. Flood, S.B. Heath and D. Lapp (eds), *Handbook of Research on Teaching Literacy through the Communicative and Visual Arts*, New York: Macmillan Publishers, pp. 181–202.

Green, J. and Dixon, C. (1993), 'Introduction to "Talking knowledge into being: discursive and social practices in classrooms"', *Linguistics and Education*, **5** (3–4), 231–9.

Green, J. and Dixon, C. (2008), 'Classroom interaction and situated learning', in M. Martin-Jones and A.M. de Majía (eds), *Encyclopedia of Language and Education: Discourse and Education*, Vol. 3, New York: Springer, pp. 3–14.

Green, J.L. and Harker, J.O. (eds) (1988), *Multiple Perspective Analyses of Classroom Discourse*, Norwood, NJ: Ablex.

Green, J. and Heras, A. (2011), 'Identities in shifting educational policy contexts: the consequences of moving from two languages, one community to English only', in G. López-Bonilla and I. Englander (eds), *Discourses and Identities in Contexts of Educational Change*, New York: Peter Lang Publishing, pp. 155–94.

Green, J.L. and Meyer, L.A. (1991), 'The embeddedness of reading in classroom life: reading as a situated process', in C. Baker and A. Luke (eds), *Toward a Critical Sociology of Reading Pedagogy*, Philadelphia, PA: Benjamins, pp. 141–60.

Green, J.L. and Wallat, C. (1981), *Ethnography and Language in Educational Settings*, Norwood, NJ: Ablex.

Green, J., Castanheira, M.L. and Yeager, B. (2011), 'Researching the opportunities for learning for students with learning difficulties in classrooms: an ethnographic perspective', in C. Wyatt-Smith, J. Elkins and S. Gunn (eds), *Multiple Perspectives on Difficulties in Learning Literacy and Numeracy*, New York: Springer Publishers.

Green, J., Franquiz, M. and Dixon, C. (1997), 'The myth of the objective transcript: transcribing as a situated act', *TESOL Quarterly*, **21** (1), 172–6.

Green, J.L., Harker, J.O. and Golden, J.M. (1987), 'Lesson construction: differing views', in G.W. Nobilt and W.T. Pink (eds), *Schooling in a Social Context: Qualitative Studies*, Norword, NJ: Albex, pp. 46–77.

Green, J.L., Skukauskaite, A. and Baker, D. (in press), 'Ethnography as epistemology: an introduction to educational ethnography', in J. Arthur, M.I. Waring, R. Coe and L.V. Hedges (eds), *Research Methodologies and Methods in Education*, London: Sage.

Green, J.L., Weade, R. and Graham, K. (1988), 'Lesson construction and student participation: a sociolinguistic analysis', in J.L. Green and J. Harker (eds), *Multiple Perspective Analysis of Classroom Discourse*, Norwood, NJ: Ablex, pp. 11–48.

Green, J., Skukauskaite, A., Dixon, C. and Córdova, R. (2007), 'Epistemological issues in the analysis of video records: interactional ethnography as a logic of inquiry', in R. Goldman, R. Pea, B. Barron and S. Derry (eds), *Video Research in the Learning Sciences*, Mahwah, NJ: Lawrence Erlbaum Associates, pp. 115–32.

Grimshaw, A., Burke, J. and Cicourel, A. (1994), *What's Going on Here?: Complementary Studies of Professional Talk*, Vol. 43, Westport, CT: Greenwood Publishing Group.

Gumperz, J. (1971), *Language in Social Groups*, Stanford, CA: Stanford University Press.

Gumperz, J. (1986), 'Interactive sociolinguistics on the study of schooling', in J.

Cook-Gumperz (ed.), *The Social Construction of Literacy*, New York: Cambridge University Press, pp. 45–68.
Gumperz, J. and Cook-Gumperz, J. (2005), 'Making space for bilingual communicative practice', *Intercultural Pragmatics*, **21** (1), 1–23.
Gumperz, J. and Cook-Gumperz, J. (2006), 'Interactional sociolinguistics in the study of schooling', in J. Cook-Gumperz (ed.), *The Social Construction of Literacy*, New York: Cambridge University Press, pp. 50–75.
Gumperz, J. and Hymes, D. (1964), 'The ethnography of communication', *American Anthropologist*, **66** (6), 127–32.
Gumperz, J.J. and Hymes, D. (1972), *Directions in Sociolinguistics: The Ethnography of Communication*, New York: Basil Blackwell.
Gumperz, J. and Levinson, S. (1996), *Rethinking Linguistic Relativity*, Cambridge: Cambridge University Press.
Guzzetti, B. and Hynd, C. (eds) (1998), *Perspectives on Conceptual Change: Multiple Ways to Understand Knowing and Learning in a Complex World*, Mahwah, NJ: Lawrence Erlbaum Associates.
Halliday, M.A.K. (1972), 'Three aspects of children's language development: learning language, learning through language and learning about language', in Y. Goodman, M. Haussler and D. Strickland (eds), *Oral and Written Language Development Research: Impact on the Schools*, Urbana, IL: National Council of Teachers of English.
Halliday, M.A.K. (1973), *Explorations in the Functions of Language*, London: Hodder.
Halliday, M.A.K. (1978), *Language as Social Semiotic: The Social Interpretation of Language and Meaning*, London: Edward Arnold.
Halliday, M.A.K. (2003), '*On Language and Linguistics*', in J.J. Webster (ed.), *The Collected Works of M.A.K. Halliday*, Vol. 3, New York: Continuum.
Hamido, G. and César, M. (2009), 'Surviving within complexity: a meta-systemic approach to research on social interactions in formal educational scenarios', in K. Kumpulainen, C.E. Hmelo-Silver and M. César (eds), *Investigating Classroom Interaction: Methodologies in Action*, The Netherlands: Sense Publishers, pp. 229–62.
Harker, J.O. (1988), 'Contrasting the content of two story-reading lessons: a propositional analysis', in J. Green, J. Harker and J. Golden (eds), *Multiple Perspective Analysis of Classroom Discourse*, Norwood, NJ: Ablex, pp. 47–78.
Heap, J.L. (1980), 'What counts as reading? Limits to certainty in assessment', *Curriculum Inquiry*, **10** (3), 265–92.
Heap, J. (1991), 'A situated perspective on what counts as reading', in C. Baker and A. Luke (eds), *Towards a Critical Sociology of Reading Pedagogy*, Philadelphia, PA: John Benjamin, pp. 103–39.
Heap, J. (1992), 'Ethnomethodology and the possibility of a metaperspective on literacy research', in R. Beach, J. Green, M. Kamil and T. Shanahan (eds), *Multiple Disciplinary Perspectives on Literacy Research*, Urbana, IL: NCRE and NCTE, pp. 25–56.
Heap, J.L. (1995), 'The status of claims in "qualitative" research', *Curriculum Inquiry*, **25** (3), 271–91.
Heath, S.B. (1982), 'What no bedtime story means: narrative skills at home and school', *Language in Society*, **11**, 49–76.
Heras, A.I. and Green, J. (2011), 'Identidades y politicas públicas educativas. Las consecuencias de cambiar de una comunidate bilingüe a inglés como única lenga instrucción', in G. López Bonilla and C.P. Fragoso (eds), *Discursos e identidades en contextos de cambio Educactivo*, Mexico: Plaza y Valdez.
Hess, R.D. and Shipman, V.C. (1966), 'Early experience and the socialization of cognitive modes in children', *Child Development*, **36**, 869–86.
Hicks, D. (1995), 'Discourse, learning and teaching', in M. Apple (ed.), *Review of Research in Education*, **21**, 49–95.
Hornberger, N. (ed.) (2008), *Encyclopedia of language and Education*, New York: Springer.
Hymes, D. (1972), 'Introduction', in C. Cazden, V. John and D. Hymes (eds), *Functions of Language in the Classroom*, New York: Teachers College Press.

Hymes, D. (1974), *The Foundations of Sociolinguistics: Sociolinguistic Ethnography, Philadelphia*, PA: University of Pennsylvania Press.

Hymes, D. (1977), 'Qualitative/quantitative research methodologies in education: a linguistic perspective', *Anthropology & Education Quarterly*, **8** (3), 165–76.

Hymes, D. (2003), *Ethnography, Linguistics, Narrative Inequality: Toward an Understanding of Voice*, London: Taylor & Francis.

Ivanic, R. (1994), 'I is for interpersonal: discoursal construction of writer identities and the teaching of writing', *Linguistics and Education*, **6**, 3–15.

Ivanic, R. (1998), *Writing and Identity: The Discoursal Construction of Identity in Academic Writing*, Amsterdam: Benjamins.

John-Steiner, V., Panofsky, C. and Smith, L. (eds) (1994), *Sociocultural Approaches to Language & Literacy: An Interactionist Perspective*, Cambridge, MA: Cambridge University Press.

Kaplan, A.S. ([1964] 1998), *The Conduct of Inquiry: Methodology for Behavioral Science*, New Brunswick, NJ: Transaction Publishers.

Kelly, G.J. and Chen, C. (1999), 'The sound of music: constructing science as sociocultural practices through oral and written discourse', *Journal of Research in Science Teaching*, **36** (8), 883–15.

Kelly, G.J., Chen, C. and Prothero, W. (2000), 'The epistemological framing of a discipline: writing science in university oceanography', *Journal of Research in Science Teaching*, **37** (7), 691–718.

Koschmann, T. (1999), 'Meaning making: a special issue', *Discourse Processes*, **27** (2).

Kress, G. and Van Leeuwen, T. (2001), *Multimodal Discourse: The Modes and Media of Contemporary Communication*, London: Arnold.

Labov, W. (1969), 'The logic of non-standard English', *Georgetown Monograph on Language and Linguistics*, **22**, 1–31.

Labov, W. (1972), *Sociolinguistic Patterns'*, Philadelphia, PA: University of Pennsylvania Press.

Lea, M.R. and Street, B. (2006), 'The "academic literacies" model: theory and application', *Theory into Practice*, **45** (4), 368–77.

Lee, C. and Smagorinsky, P. (eds) (2000), *Vygotskian Perspectives on Literacy Research: Constructing Meaning through Collaborative Inquiry*, Cambridge: Cambridge University Press.

Lee, J.S., Hill-Bonnet, L. and Gillispie, J. (2008), 'Learning in two languages: interactional spaces for becoming bilingual speakers', *International Journal of Bilingual Education and Bilingualism*, **11** (1), 75–94

Lemke, J.L. (1990), *Talking Science: Language, Learning and Values*, Norwood, NJ: Ablex.

Lemke, J.L., Kelly, G. and Roth, W.M. (2006), 'Forum: toward a phenomenology of interviews: lessons from the phenomenology of interviews', *Cultural Studies of Science Education*, **1** (1), 83–106.

Ligorio, M. and César, M. (in press), *The Interplays Between Dialogical Learning and Dialogical Self*, Information Age Publishing.

López Bonilla, G. and Englander, I. (eds) (2001), *Discourses and Identities in Contexts of Educational Change*, New York: Peter Lang Publishing.

López Bonilla, G. and Pérez Fragoso, C. (2011), *Discursos e identidades en contextos de cambio Educactivo*, Mexico: Plaza y Valdez.

MacWhinney, B. and Snow, C. (1985), 'The child language data exchange system', *Journal of Child Language*, **12** (2), 271–95.

Magalhães, M.C.C. and Rojo, R.H.R. (1994), 'Classroom interaction and strategic reading development', in L. Barbara and M. Scott (eds), *Reflections on Language Learning*, Clevedon: Multilingual Matters, pp. 75–88.

Malinowski, B. (1922), *Argonauts of the Western Pacific*, New York: Dutton.

Malinowski, B. (1967), *Diary in the Strict Sense of the Term*, London: Routledge and Kegan Paul.

80   *Handbook of qualitative research in education*

Martin-Jones, M.M. and de Mejía, A.-M. (eds) (2008), *Encyclopedia of Language and Education: Discourse and Education*, Vol. 3, New York: Springer.
Mehan, H. and Woods, H. (1983), *Reality of Ethnomethodology*, New York: Wiley.
Mercer, N. and Hodgkinson, S. (2008), *Exploring Talk in Schools*, London: Sage.
Mitchell, C.J. (1984), 'Typicality and the case study', in R.F. Ellens (eds), *Ethnographic Research: A Guide to General Conduct*, New York: Academic Press, pp. 238–41.
Moita Lopes, L.P. da (2003), 'Storytelling as action: constructing masculinities in a school context', *Pedagogy Culture and Society, Inglaterra*, **11** (1), 31–47.
Moita Lopes, L.P. da (2006), 'Queering literacy teaching: analyzing gay-themed discourses in a fifth grade class in Brazil', *Language Identity and Education*, **5** (1), 31–50.
Moll, L.C. (ed.) (1990), *Vygotsky and Education: Instructional Implications and Applications of Sociohistorical Psychology*, New York: Cambridge University Press.
Mondada, L. (2007), 'Commentary: transcript variations and the indexicality of transcribing practices', *Discourse Studies,* **9** (6), 809–21.
Moschkovich, J. (2009), 'How language and graphs support conversation in a bilingual mathematics classroom', in R. Barwell (ed.), *Multilingualism in Mathematics Classrooms: Global Perspectives*, Bristol: Multilingual Matters Press, pp. 78–96.
Moschkovich, J. (ed.) (2010), *Language and Mathematics Education: Multiple Perspectives and Directions for Research*, Charlotte, NC: Information Age Publishing.
Patai, D. (1988), *Brazilian Women Speak*, New Brunswick, NJ: Rutgers University Press.
Putney, L., Green, J., Dixon, C. and Durán, R. (2000), 'Consequential progressions: exploring collective-individual development in a bilingual classroom', in C. Lee and P. Smagorinsky (eds), *Constructing Meaning through Collaborative Inquiry: Vygotskian Perspectives on Literacy Research*, New York: Cambridge University Press, pp. 86–126.
Rampton, B. (2000), 'Continuity and change in views of change in applied linguistics', in H. Tappes-Lomax (ed.), *Change and Continuity and Applied Linguistics*, Clevedon: Multilingual Matters, pp. 97–114.
Rampton, B., Harris, R., Collins, J. and Blommaert, J. (2008), 'Language, class and education', in S. May and N.H. Hornberger (eds), *Encyclopedia of Language and Education, Volume 1: Language Policy and Political Issues in Education*, New York: Springer Science and Business Media LLC, pp. 71–81.
Rex, L.A. (2000), 'Judy constructs a genuine question: a case for interactional inclusion', *International Journal of Teaching and Teacher Education,* **16** (2), 315–33.
Rex, L.A. (ed.) (2006), 'Discourse of opportunity: how talk in learning situations creates and constrains', *Interactional Ethnographic Studies in Teaching and Learning*, Discourse and Social Processes Series, Cresskill, NJ: Hampton Press.
Roberts, C. (1997), 'Transcribing talk: issues of representation', *TESOL Quarterly*, **31** (1), 167–72.
Schiffrin, D., Tannen, D. and Schiffrin, H.E. (2003), *The Handbook of Discourse Analysis*, Malden, MA: Blackwell Publishing.
Sfard, A. (2008), *Thinking as Communicating: Human Development, the Growth of Discourses, and Mathematizing*, Cambridge: Cambridge University Press.
Sheridan, D., Street, B.V. and Bloome, D. (2000), *Writing Ourselves: Mass Observation and Literacy Practices*, Cresskill, NJ: Hampton Press.
Spolsky, B. and Hult, F. (2008), *Handbook of Educational Linguistics*, Oxford: Blackwell.
Strike, K. (1974), 'On the expressive potential of behaviorist language', *American Educational Research Journal*, **11** (2), 103–20.
Strike, K.A. (1989), *Liberal Justice and the Marxist Critique of Education: A Study of Conflicting Research Programs*, New York: Routledge.
Stubbs, M. (1976), *Language, Schools and Classrooms*, London: Methuen.
Stubbs, M. (1980), *Language and Literacy*, London: Routledge and Kegan Paul.
Stubbs, M. (1983), *Language, Schools and Classrooms*, London: Metheun.
Tuyay, S., Jennings, L. and Dixon, C. (1995), 'Classroom discourse and opportunities to learn: an ethnographic study of knowledge construction in a bilingual third grade classroom', *Discourse Processes*, **19** (1), 75–110.

van Dijk, T. (ed.) (2001), 'Studies in critical discourse analysis', Special issue of *Discourse & Society*, **4** (2), 1993, 249–83.

Vine, E. (2003), 'My partner: a five-year-old Samoan boy learns how to articulate in class through interactions with his English-speaking peers', *Linguistics and Education*, **14** (1), 99–121.

Weade, G. (1987), 'Curriculum 'n' instruction: the construction of meaning', *Theory into Practice*, **26** (1), 15–25.

Wells, G. (ed.) (2000), *Action, Talk, and Text: Learning and Teaching through Inquiry*, New York: Teachers College Press.

Wilkinson, L.C. (1982), *Communicating in the Classroom*, New York: Academic Press.

Wittgenstein, L. (1958), *Philosophical Investigations*, 3rd edn, trans. G.E.M. Anscombe, New York: Macmillan Publishing.

Wortham, S. and Rymes, B. (2003), *Linguistic Anthropology in Education*, Westport, CT: Praeger.

Wyatt-Smith, C.M. and Cummings, J.J. (Special Issue Editors). (2001), 'Examining the literacy-curriculum relationship', A special edition of *Linguistics and Education*, **11** (4), 295–312.

Yeager, E., Green, J.L. and Castanheira, M.L. (2009), 'Two languages, one community: on the discursive construction of community in bilingual classrooms', in M. Cesar and K. Kumpulainen (eds), *Social Interactions in Multicultural Settings*, Rotterdam, the Netherlands: Sense Publishers, pp. 235–68.

Zuengler, J. and Mori, J. (eds) (2002), 'Special Issue: Microanalyses of classroom discourse: a critical consideration of method', *Applied Linguistics,* **23** (3), 283–8.

6. History and ethnography: interfaces and juxtapositions

Maria Tamboukou

What is our present today? How have we become what we are and what are the possibilities of 'becoming other'? This question has triggered and underpinned my ongoing research on writing genealogies as 'histories of the present' (Foucault, 1975 [1991], p. 31). In doing this, my work has unfolded as an interface of historical and ethnographic inquiries. In this chapter, I look back in this body of work, tracing encounters between history and ethnography while framing them within the broader field of educational research.

Historical and ethnographic inquiries are wide and complex fields in themselves that have drawn on a variety of research methods and approaches depending on the epistemological and theoretical traditions that underpin them. What both fields have in common, however, is a vibrant area of 'critical studies' that keep interrogating what history or ethnography can do.[1] Researchers in educational studies have been particularly influenced by and contributed to this body of 'critical studies'. As Sue Middleton[2] has aptly put it: 'the subject "Education" has always been theoretically promiscuous and my own research toolkit includes concepts, strategies, and techniques pulled from phenomenology, neo-Marxism, and feminism, as well as Foucauldian poststructuralism' (2003, p. 38). Foucault's theories and analytical strategies have indeed been influential here, particularly in the way he has interrogated linearities and continuities in traditional historical research (Foucault, 1971 [1986]), as well as the way he has problematized the role of the human sciences in the constitution of power/knowledge regimes (Foucault, 1966 [2000]). Foucault's critique has been rigorously encompassed in his suggestion for doing genealogies and it is trails of this approach that I want to explicate and discuss in relation to my work.[3]

In Foucault's genealogical analyses, the past can never be revived or reconstructed and there is not a final destination, a place where things originated in the first place. The first task of the genealogist is therefore to turn to the past so as to excavate different layers of how human beings have created knowledge about themselves and the world. Within the genealogical framework this turn to the past is conceived as an analysis of 'descent' and 'emergence' (Foucault, 1971 [1986]). Descent moves backwards revealing numberless beginnings and multiple changes, while emergence is about the entry point of the event on the historical stage. As Foucault explains in the search for descent, it turns out that 'truth or being does not lie at the root of what we know and what we are' (1971 [1986], p. 81). The analysis of descent is about revealing the contingency of human reality, describing its complicated forms and exploring its countless historical transformations. It was in this context that in my work I looked at the formation of 'technologies of the female self' in the social milieus of education and art (Tamboukou, 2003, 2010a). In focusing on the context of the *fin de siècle*, I attempted an analysis of the specification of the female subject in a nexus of signifying genealogical events, which have constituted her public persona, but have also dissolved the frontiers between the public/political and the private/personal.

As the genealogical turn to the past can never reach an origin – it rather encounters numberless beginnings – an important task of the genealogist is to identify points of emergence, critical historical moments when 'dissonant' events erupt in the course (and discourse) of history. Emergence refers then to a particular historical moment when things appeared as events on the stage of history. It is in the context of intense power relations at play that Foucault stabilizes this 'moment of arising' (Foucault, 1971 [1986], p. 83). In this light, emergence is not the effect of individual tactics, but 'an event', an episode in a non-linear historical process. The analysis of emergence is not about why, but about how things happened; it is about scrutinizing the complex and multifarious processes that surround the emergence of the event.[4]

Locating a beginning is thus conceived as 'the researcher's cut' (Tamboukou, 2010c) in the genealogical process. In the study of women in education, my beginning was the turn of the nineteenth century. Being a period of crises and significant changes in the education of women in Europe, North America and Australia, I thought that it perfectly constituted what Foucault has defined as emergence in the genealogical analysis.

The turn of the nineteenth century has of course been the object of numerous and important studies by feminist historians.[5] These studies have often represented women in quite contradictory and often juxtaposing ways: either as heroic figures or as tragic victims within the urban spaces of modernity. Instead of being confusing, these contradictions have become highly relevant to the genealogical project. As a genealogist I was particularly intrigued to look more carefully not only into the surrounding discourses but also into the discourses of women themselves, their personal narratives through which they made sense of their lives.[6] Events are always fleeting moments in time, but they leave traces behind them in stories: tracing marks left on textual bodies, I thus chose to follow auto/biographical narratives of women in education, who moved in between different geographical, social and cultural spaces in search of a new self.

I have referred to auto/biographical narratives, but where have I looked for them? My genealogical inquiries took me to the archives, the genealogical research field par excellence. It was in the archives and in libraries that I followed traces that some of these women left in diaries, journals, letters, autobiographies and memoirs.[7] These narratives have irrevocably disrupted their image as either heroines, bearers of middle-class ideology, victims or agents of oppression. A genealogical approach to these narratives points to the fact that it is exactly when traditional history meets inconsistencies and disruptions that omissions and erasures are made for the historical linearity to be able to flow. Instead of subjects, these self-writings have therefore revealed 'nomadic subjectivities'[8] difficult to be pinned down in stable subject positions: it is upon the constitution of these subjectivities on the move that the genealogical approach has focused.

I have discussed how the genealogical turn to the past unveils power/knowledge interrelations in the constitution of truth around the self and the world. However, as I have also noted, Foucault has seen his genealogical project as 'a history of the present'. Calling into question self-evidences of the present by exposing the various ways they were constructed in the past, such histories shatter certain stabilities and help us detach ourselves from our 'truths' and seek alternative ways of existence. In my attempt to decipher the present of the genealogical project I have turned to ethnography.

WHAT IS OUR PRESENT TODAY? ETHNOGRAPHIC EXPLORATIONS

While immersing myself in the adventure of writing feminist genealogies, I am always concerned about contemporaneity: how have past formations been transposed in the constitution of the female self today? A major task of the genealogist is thus to chart the present she wants to interrogate. In the genealogical framework this is the process of constructing a *dispositif*: 'isolating a cluster of power relations sustaining, and being sustained by certain types of knowledge' (Foucault, 1980, p.196). As Deleuze has noted, in each *dispositif* it is necessary to distinguish the historical part, what we are (what we are already no longer) and the current part, what we are in the process of becoming (1992, p.164). It was therefore in the construction of the *dispositif* of my research that I turned to ethnographic practices as one of the ways I followed to relate to contemporary reality.[9] Amongst the different and diverse ethnographic studies that I have conducted, in this chapter I will discuss my work in the Massachussetts College of Art (MassArt) in Boston, USA, which I visited in March 2006 as part of my inquiries in women's art education today; my research in MassArt will further be discussed in relation to an ethnographic study of a group of women artists in Sussex, UK.

What was particularly striking with my work at MassArt was the way the history of the college is so much on the forefront of the college's identity. The following passage from an e-mail exchange with the archivist Paul Dobbs in preparation for my visit there forcefully expresses the deep historical consciousness of the people of MassArt:

> You probably know that we were the first and remain the only state-funded college of art in the states (at least the only one free-standing – not part of something else). Massachusetts industry developers and civic leaders caught wind of Thomas Cole's Kensington School and in 1870 convinced state government to mandate similar public drawing education. The state Board of Education asked Cole for help, and he sent a graduate and art school master, Walter Smith. Smith ran the Boston and Massachusetts drawing programs and in 1873 convinced the legislature to fund the Massachusetts Normal Art School (MassArt). He is often quoted for saying that he thought women were particularly well suited to art education; not an unwise move, since 60% of his enrollees were women. (E-mail communication, 16 March 2006)

What was further interesting in my work at the MassArt archives is that alongside traditional ethnographic practices[10] like participating in the everyday life of the college, attending courses, seminars and workshops and talking with students and teachers I would also work daily in its archives, which were conveniently housed in the library. Thus 'the present' and 'the past' were in a way co-existing as planes informing my research and actively interacting with each other. The case of contemporary artist May Smith was particularly illuminating in opening up an area of analysis that had not been included in my initial hypothesis and research questions: the forceful interrelation between social class and art education as conditions of possibility for women's quest for a new self (see Tamboukou, 2010d). As Pen Dalton's study has shown, in the context of the nineteenth century art education was deployed as a gendered discourse, deeply shaped by the needs of industrial modernization. In agreement with Dalton, what I have argued through my ethnographic work in MassArt is that art education has been both classed and gendered and this historical legacy has survived today, as I will further discuss.

In the context of my previous research with women teachers' narratives, art was configured as an alternative real and imaginary space, somewhere to create, but also to retreat, reflect and reinvent the self (Tamboukou,

2003). My research of writing a genealogy of women artists (Tamboukou, 2010a) has unveiled the dark side of the moon. While some women teachers have leaped into the world of art in an attempt to escape the boredom and frustration of their working lives, women artists have found in education a place to shelter themselves, as they are striving in the harsh realities of the art world.[11] There is a whole history around this reverse movement that has to be considered. The rationale for women's inclusion in all levels of education has been founded on the argument that women had to work; it was an argument revolving around the Protestant ethic of the importance of work and the evil of idleness. Art education was therefore by definition a grey area, since it could not possibly be linked to the prospect of a profession or of real work, particularly so, for working-class women.

Middle-class women as well would stay away from art education, since it carried the risk of detracting them once again from the world of professions they were striving to enter. As Dalton has noted: 'Discourses of the "lady artist" have proliferated in the modern period and are continually being reactivated. The ideology of the "lady amateur" has been synonymous with bad art; art that is unprofessional, weak, unskilled, trivial, bourgeois, merely decorative' (2001, p. 47). This forceful interrelation of art and social class that emerged from my work in MassArt was further compared and juxtaposed to ethnographic observations of a group of women artists from Brighton-Eastbourne, formed at the end of their art education degree, as the passage below from an interview with artist Pauline Crook forcefully shows:

> I belong to an art group, we are called *FrockArt* and there are seven of us, seven ladies, most of them I've known since the Certificate of Art, so that's going back to the beginning of the 1990s. And they are just lovely! They are my best friends, I just feel incredibly lucky. It's a very strong, solid women's group and we really care about each other and when we have our meetings – we usually meet and have lunch somewhere – we discuss all the things we have to discuss. They are such happy times and we laugh a lot. It's just lovely, a lovely, lovely group and they are all really good at what they do . . . And we exhibit together, usually, well this year we haven't got too many plans because we all needed, we wanted all to experiment and see what happens, so we are hoping to exhibit at the end of the year, but last year, how many times did we exhibit? Three times last year.[12]

I interviewed Pauline Crook in February 2006 as part of a multi-sited ethnographic work with groups of women artists, in Massachusetts, USA, London and Sussex, UK, Athens, Greece and Melbourne, Australia.[13] Crook's interview revealed new layers around the intersection of social class, gender and art education in the constitution of the female self in art: her story reveals that going to an art college was simply not an option for a working-class girl even in the 1970s. It was after Crook had worked as a secretary for many years and only when her children had gone to school that she became able to follow her dream: become a 'working artist', an interesting term she has chosen to describe herself:

> So I didn't go to art college, instead I did in fact what my mum wanted me to do, I learnt shorthand and typing and worked in offices, until I got married and had my first child which was . . . 27 years ago now . . . in 1979 and then I was a full time mum for quite some years and did all sorts of odd, part-time jobs and what have you to bring a little bit more money in and then when I got to 40 and when my second daughter went off to school, I just decided I wanted to do something for myself, I wanted to . . . you know, start with art up again . . . I didn't . . . I sort of didn't really think I would become *a working artist* and that I would have a studio at that stage, I just wanted to go back into that world, so what I did, I went to Brighton University and got myself on to what was in those days, called the Certificate of Art.[14]

In discussions we have held after the interview, Crook particularly emphasized and explained why she had chosen to call herself a 'working artist': 'It took me a long time to accept that I could be taken seriously by others to be an artist (and allowed myself) – that it wasn't just a hobby but what I was (and always deep down had felt I was, even as a small child). So I guess calling myself a working artist was as much for me as anyone else!'[15] What Crook's commentary powerfully highlights here is the importance of art being recognized and registered as a legitimate kind of work and not a hobby of 'the lady artist' as also noted in Dalton's (2001) study above.

What was therefore significant with my multi-sited ethnographic field work is that it opened up windows in the lives of contemporary women artists and allowed me to follow genealogical trails of entanglements between education and art.[16] It was actually material and discursive entanglements that created conditions of possibility for counter-discourses to emerge and allowed for new kinds of connectivity to be formed between social class, education and art in women's lives. Revisiting resistance within this milieu of inquiries has emerged as a rich theme of analysis (see Tamboukou, 2010e).

ETHNOGRAPHY AND GENEALOGY: SYNTHESIS AND RHYTHM

In this concluding section, I want to create a plane of thinking in which genealogy and ethnography can be brought to work (sound) together, as indeed different notes can be composed into a musical piece.[17] I suggest that working with genealogy and ethnography should be seen in the context of music and Novalis's philosophical suggestion that 'all method is rhythm' (in Bowie, 1990, p. 79). As Bowie explains in the context of the early-nineteenth-century philosophical tradition, 'rhythm, like language, is a form of meaningful differentiality; a beat becomes itself by its relation to the other beats, in an analogous way to the way in which the I of reflection is dependent upon the not-I, the signifier on the other signifiers' (1990, p. 79). In the same line of analogies, genealogical and ethnographic practices have, I suggest, the possibility of being used in the 'form of meaningful differentiality', in the sense that any single practice be it genealogical or ethnographic could be seen operating in relation to the other practices within the same analytical context. In delineating the ways in which ethnographic practices can be related to genealogical practices, it is the sound of their rhythmical movement that I have tried to listen to. What I think I have discerned in their sounding together is more like a musical piece of improvisation, notes/practices brought together only temporarily and provisionally as an effect of experimenting, inventing, inviting others to contribute, responding or playing alone.

In her ethnographic study on *Music in Everyday Life,* Tia De Nora has discussed a long theoretical tradition in the human sciences that have delineated what she calls 'the music and society nexus' (2000, p. 1). If 'musical organization is a simulacrum for social organization' (De Nora, 2000, p. 2), music I suggest, can also become an illuminating metaphor for methodological encounters in the social sciences.[18] Educational research after all is a field that has welcomed and facilitated encounters between art and sociologically driven methods of inquiry: Sara Lawrence-Lightfoot's pathbreaking work with school portraits has initiated a series of encounters between aesthetics and empiricism. Published in 1983, *The Good High School* has opened up new paths connecting epistemology and aesthetics, which Lawrence-Lightfoot has followed throughout her research; her most recent publication in this line of inquiry is *The Art and Science of Portraiture*, published in 1997. It is interesting to note here that Lawrence-Lightfoot has used the musical metaphor of 'duet' to introduce this book, which she co-wrote with Jessica Hoffmann Davis: '*The Art and Science of Portraiture* is not a solo, it is a duet' (1997, p. 15), she has written, blending portraiture and music in the ethnographer's imagination.

Situating my ethnographic work in the tradition of 'ethnographic imagination'[19] and thinking of and with music, what I have therefore suggested is the need to find a rhythm for a musical piece of genealogy and ethnography to be composed while performing together. As Ruth Boyask (Chapter 2, this volume) has cogently argued, it is important to rethink Wright Mill's (1970) notion of 'the sociological imagination' and try to view educational research within it. In this light genealogical and ethnographic practices can be deployed as meaningful differences, complementary methodological practices within a specific analytical context. Within a rhythmic configuration genealogy turns the researcher's attention to specific regimes of truth that may elude the knowledge terrain of the ethnographer, but yet they are part of the scientific discourses through which she recognizes the objects of her ethnographic inquiries and analyses their emergence, constitution and function. However, to follow the genealogical imperative of leaving aside linear and vertical causalities and start charting horizontal connections of multifarious relations between subjects and their worlds, the analyst needs descriptions both of the past and the present. While the dusty genealogical documents can offer glimpses of the past, ethnographic approaches can more effectively illuminate the present: genealogy traces the black squares in the 'order of things' (Foucault, 1966 [2000]), accommodates the invisible, creates uncertainty and points to exclusions while ethnography scrutinizes the visible. The rhythm of their sounding together resonates the contrast between visibility and invisibility, the sayable and the unsayable, pointing to what has been hidden or muted and what has been allowed to emerge or sound.

NOTES

1. See Tamboukou and Ball (2003) for an overview of critical studies. See also Boyask (Chapter 2, this volume) for a discussion of critical ethnographies in the sociology of education.
2. Sue Middleton's interdisciplinary research has made a significant contribution in the field of critical educational studies: 'for me it works to draw simultaneously on a theorist (Foucault), who posited the "death of the subject" and to employ an ethnographic life-history technique that documents how individual human subjects make meaning of their experiences and perspectives', she has written (2003, p. 38).
3. Foucault's work has been influential in a body of postructural feminist literature in ethnographic research in education. For an overview of this body of work, see St Pierre and Pillow (2000).
4. For an explication of the genealogical approach, see Tamboukou (1999, 2003).
5. For a critical overview and discussion of these studies in relation to the genealogical method, see Tamboukou (2003).
6. For further discussion of life history approaches in educational research, see Tierney and Clemens (Chapter 19, this volume).
7. See also Middleton (Chapter 21, this volume) for a detailed discussion of research in the archives with documents and particularly letters.
8. Women as nomadic subjects has been a recurring concept in my research (Tamboukou, 2003, 2009, 2010b). See also Tamboukou and Ball (2002).
9. For a detailed explication of methodological encounters between genealogy and ethnography, see Tamboukou and Ball (2003).
10. For further discussion of ethnographic practices in education as they have been transferred from the discipline of anthropology, see Mills, Chapter 3, this volume.
11. For important life history studies of art teachers, see amongst others Sikes et al. (1985).

12. Interview with Pauline Crook, 17 February 2006. I have to note here that Pauline Crook has explicitly asked me to use her real name.
13. During the British Sociological Association (BSA) annual conference in 2007, I organized an exhibition and a round table discussion with the women artists who participated in my ethnographic research. See Tamboukou, (2007).
14. Interview with Pauline Crook, 17 February 2006, my emphasis.
15. Crook, personal e-mail communication.
16. What also emerged from this ethnographic work is a dynamic interrelation between art and political activism, the discussion of which goes well beyond the limitations of this chapter.
17. In blending the boundaries between art and ethnography, I follow trends in qualitative research that incorporate arts methods in research practice. Elliott Eisner has influentially written on the value of doing it (see Eisner, 1981, 1997).
18. de Vries (Chapter 25, this volume) also uses the musical metaphor of improvisation to discuss autoethnography.
19. For significant contributions in this tradition, see Clifford and Marcus (1986), Atkinson (1990) and Willis (2000).

REFERENCES

Atkinson, P. (1990), *The Ethnographic Imagination, Textual Constructions of Reality*, London: Routledge.
Bowie, A. (1990), *Aesthetics and Subjectivity, from Kant to Nietzsche*, Manchester: Manchester University Press.
Clifford, J. and Marcus G.E. (eds) (1986), *Writing Culture: The Poetics and Politics of Ethnography*, Berkeley, CA: University of Califonia Press.
Dalton, P. (2001), *The Gendering of Art Education*, Buckingham: Open University Press.
Deleuze, G. (1992), 'What is a dispositif?', in T.J. Armstrong (ed.), trans. M. Foucault, *Philosopher: Essays Translated from the French and German by Timothy J Armstrong*, London: Harvester Wheatsheaf, pp. 159–68.
De Nora, T. (2000), *Music in Everyday Life*, Cambridge: Cambridge University Press.
Eisner, E.W. (1981), 'On the differences between scientific and artistic approaches to qualitative research', *Educational Researcher*, **10** (4), 5–9.
Eisner, E.W. (1997), 'The new frontier in qualitative research methodology', *Qualitative Inquiry*, **3** (3), 259–73.
Foucault, M. (1980), 'The confession of the flesh', in C. Gordon (ed. and trans.), *Power/Knowledge: Selected Interviews and Other Writings 1972–1977*, London: Harvester Wheatsheaf, pp. 194–228.
Foucault, M. ([1971] 1986), 'Nietzsche, genealogy, history', in Paul Rabinow (ed.), D.F. Bouchard and S. Simon (trans.), *The Foucault Reader*, Harmondsworth: Peregrine, pp. 76–100.
Foucault, M. ([1975] 1991), *Discipline and Punish*, trans. A. Sheridan, London: Penguin.
Foucault, M. ([1966] 2000), *The Order of Things: An Archaeology of the Human Sciences*, Tavistock Publications (trans.), London: Routledge.
Lawrence-Lightfoot, S. (1983), *The Good High School: Portraits of Character and Culture*, New York: Basic Books.
Lawrence-Lightfoot, S. and D.J. Hoffman (1997), *The Art and Science of Portraiture*, San Francisco, CA: Jossey-Bass.
Middleton, S. (2003), 'Top of their class? On the subject of "education" Doctorates', in M. Tamboukou and S.J. Ball (eds), *Dangerous Encounters, Genealogy and Ethnography*, New York: Peter Lang, pp. 38–55.
Mills, C. Wright (1970), *The Sociological Imagination*, Harmondsworth: Penguin (originally published in 1959).

Sikes, P., Measor, L. and Woods, P. (1985), *Teacher Careers: Crises and Continuities*, Lewes: Falmer Press.

St Pierre, E.A. and Pillow, W.S. (eds) (2000), *Working the Ruins: Feminist Poststructural Theory and Methods in Education*, London and New York: Routledge.

Tamboukou, M. (1999), 'Writing genealogies: an exploration of Foucault's strategies for doing research', *Discourse: Studies in the Cultural Politics of Education*, **20** (2), 201–18.

Tamboukou, M. (2003), *Women, Education and the Self: A Foucauldian Perspective*, Basingstoke: Palgrave Macmillan.

Tamboukou, M. (2007), 'Am I that name? Nomadic lines in becoming a woman artist', exhibition and round table discussion, British Sociological Association Annual Conference, 12–14 April, University of East London, UK.

Tamboukou, M. (2009), 'Leaving the self, nomadic passages in the memoir of a woman artist', *Australian Feminist Studies,* **24** (61), 307–24.

Tamboukou, M. (2010a), *In the Fold Between Power and Desire: Women Artists' Narrative*, Newcastle-upon-Tyne: Cambridge Scholars Publishing.

Tamboukou, M. (2010b), *Nomadic Narratives, Visual Forces: Gwen John's Letters and Paintings*, New York: Peter Lang.

Tamboukou, M. (2010c), *Visual Lives: Carrington's Letter, Drawings and Paintings*, BSA Auto/Biography Monograph Series, Nottingham: Russell Press.

Tamboukou, M. (2010d), 'Narratives from within: an Arendtian approach to life-histories and the writing of history', *Journal of Educational Administration and History*, **42** (2), 115–31.

Tamboukou, M. (2010e), 'Charting cartographies of resistance: line of flight in women artists' narratives', *Gender and Education*, **22** (6), 679–96.

Tamboukou, M. and Ball, S.J. (2002), 'Nomadic subjects: young black women in Britain', *Discourse: Studies in the Cultural Politics of Education*, **23** (3), 267–84.

Tamboukou, M. and Ball, S.J. (eds) (2003), *Dangerous Encounters: Genealogy and Ethnography*, New York: Peter Lang.

Willis, P. (2000), *The Ethnographic Imagination*, Oxford: Polity Press.

7. Feminist perspectives on qualitative educational research
Alexandra Allan

INTRODUCTION

The debates surrounding feminist research and its relationship to qualitative methods are now well worn within the social sciences. A number of established handbooks exist to guide readers through the quagmire of these discussions (Bell and Roberts, 1981; Reinharz, 1992; Ribbens and Edwards, 1992; Stanley and Wise, 1993; Maynard and Purvis, 1994; Ramazanoglu and Holland, 2002; Delamont, 2003; and Letherby, 2003). Within the field of education these discussions have also been widely rehearsed, with a number of scholars suggesting that education is one of the main fields to have benefited from, and to have contributed the most to, feminist qualitative research practice (Oleson, 2005; Skeggs, 2005). This chapter will attempt to draw together some of the major themes which have dominated feminist research in previous decades (methods, ethics, the role of the researcher and epistemology and theory) in order to ask how they have been taken up or developed within educational research; to examine what feminist qualitative educational research has entailed and what may constitute its practice in the future.

One of the major problems with an overview of this nature relates to the definition of the different concepts drawn upon. How do we attempt to understand or describe feminism, education and qualitative research when they are 'umbrella' terms which have all been used to refer to a wide range of practices, assumptions, processes and theoretical positions? Although subscribing to a basic understanding of feminism (as a political motivation to work for emancipatory reform in relation to the oppression of women), of education (*as social spaces*, both inside and outside of school, constituted by the transfer and co-construction of knowledge, Levinson, 1999) and of qualitative research (as a situated and interpretive approach to the social world, Denzin and Lincoln, 2005) this chapter will attempt to work with and highlight the multiple and complex nature of all of these terms. The chapter will utilize a wide range of research examples, all of which have been self-defined as feminist qualitative educational research; making a concerted effort not to close down discussions prematurely or to make proscriptions as to what these practices should entail (Reinharz, 1992).

A QUALITATIVE METHODOLOGY?

One of the longest running debates within feminist methodology relates to the suitability of qualitative methods for feminist research practice. Maynard (1994) is one author who proposes that these debates first arose within early second-wave feminism[1] as a response to the dominant 'value free' modes of research that existed at the time and as a critique of the exploitative relations that were commonly practised by researchers. It was a debate which was provisionally developed in opposition to positivism (a paradigmatic stance based on a core belief that the truth about the social world can be established through detached and objective observation). This so-called 'scientific' approach was rejected by many feminists who argued that it was a project that espoused a 'rationally homocentric' epistemology (Hekman, 1990, p. 8). Claiming the need for a new approach, many feminist researchers began to argue for a new post-positivist paradigm. Their argument was that this would utilize a qualitative methodology which could be used by feminist researchers to 'plug the gaps' and to contest the distortions that had been made in previous male-dominated accounts.

One, now infamous, example of such a critique can be found in Oakley's (1981) work on feminist interview methods. In this account Oakley attempted to mount a challenge against the traditional 'malestream' interview methods that dominated research practice at the time. These, she felt, were characterized by a limiting one-way process of exchange (where the researcher's purpose was just to elicit data and never respond) and by narrow attitudes to the interviewee (seeing them in an objectified manner and as simple repositories of data). Oakley's own work with women in relation to matters of health and motherhood led her to argue that such relationships were neither helpful nor desirable for feminist researchers. Indeed, her arguments relating to the use of more reciprocal and respectful interview methods led her to become seen as a key proponent for the use of qualitative methods within feminist research.

Since these early conversations it would appear that the debate has moved on considerably, away from what has often been described as a 'prescriptive', 'knitting pattern' approach and towards an acceptance of the multiple methods and epistemologies that feminists may take up (Letherby, 2004). As Dickens (1983, p. 1) explains:

Demands that feminists produce a unique methodology act to circumscribe the impact of feminism . . . we feel it is time to abandon what amounts to a defensive strategy. It has to be recognised that feminist research is not a specific, narrow, methodology, but one that is informed at every stage by an acknowledged political commitment.

Interestingly, Oakley (2000) has also revised her original line of argumentation in recent years after having gone through, what she describes as, a 'conversion experience' in relation to quantitative methods. Although Oakley does not deny the usefulness of qualitative research methods in feminist research, her work does attempt to deconstruct the discourses which have tied 'soft qualitative methods' together with femininity. Oakley argues that feminists now need to rehabilitate and reshape quantitative research methods and not to anathematize more experimental ways of knowing (Jarviluoma et al., 2003).

Feminism and Ethnography

And yet there still appears to be a great deal of sympathy amongst a number of feminist researchers for the use of certain qualitative methods and methodological approaches. One of the most commonly cited approaches is ethnography. Understood as an 'approach' to research that takes us closer to the meanings and experiences of social actors in everyday life (Denzin and Lincoln, 2005) and which utilizes a number of common methods (participant observation, informal interviewing and documentary analysis), ethnography has often been thought to have a great deal in common with feminism. These commonalities include: a focus on experience, subjectivity, meanings, participation and context (Skeggs, 2005). Ethnography is also an approach which has been understood to have been practised by female researchers for some time now (exemplified in the diaries of a number of early anthropologist's wives, Bell et al., 1993) and to have a long history in feminist research practice (demonstrated in the work of Harriet Martineau, who is widely proclaimed to be the 'mother of contemporary ethnography', Deegan et al., 2009).

Of course, as Youdell (2006) reminds us, ethnographic research is not entirely synonymous with qualitative research, for quantitative methods have often been utilized as part of the process. It is also important to note, as Skeggs (2005) does, that there is nothing inherently feminist about ethnographic research. Despite its commonalities and seeming compatibility with feminism Skeggs reminds us that ethnographic research has a basis in enlightenment imperialism (where little attention has been paid to women except, perhaps, in the classification of their bodies) and has often been used for exploitative purposes. Traditionally, Caplan (1993) suggests, ethnographic research has also been very difficult for women to conduct because its practice has been circumscribed by dogged gendered beliefs and stereotypical assumptions.

However, by arguing for ethnography to be recognized as varied in form and not simply emanating from one understanding of the social world, many feminists have continued to champion ethnography as an approach which best enables a multifaceted and in-depth understanding of women's experiences. Haraway (1998), for example, suggests that all feminist researchers should consider adopting an ethnographic approach to their research. In a similar manner, both hooks (1990) and Abu-Lughod (1986) have claimed that ethnography best enables feminists to unsettle the boundaries of traditional research practice and to gain a 'view from below'.

Feminism, Education and Ethnography

According to Delamont and Atkinson (1980, 1995) ethnography has also had a long and varied history within educational research, with many US studies having developed from cultural anthropology and most British studies tending to have originated from within the 'new' sociology of education.[2] The British strand of this research has predominantly taken place with children aged 7–16 in mainstream schooling and has involved researchers 'making the familiar' of schools 'strange', although in recent years it has increasingly been carried out in different locations and with much younger children (Delamont, 2002; James, 2005).

As Walford (2000) argues, it is feminist ethnographic research (or at least ethnographic research with a focus on gender) that has been at the forefront of the field of education for many years now. Skelton and Francis (2001) believe that this is largely due to the work of second-wave feminists who worked hard to raise awareness of the inequalities faced by girls and women in the education system. Of course, this is not to suggest that the education of girls and women was not of concern before this point (for example, see Wollstonecraft, 1792 [1975]). However, it was during the late 1970s and early 1980s that these feminist ethnographic studies began to emerge, seeking to gain a deeper insight into the actual experiences of women and girls within education. For as Llewellyn (1980) has argued, before this point we simply didn't know what girls actually did in school.

Many of these early feminist educational studies focused on issues of discrimination, 'underachievement' in maths and science, curriculum and career choices, resources (for example, textbooks) and male domination of classroom space (Stanworth, 1981; Acker, 1988; Askew and Ross, 1988; Walkerdine, 1989; Spender, 1992). One notable example of an ethnographic project which took place during this era was Clarricoates' (1980) study of four primary schools. In this project Clarricoates noted the strong sexual division of labour that occurred in these settings, the discrimination that many girls faced and the dominant 'gender codes' that were still being transmitted to the children.

In recent years feminist ethnographers have also moved on to examine a number of 'new' and different issues in relation to gender and education. These include: sexualities, sex education, academic achievement, the intersection of gender with class, gender policy and educational reform, women in further and higher education, race and ethnicity, and the informal or peer cultures that exist within educational institutions (Finders, 1997; Hey, 1997; Datnow, 1998; Francis, 1998; Holland et al., 1998, Proweller, 1998; Reay, 1998; McLeod, 2002; Weekes, 2004; Weis, 2004; Leathwood, 2005; Renold, 2005; Allan, 2010). Following the 'cultural' and 'postmodern' turn that is reported to have occurred within the social sciences, a number of scholars have also moved away from their traditional focus on classroom practice to examine processes of identity formation within wider educational institutions.

Best's (2000) ethnographic research on American high school proms is one example of such a study. In this project Best used interviews, narratives and observation in order to examine how femininity was produced and reproduced during these events. Best argues that the prom is a particularly important part of school life and a defining moment in becoming feminine. She concludes from her work that the girls she worked with took up discourses of self-transformation to give meaning to their prom practices and that it was these discourses which operated to secure their focus on constructing and reconstructing their bodies as properly feminine.

Allan's (2007, 2010) research with privately educated upper middle-class school girls also sought to examine the discursive constitution of gendered identities. Allan's research can be described as an ethnographic, longitudinal follow-up study. Alongside the traditional ethnographic methods of semi-structured interviewing and participant observation, Allan also adopted a number of visual methods in her research, including: photographic diaries, photographic workshops, photographic elicitation interviews, photomatics and collaborative film-making. These methods were thought to allow for a complex exploration of the processes of identity constitution. Rather than seeking to access the girls' 'real', 'authentic', 'static' or 'unified' identities the methods were employed because they highlighted the multiple and conflicting discursive sites that the girls negotiated. As Holliday (2000, p. 516) suggests, such methods can be regarded as particularly postmodern forms of media, allowing researchers to examine the ways in which subjects may be situated in specific configurations of discourse and making them open for examination as they recur in different images.

One further example can be witnessed in the work of Gordon et al. (2000) in a project which sought to explore citizenship, difference and marginality in four schools in Helsinki and London. The researchers were concerned with how processes of inclusion and exclusion in school produced citizens of the nation state and how gendered identities were forged during this process. Using the metaphor of 'dance' to explain how young people's identities were constituted across the official, informal and physical spaces of the school, these authors have arguably encouraged a whole new generation of feminist studies to focus on space and embodiment as important factors in the production of gendered and educational identities.

RESEARCH ON, BY AND FOR WOMEN?

Another demand made by a number of second-wave feminist researchers was for feminist research to be conducted on women, by women and for women (Stanley and Wise, 1993). This is a viewpoint which is thought to have arisen out of concerns for the visibility of women within traditional sociological studies (for example, studies where social class was often only measured in terms of the male 'breadwinner's' occupation, where research on young people solely focused on the activities of young men in gangs and street corners and where the supposedly 'private' lives of housewives were not seen to be of interest to the wider public).

Many scholars have also suggested that this was a demand that developed in conjunction with feminist standpoint theory. Although feminist standpoint theory should be recognized as a broad range of loosely related approaches, developed by a number of different scholars (including Dorothy Smith (1987), Patricia Hill-Collins (1998) and Nancy Hartsock (1998)), it is a position characterized by its concern for women's experience. Experience, in a general sense, is understood by standpoint theorists as a special form of knowledge (a tacit form of knowing only gained from situated experiences) which can be used to challenge women's oppression (Oleson, 2005).

In many of the feminist research projects which were conducted at around the time when standpoint theory was introduced, this understanding of experience often resulted in a methodological practice of 'matching' (Youdell, 2006). This was a practice involving the researcher and research participants being matched according to identity characteristics like gender, ethnicity and social class. From this viewpoint it was only possible for researchers to conduct research with groups with whom they shared a similar experience (for example, black feminists to work with other black women).

Men Doing Feminist Research

In the years since standpoint theory was first introduced it has been subject to a great deal of criticism and further debate. One particularly fierce debate to have ensued relates to the viability of men doing feminist research on women's experiences. A number of scholars have argued that this is an idea that cannot be seriously entertained owing to the very different experiences that men and women have in society (Sipilä, 1994). However, for some other scholars this should be a possibility, owing to the fact that they believe that the researcher and the researched cannot be matched in any simple way (see Probyn, 1990; Scott, 1992) and that women's oppression can only be challenged by an examination of the wider gender relations that exist in society (for example, also in relation to men and masculinities).

Les Back (1993) is one male researcher who has taken up this challenge. Although Back has outlined his own initial anxieties about engaging with feminist principles (stating that he was scared to take them up in his own practice and that he thought it was inappropriate for him to comment on them from his position as a privileged male) he has since argued for men to 'make themselves seen' in their research and for them to respond positively to the feminist research agenda. This he believes should be done without becoming 'proto-female' or 'possessing the ground of virtue in a vicarious way', but in order to accept that men are gendered subjects too and that this can have important implications for fieldwork practice.

Men, Masculinities and Educational Research

It is against the backdrop of these arguments about 'men doing feminism' that men's studies is believed to have emerged in the early 1970s, as an anti-sexist way of questioning the norms and practices that constitute masculine identities (Jarviluoma et al., 2003). Whilst such studies are not without criticism, especially because many of them are seen to be devoid of feminist analyses, they have been widely taken up by educational researchers who have become convinced of the need to examine the multiple masculinities that are produced within educational settings (Levinson, 1999).

Some of these studies have been conducted by men who claim to have been influenced by feminist principles. One example is Mac an Ghaill's (1994) study: *The Making of Men*. This was a three-year ethnographic research project which used observation, informal discussion, interviews and diaries in order to explore the construction and regulation of masculinities amongst a group of Year Eleven students (aged fifteen and sixteen). Mac an Ghaill, himself, claims that his work is 'indebted to feminist methodology', particularly to those emancipatory research methods which emphasize collaboration, reciprocity and reflexivity.

However, not all educational research on masculinity and masculine identities has been conducted by male researchers. Indeed, in an era that has been dominated by panic surrounding the supposed failure of boys in the education system, some of the most important feminist research to have been conducted by female scholars has examined the educational experiences of young men (Epstein et al., 1999). Christine Skelton's (1997) ethnographic research on how boys challenge, negotiate, reject and reconstruct masculine selves in two primary schools is one example of such a study. As a feminist researcher Skelton claims that her work is driven by the political will to gain insight into how boys engage with male power in order to add to current feminist understandings.

A FEMINIST ETHICS OF CARE?

Research ethics have also loomed large in discussions relating to feminist methodology. Often these debates have centred round notions of 'care' and 'responsibility', rather than the more traditional categories of 'outcomes' or 'rights' (Mauthner et al., 2001). Many feminists have discussed how feminist research practice should be dominated by a 'feminist ethics of care'. This is an idea that is thought to have emerged out of Carol Gilligan's (1982) work, where she is believed to have argued that women were naturally more caring than men. And although this conception of 'care' has since been criticized for relying too heavily on essentialist understandings, this communitarian ethical model is still commonly taken up by feminist researchers because of the way in which it is seen to privilege emotionality and avoid exploitation. As Ribbens and Edwards (1992) note, this is a model which appears to seek more complex answers to the conflicts that occur in research. It is not an approach which is concerned with formulating universalistic moral principles which stand outside of power relations and above context.

One of the major ethical issues to have been discussed in relation to feminist qualitative research is how power should be handled in the relationship between the researcher and the researched. This was a particular concern for Stacey (1988), who argued that even despite the emphasis placed on 'care' for participants within feminist ethnographic research, there is still a large risk that exploitation may occur because of the way in which the researcher benefits from the process at the expense of the participants. In recent years, however, a number of rejoinders have been written in response to Stacey's original article. A number of these authors have responded by suggesting that Stacey takes the argument too far; that it would never be possible to conduct a study which would be regarded as entirely ethical (Wheatley, 1994).

One further ethical concern commonly raised in feminist qualitative research relates to the representation of research data. This concern has often been described in the research literature as a 'crisis of representation', where the once widely used and esteemed realist genre of writing up research has come in for some criticism. Paralleling the work of Said (1978) in his account of Orientalism in European culture, many feminists have critiqued traditional realist research texts for inscribing a radical distinction between the observer and the observed (the author and the 'other'). Within the realist genre the author, they argue, claims a position of omniscience and the authority to speak unequivocally of the people and culture in question. It is through this process that these 'others' (often women with marginal voices) become silenced and exist only as muted objects of the researcher's scrutiny (Devault, 1990, Hammersley and Atkinson, 2007).

Representation, Reflexivity and Voice

As a result of this 'crisis' in representation many feminist scholars have argued for a need to make the previously unarticulated voices of 'other' women heard in research, producing a marked shift in the way in which feminist researchers have written up their research data. For example, some researchers have sought to move towards the practice of joint authorship in the hope that this will allow other voices to penetrate the text as a form of multivocality (Bell and Napurrula, 1989). In Fine and Weis's words (1994, p. 82), a number of feminists have pushed towards a written approach which emphasizes:

> 'contradiction, heterogeneity and multiplicity' and produce a 'cacophony of voices speaking to each other in dispute, dissonance, support, dialogue, contention and/or contradiction'.

A number of feminists have also begun to experiment with alternative forms of representation, including making use of split page narratives, ethnodrama, poetry, autoethnography and photographic essays (see, for example, Piirto, 2002; Prendergast et al., 2009). Whilst it is often recognized that these 'new' forms of representation cannot simply elide issues of authority or fully account for unequal power relations (especially if they simply provide better ways of writing about unethical projects) it is often accepted that they enable more participatory and self-conscious texts which are grounded in emotionality and lived experience (Wolf, 1992).

The crisis in representation has also led a number of feminists to become increasingly interested in reflexive research practice. Authors like De Laine (2000) and Coffey (1999) suggest that researchers need to be aware of their personal biographies, to make explicit their own location in relation to the research and to reflect on the role that they played in creating and representing the data. As Fine and Weis (1994, p. 70) explain it: researchers need to be aware of the 'hyphen at which self-other join in the politics of everyday life . . . that both separates and merges personal identities with our invention of others'.

Ethics and the Feminist Educational Researcher

Ethical questions relating to voice, representation and power have also been central to the feminist debates that have occurred within the field of education. Morris-Roberts' (2002) research on the construction and spatiality of young women's friendship groups at school is one example of a project which has further developed age-old feminist ethical concerns with 'sexist collusion'. Morris-Roberts takes up this notion in her work and explains how she was also often unwittingly party to heterosexist collusion in her own research practice. She questions whether this complicity may have further contributed to the dominant position of discourses of compulsory heterosexuality within the school, leaving even less room for girls to negotiate alternative gendered identities (also see Sikes, 2010 for a further example of work which focuses on the ethical issues researchers encounter when attempting to challenge normative notions).

Another way in which feminist researchers have taken up these ethical concerns within educational research is through the application of feminist post-structural theoretical principles to practices of representation (see, for example, Popoviciu et al., 2006). As St Pierre and Pillow (2000) suggest, researchers should now be seen to be working in the 'twilight of foundationalism', through a 'restless post-period' that troubles all of those things we once assumed were solid, substantial and whole. Many feminists have now come to question whether there is a singular reality or version of the truth which exists out there that can be easily accessed through rigorous methodological practice, and whether there is an essential human subject who remains the same throughout time (Wells et al., Chapter 8, this volume). For these feminists then, representation is no longer about:

capturing the truth already out there. It is about constructing particular versions of the truth, questioning how regimes of truth become neutralised as knowledge, and thus pushing the sensibilities of readers in new directions. If ethnography is to provide a critical space to push thought against itself, then ethnographers must begin by identifying their own textual strategies and political commitments and pointing out the differences among the stories, the structures of telling and the structures of belief. (Britzman, 2000, p. 38)

Britzman (1991) is one feminist educational researcher who has attempted to 'work the ruins' of these humanist concepts and to have represented her ethnographic work differently. Britzman's research sought to examine the multiple discourses which constituted one group of student teachers' identities during their initial year of training. Britzman's purpose was not to tell the 'real' story of what it meant to become a teacher, but rather to seek to explore the effects of discourse in this context, with the aim of imagining future worlds which could be less cruel. Britzman (2000) admits that her first attempt at writing this ethnography differently was a failure because it ended up taking a very traditional form. However, Britzman notes that as she persisted in this work she began to develop what she refers to as an ethnographic opera; a text which allowed for the plural accounts and competing stories of her participants to be told and for them to be repositioned from the site of the individual to the narrative.

Gonick (2003) and Youdell (2006) are two further authors to have taken up these principles in their representation of educational research data. Youdell describes her own techniques for representing her data as combining social transcription conventions and theatrical conventions of dramatic script. This involves Youdell representing the words of her participants in the form of dramatic scenes and episodes. This is not, she argues, to infer that they were the self-conscious performances of individuals but rather to underline the iterative and ongoing nature of discursive practice and subjectivity formation, and to leave the data open to alternative and further analysis. This she believes allows her to better examine the minutiae and complex nature of the mundane practices of schooling.

Although not using the same theatrical conventions, Gonick develops a similar approach to the representation of her ethnographic data generated with a group of young women in one American high school. In her research Gonick developed a participatory film club which she felt enabled her to explore the different ways in which the girls would use the space to try out various ways of becoming a woman. This, she believes, worked as a form of feminist critical pedagogy, where the girls could deconstruct their experiences and question their status as normal and natural. Even despite her use of these participatory methods Gonick does not make any simple claims to multivocality in her work. In fact Gonick notes how the words of one of her participants (*'I don't mean to be racist, but it's different. You can't understand. You were born here. It's different for us that just came here'*, 2003, p. 21, emphasis in original) continued to challenge her as she strove to represent her data ethically. Gonick was, however, able to address this dilemma by (re)presenting her work in the form of a 'messy text'; a text which she felt allowed for a range of different stories to be heard and for the differences between them to be made evident.

CONCLUSION

It is important to conclude by noting the inevitably partial and limited nature of the account offered in this chapter. The stories that are told here and the issues that are outlined, however dominant, can never account for the full activity of the field. What the chapter does offer, however, is a wide range of examples which have been brought together over the years under the label of feminist qualitative educational research. By drawing upon these examples it is hoped that the chapter offers readers a route into the messy and complex debates which continue to surround feminist qualitative research practice.

The chapter should not, however, be read as a simple progression story. It is not a tale which charts a singular journey from an exploitative 'malestream' tradition, to humble second-wave feminist practice, and further beyond to a complex post-structural challenge to all those things which we once held as true. For as Coffey (1999) suggests,[3] such tales gloss over the tensions, ignore the differences and do a distinct disservice to early research practice.

Rather, the account that is offered in this chapter should be recognized as a celebration of a 'highly complex, diverse and energised practice' (Britzman, 2000, p. 38). It is an account which attempts to recognize the tremendous impact that feminists have had within qualitative educational research practice (and that feminist educational researchers have had upon wider feminist qualitative research practice), where traditionally these inputs may have been overlooked or misplaced (Jennaway, 1990). It is also an account which looks to the future, in order to question how these fields may be combined in an equally fruitful manner, in order to continue this 'lusty and rigorous' methodological questioning (St Pierre and Pillow, 2000).

NOTES

1. The term 'second-wave feminism' is used in this instance to refer to a particular era of feminist thought, action and research from the 1960s and through into the late 1970s (Humm, 1992).
2. The 'new' sociology of education has been described by authors like Barton and Walker (1978) and Apple et al. (2009, p. 1) as a 'diverse and often disputatious field'. It is a field which is thought to have developed in the late 1970s with a distinct concern with social equality and for questioning the intrinsic good of schools.
3. In the article referenced here Coffey is actually referring to Denzin and Lincoln's (2005) account of the 'five moments' of qualitative research. Whilst the source being commented upon is different, I am proposing here that the argument remains the same; we cannot tell simple, singular stories about how different research practices have progressed across time.

REFERENCES

Abu-Lughod, L. (1986), *Writing Women's Worlds: Bedouin Stories*, Berkeley, CA: University of California Press.
Acker, S. (ed.) (1988), *Teachers, Gender and Careers*, London: The Falmer Press.
Allan, A. (2007), 'Struggling for success: an ethnographic exploration of the construction of young femininities in the selective, single-sex school', Unpublished PhD Thesis, Cardiff University.
Allan, A. (2010), 'Picturing success: young femininities and the (im)possibilities of academic achievement in selective, single-sex education', *International Studies in Sociology of Education*, **20** (1), 39–54.
Apple, M., Ball, S. and Armando Gadin, L. (2009), *The Routledge International Handbook of the Sociology of Education*, London: Routledge.
Askew, S. and Ross, C. (1988), *Boys Don't Cry: Boys and Sexism in Education*, Milton Keynes: Open University Press.
Back, L. (1993), 'Gendered participation: masculinity and fieldwork in a south London adolescent community', in D. Bell, P. Caplan and W. Jahan Karim (eds), *Gendered Fields: Women, Men and Ethnography*, London: Routledge, pp. 215–23.
Barton, L. and Walker, S. (1978), 'Sociology of education at the crossroads', *Educational Review*, **30** (3), 269–83.
Bell, D. and Napurrula, N.T. (1989), 'Speaking about rape is everyone's business', *Women's Studies International Forum*, **12** (4), 403–16.
Bell, D. and Roberts, H. (1981), *Doing Feminist Research*, London: Routledge.
Bell, D., Caplan, P. and Jahan Karim, W. (1993), *Gendered Fields: Women, Men and Ethnography*, London: Routledge.
Best, A. (2000), *Prom Night: Youth, Schools and Popular Culture*, London: Routledge.
Britzman, D. (1991), *Practice Makes Practice: A Critical Study of Learning to Teach*, Albany, NY: State University of New York Press.
Britzman, D. (2000), 'The question of belief', in E. St Pierre and W. Pillow (eds), *Working the Ruins: Feminist Poststructural Theory and Methods in Education*, London: Routledge, pp. 27–40.
Caplan, P. (1993), 'Learning gender: fieldwork in a Tanzanian coastal village, 1965–85', in D. Bell, P. Caplan and W. Jahan Karim (eds), *Gendered Fields: Women, Men and Ethnography*, London: Routledge, pp. 168–81.
Clarricoates, K. (1980), 'The importance of being Ernest . . . Emma . . . Tom . . . Jane: the perception and categorisation of gender conformity and gender deviation in primary schools', in R. Deem (ed.), *Schooling for Women's Work*, London: Routledge and Kegan Paul, pp. 353–64.

Coffey, A. (1999), *The Ethnographic Self – Fieldwork and the Representation of Identity*, London: Sage.
Datnow, A. (1998), *The Gender Politics of Educational Change*, London: The Falmer Press.
De Laine, M. (2000), *Fieldwork, Participation and Practice: Ethics and Dilemmas in Qualitative Research*, London: Sage.
Deegan, M.J., Hill, M.R. and Wortmann, S.L. (2009), 'Annie Marion Maclean, feminist pragmatist and methodologist', *Journal of Contemporary Ethnography*, **38** (6), 655–65.
Delamont, S. (2002), *Fieldwork in Educational Settings – Methods, Pitfalls and Perspectives*, London: Routledge.
Delamont, S. (2003), *Feminist Sociology*, London: Sage.
Delamont, S. and Atkinson, P. (1980), 'The two traditions in educational ethnography', *British Journal of the Sociology of Education*, **1** (2), 139–52.
Delamont, S. and Atkinson, P. (1995), *Fighting Familiarity: Essays on Education and Ethnography*, Cresskill, NY: Hampton Press.
Denzin, N. and Lincoln, Y. (2005), *The Sage Handbook of Qualitative Research*, London: Sage.
Devault, M. (1990), 'Women write sociology: rhetorical strategies', in A. Hunter (ed.), *The Rhetoric of Social Research: Understood and Believed*, New Brunswick, NY: Rutgers University Press, pp. 97–110.
Dickens, D. and Fontana, A. (eds) 1983), *Postmodernism and Social Inquiry*, London: University College London Press.
Epstein, D., Elwood, J., Hey, V. and Maw, J. (1999), *Failing Boys?: Issues in Gender and Achievement*, Buckingham: Open University Press.
Finders, M. (1997), *Just Girls: Hidden Literacies and Life in Junior High*, New York: Teachers College Press.
Fine, M. and Weis, L. (1994), 'Working the hyphens: reinventing self and other in qualitative research', in N. Denzin and Y. Lincoln (eds), *Handbook of Qualitative Research*, Thousand Oaks, CA: Sage, pp. 70–82.
Francis, B. (1998), *Power Plays: Primary School Children's Constructions of Gender, Power and Adult Work*, London: Trentham.
Gilligan, C. (1982), *In a Different Voice*, Cambridge, MA: Harvard University Press.
Gonick, M. (2003), *Between Femininities: Ambivalence, Identity and the Education of Girls*, New York: State University of New York Press.
Gordon, T., Holland, J. and Lahelma, E. (2000), 'Friends or foes? Interpreting relations between girls in school', in G. Walford and C. Hudson (eds), *Genders and Sexualities in Educational Ethnography, Studies in Educational Ethnography*, Volume 3, New York: Elsevier, pp. 7–25.
Hammersley, M. and Atkinson, P. (2007), *Ethnography: Principles in Practice*, London: Routledge.
Haraway, D. (1998), 'Situated knowledges: the science question in feminism as a site of discourse on the privilege of partial perspective, *Feminist Studies*, **14**, 575–99.
Hartsock, N. (1998), *The Feminist Standpoint Revisited and Other Essays*, Boulder, CO: Westview Press.
Hekman, S. (1990), *Gender and Knowledge*, Cambridge: Polity Press.
Hey, V. (1997), *The Company She Keeps*, Buckingham: Open University Press.
hooks, B. (1990), *Yearning: Race, Gender and Cultural Politics*, Boston, MA: South End Press.
Hill-Collins, P. (1998), *Fighting Words: Black Women and the Search for Justice*, Minnesota, MN: University of Minnesota Press.
Holland, J., Ramazanoglu, C., Sharpe, S. and Thomson, R. (1998), *The Male in the Head*, London: Tufnell Press.
Holliday, R. (2000), 'We've been framed: visualising methodology', *The Sociological Review*, **48** (4), 503–21.
Humm, M. (ed.) (1992), *Feminisms: A Reader*, London: Harvester Wheatsheaf.

James, A. (2005), 'Ethnography and childhood', in A. Coffey, P. Atkinson, S. Delamont, L. Lofland and J. Lofland (eds), *Handbook of Ethnography*, London: Sage, pp. 298–300.

Jarviluoma, H., Pirkko, M. and Vilkko, A. (2003), *Gender and Qualitative Methods*, London: Sage.

Jennaway, M. (1990), 'Paradigms, postmodern epistemologies and paradox: the place of feminism in anthropology', *Anthropological Forum*, **6** (2), 167–89.

Leathwood, C. (2005), '"Treat me as a human being – don't look at me as a woman": femininities and professional identities in further education', *Gender and Education*, **17** (4), 387–409.

Letherby, G. (2003), *Feminist Research in Theory and Practice*, Buckingham: Open University Press.

Letherby, G. (2004), 'Quoting and counting: an autobiographical response to Oakley', *Sociology*, **38** (1), 175–89.

Levinson, B.A. (1999), '(How) can a man do feminist ethnography of education?', *Qualitative Inquiry*, **4** (3), 337–68.

Llewellyn, M. (1980), 'Studying girls at school: the implications of confusion', in R. Deem (ed.), *Schooling for Women's Work*, London: Routledge and Kegan Paul, pp. 42–51.

Mac an Ghaill, M. (1994), *The Making of Men: Masculinities, Sexualities and Schooling*, Buckingham: Open University Press.

Mauthner, M., Birch, M., Jessop, J. and Miller, T. (2001), *Ethics in Qualitative Research*, London: Sage.

Maynard, M. and Purvis, J. (eds) (1994), *Researching Women's Lives from a Feminist Perspective*, Abingdon: Taylor & Francis.

McLeod, J. (2002), 'Working out intimacy: young people and friendship in an age of reflexivity', *Discourse: Studies in the Cultural Politics of Education*, **23** (2), 211–36.

Morris-Roberts, K. (2002), 'Individuality and (dis)identification in young women's friendships at school', PhD thesis, University of Sheffield.

Oakley, A. (1981), 'Interviewing women: a contradiction in terms?', in H. Roberts and D. Bell (eds), *Doing Feminist Research*, London: Routledge, pp. 30–61.

Oakley, A. (2000), *Experiments in Knowing: Gender and Method in the Social Sciences*, New York: State University of New York Press.

Oleson, V. (2005), 'Early millennial feminist qualitative research: challenges and contours', in N. Denzin and Y. Lincoln (eds), *Sage Handbook of Qualitative Research*, London: Sage, pp. 235–78.

Piirto, J. (2002), 'The question of quality and qualifications: writing inferior poems as qualitative research', *International Journal of Qualitative Studies in Education*, **15** (4), 431–45.

Popoviciu, L., Haywood, C. and Mac an Ghaill, M. (2006), 'The promise of post-structuralist methodology: ethnographic representation of education and masculinity', *Ethnography and Education*, **1** (3), 393–412.

Prendergast, M., Leggo, C. and Sameshima, P. (eds) (2009), *Poetic Inquiry: Vibrant Voices in the Social Sciences*, Rotterdam: Sense Publishers.

Probyn, E. (1990), 'Travels in the postmodern: making sense of the local', in L. Nicholson (ed.), *Feminism/Postmodernism*, London: Routledge, pp. 176–90.

Proweller, A. (1998), *Constructing Female Identities: Meaning Making in an Upper Middle-class Youth Culture*, New York: State University of New York Press.

Ramazanoglu, C. and Holland, J. (2002), *Feminist Methodology: Challenges and Choices*, London: Sage.

Reay, D. (1998), 'Rethinking social class: qualitative perspectives on gender and social class', *Sociology*, **32** (2), 259–75.

Reinharz, S. (1992), *Feminist Methods in Social Research*, New York: Oxford University Press.

Renold, E. (2005), *Girls, Boys and Junior Sexualities: Exploring Children's Gender and Sexual Relations in the Primary School*, London: Routledge Falmer.

Ribbens, J. and Edwards, R. (1992), *Feminist Dilemmas in Qualitative Research: Public Knowledge and Private Lives*, London: Sage.

Said, E. (1978), *Orientalism*, London: Pantheon Books.

Scott, J.W. (1992), 'Experience', in J. Butler and J.W. Scott (eds), *Feminists Theorize the Political*, New York: Routledge, pp. 22–40.

Scott, J. (1998), 'Deconstructing equality-versus-difference; or, the uses of poststructuralist theory for feminism', *Feminist Studies*, **14** (1), 33–50.

Sikes, P. (2010), 'Teacher-student sexual relations: key risks and ethical issues', *Ethnography and Education*, **5** (2), 143–57.

Sipilä, J. (1994), 'Men's studies – cracks in hegemonic masculinity', in J. Sipilä and A. Tiihonen (eds), *Constructing Man, Deconstructing Masculinities*, Tampere: Vastapaino, pp. 17–33.

Skeggs, B. (2005), 'Feminist ethnography', in A. Coffey, P. Atkinson, S. Delamont, L. Lofland and J. Lofland (eds), *Handbook of Ethnography*, London: Sage, pp. 426–43.

Skelton, C. (1997), 'Primary boys and hegemonic masculinities', *British Journal of Sociology of Education*, **18** (3), 349–70.

Skelton, C. and Francis, B. (2001), *The Sage Handbook of Gender and Education*, London: Sage.

Smith, D. (1987), *The Everyday World as Problematic: A Feminist Sociology*, Boston, MA: Northeastern University Press.

Spender, D. (1992), *Invisible Women: The Schooling Scandal*, London: The Women's Press.

St Pierre, E. and Pillow, W.S. (2000), *Working the Ruins – Feminist Post Structural Theory and Methods in Education*, London: Routledge.

Stacey, J. (1988), 'Can there be a feminist ethnography?', *Women's Studies International Forum*, **15** (1), 21–7.

Stanley, L. and Wise, S. (1993), *Breaking Out Again: Feminist Consciousness and Feminist Research*, London: Routledge and Kegan Paul.

Stanworth, M. (1981), *Gender and Schooling*, London: Hutchinson.

Walford, G. (ed.) (2000), *Gender and Sexualities in Educational Ethnography*, Oxford: Elsevier.

Walkerdine, V. (1989), *Counting Girls Out*, London: Virago.

Weekes, D. (2004), 'Where my girls at? Black girls and the construction of the sexual', in A. Harris and M. Fine (eds), *All About the Girl: Culture, Power and Identity*, London: Routledge, pp. 141–54.

Weis, L. (2004), *Class Reunion: The Remaking of the American White Working-class*, New York: Routledge.

Wheatley, E. (1994), 'How can we engender ethnography with a feminist imagination: a rejoinder to Judith Stacey', *Women's Studies International Forum*, **17** (4), 403–16.

Wolf, M. (1992), *A Thrice-Told Tale*, Stanford, CA: Stanford University Press.

Wollstonecraft, M. ([1792] 1975), *Vindication of the Rights of Woman*, Harmondsworth: Pelican.

Youdell, D. (2006), *Impossible Bodies, Impossible Selves: Exclusions and Student Subjectivities*, London: Springer.

8. Queer theory, ethnography and education

Cassandra Wells, Anna MacLeod and Blye Frank

HOW TO DO QUEER ETHNOGRAPHY IN EDUCATION?

Articulating a methodology for queer ethnography in education requires a number of contextualizing caveats regarding how its component parts have been developed and understood in academia. The process and practice of critical ethnography merits some elaboration, as do the concepts of queer studies and queer theory, not to mention an explanation of what is meant by research in education. In addition, the tools and methods of ethnographic research will need to be modified according to the requirements of the queer ethos as described. While these tasks seem straightforward, as we investigate the aims and methods of queer research and critical ethnography in the enterprise of education, the limits of each come into focus and pose irresolvable conundrums for those seeking to do queer ethnographic research. A queer ethos is oppositional and thus in a constant state of formation as it reorients to the changing discourses of 'the mainstream'. With this moving target in mind, this chapter will sketch out the borders of a queer ethnography for education, drawing on insights from critical ethnography, queer theory and 'after-queer' perspectives. While these principles will provide some direction to prospective researchers, they will also raise important and confounding questions. Therefore, we suggest that the practice of queer ethnography requires, above all, thoughtfulness and imagination.

CRITICAL ETHNOGRAPHY IN EDUCATION

Ethnography is both a product and method of social research that uses a variety of tools, including long-term observation, interviews and reflection to construct 'thick descriptions' of a particular cultural organization in order to generate insights and understandings (Anderson, 1989). 'Critical' ethnography brings a constructionist perspective to the method by rejecting traditional notions of culture as an object of nature that can be discovered and reported, seeing culture instead as an abstract concept that must be 'attributed' to a context or group by the researcher through interpretations of the material effects of behaviours, events, customs, institutions and their interrelations in everyday life (Wolcott, 1997[2001], p. 156). Influenced by interpretive sociology (which views social life and cultures as the outcome of negotiations of meanings among actors in a context), and combined with critical theories (which place inequitable power relationships based on classed, sexed and/or gendered social positions at the centre of analysis), 'critical ethnography' is understood as the study of the everyday experiences (lived experience) and social arrangements of people as they interact with the social structures of their culture (Anderson, 1989). The meeting points between people and their contexts are seen as sites where meanings that produce, reinforce or change cultures are negotiated.

Rather than dispassionate, detached and atheoretical observation, the critical turn in ethnography encouraged researchers to interrogate and theorize social arrangements. Critical ethnography, then, has been constructed as both a strategy for social scientists to probe deeply into social organization and experience, and a theory to interrogate the relationships between social structure and human agency that explains the persistence of social inequities as well as mechanisms for social transformation.

While ethnographic methods offer researchers in education rich insights, such research tends to emphasize complexity in social life and issues under examination, and does not easily offer concrete plans for educational reform or action (Anderson, 1989). Queer studies, however, include in their purpose an agenda for emancipatory change as a result of the research process (Jagose, 1996; Dilley, 1999). For this reason, queer theory offers a promising direction for action-oriented educational ethnographers.

QUEER TURN IN CRITICAL ETHNOGRAPHY

The adoption of the term 'queer', in its modern sense, has been located at some point in the early 1990s, though its origin story varies according to the aims towards which a queer approach is deployed (Jagose, 1996). In its simplest sense, 'queer' describes an oppositional difference from the mainstream culture centred on sexuality. It posits heterosexuality as dominant, and any non-hetero sexuality (gay, lesbian, bisexual, transgendered, among others) as 'other', non-dominant.

As it relates to sexual identity in this vernacular sense, 'queer' has neither a progressive nor oppressive connotation, though it has been used both to denigrate non-heterosexual desire and identification and to celebrate it. Whether 'queer' is a slur or a point of pride is a product of specific cultural and theoretical pressures bearing on debates about gay and lesbian identities (Jagose, 1996). This 'definitional indeterminacy' has inspired and required much political activity and theoretical work in the humanities, social sciences and education. For now, suffice it to say that 'queer' can refer to an identity (of a person or group) defined by their difference from 'the white heterosexual norm' (Chang, 2005, p. 172).

To further complicate its meaning, as it is used in an academic sense, queer denotes both a position (adjective) and an activity (verb) (Dilley, 1999). To take a queer position inverts the relationship between margin and mainstream, putting mainstream values and norms under examination rather than those which 'deviate' from it in whatever ways. Looking from the margins at the centre of the culture provides a vantage point from which to question the structures and processes that support and privilege heterosexuality as normative. As an activity, 'queering' is the process of analysis that deconstructs the assumptions that produce a particular social order as normal, natural or necessary. Dilley (1999) summarizes queer theory's action as a 'vigorous challenge to that which has constrained what may be known, who may be the knower, and how knowledge has come to be generated' (p. 458). Queer theory, then, draws upon postmodern views of the relationship between power and knowledge (discourse), which is implicated in the production of subjectivities that render people or groups recognizable/visible within a culture (Foucault, 1972, 1973, 1977). This movement towards critical postmodernism in educational research is outlined in Haywood and Mac an Ghaill (2003).

Discourse is both productive (it creates knowledge/subjectivities) and restrictive (in that it defines the possibilities for what can be known/how one can exist in the world). The relationship between power and knowledge is perhaps most evident in those aspects of life that are assumed as taken for granted truths, and form the basis for understanding and organizing social life. Discourses of gender and sexuality exert normative disciplinary power that produce heterosexuality as 'natural', and all other expressions of gender and sexuality as 'other', 'abnormal' or 'unnatural'. Like critical theories in general, queer theory aims to make obvious the unspoken assumptions that underwrite heterosexism, what interests are served through these assumptions, and how to reformulate social life in more inclusive possibilities for being and knowing sexuality. A pioneer in this regard is William G. Tierney (1997), whose influential *Academic Outlaws: Queer Theory and Cultural Studies in the academy* combined critical theories and political pragmatism to argue for the creation of educational communities that value difference and individuality, and against policies and practices (both institutional and personal) of cultural assimilation (the strategy of 'passing' as straight) or division (the separate-but-equal argument).

As made clear by scholars such as Tierney (1997), a 'queer' perspective has grown from political and theoretical movements concerning gay and lesbian identities, though as it is applied in academic fields, queerness has been more complexly and narrowly connected to oppositional sexualities and related struggles for social recognition and justice within a society understood as fundamentally and oppressively heterosexist (Mayo, 2006). Rather than a category into which the dominant culture lumps persons according to an erotic desire for non-heterosexual objects (identities such as gay, lesbian, bisexual, transgender, among others) in order to delegitimize them, activists and theorists have worked to 'confront what is experienced as discrimination and to commit to a collective identity based on being marginalized' (Dilley, 1999, p. 458).

At the same time, queer theory is imagined as the product of specific, historically contingent, cultural and theoretical pressures working at the limits of identity politics to interrogate and deconstruct sexual identities as fixed, universal and/or marginal (Stein and Plummer, 1994; Jagose, 1996; Dilley, 1999). Queer, then, has been used both as a construct for understanding sexual identities that are understood as located outside of cultural norms as well as a strategy for criticizing, and ultimately dismantling, the binary structures and categories (including normal/abnormal, gay/straight, female/male) that support such norms.

However, because queerness is imagined as eternally 'external' to dominant culture and committed to the destabilization of normalizing gender and sexual orientation categories, as social contexts regarding what is marginal and what is mainstream shift, so too does the definition of what is 'queer'. Queer is therefore dependent on the interrelated worlds of social politics and theory to provide the context for its work, and as such, must always be in the process of formation. This state of affairs for 'queer' may be its quintessential characteristic (Jagose, 1996, p. 1). Queer theory, therefore, must constantly be in the process of formation, as its theoretical and political efficacy depends on its resistance to definition. 'The challenge', as Chang (2005) describes it

> is to discover how epistemologies that rely on seeing and hearing, such as dominant or hegemonic ways of knowing, can be brought into dialogue with epistemologies that question what is seen and heard, such as those practices that would grow out of a concrete and active set of queer critical inquiries. In spite of this dilemma about how to act, we must bring empirical inquiry of social and institutional structures together with queer theory's critical analysis of sexual categories, in order to analyze the relevant intersections between cultural meanings and institutional structures. (p. 179)

We now turn to a consideration of the conundrums presented by Chang's challenge.

CONUNDRUM 1 – POSITION OF THE RESEARCHER

In Chapter 7 of this volume, Allan outlined some ethical debates that have shaped feminist qualitative inquiry. Connected to the 'crisis of representation' (p. 100) and the related interest in reflexive research practice (p. 101) in feminism, queer researchers have also struggled to locate themselves in both constructionism and deconstructionism. Queer theory rejects modernist tendencies for researchers to assume a position of detached objectivity relative to the research context and the researched. Instead, following postmodern influence, queer theory asserts that there is no 'objective' position from which one may impartially observe a research context, nor is there a culture that exists apart from ideologies and discourse. Researchers are always and necessarily implicated in the construction of both the research context and in the discourses that structure their own positions as researchers. Likewise, traditional ethnography asks that researchers 'bracket' their biases, to suspend the knowledge that derives from their experiences and identities, and to report on 'reality' as it exists in nature (presumably 'pre-discursively'). The critical turn in ethnography, however, revised the role of researcher as an interpreter of cultural meanings whose biases are openly incorporated into the act of ethnography (rather than a reporter of pre-discursive truths) whose purpose in the research environment is to actively question the ideologies that present themselves as natural. Both queer theory and critical ethnography, then, share the mandate for an active constructionist role for the researcher in both the framing of the research act and the production of research data and knowledge.

At the same time, both queer theory and critical ethnography involve 'deconstructionism'. As noted previously, queer theory is a de-centring theory that inverts the relationship between the mainstream and the margins of society. Queer theory interrogates the mainstream – that is, the taken-for-granted organization of a given community or context – in search of the normalizing forces that present the status quo as normal, and the silences these forces cause. In order to accomplish this, queer theory assumes a place outside of the mainstream; a 'queer' perspective from which vantage point the mainstream can be questioned. Here lies the first conundrum – how to construct and assume a 'queer' position while participating in the culture that is the subject of the ethnography? Put another way, if 'queerness' is unintelligible within mainstream culture – visible only in its absence – how can an ethnographer be incorporated into the research context while assuming a 'queer' (unknowable) position?

Youdell (2009) illustrates this problematic in her article 'Queer outings'. In it, she describes 'doing queer' as an ethnographer in an educational setting by attempting to embody 'practices that unsettle the meanings of these discourses [that construct sexual subjectivities such as hetero, gay, bisexual as unitary and complete identities] and deploy other discourses that have been subjugated or disallowed' (pp. 88). Though she attempts to construct and assume a 'queer' subjectivity and to resist the constitution of her as 'hetero in/by the heterosexual matrix of the school' (p. 95), Youdell comes to realize that 'subject-hood is dependent on our intelligibility', and that her ability to interact with the participants in her ethnographic research requires them to 'know' her (p. 88). An encounter with some students in her research setting is telling: after acknowledging 'having a boyfriend', Youdell realizes that although she made no claims to heterosexuality, 'admitting a "boyfriend" once made me that over and over again' (p. 95). When Youdell begins a sexual relationship with a woman, and again some students ask about her relationship status, she recalls: 'they put previous boyfriend together with current girlfriend and made me bisexual. I accepted that' (p. 95). At the same time as Youdell attempted to reject 'the closet', she found that the discourses of heterosexuality made her queer subjectivity nameless and thus unrecognizable. Saying nothing about it allowed her to 'pass' as hetero, naming it was necessarily a 'coming out'. 'I had followed threads of essentialism, queer theory, subjugated discourses and ethnographic field relations', Youdell explains, 'until I was bound by the impossibility of resolution' (p. 97).

CONUNDRUM 2: THE PROPER OBJECT OF QUEER ETHNOGRAPHY

Jagose (1996) suggests that the concepts of chromosomal sex, gender and sexuality constitute a kind of heterosexual triad, one that operates as a mode of social control for Western societies. She argues that queer studies are those that seek and amplify 'the incoherencies in those three terms which stabilise heterosexuality' (p. 3). Heterosexism, understood as 'an ideology that denies, denigrates, and stigmatizes any non-heterosexual form of behaviour, identity, relationship, or community' (Chang, 2005, p. 177) can be said to be the proper object for queer studies. Accordingly, the majority of qualitative queer research has focused on the following three themes, identified by Dilley (1999, p. 462):

- examination of the lives and experiences of those considered non-heterosexual;
- juxtaposition of those lives/experiences with lives/experiences considered 'normal';
- examination of how/why those lives and experiences are considered outside of the norm.

Chang (2005) adds that the production and experiences of so-called queer students and teachers dominate queer studies in education. Talburt and Rasmussen (2010) consider such recourses to non-hetero identities as objects of study a 'habit of thought' that infuses the research process in queer studies of education (p. 1) to potentially counterproductive or ironic ends. The danger in such a habit of thought is that despite queer theorists' avowals of stable identities underpinned by categorical binaries such as male/female, homo/hetero or tolerant/tolerated, a queer analysis tends to rely on social dynamics of subordination, which can reinscribe and privilege differences across identity categories, as well as hierarchical power in general (Butler, 1994; Pinar, 2003). In staking a claim to queer identities, there is the risk of normalizing 'queer' – in so doing reproducing conservative masculinist values of mainstream liberalism – and thereby emptying it of its political and theoretical utility (Butler, 1994; Jagose, 1996; Pinar, 2003; Rodriguez and Pinar, 2007). As Talburt and Rasmussen (2010) point out, the inadvertently liberal pursuit of queer subjectivities is undertaken in educational research primarily out of the activist mandate of critical queer studies. Critical pedagogy, as described by Chang (2005), seeks to 'unsettle extant power configurations' and to 'empower teachers and students to intervene in their own self-formation [and to] transform the oppressive features of the wider society that make such an intervention necessary' (p. 174). In order to enact a liberationist politics, queer research must ironically 'start from the point of assuming the existence of "lots of neoliberal subjects being hailed"' (Barnett et al., quoted in Talburt and Rasmussen, 2010, p. 7), who must be then empowered and emancipated with visions of a queer future.

A tension, therefore, exists between queer theory's acceptance of identity as unstable and inherently incomplete, on the one hand, and its tendency towards 'hailing' queer subjects into a unitary identity, on the other. Representations of 'gay' or 'lesbian' as identities, for example, acknowledge the erotic object of certain people (someone of the same sex) but it cannot encompass the experiences of gay or lesbian people who are also black or disabled or old or poor. Taking sexuality as the main theoretical construct for understanding power relations in social life may belie the postmodern position of 'identity' as a cultural fantasy, and/or reinscribe other power relations that serve to marginalize race, gender, age, class as implicit in creating and maintaining social inequalities. Arguing against 'proper objects' for feminist and queer studies, prominent queer scholar Judith Butler (1994, p. 21) writes, 'the analysis of racialization and class is at least equally important in the thinking of sexuality as either gender or homosexuality, and these last two are not separable from more complex and complicitous formations of power'. Queer projects, then, would be inconsistent with their epistemology if they took as their sole object of inquiry heterosexism, homophobia or erotic hierarchies, without considering interconnections with other social stratification systems that support and reinforce them, such as class, race, ethnicity, language, region and so on (Stein and Plummer, 1994; Chang, 2005). Rather than a narrowing of social inquiry, queer encourages a drawing out of ever more complexity, which leads it to consider all aspects of culture appropriate objects of inquiry. This requires a 'queering' of research itself, rather than producing research on 'queers' (Warner, quoted in Stein and Plummer, 1994, p. 185), which brings us to the final conundrum of queer ethnography: technique.

CONUNDRUM 3: TECHNIQUE AND QUEER ETHNOGRAPHY

Dilley (1999) argues that queer theory might enable 'the most qualitative of methodologies for collecting and analysing data' because it offers for analysis and reconstruction the very existence of 'fact' or objectivity (p. 461). An effect of such flexibility in the conception, analysis and representation of knowledge is that potentially all pedagogies, ideologies, values, institutions, practices and spaces become worthy objects and sites of analysis. Since part of the work of the queer ethnographer is to capture some of the complexity of queer and normative experiences, the seemingly inexhaustible options for inquiry can be daunting. Furthermore, the inherent contingency of both the formulation of a 'queer ethnography' and the knowledge thereby derived also raises questions of validity (for lack of better term) of the ethnographic account. That is, if a researcher approaches her or his ethnography with a queer ethos (a suspicion of dominant modes of doing, analysing and reporting research), what can be said from a queer perspective, and how might the research even begin? Are the traditional methods of ethnographic research available to the queer researcher? How might they be adapted to the ethos and purposes of queer research?

Wolcott (1997[2001]) insists that no method, alone or in some particular combination, will themselves produce an ethnography; rather than a set of investigative tools, ethnography is 'an inquiry process carried out by human beings and guided by a point of view that derives from the experience in the research setting and from the knowledge of prior anthropological research' (p. 158). This definition is helpful in that it reminds us that attentive and reflexive immersion in the field of research is the primary driving force for decisions about the research process in ethnography, and that while the hallmarks of ethnographic work – participant observation, in-depth interviews with informants and fieldnotes – are central to the success of ethnographies, there is no uniform way to apply or practice them. A 'queer ethnography' in education requires a queer approach or 'intention' in the selection and deployment of ethnographic techniques and sites. In short, this third conundrum raises questions regarding research technique and intention, and is perhaps the most important location for applying imagination towards a queering of ethnographic research in education. Keeping in mind Wolcott's emphasis on the importance of ethnography as a 'process' that requires the experience of an extended presence in the research field, this section will discuss some ways in which a queer intention can be integrated into the practice of an educational ethnography. Using the conundrums discussed so far as the starting point, we offer suggestions for queering the practice of observation, interviewing and taking fieldnotes, keeping in mind at all times that queerness in educational ethnography is a practice of thought more than method, and therefore requiring attention, reflection and imagination more than a step-by-step how-to guide.

Before we attempt to outline a practice, we should clarify how the goals of queer ethnography in education might be understood. As noted earlier, queer theory contributes to ethnography as a method by taking sexuality (particularly heteronormativity) as an issue through which society is organized and stratified. It reorients the researcher's attention from the margins to the centre, forcing a deconstruction of societal expectations for sexuality as well as apparent deviations (Stein and Plummer, 1994) and adds an emancipatory agenda to a field dominated by description (Chang, 2005). Ethnography, for its part, helps to ground queer theory in material concerns of institutional, cultural, political and social inequality along all axes of identification (intersectionality). Combining these imperatives, we can say that a queer ethnography attempts to represent the everyday culture, consciousness or lived experience of people in one or more contexts through paying attention to the structural and discursive constraints to queer expression/personhood (Chang, 2005). Queer ethnography in education has a political impetus towards reversing silences in educational contexts (not limited to schooling) and providing opportunities for action to address inequality/oppression.

In his review of critical ethnographies in education, Anderson (1989) advocates for several revisions to the practice: moving ethnographic research in education outside of classrooms and schools; using methods that enhance the ability of ethnography to empower informants; and integrating discourse analyses to 'explore how relations of domination are sustained through mobilization of meaning' (p. 263). Similarly, Chang (2005) attempts to revise critical ethnography for queer studies in education further – not by changing what is done, but rather how it is done. Chang suggests that queer ethnographies in education must be concerned with 'the deeper implications of the practices, such as the reflexive researcher's subjectivity (agency), fluid spatiality (location), and comparative historicity (time)' (p. 183). Both scholars provide insights that are compatible with each other, and which augment our conception of what a queer ethnography in education might look like. In what follows, we briefly outline these alignments under two general themes: namely, choosing sites for educational ethnography and enabling queer praxis in educational research.

SITES FOR QUEER ETHNOGRAPHY IN EDUCATION

Among the ethnographic methods available, Wolcott (1997[2001]) presumes, at the least, that an ethnographic study involves an extended presence by the researcher within a certain culture, although the precise site where that culture is best observed or available to the researcher cannot be prescribed. In educational research, the logical site for ethnographies is the school, and indeed most ethnographic investigations in the education field bear out this trend (Anderson, 1989; Chang, 2005). However, there have been calls to move education research away from an in-school focus to reflect the belief that most learning happens in other, non-formal educational settings (Anderson, 1989). While it is no doubt the case that the institutions and practices of schooling contribute to narratives and discourses of normal and abnormal sexualities, it is also apparent that schools are located within broader cultures that also have normalizing tendencies, discourses and political imperatives that contribute to the formation and maintenance of local contexts, including local subjectivities and the inequalities produced among them.

Both Chang (2005) and Anderson (1989) are concerned with taking educational ethnography out of classrooms and schools, and into contexts where broader sociopolitical forces can be examined for their impact on educational issues and relations. For Anderson, such a move acknowledges that schools are not the only – or even the primary – sites for education. Anderson argues that material and political concerns such as funding, political stewardship, internal institutional dynamics and local histories including inter-institutional relations are missed in classroom explorations of education, but have a considerable impact on the educational environment and experience. Anderson goes on to argue that the nexus of self-formation is located primarily in the relation between mass discourse and the individual, making the cultural production-reception loop another critical locus of education (Anderson, 1989, p. 249). These insights point to institutions connected to education – including government as well as non-government entities – and the mediated spaces that students and educators inhabit as important and exciting sites of ethnographic research into the ways in which queer personhood is enabled and/or constrained. Appropriate sites for queer educational ethnographies, therefore, can include schools or classrooms, but should also make connections to places where policy, curriculum, funding, political and land/space use decisions are made. Local, regional or national departments of education (or offices contained therein), community or parent-teacher associations, curriculum development agencies or education-based non-governmental organizations (NGOs), summer camps or volunteer agencies appear here, among an almost infinite number of possibilities.

For queer ethnographies, a move to researching 'educational industries' represents an opportunity to investigate how heteronormalizing knowledge is produced through relations between schools, other social institutions and the cultural ideas that circulate among them. Researchers interested in this kind of work might consider an institutional ethnographic approach as described by Dorothy Smith (2005), whose take on institutional ethnography foregrounds the ways in which people actively, though often unknowingly, engage in normalizing discourses that structure their social contexts: 'As Dorothy Smith conceives of it, the social arises in people's activities and through the ongoing and purposeful concerting and coordinating of those activities. Social life is not chaotic but is instead organized to happen as it does' (Campbell and Gregor, 2002, p. 27). As queerness is generally closeted in education, invisible in everyday life, connecting the institutional and the everyday practices that structure the closet in education is therefore an important goal of (queer) ethnography. And since education is not limited to formal schooling, queer ethnography cannot limit itself to school settings. Not only does the relationship between schooling and other social institutions warrant the attention of queer educational ethnographers, but it also creates more opportunities for investigations into the operation of normalizing powers as pedagogies.

The availability of multiple sites for queer ethnographic work is matched by the availability of multiple discourses that shape social reality within institutions of education. MacLeod (2008) understands social realities as multiple, concurrent and sometimes competing sets of ideas that help us make sense of, and create, certain ways of being in the world. In her examination of medical education, MacLeod (2008) found that the instances of disjuncture between competing discourses were especially useful in accounting for how multiple discourses, sometimes complementary and sometimes competing, are present in any given social setting, as well as the ways in which the research participants used, or were subject to, the available discourses and discursive practices. Likewise, Chang's (2005) call for 'multi-sited' fieldwork acknowledges that not only does education happen in a variety of places and spaces, multiple discourses (or 'conditions of possibility' (Foucault, 1972, 1973, 1977, 1978)) regarding sexuality also structure social reality in any given educational context or group of contexts. In Chang's view, multi-sited fieldwork is a way to better capture the complexity of queer everyday life. It insists on making connections between the institutional organization(s) connected to education, and the lived experience of the person in and affected by that organization. It requires a fluid understanding of 'sites' where education takes place, as well as the roles of the individual in self-creation and subjectivity. Queer educational ethnography, then, can also be useful for examining the cultural production/consumption loop, or the 'encode/decode' process (Mayo, 2006), whereby sexual subjectivities and narratives are produced culturally and are taken up by people or groups, interpreted, altered in relation to the self and recirculated. Following this lead, queer ethnography may be situated in mediated spaces, or 'virtual' spaces, such as web sites, social networking sites or video game environments inhabited through the computer. But a multi-sited ethnography can also move across the many spaces – material and virtual – and make connections between them, drawing out the lessons and learnings that the people inhabiting these contexts encounter, embody, create and resist.

PRAXIS AND QUEER ETHNOGRAPHY IN EDUCATION

Attending to the queer ethos in research, as mentioned earlier, requires that we consider how to take theory and research into action for social justice on queer issues. This section reviews the activities of ethnography – document analysis, observation and interviews – and imagines what a queer approach to each might look like, and how they might contribute to an agenda of emancipation from oppressive pedagogies.

Document Analysis

The enormous bureaucracies that govern educational institutions of all kinds rely on documents to accomplish their work. As such, to a large extent, documents structure the reality of educational contexts. Documents are also ubiquitous in modern institutions – choosing which documents to analyse is a decision that will be guided by the kind of research question(s) one wants to ask. Queer ethnographies of education generally ask about the ways in which sexuality is structured, presented (or hidden) and enacted in various educational sites. Documents that offer insights into these kinds of processes can refer to policy (hiring/firing, promotion/censure, social events, sports participation); curricula and textbooks (in health, science, physical education, cultural studies and so on); planning (blueprints of schools, locker rooms, community centres); communications (images/texts used in promotional materials, internal memos, inter-agency communication, and so on), among other possibilities. Some questions that may be asked of educational documents in a queer analysis are included in the list below. The important point about documents in queer ethnography is that they can offer insights into basic elements of an institution's culture, though they cannot act in and of themselves. Documents gain purchase through the work of people in context who create, interpret and promote them in specific ways. The other tools of ethnography, observation and interview, enable a fuller understanding of how educational sites/contexts are produced and governed, by whom, to what ends, and how individuals and groups (students, teachers, administrators, parents, politicians, support workers and so on) engage with them in the process of teaching and learning. Sample questions for queer document analysis:

1. Purpose of document (does it organize, direct or inform people? Who?)
2. Does the document rely on, or assume, particular identities or knowledges of the reader?
3. Does the document require or assume a sexual orientation or family organization?
4. Are stereotypes and/or assumptions regarding sexual orientation/sexual diversity presented or reinforced in the document?
5. From whose perspective is the document written? In whose interests?

Observation

Our purpose is to imagine how an observer (or participant-observer) with a queer mandate might approach observation. A clear distinction between a 'participant' and a 'participant-observer' is often impossible, as even researchers who are not directly involved in the educational or institutional process are often involved informally with those in the research setting (Baszanger and Dodier, 2004). As mentioned earlier, a queer study questions received knowledge and truth claims about sexuality, sexual identity, and related gender norms and assumptions. As such, observations made during a queer study should attempt to capture instances where such knowledges are advanced or truth claims made (in words, actions or interactions/experiences of people in context) by taking fieldnotes. However, as a queer ethos also questions the production of knowledge, even by a queer-influenced researcher, what the researcher does, thinks, says and feels should also be recorded and analysed in a journal. Fieldnotes and journals as records of observation data are discussed below.

Fieldnotes and Journals

Fieldnotes are the written records of the researcher's time 'in the field'. They are composed from the 'headnotes' and 'jottings' (Emerson et al., 1995) taken during observation, participation, interviews and reflection about the research, and expanded upon as soon as possible after they are noted. This work is explained by Emerson and colleagues (1995):

> In attending to ongoing scenes, events, and interactions, field researchers take mental note of certain details and impressions. For the most part these impressions remain 'headnotes' only. In some instances, the field researcher makes a brief written record of these impressions by jotting down key words and phrases. Jottings translate to-be-remembered observations into writing on paper as quickly rendered scribbles about actions and dialogue. A word or two written at the moment or soon afterwards will jog the memory later in the day and enable the fieldworker to catch significant actions and to construct evocative description of the scene. (Emerson et al., 1995, p. 20)

In short, fieldnotes are written accounts, filtered through the lens of the researcher, of what others in the research context do and say and form the basis for later analysis. Drawing on critical theory perspectives, queer theory asks the researcher to put power relations attached to sexuality at the forefront of her mind not only during the analysis, but also during the data collection. The fieldnotes, then, should include information about actions, dialogues, events and so on in relation to this axis of social relation. The researcher must attend in her jottings and headnotes, to what kinds of action, dialogue and experiences are banal and unremarkable, and ask at those moments about what makes them slip through the complex webs of social relations without disruption. Queer theory accepts that such interpretations by the researcher cannot represent complete or universal truth, but the aim of queer ethnographic accounts is to reverse traditional silences enforced through heteronormativity in everyday life. By this reasoning, the queer perspective will broaden, rather than shrink, our conceptual understanding of education.

Where fieldnotes account for the actors, situations and activities of others in the research context, journal entries are essential for accounting for what the researcher does, thinks, says and feels. The researcher is inextricably a part of the research findings, and therefore a high degree of reflexivity is required of her or him to provide the details of this involvement. Distinguishing fieldnotes from journal entries may be seen as a semantic choice, rather than a separate tool for conducting a queer ethnography. However it is conceptualized, the influence of the researcher on the process of inquiry and on the nature of data collected in the field is significant. Emerson and colleagues (1995) note that ethnographic data have no stable, universal meaning 'independent of *how* that information was elicited or established and by whom' (p. 12, emphasis in original). Therefore, including the personal reflections of the researcher is a means of enhancing the interpretive and analytic process. Again, it is not simply those moments of strong emotional reaction or dramatic events that need to be noted in a journal entry. Events, words, actions or experiences that strike the researcher as natural, necessary or inevitable also require examination, for it is in the deconstruction of what passes as normal that a queer ethos is at work.

Praxis

As noted earlier, and by many queer scholars and activists, queer research aims not only to contribute to knowledge in the field of education, but also to provide opportunities for transforming educational contexts, processes and practices in the direction of decreased inequalities (Anderson, 1989; Tierney, 1997; Mayo, 2006). Anderson suggests that such research 'empowers' participants in educational research by assuming they are active subjects in the creation of the self and history. '"Subjects"', Anderson tells us, 'are those who know and act; "objects" are those who are known and acted upon'. (Anderson, 1989, p. 260). The first step in developing a queer praxis to educational research is to understand research participants as rational actors in social life. This understanding of what has been called 'empowerment' is not meant to imply that a researcher is bestowing agency upon a previously disempowered or inert object. Rather, it is meant to foreground the agency already being enacted by the research participant within their context(s) of action/experience, and to signal to the researcher that her or his job is to understand the ways in which this active subject makes meaning of, engages with and contributes to their circumstances. Tierney further advocates for queer research to contribute to a community of care and connectedness as an antidote to forces that seek to define and limit individuals and groups: to 'search for connectedness while we maintain difference' (Tierney, 1997 p. 5). Educators and researchers must therefore develop an attitude of selfless love, a state he calls 'agape', in their research, teaching and indeed their lives.

It is from this understanding that a queer approach to ethnography in education may allow participants to articulate their relationship to social structures and promote action to address inequality/oppression. Such methods include: 'oral history taking' (which disperses historical authority across social actors in their own terms); 'the use of multiple informant narratives' (which is meant to reveal the 'legitimated' and 'non-legitimated' voices in social organizations, opening a window on the struggles over meaning in contexts); and 'collaborative research' (which focuses on the productive possibilities of the researcher/participant relationship to challenge hegemonic ideologies concerning the expression of personhood in everyday life) (Anderson, 1989, pp. 260–62). These suggested methods are examples of ways a queer-informed ethnographer can encourage the participation of those in the research context to articulate their own understanding(s) of their world and their place within it. Put another way, they may represent ways to access the mundane ways in which people come to terms with dominant social norms regarding sexuality.

An orientation to action, in this sense, does not guarantee a politics of anti-oppression will be enacted by research participants. Furthermore, in providing the opportunity for research participants to explicate their histories, their understandings of social structures, and the meanings of their actions/contexts with regard to sexuality and sexual orientation, there remains the theoretical connection to be made between the everyday lived experiences and understandings of the researcher/research participants and the 'macro-collective beliefs or social norms' (Chang, 2005, p. 191). This limitation of empowerment-as-action recalls the conundrum of the researcher's position in queer ethnography: the centrality of the researcher as she or he attempts to empower the researched. The ability of the researcher to control or direct participant action towards social justice on queer issues is not complete. However, the queer ethnographer must nonetheless strive to forward methods that increase the possibilities for people to make something of what's been made of them.

SUMMARY

Ethnographic methods have been advanced as appropriate tools for queer research in education to address several conundrums presented by queer theory, and to address the need for material observations and interviews in research on queer issues to date. A queer ethnography not only takes norms of sexuality and sexual personhood as the central object of questioning, but it also requires us to revisit assumptions about ethnography itself. We have argued, following Chang (2005) that a queer approach to ethnography in education

> radically inverts ethnography proper and reconsiders axiomatic assumptions of its practices: Who is the ethnographer? What is fieldwork experience? What kinds of stories count as ethnographic accounts? (p. 194)

Queer theory also requires the researcher to negotiate the politics of representation and the limits of identity in ways that resist reinscribing or reproducing marginality or universality of queer experiences and issues.

REFERENCES

Anderson, G.L. (1989), 'Critical ethnography in education: origins, current status, and new directions', *Review of Educational Research*, **59** (3), 249–70.
Baszanger, I. and Dodier, N. (2004), 'Ethnography: relating the part to the whole', in D. Silverman (ed.), *Qualitative Research: Theory, Method and Practice*, London: Sage, pp. 9–34.
Butler, J. (1994), 'Against proper objects. Introduction', *Differences: A Journal of Feminist Cultural Studies*, **6.2** (3), 1–26.
Campbell, M. and, Gregor, F. (2002), *Mapping the Social: A Primer in Doing Institutional Ethnography*, Aurora, ON: Garamond Press.
Chang, Y-K. (2005), 'Through queers' eyes: critical educational ethnography in queer studies', *Review of Education, Pedagogy, and Cultural Studies*, **27**, 171–208.
Dilley, P. (1999), 'Queer theory: under construction', *Qualitative Studies in Education*, **12** (5), 457–72.
Emerson, R., Fretz, R. and Shaw, L. (1995), *Writing Ethnographic Fieldnotes*, Chicago, IL: University of Chicago Press.
Foucault, M. (1972), *The Archaeology of Knowledge and the Discourse on Language*, New York: Pantheon Books.
Foucault, M. (1973), *The Birth of the Clinic: An Archaeology of Medical Perception*, New York: Pantheon Books.
Foucault, M. (1977), *Discipline and Punish: The Birth of the Prison*, New York: Pantheon Books.
Foucault, M. (1978), *The History of Sexuality: Volume 1: An Introduction*, New York: Vintage Books.
Haywood, C. and Mac an Ghaill, M. (2003), *Man and Masculinity: Theory Research and Social Practice*, Milton Keynes: Open University Press.
Jagose, A. (1996), *Queer Theory: An Introduction*, New York: State University of New York Press.

MacLeod, A. (2008), 'Problem-based learning and the social: a feminist poststructural investigation', PhD Thesis, University of South Australia.

Mayo, C. (2006), 'Pushing the limits of liberalism: queerness, children, and the future', *Educational Theory*, **56** (4), 469–87.

Pinar, W.F. (2003), 'Queer theory in education', *Journal of Homosexual Studies*, **45** (2), 357–60.

Rodriguez, N. and Pinar, W.F. (eds) (2007), *Queering Straight Teachers: Discourse and Identity in Education*, New York: Peter Lang.

Smith, D.E. (2005), *Institutional Ethnography: A Sociology for People*, Toronto: AltaMira Press.

Stein, A. and Plummer, K. (1994), '"I can't even think straight". "Queer" theory and the missing sexual revolution in sociology', *Sociological Theory*, **12** (2), 178–87.

Talburt, S. and Rasmussen, M.L. (2010), '"After-queer" tendencies in queer research', *International Journal of Qualitative Studies in Education*, **23** (1), 1–14.

Tierney, W.G. (1997), *Academic Outlaws: Queer Theory and Cultural Studies in the Academy*, Thousand Oaks, CA: Sage.

Wolcott, H. F. (2001), 'Ethnographic Research in Education', in C.F. Conrad, J.G. Haworth, L.R. Lattuca (eds), *Expanding Perspectives: Qualitative Research in Higher Education,* 2nd edn, pp. 155–72, Des Moins: Pearson Education. Originally published in R.M. Jaeger (ed.) (1997), *Complementary Methods for Research in Education*, Washington, DC: American Educational Research Association.

Youdell, D. (2009), 'Queer outings: uncomfortable stories about the subjects of poststructural school ethnography', *International Journal of Qualitative Studies in Education*, **23** (1), 87–100.

9. Indigenous methods in qualitative educational research
Russell Bishop

> One of the challenges for Māori researchers . . . has been to retrieve some space
> – first; some space to convince Māori people of the value of research for Māori;
> second, to convince the various, fragmented research communities of the need
> for greater Māori involvement in research; and third, to develop approaches
> and ways of carrying out research which take into account, without being
> limited by, the legacies of previous research and the parameters of both previ-
> ous and current approaches. What is now referred to as . . . Kaupapa Māori
> research is an attempt to retrieve that space and to achieve those general aims.
> (L. Smith, 1999, p. 183)

INTRODUCTION

This chapter is a retrospective account of how I developed a means of
conducting interviews in such a way that the meanings that young Māori
(the indigenous peoples of New Zealand) people constructed about their
schooling experiences were able to be brought to a wider audience, including their teachers. This chapter is based on work that I undertook in the
mid-1990s when investigating what constituted kaupapa Māori research
methods that would address Māori and other indigenous and minoritized[1] people's concerns about research into their lives (Bishop, 1996,
2005). During this research I expanded on a process of narrative analysis
termed 'collaborative storying' that we subsequently used to develop narratives of Māori student experiences (Bishop and Berryman, 2006). This
approach is very similar to that termed *testimonio* (Pérez Huber, Chapter
27, this volume) in that it is the intention of the direct narrator (research
participant) to use an interlocuter (the researcher) to bring their situation
to the attention of an audience 'to which he or she would normally not
have access because of their very condition of subalternity to which the
testimonio bears witness' (Beverley, 2000, p. 556).

These narratives of experience were used in the project in a variety of
ways. Firstly, the analysis of the narratives identified the usefulness of the
concept of discourse as a means of identifying the thoughts, words and
actions shaped by power relations; those complex networks of images
and metaphors that the various people in the stories drew upon to create

meaning for themselves about their experiences with the education of Māori students. Secondly, the interviews for the narratives were conducted in a kaupapa Māori manner in order that the participants were able to explain the meanings they constructed about their educational experiences either as or with Māori students in ways that acknowledged their self-determination. The students, for example, clearly pointed out the main influences on their educational achievement by articulating the impact and consequences of their living in a minoritized space. They explained how they were perceived in pathological terms by their teachers, and how this has had a negative effect on their lives. Thirdly, the detailed narratives of experience are used at the commencement of the professional development part of this project, this evidence being used by teachers to critically reflect upon their discursive positioning and the implications of this positioning for student learning. Sharing these vicarious experiences of schooling enables teachers to reflect upon their own understandings of Māori children's experiences and consequently upon their own theorizing/explanations about these experiences and their consequent practice. Fourthly, the students were clear about how teachers, in changing how they related and interacted with Māori students in their classrooms, could create a context for learning wherein Māori students' educational achievement could improve, by placing the self-determination of Māori students at the centre of classroom relationships and interactions. From this understanding, what has been termed the Effective Teaching Profile was developed (see Bishop et al., 2003, 2007).

The Te Kotahitanga project (Bishop et al., 2003, 2007, 2011, http://www.tekotahitanga. tki.org.nz), which is now being implemented in 49 secondary schools in New Zealand, focuses on improving the achievement of indigenous Māori students in mainstream, public secondary schools in New Zealand. The project supports teachers to create culturally responsive contexts for learning through the implementation of a pedagogy of relations within their classrooms. When this occurs, Māori students respond positively, with measurable increases being seen in terms of Māori student engagement, attendance, retention, motivation (Bishop et al., 2007, Meyer et al 2010) and achievement (Meyer et al., 2010, Bishop et al., 2011).

There were many people whose work I used when I was developing the collaborative storying approach. However, five authors stood out as providing me with crucial ideas that matched Māori understandings in ways that I was able to weave together into an approach to interviewing. These were Lather (1991), Tripp (1983), Mishler (1986), Connelly and Clandinin (1990) and Heshusius (1994). I could have 'updated' the references in this chapter as many people have developed ideas similar to these in later years, however, I have kept with these authors as their work was seminal in my thinking and in many ways this chapter is a belated opportunity to thank them for their inspiration.

Māori Peoples' Concerns About Research into their Lives

Māori people, along with many other indigenous and other minoritized peoples, are concerned that key research issues of power relations – initiation, benefits, representation, legitimization and accountability (Bishop, 2005) – continue to be dominated by the researchers' own cultural agendas, concerns and interests rather than those of the research participants (Moll, 1992; Ladson-Billings, 1995, 2000; Bishop, 1996, 2005; Deyhle and Swisher, 1997; Reyes et al., 1999; Smith, 1999; Lomawaima, 2000; Rains et al., 2000; González, 2001; and Tillman, 2002). These authors demonstrate that it is not only the research methodologies, the theories of method, that maintain the control of the culturally dominant groups' sense-making over the research outcomes, but it is also the very methods that they use that contain within them a means of maintaining researcher dominance and perpetuating the marginalization and minoritization of indigenous peoples. For example, traditional research has misrepresented Māori understandings and ways of knowing by simplifying, conglomerating and commodifying Māori knowledge for 'consumption' by the colonizers. These processes have consequently misrepresented Māori experiences, thereby denying Māori authenticity and voice. Much research has displaced Māori lived experiences and the meanings that these experiences have with the 'authoritative' voice of the methodological 'expert', appropriating Māori lived experience in terms defined and determined by the 'expert'. Moreover, many misconstrued Māori cultural practices and meanings are now part of our everyday myths of Aotearoa/ New Zealand, believed by Māori and non-Māori alike, and traditional social and educational research has contributed to this situation. As a result, Māori people are deeply concerned about to whom researchers are accountable. Who has control over the initiation, procedures, evaluations, construction and distribution of newly defined knowledge?

Traditional research epistemologies have developed methods of initiating research and accessing research participants that are located within the cultural preferences and practices of the Western world as opposed to the cultural preferences and practices of Māori people themselves. For example, the preoccupation with neutrality, objectivity and distance by educational researchers has emphasized these concepts as criteria for authority, representation and accountability and, thus, has distanced Māori people from participation in the construction, validation and legitimization of knowledge. As a result, Māori people are increasingly becoming concerned about who will directly gain from the research. Traditionally, research has established an approach where the research has served to advance the interests, concerns and methods of the researcher and to locate the benefits of the research at least in part with the researcher, other benefits being of lesser concern.

In contrast, this chapter seeks to identify how such domination can be addressed by educational researchers through their conscious participation within the cultural aspirations, preferences and sense-and meaning-making processes of indigenous people as research participants. Indigenous people understand the power of research, but remain skeptical as to the benefits that accrue to them as opposed to the researchers. This chapter details how one of the most commonly used qualitative methods, interviews, can be used in a manner that addresses issues of power over what constitutes culturally responsive research.

THE INTERVIEW AS A TOOL FOR ADDRESSING RESEARCHER IMPOSITION: SEQUENTIAL, SEMI-STRUCTURED, IN-DEPTH 'INTERVIEWS AS CONVERSATIONS'

Much has been written about how researchers can develop an enhanced research relationship with research participants through the use of in-depth, semi-structured interviews as conversations rather than through surveys or structured interviews (for example, see Bryant and Charmaz, 2007). In this way, these authors suggest that interviewers can develop a reciprocal, dialogic relationship based on mutual trust, openness and engagement where self-disclosure, personal investment and equality are promoted. However, while this might constitute a necessary condition for interviewers understanding what the lived experiences of people of another culture might mean, it is not sufficient for ensuring that the dominance of the researcher's agenda is overcome. Two very important pieces of work in the 1990s identified the sufficient conditions. The first was Patti Lather (1986, 1991) who suggested that a 'sequence' of semi-structured, in-depth interviews was necessary to maximize reciprocity through negotiation and construction of meaning, 'at a minimum this entails recycling description, emerging analysis and conclusions. A more maximal approach would involve research participants in a collaborative effort to build empirically rooted theory' (p. 61). This allows for a 'deeper probing of research issues' (p. 61) by the process of returning to topics raised in previous interviews. The topic is revisited in light of reflection undertaken by the research participants in the interim period. Adding to this understanding was the second seminal author, David Tripp (1983) who identified that while depiction of the actual words of the research participant is often insisted upon, there is a danger that this strategy may replace the search for meaning through engagement in sequential discourse with a concentration on literal representation. Often, the actual words used at a particular time may not convey the full meaning that the person wanted to express. They may be able, on reflection, to express themselves in a manner that further explains or advances their position and understanding. Hence the importance of 'sequential' interviews that are, in Lather's (1991) terms, conducted within a framework of 'dialogic reflexivity'. This method insists that the theory generated (that is, the meaning constructed/the explanations arrived at) must be a product of the interaction between the interviewer and interviewee, researcher and researched. In other words, to ensure the fair representation of the participants' views, 'negotiation of the account of meaning is essential' (Tripp, 1983, p. 39). As such, Tripp (1983) views the interview (and subsequent written transcripts) as being tools useful to help the participants to reflect, modify and reflect again on their ideas in order to present the meaning they sought so that the research participants are able to talk to the reader directly.

These two authors were challenging the notion of the interview as a data gathering tool, for as Tripp (1983) suggested, the crucial question was 'who controls what happens to the data and how' (p. 34). In other words, what considerations are given to the processing of the information, the sense-making processes and the means of constructing meaning/ seeking explanations through the interview process? Further, interviewers are being asked to consider issues of representation and legitimation by questioning who writes the account of the research interview and who judges it to be fair.

This question challenges the most commonly used data analysis process known in various guises as grounded theory, initially developed by Glaser and Strauss (1967) and expanded and detailed in many subsequent texts including *The Sage Handbook of Grounded Theory* edited by Bryant and Charmaz (2007), and also Charmaz (2006) and Clarke (2005). This process assumes that qualitative research will necessarily address issues of imposition, participation and power sharing by the formulation of themes, those recurring messages construed from the events observed and the interviews transcribed. In this process, the researchers are expected to identify ideas and code themes from the interviews that provides a structure to their subsequent writing about the interview(s). Within these structures, authors select material, often in the form of direct quotes, to illustrate the themes they have identified, which in effect as explanatory tools are theories that they have formulated to explain what the interviewee means in their interview. In this way, budding qualitative researchers are trained to develop texts that consist of themes they have identified alongside 'rich descriptions' of detail that illustrate the themes. Normally, the only part that research participants play in this process is their being provided with transcripts of their interviews, often with all the 'ums and aahs' that are common when thinking deeply about an answer, or the themes that have been developed by the researcher during their analysis. However, rarely are they offered a means whereby they can actually engage in the sense-making process of formulating themes themselves, this crucial activity being the domain of the researcher. This approach creates additional problems. The person who receives the (often huge) transcript, is obliged to spend a considerable amount of time interacting with the text. The arrival of a vast colour-coded transcript in the mail, assuming recipients are interested enough to interact at the level of concentration practised by the researcher, raises the issue of the 'response cost' in terms of the 'cost of non-compliance'. That is, the cost of resistance in terms of time and effort required may be too great for them to engage in, particularly if what they are asked to engage with is the analysis undertaken by the researcher, rather than their being asked to reflect on what they said in terms of their own analysis. Further, what happens when disagreements arise over interpretation. There is potential here for the elimination of contentious material or indeed by-passing of the concerns of the interviewee. Tripp (1983) warned that such an approach is even more problematic when researchers interview a number of participants and then intersperse interview quotations from the interviews of, for example, a dozen informants among the author's own narrative. The danger is that this approach may impose 'particular interpretations over which any one interviewee has absolutely no control' (p. 35). Qualifying or countering statements may be omitted, statements may be taken out of context and used to support the views, assumptions and aspirations of the author.

The problem will be further compounded in cases of cross-cultural translation of meaning by the researcher leaving the interview participant with an enormous task of educating the researcher into their way of making sense of the world after the fact. Being in catch-up mode is a very common experience for minoritized peoples who constantly have to correct people from the dominant culture about their understanding and interpretations. In all, a high degree of compliance with the researcher's analysis and constructions may be an inevitable, if unsuspected and invalid outcome and the benefits to the interviewee will be outweighed by those to the interviewer. Tripp (1983) emphasizes the political nature of this activity where a fundamental process of qualitative research, the interview, actually maintains power over the issues of initiation, benefits, representation, legitimation and accountability within the hands of members of the dominant group. This realization also affects cultural 'insiders' who might unwittingly use the tools designed by the dominant group, thinking that they, by their 'insider' status are going to be able to represent their own people accurately.

Whatever the case, this is not to say that one should just engage the interview participant with the text created by transcription. It is more that returning the script to the co-participant as the interview needs to be seen as a necessary part of the ongoing dialogue, for a different purpose than verifying the accuracy of transcription or the veracity of the analysis of the researcher. Engagement should be with the meaning that the research participant constructs in the text and not with the analysis done by the researcher. This is to maximize opportunities for reciprocal negotiation and a collaborative construction of meaning by the participants.

What then does this mean for the position of the researcher? If we as researchers abrogate the function of interpreter of gathered data, what is our function? Beyond participating in the research story, it would appear that our function is to act as a 'secretary' for the group, to write an account of the events as directed by the deliberations of the group (albeit of only two people) of which we are a part. In the process of developing a collaboratively constructed story, we collaboratively draw out highlights, conclusions and considerations. Such 'coding' is revisited in further interviews. Tripp (1983) also suggests that our position is not one of reflection and

> polite consideration of the opinion of others, but rather may well have become a warm argument . . . both participants . . . may be forced to take account of inconsistencies in and objections to their expressed viewpoint, and to examine and possibly change their views, rather than simply to articulate them for transcription. (p. 34)

Arguments may be put up for evaluation, probing and responding, positions may be challenged by suggesting the other person is wrong, that they have misconceptions, clouded views, blurred vision and so on. The aim of this approach is to explore the assumptions and the implications of the discursive positions taken by the research participants (including the researcher as participant).

It was the third important theorist who drew my attention to the nature of discursive positioning and its impact upon the outcomes of interviews. Mishler (1986) explained that in order to construct meaning it is necessary to appreciate how meaning is grounded in, and constructed through, discourse. Discursive practice is contextually (for example, culturally) and individually related. Meanings in discourse are neither singular nor fixed. Terms take on 'specific and contextually grounded meanings within and through the discourse as it develops and is shaped by speakers' (p. 65). Therefore a 'community of interest' between researchers and participants or among participants cannot be created unless the interview is constructed so that

> interviewers and respondents, strive to arrive together at meanings that both can understand. The relevance and appropriateness of questions and responses emerges through and is realised in the discourse itself. The standard process of analysis of interviews abstracts both questions and responses from this process. By suppressing the discourse and by assuming shared and standard meanings, this approach short-circuits the problem of meaning. (Mishler, 1986, p. 65)

This chapter therefore suggests an approach to interviewing where the 'coding' procedure is established and developed by the research participants as a process of 'storying' and 're-storying', that is, the co-joint creation of further meaning. In other words there is an attempt within the sequence of interviews, through a process of spiral discourse, to actually co-construct a mutual understanding by means of sharing experiences, thoughts and reflections. This further suggests there is the need to develop a way to conduct interviews so that the 'coding' exercise, as a product of shared meanings, becomes part of the process of description and analysis. It is suggested that sequential, semi-structured, in-depth 'interviews as conversations' conducted in a dialogic, reflexive manner need to be developed in order to facilitate ongoing collaborative analysis and construction of meaning/explanations about the experiences of the research participants. In effect, a spiral discourse that creates a qualitative shift in terms of how participants 'relate' to each other.

One way of achieving this shift is, as Connelly and Clandinin (1990) suggest, by focusing on stories and narratives of these stories. In this approach it is important first to consider in what ways those who are traditionally the passive 'researched', those who are traditionally without voice, can speak. Narrative inquiry requires a shift in the relationship between those traditionally constituted as researchers and those traditionally constituted as researched which also challenges the cultural context within which the research participants discursively position themselves, negotiate and conduct the research, that is, the interactions. In this way, the cultural context discursively positions the participants by constructing the storylines, and with them the cultural metaphors and images, as well as the 'thinking as usual', the talk/language through which research participants are constituted and researcher/researched relationships are organized. Thus the joint development of new storylines is a collaborative effort. The researcher and the researched together rewrite the constitutive metaphors of the relationship. What makes the enterprise Māori is that it is done using Māori metaphor within a Māori cultural context.

One example of how Māori metaphor sets the scene for different inter-action patterns and how these interactions address the issues of power and control is seen when researchers explain the meaning constructed of their experiences using *hui* and *powhiri* metaphors. A *hui* is a formal Māori meeting which includes a formal welcome, a *powhiri*, which is a welcome rich in cultural meaning and imagery. The *powhiri* contains cultural prac-tices that fulfil the enormously culturally important task of recognizing the relative *tapu* (potentiality for power) and *mana* (prestige) of all the participants during, as Salmond (1975) and Shirres (1982) detail, the ritualized coming together of *hui* participants. Figuratively, this is of enor-mous importance for establishing research agendas for it is here that the relationship is established and the interaction patterns that are determined by the *kawa* (protocols) of the *marae* (meeting place) are invoked. Full participation in the research requires the researcher to be able to engage meaningfully in the metaphoric *powhiri* process, and to understand the power and control issues represented and addressed, and their own part in this process. In the literal world, once the formal welcome is complete, and once the participants have been ritually joined together by the process of the *powhiri*, *hui* participants move onto the discussion of the 'take' or the matter under consideration. This usually takes place within the meeting house, a place designated for this very purpose, free of distractions and interruptions. It is also significant that such deliberations take place within a house that is symbolically the embodiment of an ancestor, further emphasizing the normality of a somatic approach to knowing in such a setting and within these processes. The participants address the matters under consideration, under the guidance of *kaumatua* (respected elders), whose primary function is to create and monitor the correct spiritual and procedural framework within which the participants can discuss the issues before them. The 'take' is laid down, as it were in front of all. Then people get a chance to address the issue without fear of being interrupted.

Generally the procedure at a *hui* is for people to speak one after another, either in sequence of left to right or of anyone participating as they see fit. People get a chance to state and restate their meanings, to revisit their meanings, and to modify, delete and adapt their meanings according to local *tikanga* (customs). The discourse spirals, in that the flow of talk may seem circuitous, opinions may vary and waver, but the seeking of a col-laboratively constructed story is central. The controls over proceedings are temporal in the form of *kaumatua*, and spiritual, as in all Māori cul-tural practices. The procedures are steeped in metaphoric meanings, richly abstract allusions being made constantly to cultural messages, stories, events of the past and aspirations for the future. They are also highly effective in dealing with contemporary issues and concerns of all kinds. As Rose Pere (1991) describes, the key qualities of a *hui* are respect, consideration, patience and cooperation. People need to feel that they have the right and the time to express their point of view. You may not always agree with the speakers, but it is considered bad form to interrupt their flow of speech while they are standing on their feet; one has to wait to make a comment. People may be as frank as they like about others at the *hui*, but usually state their case in such a way that the person being criticized can stand up with some dignity in his or her right of reply. Once everything has been fully discussed and the members come to some form of consensus, the *hui* concludes with a prayer and the partaking of food. The aim of a *hui* is to reach consensus, to arrive at a jointly constructed meaning. But the decision that this has or has not been achieved rests within the Māori culture, that is, in the *kaumatua*. This takes time, days if need be, or sometimes a series of *hui* will be held in order that the *kaumatua* monitoring proceedings can tell when a constructed 'voice' has been arrived at. At the departure from a *hui*, *poroporoaki* (ritual farewells) are said and it is often a time when new agendas or directions are set or laid out. Again used metaphorically, *poroporoaki* can well be part of a research process.

Hui as a Metaphor for Collaborative Storying

Just as story telling is a culturally located and culturally legitimated process, so the process of collaborative story construction can be understood within Māori cultural practices. Metaphorically, the concept of a Māori *hui* describes the interactions between the participants within the interviews and the process of arriving at an agreed story/write-up of the narrative. In this way, the situation of two or three people collaboratively constructing a story about their experiences within a particular research context can be understood within Māori cultural practices. Metaphorically, the concept of the *hui* (meeting) describes the interactions between the participants within the interviews and the process of arriving at an agreed collaborative story. The interviews are conducted within a context where there is a ritual of encounter, a metaphoric *powhiri* (welcome) process where *mana* and *tapu* are acknowledged and where there needs to be an expression of the 'take' (subject) under discussion. These 'take' are 'laid down' so that there has been participation by the interviewer in the activities of the researched from the outset in ways that are understandable to the researched. These interviews therefore are part of an already existing and ongoing activity. In this way, the procedure of arriving at a collaborative consensual 'story' at a *hui* is replicated in the sequence of formal semi-structured, in-depth interviews and informal 'interviews as chat' within an agreed-to agenda of *kaupapa* Māori framework of research.

One explanatory metaphor is that of the process of *whakawhanaungatanga* (establishing relationships in a Māori context) which gives voice to a culturally positioned means of collaboratively constructing research stories in a culturally conscious and connected manner. There are three major overlapping implications of *whakawhanaungatanga* as a research strategy. The first is just as establishing and maintaining relationships is a fundamental, often extensive and ongoing, part of the everyday practices of Māori people, so too it is of the research process. This involves the establishment of a *whanau* of interest (metaphorically an extended family of interest) through a process of spiral discourse. The second is that researchers are involved somatically in the research process; that is, physically, ethically, morally and spiritually and not just as a 'researcher' concerned with methodology but as a participant concerned with the well-being of the participants. Such positionings are demonstrated in the language/metaphor used by the researchers in the stories developed in the research. The third is that establishing relationships in a Māori context addresses the power and control issues fundamental to research, because it involves participatory research practices, or more correctly participant-driven research (Bishop, 1996, 2005) and calls for researcher commitment rather than for removing research bias.

CONCLUSION

This chapter has suggested that in indigenous research contexts, rather than the interview being a research tool primarily used by the researcher to gather data for subsequent processing, interviews be developed to position the researcher within co-joint reflections on shared experiences and co-joint construction of meanings about these experiences, a position where the stories of the research participants merge with that of the researcher in order to create new stories. Connelly and Clandinin (1990) term the process 'collaborative stories'. Interviews as collaborative storying goes beyond an approach that simply focuses on the cooperative sharing of experiences and focuses on connectedness, engagement and involvement with the other research participants. However, what is crucial for researching in indigenous contexts is that it necessarily will take place within the cultural worldview and discursive practices within which the research participants function, make sense of their lives and understand their experiences.

This consideration reinforces how the personal element is inextricably involved in the research process. In many types of positivistic research personal involvement is denied, and measures to control, minimize or eliminate personal individualism are instituted. In much qualitative research, the subjectivity of the researcher is acknowledged and attempts are made to acknowledge and reduce the distance between the researcher and the researched to control the effects of subjectivity. However, the crucial consideration is that the person of the researcher influences the research relationship, no matter what actions they perform, just as 'who has come' determines the quality and effectiveness of the *powhiri*. In this sense, there is no distance between the researcher and researched because distance is a construct created by researchers, who then constitute discursive practices to account and deal with distance, whether it be in terms of objectivity or subjectivity. Indeed, rather than researchers being able to determine 'distance' or the degree of their involvement, the use of Māori metaphors repositions researchers within Māori sense-making contexts such as that seen when two groups of people come together at a *hui*. The *powhiri* process initially focuses on acknowledging difference, but then becomes concerned with bringing the two parties together under the umbrella of *kotahitanga* (unity of purpose) where difference is not the issue, but rather participation as part of the new whole is crucial.

Heshusius (1994) suggested that researchers need to acknowledge their participation and attempt to develop a 'participatory consciousness'. This means becoming involved in a 'somatic, non-verbal quality of attention that necessitates letting go of the focus of self' (p. 15). Such a position stands in contrast to those who escape into objectivism, which Tripp (1983) had also challenged identifying it as 'that pathology of cognition that entails silence about the speaker, about (their) interests and (their) desires, and how these are socially situated and structurally maintained' (Gouldner, 1976, in Tripp, 1983, p. 33). Similarly, Heshusius (1994) questions what we, as researchers, do after being confronted with 'subjectivities'. 'Does one evaluate them and try to manage and to restrain them? And then believe one has the research process once again under control?' (p. 15). Both these positions address 'meaningful' epistemological and methodological questions of the researcher's own choosing. Instead, Heshusius suggests researchers need to address those questions that would address moral issues, such as 'what kind of society do we have or are we constructing?' (p. 20). For example, how can racism be addressed unless those who perpetuate it become aware through a participatory consciousness of the lived reality of those who suffer? How can the researcher become aware of the meaning of Māori schooling experiences if they perpetuate an artificial 'distance' and objectify the 'subject', dealing with issues in a manner that is of interest to the researcher, rather than of concern to the subject? The message is that you have to 'live' the context in which it happens.

In this sense, participating in the construction of the research account acknowledges what Connelly and Clandinin (1990) suggest as when 'the two narratives of participant and researcher become, in part, a shared narrative construction and reconstruction through inquiry' (p. 4). This narrative will be specific to the research participants, idiosyncratic, culturally specific to the degree of cultural consciousness of the participants and non-generalizable beyond the context of the participants. To involve another person in the process, either as a reader or as a listener, is to alter the interaction, for the next person will not see the stories as the original people do. Instead, additional people will bring themselves into a process of reconstruction of the narrative in order to address questions and raise issues that are of concern to them.

Further, rather than there being distinct stages in a research project, of 'gaining access', 'data gathering' to 'data processing' to 'theorizing', in this approach the image of a spiral, a *koru* (an opening fern frond) is suggested as one that describes the process of continually revisiting the *kaupapa* (agenda) of the research, as Heshusius (1994) suggests where 'reality is no longer to be understood as truth to be interpreted, but as mutually evolving' (p. 18). From the very first meeting, total involvement by both researcher and participant is developed. Decisions about access, description, involvement, initiation, interpretation and explanations are embedded in the very process of story telling and retelling where 'interviews are conducted between researcher and participant, transcripts are made, the meetings are made available for further discussion, and they become part of the ongoing narrative record' (Connelly and Clandinin, 1990, p. 5). In this way, the research participants can be assured that they are addressing and rectifying the traditional asymmetrical power relations over issues of initiation, benefits, representation, legitimation and accountability.

NOTE

1. 'Minoritized' is a term used in Shields et al. (2005) to refer to a people who have been ascribed characteristics of a minority. To be minoritized one does not need to be in the numerical minority, only to be treated as if one's position and perspective are of less worth; to be silenced or marginalized. Hence, for example, in schools on the Navajo reservation with over 95 per cent of the population being Navajo, or in Bedouin schools, we find characteristics of the students similar to those we may find among Māori in mainstream schools in which they are actually in the numerical minority. Also included in this category are the increasing number of migrants into European countries, populations of colour, poverty, those with different abilities and sexual persuasions.

REFERENCES

Beverley, J. (2000), 'Testimonio, subalternity, and narrative authority', in N.K. Denzin and Y.S. Lincoln (eds), *Handbook of Qualitative Research*, 2nd edn, Thousand Oaks, CA: Sage, pp. 555–65.

Bishop, R. (1996), *Collaborative Research Stories: Whakawanaungatanga*, Palmerston North, New Zealand: Dunmore Press.

Bishop, R. (2005), 'Freeing ourselves from neocolonial domination in research: a Kaupapa Māori approach to creating knowledge', in N. Denzin and Y. Lincoln (eds), *The Sage Handbook of Qualitative Research*, 3rd edn, Thousand Oaks, CA: Sage, pp. 109–38.

Bishop, R. and Berryman, M. (2006), *Culture Speaks: Cultural Relationships and Classroom Learning*, Wellington, New Zealand: Huia Press.

Bishop, R., Berryman, M. and Richardson, C. (2003), *Te Kōtahitanga: The Experiences of Year 9 and 10 Māori Students in Mainstream Classrooms*, Wellington, New Zealand: Ministry of Education, available at http:///tekotahitanga.tki.org.nz (accessed 5 September 2011).

Bishop, R., Berryman, M., Powell, A. and Teddy, L. (2007), *Te Kotahitanga: Improving the Educational Achievement of Māori Students in Mainstream Education Phase 2: Towards a Whole School Approach*, Report to the Ministry of Education, Wellington, New Zealand: Ministry of Education.

Bishop, R., Berryman, M., Wearmouth, J., Peter, M. and Clapham, S. (2011 forthcoming), *Te Kotahitanga: Improving the Educational Achievement of Māori students in English-medium Schools: Report for Phase 3 and Phase 4: 2008–2010*, Report to the Ministry of Education, Wellington, New Zealand: Ministry of Education.

Bryant, A. and Charmaz, C. (2007), *The Sage Handbook of Grounded Theory*, London: Sage.

Charmaz, C. (2006), *Constructing Grounded Theory: A Practical Guide through Qualitative Analysis*, London: Sage.

Clarke, A. (2005), *Situational Analysis: Grounded Theory After the Postmodern Turn*, Thousand Oaks, CA: Sage.

Connelly, F.M. and Clandinin, D.J. (1990), 'Stories of experience and narrative inquiry', *Educational Researcher*, **19** (5), 2–14.

Deyhle, D. and Swisher, K. (1997), 'Research in American Indian and Alaska Native education: from assimilation to self-determination' in M.W. Apple (ed.), *Review of Research in Education*, Vol. 22, Washington, DC: American Educational Research Association, pp. 113–94.

Glaser, B.G. and Strauss, A.L. (1967), *The Discovery of Grounded Theory: Strategies for Qualitative Research*, London: Weidenfeld and Nicolson.

González, F.E. (2001), '*Haciendo que hacer*- cultivating a Mestiz worldview and academic achievement: braiding cultural knowledge into educational research, policy, practice', *International Journal of Qualitative Studies in Education*, **14** (5), 641–56.

Heshusius, L. (1994), 'Freeing ourselves from objectivity: managing subjectivity or turning toward a participatory mode of consciousness?', *Educational Researcher*, **23** (3), 15–22.

Ladson-Billings, G. (1995), 'Toward a theory of culturally relevant pedagogy', *American Educational Research Journal*, **32** (3), 465–91.

Ladson-Billings, G. (2000), 'Racialized discourses and ethnic epistemologies', in N.K. Denzin and Y.S. Lincoln (eds), *Handbook of qualitative research*, 2nd edn, Thousand Oaks, CA: Sage, pp. 257–77.

Lather, P. (1986), 'Research as praxis', *Harvard Educational Review*, **56** (3), 257–74.

Lather, P. (1991), *Getting Smart: Feminist Research and Pedagogy With/in the Postmodern*, New York: Routledge.

Lomawaima, K.T. (2000), 'Tribal sovereigns: reframing research in American Indian education', *Harvard Educational Review*, **70** (1), 1–21.

Meyer, L., Penetito, W., Hynds, A., Savage, C., Hindle, R. and Sleeter, C. (2010), *Evaluation of Te Kotahitanga: 2004–2008*, Wellington, New Zealand: Jessie Hetherington Centre for

Educational Research, Victoria University, available at http://tetereauraki.tki.org.nz/Te-Kotahitanga-evaluation-report (accessed 5 September 2011).

Mishler, E.G. (1986), *Research Interviewing: Context and Narrative*, Cambridge, MA: Harvard University Press.

Moll, L.C. (1992), 'Bilingual classroom studies and community analysis: some recent trends', *Educational Researcher*, **21**, 20–24.

Pere, R. (1991), *Te wheke: A Celebration of Infinite Wisdom*, Gisborne: Ao Ako.

Rains, F.V., Archibald, J.-A. and Deyhle, D. (2000), 'Introduction: through our eyes and in our own words', *International Journal of Qualitative Studies in Education*, **13** (4), 337–42.

Reyes, P., Scribner, J. and Scribner, A.P. (eds) (1999), *Lessons from High-performing Hispanic Schools: Greater Learning Communities*, New York: Teachers College Press.

Salmond, A. (1975), *Hui: A Study of Māori Ceremonial Greetings*, Auckland, New Zealand: Reed & Methuen.

Shields, C., Bishop, R. and Mazawi, A.E. (2005), *Pathologizing Practice: The Impact of Deficit Thinking on Education*, New York: Lang.

Shirres, M. (1982), 'Tapu', *Journal of Polynesian Society*, **91** (1), 29–52.

Smith, L.T. (1999), *Decolonizing Methodologies: Research and Indigenous Peoples*, London: Zed Books.

Tillman, L.C. (2002), 'Culturally sensitive research approaches: an African-American perspective', *Educational Researcher*, **31** (9), 3–12.

Tripp, D.H. (1983), 'Co-authorship and negotiation: the interview as act of creation', *Interchange*, **14** (3), 32–45.

PART 2

NON-SCHOOL SETTINGS

10. Vocational education and training: sites for qualitative study
Jane Salisbury

INTRODUCTION

Vocational education and training (VET) can be broadly conceived as preparation and learning for the world of work. Vocational education programmes can be found in educational institutions, in workplaces and in formal training schemes run by organizations such as trades unions or private training providers. Of course professional occupations have well-regulated professional education programmes (Pugsley, Chapter 11, this volume) and the majority of these operate inside higher education (HE) where students study specialist knowledge via degrees and diplomas (Lucas, Chapter 12, this volume). Vocational training, 'on the job' also involves informal learning (Roth, Chapter 14, this volume) whereby participaton in tasks affords experiential learning. Whilst other chapters in this part of the volume cover qualitative research on the professions and HE, I will concentrate upon VET in post-compulsory education and training (PCET). In doing so, I will touch upon informal learning contexts briefly.

This chapter is concerned with identifying the ways in which apprenticeship and vocational training have been researched using qualitative methods, especially fieldwork strategies. It is not a definitive source about apprenticeship and vocational training research but a helpful starting point for those scholars interested in locating studies which have attempted thick descriptions (Geertz, 1973). The chapter draws attention to some rich and diverse studies from around the world and offers a brief commentary on how these have progressed our knowledge and understanding.

I am a committed user and teacher of qualitative research methods and keen to convince readers how exciting it can be to use them when researching lesser reported educational settings like VET! Over my career to date I have used participant observation to study social control in adult education evening classes (in French and Cookery) (Salisbury, 1991); conducted an ethnography of a university based teacher education programme (Salisbury, 1994). Most recently, and relevant for this volume,

I undertook a two-year ethnographic study of *Learning and Working in Further Education* Colleges.[1] This took me onto seven campuses and into physically diverse learning settings: engineering and construction workshops, stables, reptile hothouses, studios, Microlabs and other vocational classrooms (ESRC/TLRP, 2008, Salisbury and Jephcote, 2010). As a research site, VET is illuminating about teaching and learning generally.[2] Its relative neglect impoverishes educational research.

In the sections which follow I will answer a few framed questions to provide a structure and overview for readers and to help fight the sometimes shallow/ahistorical/reinventing wheels culture of mainstream educational research (Delamont, Chapter 1, this volume). How then have VET and apprenticeship schemes and their learning settings been studied over the last 30–40 years or so? Can we revisit older 'classic' ethnographies to illuminate methods? What recent work has been done to reduce the dearth of educational research on these learning sites?

REVISITING SOME CLASSIC ETHNOGRAPHIES OF VOCATIONAL LEARNING

Clearly some of the early studies published in Blanche Geer's (1972) edited volume *Learning to Work* depict research methods and fieldwork approaches well whilst at the same time revealing that many settings outside formal schooling and universities are the location for teaching and learning.

Our knowledge of education and training sites, however, remains limited despite British ethnographic research of the late 1980s which was published in the early 1990s. Most notably an edited volume *Youth and Inequality* (Bates and Riseborough,1993). This collection did reveal how training programmes played an important part in mediating between social class, families and careers. Inge Bates's (1990, 1991) comparative analysis of ethnographic data from two case studies of fashion design students on a diploma course and young women being trained to care for elderly and disabled people in residential settings (the 'Care girls') on a youth training scheme (YTS: a government-funded scheme for young unemployed people that ran in the UK in the 1980s), draws on interviews and fieldnotes. She shows how the differentiated demands made of students is part of their economic socialization and part of a complex process of screening for relevant social and cultural attributes. A close examination of the experience of training revealed powerful mechanisms of social reproduction.

Riseborough's (1992) colourful ethnography 'The Cream Team' resulted from participant observation and in-depth interviews with students and staff in a catering and hotel management course. Like Gary Alan Fine's (1996) closely detailed ethnography of kitchens and chefs in which as participant observer, he worked as a trainee, Riseborough too spent weeks in the hot training kitchens and service areas watching the gradual, practical accomplishment of students who were compliant strategically, but who were resentful of their intensive training.

The resistance shown in Riseborough's (1993) portrayal of 'the Gobbo Barmy Army', a group of young men on a construction studies YTS, renders visible the camaraderie, humour and crude masculinity evident in an earlier ethnographic study of British working-class boys by Paul Willis (1977) who are the *dramatis personae* of his book *Learning to Labour.*

The use of simulation and role play in vocational learning for students on a nursery nurse course was captured by Bev Skeggs (1986) who reported how the 'Care girls' resented bathing plastic baby dolls – however realistic they were. The limited curriculum and practical tasks were exposed by the in-depth observational research as training which reproduced narrow and traditional gender roles to create what Skeggs termed 'a domestic apprenticeship'. A recent Master's dissertation, 'You can't do that in the salon! An ethnographic study of a vocational course', (Clayton, 2008), reported on the use of 'blocks' (artificial heads of hair) to simulate clients' heads. The regulation and policing of the hair and beauty students' self-presentation by their teachers, Miss Snip and Miss Blush, exposed hidden curricula which was valorized over and above knowledge about hair follicles, scalp allergies and chemicals.

Secretarial studies courses, predominantly the domain of female students, have been the research focus for Linda Valli (1986) in North America and in France, Raissiguier (1994) who explored identity formation in a French vocational school. Both researchers used qualitative interviews, document analysis and observations to build up an authentic and powerful account of the ways female students learn to 'clerk' and train as secretarial service workers on courses which are often low level. In 'becoming clerical' thousands of young females participate in a well-worn gendered trajectory which feminist scholars have problematized (see Fuller et al., 2005).

Just as in compulsory schooling pupils are excluded or self absent and drop out, student exits and absences occur in VET programmes. A variety of factors shape participation and completion rates and Jonker's (2006) study of retention and drop out in a Dutch vocational school presents 'refrains of hurt and hopelessness' in students' vivid stories collected using narrative interviews. The stories were recorded over a three-year period, as part of an ethnographic study of motivation and aspiration of 150 young people at the Amsterdam School for Health Care. The combination of classroom ethnography and biographical interviewing brought Jonker close to the inside experience and outward expression of educational failure.

WHY DO WE NEED MORE CURRENT 'THICK DESCRIPTIONS'?

'Official' accounts of learning in VET emphasize the acquisition of technical skills and knowledge to foster behavioural competence in the workplace. For some 30 years or more the combination of work and learning has been a seductive idea for policy makers and governments in many Organization for Economic Cooperation and Development (OECD) countries and yet the data and evidence to support the development of VET, work-based learning and apprenticeships are not as effective as they should be (OECD, 1997; Billet, 2004; Steedman, 2010). Much of the research in this area has not been published in peer-reviewed journal articles, but in what is called in the UK the 'grey' literature of reports to sponsors and government. This material fails to acknowledge a number of important matters, not least the impact of training on apprentice or employee productivity (Wolff et al., 2010).The conditions in VET systems that provide for effective learning and the relationship between actual learning and individual identity remain largely unexplored.

According to Billet (2004, p. 149) there needs to be a reappraisal and reconceptualization of workplaces as learning environments as too little attention has been given to the intentional structuring of workplace training experiences. Being a provider of apprenticeship training rather than simply a provider of an apprenticeship workplace is a crucial differentiation that policy makers, funders and employers need to recognize (Steedman, 2010). With millions of pounds and dollars being spent on VET by governments worldwide, it is perhaps good news that some recent research has adopted in-depth qualitative approaches to explore learning and training.

Drawing on social theories of learning Fuller and Unwin (2003) set out to articulate more clearly the ways in which apprentices' workplace competence is attained through a combination of formal and informal learning. The learning sites for their project were the steel industries in England and Wales. Alongside observations and interviews with apprentices and employees, a 'learning log' proved to be an effective method to help people reflect on and record their learning activities both systematically and longitudinally. Fuller and Unwin's (2003, 2004) descriptions of 'expansive and restricted learning environments' characterized the typical affordances for apprentices' learning. Their twin concepts or continuum have been used in a set of interconnected projects and used to analyse how work organizations differ in the ways that they create and manage themselves as learning environments (Fuller and Unwin, 2004; Evans et al., 2006; Fuller et al., 2007). These writers have developed the conceptual framework of an 'expansive-restrictive' continuum of workplace factors which provides a perspective on understanding the interaction between institutional context, workplace learning environment and individual learning. This provides a useful vehicle for bringing together the pedagogical, organizational and cultural factors that contribute to learning and becoming competent or qualified.[3]

Considerable debate amongst scholars has been concerned with how to conceive 'learning' most effectively. Anna Sfard's (1998) twin metaphors for thinking about learning are a helpful tool for starting out on a study of VET and/or apprenticeship. Learning as participation (LAP) and learning as acquisition (LAC) are quite clearly, both involved in traditional VET programmes. Such programmes typically combine formal day or block release attendance at college with employment, or alternatively, significant part-time 'work experience' whilst enrolled for a college-based vocational qualification.

It would be a mistake, as Hodkinson (2005, p. 6) warns, 'to separate out either learning or the learner from the contexts in which the learning takes place as each is part of the other'. If learning is conceived as inherently embodied, social and relational, then only ethnographic approaches and case studies are fit for research on VET.

A sound example of the qualitative approach is Colley et al.'s (2003) detailed case studies of three vocational courses – in childcare, healthcare and engineering – in English further education colleges. The authors argue that in these contexts, learning is a process of becoming. The learning cultures and the vocational cultures in which students are steeped transform those who enter them. Colley et al. draw upon data from a large four-year research project (James and Biesta, 2007) and develop the concept of 'vocational habitus' to explain a central aspect of students' experience, as they have to orient to a particular set of dispositions – both idealized and realized. These authors assert that

> predispositions related to gender, family background and specific locations within the working class are necessary, but not sufficient for effective learning. Vocational habitus reinforces and develops these in line with demands of the workplace, although it may reproduce social inequalities at the same time. (Colley et al., 2003, pp. 471)

Vocational habitus is shown as involving the development not only of a 'sense' of how to be, but also a certain 'sensibility' involving requisite feelings and morals, and the capacity for emotional labour.

Many of the teachers in my own ethnographic research on teachers and students working and learning together in colleges of further education laboured emotionally for the greater good of their students. They demonstrated an ethic of care and frequently undertook pastoral work outside their official contact hours and the college day.

> 10.50 am. Arrive back in my office to find one of second years in tears – a young gentleman. Very complicated issue concerning a mental health-related problem. Student is 18 – cannot inform parents – no counsellor is available. Child protection issue could be involved here as well with a sibling. All middle management are unavailable as is the head of student services. 2.5 hours later and still with the student feeling emotionally drained after listening to all concerns from the student and supporting him as much as I could. Made him coffee in office, talked, chocolates given to him to munch with coffee. I am concerned student may harm himself – and yet there is no one to support me in this other than 1 meeting with one middle manager I located. It seems I've done everything I could here – a relief but I still feel it could have been dealt with better. No marking done in my duty time [11.00 am–2pm] as planned today. (Extract from Teacher Journal Entry 2, March 2006, Helen, College C)

In comparison with British schools and universities, little is known about what goes on in colleges of further education (tertiary colleges). The ethnographic study discussed here followed the 'journeys' of 45 students and 27 teachers over a two-year period in colleges in Wales. It recorded the various twists and turns of what went on day to day, as revealed from a range of data, some provided by the participants, others from first-hand observation. My aim was to improve our understanding of learning processes in further education and to add to knowledge of the relationships between learners and teachers and to the sorts of learning outcomes they gave rise to.

My research took me, in my ethnographer role, into different college campuses and a variety of subject courses. This generated volumes of field-notes, expanded accounts and interview transcripts from the 45 students and 27 teachers who were the 'core' participants and who also wrote six entries each for learning journals over the life of the project. As an ethnographer I discovered the special features of particular modes of study, the significance of specialist technicians in scaffolding learners, approaches to teaching and learning in different physical spaces and also identified the holistic approaches of dedicated teachers who with intensified work roles (Clow, 2001; Salisbury et al., 2009) struggled to maintain a professional identity (Gleeson and James, 2007; Jephcote et al., 2008; Jephcote and Salisbury, 2009). In participating and observing I learned alongside construction apprentices how to use a theodolyte to survey a section of a Welsh mountainside. I spent exhausting days in animal husbandry courses where I got cold and wet but learned to bandage a horse's fetlock, take rectal readings of its temperature and shampoo, de-musk and blow-dry a pungent and vicious ferret! My own experiential learning proliferated as I participated legitimately and peripherally as the token ethnographer.

The study provided a detailed ethnographic investigation of further education sites in Wales. A similar project on a much larger scale was undertaken in England (James and Biesta, 2007) and together, these projects have provided valuable knowledge about a 'Cinderella' sector of education. Of course, it goes without saying that there is a need for equivalent research which samples into the community colleges of North America, and equivalent institutions in other countries.

INFORMAL AND SITUATED LEARNING

Learning takes place in different contexts, spaces and situations and is unlikely to be provided by a single training or learning provider (Cross, 2006; Roth, Chapter 14, this volume). There have been some moves to recognize informal and non-formal learning (Eraut, 2000; Colley et al., 2002; Hodkinson and Colley, 2005) though most effort in the European Union has been focused on how to assess and certify it. Research on informal learning begins without official curriculum documents and course guides detailing aims, objectives and assessments which may be both daunting and liberating! The overarching questions framing your ethnographer's gaze will be: 'What is being learnt here? (Knowledge, skill, attitude?) How? With whom? What artefacts, or kit are used, and what stories are told?'

While skills-building approaches to vocational subjects tend to focus upon the provision of formal skills-based training, accounts of 'situated learning' (Lave and Wenger, 1991; Wenger, 1998) focus upon how tacit forms of knowledge and skill are acquired. Lave and Wenger proposed that the initial participation in a culture of practice can be looking on from the outer edge or periphery, what they term 'legitimate peripheral participation' (LPP) (Stephens and Delamont, 2010). Here the participant, a novice, moves from the role of observer, as learning and observation in the culture increase, to a fully functioning member. The progression towards fuller participation helps the learner to piece together the culture and establish their identity.

> Knowing is inherent in the growth and transformation of identities and it is located among practitioners, their practice, the artefacts of that practice, and the social organisation . . . of communities of practice. (Lave and Wenger, 1991, p. 122)

The empirical inspiration for the concepts of LPP and communities of practice (COP) derive from their observations of craft apprentices in traditional societies and though originally intended by Lave and Wenger (1991) and Wenger (1998) to help make sense of apprenticeship learning contexts, they are relevant analytic concepts for understanding the learning and working of students and their teachers. Furthermore, the paired concepts have wider application to other vocational programmes of study in both compulsory schooling and in contemporary further and higher education. *Teaching and Teacher Education* (2010, **26** (1)) (Delamont, 2010) contains 14 papers all of which use COP or LPP concepts to discuss situated learning. Anyone considering qualitative research on learning in vocational or other contexts should connect with Lave and Wenger (1991) and the papers in that special issue which demonstrates that learning occurs and is everywhere!

VET is an arena where the teacher-pupil distinction found in school ethnographies (Ball, 1980) is more complex and less clear-cut. Young people can be both teachers and learners as my fieldwork in college vocational departments revealed (Salisbury and Jephcote, 2010). Unwin (2003) has already challenged the usefulness of the 'novice expert' dichotomy in the context of apprenticeship and work-based learning. Clearly this is an oversimplification which fails to capture the more nuanced learning journeys of vocational students and apprentices. In the animal care departments I studied, students worked on farms and in hot houses for the 'exotics' (creatures such as salamanders). I observed them sharing readily their expertise and skill with their peers and specialist tutors. Analysis of observational fieldnotes, interviews and journals reveals these departments as learning arenas where 'novice to expert' trajectories are less predictable and linear. They are also spaces where teachers, technicians and students collaborate and co-participate in sharing and developing knowledge and skills.

> It sounds odd but some of the best staff development – for me personally – comes from the students. The knowhow and facts that many of them bring here to share with us all is truly amazing. (Mary, Head of Animal Care Department)

Clearly, as several researchers such as Fuller et al. (2007) and Felstead et al. (2008) have recently pointed out, student characteristics, dispositions and biographies are important influences in learning, but in seeking to demonstrate the power of individual agency, some researchers can lose sight of the contextual factors in learning settings that combine to create particular learning cultures (James and Biesta, 2007) and generate valuable learning outcomes. In sustained fieldwork I have tried not to lose sight of context. To this end I always utilize a fieldwork journal and keep a separate 'out of the field' research diary (Delamont, 2002).

During my 'first days in the field' I focused on observing the social and physical contexts for newly arrived students. I was keen to understand their 'initial encounters' with staff, peers, the campus geography and not least their classroom spaces and courses of study. Staff felt successful socialization into the student role would combat attrition and help maintain sound retention figures. Teachers recognized this phase of transition from school as having the potential to be 'pessimistic' (Ball, 1980; Salisbury and Jephcote, 2008). Furthermore this separate phase was viewed as enabling students to begin to embrace an identity as a student of a particular course or programme. Students wore with pride lab coats and waterproof gear (animal care), pink tunics and pink wheelie cases (hair and beauty), blue all-in-one boiler suits and 'toe 'tector boots' (engineering). In the canteens and coffee bars it was easy to identify new, keen students in their departmental identifiers (outfits) and importantly, to talk to them about early college experiences whilst at the same time working at rapport building and a relationship.

CONCLUDING REMARKS

Researchers who are considering undertaking a research project to look at learning on vocational training programmes or on apprenticeship schemes would of course identify a set of research questions or 'foreshadowed ideas' to help frame their study. In doing so they would be wise to revisit some of the extant literature which has thrown light on the social processes and the official and hidden curriculum of such education and training routes. Edwards and Usher (2000) argued that there is a need to move from a focus on teaching and learning as bounded practices to an examination of new and complex patterns of interconnectedness. A small number of in-depth qualitative studies have revealed that pedagogic spaces are not just mediated through teachers and trainers but through other social actors hitherto marginalized – learners, teaching assistants, assessors and technicians. Future research projects need to acknowledge this and recognize the social nature of learning and the ways students bring knowledge and expertise to the learning setting from outside it.

The affordances of using ethnographic methods to understand better such education and VET training modes is indisputable. Generating data from ethnographic observations, in-depth interviews, participant diaries and focus groups helps build up a really, really 'thick description' (Geertz,1973). When all methods, or several of them are used, triangulation between method and different data sets is possible, thereby strengthening confidence in findings (Denzin, 1978). Clearly such approaches are time-consuming. Being there and seeing – the cornerstone of ethnography – where the outsider strives for insider or emic understanding of the culture and system under scrutiny, nevertheless is a vitally important method. Combining qualitative methods in order to answer key research questions and to illuminate, for example, the what, why, when and how of apprenticeship or VET training day release schemes will provide knowledge of matters anticipated but also matters wholly unexpected. The latter are likely to have remained unearthed and invisible with conventional surveys. Thus we need more scholars to embrace qualitative multi-method research designs.

Until further ethnographic work is carried out in VET or apprenticeship settings we will remain largely in the dark about the lived experience for participants (learners, co-workers, employers, trainers, teachers and assessors) involved in such programmes. Governments and policy makers across the world emphasize increasingly the necessity of evidence-based practice in education and an emphasis on identifying 'what works' prevails (OECD, 1997). Indeed in the UK, 'Improving learning' was the key objective of a major national initiative to develop high quality research that could contribute to the improvement of learning in a range of sectors and situations. This Teaching and Learning Research Programme (TLRP) has generated a significant body of rigorous empirical work on the UK education system with several projects focusing on under-researched sectors and settings.[4] The projects on, for example, literacies for learning (Levacic et al., 2007) and bilingual literacies for learning (Martin-Jones et al., 2007) concentrate on vocational students and their teachers in further education colleges. Readers of these will gain insights into settings hitherto unresearched via the research teams' use of innovative visual methods, diaries and photo elicitation. Data uncovered reveal that young people utilize multiple literacy and textual practices at home, in work and at college and are more sophisticated and creative than is commonly recognized. This finding raises serious implications for traditional modes of assessment both for PCET and learners in schools.

The qualitative studies referred to in this chapter draw our attention to broader matters of social reproduction, inequity, gendering of vocational pathways and learning in 'authentic' learning sites beyond formal compulsory schooling. Authors, are however, often a little cautious about generalizing to other situations from studies which are modest in scale or based on just one or two VET classrooms (for example, Bates, 1990; Riseborough, 1992). The chapter has, however, identified a number of research papers which serve to celebrate the cultural uniqueness of the specific vocational learning sites! Nevertheless, the research questions and problems that these closely focused studies raise are an heuristic and provide an exciting agenda for future ethnographic research projects in diverse vocational learning settings.

ACKNOWLEDGEMENTS

Thank you to editor Sara Delamont and other contributors to this volume for constructive comments on an initial draft of this chapter and to Lesley Pugsley and Wolff-Michael Roth for sharing chapter drafts.

NOTES

1. Colleges of further education in the UK are similar to institutes of technical and further education in Australia and, to a lesser extent, community colleges in North American Colleges.
2. I have also employed qualitative methods to look inside primary and secondary school classrooms for data on gender and equal opportunities practices (Salisbury, 1996, 2000) and though this was fruitful for the UK Equal Opportunities Commission who funded the research and report, it was nowhere near as exciting as my fieldwork in non-school sites! Its sheer unfamiliarity and strangeness helped me to focus.
3. Detailed accounts of qualitative methods, learning sites and informant samples for these interconnected research projects are included in a supporting appendix in Evans et al. (2006), pp. 171–91.
4. An accessible repository – 'TLRP D space' – of all published papers, reports, project summaries and relevant bibliographies has been established and readers of this chapter are encouraged to seek out valuable related material on apprenticeship, work-based learning and further education. See TLRP home page: http://www.tlrp.

BIBLIOGRAPHY

Ball, S.J. (1980), 'Initial encounters in the classroom and the process of establishment', in P. Woods (ed.), *Pupil Strategies,* London: Croom Helm. pp. 257–9.

Bates, I. (1990), '"No roughs and no really brainy ones": the interaction between family background, gender and vocational training on a BTEC fashion design course', *Journal of Education and Work*, 4 (1), 79–90.

Bates, I. (1991), 'Closely observed training: an exploration of links between social structures, training and identity', *International Studies in Sociology of Education,* 1 (1–2), 225–43.

Bates, I. and Riseborough, G. (eds) (1993), *Youth and Inequality,* Buckingham: Open University Press.

Becker, H. (1972), 'School is a lousy place to learn anything in', *American Behavioural Scientist*, reprint in R.G. Burgess (ed.) (1995), *Howard Becker on Education,* Buckingham: Open University Press, pp. 85–105.

Billet, S. (2004), 'Learning in the workplace: reappraisals and reconceptions', in G. Hayward and S. James (eds), *Balancing the Skills Equation: Key Issues for Policy and Practice,* Bristol: Policy Press, pp. 149–70.

Clayton, A. (2008), '"You can't do that in a salon!": an ethnographic study of a vocational course', Unpublished MSc dissertation, Cardiff University.

Clow, R. (2001), 'Further education teachers' constructions of professionalism', *Journal of Vocational Education and Training*, **53** (3), 407–19.

Colley, H., Hodkinson, P. and Malcolm, J. (2002), Non-formal learning: mapping the conceptual terrain. A consultation report available from http://www.infed.org/archives/e-texts/colley_informal_learning.htm (accessed 11 March 2011).

Colley, H., James, D., Tedder, M. and Diment, K. (2003), 'Learning as becoming in vocational education and training: class, gender and the role of vocational habitus', *Journal of Vocational Education and Training*, **55** (4), 471–98.

Cross, J. (2006), *Informal Learning: Rediscovering the Natural Pathways that Inspire Innovation and Performance*, New York: Pffeifer.

Delamont, S. (2002), *Fieldwork in Educational Settings: Methods, Pitfalls and Perspectives*, 2nd edn, London: Routledge Falmer.

Delamont, S. (ed.) (2010), 'Anthropological perspectives on learning and teaching: legitimate peripheral participation revisited', *Teaching and Teacher Education* (special issue), **26** (1), 1–144.

Delamont, S. and Atkinson, P. (1995), *Fighting Familiarity*, Cresskill, NJ: Hampton Press.

Denzin, N.K. (1978), *The Research Act: A Theoretical Introduction to Sociological Methods*, New York: Mcgraw Hill.

Edwards, R. and Usher, R. (2000), *Pedagogy: Space, Place and Identity*, London: Routledge Falmer.

Eraut, M. (2000), 'Non-formal learning, implicit learning and tacit knowledge', in F. Coffield (ed.), *The Necessity of Informal Learning*, Bristol: Policy Press, pp. 12–30.

ESRC/TLRP (2008), *TLRP Research Briefing No 52: Inside Further Education: The Social Context of Learning*, Swindon: ESRC.

Evans, K., Hodkinson, P., Rainbird, H. and Unwin, L. (2006), *Improving Workplace Learning*, London: Routledge.

Felstead, A. (2008), *TLRP Research Briefing No 55: Improving Working as Learning*, Swindon: ESRC.

Fine, G.A. (1996), *Kitchens: The Culture of Restaurant Work*, Berkeley: University of California Press.

Fuller, A. and Unwin, L. (2003), 'Creating a "modern apprenticeship": a critique of the UK's multi-sector, social inclusion approach', *Journal of Education and Work*, **16** (1), 5–25.

Fuller, A. and Unwin, L. (2004), 'Expansive learning environments. Integrating organisational and personal development', in A. Fuller, H. Rainbird and A. Munro (eds), *Workplace Learning in Context*, London: Routledge, pp. 126–44.

Fuller, A., Beck, V. and Unwin, L. (2005) 'Employers, young people and gender segregation (England)', Equal Opportunities Commission Working Paper Series No. 28, Equal Opportunities Commission, Manchester.

Fuller, A., Unwin, L., Felstead, A., Jewson, N. and Kavelakis, K. (2007), 'Creating and using knowledge: an analysis of the differentiated nature of workplace learning environments', *British Educational Research Journal*, **33** (5), 743–61.

Geer, B. (ed.) (1972), *Learning to Work*, Beverley Hills, CA: Sage.

Geertz, C. (1973), *The Interpretation of Cultures*, New York: Basic Books.

Gleeson, D. and James, D. (2007), 'Professionality in FE learning cultures', in D. James and G. Biesta (eds), *Improving Learning Cultures in Further Education*, London: Routledge, pp. 126–140.

Hodkinson, P. (2005), 'Audit empiricism and bias: limiting understandings of learning', Paper presented at BERA Annual Conference, University of Glamorgan 14–17 September.

Hodkinson, P. and Colley, H. (2005), 'Formality and informality in college-based learning' in K. Kuenzel (ed.), *International Yearbook of Adult Education 31/32, 2005: Informal Learning, Self Education and Social Praxis*, Koen: Boehlau Verlag, pp. 165–82.

Hull, G.A. and Zacher, J. (2007), 'Enacting identities: an ethnography of a job training program', *Identity*, **7** (1), 71–102.

James, D. and Biesta, G. (eds) (2007), *Improving Learning Cultures in Further Education,* London: Routledge.

Jephcote, M. and Salisbury, J. (2008), 'The wider social context of learning: beyond the classroom door', *International Journal of Learning,* 15 (6), 281–8.

Jephcote, M. and Salisbury, J. (2009), 'Further education teachers' accounts of their professional identities', *Teaching and Teacher Education,* 25 (7), 966–72.

Jephcote, M., Salisbury, J. and Rees, G. (2008), 'Being a further education teacher in changing times', *Research in Post Compulsory Education,* 13 (2), 63–72.

Jonker, E.F. (2006), 'School hurts: refrains of hurt and hopelessness in stories about dropping out at a vocational school for care work', *Journal of Education and Work,* 19 (2), 121–40.

Lave, J. and Wenger, E. (1991), *Situated Learning,* Cambridge: Cambridge University Press.

Levacic, R., Edwards, R. and Satchwell, C. (2007), 'Possibilities for pedagogy in further education: harnessing the abundance of literacies', *British Education Research Journal,* 33 (5), 703–21.

Martin-Jones, M., Hughes, B. and Willams, A. (2007), 'Bilingual literacies for learning in further education', *TLRP Research Briefing No 53,* ESRC, Swindon.

Organization for Economic Cooperation and Development (OECD) (1997), *Manual for Better Training Statistics: Conceptual, Measurement and Survey Issues,* Paris: OECD.

Raelin, J.A. (2010), 'Work-based learning in US higher education policy', *Higher Education, Skills and Work-based Learning,* 1 (1), 10–15.

Raissiguier, C. (1994), *Becoming Women, Becoming Workers: Identity Formation in a French Vocational School,* New York: New York State University Press.

Riseborough, G. (1992), '"The Cream Team": an ethnography of BTEC National Diploma (catering and hotel management) students in a tertiary college', *British Journal of Sociology of Education,* 13 (2), 215–45.

Riseborough, G. (1993), 'GBH The "Gobbo Barmy Army": one day in the life of the *YTS boys*', in I. Bates and G. Riseborough (eds), *Youth and Inequality,* Buckingham: Open University Press, pp. 160–72.

Salisbury, J. (1991), 'Mucking and mixing in a cookery class', *Sociology Review,* 1 (1), 25–28.

Salisbury, J. (1994), 'There is more then one way to kill a cat: making sense of post experience professional training', in A. Coffey and P. Atkinson (eds), *Issues in Occupational Socialisation,* Aldershot: Avebury, pp. 76–115.

Salisbury, J. (1996), *Educational Reform and Gender Equality in Schools,* Manchester: Equal Opportunities Commission.

Salisbury, J. (2000), 'Beyond one border: educational reforms and gender equality in Welsh schools', in J. Salisbury and S. Riddell (eds), *Gender, Policy and Educational Change, Shifting Agendas in the UK and Europe,* London: Routledge, pp. 55–79.

Salisbury, J. and Jephcote, M. (2008), 'Initial encounters of an FE kind', *Research in Post Compulsory Education,* 13 (2), 149–62.

Salisbury, J. and Jephcote, M (2009), 'Interviews, participant journals, observations and focus groups: the affordances of using multiple methods for the study of students and teachers', Paper presented at the Annual EDUlearn Conference, Barcelona, 6–8 July.

Salisbury, J. and Jephcote, M. (2010), 'Mucking in and mucking out: vocational learning in animal care', *Teaching and Teacher Education,* 26 (1), 71–81.

Salisbury, J., Jephcote, M. and Roberts, J. (2009), 'FE teachers talking about learning', *Research Papers in Education,* 24 (4), 421–38.

Sfard, A. (1998),'On two metaphors of learning and the dangers of choosing just one', *Educational Researcher,* 27 (2), 4–13.

Skeggs, B. (1986), 'Gender reproduction and further education: domestic apprenticeships', *British Journal of Sociology of Education,* 9 (2), 131–49.

Steedman, H. (2010), 'The state of apprenticeships in 2010', available from http://cep.lse.ac.uk/pubs/download/special/cepsp22.pdf (accessed 1 February 2011).

Stephens, N. and Delamont, S. (2010), 'Roda Boa! Roda Boa!', *Teaching and Teacher Education,* 26 (1), 113–18.

Unwin, L. (2003), 'Young people as teachers and learners in the workplace: challenging the novice-expert dichotomy', Paper presented at the Annual European Educational Research Association Conference, University of Hamburg, September.

Valli, L. (1986), *Becoming Clerical Workers*, London: Routledge.

Wenger, E. (1998), *Communities of Practice: Learning, Meaning and Identity*, Cambridge: Cambridge University Press.

Willis, P. (1977), *Learning to Labour: How Working Class Boys Get Working Class Jobs*, Farnborough: Saxon House.

Wolff, A., Aspin, L., Waite, E. and Ananiadou, K. (2010), 'The rise and fall of workplace basic skills programmes: lessons for policy and practice', *Oxford Review of Education*, **36** (4), 385–405.

11. Walk this way, talk this way: qualitative research on professional education
Lesley Pugsley

Learning is not restricted to childhood, nor is education simply what occurs within the classroom. Becoming a member of a profession requires the novitiate to accept and adopt the particular mores of the group, since membership confers on the individual a degree of power within society by virtue of professional expertise. Ethnographies of professional education provide valuable insights into the ways in which knowledge is transmitted and cultural norms and values are assimilated in a variety of settings.

Professions make extraordinary demands on their members; professionals are required to master substantive amounts of specialist knowledge and technical expertise. Additionally they must engage with their own unique subcultures, each of which demands specific normative standards from its members symbolized by professional ethical codes. In the health professions, for example, these codes include strong altruistic elements. Professional standards are learned on a formal level at university and more informally in the workplace during the process of professional socialization. The transformation of novice to professional is essentially an acculturation process during which the values, norms and symbols of the profession are internalized (Merton et al., 1957; Benner, [1984] 2001). Apprentices learn to think, act and interact in increasingly knowledgeable ways by spending long periods as legitimate peripheral participants, observing and engaging with those who are expert in their chosen profession (Lave and Wenger, 1991). In consequence occupational and professional cultures are locally situated, produced and reproduced in the day to day experiences of the workforce. However, professionalism is a somewhat nebulous concept, 'like pornography: easy to recognize but difficult to define' (Swick, 2000, p. 612).

Classically divinity, law and medicine were regarded as the only professions (Clouder, 2003); however the rise of technology in the nineteenth century led to increased occupational specialization, which allowed other groups such as architects, pharmacists, teachers and nurses to claim profession status. Bucher and Strauss (1966, p. 326) attest that 'medicine is still considered the proto-type of the professions, the one upon which current sociological conceptions of professions tend to be based' and certainly much of the research in the field of professional socialization has taken medicine as its locus (Fox, 1957; Merton et al., 1957; Becker et al., [1961] 1997; Atkinson, [1981] 1997; Sinclair, 1997). However, there is a broader literature on professional learning and I have included accounts of some of these drawn from across Anglophone communities, so that the reader can appreciate the similarities and differences in these various studies.

The traditional apprenticeship system is highly successful in effecting this professional socialization, providing a programme of experiential learning, in which practices (both technical and cultural) are modelled by a master. Formal training is designed to inculcate in the novice those dispositions which embody the culture of the organization and the apprenticeship serves to dismantle the existing norms and practices of the trainee and refashion them in the image of their new professional identity. Although full acceptance into the profession will ultimately be exemplified by certification, initially the trainee tends to experience a loss of confidence and develop feelings of uncertainty. The stressful nature of the apprenticeship is well documented and is highlighted in the Australian study looking at the professional identity of nurses (MacIntosh, 2003).

During the 1950s sociological interest in the USA was directed at the ways in which doctors were trained and how they were socialized into their profession. These studies are now seminal texts (Merton et al., 1957; Becker et al., [1961] 1997) and form the bedrock of occupational socialization research. More than 60 years on, they remain germane to our understanding of the ways in which the norms and values of systems are transmitted and the ways in which novice members conform to or subvert the practices of the professional groups that they seek to access. Students wishing to research professional socialization processes need to engage with these literatures in order to appreciate the ways in which scholars have theorized the acquisition of professional knowledge.

Much of this early work supported a functionalist analysis of professionalization, wherein students were passive participants in an enculturalization process (Fox, 1957; Merton et al., 1957). Merton et al. (1957) sought to ask 'how do people become doctors' and their study at Cornell Medical School focuses on new entrants to the profession and the organizational structures of institutions which create and shape a deterministic process of learning. Their work portrays the medical school as a socializing agency in which students are merely passive recipients of the norms and values of the group to which they seek access.

In her study of medical students in the USA, Fox (1957) noted that they were challenged by the inherent uncertainties in medical knowledge and needed to come to terms with the limitations which this imposed in professional practice. However, based on his study of medical students in the UK, Atkinson (1984) contends rather that whilst there is a degree of uncertainty with regard to medical knowledge medical schools adopt a reductionist approach to the transmission of complex medical knowledge, treating it as unproblematic and requiring that students merely memorize simple facts.

Unlike the functionalist perspective of Merton et al., which sought to develop a general theory of the professions through their work in a medical setting, the symbolic interactionists' perspective encapsulated in the writing of Becker et al. ([1961] 1997), focused on the ways in which medical students 'learned the ropes' in order to 'get by'. They concentrated on things that were of interest to the students and the variations in attitudes and actions as they progressed through their training. Their study reveals the organizational hierarchies that pertain in professional education, with medical students as subordinates, constantly trying to succeed within the professional setting. It highlights the adaptations which are required in order to engage with and 'fit into' the professional culture; however it also reveals a highly active student subculture where a range of micro resistance strategies are developed. These findings challenge the earlier functionalist notion of passive acquiescence and stability within professional education.

The symbolic interactionist perspective continues to be highly significant in informing the sociology of occupations and over time has led to a series of studies which take as their focus the actions and interactions of individuals and groups as they construct and play out their professional lives and conduct, construct and reconstruct their professional careers. In the UK, it is Atkinson's ([1981] 1997) seminal study of medical training in Edinburgh, Scotland, which provides us with a benchmark for studies of this kind. His research focused firmly on the clinical context and the ways in which students interacted with patients and doctors as they learned the skills and attitudes vital to their progress into the profession. In common with the earlier work of Becker et al. (1961) and later work by Sinclair (1997), Atkinson explored the distinction between 'hot' medicine, taught in arenas such as the casualty unit, where staff are dealing with acutely ill patients and 'cold' medicine, taught in lecture theatres and during ward rounds. He identifies and illustrates the dramaturgical nature of the socialization process, illustrating the ways in which 'medical realities' are stage managed to allow students to experience different aspects of clinical practice.

Sinclair's (1997) study also helps address the lacunae of ethnographic work on medical education in the UK; focusing on medical training in a London teaching hospital the sense of theatre and the Goffmanesque front and back stage behaviours and practices are again made visible. Other studies have also focused on the socialization of doctors and nurses in the clinical context. Shapiro (1987) provides his personal reflections on being a medical student in Canada and offers a good review of other studies on the topic. He suggests that the formation of a professional identity is crucial for the medical student and contends that it is through this new identity that doctors are able to define their relationships with patients, other doctors and support staff. Faced with the complexities of their roles and an awareness of the demands imposed upon them, they cope by 'learning the ropes' and 'playing the game'. Shapiro's (1987) study also reveals the ways in which medical students engage in a form of 'one-upmanship' with their peers, suggesting that they know more, or at least something, that others in their group do not.

Bucher and Strauss (1966) looked at the ways in which doctors are socialized into the field of medical pathology, while Schatzman and Strauss (1966) studied the socialization process for trainees in psychiatry. Bucher and Stelling (1977) undertook an ethnographic study of residents in three different settings, psychiatry, biochemistry and medicine in the USA. These studies each found that while novices were in part shaped by the formal curriculum of their institution or their professional setting, they were simultaneously negotiating and creating their own professional identities through their interactions with others in their field. Haas and Schaffir (1977, 1987) used a dramaturgical lens as a means of analysis of the occupational socialization of medical students in McMaster, a new medical school in Canada with an innovative problem-based learning curriculum. Faced with this new learning format students engaged in impression management to convince others and themselves that they were competent and confident in their roles, they talked about crafting successful biographies, both to gain entry to medical school and to 'fit in' once there. The study concluded that students learned how to 'assume a cloak of competence which legitimates their presence in the clinical setting and their interactions with patients and other health care professionals' (Haas and Schaffir, 1987, p. 203).

The notion of professional identity is a consistent theme of professional socialization, which can serve to affirm group membership; the process may however prove alienating for some and educational researchers should explore these differences. This heterogeneity is highlighted in Baszanger's (1985) study of general practitioners (GPs) in France, unlike their hospital counterparts GPs (these doctors work in the community and are known as family physicians in the USA) have received little research attention. However, Baszanger's (1985) study reveals their perception of a hierarchy in the profession in which they feel marginalized from mainstream (hospital-based) medicine.

Novices are consistently seen to be developing strategies which enable them to 'learn the ropes' and 'fit in'. In a study of student nurses (Melia, 1987) exemplifies the ways in which these strategies are adopted on the wards as students learned the rules in order to gain the approval and acceptance of the qualified staff. Studies in professional socialization reveal the constant tensions inherent in the apprenticeship process. These are illustrated by Benner ([1984] 2001) in her study of students and experienced nurses in the UK. Her findings are supported by those of Phillips (2001) in her study of direct entry midwives in Wales. Howkins and Ewens's (1999) study of student nurses in the UK also illustrates how students adopt strategies to enable them to 'fit in'. The study by Du Toit (1995) in Australia looked at student nurses in two different academic settings in Brisbane and noted the transformative influence of professional socialization on identity formation. However, Du Toit argues that more research is needed on the aspects of subcultural 'deviance' which allow professionals to maintain personal identities within an adaptive education system. Roberts's (2009) ethnographic study of a pre-registration nursing programme in the UK found that the nurses felt themselves to be on the periphery of the community of practice of the qualified staff. In consequence, they formed parallel communities of students in which they used friendship groups as support networks for learning. Cant and Sharma (1998) looked at the ways in which practitioners of complementary medicine were socialized. They looked at reflexologists, homeopaths and chiropractors and saw how they perceived themselves as being constantly under threat from more orthodox medicine. However, these students too 'played the game', adopting the professional norms and practices that they had been taught when they were being supervised for professional accreditation, whilst admitting that their day to day practices remained unchanged.

The complex nature of the socialization process is further demonstrated by other studies. Clouder (2003) found that occupational therapy students still maintained individual agency whilst they were experiencing and engaging with professional socialization, She too noted that they learned to 'play the game' whereby they conformed, or at least complied, with the system. Cahill's (1999) study of students on a mortuary science programme revealed how students adopted a variety of strategies to enable them to cope with their continued exposures to the dead and the bereaved. He used Bourdieu's (1986) concept of emotional capital in order to theorize its impact on professional socialization in the reproduction of professional authority.

Studies of professional socialization have also been undertaken in a variety of settings other than medicine and whilst not so plentiful still serve to demonstrate both the ways in which novices are inculcated with the professional values and the strategies that they adopt in order to 'get by'.

There is a considerable literature on the development of professional knowledge (Schon, 1983, 1987; Eraut, 2004, 2007). Schon's work has been highly influential in fostering an understanding of professional learning and, in particular, his conceptualization of the role of reflection and reflective practice has allowed us to appreciate and problematize the complexities of teaching and learning in professional settings (Schon, 1987).This work emerged from his participant observation studies in architectural design studios at universities in several locations in the USA (Schon, 1983). His focus was on sets of architectural sketches drawn over time which illustrate the ways in which the novice architect is mentored by an expert and the reflective dialogue between novice and professional as they interrogated design decisions. Light's (1980) ethnographic study of trainee psychiatrists in the USA also highlights the key role of the mentor in the socialization process, as too does Van Maanen's (1978) ethnography of the police and Bucher and Stelling's (1977) study of how learning occurs on different professional programmes

Accountancy is another profession which has received little research attention in comparison with medicine. There are however some notable exceptions; Power's (1991) study focused on the experiences of graduate accountants preparing for the final accreditation examination. Participants reported having undergone an initiation stage in their studies for this professional examination where as novices they were informed of the need to adjust to this more 'mature' stage of their learning. They also revealed a shared student culture in which they underwent a transition in their thinking about accountancy and shifted to a more client-focused way of thinking about the profession.

Coffey's (1993) detailed study looked at the ways in which new graduate accountants are socialized into an accountancy firm. Coffey identifies a number of themes relating to the ways in which the socialization into this profession occurs and these include group formations and the dichotomous relationships that occur within them. Trainee members were both cooperative and competitive of and with each other and this duality of relationships amongst novices is a recurrent theme in the professional socialization literature (cf. Becker et al., 1961; Cohen, 1973). The study also revealed the significance of a professional dress code in the trainee accountants' socialization process. This theme of 'fitting in' and 'playing the part' has also been noted in a variety of other settings, such as nursing, with the adoption of different uniforms to denote status and medicine with its symbolic 'white coat' (Becker et al., [1961] 1997; Benner, [1984] 2001).

Theoretical and empirical work on professional socialization supports the description of professions as 'crucibles of identity formation' (Hayward and Mac an Ghaill, 1997, p. 582). Self-regulation by professional bodies enables them to control entry into the workplace and the training provided there. However, entry is not necessarily granted on the basis of qualifications alone, but may extend to include a range of expected attributes and practices, many of which are tacitly transmitted. These are intrinsically linked to identity management and the need for each professional group to ensure that it is able to recruit those who conform to the norms and values of the membership. Each profession therefore seeks to reproduce itself, maintaining the right to exert sanctions and deny entry to those who are 'other'. Access to professions remains problematic for those without the appropriate cultural capital necessary to decode the narratives that are embedded within organizational cultures (Bourdieu, 1986).

In her longitudinal study of the professional socialization of trainee solicitors in the UK, Sommerlad (2008) focused on graduates from different socioeconomic backgrounds at a 'new' university. In her study she noted the impact of their different cultural practices on the ability of some 'outsider' students to 'pass' as potential lawyers. This then is a new and subtly different focus which the ethnographic gaze can cast on the field, since it reveals strategies through which professions are still gate keeping and reproducing themselves.

The ethnographic gaze has also focused on professional socialization in academia. Becher (1989) conducted an ethnographic study looking at how academics in different departments and different subject areas adapt to the different norms and mores of their specialty fields. In their study, Delamont and Atkinson (2001) considered how doctoral students in the natural sciences are enculturated into their academic disciplines. Their work reveals the ways in which the transition from undergraduate to postgraduate status requires the students to deal with 'real life' situations. In similar vein to the dramaturgy seen in studies of medical students learning (Becker, [1961] 1997; Atkinson, [1981] 1997), these doctoral students come to appreciate the ways in which their undergraduate education was achieved via a series of carefully constructed activities. Drawn from a larger study of doctoral students in both the social sciences and the natural sciences (Delamont et al., 2000) its focus remains an under-researched area.

In his longitudinal study looking at the first three years of professional learning of nurses, engineers and trainee accountants, Eraut (2007) looked at what was being learned and the factors that were impacting on the level and direction that this learning took. As with earlier studies, his work has shown how professional knowledge has an important tacit dimension. Eraut attests that the challenge for researchers in this field is to both recognize the complexity of the different professional settings and the demands made on the professionals and to acknowledge that such complexities cannot be straightforwardly represented or understood.

The Church has been seen as one of the three traditional professions and there has been some ethnographic work on the professional socialization of novices in various religious settings. Kleinman (1984a) conducted her study of students on a divinity programme in the USA, initially focusing on the shared experiences of all the students; she soon noted a gender difference emerging in the responses of the students to their formal curriculum (Kleinman, 1984b). She found that whilst the aims and values of the programme were inclusively designed to encourage women and men to believe they would achieve equal professional status, female students felt this to be at odds with the ways in which women ministers were regarded by many parishioners and did not reflect the reality of the professional roles and status that they would experience. This work by Kleinman highlights the fact that the socialization process in professional schools does not necessarily help women address the gender-specific problems that they may encounter in their professional careers.

Campbell-Jones (1979) undertook a study of nuns from two different communities based in and around London in the UK looking at the ways in which religious organizations socialized novitiates. She identified the rituals and routines that needed to be 'endured' in order for them to acquire the group norms and values. Similarly (Welland, 1998) reported on the rituals and routines which served as an early socialization process in his study of trainee Anglican priests. While Fox (1957) also refers to occupational rituals (rituals of socialization) including symbolic actions which novices are required to undergo. This may be the cutting of hair for entry into some religious orders, donning particular uniform, a white coat perhaps as the symbolic declaration of membership, facilitating the transition from novice to professional.

In his study of trainee lawyers at the Harvard Law School, Granfield (1992) noted the shifts and accommodations made as the students attempted to fit in and adapt to the norms and values of the new roles that were being presented to them. Another study also conducted in the USA provided a comparative account of law and business students at Graham University (Schleef, 2006). Schleef's work reveals that students were initially cynical about career pathways and resistant to the advice from their respective schools. However she found this cynicism to be short-lived with students quickly adopting the norms and values of their proposed professional groupings.

There are parallels in respect of student subcultures to be found between the studies of US medical students (Becker et al., [1961] 1997) and Willis's

(1977) study of the classroom experiences of working-class boys in the UK. Each shows how students become increasingly aware of the socialization 'game'. In the Becker study, the initial idealism of a medical career is replaced by cynicism as the realities and the routines of the profession are experienced. Willis (1977) showed how the boys in his study exhibited counter-school subcultural groupings, characterized by opposition to the values and norms perpetuated throughout the school.

Lacey's (1977) study of teacher training in the UK explored the ways in which student teachers from a range of different subject specialties formed subcultures. He identified the notion of 'strategic compliance', whereby students intentionally employed strategies to enable them to conform to the social norms inherent in their training. This extended to the groups from different disciplines having shared understandings in terms of their subject areas which 'enabled them to adopt a particular stance to the ways in which their specialist subject should be taught' (p. 61). In their two-year ethnographic study Jurasaite-Harbison and Rex (2010) explored the ways in which teachers' professional learning occurred in the workplace. Drawing on data derived from a larger comparative study in Lithuania and the USA (Jurasaite-Harbison, 2009), they explored what teachers learned in these different educational cultures and settings and how they constructed and acted out their different professional identities.

The notion of reproduction of and by professional groupings is a theme that is consistently played out in a variety of studies in a range of different professional settings. In her study of high energy physicists, Traweeks (1988) found that novices soon learned what they needed to do and how they needed to behave in order to be taken seriously within their professional group. She argues that through the socialization process they became unself-conscious practitioners of the culture, developing a professional mindset such that they 'find themselves feeling the appropriate desires and anxieties and thinking about the world in a characteristic way' (Traweeks, 1988, p. 72). Again an example of an increase in professional awareness through the socialization process.

As Coffey and Atkinson (1994, p. 4) note, 'occupational and professional cultures are produced in the settings of work and education – from university departments to prisons, from accountancy firms to colleges of further education. The detailed documentation of such settings and processes remains fundamental to the sociological understanding of working life in contemporary society'. This is where ethnographic studies have proved so useful over time as they enable researchers to appreciate the routines, the rituals and the practices integral to the socialization process of novices wishing to gain access to professions and professional groupings.

These research studies are vital since researchers can render explicit the ways in which tacit, codified cultural knowledge is informally transmitted and acquired through participation in professional milieus. The recurrent themes of uncertainty – especially during periods of transition, adaption, as novices begin learning the ropes and the accommodations that are made to enable them to 'fit in' are illustrative of the socialization process in professional training. By 'learning the ropes' students generate strategies, some of which are covert, in order to succeed in their training. Ethnographic studies have allowed us to see how student subcultures develop allowing novices opportunities to exercise a degree of personal autonomy within the strictures of their learning environment and so engage as active agents in the education system. However, it is still apparent that the process of professional education and training serves to inculcate the institutional norms and values of that profession. The studies serve to emphasize the ways in which the novices are focused on doing their best and getting through their work, rather than on the final outcome of their training which is to achieve a professional qualification and the status that this confers.

A further key aspect of professional socialization revealed by these various ethnographies is the duality of the novice role. They quickly learn that while there is an idealized face of their profession and their professional role, this is set against the day to day routines as they are practised by those professionals whom they are seeking to emulate. There is clearly a performativity inherent in professionalism, as these various studies also show; professionals exhibit front and back stage, public and private behaviours as they interact with colleagues and clients in their workplaces. In medicine, for example, patients expose themselves to the clinical gaze and as professionals, clinicians are required to manage their emotions when confronted with diverse problems and conditions. The notion of professional socialization requiring novices to 'play the game' in order to fit in to their professional setting provides a good fit with the work of Bourdieu (1986) and his notion of fields. Professions can be regarded as fields in which certain stakes, interests and practices pertain. It is the habitus, the sense of what it is to be a member of a particular professional grouping that obliges its members to develop strategies to enable individual agency to be enacted within the wider socialization process. The 'rules of the game' are developed as professional codes, by the individual professions or their professional bodies, which then serve to represent, regulate and protect their membership. Those wishing to gain access need to conform to the requirements of these august bodies, just as those seeking acceptance to a golf club will observe codes, dress and patterns of behaviours, so too entry into professional groupings is monitored and managed.

Professional groups and professional cultures are often regarded as homogeneous, with shared aims and aspirations, which are reflected in the goals of the professional training schools. However, ethnographic studies can reveal individualistic and sometimes oppositional ideologies inherent in the process of professional enculturation. This chapter has attempted to illustrate this individuality in a variety of different professional settings. The twenty-first century has had huge implications in terms of techno-logical and scientific advances. Access to knowledge and a restructuring of occupational boundaries have served to redefine professions.

There is a need for new ethnographies of the socialization of profession-als and the professions, to accommodate these changes. Within medicine, for example, the fragmentation of traditional professional roles, with an emphasis on multi-professional working, has led to subspecialty roles and a changing professional profile for specialist nurse practitioners and other health care workers. Recruitment into medicine in the UK is changing as it is following the US model and increasingly looks to recruiting gradu-ate entrants into medical school. The gender balance has equalized in access to medicine worldwide and an increasingly feminized workforce has emerged which has implications for the profession and its professional status. Not only should the seminal studies of Becker and Atkinson be replicated in a variety of settings, but research attention needs to be paid to the new types of students, new curricular and new work environments facing doctors. We have no detailed ethnographies of this newly emergent medical professional to allow us to comment on the professional sociali-zation of clinicians and students ruled by shift patterns, acute, short stay admissions in hospitals, increased care in the community and the rise in the role of the expert patient. New professions have emerged as a conse-quence of recent technological advances. These too could be the subject of ethnographic inquiry in order to gain an appreciation of what it is that allows professionals to maintain their personal identities within the adaptive educational experience of professional enculturation.

The apprenticeship model of professionals 'learning on the job' is one which still pertains despite the fact that as Eraut (2004, p. 249) notes in studies on professional socialization, 'most respondents still equate learn-ing with formal education and assume that working and learning are two separate things'. The challenge to researchers is to strengthen their fields of study, by making their own education systems problematic (Delamont et al., 2010). One way is for educational researchers to cast a critical gaze on the professions in their broadest sense and to explore the ways in which professionalism is transmitted as novice professionals 'learn how to be'. Ethnographic studies can reveal valuable insights into a range of socio-cultural aspects of learning and workplace settings are integral to our understandings of how formal and tacit norms and cultures are produced, transmitted and reproduced in the professional context.

REFERENCES

Atkinson, P.A. ([1981] 1997), *The Clinical Experience. The Construction and Reconstruction of Medical Reality*, 2nd edn, Aldershot and Brookfield, VT: Ashgate.
Atkinson, P.A. (1984), 'Training for certainty', *Social Science and Medicine*, **19**, 949–56.
Baszanger, I. (1985), 'Professional socialisation and social control: from medical student to general practitioner', *Social Science Medicine*, **20** (2), 133–43.
Becher, T. (1989), *Academic Tribes and Territories*, Buckingham: Open University Press.
Becker, H., Geer, B., Hughes, E.C. and Strauss, A.L. ([1961] 1997), *Boys in White: Student Subculture in Medical School*, 5th edn, New Brunswick, NJ and London: Transaction Publishers.
Benner, P. ([1984] 2001), *From Novice to Expert: Excellence and Power in Clinical Nursing Practice*, 2nd edn, Upper Saddle River, NJ: Prentice Hall. First published Menlo Park, CA: Addison-Wesley.
Bourdieu, P. (1986), 'The forms of capital', in J. Richardson (ed.), *Handbook of Theory and Research for the Sociology of Education*, New York: Greenwood, pp. 241–58.
Bucher, R. and Stelling, J.G. (1977), *Becoming Professional*, Beverley Hills, CA: Sage.
Bucher, R. and Strauss, A. (1966), 'Professions in process', *American Journal of Sociology*, **66**, 325–34.
Cahill, S.E. (1999), 'Emotional capital and professional socialisation. The case of mortuary Science students (and me)', *Social Psychology Quarterly*, **62** (2), Special Edition, Qualitative Contributions to Social Psychology, 101–16.
Campbell-Jones, S. (1979), *In Habit: An Anthropological Study of Working Nuns*, London: Faber and Faber.
Cant, S. and Sharma, U. (1998), 'Reflexive ethnography and the professions (complementary medicine). Watching you watching me watching you (and writing about both of us)', *The Sociological Review*, 243–61.
Clouder, L. (2003), 'Becoming professional: exploring the complexities of professional socialisation in health and social care', *Learning in Health and Social Care*, **2** (4), 213–22.
Coffey, A. (1993), 'Double entry: the occupational socialisation of graduate accountants', Unpublished PhD Thesis, University of Wales, Cardiff.
Coffey, A. and Atkinson, P. (1994), *Occupational Socialisation and Working Lives*, Brookfield, VT and Gower House, Aldershot: Ashgate Publishing.
Cohen, P. (1973), *The Gospel According to the Harvard Business School*, New York: Penguin.
Delamont, S. and Atkinson, P. (2001), 'Doctoring uncertainty: mastering craft knowledge', *Social Studies of Science*, **31** (1), 87–107.
Delamont, S., Atkinson, P. and Parry, O. (2000), *The Doctoral Experience*, London: Falmer.
Delamont, S., Atkinson, P. and Pugsley, L. (2010), 'The concept smacks of magic: fighting familiarity today', *Teaching and Teacher Education*, **26** (1), 3–10.
Du Toit, D. (1995), 'A sociological analysis of the extent and influence of professional socialisation on the development of nursing identity among nursing students at two universities in Brisbane Australia', *Journal of Advance Nursing*, **21**, 164–71.
Eraut, M. (2004), 'Informal learning in the workplace', *Studies in Continuing Education*, **26** (2), 247–73.
Eraut, M. (2007), 'Learning from other people in the workplace', *Oxford Review of Education*, **33** (4), 403–22.
Fox, R. (1957), 'Training for uncertainty', in R.K.G. Merton, G. Reader and P.L. Kendall (eds), *The Student Physician*, Cambridge, MA: Harvard University Press, pp. 207–41.
Granfield, R. (1992), *Making Elite Lawyers*, New York: Routledge.
Haas, J. and Schaffir, W. (1977), 'The professionalization of medical students: developing competence and a cloak of competence', *Symbolic Interaction*, **1**, 71–88.
Haas, J. and Schaffir, W. (1987), 'Taking on the role of doctor: a dramaturgical analysis of professional socialisation', *Symbolic Interaction*, **5**, 187–203.
Hayward, C. and Mac an Ghaill, M. (1997), 'A man in the making: sexual masculinities within changing training cultures', *The Sociological Review*, **45** (4), 576–92.

Howkins, E.J. and Ewens, A. (1999), 'How students experience professional socialisation', *Journal of Nursing Studies*, **35**, 41–9.

Jurasaite-Harbison, E. (2009), 'Teachers' workplace learning within informal contexts of school cultures in the United States and Lithuania', *Journal of Workplace Learning*, **21** (4), 299–321.

Jurasaite-Harbison, E. and Rex, L. (2010), 'School cultures as contexts for informal teacher learning', *Teaching and Teacher Education*, **26** (2), 267–77.

Kleinman, S. (1984a), *Equals Before God. Seminarians as Humanistic Professionals*, Chicago, IL: University of Chicago Press.

Kleinman, S. (1984b), 'Women in seminary: dilemmas of professional socialisation', *Sociology of Education*, **57**, 210–19.

Lacey, C. (1977), *The Socialisation of Teachers*, London: Methuan.

Lave, J. and Wenger, E. (1991), *Situated Learning Legitimate Peripheral Participation*, Cambridge: Cambridge University Press.

Light, D. (1980), *Becoming a Psychiatrist: The Personal Transformation of Self*, New York: Norton.

MacIntosh, J. (2003), 'Reworking professional nursing identity', *Western Journal of Nursing Research*, **25** (6), 725–41.

Melia, K. (1987), *Learning and Working: The Occupational Socialisation of Nurses*, London: Tavistock Publications.

Merton, R.K., Reader, G. and Kendall, P.L. (1957), *The Student Physician*, Cambridge, MA: Harvard University Press.

Phillips, R. (2001), 'Doing the thing that midwives do: occupational socialisation of trainee midwives', Unpublished PhD: Thesis, Cardiff University.

Power, M. (1991), 'Educating accountants: towards a critical ethnography', *Accounting Organizations and Society*, **16** (4), 333–53.

Roberts, D. (2009), 'Friendships foster learning: the importance of friendships in clinical practice', *Nurse Education in Practice*, **9** (6), 367–71.

Schatzman, I. and Strauss, A. (1966), 'Sociology of psychiatry: a perspective and some organizing foci', *Social Problems*, **14**, 13–16.

Schleef, D. (2006), *Managing Elites: Professional Socialisation in Law and Business Schools*, Lanham, MD: Rowman and Littlefield.

Schon, D.A. (1983), *The Reflective Practitioner: How Professionals Think in Action*, Cambridge, MA: Harvard University Press.

Schon, D.A. (1987), *Educating the Reflective Practitioner*, San Francisco, CA: Jossey-Bass.

Shapiro, M. (1987), *Getting Doctored: Critical Reflections on Becoming a Physician*, Philadelphia, PA: New Society Publishers.

Sinclair S. (1997), *Making Doctors: An Institutional Apprenticeship*, Oxford: Berg.

Sommerlad, H. (2008), 'What are you doing here? You should be working in a hair salon or something: outsider status and professional socialisation in the solicitors' profession', *Web Journal of Current Legal Issues*, Web 2 (accessed 20 August 2010).

Swick, H. (2000), 'Toward a normative definition of medical professionalism', *Academic Medicine*, **75** (6), 612–16.

Traweeks, S. (1988), *Beam Times and Lifetimes: The World of High Energy Physicists*, Cambridge, MA: Harvard University Press.

Van Maanen, J. (1978), *Policing: A View from the Street*, New York: Random House.

Welland, T. (1998), 'Sleeping on the sofa: preparation for ordained ministry and the curriculum of the body', in J. Richardson and A. Shaw (eds), *The Body in Qualitative Research*, Aldershot: Ashgate, pp. 101–15.

Willis, P. (1977), *Learning to Labour*, Farnborough: Saxon House.

12. Ethnographic journeys in higher education
Lisa Lucas

ETHNOGRAPHIC STUDIES IN HIGHER EDUCATION: MAPPING THE FIELD

This chapter explores the landscape of ethnographic research within higher education, a relatively barren field compared to other areas of social life and certainly when compared to the compulsory education sector where ethnographic work is more evident (Ball, 1981; Burgess, 1983). Though there is indeed a substantial literature on students within professional disciplines and within vocational education and training and their enculturation within respective communities (see Pugsley and Salisbury chapters in this volume). However, as a relative novice who has engaged in much qualitative research into higher education but not extensive ethnographic work and who has enjoyed exploring the rich and varied literature in this area, I would argue that this is an expanding and potentially highly fruitful approach for exploring the multi-faceted and complex world of higher education. My own experiences of participant observation in academic committee meetings was illuminating and the dilemmas I faced are echoed in much of the research I discuss in this chapter (Lucas, 2006).

The main aim of this chapter is to represent the exciting and rich variety of ethnographic work in higher education, including key areas of learning and teaching, the social and learning life of students, organizational cultures, management processes and policy development and implementation within (and outside) university institutions. However, much of this cannot be addressed without at the same time engaging in the key methodological debates within ethnographic approaches on, for example, multi-sited ethnography, representation, dialogue and voice. The perceived lack of time to engage in expanded ethnographies is also shaping the debate on what counts as an ethnography. What also became apparent in my search for interesting ethnographic work was the evidence of new forms of ethnography; multi-sited ethnographies (Marcus, 1995; Wright, forthcoming), virtual ethnography, self-ethnography (Alvesson, 2003), fictional ethnography (Tierney, 1993) and ethnographic discourse analysis (Jones, 2009).

Ethnography is defined in a multitude of ways but all variously include a particular focus on culture and meaning and advocate a number of methods including, fieldwork, observation, informal and formal interviewing. Alvesson (2003) concludes that it is a study that involves

> a longer period of field work in which the researcher tries to get close to the community (organization, group) being studied, relies on their accounts as well as on observations of a rich variety of naturally occurring events (as well as on other materials, e.g. documents or material artifacts) and has an interest in cultural issues (meanings, symbols, ideas, assumptions). (Alvesson, 2003, p. 171)

However, to focus only on that research which utilizes ethnographic methods as described would miss a wealth of research that engages in the wider theoretically informed anthropological work where a key focus may be on the understanding of cultural manifestations through language and discourse and the complex ways in which subjectivity and agency are constructed and then enacted in social arenas (Shumar, 1997; Wright and Orberg, 2008).

AN ETHNOGRAPHIC UNDERSTANDING OF STUDENT LIFE, STUDENT CULTURES AND STUDENT LEARNING

> the students have no idea what the professors spend their time doing and thinking about . . . Two sophomore friends once admitted to me that they had always privately thought that 'tenure' meant that a faculty member had been around for 'ten years . . .'. (Moffatt, 1989, p. 25)

A curiosity about student life in American universities has led to two seminal texts across different time periods as well as other research that has looked at the rituals involved in the creation of student university life (Magolda, 2000). Moffatt (1989) conducted his research for *Coming of Age in New Jersey* from 1977–87 and Nathan (2005) for *My Freshman Year* during 2002–03. Both texts recognized the lack of understanding that professors have of student life similar to the misunderstanding students had about professors. Nathan (2005) maintains, 'I found out quite unwittingly that if I walked like a duck and quacked like a duck then people thought I was a duck. My fellow students began sharing opinions and gossip with me that I would never hear as a professor' (p. vii).

Nathan's (2005) research at AnyU involved her enrolling as a freshman and living in student dorms for one year. She attended classes and essentially lived the life of a student during this period and, with a few exceptions, was known only as a fellow student to those that she was researching. For this reason, she claims a high degree of familiarity with fellow students and 'authenticity' in her experiences living amongst an undergraduate community. She collected a wide variety of data sources, including the use of formal interviews and focus groups to informal conversations, observations in class, dorms and other areas of institutional life as well as artefacts such as posters, notes, graffiti and so on in order to build a complex mosaic picture of undergraduate life. Through her fieldwork, Nathan was able to provide a detailed understanding of student life in relation to their academic study, their social lives within and beyond the dormitories and their social networks and community involvement (or lack thereof). Through her view of student life she came to conclude that

> (the) undergraduate worldview, as I came to understand it, linked intellectual matters with in-class domains and other formal areas of college life, including organized clubs and official dorm programs. 'Real' college culture remained beyond the reach of university institutions and personnel, and centred on the small, ego-based networks of friends that defined one's personal and social world. Academic and intellectual pursuits thus had a curiously distant relation to college life. (Nathan, 2005, p. 100)

The official discourse of undergraduate culture linked with what was termed the 'undergraduate cynical' (Moffatt, 1989), that is, the public pronouncements of how little studying a student did and the sense that managing one's academic work was centred on finding the 'easy A' class or choosing classes that fitted with busy schedules rather than the search for a more meaningful learning experience (Nathan, 2005). However, during a more personal encounter with a fellow student, she glimpses an attitude at odds with the official discourse.

> I had just finished testing Ray on a series of vocabulary terms when he began questioning me on the past imperfect tense. 'Forget that', I responded. 'She says it's not on the test.' What he said next shocked me. 'Is it the only reason you are learning this material . . . for the test? Don't you want to learn to speak French better? Come on, do it.'
> I was mortified, really, and caught between my two roles. He was right, of course, but not from the standpoint of public student culture, which I had learned to imitate. Because we were friends, he could make that comment to me; but I had long since discovered that in the daily encounters in the dorm and the classroom, there were standard cultural conventions that marked someone as 'one of us.' (Nathan, 2005, p. 143)

She concludes, therefore, 'that the actual experience of individual students is much richer than the normative expressions of student culture' (p. 144).

A further more complex view on reality is discovered when she attempts to investigate the parameters of diversity within college life. Despite the proclamations of individual students that their friendship groups include members from different ethnic minorities, there is little evidence of this through observation and on closer examination of close friendship networks. Her questioning of students through interviews and her observation of student behaviour in the dining hall showed that whilst ethnic minority students (students of colour in American parlance) were more likely to be involved in mixed networks, this was much less likely for 'white' students. She acknowledges that her sampling was small and therefore conclusions must be tentative, however, these patterns remain to be further investigated.

In both studies, but particularly that of Nathan since her work was conducted more covertly, key ethical problems were highlighted. For Nathan, the issue of disclosure of information gathered without the knowledge of participants was an issue and affected how she chose to write up the study. Within ethnographic research, one of the key advantages is that due to the intensive nature of the research and the ability to build rapport and enter more personal domains of people's lives, a richer more nuanced picture of social domains and cultures and people's experience of them beyond the 'cultural scripts' can be accessed. However, the potentially personally intrusive nature of such research also highlights difficulties in terms of how these rich experiences can be told.

Most importantly, both of these books offer an understanding of the rites of passage into society and culture and how these are mirrored within values present in student life, which in turn play a key role in social reproduction. This ability of ethnographic work to explore the mechanisms of cultural and social reproduction are also vividly illustrated in another seminal text, which explores the important role of romantic involvement in the cultural lives of women students (Holland and Eisenhart, 1990). This research provides an in-depth study of black and white women studying at two US universities and also follows them into their transition to the world of work. The researchers interviewed and engaged in fieldwork with 23 college women. The researchers follow, 'the day to day happenings, and the everyday, often minute "choices" that paved the way into adulthood of a small number of college women in the early 1980s' (p. xi). Whilst charting the complexities of these women's lives and indeed exploring their 'dissent and moments of protest against male privilege' (p. xi), the overriding argument contained in the book is of the central importance of the culture of romantic relationships and the ability of men, in particular, to judge the attractiveness of female students. Attractiveness was seen as something that was important for both men and women. However, where men could be judged by their success in other areas such as sport or school politics, the predominant judgement of female prestige was on their attractiveness to men (Holland and Eisenhart, 1990). The significance of academic success and achievement took second place to the prestige awarded by the patriarchal judgement of attractiveness and thus romantic success based on male interest. This meant that many of the women studied did not continue in their career interests. Holland and Eisenhart (1990) argue that such patterns can be seen across the western world including countries such as the UK and Australia and so are not necessarily limited to the USA. Whether there may have been any change in these patterns has been taken up in more recent research that looks at the continuing importance of cultures of romance in university life (Gilmartin, 2005).

Further seminal texts have been produced through ethnographies conducted within medical schools focusing on medical education and student doctor cultures, in particular the classic *Boys in White* (Becker et al., 1977). The specific sociological study of *Boys in White* was focused on the nature of student culture whereas other classic studies brought the processes of teaching and learning more to the fore (Atkinson and Pugsley, 2005). These research studies are discussed in more depth elsewhere in this volume (see Pugsley chapter).

The use of ethnographic methods to research into teaching and learning in higher education has had a growing significance both in terms of utilizing ethnographic methods to explore different aspects of the teaching and learning process (Cashmore et al., 2010) and to introduce students to the practices of conducting ethnographic research (Beach and Finders, 1999). More recently, with the significant advances in new technology, a form of 'virtual ethnography' has entered the field of research into teaching and learning (Hemmi et al., 2009). These studies begin to challenge and push the boundaries of what is considered 'ethnography'. For example, Cashmore et al. (2010) collect data using 'free-form video diaries' alongside focus groups. They argue that this form of data collection can 'capture the various emotions, experiences and insights that students are feeling at particular moments in particular personal and social spaces' (p. 107). It may certainly capture the 'lived reality' of student experiences through their thoughts and feelings but where is the research-observer-interpreter in all of this? The same question may be asked of the 'virtual ethnography' methods of data collection where there seems to be a hybrid of data with forms of either formative or summative assessed work. This type of ethnography certainly provides a fascinating schema of data collection and provides insights into a new technologically complex world. In the study by Hemmi et al. (2009), they investigate traditional methods of teaching and learning via the collection of data by participant observation of classroom sessions. In parallel they also conduct a 'virtual ethnography' by collecting data from a distance-learning course via 'observation' of student interactions using, amongst others, Wiki's, Facebook and Second

Life. The participation of students in discussion sites and their use of blogs was observed and analysed. Semi-structured interviews were also conducted using either face-to-face, telephone or internet interviews as the various circumstances dictated. The researchers did acknowledge that the quality of interviews was uneven across the different media with internet interviews, in particular, plagued by technological problems (Hemmi et al., 2009). Whilst there is no doubt that this form of data collection may provide rich and in-depth understanding of student interactions via different teaching and learning modes, there is still scope to provide a convincing case of this research as ethnographic. It certainly addresses issues of identity and selfhood (particularly in the online environment) and forms of group interaction, but what of cultures and community? As this is a new field of research, there is perhaps much that is yet to be developed.

ETHNOGRAPHIC EXPLORATIONS OF UNIVERSITY AND DISCIPLINARY CULTURES

The question of university and disciplinary culture(s) is a vexed and rather under-researched and under-elaborated one. There is a relatively broad array of generic qualitative research studies that have researched this question (Becher and Trowler, 2001) but relatively few ethnographic studies. It is potentially an aspect of university life that is ripe for ethnographic investigation. So how can we explain the dearth of studies? In his book *Homo Academicus*, Bourdieu entitled the preface 'A book for burning' in order to highlight the danger of exposing the world of academia in a way that was perhaps less than flattering, potentially positioning him as a 'traitor' (Bourdieu, 1988). This problem of 'organizational loyalty' is also identified by Alvesson (2003) and the issue of not 'exposing "backstage" conditions' of academic life (p. 167). However, he also points to the difficulty of over familiarity and the possibility of academics studying academic environments with the potentially impossible task of making the 'familiar strange'.

Tierney has provided a substantive body of work to address the cultural dimensions of university life and to attempt to describe and theorize organizational cultures within institutions (Tierney, 1988; Tierney and Bensimon, 1996). Using a case study of one university in the USA, Tierney (1988) attempts to sketch an understanding of different aspects of his framework of organizational culture, including environment, mission, socialization, information, strategy and leadership. Within 'Family State College', he describes the president's use of space to effectively communicate the intended ethos of the institution.

> The president's use of space sets an example emulated by others. His open-door policy, for example, permeates the institution. Administrators either work in open space areas in full view of one another or the doors to their offices are physically open, inviting visits with colleagues, guests, or more importantly students. (Tierney, 1988, p. 15)

Following Dill (1982), Tierney argues that, '[the] management of academic culture therefore involves both the management of meaning and the management of social integration' (p. 9). The apparent openness of space and forms of interaction at 'Family State College', it is argued therefore, symbolizes the ethos of an open and responsive culture.

There exists, however, a more critical literature, which takes an anthropological perspective on the commodification, commercialization and marketization of higher education (Shumar, 1997, 1999, 2004a). Universities, Shumar (1997) argues, have been forced to 'see themselves as a business providing a product to the market' (p. 24). In looking at the commodification of culture within which universities are ensnared he attempts to analyse 'the implications this has had on intellectuals and university life in the United States' (p. 3) and in particular how 'it affects the work force in the university sector' (p. 9). Given the theoretical focus and presuppositions being brought to this research, Shumar (1997) is also keen to problematize the idea that he sees of 'being there' contained in anthropological and ethnographic research, that is, primarily the method of participant observation. He argues that 'an ethnographer not only comes to a deep knowledge and appreciation of a group of people, but s/he invents that group for the purpose of considering it and sharing the subsequent information' (p. 2).

Where there is more of a concern with the exposure of university culture(s), Alvesson (2003) advocates a form of self-ethnography. This involves, as he explains, drawing attention to 'one's own cultural context', rather than dealing with essentially personal experiences. He argues, that by engaging in a self-ethnography, the 'closeness' of the researcher to the social field ensures a degree of understanding that would potentially be lost on the 'outsider' researcher. He maintains that the problems of 'multiple cultural configurations' and 'blind spots and intellectual closures shared by people in universities also makes the project of a researcher studying a department in significant ways different from his or her own difficult' (p. 177). However, he does also point to the potential difficulties of the self-ethnographers' potential blind spots within their own department as well as the omission of 'taboo' subjects or indeed, the desire to get 'even' as the result of a negative experience within the institution. The perennial perplexities of closeness/distance and authentic/sanitized accounts continue to pervade all forms of ethnographic work.

Where particularly sensitive areas of institutional life are being investigated, the idea of 'fictional ethnographies' is proposed in order to uphold the confidentiality of anyone concerned in the research. Like a good novel, the perceived artificiality of such a form of representation may enable a 'truth' that resonates even where no attempt is made to provide a valid association with empirical accounts. This was a strategy adopted in a study of homosexuality within universities (Tierney, 1993).

The exploration of disciplinary rather than institutional cultures has been conducted extensively through sociological studies of science and in particular ethnographic studies of science laboratories. A number of classic studies investigate the cultural practices of science laboratories and attempt to understand the practices of these communities (Lynch, 1993; Knorr-Cetina, 1994). More recent research has followed these traditions in the 'culture-in-interaction' within laboratories (Benninghoff and Sormani, 2008) and the acculturation practices for the socialization of doctoral students (Holley, 2009).

AN ETHNOGRAPHIC VIEW OF HIGHER EDUCATION GOVERNANCE, POLICY DEVELOPMENT AND IMPLEMENTATION

There is a fascinating area of ethnographic research conducted which looks at both the decision-making and implementation of the educational policy-making process (Jones, 2009) and the 'lived experience' of the impacts of policy within higher education institutions (Shore and Wright, 1999; Shore, 2010). The focus, therefore, is on studying the mediation of the macro and the micro processes (Wright, forthcoming). She argues that there is a need for

> new ways of studying large scale processes of transformation – ones that include in their ambit at the one end, the national and international discourses, agencies and actors that are involved in the formulation and government of the new economic and political order, and at the other extreme, people who in their day to day activities are engaged in governance and the management of self in the fast changing conditions of their lives. (Wright, forthcoming, p. 1)

Jones (2009) in his study of European policy formulation and decision-making argues that the use of ethnographic methods and in this case an 'ethnographic discourse analysis' allows for a richness of description and allows for the ability to represent the 'being there' at a seat of decision-making, which can take one beyond what is possible from the reporting of interviews. But he also emphasizes the challenges of doing this and where elites are being studied, it can be almost impossible.

The discussion above provides the pointers to the methodological concerns of Ethnographic Discourse Analysis (EDA). Firstly, EDA is not to be considered as CDA + Ethnography. This is *ethnographic* discourse analysis and it sets out to investigate the practices of the formulation, articulation, contestation and negotiation of discourse within institutions. The position of texts is intended to be fundamentally re-orientated away from a CDA [Critical Discourse Analysis] approach and to be far more attuned to the concerns of CPE [Cultural Political Economy] and the ECM [Extended Case Method]. EDA would be mobilised as an approach to make available for investigation both the practices of actors and institutions in the production and contestation of discourse and the role of discourse in producing and re-producing those practices. (Jones, 2009, p. 237, emphasis in original)

Similarly, Wright and Orberg (2008) are researching university reform in Denmark and the mediation of such reforms through the discourse and practices of university leaders and university academics. They utilize the anthropological tools of studying 'keywords' and 'semantic clusters' to show how institutional actors utilize concepts and meanings according to their positioning and understanding, which is often more complex and difficult to predict than might be assumed.

A NEW IMPETUS FOR ETHNOGRAPHIC RESEARCH IN HIGHER EDUCATION

In this chapter I have attempted to highlight a number of aspects in the brief tour of ethnographic studies in higher education; namely, ethnographic work in different areas of higher education, different 'types' of ethnography and methodological debates and concerns.

There can be no doubt that ethnographic research and the tools of cultural anthropology more broadly have much to offer the study of higher education and indeed, there is scope to dramatically increase such research. Shumar (2004a) provides two compelling arguments for the worth of a cultural anthropological study of higher education. Firstly, he argues that contemporary anthropologists 'are in the habit of taking a step back from all interactions and institutions and asking basic questions about what these things are, why they function the way they do, and whose interests they serve. This deconstructionist spirit, coupled with the intimate knowledge that an anthropologist acquires about a group of people, can be a very powerful form of critique' (p. 36). Secondly, he sees an anthropology of higher education as 'studying up', that is, studying those in positions of power (Shumar, 2004b). The university and academics may be seen as 'the dominated dominant' (Bourdieu, 1988) but he would also advocate the need to study ourselves within the cultural and socio-political construction of the academy. As Shumar (2004b) argues, it is imperative 'that we turn our critical lens on the very institutions where many of us work and see that the forces of globalism are not only operating directly on the institutions we inhabit, they are transforming the way we produce knowledge and infiltrating our very consciousness. It is critical that we understand these processes' (p. 37). There can be no doubt that the qualitative methodological tools of anthropology alongside sociology (and debate over the similarities, differences and divergences of the two must be left for another time) are invaluable in enabling a comprehensive and compelling understanding and critique of higher education.

REFERENCES

Alvesson, M. (2003), 'Methodology for close-up studies: struggling with closeness and closure', *Higher Education*, **46**, 167–93.
Atkinson, P. and Pugsley, L. (2005), 'Making sense of ethnography and medical education', *Medical Education*, **39**, 228–34.
Ball, S. (1981), *Beachside Comprehensive: A Case Study of Secondary Schooling*, Cambridge: Cambridge University Press.
Beach, R. and Finders, M.J. (1999), 'Students as ethnographers: guiding alternative research projects', *English Journal*, **82**, 82–90.
Becher, T. and Trowler, P. (2001), *Academic Tribes and Territories: Intellectual Inquiry and the Culture of the Disciplines*, Buckingham: Open University Press.
Becker, H., Geer, B., Hughes, E.C. and Strauss, A.L. (1977), *Boys in White: Student Culture in Medical School*, Chicago, IL: University of Chicago Press.
Benninghoff, M. and Sormani, P. (2008), 'Culture in interactions: academic identities in laboratory work', in J. Valimaa and O.H. Ylijoki (eds), *Cultural Perspectives on Higher Education*, New York: Springer, pp. 109–26.
Bourdieu, P. (1988), *Homo Academicus*, Cambridge: Polity Press.
Burgess, R.G. (1983), *Experiencing Comprehensive Education: A Study of Bishop McGregor School*, London: Metheun.
Cashmore, A., Green, P. and Scott, J. (2010), 'An ethnographic approach to studying the student experience: the student perspective through free form video diaries: a practice report', *International Journal of the First Year in Higher Education*, **1**, 106–11.
Dill, D.D. (1982), 'The management of academic culture: notes on the management of meaning and social integration', *Higher Education*, **11**, 303–20.
Gilmartin, S.K. (2005), 'The centrality and costs of heterosexual romantic love among first-year college women', *Journal of Higher Education*, **76**, 609–33.
Hemmi, A., Bayne, S. and Land, R. (2009), 'The appropriation and repurposing of social technologies in higher education', *Journal of Computer Assisted Learning*, **25**, 19–30.
Holland, D. C. and Eisenhard, M.A. (1990), *Educated in Romance: Women, Achievement and College Culture*, Chicago, IL: University of Chicago Press.
Holley, K. (2009), 'Animal research practices and Doctoral student identity development in a scientific community', *Studies in Higher Education*, **34**, 577–91.
Jones, P.D. (2009), 'The European Commission and education policy in the European Union: an ethnographic discourse analysis', Unpublished PhD Thesis, University of Bristol.
Knorr-Cetina, K. (1994), 'Laboratory studies: the cultural approach to the study of science', in S. Jasanoff, G.E. Markle, J.C. Petersen and T. Pinch (eds), *Handbook of Science and Technology Studies*, London: Sage, pp. 109–26.

Lucas, L. (2006), *The Research Game in Academic Life*, Maidenhead: McGraw-Hill and Open University Press.
Lynch, M. (1993), *Scientific Practice and Ordinary Action*, Cambridge: Cambridge University Press.
Magolda, P.M. (2000), 'The campus tour: ritual and community in higher education', *Anthropology and Education Quarterly*, **31**, 24–46.
Marcus, G.E. (1995), 'Ethnography in/of the world system: the emergence of multi-sited ethnography', *Annual Review of Anthropology*, **24**, 95–117.
Moffatt, M. (1989), *Coming of Age in New Jersey: College and American Culture*, New Brunswick, NJ: Rutgers University Press.
Nathan, R. (2005), *My Freshman Year: What a Professor Learned by Becoming a Student*, Ithaca, NY: Cornell University Press.
Shore, C. (2010), 'Beyond the multiversity: neoliberalism and the rise of the Schizophrenic university', *Social Anthropology*, **18** (1), 15–29.
Shore, C. and Wright, S. (1999), 'Audit culture and anthropology: neo-liberalism in British higher education', *Journal of Royal Anthropological Institute*, **5** (4), 557–75.
Shumar, W. (1997), *College for Sale: A Critique of the Commodification of Higher Education*, London: Routledge Falmer.
Shumar, W. (1999), 'Labouring in the dream factory, part 1', *International Journal of Qualitative Studies in Education*, **12**, 239–50.
Shumar, W. (2004a), 'Global pressures, local reactions: higher education and neo-liberal economic policies', *International Journal of Qualitative Studies in Education*, **17**, 23–41.
Shumar, W. (2004b), 'Making strangers at home: anthropologists studying higher education', *Journal of Higher Education*, **75**, 23–41.
Tierney, W.G. (1988), 'Organizational culture in higher education: defining the essentials', *Journal of Higher Education*, **59**, 2–21.
Tierney, W.G. (1993), 'The cedar closet', *Qualitative Studies in Education*, **6**, 303–14.
Tierney, W.G. and Bensimon, E.M. (1996), *Promotion and Tenure: Community and Socialization in Academe*, Albany, NY: State University of New York Press.
Wright, S. (forthcoming), 'Processes of social transformation: an anthropology of English higher education policy', in J. Krejsler, N. Kryger, and J. Milner (eds), *Paedagogisk Antropologi*, Copenhagen: Danmarks Paedagogiske Universitets Forlag.
Wright, S. and Orberg, J.W. (2008), 'Autonomy and control: Danish university reform in the context of modern governance', *Learning and Teaching: International Journal of Higher Education in the Social Sciences*, **1**, 27–57.

13. Teacher education: qualitative research approaches
Mark Dressman, Wayne Journell and Jay Mann

TEACHER EDUCATION

Since the late 1980s, qualitative and ethnographic research methods have dominated inquiry across a wide range of age levels and content areas within teacher education. The complexity of teaching as a cultural activity and the individualistic quality of the profession, that is, the fact that teachers may be taught some things in cohorts but develop their habits of practice alone over extended periods of time in classrooms largely isolated from each other, has led researchers to focus on processes at local and often micro-ethnographic levels. In this chapter we focus our review of the research literature on three areas: the construction of teaching, teachers, and teacher education within North American and British/European contexts; case studies of teachers and programs; and action, or teacher-research studies conducted by teachers themselves, typically in the middle or later years of their careers. In conclusion, we consider how the application of a method originating outside education by researchers who largely see themselves as educationists first and only later as social scientists (that is, as applied anthropologists or sociologists) changes both the method and the findings that it produces.

We also offer three caveats about our review. First, our goal was not to be encyclopedic in our coverage of the research. There are many more interesting and informative studies of teacher education, both from a methodological and an issues-oriented viewpoint, than could be covered here. Rather, we chose to highlight particular studies representative of the methodological diversity in teacher education research, and to invite readers to investigate the full texts of the studies and use the references cited in them for further reference. Second, our task was to review studies of teacher education, not of teaching per se. Teacher education focuses largely on teachers' professional development, whereas teaching encompasses an enormous range of content areas, contexts, and participants. Finally and with apology, we note the limited range of national diversity in our review and what may seem to some readers to be our overemphasis on teacher education within the context of the United States. We have made a concerted effort to include major researchers and studies from other Anglophone countries, but our own backgrounds in the USA may have inevitably skewed our selection and interpretive processes.

RESEARCH ON TEACHER EDUCATION IN BRITAIN/EUROPE AND NORTH AMERICA

Twenty years ago Atkinson and Delamont (1990), in an article published in *Teaching and Teacher Education*, compared the differences between qualitative and ethnographic studies of teaching and teachers in British and North American contexts. They noted with some surprise that despite remarkable similarities in methodology and at least superficially in setting, differences in the ways that ethnographers on either side of the Atlantic wrote about teachers and teaching and the issues that they focused on were quite stark:

> For the (American) anthropologist the classroom is the site of cultural differences, often ethnic in origin, and the teacher an agent of cultural imposition. For the (British) sociologist the frame of reference is a class-based social structure, in which teachers and pupils alike are subject to the everyday disciplines of work. (p. 113)

Teachers were also 'written' differently, in their analysis. They noted that in the USA, ethnographies tended to focus on the cultural and linguistic home lives of students and the ways in which these conflicted with the culturally White, suburban orientation of teachers, whereas in Britain teachers were more often the focus of ethnographic investigation than were students, and were often presented more three-dimensionally, as people caught within conditions imposed on them by institutional and economic forces beyond their control.

To investigate whether these distinctions persist today and whether they extend to studies of teacher education, we selected at random one issue from each volume year of a major research journal in North America (*Journal of Teacher Education*) (JTE) and Britain/Europe (*European Journal of Teacher Education*) (EJTE) from 2005 to 2009 and compared their contents in terms of topic, treatment, and methodology. JTE and EJTE were selected over other major journals in the field such as *Teaching and Teacher Education* (with a broadly international focus) or *Teaching Education* (an Australian journal) because the national origins of studies published in these two journals contrasted in ways similar to the comparison made by Atkinson and Delamont.

Our analysis of studies published in JTE and EJTE shows some similarities to Atkinson and Delamont's study as well as some significant differences. In the cases of both journals, qualitative/ethnographic research methodologies predominated, with only a few quantitative or experimental studies published in EJTE or JTE. The most striking similarity, however, was the ways that teaching and teachers were constructed in Atkinson and Delamont's analysis of US studies and the ways these were constructed within recent issues of JTE. As in 1990, in 2005–09 cultural differences between the teaching force and the student population in the USA were seen as problematic. Of the 24 empirical studies published in the issues of JTE that we reviewed, seven reported on the efforts of teacher educators to raise the consciousness of largely White, female, and suburban populations of pre-service teachers to issues of linguistic and cultural diversity among the students they were or would be teaching. Implicitly and explicitly, articles with titles such as 'Teaching African American English forms to standard American English-speaking teachers: effects on acquisition, attitudes, and responses to student use' (Fogel and Ehri, 2009), 'What teacher candidates learned about diversity, social justice, and themselves from service-learning experiences' (Baldwin et al., 2007), and 'An ethics of access: using life history to trace preservice teachers' initial viewpoints on teaching for equity' (Johnson, 2007) constructed teachers and teacher candidates as not only blind to cultural and linguistic difference but resistant to learning about its implications for teaching and learning. The authoring researchers (who were typically reporting on their own work as teacher educators) often placed themselves at odds with the students/preservice teachers who were participants in their studies and their courses, and on the side of moral and ethical self-righteousness – a perspective that was reinforced by theoretical essays in the journal with titles like 'On the reasons we want teachers of good disposition and moral character' (Osguthorpe, 2008).

In contrast, neither cultural/linguistic difference nor social class was the focus of qualitative studies in EJTE within the five issues that we examined. In this journal, among 31 empirical studies published between 2005 and 2009, language education and the use of computer-based technologies predominated. Words like 'diversity,' 'equity,' and 'ethics' were absent from the titles of all articles, and there were no theoretical essays published in the journal in this period. In the case of the seven articles focusing on language education, the issue was not the politics or micropolitics of second language acquisition, as in JTE, but logistics and the development of infrastructures and more efficient and increasingly sophisticated programs for introducing foreign languages as a part of European and national language policies.

Orientations toward policy and teachers were also markedly different.

In JTE, even after we deliberately excluded themed issues on No Child Left Behind (the Bush administration's education policy) and 'Letters to the 44th President of the United States' (on the inauguration of Barack Obama) from our sample, a recurring theme was the assault on university-based teacher education programs by state and federal policy initiatives. Just as frequently, however, articles in EJTE aligned their goals and objectives with European and national educational policy, as in 'An examination of the language and interpretations of "Standard One" for initial teacher training in England' (Harrison, 2006), in which it is noted that 'While this standard is almost universally welcomed as an important component of teacher education in England, its assessment remains elusive for many teachers and tutors' (p. 431).

Teachers were also frequently depicted in alignment with the goals of government policies and teacher educators/researchers, as in this quote from the abstract of 'Bringing modern languages into the primary curriculum in England' (Macrory and McLachlan, 2009): 'The results suggest an overall positive response from trainees, but indicate a need to ensure that schools provide more explicit and targeted support when trainees are on placement' (p. 259). Overall, in EJTE, the goals and objectives of government policy, teacher educators/researchers, and teachers were depicted as reasonably well aligned, with tension arising from lack of resources and differing interpretations of policies, whereas in JTE, relations among these three stakeholders were represented as strained at best and frequently antagonistic, with teacher educators/researchers representing themselves as principled, ethical, and culturally conscious actors (often aligned with a small group of similarly enlightened teachers) against an unresponsive majority within the profession and government bureaucracy.

CASE STUDIES OF TEACHERS' PROFESSIONAL DEVELOPMENT

In an address to the American Educational Research Association shortly before the turn of the twenty-first Century, Zeichner (1999) introduced the 'new scholarship in teacher education.' Among the five approaches he described were case studies of teacher education programs, studies pertaining to learning how to teach, and examinations of the nature and impact of teacher education activities. Over a decade later, Zeichner's assessment of the field has proven prophetic. Research on teacher education and the professional development of novice teachers continues to be shaped by qualitative, single-case studies that serve to highlight the complexities of teacher training and pre-service teacher education.

For the purposes of this review, we will consider cases as research on 'bounded systems' (Stake, 1995) in which the researcher is attempting to study 'things in their natural settings, attempting to make sense of, or interpret phenomena in terms of the meanings people bring to them' (Denzin and Lincoln, 1994, p. 2). In particular, we will focus on ethnographic case studies, which use basic ethnographic methods of observation, interviewing, and artifact analysis to better understand the cultural knowledge of the individuals being studied (Spindler and Spindler, 1992; Merriam, 1998; Yin, 2008). By using such a broad definition, we can consider multiple forms of qualitative research, such as narrative inquiry (Clandinin and Connelly, 2000) and ethnography (Frank and Uy, 2004), in our analysis.

Perhaps the most prevalent types of cases found in the literature are those that describe teacher training within the context of a particular content area. In other words, the knowledge and dispositions that are needed to develop quality language arts teachers as opposed to that which is needed to develop teachers concentrating in social studies, science, mathematics, or any of the other disciplines. As Pugsley (Chapter 11, this volume) notes, the development of professional identity during teacher education programs is closely tied to norms acquired by students through immersion in the discourses of content areas in which they are specializing. These studies are just as, if not more, likely to be found in content-specific journals as they are in periodicals focusing exclusively on teacher education. Through a quick perusal of the literature, one can easily find exemplary studies that describe the specific nuances of training individuals to teach language arts (for example, Smagorinsky et al., 2007; Jones and Enriquez, 2009), social studies (for example, Yeager and Wilson, 1997; James, 2008; Monte-Sano and Cochran, 2009), science (for example, Luft, 2001; Park Rogers and Abell, 2008), mathematics (for example, Mewborn, 1999; Hill et al., 2005), and physical education (for example, Bertone et al., 2003), at both the elementary and secondary levels.

However, all pre-service and novice teachers need to develop certain knowledge and dispositions that transcend content, such as how to effectively teach for diversity and social justice. While much of the literature on teaching diverse and special needs students consists of theoretical arguments focusing on the sociocultural awareness needed by pre-service and practicing teachers, there is a growing body of qualitative research that focuses on cases of pre-service teachers learning to conceptualize difference within their teacher education programs or their first years of teaching (for example, McDonough, 2009; Pollock et al., 2009; Arndt and Liles, 2010; Castro et al., 2010). Similarly, there are numerous studies detailing how pre-service and novice teachers adapt to issues related to teaching in the twenty-first century, such as harnessing technology and working within the confines of accountability reforms (for example, van Hover, 2006; Boling, 2007).

While these examples are the most common types of qualitative cases found within the literature, one can occasionally find qualitative studies on other aspects of teacher training. For example, qualitative methods are often used to evaluate aspects of individual teacher education programs, particularly as they relate to the dispositional development of pre-service teachers (for example, Baldwin et al., 2007; Cooper, 2007). Less prevalent are qualitative longitudinal studies, such as the work done by Levin (2003), that chart the development of teachers from their pre-service experiences through the latter part of their careers. Finally, although narrative inquiry is becoming more accepted within educational research as a whole, there appears to be a lack of this methodology within the teacher education literature. While one may find articles, such as Carrillo (2010), that appear to take a narrative approach in their presentation and structure, few authors explicitly describe their studies as narrative inquiries.

In summary, our review of qualitative case studies in teacher education leads us to three observations. First, it seems clear that there is little continuity within the literature on what constitutes a 'case' when studying pre-service and novice teachers, and we posit that this ambiguity often affects the rigor of case-based research. While many single-case studies claim to use ethnographic methods, few studies appear to use these methods in concert to form thick descriptions of the case being studied. Rather, much case-based research is often limited to one or two methods of data collection, or one method of data collection is disproportionately relied upon in the analysis process. In order to achieve thick descriptions, researchers must triangulate a variety of data sources and employ rigorous analytic tools, such as meta-interviews (Clarke and Robertson, 2001), that allow for the contextualization of their findings. In short, we believe that a greater focus on ethnographic inquiry within single-case studies would produce more robust findings from which researchers and practitioners can better understand the strengths and weaknesses of teacher training programs.

Second, we share the concern voiced by Mena Marcos and Tillema (2006) that qualitative research on teacher education and practice often appears 'unfinished' in that studies tend to describe a particular problem or issue without describing possible interventions or ramifications. While single-case studies are rarely generalizable, there seems to be a need for researchers to make greater efforts to improve the validity of their interpretations through repeated studies of similar cases or by taking a longitudinal approach that studies the same case over an extended period of time. In order to use case studies as a viable way of understanding and improving teacher training, there needs to be a certain level of continuity present within the research base rather than merely a collection of various phenomena displayed for public consumption.

Finally, it seems evident that certain aspects of teacher education have been explored in greater depth than others. For example, the vast majority of studies on teacher preparation have been conducted among individuals who have received certification through traditional undergraduate teacher training programs. However, widespread teacher shortages have forced school districts to hire mid-career professionals without any teacher certification in record numbers. The experiences and training of these alternatively certified teachers who have taken non-traditional routes to the classroom represent a relatively unexplored aspect of teacher training (Zeichner and Schulte, 2001).

Similarly, the literature on preparing teachers for diversity remains largely theoretical and could benefit from a greater number of cases detailing how novice teachers respond to teaching individuals from diverse populations. We have also found that there is a noticeable lack of research on developing pre-service teachers' cultural literacy and global awareness (one noticeable exception is Merryfield, 2000, 2007). In our own work (Dressman et al., in press), we have taken steps to fill this void by studying cases of pre-service teachers' exposure to diverse cultures through the use of technology.

ACTION OR TEACHER RESEARCH

Boaz, a pre-service art teacher in a one-year teacher preparation program at Trinity University in San Antonio, Texas, noted upon the completion of a required qualitative research project, 'It was exciting . . . knowing . . . that the "jewels" were to come straight out of my hand' (Breidenstein, 2002, p. 316). These 'jewels' were mined from his own action research. An increasing number of pre-service teacher candidates and practicing educators have reaped the bounty of action research (Woods, 1985; Cochran-Smith and Lytle, 1999; Zeichner, 1999), though skeptics continue to warn that all that glitters may not be gold (Fenstermacher, 1994; Huberman, 1996).

Ernest Stringer (2007) defines 'action research' as 'a systematic approach to investigation that enables people to find effective solutions to problems they confront in their everyday lives . . . and focuses on specific situations and localized solutions' (p. 1). The researcher and the researched are inextricably linked by lived experience, and the research act is interwoven with daily practices. For teachers, the classroom/school becomes the laboratory and students and selves serve as the most intimate subjects.

The literature on action research in teacher education is considerable and varied in scope and approach. Some, like Breidenstein (2002), promote action research for self-confident pre-service teachers in their earliest formal interactions with students and teachers in school settings. Others suggest a more gradual transition to action research practices by engaging students in autobiographic narratives and ethnographic studies of culturally diverse students in a transformative experience that primes pre-service teachers for eventual action research in their own classrooms (Hale et al., 2008). On the other hand, some scholars limit pre-service teachers to traditional ethnographic projects. Woods (1985) argues that, whereas ethnographic research promotes reflection and teaches valuable observational skills during teacher preparation programs, only in-service teachers can be full 'participant-observers' in the action research process.

While there may be disagreement over the appropriate introduction of active action research in teaching practice, proponents of this methodology herald its many benefits. Zeichner (1999) considers the rise of the self-study in teacher research as the most significant development in teacher education. Action research promotes the systematic, critical examination of a teacher's self-practices and the practices of the institution where she teaches, giving rise to richer social inquiry, community knowledge, and practical classroom inquiry (Noffke and Stevenson, 1995; Noffke and Brennan, 1997; Cochran-Smith and Lytle, 1999). All teachers, whether pre-service or practicing, who participate in qualitative research projects gain a strong sense of the moral, political, and personal aspects of classroom teaching and learn to turn a critical eye inward, carrying ethnographic work to a deeply personal level (Breidenstein, 2002). Significant action research provides rich professional development opportunities for teachers and further professionalizes teaching (Cochran-Smith and Lytle, 1999). In addition, meaningful partnerships with university faculty and action researchers-teachers can provide an important voice for teachers in academic circles and affords teacher education faculty an integral, much-needed look at the professional identity development of beginning teachers (Woods, 1985; Clandinin, 1989).

Action research in teacher education is not without concern. Many scholars identify objectivity as a primary concern with this methodology (Fenstermacher, 1994; Huberman, 1996). Can teachers be objective researchers in their own classrooms and schools? Is traditional ethnographic observation by an 'impartial' researcher preferable to the conflicted position in which teachers may find themselves in action research settings? Questions of objectivity arise for teachers who engage in action research unless demonstrated interpretative inquiry techniques are preserved (Cochran-Smith and Lytle, 1999).

The concern over explicit methodology raises a second critique of action research. Woods (1985) notes that many critics find action research to be invalid, superficial, and trivial. For some, what is missing is the hard, empirical methodology that seemingly opposes interpretative research (Erickson, 1986). However, as Erickson has also noted and Atkinson and Delamont (1990) have made clear, 'The use of qualitative methods is no substitute for rigour' (p. 122). Teachers should be carefully schooled in qualitative research practices and, when possible, have the support of experienced university researchers to assist their efforts (Woods, 1985).

Learning to research qualitatively is closely related to a third and final concern about action research in the literature. Cochran-Smith and Lytle (1999) warn that haphazard, cursory introductions to teacher research can limit the potential of such projects to shape the professional lives of beginning educators. Simply making qualitative projects 'window-dressing' to the teacher education curriculum without a concerted effort to develop the deep analytic and reflection skills necessary to advance research throughout a teacher's career is without excuse.

Those who teach and practice active research have an obligation to advance the merit of this methodology with careful implementation of research plans marked by the highest caliber of qualitative research standards. The cost of not doing so is the weakened image of action research in scholarship, despite the numerous gains that are made from many well-executed studies. As a relatively new approach to interpretative research, action research places the burden of proof upon its advocates. Only then will action research assume its place as the newest jewel in the crown of qualitative research in teacher education.

CONCLUSION: METHOD AND MESSAGE

As both Atkinson and Delamont (1990) and one of us (Dressman, 2008) have noted, the widespread application of qualitative research methods to the study of educational phenomena, including teacher education, is a relatively recent development that dates to the late 1980s at the earliest. Its expansion was likely due to a combination of two factors: (1) a shift within social science as a whole away from the search for 'grand narratives' and 'laws' of social behavior to the fine-grained analysis of processes within naturalistic settings; and (2) a trend toward the democratization of graduate study in education, in which role boundaries and power relations among researchers, the researched, graduate students, and graduate faculty became more permeable.

Because the methods of qualitative, ethnographic research, such as keeping field notes; interviewing; perhaps some photography or videography; gathering documents; and then 'writing it all up,' would seem to be so straightforward that 'anyone could do it,' it often seems that everyone today in educational research *is* 'doing it,' and often with little awareness or understanding of ethnography's history, its rhetorical traditions and complexity, or its full potential. Reading through the current qualitative research on teacher education, we were repeatedly struck by several common features that seemed to limit its efficacy in producing general knowledge or improving education.

We noticed, for example, that very few studies were fully ethnographic, in that data collection seldom involved extended periods of participant observation as an outsider within a cultural field (for example, a university or alternative program; student teachers' classrooms), the making of maps or diagrams of spaces, or the interpretation of artifacts, interviews, or patterns of behavior using particular theoretical frames of reference such as structuralism, à la Lévi-Strauss (1992). Instead, researchers very often wrote about their own practice or closely related practices, their participant observation was limited to a few days or weeks in the field, and analysis often consisted of the 'coding' of interview transcripts and documents using Grounded Theory (Glaser and Strauss, 1967; Clarke, 2005; Charmaz, 2006) approaches that yielded superficial 'themes.' One consequence is that qualitative research in teacher education, even within large-scale studies, does not seem intent so much on building knowledge about the field as it does on producing informational reports of what's going on in local settings.

Moreover, the narratives produced are, to borrow a couple of Geertzian (Geertz, 1973, 1983) tropes, 'local,' but not 'thick.' They largely do not concern themselves with differences between emic and etic perspectives that would highlight differences between how phenomena might be both theoretically and practically understood, as in the 'apprenticeship as method' approach described by Roth (Chapter 14, this volume) or Nathan's (2005) year spent as an undergraduate that is described in Lucas's (Chapter 12, this volume) discussion of ethnography in higher education. Descriptions do not provide enough detail to immerse a reader in events and so produce understanding of dilemmas or situations that are almost visceral in their impact; nor do they often reference general theories of social behavior in ways that would provide connections to other studies or settings that would 'add up' or contribute to a general body of knowledge. Where connections are made to external events or conditions (most often to 'policy'), the relationship is often ideologically nuanced, as in the antagonism of studies published in JTE toward US federal policies, or the embrace of technocracy within studies published in EJTE.

Three exceptions to this within our reading would be a line of research since the late 1980s characterizing teacher education as a 'ritual process' (White, 1989; Head, 1992; McNamara et al., 2002; Cook-Sather, 2006), the work of Jennifer Gore (1992), and the work of Deborah Britzman (2003). Studies of teaching as a ritual process draw from anthropologist Victor Turner's field studies in Africa in the 1960s of initiation rites for African youth (Turner, 1969, 1982). They not only connect teacher education to the broader anthropological literature but help readers to see the education of teachers as a cultural phenomenon within (post)modern societies in ways that provide generative insights into, and that could lead to substantial improvements in, processes of professional education as a whole (but see also Pugsley's (Chapter 11, this volume) discussion of why professional education is not simply a 'rite of passage'). A second notable exception would be the highly theoretical work of the Australian researcher Jennifer Gore (1992) and in one study, her American collaborator Kenneth Zeichner (Gore and Zeichner, 1991), which has drawn from a range of theoretical resources, including Foucault (1984) and Nel Noddings (1984). Finally, Deborah Britzman's case studies of two student teachers struggling (and largely failing) to realize their expectations for teaching (*Practice Makes Practice: A Critical Study of Learning to Teach*, 2003) provides two examples of truly 'thick' and fully critical ethnographies of induction into not only the profession but the practice of teaching.

In closing, we admit that we are uncertain about how these challenges might be addressed. It is a good thing, is it not, that social science has become more self-reflexive about its claims, and that research in teacher education has become more democratic in the past two decades so that everyone involved in the process can now make a contribution? If the price of these developments for now is 'Ethnography Lite' in some arenas of publication, then we agree the price may not be too dear. But we will also hold out the possibility to researchers with the resources and an interest in basic research of an alternative methodological path that is fully ethnographic in its approach, informed by an historical and rhetorical sense of ethnography's potential, and grounded in theoretical perspectives that can structure the building of a general body of knowledge about teacher education as a cultural process.

REFERENCES

Arndt, K. and Liles, J. (2010), 'Preservice teachers' perceptions of coteaching: a qualitative study', *Action in Teacher Education*, **32** (1), 15–25.

Atkinson, P. and Delamont, S. (1990), 'Writing about teachers: how British and American ethnographic texts describe teachers and teaching', *Teaching and Teacher Education*, **6** (2), 111–25.

Baldwin, S.C., Buchanan, A.M. and Rudisill, M.E. (2007), 'What teacher candidates learned about diversity, social justice, and themselves from service-learning experiences', *Journal of Teacher Education*, **58** (4), 315–27.

Bertone, S., Meard, J. Euzet, J. Ria, L. and Durand, M. (2003), 'Intrapsychic conflict experienced by a preservice teacher during classroom interactions: a case study in physical education', *Teaching and Teacher Education*, **19** (1), 113–25.

Boling, E.C. (2007), 'Linking technology, learning, and stories: implications from research on hypermedia video-cases', *Teaching and Teacher Education*, **23** (2), 189–200.

Breidenstein, A. (2002), 'Researching teaching, researching self: qualitative research and beginning teacher development', *The Clearing House*, **75** (6), 314–18.

Britzman, D.P. (2003), *Practice Makes Practice: A Critical Study of Learning to Teach*, Albany, NY, USA: State University of New York Press.

Carrillo, J.E. (2010), 'Teaching that breaks your heart: reflections of the soul wounds of a first-year Latina teacher', *Harvard Educational Review*, **80** (1), 74–80.

Castro, A.J., Kelly, J. and Shih, M. (2010), 'Resilience strategies for new teachers in high-needs areas', *Teaching and Teacher Education*, **26** (3), 622–9.

Charmaz, K. (2006), *Constructing Grounded Theory: A Practical Guide through Qualitative Analysis*, Thousand Oaks, CA: Sage.

Clandinin, D.J. (1989), 'Developing rhythm in teaching: the narrative study of a beginning teacher's personal practical knowledge of classrooms', *Curriculum Inquiry*, **19** (2), 121–41.

Clandinin, D.J. and Connelly, F.M. (2000), *Narrative Inquiry: Experience and Story in Qualitative Research*, San Francisco, CA: Jossey-Bass.

Clarke, A. (2005), *Situational Analysis: Grounded Theory after the Postmodern Turn*, Thousand Oaks, CA: Sage.

Clarke, A. and Robertson, A. (2001), 'Lifting a corner of the research rug: a case for meta-interviews in qualitative studies', *Teaching and Teacher Education*, **17** (7), 773–82.

Cochran-Smith, M. and Lytle, S.L. (1999), 'The teacher research movement: a decade later', *Educational Researcher*, **28** (7), 15–25.

Cook-Sather, A. (2006), 'Newly betwixt and between: revising liminality in the context of a teacher preparation program', *Anthropology and Education Quarterly*, **37** (2), 110–27.

Cooper, J.E. (2007), 'Strengthening the case for community-based learning in teacher education', *Journal of Teacher Education*, **58** (3), 245–55.

Denzin, N.K. and Lincoln, Y.S. (1994), 'Introduction: entering the field of qualitative research', in N.K. Denzin and Y.S. Lincoln (eds), *Handbook of Qualitative Research*, London: Sage, pp. 1–17.

Dressman, M. (2008), *Using Social Theory in Educational Research: A Practical Guide*, New York: Routledge.

Dressman, M., Journell, W., Babcock, A., Weatherup, N. and Makhoukh, A. (in press), 'Toward technology-mediated transcultural education: learning from a discussion of politics and culture between American and Moroccan students', *International Journal of Social Education*.

Erickson, F. (1986), 'Qualitative methods in research on teaching', in M.C. Wittrock (ed.), *Handbook of Research on Teaching*, New York: Macmillan, pp. 119–61.

Fenstermacher, G. (1994), 'The knower and the known: the nature of knowledge in research on teaching', in L. Darling-Hammond (ed.), *Review of Research in Education*, Washington, DC: American Educational Research Association, pp. 3–56.

Fogel, H., and Ehri, L.C. (2009), 'Teaching African American English forms to Standard

American English-speaking teachers: effects on acquisition, attitudes, and responses to student use', *Journal of Teacher Education*, **57** (5), 464–81.

Foucault, M. (1984), 'On the genealogy of ethics: an overview of work in progress', in P. Rabinow (ed.), *The Foucault Reader*, New York: Pantheon Books, pp. 340–72.

Frank, C.R. and Uy, F.L. (2004), 'Ethnography for teacher education', *Journal of Teacher Education*, **55** (3), 269–83.

Geertz, C. (1973), *The Interpretation of Cultures*, New York, Basic Books.

Geertz, C. (1983), *Local Knowledge: Further essays in Interpretive Anthropology*, New York: Basic Books.

Glaser, B.G. and Strauss, A. (1967), *The Discovery of Grounded Theory: Strategies for Qualitative Research*, Chicago, IL: Aldine.

Gore, J.M. (1992), *The Struggle for Pedagogies*, London: Routledge.

Gore, J.M. and Zeichner, K.M. (1991), 'Action research and reflective teaching in preservice teacher education: a case study from the United States', *Teaching and Teacher Education*, **7** (2), 119–36.

Hale, A., Snow-Gerono, J. and Morales, F. (2008), 'Transformative education for culturally diverse learners through narrative and ethnography', *Teaching and Teacher Education*, **24**, 1413–25.

Harrison, J. (2006), 'An examination of the language and interpretions of "Standard one" for initial teacher training in England: professional values and practice – outcomes or opportunities?', *European Journal of Teacher Education*, **29** (4), 431–54.

Head, F.A. (1992), 'Student teaching as initiation into the teaching profession', *Anthropology and Education Quarterly*, **23** (2), 89–107.

Hill, H.C., Rowan, B. and Ball, D.L. (2005), 'Effects of teachers' mathematical knowledge for teaching on student achievement', *American Educational Research Journal*, **42** (2), 371–406.

Huberman, M. (1996), 'Moving mainstream: taking a closer look at teacher research', *Language Arts*, **73** (2), 124–40.

James, J.H. (2008), 'Teachers as protectors: making sense of preservice teachers' resistance to interpretation in elementary history teaching', *Theory and Research in Social Education*, **36** (3), 172–205.

Johnson, A.S. (2007), 'An ethics of access: using life history to trace preservice teachers' initial viewpoints on teaching for equity', *Journal of Teacher Education*, **58** (4), 299–315.

Jones, S. and Enriquez, G. (2009), 'Engaging the intellectual and moral in critical literacy education: the four-year journeys of two teachers from teacher education to classroom practice', *Reading Research Quarterly*, **44** (2), 145–68.

Levin, B.B. (2003), *Case Studies of Teacher Development: An In-depth Look at How Thinking About Pedagogy Develops Over Time*, Mahwah, NJ: Lawrence Earlbaum.

Lévi-Strauss, C. (1992), *Tristes Tropiques*, trans. J. and D. Weightman, New York: Penguin.

Luft, J.A. (2001), 'Changing inquiry practices and beliefs: the impact of an inquiry-based professional development programme on beginning and experienced science teachers', *International Journal of Science Education*, **23** (5), 517–34.

Macrory, G. and McLachlan, A. (2009), 'Bringing modern languages into the primary curriculum in England: investigating effective practice in teacher education', *European Journal of Teacher Education*, **32** (3), 259–70.

McDonough, K. (2009), 'Pathways to critical consciousness: a first-year teacher's engagement with issues of race and equity', *Journal of Teacher Education*, **60** (5), 528–37.

McNamara, O., Roberts, L., Basit, T.N. and Brown, T. (2002), 'Rites of passage in initial teacher training: ritual, performance, ordeal and numeracy skills test', *British Educational Research Journal*, **28** (6), 863–78.

Mena Marcos, J.J. and Tillema, H. (2006), 'Studying studies on teacher reflection and action: an appraisal of research contributions', *Educational Research Review*, **1** (2), 112–32.

Merriam, S.B. (1998), *Qualitative Research and Case Study Applications in Education*, San Francisco, CA: Jossey-Bass.

Merryfield, M.M. (2000), 'Why aren't teachers being prepared to teach for diversity, equity, and global interconnectedness? A study of lived experiences in the making of multicultural and global educators', *Teaching and Teacher Education*, **16** (4), 429–43.

Merryfield, M.M. (2007), 'The web and teachers' decision-making in global education', *Theory and Research in Social Education*, **35** (2), 256–76.

Mewborn, D.S. (1999), 'Reflective thinking among preservice elementary mathematics teachers', *Journal for Research in Mathematics Education*, **30** (3), 316–41.

Monte-Sano, C. and Cochran, M. (2009), 'Attention to learners, subject, or teaching: what takes precedence as preservice candidates learn to teach historical thinking and reading?', *Theory and Research in Social Education*, **37** (1), 101–35.e.

Nathan, R. (2005), *My Freshman Year: What a Professor Learned by Becoming a Student*, Ithaca, NY: Cornell University Press.

Noddings, N. (1984), *Caring: A Feminine Approach to Ethics and Moral Education*, Berkeley, CA: University of California Press.

Noffke, S.E. and M. Brennan (1997), 'Reconstructing the politics of action in action research', in S. Hollingsworth (ed.), *International Action Research: A Casebook for Educational Reform*, Washington, DC: The Falmer Press, pp. 63–9.

Noffke, S.E. and R. Stevenson (1995), *Educational Action Research: Becoming Practically Critical*, New York: Teachers College Press.

Osguthorpe, R.D. (2008), 'On the reasons we want teachers of good dispositions and moral character', *Journal of Teacher Education*, **59** (4), 288–300.

Park Rogers, M.A. and Abell, S.K. (2008), 'The design, enactment, and experience of inquiry-based instruction in undergraduate science education: a case study', *Science Education*, **92** (4), 591–607.

Pollock, M., Deckman, S., Mira, M. and Shalaby, C. (2009), '"But what can I do?": three necessary tensions in teaching teachers about race', *Journal of Teacher Education*, **61** (3), 211–24.

Smagorinsky, P., Wright, L., Augustine, S.M., O'Donnell-Allen, C. and Konopak, B. (2007), 'Student engagement in the teaching and learning of grammar: a case-study of an early-career secondary school English teacher', *Journal of Teacher Education*, **58** (1), 76–90.

Spindler, G. and Spindler, L. (1992), 'Cultural process and ethnography: an anthropological perspective', in M.D. LeCompte, W.L. Millroy and J. Preissle (eds), *The Handbook of Qualitative Research in Education*, London: Academic Press, pp. 53–92.

Stake, R.E. (1995), *The Art of Case Study Research*, Thousand Oaks, CA: Sage.

Stringer, E.T. (2007), *Action Research*, Thousand Oaks, CA: Sage.

Turner, V. (1969), *The Ritual Process: Structure and Anti-structure*, Ithaca, NY: Cornell University Press.

Turner, V. (1982), *From Ritual to Theatre: The Human Seriousness of Play*, New York: PAJ Publications.

van Hover, S.D. (2006), 'Teaching history in the Old Dominion: the impact of Virginia's accountability reform on seven secondary beginning history teachers', in S.G. Grant (ed.), *Measuring History: Cases of State-level Testing Across the United States*, Greenwich, CT: Information Age, pp. 195–219.

White, J.T. (1989), 'Student teaching as a rite of passage', *Anthropology and Education Quarterly*, **20** (3), 177–95.

Woods, P. (1985), 'Sociology, ethnography and teacher practice', *Teaching and Teacher Education*, **1** (1), 51–62.

Yeager, E.A. and Wilson, E.K. (1997), 'Teaching historical thinking in the social studies methods course: a case study', *The Social Studies*, **88** (3), 121–6.

Yin, R.K. (2008), *Case Study Research: Design and Methods*, Los Angeles, CA: Sage.

Zeichner, K. (1999), 'The new scholarship in teacher education', *Educational Researcher*, **28** (9), 4–15.

Zeichner, K.M. and Schulte, A.K. (2001), 'What we know and don't know from peer-reviewed research about alternative teacher certification programs', *Journal of Teacher Education*, **52** (4), 266–82.

14. Apprenticeship: toward a reflexive method for researching 'education in "non-formal" settings'

Wolff-Michael Roth

ed•u•ca•tion – *n.* **1.** The act or process of education or being educated. **2.** The knowledge or skill obtained or developed by such a process: LEARNING. **3.** The field of study concerned with teaching and learning pedagogy. (Webster's II, 1984, p. 418)

Everything that is internal in higher functions was necessarily once external: i.e., it was for others what today it is for itself . . . before becoming a function, it was the social relation between two people. (Vygotsky, 1989, p. 56)

INTRODUCTION

In the first introductory quote, the dictionary defines (a) active (teaching) and active/passive (being taught/learning) dimensions of education, (b) the content result from the process (that is, knowledge, skill), and (c) the field of study concerned with the items (a) and (b). The noun term is generally associated with events and products that occur in special institutional settings in which these societal practices occur. Although implied in all three dictionary senses, education as process and as product from other institutional settings and societally motivated activities – for example, workplace, playground, or leisure time – are less frequently associated with the term. How might we investigate education in such settings and activities? The answer to this question depends on how we think of education (knowledge, skill).

As a product (knowledge, skill), education is often treated as something to be found in and to be searched for in the minds of the individuals and population of interest – an attitude, as Mills (Chapter 3, this volume) suggests, perhaps more typical of North American anthropological scholarship. The second introductory quote, however, orients our gaze in a different direction. Thus, the Russian psychologist Lev S. Vygotsky (1989), grounding his method in the philosophy of Karl Marx, suggests that anything we might expect to be in the mind, the higher functions, 'were once external' and 'before becoming a function, it was the social relation between people.' Therefore, if we social scientists and educators want to understand how and what others know and learn, we do not need to find devices that allow us to get into their minds. All we need to do is study social relations between people. We are already familiar with this kind of study: ethnographers, anthropologists, and sociologists have studied social relations for a long time. However, when we look at social relations from the outside, our theoretical gaze objectifies what we see into representations (Mills, Chapter 3, this volume); what we do not get at is the way in which the practical work 'presents itself' to the practitioner (Bourdieu, 1980). The theoretical gaze does not give us an understanding of the game that the players in/on the field play: only by participating in the game will we develop this sense. Playing the two methods together and against each other promises to reveal the blind spots of each and to lead to a better understanding of education in the research site.

In this chapter, I focus on a particular combination of methods that has been shown to be very productive for studying education in a variety of non-school activities including environmental activism, informal educational settings, scientific research in laboratories and field settings, workplaces (dentistry practices, fish hatcheries, electrical construction work), and community politics. Whereas these settings and activities are non-formal 'educational' institutions, they are formal, societally motivated activities in the cultural-historical activity theoretic sense nevertheless. In all of these settings, my graduate students and I use 'apprenticeship as method' in addition to formal ethnographic and historical methods. Drawing on the two forms of ethnographic work has allowed us to engage in reflexive method for researching 'education in "non-formal" settings.'

CULTURAL HISTORY OF PARTICIPATORY METHODS

Using participation as method arose for me in the context of teaching and my experience as a head of science tasked with evaluating the teachers in my department. Being familiar with the differences between theoretical and practical understanding (Heidegger, 1977; Bourdieu, 1980), I combined formal observations of teaching with participation in the teaching of high school students. It turned out that the sense of classroom events is very different from the perspective of a participant than it is for the observer sitting in the back of the classroom – something that will also be the experience of athletes participating versus observing a game. In practice, there is a different sense because of the difference in the temporal modes that operate when there is no time out for reflecting about a next action. In praxis, each action has tremendous implications – including those of an ethical nature – whereas in theory, actions can be replayed over and over again.

Traditional ethnographic methods in formal educational settings have used participant observation (for example, Erickson, 1986), which has had and still has all the problems that come with the pretense of fly-on-the-wall approaches. After taking up a university research position, rather than using existing ethnographic methods, I developed first alone and then with a colleague 'coteaching' as a praxis of research method (Roth and Tobin, 2002). At the time I already had more than 12 years of teaching experience so that I participated in teaching together with others, which brought about learning for all teachers involved. We considered teaching as a way of learning to teach and as a way of studying teaching and learning from the inside. It turned out that from within the praxis of teaching, we came to better understand teaching through the eyes and bodies of the teachers. Rather than providing decontextualized advice about how to improve teaching, we were able to develop contextually better ways of teaching together with the regular and beginning teachers.

RESEARCHING EDUCATION IN FISH HATCHERIES

In the course of my university career, I increasingly shifted to studying 'education' (knowing, learning) outside of the formal institutions that have been developed for this purpose. Here, however, I no longer was in the position of an expert participant. My interest in active participation as a form of doing research co-occurred with my interest in cognitive apprenticeship as a form of learning. By chance, I had become familiar with and read an edited volume, *Apprenticeship: From Theory to Method and Back Again* (Coy, 1989a), which led me to bring the two interests together to evolve a new research strategy: combining traditional forms of ethnography in field settings with apprenticeship, where I learned 'the ropes' by serving as a helper in my field sites of interest. The editor's own research by means of an apprenticeship with a Tugen blacksmith (Coy, 1989b) stuck in my mind as an image that was guiding my thinking about craft, learning, and cognition. In one instance, the participation became so intensive over the course of five years that I became an active participant in the research and publication of articles on the absorption of light in the eyes of salmonid fish. Apprenticeship became a method of choice within my research team. We used the method – some of us were already practitioners, especially when university training normally is required – to study the cognitive cultures of electricians (for example, Roth in press), field ecologists (for example, Roth and Bowen, 2001), environmental activists (for example, S. Lee and Roth, 2001; Boyer and Roth, 2006), fish culturists (Y.J. Lee and Roth, 2005), dentists (Ardenghi and Roth, 2007), and ship officers (Emad and Roth, 2008).

In this method, we work together with our participants but in modes very different than the researcher-participant collaborations described in other chapters. We participate in the mundane practices of the participants, whereas Bishop (Chapter 9, this volume) and Pérez Huber (Chapter 27, this volume) have their participants become part of the mundane practices of researchers. We learn about our participants' practices as these become inscribed in our bodies, whereas Bishop and Huber have their participants contribute to and change the symbolic practices of educational research. Also to mention is the research on apprenticeship and legitimate peripheral participation (for example, Lave and Wenger, 1991, Delamont, 2010) and 'learning in likely places' (Singleton, 1998), which do not have to use apprenticeship itself as a method. As others have found out, learning an unfamiliar trade or practice is something that differs radically from the symbolic mastery that derives from observational ethnography. Thus, as a German philosopher studying Zen in the art of archery in Japan discovered, it takes years of practice before attaining practical – as opposed to symbolic – mastery (Herrigel, 1948 [1987]).

Our research on education in non-formal settings, therefore, involves two (interacting) modes. On the one hand, we participate (as helpers or replacements) in the normal operations of the site, which, in a fish hatchery, might be a monthly sampling and measurement of a fish population (Figure 14.1, right). We operate computers, slaughter fish, fertilize fish eggs, feed fish, collect 'morts' (dead fish) in the hatchery and river, and so forth. On the other hand, we interview people or videotape fish culturists at work, looking at them from the outside so to speak, attempting to interfere as little as possible in their actions (Figure 14.1, left). In the following subsections, I articulate and exemplify the two modes and how we make them interact to gain a better, reflexive understanding of education in the fish hatchery.

Apprenticeship: Learning the Ropes

Practice theorists readily accept that 'there is no manner of mastering the fundamental principles of a practice – the practice of scientific research is no exception here – than by practicing it alongside a kind of guide or coach' (Bourdieu, 1992, p. 221). Why should this be different for the social scientist, who investigates education in an 'in-formal' setting than for the people who are newcomers, legitimate peripheral participants to this same setting? That is, why should a (future) fish

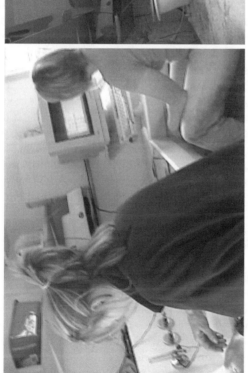

Note: On the right, the fish culturist teaches my graduate student and me how to measure and inspect the monthly sample from her coho salmon population. On the left, I videotape the fish culturist and the graduate student during a sampling episode.

Figure 14.1 Two modes of doing research: apprenticeship as method and participant observation

culturist, for example, learn through practicing the craft alongside other fish culturists who act as guides or coaches whereas a social scientist pretends that she or he will learn more by watching fish hatching from a fly-on-the-wall perspective? Would the latter not be more like reading a book or watching a documentary about the practice? To obtain an adequate understanding of the praxis of interest, one must participate in the cultural-historical activity at hand and, therefore, in the very production of the entities that this activity normally produces. In the case of fish hatching, this would mean that I participate not just like a child in a way irrelevant to the main activity but rather that my participation is legitimately peripheral, taking on all responsibilities that come with a job well done.

To study knowing and learning in fish hatcheries, I offered during the initial negotiations with the main site that we (my graduate students and I) become helpers in the various tasks that a normal hatchery operation requires. This came in particularly handy because I often had graduate students accompany me to do the research. When one of us conducted an interview with a fish culturist, another researcher would do the person's job. In the course of the five years, I have completed every standard task other than management required in the operation of a fish hatchery. In the course of the life cycle of fish, we took returning female salmon from the holding pond, killed them with a blow to the head, and opened their bellies for the harvest of the eggs. We 'cracked' (bent) a male to make the milt squirt from its belly into a plastic bag. We mixed the two in a bucket to achieve fertilization. After hatching, we participated in the transfer of fish into the different ponds, fed fish using different-sized feed depending on their age (size), sampled the fish to collect data, released the young fish ('smolt'), sampled and collected data on all fish at various places in the river and estuary, and collected the dead returning salmon that did not make it into the hatchery basin, where a new cycle began. We learned what fish culturists know in and through our participation in the living/lived work of fish culture.

Observer Participation: Studying 'Learning the Ropes'

In the observer participation mode, we are present in the site but do not participate in the work process itself. Rather, we interview members to the setting, have them do a think-aloud protocol on some formal task, videotape/photograph them at work, or conduct simple observation work. In this way, we look at the work but being in the worksite. This allows us to study education in its various forms as it occurs throughout the day – not unlike what students in a further education program on animal husbandry might experience (for example, Salisbury and Jephcote, 2010). For example, we observed the mentoring relationship of Mike, a 25-year veteran and lead fish culturist who had received national awards for his work, and Erika, a fish culturist with ten years of experience. Mike had not only done the normal work of a fish culturist but developed and conducted experiments that led to new practices, worked with research scientists helping them in developing procedures that actually worked on a hatchery scale, and had become – despite having nothing more than a high school diploma – one of the most knowledgeable fish culturist in the entire system.

We were able to see the apprentice-like relationship that Mike or Erika took with even more recent newcomers to the site or with temporary workers who, because of their occasional status, had not had as many opportunities for learning the ropes. Thus, for example, we observed Mike tutoring the seasonally working Ken how to collect the dead salmon in the river; remove and preserve multiple scales from the same fish (booklet with marked fields); measure fish size and weight; open the head to get access to, remove, and preserve the otolith; identify the presence of and remove a hair-sized coded-wire tags (length = 1.1 mm) used to identify the originating hatchery and age of the specimen; and keep proper records so that these could be used in scientific studies.

Other sites where we were able to study 'education' emerged when college students – enrolled in a fisheries and aquaculture technology program at a nearby college – came to work and learn in the hatchery as part of their 'hands-on' module. This was also an occasion for us to observe and overhear how seasoned fish culturists thought about the college education: putting abstract facts in the heads of these students, who were no better at doing the actual work then we had been when we first arrived on the site. Having learned facts about fish culture did not make these students better at the actual practice. Through their interaction with these interns, however, the seasoned fish culturists realized that 'you need some (formal) education,' but above all 'you need to know the work from/through doing it.' Mike, for example, could recognize from far away, when the identity of a fish feeder was impossible to discern, whether we looked at a very experienced, a regular, or a novice fish feeder at work. That is, even though many individuals would characterize fish feeding – which, at some times of the year, involves throwing 200 kg of fish feed with a scoop – as boring, routine, and never-changing, experienced fish culturists like Mike could see the differences in practices from far away (including whether feeders observed or did not observe the fish).

Learning to 'See' – A Case Example

Work requires particular modes of seeing, a habitus that equally underlies vision and *di*vision, which are the foundations of decisions. Learning to see is a crucial aspect of the career trajectory of a successful fish culturist. In the course of our work, we both observed and were educated in 'seeing.' There were two particular episodes that stand out for me to the present day.

The first episode concerns the classification of coho during the three-week marking program. In addition to having their adipose fins removed, a small percentage of the 4-g coho parr were also marked by means of 1.1-mm long coded wire tags that were projected into their nose by means of a special machine. At the worksite, there were three women, two operating a machine each, one placing the young coho on the half-pipes leading toward the other women or into a bucket. In fact, the different placements constituted a sorting process, and when the sorting woman 'made a mistake,' another woman would correct it by changing the placement. The different machines have different cups where the fish head is inserted, and the fish head and cup need to have a sufficient match for the marking to be successful. When I asked on what basis they classified the fish, the sorting woman told me: 'look!' I requested that she tell me, but she responded by saying that I could only learn by looking.

Feeding fish properly also required learning to see what the fish in a pond were doing and how they were moving. In my first attempts at feeding, I saw nothing at all until the point that the fish were breaking the surface when the feed from my scoop had hit the water. Mike told me that feeding this way would result in my wasting a lot of food, for he could observe that I did not see the fish and whether they were still feeding. This is a problem, for the feed that sinks to the bottom will rot, leading to an increase in bacteria, and to the infection of fish leading to higher mortality rates. It also leads to low feed conversion rates and, coincidentally, a waste of feed. Mike coached me to the point that I came to see over the five years what the fish were doing even though this mode of seeing cannot be put into words. Individuals who do not learn to see the fish behavior literally do not know what they are doing, whether they starve, correctly feed, or poison the fish.

Although learning to see was entirely learned by immanent modes, there were occasions where the invisible work of seeing was made to stand out in verbal articulation. For example, fish hatching requires identifying/classifying fish during sampling episodes. Normally, fish culturists and biologists present during such sampling episodes – designed to better understand the early migration of hatchery and wild salmon populations – have no problems identifying the fish even though for a newcomer like

Figure 14.2   A tray with different kinds of fish that are to be classified

me, even the difference between stickleback and salmon smolt was not self-evident initially. But there were times when the normally fluent classification broke down and discussions between several participants emerged – in one instance, I videotaped a 15-minute discussion between PhD scientists, field scientists, fish culturists, and the hatchery manager debating the nature of a particular sample in a collection of fish similar to the one in Figure 14.2. In the following excerpt from the transcript, Seaton, a fisheries biologist interacts with Greg, biologist and manager of the hatchery and Rick, another fish biologist (an extensive analysis of this episode can be found in Roth, 2005). They formulate what the vision involves that allows the *di*vision of specimen at hand into the various categories. Thus, Seaton states that the specimen at (in) hand has to be a chum salmon, because the sockeye salmon do not come from the lake into the estuary at that size (see preceding paragraph on categorizing fish size).

Greg rules out the category of pink salmon, but Rick responds (speaking almost inaudibly) that the fish has parr marks – he thereby articulates seeing a feature that Seaton, in another part of the entire classification episode, indicates he 'can just barely see them.' Seaton then utters what we can hear as a continuation of his earlier utterance: sockeye smolts, which spend the first year in their native lake before leaving for the ocean, are 'bigger than that (specimen).' That is, he is not just seeing the specimen but a specimen against the background of the normal sockeye size. However, Rick responds by suggesting that there are sockeye smolts that do migrate during their first year ('zero-plus') to the ocean. Thus, seeing needs to take into account the knowledge that there are not only 'one-plus' sockeye, which rules out smaller fish as sockeye, but also 'zero-plus' sockeye, which makes them the same size as other types of salmon. Vision, here, evidently is more than 'meets the eye,' and *di*vision – seeing the specimen *as* a specimen of a particular category – is the outcome of normally invisible (and nevertheless complex) work. These invisible aspects of work are made visible in moments of breakdown, when what normally works no longer does. It is precisely in/through participation in such spontaneously occurring instances of breakdown during mundane classification sessions that I learned to see the differences in the kinds of fish (salmon from stickleback) and the kinds of salmon (coho, chinook, chum, sockeye) that allowed me to properly classify them and keep the logbooks.

Cultural-Historical Contextualization

Research on education in formal institutional settings often is not only brief but also a-historical. Such research pretends to understand knowing and learning independent of the cultural-historical conditions of the particular site or of the society in which the research is conducted. Thus, in science education, for example, the same survey instruments that have been developed by researchers in Western Australia are used for the study of classroom learning environments in India, China, Korea, Malaysia, or Indonesia independent of the cultural and historical particulars of these settings. In our own work, we acknowledge that education changes with society and its culture, which undergo continuous evolution. Although it is a truism to state that work changes when there are new tools, learning in mathematics continues to be studied (and often taught) as it was some 50 years ago prior to computers and extremely cheap pocket calculators. It is equally true that changing tools require changing 'skills,' yet education research attempts to understand its objects without taking culture and history into account.

We take a different approach in our work of education in non-formal settings, where we do study both the local history of the site and the more global history of the field. Thus, in the case of the fish hatcheries, we assumed that we could understand the products and processes of 'non-formal' education in the site only if we understood its history; and we assumed that we understood the history of a hatchery only in the context of the 120-year history of salmon hatchery in British Columbia and Canada (for example, Roth et al., 2008). We chose this approach because what any individual member of a fish hatchery does is a function of the current cultural-historical state of the site, but the state of the site is a function of what the fish culturists do on a daily basis. There is therefore a mutually constitutive relation between the two levels. Similarly, the collectively motivated cultural activity of salmon hatching is concretized in different ways by each hatchery in the system ($N = 18$), but the hatcheries only exist because of a societal interest in salmon enhancement. That is, the two levels are mutually constitutive. The history of a hatchery and the history of salmon hatching at the society level are intertwined.

Enacting this approach, therefore, it was not surprising to us to find that the hatcheries differed in their practices; and with different practices, we observed different learning trajectories. A tool that was used in one side was rejected as suitable in another one. In our fish hatchery hand feeding tends to be practiced rather than machine feeding, because past experience has shown that 'machines feed the pond, people feed the fish.' We could still observe the vestiges of machine feeding in the form of rotting wooden platforms that had places where the feeding machines were attached. Human fish feeders stop throwing food into the pond when the fish stop feeding, which requires a particular perceptual skill that can only be acquired when actually feeding under the guidance of a seasoned fish culturist. During our time in the fish hatchery, we observed the adoption (by some) of a combined technique, where a homemade feed-blower was acquired in exchange for leftover feed from another fish hatchery; because it is not run independently, the operator stops feeding when the fish are satiated. In hatcheries where machine feeding is the standard practice – commercial outfits – fish culturists no longer have or learn the observational skills that were so characteristic of the 'indicator hatchery' that we studied.

Reflexivity

The different modes of research made it possible for us to study 'education in "non-formal" settings' in a reflexive way. Our primary object/ motive was the study of education, which we might have done by interviewing people and videotaping them at work. However, apprenticeship constituted a reflexive mode, as we not only came to understand the culture through participation but also, in fact, that we 'lived' the same educational process that was the object/motive of our research. We subjectively experienced the forms of education that we objectified in making it the object of our study. Moreover, by making our own experiences of education the reflexive object of our research, we had a second mode of objectifying access to it. We did not just study education, but we lived it and studied our living of it.

For my graduate students, apprenticeship as method involved another reflexive turn. On the one hand, they used apprenticeship as method for studying the practice at hand, here fish hatching. On the other hand, because we did the research together, they use apprenticeship as a method for learning how to do social science research (for example, Lee and Roth, 2005). It was by participating in an interview alongside me that they learned to interview; it was by accompanying me while videotaping a meeting or some special aspect of work that they learned camera operation and modes of videotaping as part of the ongoing work of a social science researcher.

In part because the site was about 250 kilometers from our university, the hatchery made it possible for us to sleep in one of the houses on the site. This provided us with opportunities to talk about the events of the day while preparing and eating dinner, or while meeting after dinner for a more formal data sharing and analysis session. Here, then, the students learned how to keep their research logbooks, how to move back and forth between accounts of living/lived experience and third-person observations of events from a fly-on-the-wall perspective.

TOWARD A REFLEXIVE METHOD

The traditional ethnographic methods of participant observation assumed that presence in the culture itself allows us to understand what is at stake (in our case, 'education'). But cultural-historical activity theory suggests that only when we participate in the actual (material, cultural, ideational) productions of the activity at hand does our own consciousness reflect the characteristics of the activity (Leontjew, 1982). Marxist philosophy taught us to understand that consciousness develops in and from praxis; phenomenological (ethnomethodological) studies taught us that any theoretical understanding has the practical understanding of the phenomenon as its prerequisite. It therefore does not come as a surprise to find statements to the effect that practical understanding 'precedes,' 'accompanies' and 'concludes' explanation (theoretical understanding) (Ricœur, 1991). But practical understanding is developed by explanation during interpretation. Thus, playing the two modes against each other assists us in rupturing and converting the gaze characteristic of each mode and, thereby, to engage in critical forms of research and scholarship. In everyday praxis, education neither is merely determined from the outside (pre-specified by some curriculum or historical conditions) nor merely determined by agency. Neither inside (emic) nor outside perspectives (etic) save us from ideology: only the continual melee of insights deriving from both can offer a hope of escaping the inculcating hegemonic forces of educational processes.

Critical scholars suggest that practical understanding tends to be caught up in the situation itself, never asking for the structural (historical, political, or economic) determinations of the situations, resources, discourses, practices, and so on (for example, Smith, 2005). This is so because the pre-constructed looms everywhere, for the practitioner as much as for the theoretician – the latter only is a special kind of the former (Bourdieu, 1992). We must escape from ideology, for 'a scientific practice that fails to question itself does not properly speaking, know what it does' (p. 236). To escape requires some form of radical doubt and critique of ideology. Our approach, which combines apprenticeship as method, participant observation, and historical studies of the culture allow us to identify the determinations operating in the field that are no longer evident to the practitioners and not even to participant observers concerned as they are with what can be observed. This, too, is the condition for the very methods we use – the reason for my inclusion of the history of our approach near the beginning of this chapter.

REFERENCES

Ardenghi, D. and Roth, W.-M. (2007), 'Responsibility in dental practice: an activity theoretical practice', *Journal of Workplace Learning*, **19**, 240–255.

Bourdieu, P. (1980), *Le sens pratique*, Paris: Les Éditions de Minuit.

Bourdieu, P. (1992), 'The practice of reflexive sociology (The Paris workshop)', in P. Bourdieu and L.J.D. Wacquant, *An Invitation to Reflexive Sociology*, Chicago, IL: University of Chicago Press, pp. 216–60.

Boyer, L. and Roth, W.-M. (2006), 'Learning and teaching as emergent features of informal settings: an ethnographic study in an environmental action group', *Science Education*, **90**, 1028–49.

Coy, M.W. (ed.) (1989a), *Apprenticeship: From Theory to Method and Back Again*, Albany, NY: State University of New York Press.

Coy, M.W. (1989b), 'Being what we pretend to be: the usefulness of apprenticeship as a field method', in M.W. Coy (ed.), *Apprenticeship: From Theory to Method and Back Again*, Albany, NY: State University of New York Press, pp. 115–35.

Delamont, S. (ed.) (2010), 'Anthropological perspectives on learning and teaching: legitimate peripheral participation revisited', *Teaching and Teacher Education* (special issue), **26**, 1–144.

Emad, G.R. and Roth W.-M. (2008), 'Contradictions in practices of training for and assessment of competency: a case study from the maritime domain', *Education and Training*, **50**, 260–72.

Erickson, F. (1986), 'Qualitative research on teaching', in M.C. Wittrock (ed.), *Handbook for Research on Teaching*, 3rd edn, New York: Macmillan, pp. 119–61.

Heidegger, M. (1977), *Sein und Zeit*, Tübingen: Niemeyer.

Herrigel, E. (1987), *Zen in der Kunst des Bogenschießens*, München: Otto Wilhelm Barth Verlag (first published in 1948).

Lave, J. and Wenger, E. (1991), *Situated Learning: Legitimate Peripheral Participation*, Cambridge: Cambridge University Press.

Lee, S. and Roth, W.-M. (2001), 'How ditch and drain become a healthy creek: representations, translations and agency during the re/design of a watershed', *Social Studies of Science*, **31**, 315–56.

Lee, S. and Roth, W.-M. (2005), 'Becoming and belonging: learning to do qualitative research', in W.-M. Roth (ed.), *Auto/Biography and Auto/Ethnography: Praxis of Research Method*, Rotterdam: Sense Publishers, pp. 379–402.

Lee, Y.J. and Roth, W.-M. (2005), 'The (unlikely) trajectory of learning in a salmon hatchery', *Journal of Workplace Learning*, **17**, 243–54.

Leontjew, A.N. (1982), *Tätigkeit, Bewusstsein, Persönlichkeit*, Köln: Pahl-Rugenstein.

Ricœur, P. (1991), *From Text to Action: Essays in Hermeneutics, II*, Evanston, IL: Northwestern University Press.

Roth, W.-M. (2005), 'Making classifications (at) work: ordering practices in science', *Social Studies of Science*, **35**, 581–621.

Roth, W.-M. (in press), 'Rules of bending, bending the rules: the geometry of conduit bending in college and workplace', *Educational Studies in Mathematics*.

Roth, W.-M. and Michael Bowen, G. (2001), 'Of disciplined minds and disciplined bodies', *Qualitative Sociology*, **24**, 459–81.

Roth, W.-M. and Tobin, K. (2002), *At the Elbow of Another: Learning to Teach by Coteaching*, New York: Peter Lang.

Roth, W.-M., Lee, Y.J. and Boyer, L. (2008), *The Eternal Return: Reproduction and Change in Complex Activity Systems: The Case of Salmon Enhancement*, Berlin: Lehmanns Media.

Salisbury, J. and Jephcote, M. (2010), 'Mucking in and mucking out: vocational learning in animal care', *Teaching and Teacher Education*, **26**, 71–81.

Singleton, J. (ed.) (1998), *Learning in Likely Places: Varieties of Apprenticeship in Japan*, Cambridge: Cambridge University Press.

Smith, D.E. (2005), *Institutional Ethnography: A Sociology for People*, Lanham, MD: Altamira.

Vygotsky, L.S. (1989), 'Concrete human psychology', *Soviet Psychology*, **27** (2), 53–77.

Webster's II (1984), *New Riverside University Dictionary*, Boston, MA: Houghton Mifflin.

15. Total institutions and qualitative research
Ghazala Bhatti

The term 'total institution' was first used by Erving Goffman (1959). Total Institutions can be defined as places which individuals are unable to leave easily and where they are expected to abide by strict rules which govern their behaviour. Individuals may find that they are subordinated to formal and informal sanctions, which are implemented according to a particular code of conduct. In such institutions education has the power to transform lives. However, the way in which education is imparted and knowledge acquired is quite often implicit. As organizations, total institutions function by demanding and obtaining different degrees of compliance, and ensuring adherence to a form of conduct which seeks willing or unwilling obedience to rules. These rules are not made by the majority of people living inside total institutions, who may in fact not even be consulted about them. In other words, the rules may be interpreted as duty of care by those in charge of managing total institutions, but they may be experienced as impositions, interference or obligations by those on whom they are exercised. In total institutions, it is normally the case that a few people govern the conduct of many over a long period of time. The ratio is seldom one to one. Exceptions include homes for people with severe learning disabilities and care homes for the elderly, who may have a dedicated carer working exclusively with one person at a time. There are issues of differential power (Dowding, 1996) and social control (Innes, 2003) at stake. Researchers who have studied total institutions have discovered how power is negotiated individually and collectively, how it is subverted and maintained, and how knowledge is shared or suppressed. As organizations total institutions provide naturally occurring opportunities for different kinds of learning.

Examples of total institutions which can be found in civil society are boarding schools, convents and care homes for children. Mental hospitals are total institutions where vulnerable people may be held either willingly or against their will, ostensibly for their own good, or for the protection of others in society. Mental hospitals restrain patients and care for those who may be 'sectioned'[1] for their own protection because of psychosis, for example. Others may self-harm, attempt suicide

(Crighton, 2006) or display acts of verbal or physical aggression. Most mentally ill people are far more likely to harm themselves than anyone else. They may not be aware of their own state of mind, though some troubled patients who have insight and recognize that they are unwell may try to seek help if they know how to. Vincent Van Gogh turned up at the asylum at Saint-Remy in 1889 at the height of intense depression and distress (Blumer, 2002).

ASYLUMS AND GOFFMAN

Erving Goffman's (1959) classic study of total institutions drew systematic comparisons between very different organizations. Although in *Asylums* Goffman collected his data primarily at one institution – St Elizabeth's Hospital in Washingtion, DC, which had 7000 inmates – he cited extensively from research on other institutions. These include convents, the army, monasteries, ship crews, prisons and concentration camps, where the organizational culture and conduct were quite similar to that at mental hospitals. In some ways this is surprising, as at first sight convents and hospitals might not seem to have a lot in common. The book comprises four essays which take the experiences of patients or inmates at a mental hospital as the starting point for developing sociological theory. *Asylums* is considered a classic in medical sociology, deviance and symbolic interactionism (Fine and Martin, 1995). Interactions between people are paramount both in terms of quality and content. They define the quality of daily life in the constraining, sometimes forbidding social situations which patients have to negotiate in order to survive with as much dignity as they can muster. Goffman's portrayal of mental patients is devoid of any stigmatization or stereotypical attitudes. In a sense it is obvious that any one who ends up in an asylum would be obliged to react exactly as the patients do.

> When inmates are allowed to have face-to-face contact with staff, the contact will often take the form of 'gripes' or requests on the part of the inmate and justification for the prevailing restrictive treatment on the part of the staff; such, for example, is the general structure of staff-patient interaction in mental hospitals. Having to control inmates and to defend the institution in the name of its avowed aims, the staff resort to the kind of all-embracing identification of the inmates that will make this possible. The staff problem here is to find a crime that will fit the punishment. (On the characteristics of total institutions, p. 85)

In the above quotation, mentally ill patients may as well be children at a boarding school or prisoners in jail. The power differential between the patients and staff ensures that the status quo is maintained. Goffman describes in considerable and meticulous detail how total institutions enact what he terms 'assaults upon the self', 'stripping of the self and privileges' and how a 'reassembly of the self' takes place using various 'processes of mortification'. Civilian life outside is very different to life inside a total institution, and the initiation into the process of becoming an inmate is deeply traumatic, unsettling and dislocating. When patients try to form bonds with each other inside the hospital they know that they are in a twilight zone with sometimes diffuse and sometimes rigid rules, where they do not belong either inside or outside the institution. If they are confused it will be put down to their mental illness. If they express no emotion at all, that too will be construed as odd behaviour. Goffman's analysis suggests that anyone would experience the same sense of bewildered dislocation in an identical or similar situation.

> the hospital is cut off from the outside community, becoming a world of its own, operated for the benefit of its own citizens. And certainly this moratorium is an expression of the alienation and hostility that patients feel for those on the outside to whom they were closely related. But, in addition, one has evidence of the loosening effects of living in a world within a world, under conditions which make it difficult to give full seriousness to either of them. (The moral career of the mental patient, p. 166)

Quite often patients are admitted to hospital because of the collusion/ willingness of friends and relatives. Are they being helped or were they betrayed? Goffman describes the relationship of those inside total institutions to those outside in society, as a situation of continuous conflict for which patients pay a very heavy price.

> Mental patients can find themselves in a special bind. To get out of hospital or to ease their life within it, they must show acceptance of the place accorded them, and the place accorded them is to support the occupational role of those who appear to force this bargain. This self-alienating moral servitude, which perhaps helps to account for some inmates becoming mentally confused, is achieved by invoking the great tradition of the expert servicing relation, especially its medical variety. Mental patients can find themselves crushed by the weight of a service ideal that eases life for the rest of us. (Medical model and mental hospitalization, p. 386)

In a strange way then, the lives of those inside total institutions are inextricably linked to those of us who live on the outside. We might be indifferent, oblivious or ignorant about inmates' experiences. By providing compelling evidence to educate the readers and confronting them with *Asylums* Goffman holds up a mirror to society and shatters such illusions.

HOSPITALS AS RESEARCH SITES

Attitudes towards mental illness have changed considerably over the years, from patients being confined in straitjackets to more humane methods of treatment like cognitive behaviour therapy (Mueller et al., 2010), mindfulness based cognitive therapy, mindfulness based stress reduction (Hoffman et al., 1998; Hofman et al., 2010) and other forms of 'talking therapies' which are currently in use, and which reject physical force. There are many wards in mental hospitals which cater for patients according to what the medical profession decides is best for them. Each ward has a different ethos and follows rules which are operationalized by various professionals. They educate patients about re-engaging with the world they have left outside. They also teach them ways of coping with social stigma caused by public ignorance and misinformation about mental illness (Thornicroft, 2006). Anslem Strauss et al.'s (1964 [1981]) classic study of two hospitals in Chicago *Psychiatric Ideologies and Institutions* looked critically at different professionals and their ideologies.

> Ideologies signify genuine ways of life, which is precisely why we have chosen to study psychiatric ideologies whether held by psychiatrists or . . . psychiatric aides – and in hospital settings. (Strauss et al., 1964 [1981], p. 9)

This is an interesting study on several levels. The research team was composed of three sociologists, a social psychologist and a psychiatrist. They looked at the professional identities, beliefs and ideologies of members of staff who worked at two very different hospitals – an old-fashioned large hospital and a purpose-built modern smaller hospital. The experiences and insights which the different researchers brought to bear on the data reflect their professional and personal stance. Strauss is at pains to point out that it was the collective and collaborative endeavour which enriched the research and made it whole. Researchers found that the ideologies held by various professionals operate in partial accordance with the ideologies in hospital settings. There was considerable negotiation as the professional boundaries between different personnel were not very tightly drawn. The battleground was described as 'which speciality should treat who, how and under whose aegis' (1964 [1981], p. 5). It is easy to see that behind the closed doors of the hospital, intense negotiation goes on when specialisms are emergent and therefore careers and professions are in process (Bucher and Strauss, 1961). It was found that virtually the only thing psychiatrists had in common with each other was a medical degree and interest in medical illness. There was no consensus about the kind of therapeutic care which should be offered. These were known by different names and had their origins in different knowledge bases such as somatotherapeutic, psychotherapeutic and sociotherapeutic care.

> In psychiatry, the conflict over the biological versus the psychological bases of mental illness continues to produce men who speak almost totally different professional languages. They read different journals . . . (Strauss et al., [1964] 1981, p. 7)

It can be assumed that this continues to be the case today. Strauss et al. were impressed by the way in which hospital settings generated 'influential psychiatric ideologies'. This kind of knowledge is situated in the workplace. It cannot be imparted in universities which do not have psychiatrists, nurses, psychologists, social workers and aides or ancillary staff working with actual patients in real time. Strauss et al. found a fluidity in the definition of professional boundaries. There were difficult negotiations between those who held different hierarchical positions. This can be equally true in other institutions.

Another notable study of a hospital/sanatorium *Timetables* was conducted by Roth (1963) who fell very ill with tuberculosis and had to be hospitalized. Roth tried to capture what it felt like to get through a long passage of time in *Timetables*. This was later described as 'culture bound nature of structuring the passage of time in a linear fashion' (Roth, 1974). This research inspired many studies of how time is structured in organizations and in individual careers.

BOARDING SCHOOLS

Boarding schools are total institutions which provide learning opportunities for staff and students, who have prolonged contact with each other, including time spent during leisure hours. Researchers have described different kinds of boarding schools in Britain, from one which was founded by 'feminist educational pioneers' (Delamont, 1984) who wanted to provide empowering opportunities for young women, to others where school 'Masters' actually meant men and women teachers (Walford, 1987)! This gender confusion looks misplaced and dated until the historical perspective on the main clientele of 'public school' is taken into account. (Confusingly, for an international reader, the term 'public' actually means 'fee paying and private' within the British context.) Fraser (1968) cites Thring's 'facts' about boarding schools:

> . . . Englishmen say they are fond of facts . . . Here is a fact of the greatest importance: Englishmen of the upper classes send away their children from home to

be educated by strangers. No theory which does not distinctly recognise this fact to begin with is of any value in England . . . they are sent to a place which is better than home, to be under men who train better than fathers and mothers . . . . (p. 143)

Boarding schools are the symbols of privatization and privilege (Walford, 1986, 1990) because of the amount of fees paid for children's education and because they perpetuate and reproduce social differences. Best known schools in Britain which fall in this category are Eton, Harrow, Winchester for boys and Benenden, Roedean and Cheltenham Ladies' for girls (Walford, 1990, p. 1). Not all boarding schools are 'public' schools. Lambert (1966) studied state-funded boarding schools and interestingly documented reasons why parents applied for their children to be sent there (see Lambert, 1966, appendix 3). Boarding schools have also been noted as places where homesickness abounds.

Leaving home to reside in a boarding school may be a traumatic experience for new pupils . . . homesickness . . . can impede adaptation to social and educational aspects of schools. For many pupils the experience recurs across successive school years or is so devastating that running away is seriously considered or carried out. (Fisher, 1991, p. 70)

The metaphor of escape suggests a similarity between school and prison, though this may not be strictly true of every boarding school, nor for every student. Boarding schools have been studied by researchers who have been successful in gaining access to them. Some found it much easier than others. In common with all total institutions, boarding schools too have rules and regulations. They are mostly chosen by parents for their children while the children are young, and so may not be in a position to make a choice. Although this can be equally true of other schools which are not boarding schools, children can return home from other types of schools and reconnect with life at home on a daily basis. This does not happen in boarding schools.

PRISONS AND OTHER ORGANIZATIONS

Other types of organizations such as the armed services are total institutions which civilians may join voluntarily; but once they join, they are expected to conform to strict rules and display disciplined and regimented behaviour when on duty. Individuality is not as important as observable group behaviour, conformity and team work. This is emphasized through the use of uniforms, which make the recruits identifiable and ensures that they are all seen to be obeying the same rules. Hockey's study *Squaddies* (1986) looks at the experiences of men in the armed services. As total institutions prisons are much harsher places by comparison. They are designed for people who have broken the rules and defied prevailing social norms in a given society or community. Oscar Wilde was imprisoned for homosexuality in Victorian England – something which is inconceivable today. The law decriminalizing homosexuality in the UK was passed in 1967, long after the talented English mathematician and pioneer of computer science Alan Turing had committed suicide on being identified as homosexual. Total institutions reflect social attitudes and mores.

As total institutions prisons confine people seen as criminals because they display deviant or non-conforming behaviour. Whether prisons are meant to be corrective institutions or experienced as punitive institutions depends on the particular society where they are located. Their function can change over the years. A building which is a tourist attraction today might once have held prisoners. The Tower of London is an example of this. Historically, social attitudes are always in the process of change. This means that the perception about who the prisons are for, how many and what kind of people a country holds captive, and why, can change over time to reflect changes in the law and in public perceptions. For example, stealing was considered a very serious crime which could lead to public hanging in England well into the nineteenth century. Attitudes may also change if new ways are found to deal with dangerous or unacceptable behaviour. There are different categories of prisons which detain people according to what the legal system deems appropriate for the individual and for the public good.

Wacquant's (2009) *Prisons of Poverty* looks critically at the role of prisons in society, particularly with reference to African-Americans. He suggests that urban ghettos are manufactured and continue to exist for a reason. The privatization and underfunding of public institutions cause poor people to lead denuded lives, where they are nonetheless put under surveillance. His focus on the main reason for imprisonment points at poverty as the root cause. Wacquant's (2010) article on prisoner re-entry as myth and ceremony casts a critical light on how dispossessed neighbourhoods feed poor people into the prison system where they are not helped to start a new life at all. Instead, they are fed back into the same neighbourhoods of deprivation and destitution which had led to their imprisonment in the first place. He suggests that it is not the radical critique of capitalism, but 'the neo-Durkheimian sociology of organizations and the neo-Weberian theory of the state as a classifying and stratifying agency' (2010, p. 605) which explains how very limited the lives of poor people really are in the USA. Wacquant's positioning of poverty as the main cause of social injustice provides one explanation for why prison populations will never decrease until the state is serious about tackling poverty. Wacquant's earlier work *Urban Outcasts* (2008) takes the reader into the black ghetto of Chicago's South Side and La Courneuve in Paris, using ethnography to explore life at the margins of society. He demonstrates the link between lack of educational opportunities, poverty and social inequality, all of which according to Wacquant are governed, managed and maintained by the state.

Allegations of suspected terrorism in recent years may entail incarceration for lengthy periods of time in specially designed secure exclusion units. These total institutions are impenetrable except by specially designated personnel. One example of an extreme total institution which has political implications is the geographically and socially distant Guantanamo Bay (Begg and Brittain, 2006). Should it continue to exist after the death of Bin Laden in May 2011? This shows that globally there are many kinds of total institutions which serve different purposes at different times in different countries and societies. Sometimes the lay public may not know and never find out full details regarding particular prisoners who are portrayed as very dangerous. The absence of public debate about some individual prisoners or suspects may even be enforceable by law.

The idea of a Panopticon, initiated by Bentham and illustrated by Foucault (1977), is a powerful symbol of surveillance. It denotes a heightened form of censure and self-censure which can be applied symbolically to total institutions where the occupants are not in real communication with each other. They cannot see who holds them captive, while they themselves are under constant surveillance from the watch tower in the centre which governs their very existence. It is noteworthy that Foucault depicted this well before CCTV cameras became commonplace in public spaces, giving members of the public the impression of being under constant scrutiny. One of the functions of the Panopticon is to restrict communication and collaboration among inmates, while keeping each one of them under observation.

> If the inmates are convicts there is no danger of a plot, an attempt at collective escape, the planning of new crimes for the future, bad reciprocal influences; if they are patients, there is no danger of contagion; if they are madmen there is no risk of their committing violence upon one another; if they are school children, there is no copying, no noise, no chatter, no waste of time; if they are workers there are no disorders, no thefts, no coalitions, none of those distractions that slow down the rate of work, make it less perfect, or cause accidents. (Foucault, 1977, pp. 200–1)

Within Europe it is the case that there is more public surveillance in some countries like Britain than in others like Greece and Italy. The total institutions in each country reflect differences in the social structures of those countries. Thus when it comes to studying them, location in all its manifestations is quite significant, whether it is geopolitical, socioeconomic or educational. Wherever they are located, total institutions are less transparent than other kinds of institutions, and are therefore both challenging and enticing for researchers. Each total institution has its own ethos and ground rules but as the above studies have demonstrated it is possible to research them, and to research them successfully.

ACCESSING INSTITUTIONS

As total institutions are closed spaces, not normally open to public scrutiny except by special permission granted to auditors, government inspectors or other insiders, it can sometimes be difficult to obtain first hand information as a researcher. Gilliat-Ray (2006) was barred access to a particular Deobandi Dar-ul-Uloom – a Muslim religious organization, though she was able to gain a good understanding about the training of 'Ulama' in Britain. Hawe (1995) was able to gain access to an all girls' Muslim school. It could be that gender mattered in these specific cases. It could also be that schools are on the whole more accessible than particular religious sects, which may only allow insiders to research them. Grace (2002) could write authoritatively about Catholic schools because he had insider knowledge about Catholicism and about Catholic schools, which may have made those schools more accessible.

Access depends on the qualities the researcher brings to the field as well as the institution which is accessed, whether it is a convent (Lester, 2005), the police (Katz, 2003) or a prison where prisoners agree to communicate directly with a researcher (Reuss, 2000). Access depends on who the gatekeepers are and what level of access is sought. The researcher's ethnicity, age, dress, appearance, gender, personality – everything matters. A single visit is not as risky as long-term sustained engagement with an institution, which is what ethnographers require, particularly if they wish to collect first hand original data. Normally, ethical approval has to be gained from the sponsors of the research such as a university ethics committee or other professional bodies. In Britain, in the case of medical patients the situation can become very complicated because of the Data Protection Act and demands for patient anonymity.

In principle it works like this:

- Anything that involves National Health Service (NHS) staff, patients (or human tissue/human remains), time or premises needs to go through NHS ethics approval (this is an online form, 64 pages plus a presentation to the NHS research ethics panel). The local Research Governance Office has initial guidance on this, but then it needs to be approved by the Health Trust which is responsible for a particular hospital.

- Anything involving healthy volunteers (for example, university students) and medical educators (in their teaching capacity rather than the clinical side of the job) is first considered by the School of Medicine Ethics Committee within that institution.

- Once students graduate after six years' study (post-18) and move into Foundation Training – two years of training post-qualification as doctors – the Deanery in which the hospital is located needs to approve ethical issues concerning both hospital and patient confidentiality.

Most General Hospitals are, relatively speaking, open spaces where people are admitted temporarily and then discharged as soon as possible. Patient data may be confidential but the place itself is open to visitors and different sorts of employees besides medical staff, such as gardeners, secretaries, chefs and so on. However, visiting such a space and researching it systematically poses totally different sets of questions.

ETHNOGRAPHY AND GAINING ACCESS

All qualitative researchers, and particularly ethnographers, have much to say about gaining access (Van Maanen, 1988), Walford (1987, p. 50) was interviewed by a headmaster who asked him difficult questions about the methods he was going to use to collect data – something he had not anticipated. Burgess (1987, p. 67) managed to collect data precisely because the head teacher was enabling and helpful and Burgess managed to keep in touch with him for 15 years. Serendipity is often mentioned by ethnographers, which makes it impossible to predict in advance exactly how an ethnographic journey will end. Indeed, Troman (2002) suggests that the systematic and formulaic way in which research training is provided to researchers in universities may curtail instead of enabling ethnographic creativity. For Hargreaves (1987)

> More than any other method, ethnography does not prejudge what the most important research issues are going to be . . . it does not impose its own limited frameworks of meaning and interpretation on the participants through closed schedules, attitude scales . . . based on pre-existing hypotheses. Ethnography, that is suffers little from the 'outsider's arrogance' . . . (Hargreaves, 1987, p. 24)

Access is an ongoing process throughout research. When it comes to gaining access to a particular institution, it may be the case that it is considered too secure to let researchers in. Questions might arise as to who the research would benefit and at what cost (in terms of time and money). What the short- and long-term consequences of the research might be? The information researchers seek to gain may be seen as too sensitive for the lay public. There can be many reasons for reluctance to allow a researcher in. If it is a publicly funded institution, it may be failing to make the best use of taxpayer's contributions. The institution may have had many resignations since recent change of leadership. Or, an institution may be in the midst of major change and reorganization. During the time of transition ethnographic research is bound to expose weaknesses to an impartial researcher, who might stumble upon uncomfortable truths, such as mismanagement or unhappy members of staff. This may clash with the image an institution wishes to promote about itself. Bolman and Deal's (1994) allusion to the organization as theatre is quite apt for qualitative researchers, and especially for ethnographers as they try to go backstage, to unearth what lies behind appearances. Problems with access can occur even with institutions which are not total institutions. When I tried to gain entry to a school and was barred access for doctoral research, I was told the head was 'too busy to consider' my request. Sometimes it is difficult to be certain about the reasons for refusal. Was it because I was a South Asian woman, or because I was involved in low status community education work at the time (Bhatti, 2002)? As compared to day schools, total institutions, and particularly sensitive places like prisons are more challenging to research, especially if the researcher does not normally work in one.

Gaining access to total institutions can become complicated because of the nature of the institution. If direct access is not possible, then inventive ways have to be found for accessing reliable data through other means, such as interviewing people who are more familiar with that institution. These have to be people who are able to be open and willing to share their real concerns and conflicts. They may not share everything with a researcher, but what they decide to share has to be viable and needs to have been actually experienced and not just imagined by the participants. I could not gain direct access to prisons, so I tried to access the data I needed through the teachers who taught prisoners (Bhatti, 2010). Reporting the official line about a total institution which can be accessed through publications already in the public domain, such as prospectuses, annual reports and official web pages is not particularly useful on its own. For ethnographic research this has to be substantiated by further detailed, systematic and rigorous enquiry.

Similarly, for mental hospitals, access can be gained through psychiatrists and social workers, access to young offenders' experiences can be gained through probation officers or the police. It is relatively easier to adopt the role of a teacher or a helper in a boarding school than it is to be a helper in a secure unit. In some total institutions there are not many roles that can be adopted unofficially and without formal authority. Anything that arouses suspicion is counterproductive to reliable data collection, and is therefore not worth attempting. Confidentiality is highly rated in some total institutions, and especially in places where lay people are not allowed. This has one positive aspect – in that potential ethnographers are spared the dilemmas of habitual role conflicts which are inevitable when collecting primary data in data-rich research sites. When it comes to total institutions, researchers are seldom allowed full access to everything. Total institutions are nevertheless places where rich and original ethnographic data can be collected about people whose experiences are valuable and whose voices are not often heard in the hustle and bustle of life outside. For that reason they will continue to provoke researchers' interest and curiosity, which will in turn ensure that they continue to be researched.

NOTE

1. 'Sectioned' – in Britain at present a social worker or a relative can make an application to have someone assessed, backed by two medical recommendations. Details are defined in the Mental the Health Act 1983, Department of Health, UK. Section 2 is most often used for hospital assessment, whereby patients can be detained legally for 28 days. It must be agreed that someone is so ill that they require such medical care. If a longer stay (six months) is necessary an application under Section 3 of the Mental Health Act 1983 is required.

REFERENCES

Begg, M. and Brittain, V. (2006), *Enemy Combatant*, London: Simon and Schuster.
Bhatti, G. (2002), 'On the Doctoral endeavour', in G. Walford (ed.), *Doing a Doctorate in Educational Ethnography*, Oxford: Elsevier, pp. 9–27.
Bhatti, G. (2010), 'Learning behind bars: education in prisons', *Teaching and Teacher Education*, **26** (1), 31–6.
Blumer, D. (2002), 'The illness of Vincent van Gogh', *American Journal of Psychiatry*, **159** (4), 519–26.
Bolman, L.G. and Deal, T.E. (1994), 'The organization as theatre', in T. Hardimos (ed.), *New Thinking in Organizational Behaviour: From Social Engineering to Reflective Action*, Oxford: Butterworth-Heinemann, pp. 93–107.
Bucher, R. and Strauss, A. (1961), 'Professions in process', *American Journal of Sociology*, **66**, 325–34.

Burgess, R. (1987), 'Studying and restudying Bishop McGregor School', in G. Walford (ed.), *Doing Sociology of Education*, Lewes: Falmer Press, pp. 67–94.

Crighton, D.A. (2006), 'Psychological research into reducing suicide', in G.A. Towl (ed.), *Psychological Research in Prisons*, Oxford: Blackwells, pp. 54–69.

Delamont, S. (1984), 'Debs, dollies, swots and weeds: classroom styles at St Luke's,' in G. Walford (ed.), *British Public Schools Policy and Practice*, Lewes: Falmer Press, pp. 65–86.

Dowding, K. (1996), *Power*, Buckingham: Open University Press.

Fine, G.A. and Martin, D.D. (1995), 'Humour in ethnographic writing: sarcasm, satire, and irony as voices in Erving Goffman's *Asylums*', in J. Van Maanen (ed.), *Representation in Ethnography*, London: Sage, pp. 185–97.

Fisher, S. (1991), 'Homesickness and health at boarding schools', in G. Walford (ed.), *Private Schooling: Tradition, Change and Diversity*, London: Paul Chapman, pp. 70–83.

Foucault, M. (1977), *Discipline and Punish: The Birth of the Prison*, London: Penguin.

Fraser, W.R. (1968), *Residential Education*, Oxford: Pergamon Press.

Gilliat-Ray, S. (2006), 'Educating the "Ulama" centres of Islamic religious training in Britain', *Islam and Christian-Muslim Relations*, **17** (1), 55–76.

Goffman, E. (1959), *Asylums: Essays on the Social Situations of Mental Patients and Other Inmates*, London: Anchor Books.

Grace, G. (2002), *Catholic Schools: Mission, Market, Morality*, London: Routledge.

Hargreaves, A. (1987), 'Past, imperfect, tense: reflections on an ethnographic and historical study of middle schools', in G. Walford (ed.), *Doing Sociology of Education*, Lewes: Falmer Press, pp. 17–44.

Hawe, K. (1995), 'Why Muslim girls are more feminist in Muslim schools', in M. Griffiths and B. Troyna (eds), *Antiracism, Culture and Social Justice in Education*, Stoke on Trent: Trentham, pp. 43–60.

Hockey, J. (1986), *Squaddies: Portrait of a Subculture*, Exeter: University of Exeter Press.

Hoffman, A. Goldberg, D., Bockian, N., Broadwell, S. Palmieri M.J. (1998), 'Training medical residents in mindfulness-based stress reduction: a quantitative and qualitative evaluation', *Journal of Investigative Medicine*, **46** (7), 267–77.

Hofman, S., Sawyer, A. Witt, A.A. and Oh, D. (2010), 'The effect of mindfulness-based therapy on anxiety and depression: a meta-analytic review', *Journal of Consulting and Clinical Psychology*, **78** (2), 169–83.

Innes, M. (2003), *Understanding Social Control*, Maidenhead: Open University Press.

Katz, C.M. (2003), 'Issues in the production and dissemination of gang statistics: an ethnographic study of a large Midwestern police gang unit', *Crime and Delinquency*, **3** (3), 485–516.

Lambert, R. (1966), *The State and Boarding Education*, London: Methuen.

Lester, R.J. (2005), *Jesus in our Wombs: Embodying Modernity in a Mexican Convent*, Berkeley, CA: University of California Press.

Mueller, M., Kennerley, H., McManus, F. and Westbrook, D. (eds) (2010), *Oxford Guide to Surviving as a CBT Therapist*, Oxford: Oxford University Press.

Reuss, A. (2000), 'The researcher's tale', in D. Wilson and A. Reuss (eds), *Prison(er) Education*, Winchester: Waterside Press, pp. 25–48.

Roth, J.A. (1963), *Timetables: Structuring the Passage of Time in Hospital Treatment and Other Careers*, Indianapolis and Wagatsuma: Boobs-Merrill and Hiroshi.

Roth, J.A. (1974), 'Turning adversity to account', *Journal of Contemporary Ethnography*, **3** (3), 347–54.

Strauss, A., Schatzman, L., Bucher, R., Ehrlich, D. and Sabshin, M. ([1964] 1981), *Psychiatric Ideologies and Institutions*, New York: Macmillan, Reprint of 1964 edition published by Free Press of Glencoe, New York.

Thornicroft, G. (2006), *Shunned: Discrimination Against People with Mental Illness*, Oxford: Oxford University Press.

Troman, G. (2002), 'Method in the messiness: experiencing the ethnographic PhD process', in G. Walford (ed.), *Doing a Doctorate in Educational Ethnography*, Oxford: Elsevier, pp. 99–118.

Van Maanen, J. (1988), *Tales of the Field: On Writing Ethnography*, Chicago, IL: University of Chicago Press.
Wacquant, L. (2008), *Urban Outcasts: A Comparative Sociology of Advanced Marginality*, Cambridge: Polity Press.
Wacquant, L. (2009), *Prisons of Poverty*, Minneapolis, MN: University of Minnesota Press.
Wacquant, L. (2010), 'Prisoner reentry as myth and ceremony', *Dialectical Anthropology*, **34** (4), 605–20.
Walford, G. (1986), *Life in Public Schools*, London: Methuen.
Walford, G. (1987), 'Research role conflicts and compromises in public schools', in G. Walford (ed.), *Doing Sociology of Education*, London: Falmer, pp. 45–65.
Walford, G. (1990), *Privitization and Privilege in Education*, London: Routledge.

16. In cyberspace: qualitative methods for educational research
Hugh Busher and Nalita James

INTRODUCTION

Cyberspace is an interactive site or space that is used for all computer-mediated communication (CMC). It has become a space in which people can chat and play, as well as develop online relationships and alternative forms of online identity. It has had significant impact on the conditions of social interaction, providing the opportunity for individuals to construct the reality of their everyday lives with people who are distant from them in time and space as well as those who are geographically proximate to them. In the last five years this technology has become a daily part of many people's lives rather than just a special place that they visit occasionally. It has reconfigured the way in which individuals communicate and connect with each other especially through the many social sites that now exist, such as Facebook, but also through the use of email, blogs (the Blogosphere), Twitter, bulletin boards and websites on any number of topics, such as the one for new mothers investigated by Madge and O'Connor (2005), Wikis and the blandishments of the media to contact them online. It has also become a site where the social interactions of individuals and communities can be researched and where the construction of practices, meanings and identities can be investigated, including relationships between researchers and participants, in ways that may not be possible in the physical world (Dominguez et al., 2007). In this virtual world, researchers may carry out anthropological research into the cultures of social groups in Second Life, a virtual world where people, through their avatars, engage in a range of interactions some of which may not be possible in physical life (Boellstorf, 2008).

Cyberspace has rich and complex connections with face-to-face contexts and situations (Hine, 2005). It can involve researchers becoming immersed in a virtual culture or community, adapting conventional research methods of data collection, such as interviewing or observation, to collect data in online settings possibly over a sustained period of time (Mann and Stewart, 2000). It can also be used as a research medium in the social sciences, including education, opening up innovative ways for researchers to examine human inter/actions and experiences in new contexts. For example, it offers a different space and dimension in which individuals can write about who they are and what they know.

Researching in cyberspace is marked as 'a distinct topic worthy of specific note by the introduction of new epithets to familiar methods' (Hine, 2005, p. 5). It has altered the nature of the context in which research takes place and knowledge is constructed. 'Electronic virtuality is now embedded within actuality in a more dispersed and active way than ever before' (Hammersley, 2006, p. 8). At the same time, what has emerged are a range of academic debates around the social, cultural and legal impacts of cyberspace on research methods and the implications for research. Researchers are also faced with ethical and methodological tensions and decisions about the impact of researching in cyberspace on what their participants say, how it is said and on their research practice.

This chapter will examine how online researchers can conduct their studies in cyberspace using qualitative-based methods such as interviewing to collect in-depth data. It will also consider the methodological and ethical considerations associated with this method.

USING CYBER RESEARCH METHODS

The use of online qualitative research methods in educational research has become more prevalent in the last ten years, and has included virtual ethnographies (Hine, 2000), online asynchronous (non-real-time) interviews (Orgad, 2005; James and Busher, 2006) and synchronous (real-time) online interviews (O'Connor and Madge, 2001; Bowker and Tuffin, 2004). Research using such methods has sought to examine interaction and communication online and has been interested in both what people say and the way they say it (Bryman, 2004, p. 321). However, some researchers have questioned the ways in which physical world ethnographic research methods can be applied in virtual worlds (Williams, 2007).

When interviews are conducted online, researcher and participants engage in an exchange of texts (Markham, 2004). When interviews are conducted asynchronously, this can allow for an extended and deliberate sequence of events and for researchers and participants to digest messages before replying (Kanayama, 2003). Participants have time and space to elaborate their own thinking, unhindered by the visual presence of the researchers, thus allowing for a thoughtful and personal form of conversation (Kivits, 2005).

Email is the most widely used CMC method for interviews to date. Given its asynchronous nature, participants can respond to the researcher's questions at a time and pace convenient to them. In our own research (Busher, 2001; James, 2003) this was particularly valuable. Email has been used in a variety of studies aimed at investigating Internet use and online behaviour of individuals and groups in different types of social contexts (see, for example, Hessler et al., 2003; Kivits, 2005). We chose to make use of it as an asynchronous online method of interviewing to not only meet our logistical dilemmas, but to explore whether it would generate detailed qualitative data or reflexive accounts of our participants' professional experiences and life histories in particular macro and organizational contexts in their own voices. Our choice of research method was to some extent influenced by the knowledge that all our participants had ready access to email and were familiar with using it in their professional lives.

On a practical level, we also needed a research tool that would address the problem of accessing dislocated and dispersed groups of participants (Murray and Sixsmith, 1998). We did not think that the high level of immediacy that is apparent in real-time focus groups or synchronous one-on-one interviews (O'Connor and Madge, 2003) would create the process of reflection we wanted. This was because our aim was to let our participants have time to consider their responses carefully and explicate how they 'live out their lives, find and maintain connections and seek to represent themselves to others' (Hardey, 2004, p. 195). Like Cazden (2000) we also wished to capture the different social, cultural and organizational experiences of our participants' professional life stories. To have enriched our conversations with participants, we could have used online visual methods, such as memory books (Thomson and Holland, Chapter 22, this volume) or diaries or photographic scrapbooks (Cremin et al., 2010), to supplement our participants' iterative textual exchanges with us, but considered that the iterative exchanges on their own would construct more than sufficient depth of information for our studies.

When conducting online interviews participants need to understand how they will be carried out to be reassured about their security. Researchers must decide how they are going to access the population and they must obtain informed consent from all participants. In the research design, the researcher needs to decide how to introduce the research project, its questions and how they will be delivered. In our studies, we sent participants a rubric of how the interviews would be carried out and drew on our existing personal knowledge of the participants (James and Busher, 2006). Our rubric adopted a semi-structured interview schedule in which we sent out our questions one at a time to each participant rather than sending out a large number of questions at once. This approach formed a platform from which each participant could start to write their online narratives about how they perceived their professional lives. Supplementary probes were used to explore and gain a deeper understanding of the emergent themes and issues which could be followed up in the interviews. In adopting this approach, we hoped that the email interviews would allow our participants to engage with our questions and sustain reflection on their professional lives as, 'a more immediate, continuing, dynamic and subjective self-awareness' (Finlay, 2003, p. 108).

The ability of participants to reflect on their thoughts and reactions can be enhanced through the apparent intimacy of communication facilitated by the informality of typing on the computer screen (Bowker and Tuffin, 2004). In our studies we too found that the asynchronous nature of the email communication encouraged the participants to immerse themselves in the communication taking place. By using email to interview participants on an individual basis, we carefully followed each participant's online reflections and autobiographical voices, prompting them from time to time to help the constructions of their narratives. In doing so we investigated our participants' constructed identities, the sort that Hammersley and Treseder (2007) refer to as vernacular identities rather than substantial or reflexive identities when they carried out their research on 'pro-ana' websites concerned 'with body image, diet, and eating disorders' (p. 291). This was achieved by encouraging participants to review previous events through considering texts of earlier parts of their conversations with the researchers in order to take forward their thinking on their professional practice and identity. We returned participants' texts to them as part of the normal email exchange – by not erasing messages from the exchange – leaving participants and ourselves the opportunity to interrogate participants' texts as our dialogues developed. When issues and opinions were raised in the email exchanges they did not give what they assumed was the answer we wanted to hear. Instead, they asked more questions to help their participants 'reflect on a deeper level and get to the heart of the matter' (Russell and Bullock, 1999, p. 138).

When researchers set up online synchronous interviews they need to begin by choosing a relevant software package or gain access to a chat room site to facilitate the interview. If the researcher is trying to access a community or discussion forum, they may need to mediate with a moderator or elder of that community or group (Bishop, 2006). The exchange of text in such interviews tends to involve a dynamic form of dialogue, leading to a high level of immediacy, interaction and engagement with the topic being discussed (O'Connor and Madge, 2003).

An advantage of the synchronous interview is the real-time exchanges that occur and which can lead to spontaneous responses from participants and a high level of participant involvement. Further, participants who are reticent or shy in face-to-face contexts may find that they have more confidence to 'speak' freely and have more valuable contributions to make (Rheingold, 1994, pp. 23–4). This can result in answers that are less socially desirable. The downside is that the fast paced nature of the discussion can lead to participants lagging behind. The distinction between responding and sending can also become blurred as conversational turn-taking develops into overlapping conversations. In their online synchronous interviews, Bowker and Tuffin (2004) found the delayed process of sending out questions and receiving participants' responses at a later time actually created less opportunity to relate to participants by reciprocating disclosure of experiences, although they met with participants offline prior to the commencement of the interviews to overcome this problem. Responses from the participants were brief, and made up of very few words.

DEVELOPING RELATIONSHIPS IN CYBERSPACE

The quality of relationships researchers build with participants in qualitative research is very important to the success of that process, whether research is conducted face-to-face or online. The researcher needs to work hard to establish a research relationship in which the participant feels safe enough to be able to discuss freely their experiences and feelings. As Kivits (2005, p. 38) notes

> As with face-to-face interviews, where the success of the interaction is a matter of personal affinities, online and email interview relationships will be differently experienced, and hence valued, according to the individual subjectivities involved.

Online, research interviews are devoid of the normal social frameworks of face-to-face encounters between researchers and participants, in which both interpret the social characteristics of the other, either verbally or non-verbally through gesture, tone of voice and facial expressions (James and Busher, 2007). However, Kendall (2000) noted in her research of the BlueSky social forum that people made the same gendered interpretations of other people's posts as they would have made of their offline comments. These interpretations drew on people's cultural knowledge derived from the offline cultures they inhabited. Further, if researchers are visually and physically absent in online research projects other participants can have a sense of marginality, feeling deprived of a sense of engagement in a human conversation and, so, of a sense of power to present their own voice. Such a sense of marginality can lead to a lack of sense of commitment to a research project and to participants taking a limited part or dropping out altogether (James and Busher, 2006).

In our studies much depended on the personal relationships we developed with our participants that allowed them to trust us. However, the framework we sent our participants setting out how our studies would be carried out did not fully assuage some of our participants' fears about protecting their privacy (James and Busher, 2006). In telling us their stories, some of our participants revealed concerns about protecting their privacy and anonymity online, an issue we return to later in the chapter, especially as they were revealing personal (and sometimes sensitive) information about their professional lives and identities. Whilst not questioning our integrity as researchers, some participants expressed concerns about the nature of email as a medium, the ability for communication to be passed on inadvertently and the risk this posed to their privacy, so that they could make an informed choice about whether or not to participate. Despite the professional relationships we had already developed with our participants offline, which had created some elements of rapport and trust, we still had to work hard to build a research relationship online that would reassure our participants of the sincerity of our intentions.

Whether participants are engaged in synchronous discussion groups or asynchronous email interviews, researchers need to construct an anonymous and non-threatening environment space, that minimizes the risk to participants' privacy and anonymity in order to construct a creative, collaborative relationship with other people online (Orgad, 2005, p. 55). This can be achieved through repeated interaction and mutual disclosure which create a context of trust (Mann and Stewart, 2000). The 'stage of mutual self-disclosure' (Kivits, 2005, p. 40) is essential in sustaining the research relationship. In James's (2007) research, the researcher wanted to acquire an 'understanding of her participants' perspective through an open and honest dialogue'. She invested her own identity into the research relationship in an attempt to democratize narrative exchanges and construct a more equal interaction and a dialectical relationship (Illingworth, 2001). The following email exchange gives an example of this:

P: '. . . My experiences as an academic psychologist have shaped my professional identity in that I am acutely aware of the rigour with which research is carried out and so feel able to lend some authority to observations/judgments based on the robustness of empirical inquiry . . .'

R: 'I think that's interesting. In considering the issue myself I have found that my professional identity is linked not only to the working context and the culture within which I work but other identities, which are important to me . . . These identities merge with each other and are influenced by each other in terms of how I live my life as a whole . . .'

P: 'I absolutely agree with you. For instance, I teach gender and Psychology and regard myself as a feminist, so this has a bearing on how I deliver psychological material and how I am perceived. Similarly I am a parent so when talking about socialisation I feel I can lend some credibility from my own experience. My professional identity is completely bound up with my personality . . .'

The development of such collaborative discourses constitute the creation of a particular or small culture (Holliday, 1999), in which researchers and participants construct shared meanings and practices during the course of each project, gradually replacing the dominant discourses of the research-ers who began the studies. The virtual setting of email research interviews is akin to the liminal or third spaces (Bhabha, 1994) which novices to an institution inhabit when they join it and interact with participants with different perspectives to begin to construct new or transient communities.

Online research can be devoid of the tensions, restrictions and expecta-tions of the offline world (Illingworth, 2006, online). Most participants in online spaces will not have met face-to-face. Indeed, instigating face-to-face interactions may actually threaten participants' experiential under-standing of their online world (Orgad, 2005, p.53). In online research, participants and researchers are hidden from each other by the 'smoked mirror' of the Internet as a consequence of the visual anonymity and pseudonymity. These can disguise participants' identities and thus make it easier for people to play with their views and perspectives (Jacobson, 1999). However the identities which participants and researchers project on to the other is problematic (Hammersley and Treseder, 2007) and related to their offline cultural experiences (Kendall, 2000). The under-standings of identity that participants are using will affect the research methods being used (Hammersley and Treseder, 2007). Participants' pres-entation of self whether playful, superficial or written in an engaged way makes a considerable difference to the quality of a research project and the trustworthiness of its outcomes (James, 2003).

Online silences too can represent a number of scenarios but without the visual cues can make interpretation unclear. James (2003) asked one of her participants: 'Haven't heard from you in a while. I wondered if you still wished to continue the interview?' Such silences can occur because the participant is thinking through their response. It might also be inter-preted as a means whereby they are withdrawing their consent to continue with the interview because they feel uncomfortable about telling their stories, despite the researcher's investment in the relationship. As Busher (2001) found in his study, sometimes slow responses by the researcher to participants' queries about the research process or the meaning of some questions tended to deprive participants of a sense of engagement in a human conversation and of a sense of security of knowing, even if incorrectly, who were the researchers socially. This points to the need for researchers to identify the existence of 'strategies of visibility . . . which make up for the lack of traditional social cues and which indeed permit the development of a status differentiation' (Paccagnella, 1997, online) to build trust and to encourage participants to 'disclose'. In turn, participants can take advantage of the freedom of expression that the anonymity of the online interview allows.

On the other hand, time and space can also be used to 'insert the online world of the Internet into offline contexts, and vice versa' (Hine, 2000, p. 115). For example, in one of Hine's (2000) studies, one participant mentioned in her email interview that she was concerned about losing her academic identity. When the researcher met up with the participant at a meeting they were both attending, the participant talked about her experiences again. Later, when the email interview resumed, the researcher probed some more by linking to things that had been raised in their face-to-face conversations. The move between online and offline interaction then can sensitively 'capture the multifaceted nature of participants' experiences and encompass "both sides of the screen"' (Orgad, 2005, p. 53) as well as combine online and offline research methods.

BEING IN/VISIBLE IN CYBERSPACE

When research is carried out in cyberspace, researchers encounter conflicts between the requirements of research and its possible benefits, on the one hand, and human subjects' rights to and expectations of autonomy, privacy and informed consent (Ess and the Association of Internet Researchers (AoIR), 2002, p. 2). As in offline research, when negotiating entry into an online research project, researchers need to make clear to participants how they and other people might benefit from the research in which they are being invited to take part (Robson and Robson, 2002).

Whilst the ethical issues for online research are the same as those for face-to-face (onsite) research, the Internet has provided 'a virtual sphere of existence separate from the real [*sic*] world' (Hine, 2000, p. 118) in which humans can interact as themselves or through their avatars and which researchers can investigate. This sphere presents additional challenges for constructing ethical research that guards participants' privacy and confidentiality and gains their informed consent to participate (Ess and the AoIR, 2002). For example, gaining informed consent online is potentially more problematic than in physical life as participants in online research projects can, arguably, more easily deceive researchers about their identity. Some researchers think that the nature of online interactions makes it more difficult for researchers to assure and ascertain the trustworthiness and authenticity of data (Ess and the AoIR, 2002), raising 'new problems in judging what is authentic' (Hine, 2000, p. 118). However, the authenticity of online research conversations and participants' identities can be addressed through considering the extent to which researchers and participants construct credible and consistent stories in the course of their text-based exchanges (Clandinin and Connelly, 2000; Lee, 2006).

On the other hand, to some extent CMC facilitates the construction of voluntary participation in research projects as, particularly in asynchronous interviews, participants can respond as and when it suits them irrespective of reminders by researchers (James and Busher, 2009). 'Silence' or lack of obvious response by participants might also be interpreted as an indication that they are, perhaps temporarily, withdrawing their informed consent to participate (James and Busher, 2006). The reasons for participants dropping-out of research may not be transparent to researchers or amenable to investigation. This emphasizes that informed consent is not something only garnered at the start of a study but must be sustained throughout it, allowing participants to withdraw consent when they wish. Further, the absence of the physical presence of a researcher sometimes makes it easier for some participants to commence their discussions, especially in online interviews where there is no moderator present.

Another aspect of the ethical problems faced in online research is knowing what constitutes private and public conversations. Although an online discussion group might be accessible to the public the conversations taking place might be confidential to the participants. Another component is the topic being discussed and the extent to which it represents personal information that individuals may not want to have shared in the public domain (Elgesem, 2002). Some researchers see online texts as both publicly private and privately public (Waskul and Douglass, 1997). This is because on the Internet, 'privacy need not be expressly linked to concealment' (Joinson, 2005, p. 26). Further, inviting participants of a discussion forum to join a research project might be perceived by them as an invasion of private space because the posting is not perceived as relevant to the focus of the discussion. Ethical practice in the last case would be to approach the moderator of the discussion forum and wait for her or him to discuss the request to conduct research to be debated by members of the forum.

For participants of online discussions this makes it problematic to know to what extent they should divulge personal information because they are not sure to what extent that information will be broadcast in an even more public domain. It is for this reason that Ess and the AoIR (2002) argue that researchers are more likely to persuade participants to disclose personal information if they establish a safe online environment, such as a dedicated project website. In asynchronous focus group interviews using regular listserv or bulletin boards, the interaction will be less private and this may lead participants to be less candid than in email interviews. Even email records of conversations might make participants visible. The apparent privacy of participants – they seemed to be unseen to each other and the researchers – is instantly breached by some of the characteristics of the medium of email-based discussion unless research records are curated in ways that avoid participants' email addresses being stored with their real names.

The grounds for informed consent in face-to-face research also apply to online environments. In our research, we had to gain participants' informed consent to take part in research as part of establishing the online research project. We had to identify ourselves and our purposes. We also needed to construct a means through which participants could check and confirm the meaning of their texts/speech acts before they were used outside the conversations of the project communities for which they were originally intended. So, in agreeing the accuracy of the records of our participants' conversations and reflecting on the credibility of our interpretations of these conversations, we were never entirely sure to what depth the participants had actually agreed to these records. For example, one participant pointed out that 'in email communication clarification is not always easy' especially if there are time lapses in message exchanges and participants could not remember what they had said previously. However, the linkage between the participants' voices and the researchers' interpretations of the themes emerging in them was reflected in the conceptual models that emerged from our studies (James and Busher, 2006).

Protecting participants' privacy is a particular issue in online interviews that seek to gather personal or sensitive data. The extent to which participants may be willing to be open and honest with researchers is likely to depend heavily on the extent to which the researchers can construct a secure environment for communication and one which protects participants' anonymity. This allows participants to feel confident that their privacy is protected and the risk of harm to them is minimized to a level acceptable to them.

Much depends on the personal relationships researchers are able to develop with participants that allow them to build trust. This could include developing offline relationships first. It also involves being culturally sensitive to issues of privacy as participants perceive them if they are to be willing to 'open up'. In our studies we carefully constructed an online research setting that decreased their vulnerability. We wanted our participants to feel confident that their privacy was adequately protected 'in their eyes' if they self-disclosed, and the risk of harm to them or their communities was minimized to a level acceptable to them (James and Busher, 2006). However, as our projects were conducted via email using our university website, rather than a dedicated project website, we had to make the participants aware that their conversations with us were not taking place in a private setting (Barnes, 2004), allowing them to make an informed choice about whether or not to participate. Whether research interviews are conducted asynchronously or synchronously, researchers have responsibility to ensure that privacy and data security is adequate for the research.

CONCLUSION

Cyberspace has altered the nature of the way in which everyday life activities are performed, the context in which research can take place and how knowledge is constructed. It has provided both a 'constructed' and 'cultural' context in which researchers and participants can interact and communicate and a site where the self is expressed through a process of reflection and interaction.

When online research interviews are conducted in cyberspace, the methodology has to be consistent with the integrity of the research topic and context, When the researcher enters the online setting, they have to think carefully about how to convey 'the same level of confidence, commitment, privacy and trustworthiness in a "body-less medium"' (Seymour, 2001, p. 161). One solution is for researchers to 'see and sense' online interactions, as both analyst and experience-participant. This may help to remove the aura of suspicion surrounding stranger-to-stranger communication in cyberspace (Smith, 1997, p. 40). Researchers can have an active involvement rather than being a detached observer. This can lead to a sense of online belonging, and through that, a shared identity with their participants. This approach can also allow online researchers to delve into the everyday experiences of research participants, and attend to their voices, actions and emotions (and can be usefully employed in the online setting, particularly when researching sensitive discussion involving online groups). Although researchers and other participants cannot avoid interpreting the identities of the other during online research, the interpretations they choose will affect their choice of research methods as well as the outcomes of the research (Hammersley and Treseder, 2007). However, it also indicates how hard researchers have to work to understand how their participants live and interact.

Online research is a useful additional method for researchers but will not suit every research project. Drawing on the preceding discussion, the remainder of this section suggests ways in which researchers can enact online qualitative research in an ethical manner.

For research design researchers need to:

- Consider carefully the advantages and challenges of using online methods instead of face-to-face ones for the specific topic being investigated.
- Ensure the research aims and design reflect the cultural contexts in which participants are embedded.
- Provide clear justification for the methods of data collection and analysis to answer the questions you have posed and explain this to participants.
- Select synchronous or asynchronous modes of interviews depending on the purposes of the research project as well as the characteristics of your participants' lives.
- Review the research relationship to make sense of the social space of the online communication and interaction and reassure participants.
- Discover what time zones your participants inhabit and the extent to which their patterns of work mirror yours.
- Discover when it is most convenient for your participants to respond to your questions.

For Online research relationships researchers need to:

- Reflect on ways that researchers come to know their participants both online and offline.
- Consider whether combining online and offline interviews serves the purposes of the research project as well as the characteristics of the project's potential participants' lives.
- Think about what is lost/gained in the move from online to offline interactions, and vice versa.
- Consider how they will respond to online and offline interviews as these present two different types of discourses and need to be carefully analysed.

For ethical practice researchers need to:

- Think carefully about how to assure participants' safety, privacy and trustworthiness of the faceless medium.

- Explore their participants' cultural understandings, hopes and fears of Internet communication.
- Act respectfully and ethically when engaging with online communities and acknowledge their peripherality when trying to join an existing online community for research purposes.
- Remember the international frameworks of Internet communications.
- Make your communication sites as secure as possible.
- Gain participants' informed consent to take part in research right from the beginning of a study, that is, from the time that they join or the researcher sets up an online community of some sort.
- Identify themselves and their purposes when they begin their studies.
- Define what texts will be stored and saved for a research project and in what way they will be used.
- Construct a means with participants through which members can check and confirm the meaning of their texts/speech acts before they are used outside the conversations of the communities for which they were originally intended.
- Explain clearly to their putative participants how participants' identities and, possibly that of the online community too, will be disguised to avoid the privacy of themselves and their correspondents being infringed.
- Make clear to participants in online research how they and other people might benefit from the research in which they are being invited to take part.

REFERENCES

Barnes, S.B. (2004), 'Issues of attribution and identification in online social research', in M.D. Johns, S.L.S. Chen and G.J. Hall (eds), *Online Social Research: Methods, Issues and Ethics*, Oxford: Peter Lang Publishing, pp. 203–22.

Bhabha, H. (1994), *The Location of Culture*, London: Routledge.

Bishop, J. (2006), 'Increasing participation in online communities: a framework for human–computer interaction', *Computers in Human Behavior*, **23** (4), 1881–93.

Boellstorff, T. (2008), *Coming of Age in Second Life: An Anthropologist Explores the Virtually Human*, Princeton, NJ: Princeton University Press.

Bowker, N. and Tuffin, K. (2004), 'Using the online medium for discursive research about people with disabilities', *Social Science Computer Review*, **22** (2), 228–41.

Bryman, A. (2004), *Social Research Methods*, 2nd edn, Oxford: Oxford University Press.

Busher, H. (2001), 'Being and becoming a doctoral student: culture, literacies and self-identity', Paper presented at TESOL Arabia Conference, 14–16 March.

Cazden, C. (2000), 'Taking cultural differences into account', in B. Cope and M. Kalantis (eds), *Multi-literacies: Literacy, Learning and the Design of Total futures*, London: Routledge.

Clandinin, D.J. and Connelly, F.M. (2000), *Narrative Inquiry: Experience and Story in Qualitative Research*, San Fransciso, CA: Jossey Bassey.

Cremin, H., Mason, C. and Busher, H. (2010), 'Problematising pupil voice using visual methods: findings from a study of engaged and disaffected pupils in an urban secondary school', *British Educational Research Journal*, **37** (4), 585–603.

Dominguez, D., Beaulieu, A., Estalella, S., Gomez, E., Schnettler B. and Read, R. (2007), 'Virtual ethnography', *Forum: Qualitative Social Research*, **8** (3), available at http://www.qualitative-research.net/index.php/fqs/article/viewArticle/274/601 (accessed 5 September 2011).

Elgesem, D. (2002), 'What is special about the ethical issues in online research?', *Ethics and Information Technology*, **4**, 195–203.

Ess, C. and the Association of Internet Researchers (AoIR) (2002), 'Ethical decision-making and Internet research', available at http://www.aoir.org/reports/ethics.pdf (accessed 5 September 2011).

Finlay, L. (2003), 'Through the looking glass: intersubjectivity and hermeneutic reflection', in O. Finlay and B. Gough (eds), *Reflexivity: A Practical Guide for Researchers in Health and Social Sciences*, London: pp. Blackwell, 105–19.

Hammersley, M. (2006), 'Ethnography: problems and prospects', *Ethnography and Education*, **1** (1), 3–14.

Hammersley, M. and Treseder, P. (2007), 'Identity as an analytic problem: who's who in "pro-ana" websites?', *Qualitative Research*, **7** (3), 283–300.

Hardey, M. (2004), 'Digital life stories: auto/biography in the information age', *Auto/Biography*, **12**, 183–200.

Hessler, R.M, Downing, J., Beltz, C., Pellicio, A., Powell, M. and Vale, W. (2003), 'Qualitative research on adolescent risk using email: a methodological assessment', *Qualitative Sociology*, **26** (1), 111–24.

Hine, C. (2000), *Virtual Ethnography*, London: Sage.

Hine, C. (2005), *Virtual Methods. Issues in Social Research on the Internet*, Oxford: Berg.

Holliday, A.R. (1999), 'Small cultures', *Applied Linguistics*, **20** (2), 237–64.

Illingworth, N. (2001), 'The internet matters: exploring the use of the internet as a research tool', *Sociological Research Online*, **6** (2), http://www.socresonline.org.uk/6/2/illingsworth.html (accessed 5 September 2011).

Illingworth, N. (2006), 'Content, context, reflexivity and the qualitative research encounter: telling stories in the virtual realm', *Sociological Research Online*, **11** (1), http://www.socresonline.org.uk/11/1/illingworth.html (accessed 5 September 2011).

Jacobson, D. (1999), 'Doing research in cyberspace', *Field Methods*, **11** (2), 127–45.

James, N.R. (2003), 'Teacher Professionalism, Teacher Identity: How Do I See Myself?', Unpublished Doctorate of Education Thesis, University of Leicester, School of Education, July.

James, N. (2007), 'The use of email interviewing as a qualitative method of inquiry in educational research', *British Educational Research Journal*, **33** (6), 963–76.

James, N. and Busher, H. (2006), 'Credibility, authenticity and voice: dilemmas in web-based interviewing', *Qualitative Research Journal*, **6** (3), 403–20.

James, N. and Busher, H. (2007), 'Ethical issues in online educational research: protecting privacy, establishing authenticity in email interviewing', *International Journal of Research & Method in Education*, **30** (1), 101–13.

James, N. and Busher, H. (2009), *Online Interviewing*, London: Sage.

Joinson, A.N. (2005), 'Internet behaviour and the design of virtual methods', in C. Hine (ed.), *Virtual Methods: Issues in Social Research on the Internet*, Oxford: Berg, pp. 21–34.

Kanayama, T. (2003), 'Ethnographic research on the experience of Japanese elderly people online', *New Media & Society*, **5** (2), 267–88.

Kendall, L. (2000), '"OH NO! I'M A NERD!": hegemonic masculinity on an online forum', *Gender & Society*, **14**, 256–74.

Kivits, J. (2005), 'Online interviewing and the research relationship', in C. Hine (ed.), *Virtual Methods: Issues in Social Research on the Internet*, Oxford: Berg, pp. 35–50.

Lee, H. (2006), 'Privacy, publicity and accountability of self-presentation in an online discussion group', *Sociological Inquiry*, **76** (1), 1–22.

Madge, C. and O'Connor, H. (2005), 'Mothers in the making? Exploring notions of liminality in hybrid cyberspace', *Transactions of the Institute of British Geographers*, **3** (1), 83–97.

Mann, C. and Stewart, F. (2000), *Internet Communication and Qualitative Research. A Handbook for Researching Online*, London: Sage.

Markham, A.N. (2004), 'Representation in online ethnography', in M.D. Johns, S.L.S. Chen and G.J. Hall (eds), *Online Social Research: Methods, Issues and Ethics*, Oxford: Peter Lang Publishing, pp. 141–57.

Murray, C. and Sixsmith, J. (1998), 'Email: a qualitative research medium for interviewing?', *International Journal of Social Research Methodology*, **1** (2), 103–21.

O'Connor, H. and Madge, C. (2001), 'Cybermothers: online synchronous interviewing using conferencing software', *Sociological Research Online*, **5** (4), http://www.socresonline.org.uk/5/4/o'connor.html.

O'Connor, H. and Madge, C. (2003), 'Focus groups in cyberspace: using the Internet for qualitative research', *Qualitative Market Research. An International Journal*, **6** (2), 133–43.

Orgad, S. (2005), 'From online to offline and back: moving from online to offline relationships with research participants', in C. Hines (ed.), *Virtual Methods: Issues in Social Research on the Internet*, Oxford: Berg, pp. 51–66.

Paccagnella, L. (1997), 'Getting the seats of your pants dirty: strategies for ethnographic research on virtual communities', *Journal of Computer-Mediated Communication*, **3** (1), http://www.ascusc.org/jcmc/vol3/issue1/paccagnella.html.

Rheingold, H. (1994), *The Virtual Community: Finding Connection in a Computerised World*, London: Secker and Warburg.

Robson, K. and Robson, M. (2002), 'Your place or mine? Ethics, the researcher and the Internet', in T. Welland and L. Pugsley (eds), *Ethical Dilemmas in Qualitative Research*, London: Ashgate.

Russell, T. and Bullock, S. (1999), 'Discovering our professional knowledge as teachers: critical dialogues about learning from experience', in J. Loughran (ed.), *Researching Methodologies and Practices for Understanding Pedagogy*, New York: The Falmer Press.

Seymour, W. (2001), 'In the flesh or online. Exploring qualitative research methodologies', *Qualitative Research*, **1** (2), 147–68.

Smith, C. (1997), 'Casting the net: surveying an internet population', *Journal of Computer Mediated Communication*, **3** (1), http://jcmc.huji.ac.il/vol3/issue1/smith.html.

Waskul, D. and Douglass, M. (1997), 'Cyberself: the emergence of self in on-line chat', *Information Society*, **13** (4), 375–98.

Williams, M. (2007), 'Avatar watching: participant observation in graphical online environments', *Qualitative Research*, **7** (1), 5–24.

RECOMMENDED READING

Fielding, N., Lee, R.M. and Blank, G. (2007), *The Sage Handbook of Online Research Methods*, London: Sage.

James, N. and Busher, H. (2009), *Online Interviewing*, London: Sage.

Kendall, L. (2002), *Hanging Out in the Virtual Pub: Masculinities and Relationships Online*, Berkley, CA: University of California Press.

PART 3

DATA COLLECTION

17. Schools in focus: photo methods in educational research

Louisa Allen

Picture methods are diverse and can include the use of cameras (Dixon, 2008), drawings (White et al., 2010), cartoons (Warburton, 1998), videos (Holliday, 2004; White, Chapter 23, this volume) and diagrams (Crilly et al., 2006). This chapter is concerned with photo methods as one form of picture method within educational research. Although photo methods have been an increasingly popular strategy for social scientists over the past ten years (Clark-Ibanez, 2004), their use in educational research has been piecemeal and largely unchartered. Rather than mapping a comprehensive history, this chapter seeks to illuminate aspects of the landscape of photo methods in education. It addresses some key questions about this method within the specific setting of schooling. The chapter asks what is distinctive about photo methods compared with conventional research methods? For what purpose and how have photo methods been employed by educational researchers? And, what challenges do researchers wishing to employ photo methods in education face?

SITUATING PHOTO METHODS WITHIN VISUAL RESEARCH

Vision is a predominant way of knowing in contemporary western society that is largely taken for granted (Hansen-Ketchum and Myrick, 2008). As Berger (1977) has famously noted, 'Seeing comes before words . . . and establishes our place in the surrounding world'(Berger, 1977, p. 7). A prioritization of the visual is evidenced in what has been conceptualized as 'the bombardment and saturation of contemporary societies with images'(Fischman, 2001, p. 29). This phenomenon is partly due to the increasing availability of visually sophisticated technologies such as digital cameras, internet and camera phones, enabling the immediate capture and dissemination of images. Others attribute this inundation of images theoretically to postmodernism where 'the visual has become more important as a pivotal aspect of social life' (Emmison and Smith, 2000, p. ix). This theoretical interest has engendered a 'pictorial turn' (Mitchell, 1987) in social science research invoking a concern with producing accounts of the texture of social life that reach beyond words (Knowles and Sweetman, 2004).

Within the social sciences visual research is grounded in the idea that 'scientific' insight can be acquired 'by observing, analysing and theorizing its [that is, society's] visual manifestations; behaviour of people and material products of culture' (Pauwels, 2010, p. 546). That the visual might constitute legitimate research 'evidence' remains a controversial idea for some academic disciplines (Kaplan et al., 2007). A reliance on words and numbers in educational research has often resulted in the dismissal of images as legitimate data (Fischman, 2001). The use of cameras and photos as tools for producing knowledge can invoke particular suspicion. Cameras are perceived to invade privacy, objectify and distort 'reality'. In their discussion of authors' and editors' reluctance to include photographs in published works Emmison and Smith (2000) cast this suspicion as a 'double standard'.

> What is ironic . . . is that whilst photographs are often deemed to be unacceptable by authors and editors, textually explicit descriptions of morally suspect materials are considered less so . . . Whilst texts are associated with reason and higher mental faculties, images are seen as subversive, dangerous and visceral. (Emmison and Smith, 2000, p. 14)

Those who support the visual as a data source maintain that 'any account whether it involves photographs or not is constructed' (Chaplin, 1994, p. 206). It is how methods are operationalized and data subsequently reported which determines whether it is objectifying and/or privacy breaching.

Given this controversy why might educational researchers employ photo methods? A key reason is the belief that photo methods have the potential to capture and generate qualitatively different data (Walker, 1997). Chaplin (1994) argues that visual methods can 'tap into existing resources which would otherwise lie dormant, unexplored and unutilized' (Chaplin, cited in Packard, 2008, p. 63). A distinctive quality of photo methods is their ability to foreground the material and corporeal (Thomson and Holland, Chapter 22, this volume). This was the reason I employed photo methods in my research into the 'sexual cultures' of schooling (Allen, 2009b). The sexualization of school space has largely been neglected because it is difficult to capture and articulate through traditional research techniques. In the risk-adverse setting of schooling (Jones, 2001) asking students about sexual embodiment can prove uncomfortable and position researchers as 'dangerous'. However, when this topic is introduced on participants' own terms via photographs they have taken, space for talk about bodies emerges.

The ability of photo methods to capture the material gives them a distinctive quality as a data collection strategy. The potential indexical character of photos and their representation of tangible objects arguably constitutes them as persuasive forms of data (Hurdley, 2007). Becker (2002) explains how images can lend support to participants' accounts in ways talk cannot.

> What can you do with pictures that you couldn't do just as well with words (or numbers)? The answer is that I can lead you to believe that the abstract talk I've told you has a real, flesh and blood life, and therefore is to be believed in a way that is hard to do when all you have is the argument and some scraps and can only wonder if there really is anyone like that out there. (Becker, 2002, p. 11)

Croghan et al., (2008) provide an example of this phenomenon in their research examining how the construction of youth identity intersects with patterns of consumption. In this study, 14-year-old Keith's talk constituted him as a street-wise rock fan and member of a particular music-based male-oriented style. Given Keith's age and claim to an older 'scene', researchers were unsure whether the identity he projected was one he aspired to, or actually lived. Via photo elicitation, however, Keith produced photos revealing himself sitting amidst a popular rock band. Placing himself with the band (with their apparent permission) creates an association that verbal claims cannot. As the researchers explain Keith 'is demonstrably, and through the fixed image permanently, associated with the band, and with the identities that his association invokes (Croghan et al., 2008, p. 353). Whether or not researchers want to claim photographs depict 'a truth', photographs can more convincingly display tangible forms that written and verbal text can only reference.

Photographs can also reveal things that are elusive to articulate or write about. Rose (2007) proposes that cameras can record what might be conceptualized as a location's 'texture' or 'atmosphere', that is, the 'feeling' or 'sense' of a space. Tim Edensor's (2005) study of industrial ruins provides an example of such 'texture' where photographs convey an atmosphere of 'decay', 'abandonment' and 'eeriness'. Explaining this experiential quality of photos, he says:

> Photographs are never merely visual but in fact conjure up synaesthetic and kinaesthetic effects, for the visual provokes other sensory responses. The textures and tactilities, smells, atmospheres and sounds of ruined spaces, together with the signs and objects they accommodate, can be empathetically conjured up by visual material. (Edensor, 2005, p. 16)

This immediate sensory invoking potential means images can also elicit memories, feelings and conflicts forgotten or unacknowledged (Mahruf et al., 2007). When participants are emotionally invested in something their accounts often prove richer and more expansive. The particular emotive and evocative quality of images means they can be useful stimulants in this regard (Knowles and Sweetman, 2004). Mahruf et al. (2007) described students' talk as scant in conventional interviews during their study of student transition from non-formal primary to formal high schools in Bangladesh. When digital photos were displayed on a laptop during subsequent interviews however, they invoked feelings of nostalgia that increased participant talk.

TYPES OF PHOTO METHODS

An important question for visual researchers is what purpose will photos serve? Historically, photos have constituted sources of data in their own right. Shaped by a scientific realist paradigm photographs were utilized in the nineteenth and early twentieth centuries to capture 'scientific' and 'objective' data (Collier, 1967). This inventory capacity to reflect 'the truth' about material existence was characteristic of early anthropological studies where researchers took photos to document cultural communities (Bateson and Mead, 1942).

The idea that photographs represent authentic records of material exist-ence is now highly contested. The advent of post-structuralism has gener-ated considerable scepticism about a pre-existing material reality (Foucault, 1976) and photographic ability to accurately capture it. As Baudrillard comments, it is no longer possible to make a distinction between the real and the unreal, as the ability to digitally create and change photographs means the connection between 'image' and 'truth' has been intermin-ably severed (Baudrillard, 1988). Images therefore 'are never transparent windows into the world' but instead interpret and depict it in particular ways (Rose, 2007, p. 2). This situation occurs because images are perceived to be socially constructed at the site of production and reception (Banks, 2001). A photographer's decisions about what falls in and out of frame mean the image is always a selection and construction (Thomson, 2008). In addition, 'the reality the researcher . . . [and participant] sees in the image is framed by her or his own culturally and individually specific subjectivity' (Pink, 2007, p. 124). Meanings of photographs are thus polysemic, a capac-ity which photo essays unaccompanied by explanatory text capitalize upon (see Margolis, 2007).

Another purpose photographs can serve is to stimulate discussion. In this case, data does not have to be found in the photographs themselves but can be generated through talk about them. Wright et al. (2010) employed photographs to foster talk in research around African-Carribbean youth's experience of exclusion. Researchers anticipated traditional one-to-one interviewing would prove inhibitive for these youth who were 'likely to have experienced many interview situations where the aim was to "prove" their responsibility for exclusion' (Wright et al., 2010, p. 544). Instead, participant photography was employed to encourage young people to frame talk about exclusion in their own terms.

Photo elicitation involves stimulating dialogue during individual or group interview through photo prompts (Pink, 2007). Collier (1967) explains photos can have a 'can-opener' effect opening conversations between people. Clark-Ibanez (2004) notes photo prompts work well when interviewing children by helping to overcome barriers like 'level of linguistic communication, cognitive development, the question-and-answer setting, and the accentuated power dynamics of the adult interviewing a child' (Clark-Ibanez, 2004, p. 1512). Introducing participant generated photographs may stimulate participants' talk because the children are knowledgeable about and invested in the photos displayed.

Another important decision is whether images are sourced by the researcher or participant, and if these are 'found' or 'generated'. 'Found' images comprise pre-existing or societal imagery (family pictures, advertisements, postcards, paintings, feature and documentary film) with potentially no known origin (Pauwels, 2010). 'Participant found' images may be useful when a participant seeks to authenticate or embellish stories. For example, by illustrating talk about their schooling experiences with a school picture of themselves. Another example of 'found' images comes from New Zealand-based research exploring 11–13-year-old girls' sexual subjectivities. Young women at school were asked to make a collage reflecting how they understood themselves as sexual (Ingram, 2011). Collage images were predominately sourced from magazine photos and used to launch individual interview discussion.

Researcher 'found' or 'generated' images can be useful when conducting theory-driven research. A researcher may introduce participants to conceptual understandings in existing literature by showing images intended to probe an issue. For example, to explore the notion of schools as sites for social (re)production I have shown first year university students images from the DVD 'Another Brick in the Wall' by 1970s band Pink Floyd. These offer students the opportunity to reflect on whether their experience of schooling made them metaphorically 'bricks' in 'the wall', or conforming citizens in the social fabric of society. Researcher generated images were also employed by Mahruf et al. (2007) in phase one of their study of Bangladeshi students' school transition experiences. These researchers took photographs of a range of educational settings students might experience in primary and high school. During phase two of the fieldwork participants were shown images during interviews to encourage talk about personal experiences of school transition.

There may be caveats in using researcher 'found' and 'generated' images however. Images sourced by the researcher can structure and dominate subsequent discussion. When empowering participants and centring their concerns is paramount, such an approach may be prohibitive. Visual researchers also caution against researchers' tendency to capture 'visually arresting' images rather than what might hold meaning for participants. Clark-Ibanez (2004) notes how she found herself taking photos of things she viewed as unique and beautiful as an outsider to the Los Angeles area where she was working in two schools. These shots included a Domino's Pizza deliveryman on a bicycle and meat store mural which she realized lacked meaning for the children in her study. To ensure images reflect participant interests participant generated photos may be preferred.

The use of participant generated images in educational research has been diverse. One method has been to invite students to undertake photo diaries. This approach was taken by Allan (2005) while examining how high achieving girls in Britain manage and negotiate gendered and academic identities. Junior school girls created photographic diaries expressing their identities and experiences and then explored these through photo elicitation. In another Australian-based project (Carrington et al., 2007), students produced digital photographs representing their views of inclusion and exclusion in their school community. The process was not to 'diarize' each experience, but to select a set of photographs that were representative of them. Participants could choose to take photographs individually or as a group. A benefit of this approach is encouraging group work as participants negotiate what and how photos are taken (Kaplan and Howes, 2004; Abrahams et al., 2006; Moss et al., 2007). In Carrington et al.'s (2007) research participant photographs were displayed on classroom notice boards allowing discussion with fellow students about which best represented their collective ideas. This approach offers a 'public' and collective production of images (as opposed to an individualized photo diary) where what is displayed has significance (although not necessarily in the same way) for all group members.

POSSIBILITIES AND LIMITS OF PHOTO METHODS IN EDUCATION

Particular types of educational research appear more readily drawn to photo methods as a consequence of its perceived possibilities and limits. Often this research has a social justice agenda and is focused on implementing change. Photo methods are popular in studies of educational inclusion and exclusion where the aim is to engender the former (Carrington et al., 2007; Kaplan et al., 2007; Moss et al., 2007; Prosser and Loxley, 2007; Wright et al., 2010). A social change agenda is apparent in photo method research concerning student safety (Abrahams et al., 2006), supporting student success (Marquez-Zenkov, 2007) and increasing educational participation (Dean, 2007). This capacity for social action is presumed possible by the way 'the camera is a distancing object' (Radley and Taylor, 2003, p. 97). Taking a photo of something can bridge the flow of everyday experience, encouraging critical reflection about taken-for-granted practices. In this way, photo methods can help create a social conscience and stimulate social action. Foster-Fishman et al. (2005) suggest that photo methods can have intervention-like impacts for participants, such as increased self-competence, emergent critical awareness of one's environment and the cultivation of resources for social and political action (Foster-Fishman et al., 2005, p. 281).

Another reason photo methods have proved attractive to educational researchers is because participants can wield authority over the content and composition of images. According to Pink (2001) 'visual methodologies have the potential to challenge existing approaches' by inviting participants to 'tell their stories' in ways they have literally 'framed' (p. 10). This increased agency and opportunity to speak for themselves is thought to help diminish traditional power imbalances between researcher and participant (Phoenix, 2010). I employed participant generated photo diaries in my research because it seemed commensurate with a critical youth studies perspective concerned with centring and prioritizing young people's concerns (Allen, 2009b). Giving young people disposable cameras to take photos of how they learned about sexuality at school enabled them to decide what they deemed important.

Whether photo methods can successfully give participants 'voice' and reduce unequal research relations is contentious (Piper and Frankham, 2007). While young people in my research were able to exercise agency in relation to the research task (see Allen, 2008) the potential for addressing researcher/participant power imbalances was curtailed by ethics committee regulations. Concern that young people would use cameras inappropriately meant restrictions were placed on what photos they could take and where (for example, only in places of normal public access and no naked body parts). The effect was to erode young people's agency to tell their story in their own way (Allen, 2009a). Packard (2008) offers a similar caution about photo methods as 'the cure-all' for research power imbalances. In his study of homeless people in Tennesse a participatory photo method was implemented as 'a tool of empowerment enabling those with little money, power or status to communicate' (Hurworth, 2003 p. 3). However, because homeless participants were unused to operating cameras and 'being heard', the method's power-levelling potential was unrealized. One participant, for instance, obscured information in his images often by catching his thumb in frame, because he didn't want to ask for help using the camera. For this participant, 'feelings of shame and embarrassment' about his photo skills inhibited him from communicating his perspective (Packard, 2008, p. 71). Packard concludes that 'the main strength of my method – giving voice to the voiceless – was undermined because of the extreme marginality of my participants' (Packard, 2008, p. 74).

Another challenge for photo methods can be gaining ethics committee approval and access to schools. Fears that cameras are more 'exposing' and therefore 'dangerous' than text-based methods can engender reluctance to sanction their use (Prosser and Loxley, 2007; Pauwels, 2010). It took seven months to gain ethics approval for my project around the sexual cultures of schooling (for details see Allen, 2009a). Several schools refused participation on the grounds that the research was 'too risky'. A number of high profile media cases involving students taking photos on mobile phones and distributing them via the internet had preceded my fieldwork (Netsafe, 2005). These had resulted in some schools enforcing strict rules around camera phones and punishing students for inappropriate use. Using cameras in research was subsequently perceived as too perilous and as undermining school authority. Potential negative publicity from the study and an increase in workload for teachers fielding parental questions about it were also a disincentive to participate. This risk-adverse and image-conscious context of schooling can make it more difficult for photo methods to be sanctioned and operationalized.

Assigning anonymity to photographed subjects can be another dilemma. Warping or cropping images offers one way to protect participant anonymity but can have undesired effects. In a bid to abide by ethics committee regulations around anonymity, participants in my research (Allen, in press) often took photos that removed identifying features such as an individual's face. Instances of 'head cropping' resulted in body shots (that is, of a female student's chest only) which ironically had the objectifying and sexualizing effect the ethics committee wanted to avoid (Allen, 2009a). Researchers have noted other attempts at maintaining anonymity, such as face blurring, can dehumanize the subject and interfere with the photographer's intended meaning (Pole, 2007).

CONCLUSION

Most photo method research undertaken by educationalists is not located in educational journals, but in visual sociology (O'Donoghue, 2007 as an example). The aim of this chapter has been to address this phenomenon by drawing together photo method research within the field of education. Given that use of photo methods as a data collection technique is relatively new in education, it is hoped this chapter ignites a broader and more in-depth conversation amongst educationalists about their use. While this chapter has sketched some of the contours and concerns of photo methods in educational research some important issues have not been addressed. To realize the full potential of photo methods it is imperative to be able to articulate what photo data 'means'. One of the key questions left unanswered by this chapter and with which those who employ photo methods must grapple is how to analyse images and their relationship to text (see Chaplin, 2005; Piper and Frankham, 2007; Pink, 2007; Rose, 2007; Allen, in press; Reader, Chapter 30, this volume).

REFERENCES

Abrahams, N., Mathews, S. and Ramela, P. (2006), 'Intersections of sanitation, sexual coercion and girls' safety in schools', *Tropical Medicine and International Health*, 11 (5), 751–6.

Allan, A. (2005), 'Using photographic diaries to research the gender and academic identities of young girls', in G. Troman, B. Jeffrey and G. Walford (eds), *Methodological Issues and Practices in Ethnography* (Studies in Educational Ethnography), Oxford: Elsevier, pp. 19–36.

Allen, L. (2008), 'Young people's agency in sexuality research using visual methods', *Journal of Youth Studies*, 11 (6), 565–78.

Allen, L. (2009a), '"Caught in the act": ethics committee review and researching the sexual culture of schools', *Qualitative Research*, 9 (4), 395–410.

Allen, L. (2009b), '"Snapped": researching the sexual culture of schools using visual methods', *International Journal of Qualitative Studies in Education*, 22 (5), 549–61.

Allen, L. (in press), 'The camera never lies?: Analysing photographs in research on sexualities and schooling', *Discourse: Studies in the Cultural Politics of Education*.

Banks, M. (2001), *Visual Methods in Social Research*, London: Sage.

Bateson, G. and Mead, M. (1942), *Balinese Character: A Photographic Analysis*, New York: New York Academy of Sciences.

Baudrillard, J. (1988), *Selected Writings*, Cambridge: Polity Press.

Becker, H. (2002), 'Visual evidence: a Seventh Man, the specified generalization, and the work of the reader', *Visual Studies*, 17, 3–11.

Berger, J. (1977), *Ways of Seeing*, London: Penguin.

Carrington, S., Allen, K. and Osmolowski, D. (2007), 'Visual narrative; a technique to enhance secondary students' contribution to the development of inclusive, socially just school environments – lessons from a box of crayons', *Journal of Research in Special Educational Needs*, 7 (1), 8–15.

Chaplin, E. (1994), *Sociology and Visual Representation*, London: Routledge.

Chaplin, E. (2005), 'The photograph in theory', *Sociological Research Online*, 10 (1), 1–37.

Clark-Ibanez, M. (2004), 'Framing the social world with photo-elicitation interviews', *American Behavioral Scientist*, **47** (12), 1507–27.

Collier, J. (1967), *Visual Anthropology: Photography as a Research Method*, New York: Holt, Rinehart and Winston.

Crilly, N., Blackwell, A. and Clarkson, J. (2006), 'Graphic elicitation: using research diagrams as interview stimuli', *Qualitative Research*, **6** (3), 341–66.

Croghan, R., Griffin, C., Hunter, J. and Phoenix, A. (2008), 'Young people's constructions of self: notes on the use and analysis of the photo-elicitation methods', *International Journal of Social Research Methodology*, **11** (4), 345–56.

Dean, C. (2007), 'Young travellers and the Children's Fund: some practical notes on an experimental image-based research project', *Journal of Research in Special Educational Needs*, **7** (1), 16–22.

Dixon, M. (2008), 'Images of teacher and student positionings: storylines from speech acts to body acts', in J. Moss (ed.), *Researching Education: Visually – Digitally – Spatially*, Rotterdam: Sense Rotterdam, pp. 87–106.

Edensor, T. (2005), *Industrial Ruins: Space, Aesthetics and Modernity*, Oxford: Berg.

Emmison, M. and Smith, P. (2000), *Researching the Visual: Images, Objects, Contexts and Interactions in Social and Cultural Inquiry*, London: Sage.

Fischman, G. (2001), 'Reflections about images, visual culture and educational research', *Educational Researcher*, **30** (28), 28–33.

Foster-Fishman, P., Nowell, B., Deacon, Z., Nievar, M. and McCann, P. (2005), 'Using methods that matter: the impact of reflection, dialogue and voice', *American Journal of Community Psychology*, **36** (3–4), 275–91.

Foucault, M. (1976), *The History of Sexuality, Volume 1*, trans. R. Hurley, Harmondsworth: Penguin.

Hansen-Ketchum, P. and Myrick, F. (2008), 'Photo methods for qualitative research in nursing: an ontological and epistemological perspective', *Nursing Philosophy*, **9**, 205–13.

Holliday, R. (2004), 'Reflecting the self', in C. Knowles and P. Sweetman (eds), *Picturing the Social Landscape: Visual Methods and the Sociological Imagination*, London: Routledge, pp. 49–64.

Hurdley, R. (2007), 'Focal points: framing material culture and visual data', *Qualitative Research*, **7** (3), 355–74.

Hurworth, R. (2003), 'Photo-interviewing for research', *Social Research Update*, **40**, 1–4.

Ingram, T. (2011), 'Negotiating girlhood: girls' understanding of themselves as sexual subjects', Unpublished Master's Thesis, Faculty of Education, University of Auckland.

Jones, A. (ed.) (2001), *Touchy Subject: Teachers Touching Children*, Dunedin: Otago University Press.

Kaplan, I. and Howes, A. (2004), '"Seeing through different eyes": exploring the value of participative research using images in schools', *Cambridge Journal of Education*, **34** (2), 143–55.

Kaplan, I., Lewis, I. and Mumba, P. (2007), 'Picturing global educational inclusion? Looking and thinking across students' photographs from the UK, Zambia and Indonesia', *Journal of Research in Special Educational Needs*, **7** (1), 23–35.

Knowles, C. and Sweetman, P. (2004), *Picturing the Social Landscape: Visual Methods and the Sociological Imagination*, London: Routledge.

Mahruf, M., Shohel, C. and Howes, A. (2007), 'Transition from nonformal schools: learning through photoelicitation in educational fieldwork in Bangladesh', *Visual Studies*, **22** (1), 53–61.

Margolis, E. (2007), 'Special issue on education', *Visual Studies*, **22** (1), 1–12.

Marquez-Zenkov, K. (2007), 'Through city students' eyes: urban students' beliefs about school's purposes, supports and impediments', *Visual Studies*, **22** (2), 138–54.

Mitchell, W. (1987), *Iconology*, Chicago, IL: University of Chicago Press.

Moss, J., Deppeler, J., Astley, L. and Pattison, K. (2007), 'Student researchers in the middle: using visual images to make sense of inclusive education', *Journal of Research in Special Education Needs*, **7** (1), 46–54.

Netsafe, The Internet Safety Group (2005), 'The text generation mobile phones and New Zealand youth: a report of results from the Internet Safety Group's Survey of teenage mobile phone use', available from http://www.netsafe.org.nz (accessed 7 September 2011).

O'Donoghue, D. (2007), '"James always hangs out here": making space for place in studying masculinities at school', *Visual Studies*, **22** (1), 62–73.

Packard, J. (2008), '"I'm gonna show you what it's really like out here": the power and limitation of participatory visual methods', *Visual Studies*, **23** (1), 63–77.

Pauwels, L. (2010), 'Visual sociology reframed: an analytical synthesis and discussion of visual methods in social and cultural research', *Sociological Methods and Research*, **38** (4), 545–81.

Phoenix, C. (2010), 'Seeing the world of physical culture: the potential of visual methods for qualitative research in sport and exercise', *Qualitative Research in Sport and Exercise*, **2** (2), 93–108.

Pink, S. (2001), *Doing Visual Ethnography*, 1st edn, London: Sage.

Pink, S. (2007), *Doing Visual Ethnography: Images, Media and Representation in Research*, 2nd edn, London: Sage.

Piper, H. and Frankham, J. (2007), 'Seeing voices and hearing pictures: image as discourse and the framing of image-based research', *Discourse: Studies in the Cultural Politics of Education*, **28** (3), 373–87.

Pole, C. (2007), 'Researching children and fashion: an embodied ethnography', *Childhood*, **14** (1), 67–84.

Prosser, J. and Loxley, A. (2007), 'Enhancing the contribution of visual methods to inclusive education', *Journal of Research in Special Educational Needs*, **7** (1), 55–68.

Radley, A. and Taylor, D. (2003), 'Images of recovery: a photo-elicitation study of the hospital ward', *Qualitative Health Research*, **13** (1), 77–99.

Rose, G. (2007), *Visual Methodologies: An Introduction to the Interpretation of Visual Materials*, 2nd edn, London: Sage.

Thomson, P. (2008), 'Children and young people: voices in visual research', in P. Thomson (ed.), *Doing Visual Research with Children and Young People*, Oxon: Routledge, pp. 1–20.

Walker, R. (1997), 'Finding a silent voice for the researcher: using photographs in evaluation and research', in M. Schratz (ed.), *Qualitative Voices in Educational Research*, London: The Falmer Press, pp. 72–93.

Warburton, T. (1998), 'Cartoons and teachers: mediated visual images as data', in J. Prosser (ed.), *Image-based Research: A Sourcebook for Qualitative Researchers*, London: Routledge Falmer, pp. 252–62.

White, A., Bushin, N., Carpena-Mendez, F. and Ni Laoire, C. (2010), 'Using visual methods to explore contemporary Irish childhoods', *Qualitative Research*, **10** (2), 143–58.

Wright, C., Darko, N., Standen, P. and Patel, T. (2010), 'Visual research methods: using cameras to empower socially excluded black youth', *Sociology of Health and Illness*, **44** (3), 541–58.

18. Mobile methods
Margarethe Kusenbach

INTRODUCTION

Research based on so-called mobile methods promises innovative insights into issues of identity, interaction, structure, and power within modern bureaucracies. However, to my knowledge, mobile methods – meaning techniques of data collection during which researchers move alongside participants – have yet to be used and reflected upon in the field of education. Nonetheless, there are mobile studies of children and youth (for example, Hall, 2009; Ross et al., 2009) and discussions of mobile methods in related fields (such as social work, cf. Ferguson, 2011) which might give education researchers some initial directions. In what follows, I provide a general overview of mobile methods research in order to familiarize education students and scholars with this new and original methodological trend.

Currently, several dozen scholarly publications based on and about mobile methods are available on the academic market. Those include several books (Bærenholdt et al., 2004; Czarniawska, 2007; Elliott and Urry, 2010; also see Pink, 2009a), a good number of journal articles and chapters (see below), as well as various dissertations and research reports which are not mentioned in this overview. Three edited volumes specifically devoted to mobile methods (Ingold and Vergunst, 2008; Fincham et al., 2009; Büscher et al., 2011), the quarterly Routledge journal *Mobilities*, and the last 2010 issue of the journal *Visual Studies* also include many relevant pieces. Academic work on mobile methods has been conducted and published in both North America (USA and Canada) and Europe (predominantly in the UK). Contributors are notably interdisciplinary and include sociologists, geographers, scholars in transportation, health, and social work, as well as representatives of cultural disciplines.

The subject of interest is quite new, less than ten years old. While there are some 'classic' examples of scholars using, in effect, mobile methods in the twentieth century (for example, Lynch, 1960; Kozol, 1995), systematic applications and reflections from a methodological point of view are more recent, with the earliest articles of this sort surfacing in 2003 and 2004 (Kusenbach, 2003; Anderson, 2004; Ingold, 2004). The dynamic and sprawling nature of the field makes it difficult to summarize with some authority. And because I am one of the early contributors, my views may differ from the ones of others who are fellow members of the quickly growing mobile methods community.

BACKGROUND

I begin by briefly sketching the academic milieus that gave rise to the interest in mobile methods. Two contexts are especially noteworthy in this respect, (a) the Mobilities Paradigm, and (b) qualitative researchers' interest in phenomenology and methodological innovation.

The Mobilities Paradigm

Over a series of publications, UK-based scholars John Urry, Monika Büscher, Mimi Sheller, and Katian Witchger have sketched out the contours of a new Mobilities Paradigm which, in turn, is rooted in the broadly proclaimed 'Spatial Turn' in the social sciences. Put simply, the Mobilities Paradigm draws theoretical and empirical attention to the many forms of travel that characterize modern societies: movements of people, goods and objects, images, ideas, and communication in general. The substantial increase of these mobilities is, in part, a result of new technologies and other innovations and, in part, due to a general expansion of human networks and social systems. As social life and societies become more mobile, social scientists are well advised to develop new forms of research and representation that appropriately reflect this change, giving rise to what is often called mobile methods (Sheller and Urry, 2006).

At its best, mobility research sheds new light on issues of power and social structure. According to its founders, the Mobilities Paradigm signifies an ideological trend away from longstanding 'sedentary' tendencies in academia, in theory as well as in research. Mobility researchers take a position against static world views defined by territorialism, nationalism, and immobile structures, and move towards developing perspectives that transcend disciplinary and geographical borders, and that prioritize dynamism and social change.

In a somewhat critical article, Hall (2009) points out that the increased mobility proposed by the new paradigm does not erode the importance of place. It could even be that new mobilities amplify the significance and awareness of the local. Hall (2009, p. 575) further explains that, ironically, 'staying put, as any fieldworker can tell you, involves moving around.' He thereby draws attention to everyday spatial routines which may have not changed as dramatically as other movements, and which are not the primary focus of mobility researchers – even though they acknowledge that not everything is on the move, and that it is also important to investigate patterns of access and exclusion.

Phenomenology and Methodological Innovation

Many scholars contemplating and using mobile methods draw on the works of phenomenologically minded philosophers (for example, Casey, 1993), geographers (Relph, 1976; Tuan, 1976), sociologists (Georg Simmel; Michel de Certeau), and others who have emphasized the importance, and even primacy, of the spatial environment in human experience and social life. Casey (2001, p. 684), for instance, speaks of a 'constitutive coingredience' of self and place and claims that 'each is essential to the being of the other.' The argument goes that if place and environment are fundamental features in human experience and social life, they have to play an integral part in scholarly investigations and representations of these matters.

Phenomenologically informed critiques often discuss the limits of 'traditional' qualitative methods such as observation and interviewing (Kusenbach, 2003; Carpiano, 2009). On the one hand, ethnographers have pondered the shortcomings of the observational method, for instance, in comparison with interviews (Kleinman et al., 1994). Ethnography is increasingly understood as a multi-sited (Marcus 1995; Duneier, 1999) or even global (Burawoy et al., 2000) enterprise requiring researchers to move around and go where the flow of the field takes them (see Chapter 3, this volume, for more details on mobile ethnography). It might be high time to replace the early twentieth-century metaphor of the 'dirty pants,' from sitting on street corners, with one involving 'shoe leather' (Duneier, 2004) as central to the work of ethnographers.

On the other hand, qualitative researchers who predominantly use interviews have lamented the lack of 'emplacement' of this method, leading them to include detailed observations of what Elswood and Martin (2000) have called the 'micro-geographies' of interviews (cf. also Sin, 2003; Brown and Durrheim, 2009; Riley, 2010). The result is a trend toward more dynamic and place-sensitive interviewing techniques. Jones et al. (2008, p. 8) note that mobile interviewing provides 'a means to take the interviewing process out of the "safe" confines of the interview room and allow the environment and the act of walking itself to move the collection of interview data in productive and sometimes entirely unexpected directions.' In short, interest in innovative and phenomenologically sensitive forms of data collection was building up in various methodological contexts. The outlined critiques met in the development of hybrid mobile methods that include elements of both observations and interviews, as well as new procedures and technologies.

Going beyond these two fields of origin, Büscher and Urry (2009), Hein et al. (2008), Sheller and Urry (2006), and others discuss additional contexts that have undoubtedly spurred an interest in mobile methods: theories of the body, science and technology studies, social network theories, and other approaches not described in this overview. Lastly, some advocates of mobile methods were inspired by historical and literary scholars such as Walter Benjamin (Jenks and Neves, 2000) or by contemporary artists such as Sophie Calle. There are also films and other works of high and popular culture that have stimulated the creative development of mobile research methods (for example, Pink et al., 2010).

DEFINITION

The term mobile methods is currently used as a label for a wide variety of research activities, and the goal of this section is to develop a crisp definition of the term.

In the interest of precision, I suggest that the term mobile methods be reserved for 'methods of participating in patterns of movement while conducting research' (Büscher et al., 2011, p. 8), and that a more inclusive concept, for instance, mobility methods, be applied to other technologies and techniques named and described by John Urry and his colleagues throughout several publications. Such a focused understanding of the term harmonizes with Hein's conception of mobile methods as instances where 'research subject and researcher are in motion in the 'field'' (Hein et al., 2008, p. 1276). Further, it capitalizes on Marcus's (1995) idea of 'following the people' as one strategy of doing multi-sited ethnography.

At this point in time, mobile methods are overwhelmingly qualitative which means these techniques produce intensive, non-numerical data sets. Mobile methods are tools for describing and understanding, rather than for explaining and predicting, patterns of human travel. Material aids and technologies (such as maps, photographs, GIS, GPS) certainly can be used in supportive and creative ways while researchers follow people, yet their use alone does not constitute a mobile method.

Building on these initial clarifications, I further define mobile methods as research techniques displaying the following five characteristics: they are (a) person centered, (b) interactive, (c) data set driven, (d) metaphoric, and (e) place based.

Mobile Methods are Person Centered

The primary goal of the use of mobile methods is to understand and theorize aspects of human experience and social action, thus issues that always originate with socialized individuals, or persons. Mobile methods researchers are interested in objects and environments, and in objectified structures, only inasmuch as they become part of individual or social experiences, or, in other words, as they are bestowed with meaning.

Mobile Methods are Interactive

Mobile methods researchers interact with those being researched. These interactions best occur face-to-face, in real time and place, in what Sheller and Urry (2006, p. 218) have called 'co-present immersion.' Mediated interactions are not unthinkable, yet they typically do not produce the same depths of data and insights. Stated otherwise, mobile methods are ethnographic methods in which social interactions and personal relationships are critical instruments of data collection (Coffey, 1999).

Mobile Methods are Data Set Driven

They seek to assemble a cohesive set of data. The richness of the data lies in the density and diversity of other people's reconstructed experiences. Similar to interview studies, mobile methods require a systematic 'sampling' of participants, followed by the repetition of a relatively focused research activity with each. This is different from gaining ethnographic entry into a field, and it goes beyond episodes of 'hanging out' with a small number of key informants that typically occur in fieldwork.

Mobile Methods are Metaphoric

At their best, mobile researchers develop a metaphoric understanding of mobility: they register phenomena that transcend the mechanics of physical bodies in material environments. As people move through their everyday rounds, they engage in both mundane and significant 'metamorphoses' of the self (Katz, 1999). Mobile methods allow glimpses into how people experience and navigate symbolic personal and social landscapes as well as natural and built environments.

Mobile Methods are Place Based

This means that mobile methods practitioners view place and environment as important, indeed essential, aspects of human experience. Participants in mobile methods not only face each other but they also unite in facing a third dimension, the outside world. Or, to say it with Hall (2009, p. 582), mobile researchers engage in 'three way conversations.' The social geographer Seamon (1979) suggested that human engagement with the environment unfolds on an 'awareness continuum' spanning between separation at the one end and complete mergence at the other. Mobile methods produce insights into the qualities of such engagement, of Casey's 'coingredience' of selves and places.

Methods displaying the above qualities go by many names, including 'bimbling,' 'participation while walking,' 'walking probes,' and 'mobile narratives.' The ones I find most useful are the older 'go along' and the newer 'shadowing,' because of their freshness and brevity, and because they do not limit the alongside mode of mobility to walking only. However, more important than finding the ultimate name is the conceptual distinction of two basic types of mobile methods, which, for now, I call 'trails' and 'tours.'

TRAILS AND TOURS

Trails

I define trails as 'natural' go alongs (Kusenbach, 2003, p. 463), or as instances of what Czarniawska (2007) and Jirón (2011) call 'shadowing,' meaning examinations of mobile activities that existed before researchers entered the scene and will continue to exist after researchers depart. The bulk of human mobility is composed of predictable and regular local outings, such as commuting to work or school, walking the dog, shopping for food, or seeking sociability and entertainment, and many of these outings can be trailed quite easily.

An intensive use of trails can be found in the work of Jirón (2007, 2011), who engaged in extended natural observations of people in Santiago de Chile while following them from home to work and back over the course of an entire day. Shadowing periods were accompanied by extensive interviews which Jirón conducted before and after her days in the field. In a recent study, Hall (2009) followed social outreach workers around in the city of Cardiff, UK. He sought to understand how these workers find needy people and 'read clues' of their presence in the environment. Riley

(2010) also used trails in his interviews with farmers, accomplished while he accompanied them as they fed their animals and tended to other duties. Lastly, Anderson (2004) used more or less natural go alongs during spontaneous walks with his social activist subjects.

Tours

In contrast, tours are 'contrived' or 'experimental' go alongs (Kusenbach, 2003, p. 464). Until several years ago, I was unsure which insights tours could provide into everyday social realities in comparison with trails, yet I became deeply impressed by the sophistication of tour-based studies conducted within the last few years. My most recent study of mobile home communities in Florida therefore included systematic go alongs of the tour type for better comparison, instead of more natural yet difficult-to-analyse trails.

One issue that shall not complicate the basic distinction is the fact that tours can be first-order phenomena. Some people give tours all the time, most obviously those who are doing it for money. Lately, tour professionals have garnered the scholarly attention of researchers utilizing mobile methods (Farias, 2010; Wynn, 2011). Yet natural tours are not limited to professionals, as they often occur in informal social contexts as well. According to DeLeon and Cohen (2005, p. 203), it is crucial that tours follow informants to environments and places that have personal meaning to them. The task then is to 'simply . . . walk around and encourage the informant to talk about past and current associations with the physical surroundings.'

There are many interesting examples of tours of which I can only mention a few. Carpiano (2009) provides a very insightful discussion of his use of neighborhood tours while examining health issues in a low income community. Jones et al. (2008) report on their experimenting with different types of tours while following subjects into urban environments. Further, Pink (2009b) describes a series of tours given to her by employees and activists of Flintshire, a town in Wales which is a member of the 'slow city' movement. Lastly, Hall (2009) reports on the mobile narratives of young people whom researchers accompanied to places that were important to the youth.

In short, in the literature, tours range from unstructured prompts to walk around, over participant planned and led visits of one or more significant places, to fixed routes designed by researchers who then prompt subjects to follow them. In other words, tours fluctuate between highly controlled and experimental events on the one hand, and almost natural outings on the other, depending on the degree of planning and intervention by the researchers before and while they engage participants.

ISSUES AND CHOICES

When using mobile methods, researchers have important issues and choices to consider. One vital consideration concerns the mode of transportation while following people. There currently is a bias toward walking as the most commonly used mobile method (for example, Lee and Ingold, 2006). Even though some of the advantages of walking are obvious (it is slow, easy, flexible), other forms of natural, or slightly arranged, travel need not be excluded from mobile research approaches (Kusenbach, 2003). A notable exception is the work of Eric Laurier (Laurier, 2004; Laurier et al., 2008) on everyday driving, yet there are many other vehicles (from wheelchairs over subways to airplanes) and movements that present nearly uncharted territories and opportunities for mobile researchers.

Second, there is the question of how researchers engage subjects in talk and reflection while following them around. Approaches here can range from using highly structured interview guides to completely open conversations with no or few prompts by the investigator. Most mobile researchers prefer a hybrid approach in which they ask some questions yet leave plenty of room for participant-initiated talk. Depending on the researchers' goals and preferences, mobile methods can therefore resemble unstructured field observations as well as relatively structured interviews. There is no right choice, of course, yet it is important to reflect on the type of data, as well as the omissions, that result from the decisions that have been made regarding the structure and rigidity of one's approach.

A third important issue which has not received sufficient attention in the past (for exceptions see Jones et al., 2008; Carpiano, 2009) is the question of adequate documentation (see Chapter 36, this volume, for details on writing and analysing observational fieldnotes). Practitioners of mobile methods need a system of recording their movements, observations, and conversations. Records of spatial activities need to be synchronized with records of conversations, and talk needs to be spatialized or geo-coded, in order to allow for maximum insights. Researchers have begun experimenting with combinations of mobile methods and new technologies (such as GIS and GPS) that go beyond paper and pencil, voice recorder and camera (for example, Pink, 2007). Hein and colleagues (2008, p. 1280) correctly note that 'mobile methods represent an almost unique opportunity to explore cutting edge theory and technology simultaneously.' Much remains to be discovered and accomplished in these respects.

A fourth and, for now, last issue of importance is the question of triangulation. How can we best combine mobile methods with other data collection techniques? How can we compare and integrate the resulting multiple data sets? Ultimately, questions regarding triangulation are questions about epistemology. What kind of knowledge do mobile data sets represent or produce? How should we evaluate this knowledge in relation to other kinds of evidence and insight? The literature features initial, interesting steps toward methodological mixing and integration (for example, Carpiano, 2009; Jirón, 2011), yet these and other questions regarding triangulation demand further consideration in the future.

CONCLUSION

I begin this final section by briefly considering the limitations and advantages of mobile methods. Carpiano (2009) already offers an excellent discussion of the pros and cons that I shall not replicate here.

First, there are limitations. Like any social research method, mobile methods are limited by thematic, practical, and interpersonal aspects. Thematically, in order for mobile methods to gain traction, research subjects must display a minimal degree of environmental engagement (Seamon, 1979), something routinely occurring when people are on the move. Such engagement may also be evident during less mobile and even stationary activities, such as waiting for the bus, eating, talking on the phone, or perhaps even watching TV or a movie. Yet mobile methods are not useful for a study of meditation. On the other hand, subjects' engagement with the environment must allow for third-party observation and leave some room for conversation and reflection. Some mobile activities (for example, extreme sports) might be too engaging, too dangerous, or too private to be studied via the methods described here.

Next, there are important practical circumstances – including lighting conditions, weather and temperature, physical access, and bodily capabilities – which may limit research subjects, researchers, or both in their ability to engage in mobile research. The idea of employing mobile methods to investigate, for instance, walking routines of seniors in Chicago during the winter, or in Miami during the summer, is a bad one, for obvious reasons.

Lastly, there are social complexities which may diminish the utility of mobile methods. Mobile methods are, in essence, social interactions embedded in larger fieldwork relationships (Coffey, 1999). In order for these relationships to work, researchers and subjects must have a positive connection, and they must be willing and able to communicate in meaningful ways. As with all methods, mobile methods require understanding and consent from research participants, and a commitment by researchers to avoid or minimize harm. Generally speaking, the conditions for the successful use of mobile methods do not differ much from the ones of studies based on either observations or interviews. Yet because mobile methods combine elements of both, there might be more topics and situations that pose limits to their application.

I can only touch upon the most notable advantages and opportunities of mobile methods here. One entirely positive aspect of mobile methods is their ability to build bridges to, and rapport with, research participants who might not be as easy to recruit otherwise. Going along with someone creates a 'distinct sociability' (Lee and Ingold, 2006) – a special connection resulting from sharing space, time, and experience – that helps researchers forge positive relationships with others, especially with those who are socially different from themselves (Carpiano, 2009).

The second and probably most important advantage of mobile methods over either lonely observations or sit down interviews is the access they provide to otherwise unnoticed or distorted aspects and patterns of individual and social life. For instance, mobile methods offer unique and powerful views into routine perceptions and movements, personal biographies, as well as into community social structure and culture (Kusenbach, 2003). The general point is that, when used sensibly, mobile methods can provide scholarly knowledge that is 'truer to life' (Hall 2009, p. 582). Anderson (2004, p. 58) emphasizes their potential for discovery in explaining that mobile methods help 'excavate levels of meaning both the researcher and researched may theretofore have been unaware of.' Because, unlike in interviews, there is less pressure to fill silences, mobile methods allow exploring 'non-verbalized' knowledge and practices (Riley, 2010). At the minimum, mobile interviewing gives interviewers more time to formulate better questions and follow-ups (Riley, 2010), and it gives ethnographers access to taken-for-granted and non-situational aspects of daily life that simply cannot be observed.

A third major advantage is that mobile methods are typically more participatory and democratic than other qualitative methods in allowing research subjects to set important parameters of the research. Because they engage participants where they 'already are' and encourage reflection, mobile methods have the potential of initiating or advancing personal growth and social change (Carpiano, 2009). They can be incorporated productively in applied research designs and therefore have the potential of making a difference in public opinion and policy. In sum, mobile methods have characteristics that make them suitable tools of a public and engaged social science.

In closing, while mobile methods are an active and productive methodological subfield, we are far away from reaching, or even under-standing, their full potential in social research. Much exciting conceptual and empirical work remains to be done. For instance, one innovative suggestion (Carpiano, 2009) is the fusion of focus groups and mobile methods into something like 'focus group tours.' Another promising future expansion would be the use of mobile methods to explore how people navigate 'social' territories and regions of the self – meaning step-ping away from mobile methods as a tool of physical mobility research, toward a creative adaption of this tool in research on identity, relation-ships, institutions, and social structures within other subfields of sociol-ogy. What I find most promising is the apparent ability of mobile methods to spark exchanges between typically (more or less) disconnected groups of social scientists, such as Europeans and North Americans; senior and junior scholars; members of different disciplines such as sociology, geog-raphy, and cultural studies; proponents of interpretive, critical, and post-modern approaches; and so on. And I also hope that the incorporation of new technologies in mobile methods research will help topple the stifling barrier that continues to divide qualitative and quantitative methods of social research.

REFERENCES

Anderson, J. (2004), 'Talking whilst walking: a geographical archeology of knowledge', *Area* **36** (3), 254–61.
Bærenholdt, J.E., Haldrup, M., Larsen, J. and Urry, J. (2004), *Performing Tourist Places*, Aldershot, UK: Ashgate.
Brown, L. and Durrheim, K. (2009), 'Different kinds of knowing: generating qualitative data through mobile interviewing', *Qualitative Inquiry*, **15** (5), 911–30.
Burawoy, M. Blum, J.A., George, S. et al. (2000), *Global Ethnography*, Berkeley, CA: University of California Press.
Büscher, M. and Urry, J. (2009), 'Mobile methods and the empirical', *European Journal of Social Theory*, **12** (1), 99–116.
Büscher, M. Urry, J. and Witchger, K. (eds) (2011), *Mobile Methods*, New York: Routledge.
Carpiano, R.M. (2009), 'Come take a walk with me: the "go-along" interview as a novel method for studying implications of place for health and well-being', *Health & Place*, **15** (1), 263–72.
Casey, E.S. (1993), *Getting Back Into Place*, Bloomington and Indianapolis, IN: Indiana University Press.
Casey, E.S. (2001), 'Between geography and philosophy: what does it mean to be in the place-world?', *Annals of the Association of American Geographers*, **91** (4), 683–93.
Coffey, A. (1999), *The Ethnographic Self: Fieldwork and the Representation of Identity*, London: Sage.
Czarniawska, B. (2007), *Shadowing and Other Techniques for Doing Fieldwork in Modern Societies*, Malmo, Sweden: Liber.
DeLeon, J.P. and Cohen, J.H. (2005), 'Object and walking probes in ethnographic interview-ing', *Field Methods*, **17** (2), 200–204.
Duneier, M. (1999), *Sidewalk*, New York: Farrar, Straus & Giroux.

Duneier, M. (2004), 'Scrutinizing the heat: on ethnic myths and the importance of shoe leather', *Contemporary Sociology*, **38** (2), 139–50.
Elliott, A. and Urry, J. (2010), *Mobile Lives*, New York: Routledge.
Elswood, S.A. and Martin, D.G. (2000), '"Placing" interviews: location and scales of power in qualitative research', *Professional Geographer*, **52** (4), 649–57.
Farias, I. (2010), 'Sightseeing buses: cruising, timing and the montage of attractions', *Mobilities*, **5** (3), 387–407.
Ferguson, H. (2011), 'Mobilities of welfare: the case of social work,' in M. Buescher, J. Urry and K. Witchger (eds), *Mobile Methods*, New York: Routledge, pp. 72–87.
Fincham, B., McGuiness, M. and Murray, L. (eds) (2009), *Mobile Methodologies*, Basingstoke: Palgrave Macmillan.
Hall, T. (2009), 'Footwork: moving and knowing in local space(s)', *Qualitative Research*, **9** (5), 571–85.
Hein, J.R., Evans, J. and Jones, P. (2008), 'Mobile methodologies: theory, technology, and practice', *Geography Compass*, **2** (5), 1266–85.
Ingold, T. (2004), 'Culture on the ground: the world perceived through the feet', *Journal of Material Culture*, **9** (3), 211–40.
Ingold, T. and Vergunst J.L. (eds) (2008), *Ways of Walking: Ethnography and Practice on Foot*, Aldershot: Ashgate.
Jenks, C. and Neves, T. (2000), 'A walk on the wild side: urban ethnography meets the flaneur', *Cultural Values*, **4** (1), 1–17.
Jirón, P. (2007), 'Unravelling invisible inequalities in the city through urban daily mobility: the case of Santiago de Chile', *Swiss Journal of Sociology*, **33** (1), 45–68.
Jirón, P. (2011), 'On becoming "la sombra/the shadow"', in M. Buescher, J. Urry and K. Witchger (eds), *Mobile Methods*, New York: Routledge, pp. 36–53.
Jones, P., Bunce, G., Evans, J., Gibbs, H. and Hein, J.R. (2008), 'Exploring space and place with walking interviews', *Journal of Research Practice*, **4** (2), Article D, available from http://snp.icaap.org/index.php/jrp/article/view/150/161 (accessed 9 September 2011).
Katz, J. (1999), *How Emotions Work*, Chicago, IL: University of Chicago Press.
Kleinman, S., Stenross, B. and McMahon, M. (1994), 'Privileging fieldwork over interviews: consequences for identity and practice', *Symbolic Interaction*, **17** (1), 37–50.
Kozol, J. (1995), *Amazing Grace: The Lives of Children and the Conscience of a Nation*, New York: Perennial.
Kusenbach, M. (2003), 'Street phenomenology: the go-along as ethnographic research tool', *Ethnography*, **4** (3), 455–85.
Laurier, E. (2004), 'Doing office work on the motorway', *Theory, Culture, Society*, **21** (4–5), 261–77.
Laurier, E. (with 13 other authors) (2008), '"Driving" and "Passengering" notes on the ordinary organization of car travel', *Mobilities*, **3** (1), 1–23.
Lee, J. and Ingold, T. (2006), 'Fieldwork on foot: perceiving, routing, socializing', in S. Coleman and P. Collins (eds), *Locating the Field: Space, Place and Context in Anthropology*, Oxford: Berg, pp. 67–87.
Lynch, K. (1960), *Image of the City*, Cambridge, MA: MIT Press.
Marcus, G.E. (1995), 'Ethnography in/of the world system: the emergence of multi-sited ethnography', *Annual Review of Anthropology*, **24**, 95–117.
Pink, S. (2007), 'Walking with video', *Visual Studies*, **22** (3), 240–52.
Pink, S. (2009a), *Doing Sensory Ethnography*, London: Sage.
Pink, S. (2009b), 'An urban tour', *Ethnography*, **9** (2), 175–96.
Pink, S., Hubbard, P., O'Neill, M. and Radley, A. (2010), 'Walking across disciplines: from ethnography to arts practice', *Visual Studies*, **25** (1), 1–7.
Relph, E.C. (1976), *Place and Placelessness*, London: Pion.
Riley, M. (2010), 'Emplacing the research encounter: exploring farm life histories', *Qualitative Inquiry*, **16** (8), 651–62.
Ross, N.J., Renold, E., Holland, S. and Hillman, A. (2009), 'Moving stories: using mobile

methods to explore the everyday lives of young people in public care', *Qualitative Research*, **9** (5), 605–23.

Seamon, D. (1979), *A Geography of the Life World*, New York: St Martin's Press.

Sheller, M. and Urry, J. (2006), 'The New Mobilities Paradigm', *Environment and Planning A*, **38**, 207–26.

Sin, C.H. (2003), 'Interviewing in "place" the socio-spatial construction of interview data', *Area*, **35** (3), 305–12.

Tuan, Y.F. (1976), *Space and Place*, Minneapolis, MN: University of Minnesota Press.

Wynn, J. (2011), *The Tour Guide: Walking and Talking New York*, Chicago, IL: University of Chicago Press.

19. The uses of life history
William G. Tierney and Randall F. Clemens

Life history has a long, rich tradition in the social and psychological sciences. Scholars have established the method in several disciplines, ranging from the first sociological life history, Thomas and Znaniecki's (1918–20[1958]) *The Polish Peasant in Europe and America*,[1] to the popular psychobiography, Erikson's (1969) *Gandhi's Truth: On the Origins of Militant Nonviolence*. The approach has also appeared in multiple forms. The influential *Son of Old Man Hat* (Left Handed, 1938), for example, is a comprehensive account of one Native American's life, whereas 'Adequate schools and inadequate education: the life history of a sneaky kid' (Wolcott, 1983) is an edited account of one homeless youth's life. The former is composed entirely of the subject's own words whereas the latter contains a mix of the subject's words and the researcher's interpretation and analysis. *Translated Woman* (Behar, 2003) is an experimental life history in format and tone, and Gelya Frank would not even characterize *Venus on Wheels* (2000) as a life history, although its roots and framework spring from life history.

Another important characteristic of life histories is that oftentimes they contain no overt theoretical framework – a tradition beginning with the first texts (see Radin, 1926; Left Handed, 1938). This has been a point of contention for many methodologists, who question the merit and scientific rigor of the approach (Watson and Watson-Franke, 1985). Yet, after nearly a century, the method is experiencing a renaissance as individuals' acknowledge its flexibility and usefulness (Frank, 1995). While the pan-disciplinary nature and ever-evolving form of life history has resulted in definitional debates among methodologists (Denzin, 1989), we suggest these characteristics are a testament to the method's adaptability and the methodologist's creativity. In addition, while we acknowledge critiques that focus on lack of criteria, scientific rigor, and ill-defined uses, critics ought not disavow the method simply because it does not comply with positivist standards (Phillips, 1994; Hatch and Wisniewski, 1995).

In what follows, we address recurring methodological issues, including definitions and uses of life history as well as criteria to judge it. The major focus of the chapter, however, is to provide a brief, accessible introduction to the practical issues of conducting a life history.[2] We focus on four stages of research: design, collection, analysis, and presentation. Our framework is largely anthropological, and we refer to assorted approaches such as semiotics, hermeneutics, phenomenology, ethnomethodology, discourse theory, and symbolic interactionism.

DEFINING LIFE HISTORY

Life history resides within the larger category of narrative research. Narrative research comprises multiple and oftentimes overlapping variations, including autoethnography, biography, cultural biography, life story, oral history, and testimonio.[3] The differences vary from distinct to subtle, and perhaps all can be considered derivations of biography (Smith, 1994).[4]

To illustrate the complexity of defining approaches, we start with the closest relative of life history, life story. Plummer (2001) states that a life story is 'an account of one person's life in his or her own words. Life stories come through many blurred sources: biographies, autobiographies, letters journals, interviews, obituaries' (pp. 18–19). He identifies life story as the approach and biographies and autobiographies as sources. Plummer's definition, 'an account of one person's life in his or her own words,' is considerably general.

Atkinson (2001) adds to the above definition: 'A life story is the story a person chooses to tell about the life he or she has lived, told as completely and honestly as possible, what the person remembers of it and what he or she wants others to know of it, usually as a result of a guided interview by another' (p. 125). Most notably, he inserts the interviewer into the process. At this point, a simple definition of life history, an 'account of a life based on interviews and conversations' (Denzin, 1989, p. 48), may help to emphasize the challenge of categorization. We hope the similarities between 'story' and 'history' are obvious; when catalogued and compared the differences between the two become more a matter of word choice than a generalizable rule (Frank, 2000).

The terms life story and history are seldom distinct. To one researcher, biography, life story, and life history may be perfect synonyms; to another, interchanging the terms may indicate methodological laziness. In contemplation of seemingly minute, but important, issues, the researcher's awareness of his or her own position becomes paramount. Consider, for example, Peacock and Holland's (1993) explanation for selecting life 'story' over 'history': 'Rather than "life-history," we prefer the term "life story." By "life story" is meant simply the story of someone's life. For our purposes, "story" is preferable to "history" because it does not connote that the narration is true, that the events narrated necessarily happened, or that it matters whether they did or not' (p. 368). When approaches are contested and problematized, the duty to express clearly a methodological stance falls on the researcher. Whether a person selects life story or history, he or she needs to communicate a specific definition of the approach and its place in a broader constellation of definitions.

Our definition builds on three well-known articulations of the method:

1. 'Life history will be used in this book to refer to an extensive record of a person's life as it is reported either by the person himself or by others or both, and whether it is written or in interviews or both' (Langness, 1965, p. 4).
2. 'The life history, like the autobiography, presents the subject from his own perspective. It differs from the autobiography in that it is an immediate response to a demand posed by an Other and carries within it the expectations of that Other. It is, as it were, doubly edited, during the encounter itself and during the literary re-encounter' (Crapanzano, 2009, p. 4).
3. 'Life histories are distinguished from biographies in fields other than anthropology such as history or literature by choice of subject (usually ordinary people, rather than public figures, often nonliterate members of traditional societies, ethnic minorities, or urban sub-cultures); by fieldwork methods involving face-to-face interaction (collaboration with a living subject through interviews that are usually tape-recorded and transcribed and the use of observations and sometimes personal documents, such as diaries or historical records); and formal attention to topics of theoretical interest in the discipline (such as how individuals acquire a particular cultural, gender, or political identity)' (Frank, 1996, p. 705).

All three definitions provide logical starting points. Langness (1965) offers a basic definition, similar to the previous definitions of life story. Crapanzano (2009) displays his anthropological roots as well as a turn towards the post-modern. He discusses not only the expectation of the other but also the joint process of construction. Lastly, Frank (1996) provides the most technical definition and the need for a theoretical framework.

We present a composite of all three definitions with the addition of some features garnered from practical experience. Hence, life history is a dynamic and recursive process between researcher and participant. The two parties jointly construct a narrative via multiple data sources, including interviews and documents. Data collection and analysis occur simultaneously wherein the researcher develops and tests codes, categories, and theories. The final document is a contextually bound representation of the life of the participant along with his or her relationship with the researcher. In addition, the explicit inclusion of theory, analysis, and inter-pretation is not necessary in the life historical product; however, in order to improve scientific rigor, the researcher needs to have systematically and exhaustively fulfilled and documented every step of the research process (Guba, 1981; Lincoln and Guba, 1985).

FOUNDATIONAL EXAMPLES OF LIFE HISTORY

Before proceeding to practical considerations, we present examples of three exceptional life histories. They represent entry points to three differ-ent eras of the approach.[5] For each exemplar, we provide a brief descrip-tion of the text as well as its significance.

Crashing Thunder (1926)

'The value and significance of the autobiography that follows does not simply lie in the fact that it is a document absolutely unique of its kind – the only account that has ever been obtained from a so-called "primitive" man' says Paul Radin (1926) as he introduces the narrative of Crashing Thunder, 'but in the fact that this particular individual took his task liter-ally and attempted to give an absolutely and bewilderingly honest account of his life' (pp. xvi–xvii). So begins Radin's foundational text, typically thought of as the first serious life history by an anthropologist (Langness and Frank, 1981). While Radin began field work in 1909 and spent con-siderable time with the Winnebago tribe, located just south of Sioux City, Iowa, the biography is mostly the product of a 48-hour time period, when Crashing Thunder recounted his life's story in written form and in a lan-guage other than English.

The significance of the biography is twofold: first, *Crashing Thunder* is the life history of one normal person intended to provide entree into the Winnebago culture. Unlike previous anthropological texts, the focus is on one specific person, not all of the community. Second, in the Franz Boas tradition, Radin focused on collecting and recording data rather than on interpreting and analysing it (Langness and Frank, 1981). The entire text contains no explicit interpretation or analysis.

Children of Sánchez (1961)

Oscar Lewis begins his innovative life history by writing, 'My purpose is to give the reader an inside view of family life and of what it means to grow up in a one-room home in a slum tenement in the heart of a great Latin American city which is undergoing a process of rapid social and economic change' (p. xi). He does so by recording and presenting the self-reported stories of Jesús Sánchez and his family. The stories are in-depth, sometimes even confessional; consider the first words of Jesús's daughter, Marta: 'My childhood was the happiest any girl could have. I felt free . . . Nothing tied me down, absolutely nothing' (p. 133).

The significance is threefold: first, Lewis solidifies life history as literary genre (Watson and Watson-Franke, 1985). Second, by presenting multiple histories, he skirts some of the sampling criticisms of life history and also reduces researcher bias. Third and last, his account of the Mexican family resulted in the phrase 'culture of poverty,' which Lewis (1966) describes as 'a way of life handed on from generation to generation along family lines' (p. 19). While Lewis intended the phrase to convey the unique cultural features of a specific group, the term became controversial and synonymous with indolence and deprivation. Despite criticisms of Lewis's model (Leacock, 1971), his portrayals of the poor greatly influenced public policy in the 1960s.

Venus on Wheels (2000)

'From the moment I met Diane,' Gelya Frank (2000) states, 'she inverted and subverted the predictable dynamics of power implied by our relative social positions' (p. 18). For Frank, the unique power relationship between researcher and subject is worthy of constant examination. *Venus on Wheels* is an account of the 20-year relationship between Diane DeVries, a woman born with no arms or legs, and the researcher, Gelya Frank. A significant amount of information is provided not only about the research subject but also the role of the researcher. Importantly, Frank refers to her text not as life history, but as cultural biography, 'a cultural analysis focusing on a biographical subject that makes use of ethnographic methods, along with life history and life story, and that critically reflects on its methodology in action as a source of primary data' (Frank, 2000, p. 22). We include the cultural biography here because the text is a logical extension of the life history with clear antecedents.

The significance of Frank's cultural biography is twofold: first, unlike *Crashing Thunder* and *Children of Sánchez*, the imprint of the author is apparent in the text. Not only is the researcher present, but the text is jointly constructed through the interactions between Frank and DeVries. Second, data, theory, interpretation, and analysis are interspersed throughout the text. While *Venus on Wheels* is certainly not the first example of a mixture of data and theory, it does provide a useful example of how one author navigated the challenges of presentation.

These three examples – *Crashing Thunder*, *Children of Sánchez*, and *Venus on Wheels* – present valuable models for the novice and experienced life historian alike.

CONDUCTING A LIFE HISTORY

Along with being students and advocates of the approach, we have also used life history in our work. Tierney conducted a life history of a Native American dying of AIDS (Tierney, 1993) and of a young Malaysian facing the forces of globalization in a developing country (Tierney, 2010a). We have both written life histories of first generation college students (Clemens, May, 2010; Tierney, May, 2010), and Tierney and Colyar (2009) edited a book of life histories of high school students applying to college. The remaining text highlights important considerations from our own research and experience.

MODES AND TOPICS OF STUDY

Disputes occur between quantitative and qualitative methodologists about the 'best' approach to study education problems. With the current policy climate, legislators and policy-makers clearly favor experimental and quasi-experimental research (Tooley, 2001; Shavelson and Towne, 2002; Slavin, 2002). Such resolute predilections, however, often ignore a central tenet of research design: research questions dictate modes of inquiry.

As we have noted previously (Tierney and Clemens, 2011), well-designed quantitative and qualitative studies both have merit; the two should be viewed as complementary, not adversarial. A large experimental study to measure the effect of a reading intervention on elementary school students elucidates one aspect of the educational experience. Similarly, a qualitative study to account for the socio-economic challenges of a small group of children whose parents are undocumented workers in the United States highlights another component of the educational experience. Life history more closely resembles the second study.

The value of life history is to provide a portrait of lives over time. Paul Radin (1913), describing his dissatisfaction with traditional methodologies, states: '[T]hey represented but the skeleton and bones of the culture they sought to portray; that what was needed, if we were ever to understand the Indian, was an interpretation of his life and emotions from within' (p. 293). He then explains the origins and purposes of his method:

> I happened to run across one of those serious and sedate middle-aged individu-
> als whom one is likely to meet in almost every civilization, and who, if they
> chose to speak in a natural and detached manner about the culture to which
> they belonged, could throw more light upon the workings of an Indian's brain
> than any mass of information systematically and carefully obtained by an
> outsider. (pp. 293–4)

Radin's point of view, nearly one century later, still captures the benefits of life history. The goal of the anthropological life history is to
provide a venue for the ignored, forgotten, or voiceless. Just as Vincent
Crapanzano's (1980) detailed, expressive life history offers a glimpse into
the world of Tuhami, a Moroccan tilemaker, so too can a well-conceived
and enacted life history of an undocumented youth inform the reader
about the inherent struggles to obtain a high school education.

DATA SOURCES

Like the myriad forms of life history, potential data sources are equally
varied. We suggest here the sources and tools a life historian is most likely
to use and/or encounter.

Interviews

For the majority of life histories, interviews form the core of data collection (Elliott, Chapter 20, this volume; Helling, 1988). It is useful to
consider the role of the interviewer and purpose of the interview. Kvale
(2007), using metaphor, describes the epistemological underpinnings
of two types of interview styles: the interviewer as time-traveler versus
excavator (Kvale, 2007). The time-traveler views the interview as a co-
constructed experience during which interviewer and interviewee go on a
journey together; the excavator views the interview as a procedure during
which the interviewer unearths data from the interviewee. Both ideal types
are useful to begin thinking about interviewing.

While this text is not meant to provide a comprehensive guide to
interviewing,[6] we offer several considerations for those who undertake
life histories: first, creating interview protocols for a short study with an
unfamiliar subject is drastically different than creating protocols for a long
study with a familiar subject. Second, although the interviewer should
create a semi-structured protocol based around themes, he or she should

also be unafraid to allow the subject to guide topic selection during the interview. Lastly, the interview is a skill and an art. Always be aware of the arc of the interview protocol and conclude the interview by allowing the subject to add anything they feel either party has omitted.

Observations and Settings

Insofar as a life history is likely to extend over time, the researcher has the potential to observe the informant in multiple settings. Unlike some interviews that may be brief and held in an interviewee's office, the life history is an undertaking where the informant has the ability to show the researcher multiple locations that have some sort of meaning to the individual. Oscar Lewis, for example, conducted his study in the village and home of his informants. The life history of the Malaysian (Tierney, 2010a) that one of us did occurred in a variety of locales where the individual was able to explain various aspects of working-class life in Malaysia. The life history of the man dying of AIDS (Tierney, 1993) was more circumscribed, due to his illness, but the setting could not be ignored. Our point here is that with a life history the setting is likely to add observational data.

Documents

In this wide-ranging category, we include documents such as diaries, letters, photographs, and fieldnotes from observations (Denzin, 1970; Plummer, 2001). Additional but infrequently used sources include obituaries, questionnaires, newspaper articles, and artifacts from educational or professional settings, such as essays or performance reviews.[7]

The use of documents is only limited by the researcher's imagination. While interviews provide insider accounts, documents provide alternative perspectives of the subject's life and access to multiple settings. For instance, a twelfth-grader's English essay not only displays a component of the subject but also the comments may explain her interactions with the teacher. In addition, an interviewer may not be able to gain access to a work-site; however, photographs may allow for a substitute understanding of that setting.

Digital Sources

In 1961, Oscar Lewis wrote, 'The tape recorder, used in taking down the life stories in this book, has made possible the beginning of a new kind of literature of social realism' (p. xii). Certainly, with the advent of the digital age, additional data collection techniques exist. The researcher now has diverse options, including social media (such as Facebook, Twitter, Yelp, YouTube, and Wordpress), e-mail, and text messages. These sources should not be viewed as novelty; rather, they are changing the way individuals communicate and think. A life history about a teenager that does not account for social media or text messages is most likely insufficient. In addition, technology increases the number of potential interactions and removes spatial boundaries. A researcher and subject can now communicate from disparate locations via video chat, text message, and e-mail.

DATA ANALYSIS

Data analysis is an ongoing, recursive process that occurs simultaneously with data collection.[8] As Cortazzi and Jin (Chapter 35, this volume) suggest, analysis involves questioning. The researcher creates and tests codes, categories, and, if employed, theoretical frameworks. He or she constantly compares data with alternative cases (Glaser and Strauss, 1967; Charmaz, 2006) as well as consults with the subject about the accuracy of data and interpretation (LeCompte and Goetz, 1982). The researcher may use technology to assist with analysis. Just as technology has created more data collection sources, it has also generated numerous options for analysis. Computer assisted qualitative data analysis software (CAQDAS) organizes, stores, presents, and maps data efficiently and uniquely.[9] Software is most useful for organization; however, it does not replace the interpretive nature of qualitative research (Lincoln and Guba, 1985).

A concern for all stages of research – analysis in particular – is thoroughness. One critique of life history has been its lack (or perceived lack) of scientific rigor. Watson and Watson-Franke (1985) state:

> The life history has meant entirely different things to its various proponents. In the past, investigators used life histories for any purpose that suited their individual research needs or the requirements of a theory subscribed to at the time . . . Unfortunately, the result is that the usefulness of life history analysis is difficult to see from either a scientific or humanistic perspective. (p. 16)

This is not to imply criteria for the judgment of life history do not exist. The first attempt to define criteria for life history occurred in 1935. John Dollard, in *Criteria for the Life History*, presented criteria that reflected the trend of using life history to understand culture, for instance, 'The subject must be viewed as a specimen in a cultural series' (p. 8). While Dollard's criteria are now antiquated, at the time, he provided direction to an otherwise informal method (Langness and Frank, 1981) and led a movement to create rigorous standards (see Allport, 1942; Kluckhohn,

1945).[10] And yet, due to reasons we have already discussed, namely the method's resistance to definition, no single standard for rigorous research has been adopted by all life historians.

Nonetheless, the need for criteria to judge scientific rigor is clear. We proffer a few suggestions to improve the trustworthiness of data: first, constant comparisons of data to other cases as well as member checks improve the accuracy and analysis and interpretation of data. Allowing peers to review the researcher's work also improves trustworthiness and, in relation to the final presentation, minimizes the potential for interpretive differences of the text by writer and reader (Wolcott, 1990). Next, Tierney and Clemens (2011) propose additional criteria for conducting policy-oriented research, such as 'thick description' (Geertz, 1973), offering multiple interpretations with a clear justification for the primary exegesis, and presenting data in a compelling, appropriate manner. Finally, the researcher should complete a research audit – an archive of raw data and documentation of each step of inquiry – for the entire process of the study (Lincoln and Guba, 1985). If an individual questions data or interpretations, the researcher ought to be able to logically trace the original kernel to the final presentation of data. As Langness and Frank (1981) affirm, 'Only insofar as you can understand all of the steps in your analysis, and communicate them to others, can you be said to have completed a useful or meaningful life history' (p. 86).

DATA PRESENTATION

Perhaps more than other genres, the life historian places a great deal of focus on the construction of the text. Insofar as the interaction between the historian and the informant is more intense than a typical interview or focus group, the author takes into account his or her role in the undertaking as well as how the research subject helped shape the text. Although most of qualitative research projects deal with such issues in one manner or another, they are particularly critical in a life history. The researcher's relationship and subject position are central to the reader's understanding of how the data were developed and constructed. Similarly, the informant's ability to comment on his or her circumstances goes well beyond what one might expect from a series of interviews or a case study.

To understand the compound variables of performing a life history, Pamphilon (1999) provides a useful analytic tool. The zoom model analyses four levels, or perspectives: the macro, meso, micro, and interactional. Each level illuminates a unique perspective of the research process. The macro level focuses on socio-historical aspects. The meso level pertains to the themes that develop from the stories of the participants. The micro level highlights the oral components of life history, and the final level, the interactional-zoom, places the focus on the researcher's role in conducting and reporting the life history. These four levels create a useful framework, or typology, for understanding the variables involved in research; they also merit address in the historical document.

The last level of Pamphilon's (1999) typology, the researcher's role, is a critical component of life history – and one that is often underemphasized. The biographer throughout the process is integral. Recall the end of Vincent Crapanzano's (2009) definition of life history – 'it is, as it were, doubly edited, during the encounter itself and during the literary re-encounter' (p. 4). One challenge of conducting and then writing life history is the translation of researcher to writer (Tierney, 1998). The researcher is not simply a recorder and projector; rather, he or she constantly editorializes. Not only does life historian fulfill the multiple roles of researcher and author, but the researcher is also most likely a character in the text.

ETHICS AND RELATIONSHIPS

Our final point is the ethics of and relationships developed during life history. We have undertaken several life history projects, which are usually classified as exempt by our university's institutional review board, the governing body of ethics and research as well as with federal agencies. The reason is straightforward: given the federal definition of research – 'a systematic investigation, including development, testing, and evaluation, designed to develop or contribute to generalizable knowledge' (Department of Health and Human Sciences, 2009; Office for the Protection of Research Subjects, 2010) – life history does not qualify as 'research.' Does this mean no ethical implications for life history research exist? The answer is resolutely 'no.' In an attempt to come to terms with the subject's version of reality, the researcher and subject often navigate difficult and emotional topics.

The relationship between the two is the core of life history. Thoughtfulness, rapport, privacy, and trust are all critical concerns of the life historian (Langness and Frank, 1981). Earlier in the chapter, we touched on the epistemological underpinnings of interviewing. That is, is the interview process a joint discovery or unitary extraction (Kvale, 2007)? Both choices include important ethical concerns, and the researcher needs to prepare for the unexpected consequences of investigating challenging subjects. Ponder a scenario in which a subject admits to being physically abused by a parent. In contemplation of emotional well-being, this instance could be hugely damaging to the informant and the role of the researcher could either alleviate or exacerbate an issue (Tierney, 2010b).

In addition, the benefits from conducting a life history should not only aggregate to the researcher. Some form of reciprocity must occur, whether it includes helping a student with school work or exploring and communicating intricate crises.

Based on our past field experiences, we suggest five considerations for the life historian:

1. Explain clearly and exactly the purposes of and time commitment necessary for the research project and include all information in a consent form, of which the informant and researcher keep signed copies.
2. Recognize that power dynamics exist between researcher and subject. Do not coerce or place the subject in difficult circumstances by developing a reflexive relationship.
3. Prioritize the subject's well-being above the research project.
4. Protect the subject's identity and privacy.
5. Present data accurately and obtain feedback from the subject throughout the writing of the text.

CONCLUSION

During its long existence, life history has been purposed and re-purposed (Tierney, 2000). Scholars have thought of the approach as a way to understand a culture, as a co-constructed text that brings into question issues such as what is meant by identity or culture, or as little more than a story that reveals a singular tale. Others have used life history as a way to explain a particular theoretical conundrum or to shed light on a little-studied problem (see Heyl, 1977; Middleton, 1987). As a result, consensus about the uses of or criteria for life history does not exist. The need for researcher awareness and thoughtfulness when adopting any method is vital, but we are suggesting that such a point is especially germane with life history insofar as it is so methodologically fragile. While we have intended to impart some of the dilemmas of life history, our purpose also has been to underscore our admiration for, and belief in, the potential of the approach. In her landmark text, Frank (2000) highlights the liberatory power of life history: 'The life history method, through which individuals tell their own stories, is more than a tool for salvaging memories. Unlike most reports by social scientists or those found in commercial media, first person narratives have the power to "liberate the subject" of history to express and represent herself in her own terms' (p. 9).

Not only can a life history transform participants, it too can inform public policy. Life history provides detail and the thickest of descriptions (Geertz, 1973) often lacking in large, empirical studies. Like Oscar Lewis's *Children of Sánchez* (1961) illustrates, life histories have the potential to illuminate social issues and move individuals to action (McCall, 1985). In doing so, the approach highlights the often overshadowed lives of historically marginalized individuals.

NOTES

1. Two Chicago School works – *The Polish Peasant in Europe and America* and Clifford Shaw's (1930 [1966]) *The Jack-roller*, the story of Stanley, a juvenile delinquent – were critical to establishing the method in sociology (Plummer, 2001). Of note, a testament to the important role of the subject in life history, Stanley's story was updated 50 years later in Jon's Snodgrass's (1982) *The Jack-roller at Seventy*.
2. For a more comprehensive introduction to life history, several definitive texts exist, including Denzin's (1989) *Interpretive Biography*, Langness and Frank's (1981) *Lives: An Anthropological Approach to Biography*, and Plummer's (2001) *Documents of Life 2: An Invitation to a Critical Humanism*.
3. The purpose of the text is not to review each type of narrative; however, here are a few introductory texts for an assortment of narrative forms: *Narrative Analysis* (Riessman, 1993), *The Narrative Study of Lives* (Josselson and Lieblich, 1993), 'The new narrative research in education' (Casey, 1995–96), *Storied Lives: The Cultural Politics of Self-understanding* (Rosenwald and Ochberg, 1992), 'Autoethnography, personal narrative, reflexivity: researcher as subject' (Ellis and Bochner, 2000), *The Ethnographic I: A Methodological Novel About Autoethnography* (Ellis, 2004), *Ethnographically Speaking: Autoethnography, Literature, and Aesthetics* (Bochner and Ellis, 2002), 'Biographical method' (Smith, 1994), *Writing Lives: Principia Biographica* (Edel, 1984), 'Disrupting apartheid of knowledge: *testimonio* as methodology in Latina/o critical race research in education' (Pérez Huber, Chapter 27, this volume) and 'Testimonio, subalternity, and narrative authority' (Beverley, 2000).
4. Denzin (1989) provides a helpful overview and typology of the variants of biography.
5. For a longer list of notable life histories, consult *Documents of Life 2: An Invitation to a Critical Humanism* (Plummer, 2001, p. 21).
6. For an introduction to interviewing in particular and qualitative methods in general, see *Doing Interviews* (Kvale, 2007), *Interviewing as Qualitative Research: A Guide for Researchers in Education and the Social Sciences* (Seidman, 2006), *Introduction to Qualitative Research Methods* (Taylor and Bogdan, 1998), *Qualitative Inquiry and Research Design: Choosing Among Five Approaches* (Creswell, 1998), *Qualitative Evaluation and Research Methods* (Patton, 1990), and *The Research Act: A Theoretical Introduction to Sociological Methods* (Denzin, 1978).
7. For further discussion of documents, see Middleton's (Chapter 21, this volume). 'Jane's three letters: working with documents and archives.'
8. For descriptions of data analysis, consult the introductory qualitative research texts that we cite for interviewing. In addition, see *Naturalistic Inquiry* (Lincoln and Guba, 1985), *The Discovery of Grounded Theory: Strategies for Qualitative Research* (Glaser and Strauss, 1967), *Situational Analysis: Grounded Theory After the Postmodern Turn* (Clark, 2005), *Constructing Grounded Theory: A Practical Guide Through Qualitative*

278   *Handbook of qualitative research in education*

Analysis (Charmaz, 2006), and 'Analysing narratives: the narrative construction of identity' (Watson, Chapter 34, this volume).
9.   Examples of CAQDAS include Atlas.ti, NVivo, HyperRESEARCH, and MAXQDA.
10. For a more contemporary discussion of criteria for life history and narrative research – including verisimilitude, believability, trustworthiness, and explanatory power – and a list of further references, see Hatch and Wisniewski (1995, p. 129).

REFERENCES

Allport, G. (1942), 'The use of personal documents in psychological science', Bulletin 49, Social Science Research Council, New York.
Atkinson, R. (2001), 'The life history interview', in J.F. Gubrium and J.A. Holstein (eds), *Handbook of Interview Research: Context & Method*, Thousand Oaks, CA: Sage, pp. 121–40.
Behar, R. (2003), *Translated Woman: Crossing the Border with Esperanza's Story*, Boston, MA: Beacon Press.
Beverley, J. (2000), 'Testimonio, subalternity, and narrative authority', in N.K. Denzin and Y.S. Lincoln (eds), *Handbook of Qualitative Methodology*, 2nd edn, Newbury Park, CA: Sage, pp. 555–565.
Bochner, A.P. and Ellis, C. (eds) (2002), *Ethnographically Speaking: Autoethnography, Literature, and Aesthetics*, Walnut Creek, CA: AltaMira Press.
Casey, K. (1995–96), 'The new narrative research in education', *Review of Research in Education*, **21**, 211–53.
Charmaz, K. (2006), *Constructing Grounded Theory: A Practical Guide Through Qualitative Analysis*, Thousand Oaks, CA: Sage.
Clark, A. (2005), *Situational Analysis: Grounded Theory After the Postmodern Turn*, Thousand Oaks, CA: Sage.
Clemens, R.F. (May, 2010), '"Oh my God, I'm the only Latina and with an accent!": The life history of a good, hardworking immigrant', Paper presented at the annual meeting of the American Educational Research Association, Denver, Colorado.
Crapanzano, V. (1980), *Tuhami: Portrait of a Moroccan*, Chicago, IL: University of Chicago Press.
Crapanzano, V. (2009), 'The life history in anthropological fieldwork', *Anthropology and Humanism Quarterly*, **2** (2–3), 3–7.
Creswell, J.W. (1998), *Qualitative Inquiry and Research Design: Choosing Among Five Approaches*, Thousand Oaks, CA: Sage.
Department of Health and Human Sciences (2009), 'Protection of human subjects', available from http://www.hhsgov/ohrp/humansubjects/guidance/45.fr46.html#46.102 (accessed September 2011).
Denzin, N.K. (1970), 'The life history method', in *The Research Act*, Chicago, IL: Aldine Company, pp. 219–59.
Denzin, N.K. (1978), *The Research Act: A Theoretical Introduction to Sociological Methods*, New York: McGraw-Hill.
Denzin, N.K. (1989), *Interpretive Biography*, Newbury Park, CA: Sage.
Dollard, J. (1935), *Criteria for the Life History, with Analysis of Six Notable Documents*, New Haven, CT: Yale University Press.
Edel, L. (1984), *Writing Lives: Principia Biographica*, New York: W.W. Norton & Company.
Ellis, C. (2004), *The Ethnographic I: A Methodological Novel About Autoethnography*, Walnut Creek, CA: Altamira Press.
Ellis, C. and Bochner, A.P. (2000), 'Autoethnography, personal narrative, reflexivity: researcher as subject', in N.K. Denzin and Y.S. Lincoln (eds), *Handbook of Qualitative Methodology*, 2nd edn, Newbury Park, CA: Sage, pp. 733–68.

Erikson, E. (1969), *Gandhi's Truth: On the Origins of Militant Nonviolence*, New York: Norton.

Frank, G. (1995), 'Review: Anthropology and individual lives: the story of the life history and the history of the life story', *American Anthropologist*, **97** (1), 145–8.

Frank, G. (1996), 'Life history', in D. Levinson and M. Ember (eds), *Encyclopedia of Cultural Anthropology*, Vol. 2, New York: Henry Holt.

Frank, G. (2000), *Venus on Wheels: Two Decades of Dialogue on Disability, Biography, and Being Female in America*, Berkeley, CA: University of California Press.

Geertz, C. (1973), 'Thick description: toward an interpretive theory of culture', in *The Interpretation of Cultures: Selected Essays*, New York: Basic.

Glaser, B.G. and Strauss, A.L. (1967), *The Discovery of Grounded Theory: Strategies for Qualitative Research*, Chicago, IL: Aldine.

Guba, E.G. (1981), 'Criteria for assessing the trustworthiness of naturalistic inquiries', *Educational Communication and Technology*, **29** (2), 75–91.

Hatch, J.A. and Wisniewski, R. (1995), *Life History and Narrative*, London: The Falmer Press.

Helling, I.K. (1988), 'The life history method: a survey and discussion with Norman K. Denzin', *Studies in Symbolic Interaction*, **9**, 211–43.

Heyl, B.S. (1977), 'The madam as teacher: the training of house prostitutes', *Social Problems*, **24** (5), 545–55.

Josselson, R. and Lieblich, A. (eds) (1993), *The Narrative Study of Lives*, Newbury Park, CA: Sage.

Kluckhohn, C. (1945), 'The personal document in anthropological science', in L.R. Gottschalk, C. Kluckhohn and R. Angell (eds), *The Use of Personal Documents in History, Anthropology, and Sociology*, New York: Social Science Research Council, pp. 78–193.

Kvale, S. (2007), *Doing Interviews*, Thousand Oaks, CA: Sage.

Langness, L.L. (1965), *The Life History in Anthropological Science*, New York: Holt, Rinehart and Winston.

Langness, L.L., and Frank, G. (1981), *Lives: An Anthropological Approach to Biography*, Novato, CA: Chandler & Sharp Publishers.

Leacock, E.B. (ed.) (1971), *The Culture of Poverty: A Critique*, New York: Simon and Schuster.

LeCompte, M.D. and Goetz, J.P. (1982), 'Problems of reliability and validity in ethnographic research', *Review of Educational Research*, **52** (1), 31–60.

Left Handed (1938), *Son of Old Man Hat: A Navaho Autobiography Recorded by Walter Dyk*, New York: Harcourt, Brace and Company.

Lewis, O. (1961), *The Children of Sánchez: Autobiography of a Mexican Family*, New York: Random House.

Lewis, O. (1966), 'The culture of poverty', *Scientific American*, **215** (4), 19–25.

Lincoln, Y.S. and Guba, E.G. (1985), *Naturalistic Inquiry*, Beverly Hills, CA: Sage.

McCall, M. (1985), 'Life history and social change', *Symbolic Interaction*, **6**, 169–82.

Middleton, S. (1987), 'Schooling and radicalisation: life histories of New Zealand feminist teachers', *British Journal of Sociology of Education*, **8** (2), 169–89.

Office for the Protection of Research Subjects (2010), 'Is your project human subjects research: a guide for investigators', available at http://www.usc.edu/admin/provost/oprs/private/docs/oprs/NHSR_3_6_06_WEB.pdf (accessed 20 July 2010).

Pamphilon, B. (1999), 'The zoom model: a dynamic framework for the analysis of life histories', *Qualitative Inquiry*, **5**, 393–410.

Patton, M.Q. (1990), *Qualitative Evaluation and Research Methods*, 2nd edn, Newbury Park, CA: Sage.

Peacock, J.L. and Holland, D.C. (1993), 'The narrated self: life stories in process', *Ethos*, **21** (4), 367–83.

Phillips, D.C. (1994), 'Telling it straight: issues in assessing narrative research', *Educational Psychologist*, **29** (1), 13–21.

Plummer, K. (2001), *Documents of Life 2: An Invitation to a Critical Humanism*, London: Sage.

Radin, P. (1913), 'Personal reminiscences of a Winnebago Indian', *Journal of American Folklore*, **26**, 293–318.

Radin, P. (1926), *Crashing Thunder: The Autobiography of an American Indian*, New York: D. Appleton and Company.

Riessman, C.K. (1993), *Narrative Analysis*, Newbury Park, CA: Sage.

Rosenwald, G.C. and Ochberg, R.L. (eds) (1992), *Storied Lives: The Cultural Politics of Self-understanding*, New Haven, CT: Yale University Press.

Seidman, I. (2006), *Interviewing as Qualitative Research: A Guide for Researchers in Education and the Social Sciences*, New York: Teachers College Press.

Shavelson, R.J. and Towne, L. (2002), *Scientific Research in Education*, Washington, DC: National Academy Press.

Shaw, C.R. ([1930] 1966), *The Jack-roller: A Delinquent Boy's Own Story*, Chicago, IL: University of Chicago Press.

Slavin, R. (2002), 'Evidence-based policies: transforming educational practice and research', *Educational Researcher*, **31** (7), 15–21.

Smith, L.M. (1994), 'Biographical method', in N.K. Denzin and Y.S. Lincoln (eds), *Handbook of Qualitative Methodology*, Newbury Park, CA: Sage, pp. 286–305.

Snodgrass, J. (1982), *The Jack-roller at Seventy: A Fifty-year Follow-up of 'a Delinquent Boy's Own Story'*, Lexington, MA: Lexington Books.

Taylor, S.J., and Bogdan, R. (1998), *Introduction to Qualitative Research Methods*, 3rd edn, New York: John Wiley & Sons.

Thomas, W.I., and Znaniecki, F. ([1918–20] 1958), *The Polish Peasant in Europe and America*, New York: Dover Publications.

Tierney, W.G. (1993), 'Self and identity in a postmodern world: a life story', in D. McLaughlin and W.G. Tierney (eds), *Naming Silenced Lives: Personal Narratives and the Process of Educational Change*, New York: Routledge, pp. 119–34.

Tierney, W.G. (1998), 'Life history's history: subjects foretold', *Qualitative Inquiry*, **4**, 49–70.

Tierney, W.G. (2000), 'Undaunted courage: life history and the postmodern challenge', in N.K. Denzin and Y.S. Lincoln (eds), *Handbook of Qualitative Methodology*, 2nd edn, Newbury Park, CA: Sage, pp. 516–28.

Tierney, W.G. (2010a), 'Globalization and life history research: fragments of a life foretold', *International Journal of Qualitative Studies in Education*, **23** (2), 129–46.

Tierney, W.G. (2010b), 'Life history and voice: on standpoints and reflexivity', in M. Gasman (ed.), *The History of U.S. Higher Education: Methods for Understanding the Past*, New York: Routledge, pp. 122–34.

Tierney, W.G. (May, 2010), 'The method of life history: uses and abuses for understanding the lives of first-generation students', Paper presented at the annual meeting of the American Educational Research Association, Denver, Colorado.

Tierney, W.G. and Clemens, R.F. (2011), 'Qualitative research and public policy: the challenges of relevance and trustworthiness', in J. Smart and M.B. Paulsen (eds), *Higher Education: Handbook of Theory and Research*, Vol. 26, New York: Agathon Press, pp. 57–83.

Tierney, W.G. and Colyar, J.E. (eds) (2009), *Urban High School Students and the Challenge of Access: Many Routes, Different Paths*, revised edn, New York: Peter Lang.

Tooley, J. (2001), 'The quality of educational research: a perspective from Great Britain', *Peabody Journal of Education,* **76** (3), 122–40.

Watson, L.C. and Watson-Franke, M. (1985), *Interpreting Life Histories: An Anthropological Inquiry*, New Brunswick, NJ: Rutgers University Press.

Wolcott, H.F. (1983), 'Adequate schools and inadequate education: the life history of a sneaky kid', *Anthropology and Education Quarterly,* **14** (1), 3–32.

Wolcott, H.F. (1990), 'On seeking – and rejecting – validity in qualitative research', in E.W. Eisner and A. Peshkin (eds), *Qualitative Inquiry in Education: The Continuing Debate*, New York: Teachers College Press, pp. 121–52.

20. Gathering narrative data
Jane Elliott

INTRODUCTION: DEFINING NARRATIVE AND UNDERSTANDING ITS IMPORTANCE IN RESEARCH

Perhaps the most concise definition of narrative is that it is a story with a beginning, a middle and an end – this description has been traced back to Aristotle in his *Poetics* (Chatman, 1978; Martin, 1986). Temporality is certainly widely accepted as a key feature of narrative form. In an influential paper, Labov and Waletzky (1997)[1] stated that narrative provides a 'method of recapitulating past experiences by matching a verbal sequence of clauses to the sequence of events that actually occurred' (p. 12). The placing of events in a sequence is therefore considered by many to be the defining feature of narrative, and it is this that perhaps best characterizes the use of narrative in many research interviews.

However, a successful narrative is more than just a sequence or chronicle of events. Indeed, Labov and Waletzky (1997) suggested that although a minimal narrative is composed of a sequence of actions such a narrative is 'abnormal: it may be considered as empty or pointless narrative' (Labov and Waletzky, 1997, p. 13). They described fully formed narratives as having six separate elements: the abstract (a summary of the subject of the narrative); the orientation (time, place, situation, participants); the complicating action (what actually happened); the evaluation (the meaning and significance of the action); the resolution (what finally happened); and lastly, the coda, which returns the perspective to the present (see Cortazzi and Jin, Chapter 35, this volume for a more detailed discussion of this). Labov and Waletzky (1997) argued that these structures are typically used by the teller to construct a story out of past experiences, and to make sense of those experiences both for himself or herself and for the audience. Although not all narratives necessarily include all of these six elements, at a minimum a narrative must include the complicating action, that is, a temporal component, while it is the evaluation that has been highlighted as crucial for establishing the point or the meaning of the story. Given the specific interest for many qualitative researchers in understanding the meanings of events and experiences from an individual's perspective, it is clear why narrative can be seen as a powerful and useful tool for the collection of information in research.

Over the past two decades, the awareness of the importance of narrative among qualitative researchers has spread through a wide range of different substantive areas. Within the field of education, for example, in Britain Martin Cortazzi (1991) used narrative in his research on the experiences of primary school teachers and Smith (1996) emphasized that she was interested in listening to women's stories in interviews about their experiences of returning to education as mature students in order to understand more about the support or barriers presented by their husbands and partners. In North America too, those in the field of education have found the use of narrative very fruitful in their research (Connelly and Clandinin, 1999; Clandinin and Connelly, 2000).

In addition, in the sociology of health there has been a focus on lay perspectives on disease and patients' own experiences of ill health. In particular for those suffering from chronic disease the idea of an 'illness career' has been a useful analytic tool and this can be readily expressed in the form of a narrative. Researchers such as Kleinman (1988), Charmaz (1991), Kelly and Dickinson (1997) and Williams (1997) have therefore written about the impact of chronic ill health on individuals' sense of identity. Narrative has also surfaced in the literature on health behaviour and health education, for example, in the work of Moffat and Johnson (2001) and Workman (2001).

In 2006, a special issue of the journal *Narrative Inquiry* was edited by Michael Bamberg. Entitled 'Narrative – State of the Art', the special issue included 24 articles by authors from different disciplines with the aim of generating new discussions and promoting innovative work in the field. This therefore provides a helpful resource for those wanting an introduction to recent work in the area. In particular the paper by Stephanie Taylor on 'Narrative as construction and discursive resource' and the paper by Atkinson and Delamont 'Rescuing narrative from qualitative research' provide a helpful contribution to a key debate around the extent to which narratives produced in the context of a research interview might be thought of as representing memories, as an unproblematic 'vehicle for personal or private experience', or whether they should be more properly understood as a very specific and situated social construction. In this second, discursive, approach a central assumption is that 'talk and language are not directly referential, conveying meanings which are "out there" in the world, but, rather, that these meanings are constituted within talk' (Taylor, 2007, p. 4). These different approaches to understanding narrative in a research context form the dimensions of an important continuing debate, and this I will return to in the concluding section of this chapter.

Narrative Research in Different Cultural Contexts

In addition to having a clear chronological dimension, narratives are inherently social – they are told for a specific audience and they draw on the models and genres that are culturally available to the individual narrator. This means that the structures and functions of narratives may well vary across cultures (Cortazzi, 1993, pp. 102–8). There are perhaps four ways in which narratives may vary across cultures. First, the way in which the evaluative elements of the narrative are communicated may be different in different cultural contexts. Second, the degree of collaboration expected between narrator and audience may be very different. Third the appropriate occasion for certain types of narrative may vary. Cortazzi and Jin (2006) highlight, for example, that the narratives provided by East Asian applicants for British Masters degree courses are very different from the types of narratives that British students would include in similar letters of application. The East Asian applicants use the narratives to establish themselves as moral persons with sound family backgrounds – characteristics that would be understood as less salient for successful application by British students. As Cortazzi and Jin explain, 'The British Reader might read this very positive personalisation as over-claiming through exaggerated boasting or poetic irrelevance; conversely, a Chinese reader of a typical British application letter might wonder why the expected exposition of the moral identity of the person is absent' (Cortazzi and Jin, 2006, p. 38). A fourth aspect of narrative variability across cultures concerns the actual performance of the narrative. Minami (2002), for example, has shown cross-cultural variation in children's stories with Japanese children telling much more succinct accounts of personal events and American children giving more elaborated accounts of single events.

There is not space here to give a comprehensive review of the ways that narrative has been used by social scientists – the aim has been to highlight the broad range of subject areas that are amenable to a narrative approach. Some of the common themes that run through research that pays attention to narrative in respondents' accounts are:

1. An interest in people's lived experiences and an appreciation of the temporal nature of that experience.
2. A desire to empower research participants and allow them to contribute to determining what are the most salient themes in an area of research.
3. An interest in process and change over time.
4. An interest in the self and representations of the self.
5. An awareness that the researcher himself or herself is also a narrator.

In this chapter the focus will be on verbal narratives collected in the context of research interviews. In particular I will discuss the different ways of eliciting narratives from research participants and the practicalities of carrying out effective interviews. The interview is perhaps the main information gathering tool for the social sciences. Holstein and Gubrium (1995, p. 1) suggest that the vast majority (perhaps 90 per cent) of all social science research uses interview data. However it should also be recognized that some researchers employ visual narrative techniques such as drawing and photography and that these can be particularly effective in school settings (see, for example, Prosser, 2007; Carrington et al., 2007). This chapter will draw on recent experiences of conducting interviews with a narrative structure as part of the social participation and identity project. As will be discussed below these interviews also made some use of visual techniques but the main emphasis was on verbal narratives.

THE PRACTICALITIES OF NARRATIVE INTERVIEWING

Asking the 'Right' Questions

Authors such as Graham (1984), Mishler (1986) and Riessman (1990) have each emphasized that interviewees are likely spontaneously to provide narratives in the context of interviews about their experiences, unless the structure of the interview itself or the questioning style of the interviewer suppresses such stories. Most people enjoy telling stories, and, with a little encouragement, will provide narrative accounts of their experiences in research interviews. For example, Mishler explicitly links the notion of obtaining narratives in interviews to the aim of empowering respondents as he succinctly explains:

> Various attempts to restructure the interviewer-interviewee relationship, so as to empower respondents, are designed to encourage them to find and speak in their own 'voices.' It is not surprising that when the interview situation is opened up in this way, when the balance of power is shifted, respondents are likely to tell 'stories.' In sum, interviewing practices that empower respondents also produce narrative accounts. (Mishler, 1986, pp. 118–19)

However, in contrast to this view that narratives will emerge naturally during in-depth interviews (if only researchers are prepared to hear them), some authors have described situations in which they failed to obtain narratives from respondents even though this was the primary aim of the interview. This raises questions about the most effective ways of encouraging respondents to provide detailed storied accounts of their experiences in interviews.

Qualitative researchers generally agree that questions in interviews should be framed using everyday rather than sociological language. Chase (1995) provides a telling account of how the failure to adhere to this principle prevented respondents from providing the narratives about their work experiences that she was hoping for. In a research project on women's experiences in the white- and male-dominated profession of public school superintendents in the United States, Chase, and her co-researcher Colleen Bell, wanted to hear about the concrete experiences of women school superintendents. In the early interviews they included a series of questions specifically about what it is like to be a woman in a male-dominated profession and, in the spirit of developing an egalitarian relationship with these women professionals, these questions were introduced with a few statements about the sociological thinking behind them. Chase describes how eventually they realized that they needed to drop these 'sociological questions' in favour of asking much more straightforward and simple questions. For example, a brief request for an individual's work history proved to be effective in encouraging the respondents to tell stories about their professional lives. Chase explains that the problem with sociological questions is that 'they invite reports. They do not invite the other to take responsibility for the import of her response because the weight of the question lies in the sociological ideas' (Chase, 1995, p. 8). From her own experiences of interviewing, Chase therefore concludes that we are most likely to succeed in eliciting narratives from our research subjects when we ask simple questions that clearly relate to their life experiences.

Hollway and Jefferson (2000) also describe their unsuccessful attempts to get interviewees to give narrative responses in their pilot interviews for a study on the fear of crime. They suggest that although their questions were open-ended and framed in everyday language they were still too focused on the interests of the researcher and were not broad enough to allow respondents to provide the detailed narrative accounts they were hoping to elicit. Following careful analysis of the transcripts of pilot interviews, Hollway and Jefferson revised their interview guide to make the questions more open. They argue that the best questions for narrative interviews invite the interviewee to talk about specific times and situations, rather than asking about the respondent's life over a long period of time, and provide helpful examples of the questions they used (Hollway and Jefferson, 2000).

In addition to asking appropriate questions, the interviewer who wants to encourage the production of narratives during an interview must clearly also be a good listener. Paul Thompson argues that, in oral history interviewing, the interviewer should 'Wherever possible avoid interrupting a story. If you stop a story because you think it is irrelevant, you will cut off not just that one but a whole series of subsequent offers of information which will be relevant' (Thompson, 1978, p. 172). This is consonant with Elliot Mishler's suggestion that a process takes place at the beginning of a research interview that might be thought of as the interviewer training the interviewee to give appropriate responses. It is widely recognized in the social sciences that the subjects of research are eager to comply with the wishes of the researcher and to provide the type of responses that the researcher is looking for. If the researcher implicitly communicates that narrative responses are not what is wanted, by interrupting the interviewee's stories, for example, this in some senses 'trains' the respondent to provide a different type of information.

Collecting Life Histories – the Use of a Life History Grid

If the primary aim of carrying out qualitative biographical interviews is to obtain individuals' own accounts of their lives, it is clearly important not to impose a rigid structure on the interview by asking a standardized set of questions. However, it is also important to be aware that some individuals might find it very difficult to respond if asked to produce an extended narrative. This is a particular problem if the focus of the research is on the broad life course or on experiences (such as education and training or employment) that may span a great many years. Respondents are likely to find it easier to talk about specific times and situations rather than being asked about a very wide time frame. One approach is therefore to make use of a pre-prepared life history grid at the beginning of the interview. The life history grid can have a number of different formats. The 'Balan' type of grid, discussed by Tagg (1985), has a row for each year, and the respondent's age is entered in the left hand column. The remaining columns are used to record major events under a number of different headings such as education history, work history, housing history and family history. Clearly these categories will vary somewhat depending on the exact focus of the research. For example, research on the experiences of mature students might include a column for events related to education and training, and research in criminology may have a column for arrests and incarcerations. Completing the grid will ideally be a joint task undertaken by the interviewer and interviewee at the beginning of the interview. By moving backwards and forwards between the different areas of the respondent's life, the memory is stimulated. For example, an individual may have no difficulty remembering the year when their first child was born but may not remember the date when they returned to college as a mature student.

However if they remember that this occurred the year after their child was born the life history grid helps to locate this educational event. Once the grid is completed, the respondent can be asked to use it to help guide them as they recount the story of their life, starting from whatever point is most appropriate for them as an individual or for the purposes of the research.

The Length of Narrative Interviews

The emphasis within in-depth interviews on allowing the respondents to set the agenda and on listening to, rather than suppressing, their stories also raises practical questions about the appropriate length for these type of interviews. For example, Riessman discusses how a research project that was originally conceived as using a structured interview to examine the differences between the post-separation adaptation of men and women was modified to allow interviewees more of an opportunity to talk and to tell the story of how their marriage had ended (Riessman, 1990). She explains that in the pilot phase of the study, the structured interviews typically took under two hours to complete, but in the research itself, when interviewees were allowed to tell their stories, many of the interviews lasted for up to six hours. Several authors suggest that 90 minutes is the optimum length for a qualitative research interview (Seidman, 1998; Hermanowicz, 2002). If the quantity of material to be covered in an interview is judged to need more than two hours then the most practical solution is to conduct a second and even a third interview. Regardless of decisions about the exact length of the interview, what is important is to make the timing clear to the interviewee from the start. In my own research with graduate women in their forties (Elliott, 2001), I suggested to interviewees that the interview would probably last for approximately an hour and a half, but might go on as long as two hours. This appeared to be helpful to interviewees as it gave them a sense of how much detail to provide. Interviews of this length yield transcripts of approximately 20 to 30 pages of text (or approximately 15 000 to 20 000 words). In terms of the task of analysis this clearly provides a wealth of material to examine.

Repeated Interviews

A further practical consideration when using the method of narrative interviews is whether to rely on a single interview or whether to conduct a series of interviews with each respondent, and practice among researchers is very variable in this respect. Seidman (1998) makes a persuasive case for conducting a series of three interviews with each respondent. He suggests that the first interview should focus on the life history of the respondent, who should be asked to provide an account of his or her past life leading up to the topic or event of interest. The second interview should then focus on the concrete aspects of the respondent's present experiences, and Seidman advocates encouraging the respondent to tell stories as a way of eliciting detailed information. In the final interview, the researcher can then move on to encourage the respondent to reflect on their understandings of those experiences. Seidman argues that this three-interview structure also helps with establishing the internal validity of the findings as the researcher can check that the respondent is consistent across the three separate interviews. Tierney and Clemens (Chapter 19, this volume) also suggest that when collecting information in order to produce a life history (that is, a particular type of narrative research approach), it is likely that the interview process will extend over time and this may also allow the informant to show the researcher specific locations that have a particular meaning for the individual. In this case the settings for the series of interviews may well provide additional observational data for the researcher.

Hollway and Jefferson also give a helpful account of the process surrounding the use of two interviews in their research on the fear of crime in a British city (Hollway and Jefferson, 2000). Between the first and the second interview, a week later, the researchers together listened carefully to the recording of the first interview and discussed the material covered. The comments and analysis of the researcher who had not carried out the initial interview were valuable in that they provided a slightly more detached perspective on the interview. The notes taken during this process would then lead to the construction of further narrative questions to ask in the second interview. The use of two interviews also enabled the researchers to build up a trusting relationship with the interviewees and to demonstrate that they were interested in hearing about their experiences. Hollway and Jefferson argue that it enabled the interviewee to build up confidence that stories were what the researcher wanted. Because the narrative approach to interviewing differs from individuals' usual expectation that researchers ask lots of closed questions, it can take time to build up a respondent's confidence that telling stories about their experiences is valid within the interview context (Hollway and Jefferson, 2000, p. 44).

Recording Narrative Interviews

Given the focus in in-depth narrative interviews on the interaction between the interviewer and interviewee and on the form of the narratives provided rather than simply on the content, it is clearly very useful to be able to record the interview. This also allows the interviewer to give full attention to the interviewee rather than pausing to take notes. For interviews lasting 90 minutes or more it would be impractical to try and remember the interviewee's responses and make detailed notes at the end of the interview. Recording is therefore now generally thought to be good practice in all qualitative interviewing (Hermanowicz, 2002). Without tape-recording all kinds of data are lost: the narrative itself, pauses, intonation, laughter. In particular if the interview is understood as a site for the production of meanings, and the role of the interviewer is to be analysed alongside the accounts provided by the interviewee, it is important to capture the details of the interaction.

Having discussed the practicalities of conducting interviews that seek to elicit narratives from respondents, the next section provides a description of a specific research project that aimed to collect narrative biographical information from individuals who are part of an existing longitudinal 'cohort study'.

THE SOCIAL PARTICIPATION AND IDENTITY PROJECT

The aim of the social participation and identity project was to carry out qualitative biographical interviews with a subsample of approximately 180 individuals at age 50, who were all members of the 1958 British Birth Cohort study, also known as the National Child Development Study (NCDS). This is a longitudinal study that has followed individuals since they were born, through childhood and into adult life. As has been discussed elsewhere, cohort studies can be thought to have clear narrative properties (Elliott, 2008). They enable us to follow individual lives through time and encourage quantitative analysis that focuses on how early life experiences and environments may impact on later outcomes. However, the quantitative data collected as part of a cohort study could be thought of as being closer to a chronicle than a narrative. Events, experiences and dates are recorded but the individual respondents are not typically asked to make meaning out of this information, or to provide their own narrative account of their life. Rather narratives may be constructed by researchers who aim to make sense of the detailed data from a large sample within the framework of their own research questions. By carrying out more qualitative interviews with cohort members it was intended to give the respondents themselves an opportunity to provide a narrative account of their life which would complement the quantitative data that has been collected from and about them ever since they were born. The interviews were in six main sections and focused on: (1) neighbourhood and belonging; (2) leisure activities and social participation; (3) personal communities; (4) life history; (5) identity; (6) reflections on being part of the NCDS. Each section included a number of questions that were open-ended and allowed for, or positively encouraged, a narrative response from the cohort member. For example, one focus of interest within the project was how the geographical location of the individual cohort member might impact on their opportunities for social participation. In particular, how they viewed their local neighbourhood or community and how well they were integrated with those who lived in close proximity. When designing the topic guide it was decided to ask questions about locality, neighbourhood and belonging at the beginning of the interview. Similar questions had been asked in a previous research project and had been found to be relatively straightforward and non-threatening for interviewees to answer. In line with the experiences of Chase and Bell, discussed above, these brief factual questions frequently elicited narrative responses as is shown in the extract below.

> *Q:* In terms of where you live now could you tell me a little bit about how long you've lived where you live and how you came to live there?
> *A:* Okay. I've lived there almost . . ., it'll be five years actually in May next year and I was in a flat before that, that was a year before that, a private flat. Where I am now is social housing in a council tenancy. I'm basically . . ., my marriage broke down after 22 years I think and, hmmm, I feel I had no choice, I had to . . ., I left the family home really. My salary at the time was about 700 pound and my rent in the private house, private flat, was 650, so, but it gave me a sanctuary but it was only a tenancy for six months and they extended it to a year 'cause my boy was 12 at the time, 11 or 12, so I wanted somewhere that felt safe for both of us. And then when that tenancy finished I got halfway through the second tenancy, I got offered this council property and that brought up a lot of things, particularly from my childhood about going back into social housing or council housing 'cause I spent all of my adult life trying never to go back to what I'd come from. So I've been in this flat about four and a half, four and a three quarter years and I've never settled in it.

In this extract the respondent is very candid and gives an elaborated narrative response. There is a clear temporal dimension here, together with concrete references to durations and age – a chronicle is provided of a marriage that ends after 22 years, the need to leave the family home, time spent in a private flat and then a reluctant move to council housing. However, what makes this more than chronicle is the evaluative elements, the reflexivity of the interviewee who talks both about the constraints she has faced (the need to leave the family home, the lack of money, the need for a sanctuary or somewhere that feels 'safe'), her resistance to move back to council housing and her antipathy towards her current home. This therefore provides an example of the way in which a brief factual question can elicit a narrative within a qualitative interview, and of the way in which Labov and Waletzky's narrative structure may be applied in order to begin an analysis of the elements of individual accounts.

Later in the interview, respondents were more explicitly asked to provide an extended narrative. In section 4 of the interview cohort members were asked to provide their 'life story'. The question was framed as follows (and the bold text was used to indicate to interviewers phrases that should be used consistently across all the interviews):

> The **National Child Development Study** has collected a lot of detailed information about you in recent years. But we'd now like to give you a chance to say what has been important in your life from your own perspective. So could you talk me through your **life story** as you see it?

It was striking how many cohort members were taken aback by this question, and responded by laughing or exclaiming 'Oh my God!' or 'Oh Goodness me!', although in almost all cases were then able and prepared to go on and provide an account of their life so far. As a follow up to this question, respondents were then asked:

> Have you covered all of the major points you want to cover? What would you say have been the **key influences and turning points?**

As the final part of this stage of the interview, respondents were asked to complete a 'life trajectory' diagram. They were asked to select one from eight 'life diagrams' (taken from Ville and Guérin-Pace, 2005) which best represented their own life to date, or if none were applicable, to draw one of their own (Figure 20.1).

Respondents generally found this task interesting and straightforward to complete. Two 'positive' trajectories, diagram three and diagram seven (Figure 20.1), were the most popular and approximately a third of respondents chose to draw their own trajectory. These drawings were, however, usually a variation of trajectory three or seven, with different spacing between the 'ups and downs' that have been experienced through life. These life diagrams could perhaps be thought of as simple visual narratives, where the horizontal axis represents the passage of time and the trajectory line provides a summary representation of an individual's life trajectory. From an analytic perspective it is not just which diagram that is chosen that is of interest but also the way in which the respondent discusses his or her choice with the interviewer. This type of visual or diagramatic exercise could therefore be thought of as an additional way of eliciting and encouraging narrative information in an interview setting.

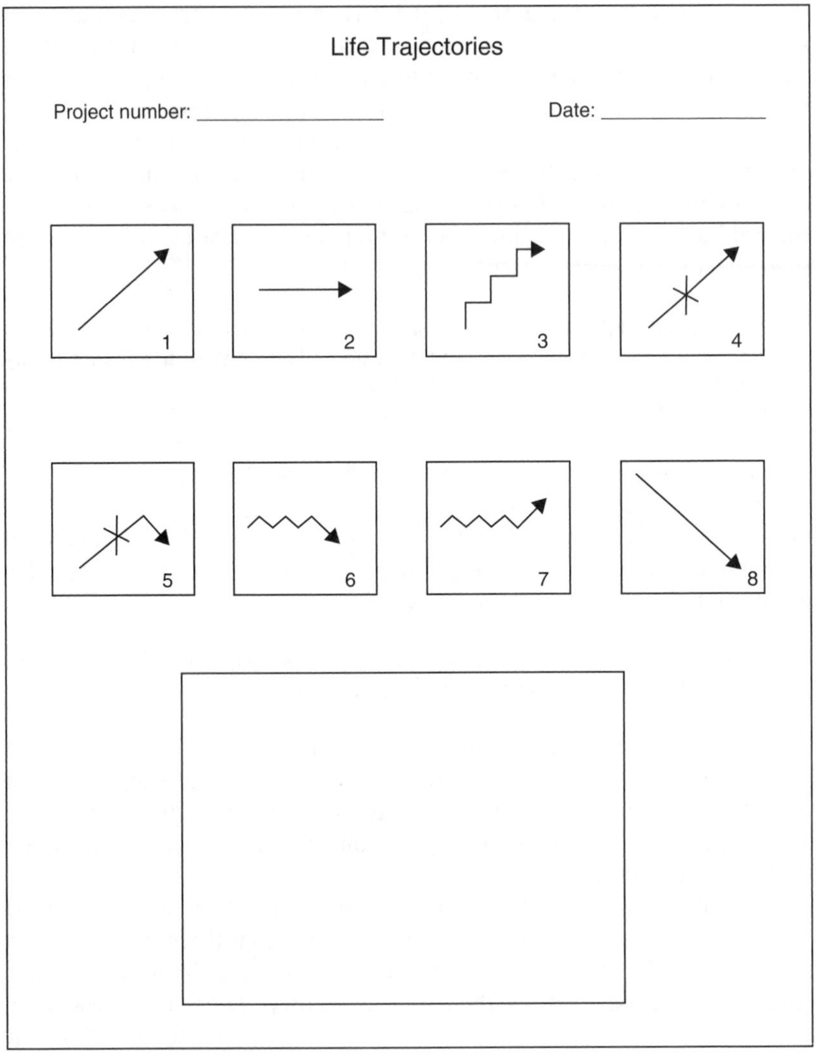

Life Trajectories

Project number: _____   Date: _____

Figure 20.1   Life trajectory diagrams

The researchers on the project were specifically interested in the nar-ratives provided by cohort members and analysis frequently focuses on these narrative aspects (see, for example, Miles et al., 2011). However, the structure of the interview was rather different from that used by others who work in the field of biographical narratives. For example, the

Biographic Narrative Interpretive Method (BNIM) of Interviewing advocated by Wengraf (2001) is much less structured than the interview schedule described above. BNIM focuses much more explicitly on helping the respondent to tell his or her life story, rather than the request for the life story to be embedded within a wider set of open-ended questions. There is no single correct method for conducting interviews informed by an interest in narrative, rather it is important for each researcher to be clear about the research questions and themes that motivate their work and to tailor their approach to fit this.

THE NATURE AND STATUS OF NARRATIVES WITHIN RESEARCH INTERVIEWS

The discussion above has aimed to provide an outline of practical questions to consider when aiming to collect narrative information in the context of a research project. However this focus on practical issues, at the level of method, runs the risk of neglecting to address debates around more methodological and epistemological aspects of narrative research. In relation to this it is important to highlight a debate which emerged about the use of narrative at the end of the 1990s and that continued through the 2000s. The central question is the extent to which narrative can be understood as providing a transparent window to a pre-existing reality or is better understood as a form of social action that should be the focus of research in its own right (Atkinson and Delamont, 2006). In a key paper, published in *Qualitative Inquiry*, Atkinson and Silverman (1997) highlighted the increasing dominance of the type of research interview that adopts 'a confessional mode of discourse and has as its goal the revelation of private experience' (p. 310). They argued that this conceptualization of the interview as an arena where authentic information can straightforwardly be collected/gathered from the respondent or interviewee is an overly naive one. It privileges the notion of the romantic subject, the self that is fully formed and unproblematic and who can be called upon to report reliably on past experiences, emotions and encounters. This questioning of the status of interview accounts as representing authentic and direct contact with the experiences and realities of interviewees echoes the concept of the 'Active Interview' in which both interviewer and interviewee should be understood as 'Active' participants (Holstein and Gubrium, 1995). As Denzin has also argued by understanding the interview as a joint performance it is recognized that 'there is no essential self or private, or real self behind the public self. There are only different selves, different performances, different ways of being a gendered person in a social situation. These performances are based on different narrative and interpretive practices' (Denzin, 2001, pp. 28–9). The role of the reflexive interviewer is therefore to deconstruct the uses and abuses of the interview. This approach to narrative interviewing involves a shift in the focus of research from 'roughly what lies beneath talk to what is happening now; in other words to actions and practices in their social context' (Taylor, 2007, p. 118). While this is an important corrective to an approach that assumes that an experienced reality can be straightforwardly read off from the narratives provided by respondents in research interviews, these more social constructionist and discursive approaches to research have been criticized for underplaying the coherence and continuity of the narrative structure of normal human experience and overemphasizing 'flux, disorderliness and incoherence' (Crossley, 2000, p. 528). In addition there is an argument that research that only focuses on an analysis of the interview encounter will not be successful in describing and seeking to understand individuals' lived experiences or addressing the substantive empirical questions which provided the original motivation for the research.

The key message here is that researchers should be clear about their theoretical and ontological perspective, as well as their research questions, when planning their research, so that the methods and approaches used for generating and recording information during the interview should be consistent with the analysis that is planned. For example, those whose purpose is primarily to explore the production of narratives as a discursive co-production shared by interviewer and interviewee need to ensure that material is recorded and then transcribed in enough detail to allow for the analysis of the discursive interaction, including interruptions, pauses, hesitations and overlapping speech. In other words, that the presence and role of the interviewer is as apparent as that of the interviewee. However, even for those whose primary interest is in the content of the narratives produced and who want to focus analytic attention on the experience that lies behind the talk, it is important to be aware of the way in which the interviewer and the social context of the interview will shape the telling and apparent meaning of those experiences.

THE ADVANTAGES AND DISADVANTAGES OF A NARRATIVE APPROACH TO INTERVIEWING

Over the past three decades there has been an explosion of interest in narrative within the social sciences, and many researchers are exploring innovative ways of encouraging respondents to provide narrative materials for the purposes of research, including the use of more visual methods.

In one of the earliest texts advocating narrative interviewing Mishler argued strongly that narrative approaches to data collection are more ethical in that they transfer power from the researcher to the respondent or participant in the research. He explicitly stated that 'A central task in what follows is to find ways to empower respondents so that they have more control of the processes through which their words are given meaning' (Mishler, 1986, p. 118). In very practical terms, as Cortazzi and Jin, (Chapter 35, this volume) explain, because stories are difficult to interrupt once they have begun, they enable speakers to 'hold the floor' and temporarily allow the narrator to control the conversation. However, there are perhaps two main critiques of the view that narrative interviewing necessarily is more empowering than other forms of data gathering in research. First, it should be recognized that the narrative genres or narrative forms that are available to individuals within a specific cultural context are likely to constrain the type of narratives that can most easily be told (Heilbrun, 1988; Plummer, 1995). Indeed one argument is that the narrative form actually does violence to individual experiences by imposing an appropriate way of recounting those experiences (see Watson, Chapter 34, this volume for further discussion of this). Second, the suggestion that narrative methods of data collection empower respondents relies on the tacit implication that the researcher is the super ordinate who has power to bestow on or donate to the, relatively powerless, interviewee. In contrast to this, Scheurich (1995) develops a more postmodern view of the power relationship between researcher and respondent that highlights the possibilities and opportunities for resistance and disruption within the research interview. The notion that narrative is by definition empowering is therefore over-simplistic and can obscure the complexities and uncertainties of interactions within research interviews, which themselves merit further investigation and representation within the finished research account.

Linked to these issues around power relationships within interviews, it should also be recognized that there is likely to be a great deal of heterogeneity between research participants in terms of their ability and willingness to give narrative accounts of their experiences. As has been discussed above, there are approaches to interviewing that can help, or hinder, the production of narrative, but even with the most skilled interviewer it is unlikely that every participant will produce the same number or quality of narratives in response to the same research interview. Indeed one approach to narratively informed research would be to focus on the question of why some individuals are more willing, or able, than others to provide narrative accounts within specific contexts. One danger of conducting research underpinned by an interest in narrative is that by definition it will tend to concentrate analytic attention on the narratives within interviews and to focus on those individuals within the group of respondents who were most successful at producing narrative accounts of their experiences. This runs the risk of failing to ask questions about that which is not narrated.

This chapter has focused on narrative data collection and in particular has discussed research interviews. However, as has been highlighted above, the decisions made by researchers about how to collect narrative information cannot be separated from decisions about approaches to analysis and to presenting research findings. In addition, depending on the perspective taken on the construction of narrative within the research, the level of detail preserved when recording narratives will be important. Chapters 34, 19 and 35 on the narrative construction of identity, life stories and 'Approaching narrative analysis with 19 questions' therefore all provide additional material that is centrally relevant to the questions raised here.

NOTE

1. A discussion of the impact of this article formed the basis of a whole volume of the *Journal of Narrative and Life History* (Volume 7, 1997). The original Labov and Waletzky paper from 1967 was reprinted as the first paper in this 1997 volume and the page numbers provided will refer to this later edition.

REFERENCES

Atkinson, P. and Delamont, S. (2006), 'Rescuing narrative from qualitative research', *Narrative Inquiry*, **16**, 164–72.
Atkinson, P. and Silverman, D. (1997), 'Kundera's immortality: the interview society and the invention of the self', *Qualitative Inquiry*, **3** (3), 304–25.
Carrington, S., Allen, K. and Osmolowski, D. (2007), 'Visual narrative: a technique to enhance secondary students' contribution to the development of inclusive, socially just school environments. Lessons from a box of crayons', *Journal of Research in Special Educational Needs*, **7** (1), 8–15.
Charmaz, K. (1991), *Good Days Bad Days: The Self in Chronic Illness and Time*, New Brunswick, NJ: Rutgers University Press.
Chase, S.E. (1995), 'Taking narrative seriously: consequences for method and theory in interview studies', in R. Josselson and A. Lieblich (eds), *Interpreting Experience: The Narrative Study of Lives*, Thousand Oaks, CA: Sage, **3**, pp. 1–26.
Chatman, S. (1978), *Story and Discourse: Narrative Structure in Fiction and Film*, Ithaca, NY: Cornell University Press.
Clandinin, D.J. and Connelly, F.M. (2000), *Narrative Inquiry: Experience and Story in Qualitative Research*, San Fransisco, CA: Jossey-Bass.
Connelly, F.M. and Clandinin, D.J. (1999), *Shaping a Professional Identity: Stories of Educational Practice*, New York: Teachers College Press.
Cortazzi, M. (1991), *Primary Teaching How It Is: A Narrative Account*, London: David Fulton Publishers.
Cortazzi, M. (1993), *Narrative Analysis*, London: Falmer Press.

Cortazzi, M. and Jin, J. (2006), 'Asking questions, sharing stories and identity construction: socio-cultural issues in narrative research', in S. Trahar (ed.), *Narrative Research on Learning: Comparative and International Perspectives*, Oxford: Symposium Books, pp. 25–43.

Crossley, M.L. (2000), 'Narrative psychology, trauma and the study of self/identity', *Theory and Psychology*, **10** (4), 527–46.

Denzin, N. (2001), 'The reflexive interview and a performative social science', *Qualitative Research*, **1** (1), 23–46.

Elliott, J. (2001), 'Success stories: narrative representations of women's lives', PhD Thesis, Department of Sociology, Manchester.

Elliot, J. (2008), 'The narrative potential of the British Birth Cohort Studies', *Qualitative Research*, **8** (3), 411–21.

Graham, H. (1984), 'Surveying through stories', in C. Bell and H. Roberts (eds), *Social Researching*, London: Routledge and Kegan Paul, pp. 104–24.

Heilbrun, C. (1988), *Writing a Woman's Life*, New York: Ballantine.

Hermanowicz, J.C. (2002), 'The great interview: 25 strategies for studying people in bed', *Qualitative Sociology*, **25** (4), 479–99.

Hollway, W. and Jefferson, T. (2000), *Doing Qualitative Research Differently: Free Association, Narrative and the Interview Method*, London: Sage.

Holstein, J. and Gubrium, J. (1995), *The Active Interview*, Thousand Oaks, CA: Sage.

Kelly, M.P. and Dickinson, H. (1997), 'The narrative self in autobiographical accounts of illness', *Sociological Review*, **45** (2), 254–78.

Kleinman, A. (1988), *The Illness Narratives: Suffering, Healing, and the Human Condition*, New York: Basic Books.

Labov, W. and Waletzky, J. (1997), 'Narrative analysis: oral versions of personal experience', *Journal of Narrative and Life History*, **7** (1–4), 3–38; Reprinted from J. Helm (1967), *Essays on the Verbal and Visual Arts*, Seattle, WA: University of Washington Press, pp. 12–44.

Martin, W. (1986), *Recent Theories of Narrative*, Ithaca, NY: Cornell University Press.

Miles, A., Savage, M. and Bühlmann, F. (2011), 'Telling a modest story. Accounts of men's upward mobility from the National Child Development Study', *British Journal of Sociology*, **62** (3), 418–41.

Minami, M. (2002), *Culture-specific Language Styles: The Development of Oral Narrative and Literacy*, Clevedon: Multilingual Matters.

Mishler, E.G. (1986), *Research Interviewing: Context and Narrative*, Cambridge, MA: Harvard University Press.

Moffat, B.M. and Johnson, J.L. (2001), 'Through the haze of cigarettes: teenage girls' stories about cigarette addiction', *Qualitative Health Research*, **11** (5), 668–81.

Plummer, K. (1995), *Telling Sexual Stories: Power, Change, and Social Worlds*, London: Routledge.

Prosser, J. (2007), 'Visual methods and the visual culture of schools. Special edition "The Visible Curriculum"', *Visual Studies*, **22** (1), 13–30.

Riessman, C.K. (1990), *Divorce Talk*, New Brunswick, NJ: Rutgers University Press.

Scheurich, J. (1995). 'A postmodernist critique of research interviewing', *Qualitative Studies in Education*, **8** (3), 239–52.

Seidman, I. (1998), *Interviewing as Qualitative Research*, New York: Teachers College Press.

Smith, S. (1996), 'Uncovering key aspect of experience: the use of in-depth interviews in a study of women returners to education', in E.S. Lyon and J. Busfield (eds), *Methodological Imaginations*, Houndmills: Macmillan, pp. 58–74.

Tagg, S.K. (1985), 'Life story interviews and their interpretation', in M. Brenner, J. Brown and D. Canter (eds), *The Research Interview: Uses and Approaches*, London: Academic Press, pp. 162–200.

Taylor, S. (2007), 'Narrative as construction and discursive resource', in M. Bamberg (ed.), *Narrative – State of the Art*, Benjamins Current Topics 6, Amsterdam: John Benjamins Publishing, pp. 113–22.

Thompson, P. (1978), *The Voice of the Past: Oral History*, Oxford: Oxford University Press.

Ville, I. and Guérin-Pace, F. (2005), 'Identity in question: the development of a survey in France', *Population*, **3**, 231–58.

Wengraf, T. (2001), *Qualitative Research Interviewing: Biographic, Narrative and Semistructured Method*, London: Sage.

Williams, G. (1997), 'The genesis of chronic illness: narrative reconstruction', in L.P. Hinchman and S.K. Hinchman (eds), *Memory, Identity, Community: The Idea of Narrative in the Human Sciences*, Albany, NY: State University of New York Press, pp. 185–212.

Workman, T.A. (2001), 'Finding the meanings of college drinking: an analysis of fraternity drinking stories', *Health Communication*, **13** (4), 427–47.

21. Jane's three letters: working with documents and archives
Sue Middleton

Over half a century ago, sociologist C. Wright Mills advised research students 'that the most admirable thinkers within the scholarly community you have chosen to join do not split their work from their lives. They seem to take both too seriously to allow such dissociation, and they want to use each for the enrichment of the other' (1959, p. 215). A social scientist's creativity (or sociological imagination) might be inspired when what at first may seem merely 'personal troubles of milieu' are reconceptualized as also wider 'public issues of social structure' (1959, p. 14). Accordingly, this chapter on the use of documents as resources for educational (and wider) qualitative research takes as an exemplar the story of how my vague and long-held personal curiosity about my mother's family was transformed into a five-year study of the writing of a small group of 'labouring poor' involving close study of documents in 12 repositories in Britain and New Zealand. As Prior (Chapter 31, this volume) also argues, documents can be interrogated in multiple ways. I describe how my readings of the letters and of archival resources pertaining to their wider contexts generated ever-changing questions, lines of inquiry and conceptual voyages through historical, sociological, geographical and educational theory.

INTRODUCING JANE

It all began at a family reunion at which I received copies of two letters written by my mother's paternal great grandparents, Jane and Samuel Retter. I was informed that Jane and Samuel had been servants employed at Ham House (in the village of Ham, near Richmond, in Surrey), that this house was now a National Trust property open to the public and that in 1841 Jane and Samuel had set sail for Wellington on the barque *Lord William Bentinck* with their two little boys, Jane pregnant with her third child. The two letters had been written in Wellington in 1844, just four years after Britain's annexation of New Zealand as a crown colony. The first letter began (for references to individual letters, see Middleton, 2010a, 2010b):

May 15, 1844.
MY DEAR MOTHER,-With pleasure I once more take my pen in hand to write to you, hoping it will find you in a good state of health, as, thank God, it leaves me and mine at present. My dear mother, I heard from you when my brother John received a letter from Henry, and was very sorry to hear that you had been very ill.

In this way I learned that Jane had a brother, John, also in New Zealand. Her second letter, dated 8 October 1844, was addressed to their brother Henry, who was still in Surrey:

... My dear brother, I am happy to inform you that I am happy and comfortable. My husband is in a constant place, where he has been these two years, under the sheriff of Wellington. Wages are reduced; my husband gets only a pound per week, but we have not lately interfered with his weekly money, for we have made the produce of the two cows keep us. We sell new milk at 6d. per quart, skim milk at 4d. per quart; fresh butter at two shillings per pound. Both our cows are within three months of calving: my heifer grows a fine little beast. Don't forget the seeds I mentioned in my other letter. Please to send me a few furze seed, and some damson, and some white bullace ...

My feminist curiosity was immediately aroused: Jane was a subsistence farmer, gardener and trader supporting her family and accumulating her husband's wages as capital. Were these domestic and economic arrangements typical of Jane's class at her time and place? My background in geography raised further questions: in importing the seeds of English plants (one of which, furze or gorse has since become an invasive and noxious weed in New Zealand), Jane was active in the (colonial) reinscription of a 'wild' southern landscape according to an English template.

Jane described the family's relations with indigenous Māori: 'we have found the natives very civil . . . If we can get the land claim settled, we are in hopes that the place will flourish both for the poor and rich.' Were Jane's seemingly liberal attitudes to Māori characteristic of labouring immigrants to Wellington in the early 1840s? What were these land claims? Would Jane's vision of a society where both rich and poor, British and Māori might all prosper have been 'possible' in the rural situation from which she had emigrated? And if not, how had this sense of possibility emerged? What were the conceptual and linguistic resources available to Jane and her contemporaries to 'think with'? How might Jane have learned to read and write? Was her 'liberalism' a product of her upbringing and schooling or did it emerge after and in spite of these?

In her letters Jane maintained family and wider village networks. They included references and messages to third parties in and around Ham:

Here we have so many barbers, tailors, ribbon- weavers, button-makers. Please to tell Mr. Tollemache they are not farmers, and we want farmers in a new colony; these are useful members. We have far too many lawyers; I believe some of them are going home in the same ships they came out by. Retter says he should like to see Mr. Tollemache at New Zealand.

The 'Mr Tollemache' suggested someone 'above' her in the social scale. From Wellington Jane was asking her 'betters' to recruit labour and capital for the colony. Did this signify some sort of radical shift in social relations after migration?

The copies of these letters circulated at the reunion had been typed onto a computer by an unknown relative, who had transcribed them from a publication called the *New Zealand Journal*. What was the *New Zealand Journal*? How did its editors get hold of Jane's personal letters, addressed to her mother and brother in Surrey? Whose interests were served by their publication? Who read them in their printed form? Did Jane consent to their publication? The letter from Jane to her brother was entitled 'Extracts of a letter from Wellington': who had done the 'extracting'? Was it Jane's voice alone I was hearing, or were other, editorial voices echoing through these printed versions of her texts? . . . But after the reunion I had to suspend curiosity to concentrate on my teaching and my 'real' research on a completely different topic. . . .

Six years later, I was granted research leave in London. Weary of decades of interview-based education policy research, I wanted a change in topic and methodology. I wanted to learn how to use the great research libraries of London and to immerse myself in old documents. My fore-bears had emigrated to Wellington during the first years of Edward Gibbon Wakefield's New Zealand Company commercial colonization scheme: might Jane's letters lead me to something academic? Allured by the British Library's vast manuscript collections, I determined to begin there with Wakefield's family correspondence.

Shortly after my arrival in London, I paid a tourist visit to Ham House. On the ticket office was a notice inviting visitors with 'historical connec-tions with the house' to make themselves known to staff. I did so and suddenly my private fascination as a descendant of servants crossed over into my professional life as a social historian of education and my reading of the Wakefield correspondence in the British Library. The bridge was a local history written by Evelyn Pritchard (2003), a National Trust volun-teer. Her book explained how the Retters had been part of a group of four families and three single men sponsored to Wellington as part of the New Zealand Company scheme by their employers, the owners of the Ham estates, the Tollemache brothers. One of them was the 'Mr Tollemache' in Jane's letter.

Pritchard's text identified further letters in the *New Zealand Journal* (NZJ) sent to their families or to the Tollemaches by members of this group. In the National Archives' Public Record Office at Kew, I pored over the 1840–45 issues of the NZJ. It was a London-based newspaper closely aligned with (but not owned by) the New Zealand Company. I found eight letters in total from the Ham group. A new research project had begun. I would begin with an investigation of the NZJ itself. Who was its editor? What were its purposes and policies? How were letters from labouring poor in Wellington obtained from their recipients in Surrey for reprinting in this London paper? How might these letters have been selected or modified by the editing process? And what value might they have as resources for researchers? This 'detective work' would immerse me in hundreds of documents. But, before recounting my detective story, I consider some uses of documents in qualitative research more broadly.

DOCUMENTS IN QUALITATIVE RESEARCH

Qualitative research records, interprets and explains the rhythms, colour and dynamics of everyday experience. Qualitative projects almost always include some engagement with documents: printed or handwritten, electronic or on paper, published or unpublished, public or private, contemporary or historical. As Prior describes (Chapter 31, this volume), they may be textual and/or visual (flowcharts, graphs, architectural blueprints, floor-plans and so on). They may be 'public' (official) or 'private' (personal) texts. Some documents combine textual/verbal and visual/pictorial elements (Thomson and Holland, Chapter 22; Tamboukou Chapter 6, this volume).

Public documents range in size and scope: macro, meso and micro. Macro-level documents include policy statements of governments, ministries, private sector or multinational organizations. They include reports of and submissions to committees of inquiry, national curriculum statements, statutes and regulations. Current policy texts are usually accessible through the organization's websites. Historical policy texts are archived in national, regional or institutional repositories. A National Archive is the official memory of a government. Private providers of education (such as church or charitable trusts) often have their own archives.

Researchers read documents according to disciplinary orientation and the purposes of the project. An official document may be read in its entirety or selectively mined for the secondary (including statistical) data it contains on a topic, such as examination pass rates of particular schools or children or regions (Gorard, 2010). Policy texts may be regarded as sources of empirical historical information: this was the policy, these were the debates about it and these were its results. Prior (Chapter 31, this volume) categorizes these approaches as 'content analyses'. Alternatively, as discussed below, they may be studied as discourse (with language the focus of inquiry).

'Meso-level' documents translate or operationalize macro-level policies for everyday implementation: the speech notes of politicians, the public notices in government gazettes or memoranda to teachers. Influenced by Marx's idea of a 'social relation', sociologist Dorothy Smith incorporates meso-level texts in what she terms 'institutional ethnographies' (Smith, 2002). In institutions such as schools documents are '"active" in co-ordinating what we are doing with another or others' (p. 102) and 'the text coordinates a local and particular course of action with social relations extending both temporally and spatially beyond the moment of the text's occurrence' (p. 103). To illustrate: lists of 'core competencies' or 'national standards' mediate between a distant (or 'extra-local') Ministry of Education and the teaching activities that give shape to children's classroom activities. These generate 'micro-level' public documents: teachers' assessments of children's progress or development and the children's own written, numeric, artistic or practical productions.

Since the 1980s, many educational researchers have included macro- and/or meso- and micro-level documents in various forms of discourse analysis. Although influenced by different theorists (including Bhaktin, Derrida and Foucault) discourse analyses share an emphasis on the 'language' of documents (Luke, 1995). An early compilation of such work, entitled *Changing the Subject*, explored how psychology 'regulates' social institutions, including schools (Henriques et al., 1982). Valerie Walkerdine's chapter (1982) studied how Piagetian developmental psychology was 'performed' in teachers' surveillance, monitoring and discipline of children. The arrangement of classroom furniture, the apparatus, the grouping and activities of children, and the templates for assessment all 'normalized' or 'pathologized' children according to Piagetian 'stages of development'. The textually created subject-positions (identities or personae) of the 'normally' (and abnormally) developing child were 'produced' by developmental psychology. A discourse 'produces its own object' (Butler, 1997). Documents are intrinsic to this, as Foucault explained:

> The examination that places individuals in a field of surveillance also situates them in a network of writing; it engages them in a whole mass of documents that capture and fix them. The procedures of examination [are] accompanied . . . by a system of intense registration and of documentary accumulation. A 'power of writing' [is] constituted as an essential part in the mechanism of discipline. (1977, p. 189)

As with other social sciences, research literature in education includes countless examples of Foucauldian discourse analyses that combine macro-, meso- and micro-level public documents with ethnographic data. Useful selections include those edited by Ball (1990), Popkewitz and Brennan (1998) and Tamboukou and Ball (2003).

While the public documents of policy and/or institutions have long-standing respectability as objects of social scientists' attention, private documents were once deemed the domain of the amateur (the local or family) historian: the births, deaths and marriage records used in family tree genealogies and family treasures such as 'old photographs, diaries and letters' (Fitzpatrick, 1994, p. viii). Ken Plummer (2001) describes these as 'documents of life'. If viewed as what Liz Stanley refers to as 'referential' texts (2004), they have sometimes been used as historical equivalents to the ethnographic data created in interviews or observational methods (see also Prior, Chapter 31, this volume; Thomson and Holland). However, as Stanley and others warn us, these texts should not be regarded as windows opening onto a past everyday reality. As with a qualitative researcher's interview transcripts or fieldnotes, letters and diaries are not simply conduits of information: their language, preservation and reproduction are themselves social phenomena worthy of study (see Tierney and Clemens, Chapter 19, this volume). Letters bear traces of the biographical, discursive (linguistic), spatiotemporal, social, economic and cultural conditions of their production (Earle, 2005; Gerber, 2005).

Private documents are often found in the manuscript collections of archives. But an archive stores only those deemed important enough to keep and the categories according to which they are catalogued signify themes envisaged as likely to interest researchers. It is also useful to consider the 'absences' of certain kinds of text. Families who 'gifted' personal documents to libraries were more likely to be those with education and/or to have attained social prominence. In the case of nineteenth-century colonial migration to New Zealand, the diaries and letters of colonial officials and prominent citizens were often kept, but 'correspondence from those who sailed steerage or were at the wage-earning end of colonial society' is scarce' (Macdonald, 2006, p. xiii). As with oral life-history studies that record the voices of living members marginalized or forgotten populations (see Tierney and Clemens, qv), the early nineteenth-century labourers' letters published in the NZJ might add to understanding of labouring poor in the initial phases of colonization. It was important to evaluate their nature and value as research data.

In the study of letters any distinction between public and private documents breaks down. The content, style and timbre of a letter is oriented towards its addressee (parent, lover, friend, colleague and so on) (see

Tamboukou, 2010a, 2010b). As with contemporary e-mails, in the nineteenth century letters were often passed around families or villages. This practice was understood, accepted and exploited by letter-writers, whose writing constructs and projects semi-public personae or 'epistolary selves' (Stanley, 2004). The same writers might project different 'selves' in letters intended for officials or newspaper editors: anticipated readers, then, are in a sense co-authors (Tamboukou, 2003). The publication of the 'personal' letter (addressed to 'My dear mother' or 'My dear brother') in a newspaper turns it into a different kind of text. Liz Stanley describes these as '"ur-letters" produced by transcribing, editing or publishing activities' (Jolly and Stanley, 2005, p. 100; see also Stanley, 2004).

New Zealand historian Erik Olssen (1992, p. 73) suggested that 'only by excavating the tropes of nineteenth century language can we start reconstructing the immigrants' psychic and mental maps and relating them to their new landscapes'. The 'mental maps' of my letter-writing labourers were enabled and constrained first by the conceptual, educational and material resources available to them in rural England. I would need evidence of my letter-writers' literacy and any schooling they or their children might have received. But what was it that made these farm labourers and servants 'recruitable' as participants in the New Zealand Company's systematic colonization scheme? I would first need background knowledge of Wakefield's theory of 'systematic colonization', the policies of the New Zealand Company, and British colonial policies more broadly.

JANE'S LETTERS AS PEDAGOGICAL PHENOMENA

My reading of Wakefield's family correspondence in the manuscript collections in the British Library was a useful introduction to the large secondary literature on his 'systematic colonization scheme'. I read biographical and historical studies of Wakefield, his theories and Company practices. In Archives New Zealand's Wellington branch I studied local 'meso-level' (or in Smith's terms, 'co-ordinating') documents: reports and regulations of the New Zealand Company and announcements in Wellington newspapers about its activities there. When Jane asked her brother to send seeds, or Mr Tollemache to recruit immigrants with agricultural skills, she actively participated in Wakefield's 'systematic colonization scheme' specifically and, more broadly, in the 'wider world system of production and consumption and exchange, not simply in limited economic terms, but also in social and cultural terms' (Gibbons, 2003, p. 41; see also Smith, 2002; Caruso, 2008). Jane and her peers were complicit in the colonial reinscription of landscape or, in Lefebvre's terms (1991), in 'the production of space' (see Middleton, 2010a).

Influenced by political economists (including Adam Smith and John Stuart Mill), Wakefield had envisaged a colony that, while modelled on the best features of English society, would avoid its pauperized and aristocratic extremes. Land would be sold at a 'sufficient price' allowing accumulation of a surplus with which to sponsor the emigration of labouring families. Algernon and Lionel Tollemache had been shareholders, directors and major investors in the New Zealand Company from its beginnings. They had purchased large acreages of land in and around Wellington at the first land ballot. They had paid the passages of the four families and three single men from their estate. The land price would be high enough to necessitate working for wages for several years, but low enough to make land or business ownership realizable for emigrating labourers.

But the land must first have been fairly purchased from local Māori. Consistent with Victorian 'stadial' ethnographic theories of racial development, Wakefield viewed Māori as 'superior natives' capable of civilization. Jane wrote that 'the natives are civilised'. Wakefield's aim was to integrate Māori throughout the hierarchies of his new colonial society. Māori traditions of communal land use would be supplanted by the British/capitalist system of individualized property ownership. But, as in Jane's letter, company 'purchases' from Māori were soon disputed. Jane saw this as unjust: 'If we can get the land claim settled, we are in hopes that the place will flourish both for the poor and rich.'

In its 'Regulations for labourers wishing to emigrate to New Zealand' (disseminated widely through billboards and newspapers) the Company listed occupations and character traits required of immigrants. To be considered for free passages (sponsored by the Tollemaches) my letter-writing labourers had to have met these criteria. The Company promised that 'every one of them who is industrious and thrifty, may be sure to become not merely an owner of land, but also in his turn an employer of hired labourers, a master of servants'. Here the Company projected a 'subject-position'. Jane's 'epistolary self' – her textual persona – was consistent with this: industrious (a farmer, gardener and trader), thrifty (saving her husband's wages) and a landowner.

So how did the tropes in Jane's letters (civilization and savagery, capital and labour, thrift and hard work) come to align so closely with the Company's scripts? This generated three simultaneous lines of inquiry. The first addressed the literacy and schooling of my individual letter-writers and their children (in Surrey and in Wellington) and of those of their class more generally (Middleton, 2008, 2011). The second was to identify editorial interventions in, or over-writing of, the letters in their published form (Middleton, 2010b). And the third focused on the transformation of 'servants' (most of them were farm labourers) in Surrey's lower orders into the self-sufficient colonial subjects desired for Wellington's conditions (Middleton, 2010a).

There was a large monitorial school in Ham, run by the Church of England's 'National Society for the Promoting the Education of the Poor in the Principles of the Established Church' with the expressed intention of teaching the lower orders to accept their allotted 'place'. I located the Ham National School's timetable in the Church of England's Lambeth Palace Library and copies of its textbooks in the British Library, St Pancras. While tropes of Empire, civilization and savagery were evident, the liberal promise of 'bettering oneself' had not entered the lexicon for pupils of the lower orders (Middleton, 2010b). The sense of possibility of social mobility through emigration would have to have come from elsewhere. Might this have been the Company itself?

Turning to Basil Bernstein's (2000) sociology of education for conceptual resources, I interrogated the New Zealand Company itself as a 'pedagogical device' (Middleton, 2010a). A pedagogic device is 'there for one purpose: to transmit criteria' (Bernstein, 2000, p. 78) according to which 'acquirers' (of knowledge, information or skills) are evaluated. It projects the 'external' identities (or subjectivities) desired by 'providers and evaluators': traits of character, physique or labour skills. Direct teaching is not necessarily involved. Pedagogical devices define the system's 'evaluative rules' and 'provide for acquirers the principles for the production of what counts as the legitimate text. The legitimate text is any realisation on the part of the acquirer which attracts evaluation' (Bernstein, 2000, p. 78). Here a text is anything read for evaluation – a document, a body type, spoken responses in an interview, a demonstration or a testimonial from a third party.

As a pedagogical device, the Company 'projected' criteria for desirable emigrants. Applicants had to exhibit these qualities. Jane and the other letter-writers were recruited, selected, transported and managed as part of this scheme. Landless labourers were to transform (or present) as self-sufficient, enterprising colonial subjects. The selection of the labourers' letters for publication accorded them the status of legitimate texts and their writers as having internalized the desirable colonial identification. Jane's letters presented her family as having these qualities.

But to what extent might her published letters have been invented or over-written by the editor of the NZJ? In Wellington's Turnbull Library I found correspondence between the editor of the NZJ in London (H.S. Chapman) and his friend Samuel Revans, the editor-proprietor of Wellington's first newspaper. In these exchanges, Revans frequently berated Chapman for unauthorized publication of personal letters sent 'Home' by prominent Wellington families and, as was the custom, copied and shared. There was no mention, however, of the letters of labourers.

JANE'S THIRD LETTER

There was widespread suspicion amongst historians that the letters from emigrants published in British newspapers could be editorial inventions or 'edited and excised to the extent that textual analysis had become unfeasible' (Fitzpatrick, 1994, p. 26). Some suggested that they had been editorially crafted 'to appear to be personal documents, when they actually were composed for use as propaganda, for or against emigration' (Gerber, 1999, p. 37). Before using the letters as data, I would have to prove authorship and trace the extent of editorial intervention. This would legitimate their value as documents by and about a class of people otherwise almost invisible in New Zealand's archival resources on the early 1840s.

I now had eight letters published in the NZJ under the names of four different members of the Ham group. I knew that the writers and the people they wrote about were genuine historical figures. While the genealogical trees in Pritchard's local history had provided a starting point, further family history material found me in unexpected ways. The curator at Ham House received inquiries from descendants of its former staff and of its aristocratic owners and forwarded these to me. Webs of electronic correspondence soon linked my research in Hamilton, New Zealand, with interested descendants of the letter-writers and their sponsors in New Zealand, the UK, Switzerland and Spain.

So I was confident about the authenticity of these letters. Their writers, recipients and contents were historically 'real'. My study of the NZJ's editorial policies and practice suggested that, although copying and 'correcting' might have been common, the letters' substance and authorship were genuine. The letters' routes from their village recipients into the pages of the NJZ seemed clear: two letters were addressed to the Tollemaches and others urged recipients to pass messages to them. As a Member of Parliament, Frederick Tollemache was often in London, and close to Company circles. And people with such connections often passed copies of emigrants' letters to the editor of the NZJ.

So I wrote and submitted a paper to a history journal. In writing, researchers, reviewers and publishers 'co-construct' not only a new text (the scholarly article) but also legitimate an authorial 'self' (Thomson and Walker, 2010; Thomson and Holland, qv). I was used to writing for sociological journals, but with this material it was an audience of historians that I needed to convince. The documents of reviewing are not only summative – they are formative. One reviewer's text was scathing: 'I am not convinced . . . that any part of the published letters was actually written by the working people credited with their authorship.' To render my research (and myself as historian) legitimate, I would have to locate an unpublished 'original' letter by at least one of the four Ham writers. Pritchard's book contained paraphrased extracts from a third, unpublished letter from Jane Retter and I had cited this as evidence. But the reviewer dismissed Pritchard's local history as evidence. Pritchard could not be contacted as she had recently died.

Her book mentioned that a typed transcript of this original had been sent to her by Kay (name changed to protect privacy), an Auckland descendant of Jane's mother (Mrs Philp, the letter's recipient). I had tried, but failed to trace Kay. But Pritchard had left one further clue: Kay had received the transcript from Barbara, another descendant resident in Madrid. Barbara had an uncommon surname. In desperation, I typed this name into Google. This linked to Barbara's old holiday photos on a social networking site and an e-mail address I deemed unlikely to be still active . . . I sent a message and went to bed . . .

The next morning a scanned image of Jane's handwritten letter appeared on my screen! Barbara wrote: 'My uncle showed me the letter in the late 1980's (it was found in my grandmother's belongings when she died). I don't have the original – which possibly is in my cousin's possession . . . but luckily I was given a photocopy years ago, which I reproduce here in PDF.' In days before the availability of scanners, Pritchard had worked from a typed transcript made from a photocopy of Jane's handwriting. Digital enhancement of the pdf scan made it possible for me to decipher most of the missing phrases in the transcription supplied to Pritchard.

Dated 8 October 1844, Jane's third letter – kept for generations within her mother's family – was written on the same day as her published letter to her brother. I could compare their content and language. Maternal and fraternal relationships affected the timbre of Jane's texts. Her tone was businesslike towards her brother, requesting him to solicit capital and labour in Ham through Mr Tollemache. It was highly emotional towards her mother, grieving the death of a baby, rejoicing in the birth of another and her pleasure in her four surviving children. But Jane's 'factual' descriptions of Samuel's work and wages, their land and cows were identical in the two letters. Her grammar and spelling had been lightly 'cleaned up' in the published version. I revised the paper, which was subsequently published (Middleton, 2010b). This publication legitimized these letters' 'provenance' and I could now use these documents as 'data' in wider sociological analyses (Middleton, 2010a, 2011).

CONCLUSION

This account of how a personal family puzzle was transformed into a cross-disciplinary research project set out to render problematic the qualitative, textual and visual resources social scientists treat as data. It demonstrated how a researcher's topic, questions and theoretical background inform the selection and screening of the materials available, enabling me to assemble 'an archive of my own – an assemblage of . . . textual and visual narratives' (Tamboukou, 2010b, p.165). I argued that, in the case of my immigrants' letters, it was essential to validate them as useful data by interrogating the circumstances of their production, reproduction and dissemination. The letter-writers' 'epistolary selves' were not only performances of personal attributes or familial roles, but were also enactments of broader 'tropes of nineteenth century language'. They could usefully be viewed as projections of the 'external identities' scripted by the New Zealand Company specifically and the utilitarian/liberal philosophy of the early Victorian era more generally. The New Zealand Company scheme offered labouring emigrant poor tropes of individual enterprise and social mobility – thoughts previously suppressed amongst those at the bottom of Surrey's rigid rural social order. As Maria Tamboukou expressed it, writing letters helped them to 'work upon themselves in search of a new mode of being or rather of becoming' (2010a, p. 6).

Researching and writing similarly produces new selves. As this story's researcher-writer, what had been disparate strands of interest and expertise coalesced and produced me as a different type of (cross-disciplinary) researcher, thinker and writer. Research produces its subjects (researchers) as much as it does its objects of inquiry. As with other kinds of 'data', documents continue to 'work' on and produce their researcher-readers.

REFERENCES

Ball, S. (ed.) (1990), *Foucault and Education*, London and New York: Routledge.
Bernstein, B. (2000), *Pedagogy, Symbolic Control and Identity: Theory, Research, Critique*, Lanham, MD: Rowman and Littlefield.
Butler, J. (1997), *The Psychic Life of Power: Theories in Subjection*, Stanford, CA: Stanford University Press.
Caruso, M. (2008), 'World systems, world society, world polity: theoretical insights for a global history of education', *History of Education*, **37** (6), 825–40.

Earle, R. (ed.) (2005), *Epistolary Selves: Letters and Letter-writers, 1600–1945*, Aldershot: Ashgate.

Fitzpatrick, D. (1994), *Oceans of Consolation: Personal Accounts of Irish Migration to Australia*, Ithaca, NY and London: Cornell University Press.

Foucault, M. (1977), *Discipline and Punish*, Harmondsworth: Penguin.

Gerber, D. (1999), 'The immigrant letter between positivism and populism: American historians' uses of personal correspondence', in R. Earle (ed.), *Epistolary Selves: Letters and Letter-writers, 1600–1945*, Aldershot: Ashgate, pp. 37–58.

Gerber, D. (2005), 'Acts of deceiving and withholding in immigrant letters: personal identity and self-representation in personal correspondence', *Journal of Social History*, **39** (2), 315–30.

Gibbons, P. (2003), 'The far side of the search for identity: reconsidering New Zealand history', *New Zealand Journal of History*, **37** (1), 38–49.

Gorard, S. (2010), 'Doing data analysis', in P. Thomson and M. Walker (eds), *The Routledge Doctoral Students' Companion*, London and New York: Routledge, pp. 221–30.

Henriques, J., Hollway, W., Urwin, C., Venn, C. and Walkerdine, V. (1982), *Changing the Subject*, London: Macmillan.

Jolly, M. and Stanley, L. (2005), 'Letters as/ not a genre', *Life-writing*, **1** (2), 75–101.

Lefebvre, H. ([1974] 1991), *The Production of Space*, transl. D. Nicholson-Smith, Oxford: Blackwell.

Luke, A. (1995), 'Text and discourse in education: an introduction to critical discourse analysis', in M. Apple (ed.), *Review of Research in Education*, Washington, DC: American Educational Research Association, pp. 3–48.

Macdonald, C. (2006), 'Introduction', in C. Macdonald (ed.), *Women Writing Home 1700–1920, Vol. 5 New Zealand*, London: Pickering and Chatto, pp. xi–xxix.

Middleton, S. (2008), 'Schooling the labouring classes: children, families and learning in Wellington, 1840–1845', *International Studies in Sociology of Education*, **18** (2), 135–47.

Middleton, S. (2010a), 'Labourers' letters from Wellington to Surrey, 1840–1845: Lefebvre, Bernstein and pedagogies of appropriation', *History of Education*, **39** (4), 459–79.

Middleton, S. (2010b), 'The seven servants of Ham: labourers' letters from Wellington in the New Zealand Journal, 1840–45', *New Zealand Journal of History*, **44** (1), 54–75.

Middleton, S. (2011), 'Schooling of labouring migrants, Surrey to Wellington 1841–1844', *History of Education Review*, **40** (2), 108–26.

Mills, C. Wright (1959), *The Sociological Imagination*, Harmondsworth: Penguin.

Olssen, E. (1992), 'Where to from here? Reflections on the twentieth century historiography of nineteenth century New Zealand', *New Zealand Journal of History*, **26** (2), 54–77.

Plummer, K. (2001), *Documents of Life 2: An Invitation to Critical Humanism*, London: Thousand Oaks.

Popkewitz, T. and Brennan, M. (eds) (1998), *Foucault's Challenge: Discourse, Knowledge and Power in Education*, New York: Teachers College Press.

Pritchard, E. (2003), *The 1841 Emigrants from Ham to New Zealand Sponsored by Algernon Tollemache of Ham House*, Richmond, Surrey, UK, privately published by Evelyn Pritchard.

Smith, D. (2002), 'Institutional ethnography', in T. May (ed.), *Qualitative Research in Action*, London: Sage, pp. 17–52.

Stanley, L. (2004), 'The epistolarium: on theorising letters and correspondences', *Auto/ Biography*, **12**, 201–35.

Tamboukou, M. (2003), *Women, Education and the Self: A Foucauldian Perspective*, Houndmills, Basingstoke: Palgrave Macmillan.

Tamboukou, M. (2010a), *In the Fold Between Power and Desire: Women Artists' Narratives*, Newcastle Upon Tyne: Cambridge Scholars Publishing.

Tamboukou, M. (2010b), *Nomadic Narratives, Visual Forces: Gwen John's Letters and Paintings*, New York: Peter Lang.

Tamboukou, M. and Ball, S. (eds) (2003), 'Dangerous encounters: genealogy and ethnography', in E. McWilliam (ed.), *Eruptions: New Thinking Across the Disciplines*, Vol. 17, New York: Peter Lang.

Thomson, P. and Walker, M. (2010), 'It's been said before and we'll say it again – research is writing', in P. Thomson and M. Walker (eds), *The Routledge Doctoral Students' Companion*, London and New York: Routledge, pp. 149–60.

Walkerdine, V. (1982), 'Developmental psychology and the child-centred pedagogy', in J. Henriques, W. Hollway, C. Urwin, C. Venn and V. Walkerdine, *Changing the Subject*, London: Macmillan. pp. 132–202.

22. Memory books as a methodological resource in biographical research
Rachel Thomson and Janet Holland

In this chapter we explore our use of memory books in a qualitative longitudinal study of transitions to adulthood (Henderson et al., 2007).[1] The idea of using a memory book emerged from several sources. We wanted to document young people's changing constructions of self over time, and were aware of the limitations of the interview method. Anthony Giddens's (1991) theoretical model of the reflexive project of self, in which a biography is organized in terms of flows of social and psychological information about possible ways of life, provided a starting point (Plumridge and Thomson, 2003, p. 214). But we were aware of the need to ground what is primarily a symbolic theoretical account of identity (McNay, 2000) as well as allowing for less coherent expressions of self. We also wanted to understand the resources the young people draw on in this identity work, which we conceptualized in Foucault's terms as 'technologies of the self': historically and culturally specific practices through which the 'individual acts upon himself' (sic) (Martin et al., 1988, p. 19). Although it is possible to access these technologies empirically through the narratives that young people construct in interviews, we also wanted to explore the potential for a more embodied and visual methodology that young people could engage with outside the interview setting.

Other methodological strategies have been used to disrupt a purely narrative presentation of self in interviews such as photographic albums in oral history and cultural studies (Seabrook, 1991; Walkerdine, 1991); and photographs in autobiographical and identity work with young people (Towers, 1986; Cohen, 1989; Allen, Chapter 17, this volume). One method employed in child therapy captured our attention – young people were encouraged to compile memory boxes to create a resource for the maintenance of a coherent sense of self in the face of parental bereavement, adoption and fostering (Jones, 1985; Barnardos, 1992; Harper, 1996). We hoped that young people in our study would bring records of their experiences to their memory books and material they saw as relevant to their current and future identities. We thought that asking young people to document themselves using 'memorable' material, away from the demands of the interview might facilitate the production of different and complementary expressions/constructions of self.

313

DEVELOPING THE METHOD

Our plan was to use the memory books as a basis for the second of three interviews, nine to twelve months apart. The first step involved creating our own memory books, which helped to provide an expectation of what might be produced and alerted us to ethical issues involved. Each member of the research team attempted to document their everyday life and sense of self over a three-month period. In sharing the results we found each had approached the task very differently. One had created an elaborate 'self book' organized around themes using pictures, writing and graphics. Another had kept a daily diary. Others had a disorganized collection of paraphernalia of everyday life. We felt exposure in sharing our books, guilt (at having 'failed' at the task'), envy (ours was not as 'good' as others) and embarrassment (revelation of the intimate), alerting us to advantages and disadvantages of the method. The realization that young people might be intimidated by the task encouraged us to introduce more structure for those who wished it. We also recognized that ownership and confidentiality would be important for those who created memory books.

Whilst experimenting ourselves we also consulted the young people on the method by post, eventually producing a small book that could be used as a diary or scrapbook, with stickers providing headings for entries, including 'adult', 'change', 'problems', 'sex', 'myself', 'relationships', 'love' and 'career'. We provided folders (to hold paraphernalia), glue and disposable cameras. A leaflet explaining what we expected from the memory books, commenting on issues of ownership and confidentiality and reflecting on our own experience of keeping them was included.

The memory book package was given to the young people at the end of the first interview, and they were asked to keep it in any way they liked and bring it back for the second. We explained that the books belonged to them, but we would like to copy extracts with their permission. These are the instructions:

In your book you could do any combination of the following:
- Write
- Draw
- Stick on photos
- Stick in magazine or newspaper cuttings
- Stick in things that remind you of something – tickets from events you have been to, postcards, etc.

You will see that we've included a set of stickers with 'trigger' words to get you started – and some blank stickers to write any other suggestions of your own.

You can change your style whenever the mood takes you. The most important thing is that whatever you put in is about you and your life: for instance your plans; your friends; your hopes and fears as well as the more day-to-day things you do.

It is good to put things in when they are fresh in your mind, but you can always add things later. Some of you may want to add something to the book every couple of days, others may use it every week, month . . . or whenever suits you. Try to remember to date your entries – it makes it a lot more interesting when you look back.

Before distributing the books to participants we piloted the memory book interview with one young person and notes on how the interview went were fed back to the other interviewers. We were delighted and surprised that 49 young people (of 98) brought their memory books to the second interview. A few had completed memory books but decided that they were too personal and would not share. The length ranged from three to fifty pages. Reasons given for not bringing a memory book included: the book had become too private; it was too risky to write things down where others could find it; it was not their style to write things down; and that they had lost the book, or forgotten to bring it along. We were flexible about the young people's use of the memory book, if there was one we used it as a basis for a subject-led dialogue or stimulus in the interview, if not we had an agenda to pursue.

In the interviews some young people revealed how uncomfortable they felt expressing themselves through writing. Others felt that nothing happened in their life that was worth writing about or so much happening that they had no time to do it. As one young man explained:

I don't know if it was my dyslexia, I couldn't write it, I felt they are going to see this diary, if they're going to see my handwriting and everything you know there's no way they're going to be phoning me up asking what does this say. (Owen)

Several commented on their unfamiliarity with the diary format, yet battled on and created some highly personal and articulate accounts of their lives. Martin's memory book is an amusingly written account of a club 18–30s holiday in Tenerife with his mates, and his first few days at university. 'It's certainly different because I haven't done any diary or any thing like that before, I suppose it's a little bit difficult remembering to write things down . . .'.

Although they complied with the task some nevertheless found the method constraining. Joss observed 'I don't really like diaries. It just lets you go back and relive your failures. Usually you write about failure', and Valerie commented 'it's like writing what you already know so it seems pointless'.

MAPPING THE STYLE AND CONTENT OF MEMORY BOOKS

It was not always realistic for researchers to copy entire memory books, and a checklist was created in which they noted the basic elements of style and content, whether copies had been made and how they reflected the character of the overall material. Original memory books were then returned to the young people. These checklists enabled us to create an initial mapping of the form and content of the books (Prior, Chapter 31, this volume).

Diary and scrapbook were the major forms of memory books, and the young people often used the stickers provided to structure their entries, sometimes adding themes of their own. A range of material could be included in the scrapbook, for example: print outs of emails, valentine cards, love letters and postcards (including from the research team),[2] a personal testimony (of a religious conversion), a family tree, autographs, train tickets, exam results, club flyers, stickers, tickets for cultural events, party invites, newspaper cuttings, artwork, poems, song lyrics, entries by friends, lists (of friends, of favourites and so on), pub mats, brochures and a hair extension. Many memory books combined elements of both diary and scrapbook. Ten young people produced memory books with only writing, and three with no writing. Many young people included photographs of friends, family and the spaces they inhabit. They also wrote about what was happening to them; their thoughts and feelings, and 'critical moments' in their lives (Thomson et al., 2002). More younger than older and more young women than men completed the books (37:12). More young women than young men favoured the 'Dear Diary' approach.

Memory books encouraged the young people to reflect on changes over time, and those who embraced the method remarked on how they enjoyed this process. One saw it as a continuous assessment of her life, and some used it as a repository for confidences. Paula, who had never written a diary, produced a very detailed memory book diary which provided her with a creative outlet when she went to college. For some keeping the memory book became extremely important, and they planned to continue the process; one felt so strongly that he had made provision in his will for it to be given to a close friend in the event of his death. The field note extract below captures the feeling of many of the comments made:

> R said she enjoyed keeping the diary very much, she liked being able to look back at what she had done, what she was thinking, and how she was feeling at different times. She didn't like to keep the memory book out in the open in her bedroom for fear any one else would read it, so when it wasn't in view she sometimes forgot about it. . . . Her general evaluation of being involved in the

project was very positive. She found that she thought more about what she was doing, keeping the diary helped her work through things in her head and she enjoyed meeting up and having the chance to talk over things. She valued the opportunity to reflect (not her term). She said that after the meetings she would go home and think about what she had talked about and what was happening. (Sheena, February 2002)

AUDIENCES AND PRIVACY

In attempting to make sense of the memory books it is important to consider the audience that young people might have expected or intended. Imagined audiences may be multiple and fluid, changing over time as is demonstrated by those who created a memory book but decided not to share it with researchers. Notions of privacy are also complex and mediated by information and communication technologies. They mean something different for adults and young people, who have few spaces that they control (Henderson et al., 2003). For young people in particular, the expression or creation of intimacy may not be coterminous with either the 'private', privacy or confidentiality (Thomson, 2009).

Several of those who completed diaries noted that although they kept them hidden from their family, they were happy for the researchers to read them. For others their memory book was more public and they showed it to their siblings or parents, friends and boy/girlfriend. Monica explained that she used her memory book as a way of communicating with her boyfriend. She gave him the book to read because it explained how she felt about things that had happened in their relationship that she found difficult to talk about to him.

Memory books varied then in terms of their tone and the audience for whom they appeared to be written. Some of the young people explained that they already kept a personal diary and so their memory books were more public. For others the books seemed to be quite personal, written as 'a conversation with oneself', although offered up to the researchers' gaze. Memory books also differed in how explicitly they referred to the research team as an audience. At one extreme Dear Diary entries were made directly to a named researcher, and at the other memory books took the style of a secret and private space, all, or much, of which was not shown to the researcher. Most commonly books slipped between styles. One young woman's memory book opens with a photograph and a formal introduction of herself, and includes musings on what is expected of her in the research. A few entries later she reveals that her parents have just split up and from this point her book moves into a much more informal style in which she expresses her day-to-day anxieties about what is happening in her life. As the style changes so the entries become less formal, with increasingly messy handwriting. Yet we are reminded of the researchers' gaze by a note at the bottom of one page (in a different coloured pen suggesting that the author has annotated the text) apologizing for the quality of the handwriting.

Kehily et al. (2002) suggests that private diaries can be understood as 'conceits', written to an imaginary audience underpinned by the possibility of exposure. In most cases the young people were happy to have their books looked at and copied, and few made any provisions about areas of content that they wanted to be kept confidential. But exposure can be negotiated. Young people were able to claim confidentiality in the way that they presented their memory book in the interview. Some edited as they talked through them, skimming over pages, and not referring to some of the material written or displayed.

The research team were aware that young people had entrusted us with their memory books without the benefit of *our* understanding of the audiences involved in academic production. This gave us a troubling sense of responsibility as captured in the following field note:

> I did not realise we wanted examples from all diaries. So I didn't ask R for a copy of her diary, or to copy different pieces, neither did I ask her how she would feel about me doing so. This is probably my own projection, but I have to say that it did feel that it would be a bit of an intrusion to do so. (Sheena, February 2000)

Understandably young people were most concerned about confidentiality in relation to the known audiences of their social worlds, yet the styles that they adopted suggest an awareness of a wider public as well as being cultural references to particular social locations. For example, one young man used his memory book as a vehicle for his own creative writing, producing what the researcher called an 'Adrian Mole' account of some 50 pages that was witty and journalistic. This and a number of other books showed the marks of deliberation and editing and contrast with a more informal, raw 'confessional style'. This raises interesting questions about the relationship between literary styles and the (production of) authenticity. Clearly some styles suggest a more mediated and crafted approach than others. However, we must assume that all the material produced for memory books are crafted. What then becomes interesting is the exploration of the particular styles that young people adopted and how these might relate to the wider cultural resources and textual styles to which they have access.

USING THE MEMORY BOOK DATA

In a discussion of the use of diaries, biographical objects and visual data as 'documents of life' Plummer (2001) distinguishes the role that such data may play in terms of 'documentation', acting as 'resources' for further explanation and as a 'critical' tool for understanding identity (Prior, Chapter 31, Reader, Chapter 30, Middleton, Chapter 21, this volume). We have found these three terms useful as a means of reflecting on the different ways that we have drawn on the memory book data in our work.

Documentation

The life story interviews that we conducted inevitably led to a high level of glossing in young people's accounts of the period of their lives between interviews. Recent events and preoccupations tended to dominate the accounts, and our interview agenda encouraged young people to focus on key moments of change and transition rather than the everyday activities and feelings that make up the fabric of everyday life. Memory books could document the more mundane aspects of teenage life, drawing us into a more immediate time frame of contemporaneous events. This was particularly so where young people had approached the task of keeping the books on a regular basis. Thus we gained insights into the temporal intricacies of friendships, romances, nights out, moments of boredom and insecurity that might otherwise have eluded us. Even where young people kept their memory books more sporadically, they might gloss over the period since they had last written, but then engage in detailed discussions of activities such as a recent holiday, the millennium, waiting for GCSE examination results and other events that would have received only cursory attention in an interview.

Things were recorded in memory books that were not mentioned in interviews. For example, when putting together a case study of one young man over a period of four interviews, we found that he had never been asked about his first sexual experience. This information was in his memory book, where a photograph of a hotel was accompanied by the handwritten text 'the place where I lost my virginity'. In many cases we observed that young people expressed 'a different voice' in their memory books, reflecting aspects of their character not evident in their interviews. Seemingly quiet, shy and serious young people sometimes presented us with highly comic portraits of self. Others created memory books in which otherwise hidden emotional depth and reflexivity were displayed. We do not wish to suggest, however, that the voices captured in the memory books are more authentic than those expressed in interviews, rather that the medium enriches and complicates the picture that we are able to build of the young person concerned.

The inclusion of biographical objects was an important aspect of some (but not all) of the memory books. These objects included photographs (both those that young people had taken themselves and those they had cut out from magazines or postcards and elsewhere), but also material: ticket stubs from leisure events and journeys, a pom pom from the night of the millennium, records of examination scores and other items. Such objects can be understood as 'documentation' of the stories that they accompanied, alerting us to those things that young people were proud of, but also echoing the records of achievement that they compile as part of GCSE course work (Prior, Chapter 31; Reader, Chapter 30, this volume).

The inclusion of visual data in memory books also provides an important document of participants' changing embodiment over the course of the study. Where young people included photographs in their memory books they provide an enduring record of bodies at particular moments. School photographs, pictures of them in newly acquired braces, a hair extension and photos of new tattoos and piercings all bring the body into the foreground within a methodology otherwise dominated by text and discourse. Likewise, pasted-in pictures and drawings all provide a sense of the visual cultures within which young people construct their identities.

Resource for Further Explanation

One of our aims in developing the memory book method was to facilitate the second interview, enabling an approach less driven by our research agenda and more by the young person. We hoped that the memory books would serve to de-centre the interview process, bringing aspects of the young person's experience outside the room into the encounter. The memory books certainly changed the character of the interviews of which they were part, both in terms of the dynamics and the type of data generated. This extract from field notes from the pilot interviews gives a taste of the impact that memory books had on the researchers involved:

> Initially when L came in with her memory book and photos I was a bit thrown. She immediately placed them all on the table and said something like 'here they are' in a way that suggested that she felt like she had done her homework – fulfilled her obligation to the project, that the purpose of our meeting was just to look at the memory book . . . I suppose that I should not have been all that surprised that she had the MB with her – the info I sent her in the letter accompanying the memory book, and the info sheet itself, outlined the method as just that – fill in the memory book, and bring it to the interview. After the initial reaction, I enjoyed the session with the memory book. It felt like we got onto

a different level of intimacy – but still fairly boundaried and safe. The method felt like the kind of thing you might do with a close friend – show them bits of your life, share holiday snaps, and info on people in the snaps. Time – it took much longer than the other interviews, and could have gone on longer. Much easier to go off on tangents – lots of pieces and snippets are thrown up. It's very tempting to pursue all, but it would be impossible. (Sheena, memory book pilot, October 1999)

Researchers struggled to find ways of engaging with the memory book material, and in practice developed a flexible approach, inviting young people to talk them through their memory books and moving between a discussion of the books and the interview agenda. From the transcripts it is difficult to get a feel for whether the memory book gave the research subject more control or not. The memory book part of the interview varied from a few lines to half of the interview. In these interviews a segment, usually the first, was spent examining the book, involving both the interviewer and/or the young person using cues from the books for a much fuller description of events and feelings. Given that the researchers had no time before the interview to read the books and to absorb their contents, the extent to which the material within the books influenced the interview itself depended in part on the willingness of the young person to refer to the memory book during the interview, and the extent to which the researcher was able to weave between the memory book material and the interview schedule. Where young people presented highly visual material with clear thematic headings and use of stickers this might be easier than where the books were dominated by text.

A Critical Tool for Understanding Identity

It was only after the second interview was complete that researchers were in a position to read the memory books and to copy sections of them for record. At this point the books became available to the whole research team and were subject to the mapping analysis described earlier, exploring questions of style, audience and content. Although it was interesting to see the range of ways that young people approached the task of compiling the memory book and the variety of cultural forms they drew on in this process, it was only when we began to develop in-depth individual case studies that the memory book data really came into its own. Memory books became an extremely valuable part of individual data archives, providing insights into the cultural resources and technologies that underpin young people's projects of self. The mediation of identity work through cultural resources becomes apparent in the memory books, where, for example, a classed and gendered identity may be claimed through the adoption of a particular literary style, or a mimetic relationship between self and other may be mediated through visual images literally cut and pasted from popular culture (Willis, 1990; Lury, 1998). We do not have space here to provide examples of these extended individual case studies, other than to say that it is through case histories that we can explore how an individual's project of self unfolds over time, drawing on specific cultural and social resources, situated within particular social horizons (Ortner, 2003; Thomson, 2009).

CONCLUSION

In this chapter we have described the development of an innovative method, the memory book, and its use with biographical interviews. We have placed ourselves within this account, described how young people responded to the challenge of creating their own memory books and mapped some of the elements of the form and content of the books that they allowed us to see. We have distinguished between their function as sources of documentation, resources for elaboration and as critical tools for the understanding of identity. We hope to have shown the importance of memory book data as a means to bring embodiment and the visual into a method dominated by text and a theoretical frame dominated by narrative. We also have shown how memory books facilitate the introduction of a range of different voices which disrupt cohesive narrative presentations and theorizations of self. These voices are diverse, but tend to be embedded within a more contemporaneous time frame than interview narratives. While they appear to be less 'public' accounts of self than those produced in interviews, they are far from simply 'private' and we have suggested that an exploration of audience and literary/visual style can be productively pursued as a way of understanding the cultural resources on which young people draw in the process of inventing themselves.

The memory books have proved to be a rich and provocative resource, which as researchers we feel privileged to access. We are being very careful about how we use them, intending to ensure that we respect young people's privacy and generosity. In much the same way as private letters and diaries, memory books are compelling, providing access into an extremely intimate space that has the danger of inciting voyeurism and a prurient fascination. It is then a continuing challenge to us to use the memory book data in an ethical way that honours the trust that young people placed in us by both creating them in the first place, and then sharing them with us.

Memory books are not simply records of daily life but are self-conscious repositories of memorabilia. Rather than simply understanding the memory books and the images within them as a document of the self, we could also see the books themselves as a technology – the means and the medium for inventing the self. In our view there is potential for the use of memory books with a range of different research subjects, with a view to gaining insight into periods of personal change.

NOTES

1. The Inventing Adulthood projects ran between 1996 and 2005, funded in consecutive studies by the Economic and Social Research Council. The data set has now been digitalized and archived and is available for secondary analysis. A full account of the methodology, including a showcase of the data set, can be found at http://www.lsbu. ac.uk/inventingadulthoods, or accessed through Qualidata, the UK data archive at Essex University. Also in the Timescapes Archive: http://www.timescapes.leeds.ac.uk.
2. Researchers sent various types of postcards to the young people as part of keeping in touch. Holiday postcards were also included in the memory books.

REFERENCES

Barnardos (1992), *The Memory Store*, London: Barnardos.
Cohen, P. (1989), *Really Useful Knowledge: Photography and Cultural Studies in the Transition from School*, London: Trentham Books.
Giddens, A. (1991), *Modernity and Self Identity: Self and Society in the Late Modern Age*, Cambridge: Polity Press.
Harper, J. (1996), 'Recapturing the past: alternative methods of life story work', *Adoption and Fostering*, **20** (3), 21–8.
Henderson, S., Taylor, R. and Thomson, R. (2003), 'In touch: young people, communication and technologies', *Information, Communication and Society*, **5** (4), 494–512.
Henderson, S., Holland, J., McGrellis, S., Sharpe, S. and Thomson, R. (2007), *Inventing Adulthoods: A Biographical Approach to Youth Transitions*, London: Sage.
Jones, A.M. (1985), *The Foster Child, Identity and the Life Story Book*, Bangor: University College of North Wales.
Kehily, M.J., Mac an Ghaill, M., Epstein, D. and Redman, P. (2002), 'Private girls and public worlds: producing femininities in the primary school', *Discourse*, **23** (2), 167–78.
Lury, C. (1998), *Prosthetic Culture: Photography, Memory and Identity*, London: Routledge.
Martin, L.H., Gutman, H. and Hutton, P. (1988), *Technologies of the Self: A Seminar with Michel Foucault*, London: Tavistock.
McNay, L. (2000), *Gender and Agency: Reconfiguring the Subject in Feminist and Social Theory*, Cambridge: Polity Press.
Ortner, S.B. (2003), *New Jersey Dreaming: Capital, Culture and the Class of '58*, Durham, WC and London: Duke University Press.
Plummer, K. (2001), *Documents of Life 2: A Critical Invitation to Humanism*, London: Sage.
Plumridge, L. and Thomson, R. (2003), 'Longitudinal qualitative studies and the reflexive self', *International Journal of Social Research Methods – Special issue on Longitudinal Qualitative Methods*, **6** (3), 213–22.
Seabrook, J. (1991), 'My life in that box', in J. Spence and P. Holland (eds), *Family Snaps: The Meaning of Domestic Photography*, London: Virago: pp. 171–85.
Thomson, R. (2009), *Unfolding Lives: Youth, Gender and Change*, Bristol: Policy Press.
Thomson, R., Bell, R., Henderson, S., Holland, S., McGrellis, S. and Sharpe, S. (2002),

'Critical moments: choice, chance and opportunity in young people's narratives of transition to adulthood', *Sociology*, **6** (2), 335–54.

Towers, T. (1986), 'Introduction', in T. Pateman (ed.), *Autobiography and Education*, University of Sussex Education Area Occasional Paper 13.

Walkerdine, V. (1991), 'Behind the painted smile', in J. Spence and P. Holland (eds), *Family Snaps: The Meaning of Domestic Photography*, London: Virago, pp. 35–45.

Willis, P. (1990), *Common Culture: Symbolic Work at Play in the Everyday Cultures of Young People*, Buckingham: Open University Press.

23. Turning the camera on yourself: digital video journals in educational research
ML White

INTRODUCTION

This chapter explores the use of digital video[1] and in particular digital video journals[2] in educational research. In the research project discussed here I chose to adopt a broadly ethnographic methodology using digital video as a way of practising and presenting educational research. In this research digital video was conceived and practised in the research process for documentation, representation, collaboration and reflection. The research style has much in common with visual ethnography (cf. Morphy and Banks, 1997; MacDougall, 1998; Ruby, 2000; Grimshaw, 2001), where video, film and photography along with other electronic media are viewed and created as cultural texts; representations of ethnographic knowledge and 'sites of cultural production, social interaction and individual experience that themselves form ethnographic fieldwork locales' (Pink, 2001, Introduction).

In the research the digital video journal was one of five categories of digital video and it is important to locate its use within a theoretical framework incorporating traditional (written) and digital text. The digital text included still images, electronic communication and five kinds of digital video: narrative orientated, episode orientated, interview focused, digital video directed by young people and my digital video journal. The digital texts provide multiple perspectives and multiple representations of the research process creating a richer, more complex research picture (Lincoln and Guba, 1985; Weis and Fine, 2000), and as I suggest elsewhere (White, 2009) a new ethnographic practice. In this research the use of digital video was a central research method and rather than report on the research findings, in this chapter I draw on the experience of the research process in order to consider the use of digital video journals in educational research and the challenges and success of the method. I begin by outlining the research context and the practical details of digital video use before going on to explore the processes, the possibilities and the dilemmas of using digital video journals in educational research.

THE RESEARCH CONTEXT

This chapter draws on ethnographic educational research that took place at Educational Video Center (EVC), a non-profit media education centre in New York City (NYC). Using words, images and digital video, recorded as part of the research process and the EVC curriculum, the research explored how young people represented themselves and their experiences of digital video production in a third space (Bhabha, 1994). Coffey et al. (2006) remind us that 'ethnographic and qualitative research is now situated within a world increasingly saturated by multimedia technologies' (p. 15), and this is true in the research setting where young people produce a documentary and digital video is used as part of a pedagogical practice and in the process to achieving an educational goal. At EVC young people experience how digital video can be used to negotiate identity (Dyson, 1997; Fisherkeller, 2002), and that their real world experiences, as film and television viewers, in their communities and as learners, has value (Buckingham, 1996; Tyner, 1998; Goodman, 2003; Kist, 2005).

While Lomax and Casey (1998) suggest that 'the camera . . . is socially significant' (p. 6), and Bogdan and Biklen (1998) believe that the presence of a video camera in the classroom causes students to behave differently, at EVC the digital video camera (and digital stills camera) were familiar and much used pieces of technology and young people become familiar with visual representations of themselves through the process of documentary production (Goodman, 2003). This limited their 'reactivity' to the digital video camera (McCarty, 1995), described by Stigler et al. (2000) as the 'camera effect' and changed how they created and viewed digital representations of themselves. In other research settings the use of digital technology might be more problematic and there are instances when video is rejected as a method when it is considered a distraction for those involved (cf. Mousley, 1998).

The research then is both anthropological in that it is focused on social relationships and culture and ethnographically styled as it attends to the social contexts of contemporary digital video production. The research attempts to understand the value and impact of specific educational experience rather than generate a 'thick' description (Geertz, 1973), of young people's cultures. Considering that conventional writing presents a 'thin' description, multi-media and multi-modal texts were included to counter the representation of a single implicit point of view that does not do justice to the complexity of the experience. In other work (White, 2009) I use the term Ethnography 2.0[3] because I believe that the development and availability of digital technology and its collaborative affordances has changed ethnographic research practices. While in the past anthropologists and ethnographic researchers have utilized analogue technologies (Coffey et al. 1996), today digital technology changes the materiality of texts, transforming communication (Kress and Van Leeuwen, 2001; Kress, 2003), and developing new possibilities for research practice (Tierney and Clemens, Chapter 19, this volume). In the research I argue that digital technology changes the relationships between text, author-producer and audience and have come to agree with Illich (1973) who believed that 'tools are intrinsic to social relationships. An individual relates himself in action to his society through the use of tools that he actively masters . . .' (p. 21). In this research the data of digital video becomes a basis for telling stories that are central to the dialogical process of research.

'I'M TURNING THE CAMERA ON . . .'

> An ethnographer going into the field ten or twenty years from now may take along as equipment a video camera, one or two microphones, a computer, disks, or tape for storage, a printer, paper and maybe some lights. (Seaman and Williams, 1992, p. 306)

While researchers have warned against an obsession with technology (Collier and Collier, 1986; Hammersley and Atkinson, 1995), relatively little is written about the choice of technology (Ratcliff, 1999) or its use and potential in educational research (Walker, 2004). Much of what is available addresses the use of digital technologies and hypermedia construction in research practice (cf. Coffey et al., 2006), and does not employ the technologies they are concerned with[4] (Moores, 1993, p. 3). As the cost of computer hardware and editing software has fallen digital video use has become a viable option in research methodologies (Pea, 1999; Walker, 2002), and more researchers have begun to think about their relationship with technology and its relationship to education and culture and the contribution it might make to research (Weaver and Atkinson, 1994; Dicks and Mason, 1998; Coffey et al., 2006). Recognising the need for the modes of representation to reflect the modes of enquiry I purposefully sought out multiple modes and multiple media to tell the research story. In any research it is important to remember that the choice and use of equipment inevitably influences the outcomes (Prosser, 1998; Ratcliff, 1999; Pink, 2001; Grady, 2004), and in this section I describe my equipment choices before going on to detail the theoretical framework, the processes involved in using digital video use and the ethical dilemmas that emerged.

Before travelling to EVC I purchased a mid-sized digital video camera, a lavaliere or clip-on microphone and headphones for exclusive use in the research project. Ratcliff (1999) travelled to his research site (an

American elementary school[5]), each day with a VHS and a VHS-C camcorder (the latter was used by a research student who often accompanied him and recorded Ratcliff recording students), two tripods, two pairs of headphones, microphones, tape and power supplies. Travelling to a location where digital video equipment was available to both purchase and borrow, I travelled to New York with only items that I considered to be essential to the research process and technology I needed to be familiar with in order to operate it successfully. I did not take extra equipment in part because I was limited to what I could travel with but also because I did not want to stand out in the research setting. Unlike Ratcliff (1999), I did not record myself recording others and I only ever used one digital video camera at any one time. My choice of equipment was influenced by my experience using technology and I wanted a 'prosumer'[6] camera that would provide good picture quality but was not physically large. I purchased a Panasonic NV400; a mid-sized 3CDD[7] miniDV[8] camera which is not too big to stand out nor too small to be fiddly to operate. While my digital video camera might have been more economically purchased in NYC, the broadcast standards in Europe and the USA and Japan are different and a NTSC (USA/Japan) digital video camera would not be compatible with a UK television set (for playback), or easily edited.[9] More importantly, I knew that it was important to familiarize myself with the digital video camera and its functions before using it in a research setting. Looking back, the technical preparation time was important to my confidence at EVC where all members of staff were technically proficient and when I arrived at EVC I did not have to focus on the mechanics of digital video use which might have taken my focus away from what was happening and affected my early interactions with young people and staff. If I purchased the research equipment today I would undoubtedly make different choices and with smaller, cheaper equipment available would likely choose a digital video camera that recorded directly onto a hard drive.[10]

VIDEO IN RESEARCH

While much of the literature concerning the use of video comes from the fields of anthropology and ethnography, the view that 'film and video have become essential for the study of human behaviour' (Collier and Collier, 1986, p.139), and that there are 'understandings that may be accessible only through non-verbal means' (MacDougall, 1997, p. 292), is developed in a number of education studies (cf. Allen, Chapter 17, this volume). Video is used in teacher education (Stigler et al., 2000), to record classroom behaviour for later analysis (Goldman-Segall, 1998), to record the research process (Ratcliff, 1999), and as a tool for self-reflection and coaching (Hopkins, 2001; Sherin and Han, 2004). Studying peer culture in the classroom, Beresin (1993), used video to record student interactions. After each lesson she asked classroom teachers to view video recordings and compared their understanding of events with her own analysis of what was taking place. Harel (1991), studying children's classroom behaviour, described the video camera on a tripod as 'a silent observer' (p. 449) and used it when she could not take part in activities because she was in another part of the room. While Bowman (1993) used video to record students as they played computer games and considered that what he saw helped him to plan future observations. Commenting on the use of video in classrooms, Lampert (2000) notes that 'video makes it possible to have a running image of the teacher-student-subject interaction' (p. 68).

VIDEO DIARIES

In educational research video diaries have been used to explore learning dispositions adding 'to what is already accessible in the classroom' (Noyes, 2004, p.195) and to document the experience of learning in a technology rich environment (Quadri et al., 2007). In other research Holliday (2004a) used video diaries to examine the performative nature of queer identities and to evaluate their potential 'for capturing some of the complex nuances of the representation and display of identities' (p. 1597). Giving participants video cameras, Holliday asked adults to represent themselves in their everyday environments at 'work, rest (home), and play (the scene)' (p. 1598). Reflecting on the experience, Holliday (2004b) believed that through the process of video production 'the diarists' selves and their reflections seem to be much more present . . . through video than if I were simply reciting their accounts in my own words' (p. 60).

In the research at EVC young people did not produce a digital video diary and they were not asked to although they did use digital video technologies 'to construct accounts of their lives in their own terms' (Holloway and Valentine, 2000, p. 8). Asking someone to produce a digital video diary is to ask them to interpret what a diary is. Rather than offering 'a more direct understanding of people' (Rich et al., 2000, p. 156), what is produced might be more accurately considered 'a kind of performance' (Latham, 2003, p. 2002).

Central to using digital and video technologies is the relationship between what we see and what was recorded. In other words, asking the questions: who has selected, framed and edited what we see and how much can we trust of what we see of these digital video events?[11] The tendency to treat visual texts as 'visual evidence' is problematic (Davies, 1999, p.120) and Flick's (1998) view of 'visual media for research purposes' as 'second hand observation' (p.151) is misleading because the process involves selection of frame and focus, editing and interpretation. Like MacDougall (1997), I recognize that the perspective afforded by the digital video camera is not an objective one and focusing on one thing means that something else is out of focus (Young, 1975). While the objectivity/subjectivity debate is an important consideration in any research, as Pink (2006) notes it is a historical debate. Like Banks who asserts that '[all] image production by social researchers in the field, indeed all first hand social research of any kind, must be collaborative to some extent' (2001, p. 119), I recognize my subjectivity in the research and I have endeavoured to produce a reflexive, theoretically informed account. In this research someone always operated the digital video camera (myself or a young person at EVC), and its position and a frame was chosen to record particular events and action. Unlike ethnographic film (cf. Ruby, 2000), the digital video extracts (and the digital video journals) of the research do not present a linear story, nor are they intended to as they represent the complexities of the research task, of the human experience and of multiple points of view in the research process. What is recorded and how it is recorded reveals the situated nature of the technology, within the physical space and within wider society.

THEORETICAL FRAMEWORK – FIVE CATEGORIES OF DIGITAL VIDEO

Throughout the research period at EVC I developed a theoretical frame broadly defining five categories of digital video use: narrative orientated digital video, episode orientated digital video, interview focused digital video, digital video directed by young people and my digital video journal. The identification of each category was developed at EVC as a way of making sense of digital video use and as an acknowledgement that digital video (and other digital media) are created as cultural texts and representations of new ethnographic knowledge. In this section I discuss the possibilities and the dilemmas of each digital video category and provide detail of when they were each used.

Source: ML White, 2005.

Figure 23.1   *Digital video still of the EVC classroom*

Narrative Orientated Digital Video

As viewers of television and film we borrow the visual and textual codes we are most familiar with. Made up of a variety of different shot types we are used to seeing very brief images, which change in order to create a story, a mood or provide information. Narrative orientated digital video is the form that is most similar to this style and at the start of the research process was the form I used most. Narrative orientated digital video included recordings of the different locations at EVC (the office space, classroom and common areas), and included both structured, formal curricular and informal events (Figure 23.1). While the narrative orientated recordings were observational they did not record whole events or episodes of life at EVC. Narrative orientated recordings tended to be shorter in length and included a wide range of locations and activities that edited together would create a mosaic portrait of EVC and not a structured narrative.[12] Grosz (1995) reminds us that a particular reading is never guaranteed and, like the edited montage where meaning is made when the audience interprets what they see and from the order and relationship of shots, narrative orientated observation presents only one point of view.

The use of digital video complicates the process, the presentation, the reading and the representation of research and requires that the reader 'is put in a role that requires active engagement' (Walker, 2002, p.120) with the text. The view that 'representations, once made, are open to re-representation, misrepresentation and appropriation' (James et al., 1997, p.13) is especially true when using digital video as even the original media form is not clear and what we see can be 'faked' with digital tools changing 'the way it was'[13] (Pea, 1999, p. 353). As Berger ([1972] 1977) stated, 'the relation between what we see and what we know is never settled' (p.7).

Episode Orientated Digital Video

Episode orientated digital video included long unbroken recordings of classroom sessions where young people were engaged in EVC activities, including video production and interview exercises that took place both inside and outside the building. Like Strandell (1994, p. 32), I defined an episode as a course of events limited by time and space and a particular group of people. A new episode began when young people moved from the classroom to the street or when a new activity began. Episodic recordings were framed to include as much of the area as possible and rarely involved a change of camera shot type or location. This kind of digital video recognizes that any digital video recording involves selection (Collier and Collier, 1986) and subjectivity, where to position the digital video camera and what to record.

Interview Focused Digital Video

The digital video camera was also used to record interviews and I always asked both young people and staff to choose their interview location and offered them the opportunity to frame themselves using the LCD screen, which when turned 360 degrees allowed people to view themselves 'on screen' and gave them the opportunity to make changes to the framing of the shot. Without exception everyone chose mid shots and placed themselves at the centre of the frame. Ruby (1995) suggests that posed photography provides an indication of how people want to be seen by others. Interview focused digital video was staged in the same way that a photograph is set up and on a number of occasions interview times were changed when young people said that they were unhappy with what they were wearing, did not think that they looked 'good enough' (to be recorded) or simply did not want to be filmed. In a digital video interview Jessica is seen to pull her hood over her head saying 'I didn't do my hair today', indicating her awareness and control of the represented self. When interview times were changed I considered that participants should have 'some say in the construction of their image' (Ruby, 2000, p. 219) and to choose how they wanted to look. While I consider that my research approach was collaborative I recognize that 'we are, as researchers socially located and frequently privileged' (Raby, 2007, p. 55) and I worked hard to ensure that agency was shared.[14]

Digital Video Directed by Young People

The fourth kind of digital video was that recorded by young people at EVC, both as part of the curriculum and when 'playing', during breaks and when 'off task'. While I planned to use digital video recorded and produced by young people as part of the EVC curriculum and directed by the EVC methodology, a more informal digital video use developed during the research process.

At EVC there were often a number of digital video cameras 'on' – in the classroom, outside on the city street and when visiting a new location to record an interview (Figure 23.2). If my camera was not already being used as part of the research process young people sometimes used the digital video camera to record others working, city scenery or when 'playing' and taking a break. Looking through a digital video tape after class one day I watched and listened to Veridiana interview four young people, asking them to talk about what they were doing and how they felt about EVC (something I had asked her previously). Veridiana provided a commentary to the classroom shots and told me that I had not 'missed anything' by being away from class.

Digital video recorded by young people provides an important point of view and develops the collaborative nature of the research. What young people choose to record, how they frame shots and what they say or do not say in the voice over and to each other communicates in a meaningful way about their cultures and communities, their identities and their educational experiences. In this research 'playing' with the digital video camera is understood as a process in which the self is produced (Butler, 1990) and like Niesyto (2000) I believe that to understand 'youth's ideas, feelings, and their ways of experiencing the world, he or she should give them a chance to express themselves also by means of their own *self-made* media products' (p. 137, original emphasis).

Source: ML White, 2005.

Figure 23.2   Digital video still of a filming trip

Digital Video Journal

The final kind of digital video was my own digital video journal (Figure 23.3). Pink (2001) suggests that 'video can serve as ethnographic diary keeping' (p. 88), and I used the digital video camera in the construction and the presentation of my research self. Like the video diary form (first identified in the 1990s when Video Nation was broadcast on BBC2), through the digital video journal 'an autobiographical self can be talked into being' (James, 1996, p.125) and my digital video journal is one representation of the 'contemporaneous flow of public and private events' (Plummer, 1983, p.170). While the use of written diaries as a research method is well documented (Corti, 1993), I used the digital video camera to record my reflections on the research experience as it took place, providing 'the opportunity for the recording of events and emotions in their social context' (Meth, 2003, p. 200).

I began my digital video journal before travelling to EVC and in those early recordings I explored the theoretical considerations of the research

Source: ML White, 2007.

Figure 23.3 A still from my digital video journal

and my personal concerns. Talking to 'an absent, imaginary other . . . effectuated by the technology' (Renov, 1996, pp. 88–9) I acknowledged my self and my fears in order to develop a critical reflexive perspective. The digital video journal offers a self-revelatory narrative (Atkinson and Silverman, 1997) and through its construction adds 'critical reflection to our ongoing task of making sense out of who we are and what it is we do' (Agar, 1986, p. xi). Through the experience of recording myself and keeping a digital video journal I considered the objectifying potential of technology use and I learnt first hand the need to note and reflect on the conditions of production. When I later used a digital video camera at EVC I did not ask anyone to act differently as I understood that asking people to 'act naturally' is to ask them to objectify themselves and to perform for their own gaze. Keeping a digital video journal I found it difficult to 'be myself' and to reflect on my hybrid researcher-teacher-participant identity. The digital video journal requires that the researcher be comfortable with technology, the sound of their own voice and their represented image. Viewing extracts 'after the fact' (Geertz, 1995) I was very aware of how I looked (very tired), and sounded (very Scottish), and was not comfortable showing the digital video to others. This caused me to question my own ethical position and consider whether it was acceptable to record others when I was hesitant to record myself.[15]

CONCLUSION

For Ruby (2000), a reflexive approach is an ethical approach and it is especially important when using digital video to note and reflect on the conditions of recording and of production. MacDougall (1998) differentiates between deep reflexivity when video records the research encounter and explanatory reflexivity common in written texts about the research experience and produced after the event. The digital video journal occupies a hybrid space between the two and this must be acknowledged.

In any research project our ethical stance and the challenges that emerge pervade all that we do and every decision we make: whom we speak with; how we behave; the questions we ask; the technology we use and how we publicize our work. While I am not suggesting that a digital video camera in the hands of young people naturally makes for an empowering experience, I have endeavoured to work honestly and the five categories of digital video ensure 'that power dynamics are not hidden and that efforts at democratizing power take place to the extent possible' (Cheatham and Shen, 2003, pp. 318–19). Like Best (2000), who visited high schools and interviewed young people as they prepared for their high school prom, Hey (1997), who studied female friendships in a secondary school, and Pascoe (2007), who experienced 'moment[s] of misidentification' (p.177) in her study of masculinity and sexuality in a high school, I tried to balance the ethical considerations of research 'with' young people and the (re)presentation of personal experiences. To protect the identity of participants Best (2000), Hey (1997) and Pascoe (2007) changed the names of people and the places involved.[16] In this research the use of digital video makes such anonymity impossible and I am acutely aware of my responsibility representing the lives of others. While Mitchell (2005) argues that the 'life of images is not a private or individual matter. It is a social life [of] . . . the worlds they represent' (p. 93), I feel responsible for the visual material that I have and indebted to protect it. While everyone who took part in this research project agreed to participate and I have signed consent forms, the inclusion of a digital video and my digital video journal requires more than talking to the camera and researchers must consider the ethics of research practice and how digital video impacts on them. Digital video is neither produced nor 'read' in isolation and while 'the data produced are unashamedly complex . . . therein lies an advantage' (Noyes, 2004, p. 207).

I am grateful to the young people and staff at EVC (http://www.evc.org) for their participation in this research.

NOTES

1. I distinguish between film, video and digital video to develop the view that 'new' technology requires new methods of research (Pink, 2001). While film and (analogue) video is considered a recording tool, which is later read, digital video is concerned with collaborative knowledge construction and a new digital discourse. Digital technology changes the nature and possibilities of research methods 'facilitating direct exchanges and communication across great distances, thus creating new possibilities for dialogue with audiences' (de Block, et al., 2005, p. 77).

2. In this chapter the term diary refers to a personal record concerned only with the detail of what took place while a journal is a reflexive text not restricted by form, structure or content.

3. O'Reilly (2004) pioneered the use of the suffix 2.0 when he used the term 'Web 2.0' to refer to the collaborative nature of the Internet.

4. One of the ironies of the research and the chapter is that the medium of print is not particularly effective in communicating the content and process of the research experience or in the consideration of digital video use in ethnographic research.

5. The first stage of compulsory education: in the UK this is referred to as primary school.

6. This term was first coined by Toffler (1980), as a contraction of 'producer' and 'consumer' and describes the complex relationship between professional and amateur producers.

7. The visual quality of digital video is directly related to the camera lens quality and the processing power of the Charged Coupled Device (CCD). The Panasonic NV400 has a Leica Dicomar lens and a 3CCD system that uses 1 070 000 pixels times three.

8. MiniDV refers to the recording device (the tape) that stores the video. MiniDV is one of three common digital formats used to record sound and images.

9. While it is possible to edit different formats of DV in iMovie (the Apple editing software I used), I did not want to be restricted to either a software package or only one digital video camera in case of technical failure.

10. This would avoid the need to purchase and use DV tapes, which have a limited life span and are more difficult to secure. Recording directly onto a hard drive would also eliminate the need to import digital video, which is a time consuming task.

11. It should be noted that it is not the use of digital technology that prompts these questions. For example, the Yanomami series of ethnographic films produced by Nepoleon Chagnon in collaboration with Tim Asch continue to be controversial after the publication of Tierney's (2000) *Darkness in El Dorado*. Drawing on the Yanomami controversy, Borofsky (2005) considers the ethical and controversial questions critical to the field of anthropology and the practice of fieldwork.

12. Reader (Chapter 30, this volume) describes a similar process with images that he calls juxtapositioning.

13. Whether anything can ever be represented 'the way it was' is not addressed in this study.

14. (Re)presenting images form the research here I recognize the ethical contradictions. While I have permission for the reproduction of this material I am choosing what to share.

15. My digital video journal was recorded at EVC, in the library, the apartment I was living in and in other locations I chose to represent the research experience. While I wrote my research journal in a wider variety of places I was very conscious of being 'seen' recording my digital video journal and for this reason it feels less authentic and more staged.

16. Although Best (2000) includes images she does not provide references.

REFERENCES

Agar, M. (1986), 'Foreword' in T.L. Whitehead and M.E. Conway (eds), *Self, Sex And Gender in Cross Cultural Fieldwork*, Urbana, IL: University of Illinois Press, pp. ix–xi.

Atkinson, P. and Silverman, D. (1997), 'Kundera's immortality: the interview society and the invention of the self', *Qualitative Inquiry*, **3** (3), 304–25.

Banks, M. (2001), *Visual Methods in Social Research*, London, Thousand Oaks, CA and New Delhi: Sage.

Beresin, A.R. (1993), 'The play of peer cultures in a city school-yard', Unpublished Doctoral Dissertation, University of Pennsylvania (University Microfilms No. 9331755).

Berger, J. ([1972]1977), *Ways of Seeing,* London: BBC, Penguin.

Best, A. (2000), *Prom Night: Youth, Schools, and Popular Culture*, New York: Routledge.

Bhabha, H.K. (1994), *The Location of Culture*, New York: Routledge.

Bogdan, R. and Biklen, S. (1998), *Qualitative Research for Education: An Introduction to Theory and Methods*, Boston, MA: Allyn and Bacon.

Borofsky, R. (2005), *Yanomami: The Fierce Controversy and What We Can Learn From It* (California Series in Public Anthropology), Berkeley, CA: University of California Press.

Bowman, M.D. (1993), *Children's Use of Computer-based Interactive Stories* (Research report), Ayr, Scotland: University of Paisley.

Buckingham, D. (1996), *Moving Images: Understanding Children's Emotional Responses to Television*, Manchester: Manchester University Press.

Butler, J. (1990), *Gender Trouble*, London: Routledge.

Cheatham, A. and Shen, E. (2003), 'Community based participatory research with Cambodian girls in Long Beach, California: a case study', in M. Minkler and N. Wallerstein (eds), *Community Based Participatory Research for Health*, San Francisco, CA: Jossey-Bass, pp. 316–31.

Coffey, A., Holbrook, B. and Atkinson, P. (1996), 'Qualitative data analysis: technologies and representations', *Sociological Research Online*, **1** (1), http://www.socresonline.org.uk/1/1/4.html

Coffey, A., Renold, E., Dicks, B., Soyinka, B. and Mason, B. (2006), 'Hypermedia ethnography in educational settings: possibilities and challenges', *Ethnography and Education*, **1** (1), 15–30.

Collier, J. Jr and Collier, M. (1986), *Visual Anthropology: Photography as a Research Method*, Albuquerque: University of New Mexico Press.

Corti, L. (1993), 'Using diaries in social research', *Social Research Update*, Issue 2. UK, Department of Sociology, University of Surrey, available at http://www.soc.surrey.ac.uk/sru/SRU2.html (accessed 12 August 2006).

Davies, C.A. (1999), *Reflexive Ethnography: A Guide to Researching Selves and Others*, London: Routledge.

De Block, L., Buckingham, D. and Banaji, S. (2005), *Children in Communication about Migration* (CHICAM), final project report.

Dicks, B. and Mason, B. (1998), 'Hypermedia and ethnography: reflections of a research approach', *Sociological Research Online*, **3** (3) http://www.socresonline.org.uk/socresonline/3/3/3.html (accessed 12 April 2006).

Dyson, A. (1997), *Writing Superheroes: Contemporary Childhood, Popular Culture, and Classroom Literacy*, New York: Teachers College Press.

Fisherkeller, J. (2002), *Growing Up with Television: Everyday Learning Among Young Adolescents*, Philadelphia, PA: Temple University Press.

Flick, U. (1998), *An Introduction to Qualitative Research,* London: Sage.

Geertz, C. (1973), 'Thick description: toward an interpretive theory of culture', in C. Geertz, *The Interpretation of Cultures*, New York: Basic Books, pp. 3–32.

Geertz, C. (1995), *After the Fact: Four Decades, Two Countries, One Anthropologist*, Cambridge, MA: Harvard University Press.

Goldman-Segall, R. (1998), *Points of Viewing Children's Thinking: A Digital Ethnographer's Journey,* Mahwah, NJ: LEA.

Goodman, S. (2003), *Teaching Youth Media: A Critical Guide to Literacy, Video Production and Social Change*, New York: Teachers College Press.

Grady, J. (2004), 'Working with visible evidence: an invitation and some practical advice', in C. Knowles and P. Sweetman (eds), *Picturing the Social Landscape: Visual Methods and the Sociological Imagination*, London: Routledge, pp. 18–33.

Grimshaw, A. (2001), *The Ethnographer's Eye: Ways of Seeing in Anthropology*, Cambridge: Cambridge University Press.

Grosz, E. (1995), *Space, Time, and Perversion*, New York: Routledge.

Hammersley, M. and Atkinson, P. (1995), *Ethnography: Principles in Practice*, 2nd edn, London: Routledge.

Harel, I. (1991), 'The silent observer and holistic note taker', in I. Harel and S. Pupert (eds), *Constructionism,* Norwood, NJ: Ablex, pp. 449–64.

Hey, V. (1997), *The Company She Keeps*, Milton Keynes: Open University Press.

Holliday, R. (2004a), 'Filming "the closet": the role of video diaries in researching sexualities', *American Behaviour Scientist*, **47** (12), 1597–616.

Holliday, R. (2004b), 'Reflecting the self', in C. Knowles and P. Sweetman (eds), *Picturing the Social Landscape: Visual Methods and the Sociological Imagination*, London: Routledge, pp. 49–64.

Holloway, S. and G. Valentine (2000), *Children's Geographies,* London: Routledge.

Hopkins, P. (2001), *The Role of Video in Improving Teaching and Learning*, London: TTA Publications.

Illich, I. (1973), *Tools for Conviviality*, New York: Harper and Row.

James, A., Hockey, J. and Dawson, A. (1997), *After Writing Culture: Epistemology and Praxis in Contemporary Anthropology*, London: Routledge.

James, D.E. (1996), 'Lynn Hershman: the subject of autobiography', in M. Renov and E. Suderberg (eds), *Resolutions: Contemporary Video Practices*, Minneapolis, MN: University of Minnesota Press, pp. 124–33.

Kist, W. (2005), *New Literacies in Action: Teaching and Learning in Multiple Media*, New York: Teachers College Press.

Kress, G. (2003), *Literacy in the New Media Age,* London: Routledge.

Kress, G. and Van Leeuwen, T. (2001), *Multimodal Discourse: The Modes and Media of Contemporary Communication*, London: Arnold.

Lampert, M. (2000), 'Knowing teaching: the intersection of research on teaching and qualitative research', in B.M. Brizuela, J.P. Stewart, R.G. Carrillo and J.F. Berger (eds), *Acts of Inquiry in Qualitative Research*, Reprint Series No. 34, Cambridge, MA: Harvard Educational Review, pp. 61–72.

Latham, A. (2003), 'Research, performance, and doing human geography: some reflections on the diary-photograph, diary-interview method', *Environmental Planning A*, **35** (11), 1993–2017.

Lincoln, Y. and Guba, E. (1985), *Naturalistic Inquiry*, New York: Sage.

Lomax, H. and Casey, N. (1998), 'Recording social life: reflexivity and video methodology', *Sociological Research Online*, **3** (2), http://www.socresonline.org.uk/socresonline/3/2/1.html (accessed 29 October 2007).

MacDougall, D. (1997), 'The visual in anthropology', in H. Morphy and M. Banks (eds), *Rethinking Visual Anthropology*, New Haven, CT: Yale University Press, pp. 276–95.

MacDougall, D. (1998), *Transcultural Cinema*, Princeton, NJ: Princeton University Press.

McCarty, M. (1995), 'McCarty's law and how to break it', in P. Hockings (ed.), *Principles of Visual Anthropology*, 2nd edn, The Hague: Mouton, pp. 45–51.

Meth, P. (2003), 'Entries and omissions: using solicited diaries', *Geographical Research Area*, **35** (2), 195–205.

Mitchell, W.J.T. (2005), *What Do Pictures Want: The Lives and Loves of Images*, Chicago, IL: University of Chicago Press.

Moores, S. (1993), *Interpreting Audiences: The Ethnography of Media Consumption*, London: Sage.

Morphy, H. and Banks, M. (1997), 'Introduction: rethinking visual anthropology', in

H. Morphy and M. Banks (eds), *Rethinking Visual Anthropology*, New Haven, CT: Yale University Press, pp.1–35.

Mousley, J. (1998), 'Ethnographic research in mathematics education: using different types of visual data refined from videotapes', in C. Kanes, M. Goos and E. Warren (eds), *Teaching Mathematics in New Times*, Brisbane: Mathematics Education Research Group of Australia, pp. 397–403.

Niesyto, H. (2000), 'Youth research on video self-productions: reflections on a social-aesthetic approach', *Visual Sociology*, **15**, 135–53.

Noyes, A. (2004), 'Video diary: a method for exploring learning dispositions', *Cambridge Journal of Education*, **34** (2), 193–210.

O'Reilly, T. (2004), 'What is Web 2.0?', available at http://conferences.oreillynet.com/web2com/ (accessed 15 November 2006).

Pascoe, C.J. (2007), *Dude, You're a Fag: Masculinity and Sexuality in High School*, Berkeley, CA: University of California Press.

Pea, R. (1999), 'New media communication forums for improving education research and practice', in E. Lagemann and L. Shulmand (eds), *Issues in Educational Research: Problems and Possibilities*, San Francisco, CA: Josey-Bass, pp. 336–70.

Pink, S. (2001), *Doing Visual Ethnography: Images, Media and Representation in Research*, London: Sage.

Pink, S. (2006), *The Future of Visual Anthropology: Engaging the Senses*, London: Routledge.

Plummer, K. (1983), *Documents of Life*, London: George Allen and Unwin.

Prosser, J. (ed.) (1998), *Image-based Research: A Sourcebook for Qualitative Researchers*, London: Falmer Press.

Quadri, N., Bullen, P. and Jefferies, A. (2007), 'Student diaries: using technology to produce alternative forms of feedback', *Proceedings of the 2nd International Blended Learning Conference*, University of Hertfordshire pp. 214–222, available at https://uhra.herts.ac.uk/dspace/bitstream/2299/1720/1/901871.pdf (accessed 11 November 2007).

Raby, R. (2007), 'Across a great gulf? Conducting research with adolescents', in A. Best (ed.), *Representing Youth: Methodological Issues in Critical Youth Studies*, New York: New York University Press, pp. 39–59.

Ratcliff, D. (1999), 'Qualitative research resources', available at http://don.ratcliffs.net/ (accessed 27 January 2005).

Renov, M. (1996), 'Video confessions', in M. Renov and E. Suderberg (eds), *Resolutions: Contemporary Video Practices*, Minneapolos, MN: University of Minnesota Press, pp. 78–101.

Rich, M., Lamola, S., Gordan, J. and Chalfen, R. (2000), 'Video intervention/prevention assessment: a patient-centered methodology for understanding the adolescent illness experience', *Journal of Adolescent Health*, **27**, 155–65.

Ruby, J. (1995), *Secure the Shadow: Death and Photography in America*, Boston, MA: MIT Press.

Ruby, J. (2000), *Picturing Culture: Explorations of Film and Anthropology*, Chicago, IL: University of Chicago Press.

Seaman, G. and Williams, H. (1992), 'Hypermedia in ethnography', in P.I. Crawford and D. Turton (eds), *Film as Ethnography*, Manchester: Manchester University Press, pp. 300–311.

Sherin, M.G. and Han, S. (2004), 'Teacher learning in the context of a video club', *Teaching and Teacher Education*, **20**, 163–83.

Stigler, J.W., Gallimore, R. and Hiebert, J. (2000), 'Using video surveys to compare classrooms and teaching across cultures: examples and lessons from the TIMSS video studies', *Educational Psychologist*, **35** (2), 87–100.

Strandell, H. (1994), *Sociala mötesplatser för barn Aktivitetsprofiler och förhandlingskulturer på daghem* (Children's social meeting places), Helsinki: Gaudeamus.

Tierney, P. (2000), *Darkness in El Dorado: How Scientists and Journalists Devastated the Amazon*, New York: Norton.

Toffler, A. (1980), *The Third Wave: The Classic Study of Tomorrow*, New York: Bantam.

Tyner, K. (1998), *Literacy in a Digital World: Teaching and Learning in the Age of Information*, Mahwah, NJ: Lawrence Erlbaum Associates.

Walker, R. (2002), 'Case study, case records and multimedia', *Cambridge Journal of Education*, **32** (1), 109–27.

Walker, R. (2004), 'Editorial', *Cambridge Journal of Education*, **34** (2), 139–42.

Weaver, A. and Atkinson, P. (1994), *Microcomputing and Qualitative Data Analysis*, Aldershot: Avebury.

Weis, L. and Fine, M. (eds) (2000), *Speed Bumps: A Student Friendly Guide to Qualitative Research*, New York: Teachers College Press.

White, ML (2009), 'Ethnography 2.0: writing with digital video', *Ethnography and Education*, **4** (3), 389–414.

Young, C. (1975), 'Observational cinema', in P. Hockings (ed.), *Principles of Visual Anthropology*, Chicago, IL: Aldine, pp. 65–80.

24. 'Traditional' ethnography: peopled ethnography for luminous description
Sara Delamont

INTRODUCTION

The term 'traditional' ethnography as used here is broadly similar to Adler and Adler's (2008) 'classical and mainstream'; what Fine (2003) termed 'peopled' and what Katz (2001, 2002) sees as producing 'luminous description'. The chapter sets out what is meant by ethnography, contrasts sociological and anthropological ethnography of education and describes how ethnography is done and written up, drawing on a current project (Delamont, 2009), on *capoeira*, the Brazilian martial art.

ETHNOGRAPHY, FIELDWORK AND PARTICIPANT OBSERVATION DEFINED

There are three closely related terms: ethnography, fieldwork, participant observation: all of which are part of the wider category, qualitative research. The majority of qualitative studies conducted in disciplines other than anthropology draw on interviews rather than ethnography. This chapter is about participant observation done during fieldwork, where any interview in data collected are supplementary to the observation (see Hammersley and Atkinson, 2007).

Participant observation, ethnography and fieldwork are used interchangeably in the literature; spending long periods watching people, coupled with talking to them about what they are doing, thinking and saying, designed to see how they understand their world. Ethnography as the most inclusive term, with participant observation and fieldwork being useful descriptions of the data collection technique and the location. Fieldwork is the data collection phase of a research process: an investigator doing participant observation and ethnographic interviewing, in a factory, a hospital, a village in Portugal or a school. The term can cover collecting quantitative data (for example, a census) if these data are collected 'in the field', especially during a period of ethnographic observation.

The researchers' aim is to understand how the cultures they are studying 'work': that is, to grasp what the world looks like to the people who live in the fishing village, boarding school or mining community. Researchers discover what 'their' people believe; what they do at work and in their leisure time; what makes them laugh, cry and rage; who they love, hate and fear; and how they choose their friends and endure their relations. This is done by living with the people being studied, watching them work and play, thinking carefully about what is seen, interpreting it and talking to the actors to check the emerging interpretations. The term 'participant' observation does not usually mean real participation: researchers do not usually catch fish, teach classes or dig coal, rather they watch these things being done, and 'help' occasionally. It is important to participate enough to be able to write feelingly about the nature of the work; its pains and pleasures; smells and sounds; physical and mental stresses. However, the researcher cannot actually spend the whole time fishing, teaching or digging coal, because that would prevent both studying other members of the social world and, perhaps more vitally, time spent writing the field-notes, thinking about the fieldwork, writing down those thoughts and sys-tematically testing the initial insights in the setting. So 'participant' does not mean doing what those being observed do, but interacting with them while they do it.

There are the two main types of fieldwork which we can gloss as total immersion and partial immersion. In anthropology researchers have tradi-tionally moved to live at the fieldsite: immersed in the culture under study 24 hours a day. Most observational research in education is based on a more partial immersion; researchers eat, sleep and relax at home but spend a chunk of the day observing in the fieldsite.

ETHNOGRAPHY IN ANTHROPOLOGY AND SOCIOLOGY

Ethnography has a long history in both anthropology and in sociology. Anthropologists still like to claim that they have the exclusive custody of the real, true ethnography (Delamont, Atkinson and Parry, 2000) and rely on their use of the method to distinguish themselves rhetorically from other social scientists. Hirsch and Gellner (2001) feel able to state that while other disciplines may do or claim to do ethnographic field-work, the term 'an ethnography' to refer to a monograph 'is confined to anthropological circles' (p. 1). Anthropologists have used ethnography as their main method, and believe that no other technique has ever rivalled it (Mills, Chapter 3, this volume). Anthropologists have used some other techniques as subsidiaries to living in a culture full time, but only as subsidiaries (Faubion, 2001; Macdonald, 2001). In the USA Boas is seen as the pioneer of fieldwork, inspiring disciples including Ruth Benedict, Zora Neale Hurston and Margaret Mead (see Behar and Gordon, 1995). In the UK, Malinowski is usually credited with inventing fieldwork, and his disciples included Audrey Richards and Camilla Wedgwood (Leach, 1984; Lutkehaus, 1986).

Sociology has used ethnography as long as anthropology: that is, since the 1890s: but it has often been unfashionable, a minority pursuit. Ethnography has never had the status, and sole domination, in sociology that it had, and has, in anthropology (Boyask, Chapter 2, this volume). Sociological ethnography, and other qualitative methods were pioneered at Chicago, alongside survey and statistical techniques. Chicago sociology was robustly empirical, and this empiricism spread to other centres of sociology in the USA (Deegan, 2001). At Chicago, ethnographic methods fell out of fashion in the early 1960s (Platt, 1995; LeCompte, 2002). Since the mid 1970s there has been a rebirth of qualitative methods in sociology and a rapid growth in their popularity in education (see Atkinson, Coffey, Delamont, Lofland and Lofland, 2001). This growth has not, however, united sociological and anthropological uses of the method (Delamont and Atkinson, 1995). In the past decade there have been several apocalyptic statements that traditional ethnography is dead. That is simply wrong, but in this chapter there is no space to rehearse the arguments which are covered elsewhere (Delamont, Coffey and Atkinson, 2000; Atkinson, Coffey and Delamont, 2003; Atkinson, Delamont and Housley, 2008).

BEFORE THE FIELDWORK

Good fieldwork comes from being interested in some aspects of the setting and its actors, and on having some foreshadowed problems grounded in social science. The more thinking, writing and reading that has gone into developing the foreshadowed problems, the better: but no one should think, write and read rather than go into the field and start observing. A pilot site is useful to practice a bit of observation too. It is vital to 'abandon' the foreshadowed problems if they are impeding the collection of good data: or if not to abandon them, to put them to one side to focus on the core issues that are staring the researcher in the face.

My current *capoeira* fieldwork began, by accident, in November 2002 ten years after I first thought of the research. I teach a module on Brazil, and read an ethnography about *capoeira* in Salvador de Bahia, Brazil, by Lewis (1992), which made it sound fascinating, both in its own right and as an 'educational' setting. There were no classes near Cardiff in 1993, so

I put the idea 'on hold'. In 2002 students told me of a *capoeira* class in a youth centre: a site I could get to. I went along to see what *capoeira* was, partly out of curiosity and partly to find something interesting to do 'educational' fieldwork on. The class turned out to be fascinating, included a colleague Neil Stephens among the students, and my diary records my excitement at discovering 'a great fieldsite'. Of course I did not understand most of what I saw and heard, but I could see why Lewis (1992) had been captivated by *capoeira*. Those classes folded, and both my research, and Neil Stephens's apprenticeship in *capoeira,* ended. I was disappointed, and started to look for other things to study. In 2003 another teacher, Achilles,[1] began to teach in Cardiff. I went to meet him, and Achilles was happy to be observed and my co-author Neil Stephens was there.

It does not matter where the initial decision to try a fieldsite for 'fit' comes from. However it is important to be reflexive about personal, biographical, financial and academic reasons for the choice, and to record these reflections systematically. It is vital to think about the access and the ethics, and to begin to write the reflexive 'diary' or its equivalent. As soon as a possible fieldsite opens up it is necessary to negotiate access, and submit the proposed research to an ethics committee.

HOW TO OBSERVE AND RECORD

Novice researchers are often very unclear about what they should be looking at, what sort of looking or watching becomes 'observation', and how to judge whether or not they are doing it 'right'. Precisely what to watch is often unclear. The textbooks are rarely specific enough and the 'confessional' or autobiographical accounts overemphasize disasters and faux pas or danger and risk (see de Marrais, 1998; Nordstrom and Robben, 1995, for example). It is valuable to read about doing ethnography on oil rigs or container vessels (Sampson, 2004), in opium dens or war zones, but they do not provide much practical help about what to look for in a school mathematics lesson or a university chemistry lecture on a wet Wednesday.

Observation in educational settings can be dangerous, but in general the problems are over-familiarity and boredom. Because educational researchers have been pupils and students, and very often teachers and lecturers, it is hard to concentrate and 'see' things there. Going into schools in a different country provides instant 'strangeness', but in our own it is hard to force oneself to focus on what is happening rather than what one 'expects', 'knows' and is familiar with (see Delamont, 2002, pp. 46–55, 2008; Delamont, Atkinson and Pugsley, 2010). It is also hard not to judge.

The researcher's job is to find out what the participants think is going on, what they do, why they do it, how they do it and what is 'normal' and 'odd' for them. Much educational research rushes to judgement about the 'quality' of the teaching or the attitudes of pupils.

Good observers are systematic about observing, and recording. In a school I sketch every 'room' or space entered for the first time; classrooms, labs, staffrooms, library, changing rooms, hockey pitch, sickroom, stock-cupboard, gym, swimming pool, space for the bicycle racks and so on and thereafter note where in that space the key actions take place. I note what is displayed on the walls and door and noticeboards, officially and unofficially (for example, 'No Food or Drink to be Consumed in this Room' and the graffiti that states 'Robbie is fit' or whatever). The nature, location and condition of the furniture and fittings needs attention, as do the smell of any space (does the boys' changing room smell of hash, socks or chlorine?), and whether it is noisy or quiet (can you hear traffic, or bird song, or the dinner ladies clearing away lunch?). So observation is about using all the senses: not just sight.

Try to observe from different places or angles in the spaces you visit regularly: in the lecture hall sit in different places; in the staffroom spread yourself around among various cliques. Many ethnographers 'fall in with' one subset of pupils or students or staff and only observe and interact with them, as Cusick (1973) did. Where institutions have clerical staff, technicians, manual workers, their daily lives may provide real insights into the whole place: even if they are not the main focus, time with them can be rewarding. A day spent in one place, followed by a day following someone around will give good contrasts. Time matters – observe, and record, when things happen and how long they take: how long does it take to get coffee in the staffroom at morning break? How long to return a DVD to the library? How much time in a gym lesson do a keen boy and a reluctant one actually spend moving and how much queuing up or sitting? What percentage of the talk in the Spanish conversation class is in Spanish?

The most important things are to be reflexive, and not to slide into familiarity. Force yourself to think hard about what effect you are having, on what you need to know, on how to find out what you need to know, on changing your focus so the angles you get shift. Think about, and record, your strategies for staying alert, for making the familiar strange. Record whether you are too hot or too cold, whether it is quiet or noisy, what you could and could not do. Then think about how that affected what you could see, and what you understood of what you saw. Geer (1964, p. 382) stressed that if a process is a mystery, then sustained observation will clear it up. Note that this is a process: the longer you observe the more your understanding should grow and develop.

WHAT TO OBSERVE AND RECORD

All these observations and reflections are only useful if they are recorded: everything needs to be written down, in one large record, or several smaller differentiated ones. My emphasis is always on the concrete, because that is what fades. We all remember the emotions and outbursts – the delight, the anger, the embarrassment – but are likely to forget the details that are needed to write good ethnographic texts. So count things: how many pupils in the class? Males? Females? British Asian? African-Caribbean? Turkish? Somali? Are there enough Bibles in religious education for every pupil to have one? How many of the Bunsen burners are working? Bodies matter: how are staff and students dressed? Who is clean, who smells? What is the state of people's teeth? What youth fashions are in vogue and do they mark out cliques? How many people have all the necessary 'kit'?

In the Oracle project (Delamont and Galton, 1986) in the Coalthorpe schools, the only boys who had perfect, complete kit for everything from rugby to art, from woodwork to swimming, were those from the local authority children's home. They had everything, it was all new, all fitted, and was all name marked with woven name tapes. Everyone else had some missing items, hand-me-downs, homemade items, things that were too big, or already too small, or were adapted – their art apron, for example, was an old shirt of their father's. What bodily skills are expected of students and pupils? Are nine year olds required to sit still for 40 minutes, to manage without lavatory visits for whole lessons, to use pens with liquid ink in? How many people have pierced ears, navels, lips, tongues, noses? In some settings the researcher does not just observe, but talks to people in the setting, or even undertakes the activities themselves. Appropriate behaviour in a mathematics lesson would be inappropriate at the school fete, and vice versa; a chemistry lesson is different from the bus trip to an 'away' rugby game.

WHAT TO WRITE DOWN

Fieldwork is only as good as the fieldnotes: the fieldnotes are only as good as the way(s) they are written, written up and analysed. In classrooms, or other pedagogical settings, such as *capoeira* classes, it is usually possible to write as I observe. *In situ* I write scribbled notes in spiral-bound 'reporters'' notebooks – I use abbreviations and mnemonics which I can decipher, and aim to record as much as I can. I do not try to write legibly, they are only an aide-memoire for me. An illegible handwriting style and personal shorthand afford the research some privacy, in case someone looks at the notebook. I date each entry, record the time down the left-hand side every four to six minutes, and scribble furiously. A 90-minute class might cover 12 to 20 sides of such a pad. As soon as I get 'home', I write up those notes into an A4 spiral-bound book. This is a much more detailed account, based on the fieldnotes, but amplified, and with some reflections, commentary and cross-referencing added. Twelve sides of the reporter's notebook will take 20 to 30 A4 sheets when expanded. These notes will not be in beautifully grammatical English, but there will be sentences. There is an example of an equivalent set of notes written in real time, and then written up out of the field in Delamont (2002, pp. 60–4) about a cookery class for a group of slow learners.

This strategy only works if the abbreviated, scribbled notes are written up very soon after they are made. I try to write up within 24 hours of the class, while everything is fresh in my mind. If the longer version is written quickly I can still understand my own scribble. If I leave the task for a few days it is hard, if not impossible to fill in all the mundane events, and even, arguably, slightly dishonest, to try to.

Quotes from my fieldnotes in publications (for example, Stephens and Delamont, 2010) are from amplified versions in the A4 book and they are the record I can read years later and still make sense of. As the books fill up I separate them, storing the reporters' notebooks in work and the A4 ones at home, in case of fire, flood or theft. I number the books, and keep a record of which book covers a specific date range so I know that Book 63 starts on 10 October 2010 and ends on 31 October 2010. These books are 'factual'. Other researchers, who want their bodily sensations, thoughts and feelings to be rolled up into their fieldwork might only keep one multi-faceted record.

I keep both my original scribbled, abbreviated notes and my written up 'out of the field' notes in handwriting, because that is how I work best. If I were more technologically innovative, or richer, I could work differently. There are other ways to keep the records. Many ethnographers dictated their fieldnotes: traditionally onto tape to be transcribed by a secretary, but today most researchers will use voice recognition software, or word-process them. Taking a laptop into the field and typing the notes straight in works indoors, in dry places and safe spaces. A project on chemistry lectures could be recorded on a laptop, while one on swimming teachers, or outreach work in high crime neighbourhoods could not be. In some settings the fieldnotes could be spoken into a digital recorder which would enable them to be turned to written text rapidly. Having them in machine-readable form means that it is easy to index and code them, and to prepare them for an analytic software package (CAQDAS) (Fielding, 2001; Stewart, Chapter 37, this volume). If you want to mix 'facts' and reflection, then it is sensible to use a software package that allows you to tag and mark passages to help keep different types of text clearly labelled for your own clarity. Geer (1964, p. 372) used the 'comments' she had recorded during her early fieldwork to explore how foreshadowed problems are refocused and reframed in the beginning of a project. She spent six hours a day in the field, then dictated her notes, adding some comments or 'an interpretive summary' (p. 373).

TYPES OF RECORD

I try to keep my commentary separated from the 'factual' record in the A4 books, by ruling lines across the text and marking off comments physically. These though are usually not autoethnography or reflections or confessions, but rather low level. So I might, when writing up put in:

> Sicinnus *never* demonstrated with a woman tonight, and I found the whole class on the aggressive side – more like the ones in New Zealand than Achilles's usual sessions.

Or

> I was surprised by the large number of students in the advanced class who could sing verses, even though they weren't, as far as I can see, Brazilian or Portuguese. I wonder if Sicinnus has singing classes, or requires singing verses for belts?

These comments are the topics I try to explore in future observations, in informal and formal interviews, and in discussions with Neil Stephens especially when we write papers (for example, Stephens and Delamont, 2009). My more reflexive, self-critical and confessional comments are kept physically separate from the ongoing fieldnotes, in other types of notebook. An A5 spiral-bound book is used for keeping reflections in tranquillity: ideas I am having, things to follow up, possible papers to write, items to read, theory and self-criticism. There I would write: 'I must sort out the belt order in Sicinnus's group – why do I *always* leave it till after fieldwork, instead of sorting it out *before* I observe?', or

> I wonder why 1 always feel sick and scared before 1 walk into a new class – even when I know rationally that Sicinnus would be cheerful when I arrived, and his students would be cool about my presence. I've *never* had a hostile reception – typically the teacher sees me, and a big smile appears – so why do I dread the entrance?

Or

> I wonder if I can use Loic Wacquant's idea of the pugilistic habitus to make sense of Sicinnus's classes – Perseus's don't feel pugilistic but his *do*. If I had Bourdieu's advice on that . . ..

I keep a fourth type of notebook – again the reporter style but with different cover designs – in which I put notes from academic sources, lists of the pseudonyms and any phrases from the data or the literature that might make catchy titles for papers.

WHAT TO DO WITH THE DATA

Novices often separate data analysis from data collection. Coffey and Atkinson (1996) aimed their book on analysis at such unfortunate people, who have mistakenly allowed their data to pile up unanalysed because they separated the two activities. It is absolutely fatal to separate analysis and writing up from the fieldwork. My A5 notebook is, essentially, the beginning of the analysis and the genesis of the publications. The analytic themes and categories, arising from the data, from literature, from one's own head, are constantly interacting with the data as they are collected: the ongoing research is led by, and leads, the theorizing and vice versa. When I watched Sicinnus's class I wrote in my original notes:

> 10.20 The *roda*[2] goes on. Two men are playing, or rather competing. It is fierce. Sicinnus does not signal to them to tone it down, or stop them, or warn them of danger or anything. Unlike Achilles or Perseus, this is tough. Gladstone buys the game, and it gets even fiercer. I stop clapping and put my arms and hands up in the classic defensive position both so I won't get kicked, *and* so I signal to Sicinnus and anyone else who notices that I understand that standing in the *roda* can be dangerous and I am (a) experienced and (b) alert.

It was after this lesson I wrote in the A5 book the question about Loic Wacquant's (2004) notion of the pugilistic habitus quoted earlier, followed by a note to myself to discuss the concept with Neil Stephens and see if it could be developed further. If I want to develop ideas of 'aggression' I go back through the 60 plus A4 books and search for all the examples of aggression in *rodas*, and 'code' them, looking to see if my impression of Sicinnus's class is supported by the data. My coding is very old-fashioned – I use colours, and stick removable coloured labels on the pages where themes occur – so where I have something coded as 'authenticity claim' or 'Brazilian-ness' or 'Inversions', for example, there are red, green and lilac coloured markers. I do not use highlighters or coloured ink to mark the actual text, because I want to be able to remove codes and recode the same, handwritten text. I could get the A4 books word-processed and use a software package. So if I want to look back over the fieldnotes from 500 lessons and explore the concept of 'pugilistic habitus' or, more sensibly, because it is a broader category, 'aggression: used and prevented', I will choose a colour, say pink, and code incidents of it, or comments on it, from October 2002 to the present. I generally start at October 2002, and come forward, through the fieldwork period. The main reason for analysing data is, of course, to write about them, and that is the best bit.

WRITING: THE BEST BIT

There is no point in doing research unless it is turned into a report, a thesis, an article, a set of papers, a book, or all five. There are three 'tricks': first, start 'writing up' from the very beginning; second, accept the pleasures of drafting; and third, write regularly. To take these in reverse order, I try to write 500 words every day of the week, and when I miss a day, I make it up as soon as possible. Writing means multiple drafts – but drafting, polishing, redrafting, scrapping rough bits are pleasures. Screwing up a piece of paper and throwing it away is fun. I write in biro on paper. The amount in the waste paper basket – and I use a huge log basket as a waste paper basket – is an indication of the draft improving. Third, thinking about the writing from the beginning is important. The notebooks where I start putting possible titles, and the A5 notebooks with ideas about what might be written (and journals where the writing might go) are vital parts of the research process.

The whole rationale of ethnography is that there are not discrete 'stages', but rather a continuous abductive, iterative process. As I stand in a corner of the gym in Fordhampton and watch Sicinnus teach I am not only doing fieldwork, I am also thinking about analysing the data and about what publications will emerge from the data collection.

NOTES

1. All names of *capoeira* teachers and students are pseudonyms.
2. The ring in which *capoeira* is played.

REFERENCES

Adler, P.A. and Adler, P. (2008), 'Of rhetoric and representation: the four faces of ethnography', *The Sociological Quarterly*, **49** (1), 1–30.

Atkinson, P.A., Coffey, A. and Delamont, S. (2003), *Key Themes in Qualitative Research*, Walnut Creek, CA: Alta Mira Press.

Atkinson, P.A., Delamont, S. and Housley, W. (2008), *Contours of Culture*, Lanham, MD: Alta Mira Press.

Atkinson, P.A., Coffey, A., Delamont, S., Lofland, J. and Lofland, L. (eds) (2001), *Handbook of Ethnography*, London: Sage.

Behar, R. and Gordon, D. (eds) (1995), *Women Writing Culture*, Berkeley, CA: University of California Press.

Coffey, A. and Atkinson, P.A. (1996), *Making Sense of Qualitative Data*, Walnut Creek, CA: Sage.

Cusick, P. (1973), *Inside High School*, New York: Holt, Rinehart and Winston.

Deegan, M.J. (2001), 'The Chicago School of ethnography', in P.A. Atkinson, A. Coffey, S. Delamont, J. Lofland and L. Lofland (eds), *Handbook of Ethnography*, London: Sage, pp. 11–25.

Delamont, S. (2002), *Fieldwork in Educational Settings*, London: Falmer.

Delamont, S. (2008), 'For lust of knowing: observation in educational ethnography', in G. Walford (ed.), *How to do Educational Ethnography*, London: Tufnell Press, pp. 39–56.

Delamont, S. (2009), '"The only honest thing": autobiography, reflexivity and small crises in fieldwork', *Ethnography and Education*, **4** (1), 51–64.

Delamont, S. and Atkinson, P.A. (1995), *Fighting Familiarity*, Cresskill, NJ: Hampton Press.

Delamont, S. and Galton, M. (1986), *Inside the Secondary Classroom*, London: Routledge.

Delamont, S., Atkinson, P. and Parry, O. (2000), *The Doctoral Experience*, London: Falmer.

Delamont, S., Coffey, A. and Atkinson, P.A. (2000), 'The twilight years', *Qualitative Studies in Education*, **13** (3), 223–38.

Delamont, S., Atkinson, P.A. and Pugsley, L. (2010), 'The concept smacks of magic: fighting familiarity today', *Teaching and Teacher Education*, **26** (1), 3–10.

de Marrais, K.B. (ed.) (1988), *Inside Stories*, Mahwah, NJ: Erlbaum.

Faubion, J.D. (2001), 'Currents of cultural fieldwork', in P.A. Atkinson, A. Coffey, S. Delamont, J. Lofland and L. Lofland (eds), *Handbook of Ethnography*, London: Sage, pp. 39–59.

Fielding, N. (2001), 'Computer applications in qualitative research', in P.A. Atkinson, A. Coffey, S. Delamont, J. Lofland and L. Lofland (eds), *Handbook of Ethnography*, London: Sage, pp. 453–67.

Fine, G.A. (2003), 'Towards a peopled ethnography', *Ethnography*, **1**, 41–60.

Geer, B. (1964), 'First days in the field', in P. Hammond (ed.), *Sociologists at Work*, New York: Anchor, pp. 372–98.

Hammersley, M. and Atkinson, P.A. (2007), *Ethnography*, London: Routledge.

Hirsch, E. and Gellner, D.N. (2001), 'Introduction', in D.N. Gellner and E. Hirsch (eds), *Inside Organizations*, Oxford: Berg, pp. 1–15.

Katz, J. (2001), 'From how to why (Part 1)', *Ethnography*, **2** (4), 443–73.

Katz, J. (2002), 'From how to why (Part 2)', *Ethnography*, **3** (1), 63–90.

Leach, E.R. (1984), 'Glimpses of the unmentionable in the history of British social anthropology', *Annual Review of Anthropology*, **13**, 1–23.

LeCompte, M. (2002), 'The transformation of ethnographic practice: past and current challenges', *Qualitative Research*, **2** (3), 283–99.

Lewis, J.L. (1992), *Ring of Liberation*, Chicago, IL: University of Chicago Press.

Lutkehaus, N. (1986), '"She was very Cambridge". Camilla Wedgwood and the history of women in British social anthropology', *American Ethnologist*, **13** (4), 776–98. Reprinted in S. Delamont and P. Atkinson (eds), *Gender and Research*, Vol. I, 2008, London: Sage, pp. 122–51.

Macdonald, S. (2001), 'British social anthropology', in P.A. Atkinson, A. Coffey, S.

Delamont, J. Lofland and L. Lofland (eds), *Handbook of Ethnography*, London: Sage, pp. 60–79.

Nordstrom, C. and Robben, A.C.G.M. (eds) (1995), *Fieldwork Under Fire*, Berkeley, CA: University of California Press.

Platt, J. (1995), 'Research methods and the Second Chicago School', in G.A. Fine (ed.), *A Second Chicago School?* Chicago, IL: University of Chicago Press, pp. 82–107.

Sampson, H. (2004), 'Navigating the waves: the usefulness of a pilot in qualitative research', *Qualitative Research*, **4** (3), 383–402.

Stephens, N. and Delamont, S. (2009), 'They start to get *malicia*', *British Journal of Sociology of Education*, **30** (5), 537–48.

Stephens, N. and Delamont, S. (2010), '"*Roda Boa!*" "*Roda Boa!*"' *Teaching and Teacher Education*, **26** (1), 113–18.

Wacquant, L. (2004), *Body and Soul*, New York: Oxford University Press.

25. Autoethnography
Peter de Vries

DIALOGUE BETWEEN SELF NOW (PETER2010) AND SELF THINKING ABOUT UNDERTAKING A PHD (PETER1996)

Peter2010: So you're thinking about doing a PhD are you Peter?

Peter1996: Yes Peter, I am.

Peter2010: On what topic?

Peter1996: Me.

Peter2010: You?

Peter1996: Yes, me. Well actually about me as a music teacher.

Peter2010: Why would you do that?

Peter1996: To learn more about my practice as a teacher and to learn more about me. And I guess for other people – other teachers, educators, parents – to understand how difficult, how isolating and how important this job is.

Peter2010: Oooh, you're sounding a bit political there.

Peter1996: Yes, there's a lot of misunderstanding about what music teachers actually do and the kinds of dilemmas we face which are unique to being a primary school music teacher.

Peter2010: So it sounds like you want to conduct an autoethnography.

Peter1996: I do?

Peter2010: I think so. I mean, you like to write – you've published poetry, short stories, even a children's book.

Peter1996: True. But how is that related to a PhD and to autoethnography?

Peter2010: Autoethnography embraces writing that moves beyond the confines of academic writing. Autoethnographers write poetry, short stories, conversations with themselves like the one we're having right now, play scripts, you name it. It's about being a boundary-crosser (Reed-Danahay, 1997) – and one of those boundaries us autoethnographers cross are the boundaries of writing genres.

Peter1996: Okay, but you still haven't told me what autoethnography is.

Peter2010: Well it's not that easy. Like Delamont (2009, p. 58) writes, there's no agreed set of definitions of autoethnography . . . but what I can say is that autoethnography is inward looking, it's a narrative of the self.

Peter1996: Like an autobiography?

Peter2010:   Kind of. Well not really, actually, because it's also about connecting the self to the culture you live in, or as Hamilton, Smith and Worthington (2008, p. 21) put it, autoethnographers emphasize 'the larger social context'.

Peter1996:   Which means?

Peter2010:   Which means focusing on 'the social and cultural aspects of the personal' (Hamilton, Smith and Worthington 2008, p. 24). And by doing this, rather than just writing about yourself, you start to question what happens to you and why it's happening. And better still, when you write about this and other people read what you've written you're creating a 'space of dialogue, debate, and change' (Holman Jones, 2005, p. 764).

Peter1996:   I like the sound of that. Not just researching me, but looking at the bigger picture and pointing to the flaws, the inequities in the education system I'm working in as a music teacher.

Peter2010:   You're sounding excited – so this might be the right fit for you.

Peter1996:   I'm thinking so. But I was talking to one of my old university lecturers, who said when I was talking to him about maybe enrolling in a PhD and about what I was interested in researching that self-study was what I was describing.

Peter2010:   Wow – that was a long, grammatically convoluted sentence you just spoke.

Peter1996:   That's because I thought it and spoke it like that – that's how people speak.

Peter2010:   I know, I know – you are so going to enjoy the freedom in writing that autoethnography provides and celebrates.

Peter1996:   But what about self-study?

Peter2010:   So we're talking mid 1990s . . . Mmmm, self-study, particularly in teacher education, is starting to gain momentum, so I'm not surprised it's been mentioned in relation to your research ideas. Like autoethnography, you're the main focus of a self-study. But in self-study the focus is narrower than autoethnography – it's about you in action (Hamilton, Smith and Worthington, 2008, p. 17), so you as a teacher. It's about focusing on your practice as a teacher.

Peter1996:   That's a good thing, that's what I'm interested in.

Peter2010:   Of course it is. You reflect on your practice as a teacher so that your teaching improves.

Peter1996:   I kind of do that now.

Peter 2010:   Sure, but I know you – you don't do it in the systematic way that self-study would have you do this.

Peter 1996:   Self-study and autoethnography still sound very similar.

Peter2010:   They are, but whereas self-study focuses on your practice as an educator, autoethnography looks far wider, towards the broader culture that you're working and living in. Self-study will often start with the researcher identifying a specific problem in their practice and work towards addressing that problem. Self-study foregrounds reflective practice, which is a key driver for undertaking self-study. That's not the case in autoethnography. And self-study is quite clear about using multiple methods to collect data (LaBoskey, 2004), whereas this is not always the case in autoethnography. You like jazz, right?

Peter1996:   You know I do.

Peter2010:   Well think of autoethnography as a long improvisation – it takes you to places you didn't plan to go to and it allows you to really explore these places. Or as Carolyn Ellis (1999, p. 669) says, autoethnography 'celebrates concrete experience and intimate detail; examines how human experience is endowed with meaning; is concerned with moral, ethical, and political consequences; encourages compassion and empathy; helps us know how to live and cope; features multiple voices and repositions readers and 'subjects as coparticipants in dialogue'.

Peter1996:   I like that – it's a bigger picture.

Peter2010:   Ultimately yes, but it starts with you, your own experience in a culture looking reflexively at 'self-other interactions' (Holt, 2003, p. 19). So it's not all you-you-you, but about you in relation to others.

Peter1996:   So for me this could be how I work and have worked with children, other teachers, school administrators, my family, my girlfriend and how all these people have impacted on who I am as a teacher.

Peter2010:   Yes, but you can go beyond that to looking at your place as a teacher in the 1990s, in Australia, coming from an education at university and then a year at teachers' college.

Peter1996:   So it really is about me in relation to the culture I have grown up in and lived as a teacher.

Peter2010:   Yes. Are you convinced?

Peter1996:   I'm getting there. But tell me about how you'd actually do autoethnographic research.

Peter2010:   There's no one way to conduct this kind of research.

Peter1996:   So I could just sit down and start writing?

Peter2010:   You could.

Peter1996:   So I could write, say, a novel about my life as a teacher.

Peter2010:   You could. But don't focus on the actual genre of writing to begin with. For a starting point I'd look to Carolyn Ellis (1999, p. 671) again: 'I start with my personal life. I pay attention to my physical feelings, thoughts, and emotions. I use what I call systematic sociological introspection and emotional recall to try to understand an experience I've lived through. Then I write my experience as a story.'

Peter1996:   I like that, so it's not just an outpouring of feelings and thoughts.

Peter2010:   Exactly. Although that could be the starting point – like you are journaling, just jotting down thoughts and ideas that you then go back to explore in greater detail. But this is research, so as a number of authors who have written about autoethnography have stressed, this research has to be scholarly. Duncan (2004, p. 5), for example, stresses that autoethnography must draw on multiple sources of evidence, like 'participant observation, reflective writing, interviewing, and gathering documents and artifacts'. Hamilton, Smith and Worthington (2008, p. 22) also stress this, highlighting research strategies like 'note-taking, memory work, narrative writing, observation, and interview'.

Peter1996:   So I might start off with some memory work, writing down my experiences as a music teacher since I entered the profession. Maybe I could observe another teacher teach, then have that person observe me, then we have a conversation about our teaching. Maybe I could interview key people who have been part of my teaching life. Then I could go back through all the yearbooks and cuttings I've collected over the years teaching and use these too.

Peter2010:   Now you're talking. And you'd draw this all together in the form of a narrative, a story.

Peter1996:   So as this is about me I'm assuming I'd write this in the first person.

Peter2010:   Correct.

Peter1996:   And I'd write it like I'm having a conversation with whoever might read what I've written?

Peter2010:   Absolutely – you want to really engage the reader, invite them into your world.

Peter1996:   And because I've got carte blanche to cross writing genres I might employ fiction in my narrative?

Peter2010:   Correct. But there are no hard and fast rules.

Peter1996:   But what about literature reviews? Surely I can't just write – I've got to demonstrate that what I'm saying relates to what other researchers have found or contradicts what other researchers have found?

Peter2010:   Of course. And that can be done in any number of ways. It could be quite traditional, where the written narrative begins with a section that reads like the sort of literature review that occurs early on in many academic journal articles. Nicholas Holt (2003) does this in his autoethnographic writing story. Or it may come at the end of the narrative writing, like Lee (2010) did with her autoethnography about being confined to bed following laser eye surgery.

Peter1996:   What about no reference to literature?

Peter2010:   That's tricky, and it's something I have done when I published a poem in an academic journal (de Vries, 2006) – I thought of it and conceptualized it as an autoethnography.

Peter1996:   What was it about?

Peter2010:   Ultimately that's up to the reader, which is why I like using poetry, it really is open to so much interpretation. But the core of the poem was about constantly being under pressure to apply for research grants as an academic. To try and make my point I used absurdist humour, bringing in real characters from the past and present (Bob Dylan, William Shakespeare). I'll give you a taste . . .

> *as he [Shakespeare] sat at his laptop*
> *applying for more and more*
> *grants*
> *from private and public*
> *bodies*
> *spending so much time writing these*
> *things*
> *these new forms of*
> *communication*
> *that*
> *he truly believed*
> *he was turning into*
> *Harold Pinter.*
> *Of course the irony was that Bill*
> *the Shakespeare Bill*
> *became so good at writing these 'artforms' that*
> *he published books and plays and sonnets about*
> *writing grants*
> *and spent little time writing anything else.*
> *But in the end*
> *he didn't care because*
> *he was so busy he had no time*
> *to navel-gaze*
> *about the meaning of life etc*
> *it was all grant writing*
> *for research projects about the effects of*
> *grant writing*
> *on grant writers*
> *both successful, semi-successful and failed*
> *and of course*
> *Bill intended to be a great innovator by writing up his*

'results'
in a creative way
like maybe in a multi-coloured numerical table
because if Bill had learnt one thing
it was that good-looking quantification
was most valued in the academy
and in the soundbyting
MEDIA
who only wanted to quote
statistics
to make a point
accompanied by footage
of atrocities about
the sad/rotten state of everything
(including Denmark).

Peter1996:   So this was your experience, channelled through a ficitonalized Shakespeare?

Peter2010:   My experiences and what I had observed other academics experiencing and talking about at the time of writing.

Peter1996:   So it connects your experience as an academic to the broader culture of working as an academic in a university?

Peter2010:   Yes. I view the poem as an autoethnography. I wrote down my observations, my feelings towards this issue, I wrote down the conversations I'd had with colleagues on the topic, and then fashioned this poem.

Peter1996: With no reference to literature?

Peter2010:   No. This was a standalone poem. Which I pass on to other academics, which I've even performed in research seminars. And it always gets people talking, and hopefully questioning the nature of an academic's work. Leavy (2010, p. 240) says that poetry can 'play with, expose, highlight, and undermine power'. I like to think that this poem goes some way to doing this.

Peter1996:   Nice – but I can't see myself writing a poem as a PhD.

Peter2010:   Well, you didn't. Let me tell you about what you are about to undertake, the autoethnography of your life as a primary school music teacher . . .

Dear Peter1996,
Just a taste of what you are about to embark on . . . a) you will write a novel – about your life as a teacher; b) you will analyse this novel and draw out core themes and issues about your lived experience as a teacher and about the teaching profession; c) you will then write in further depth about these

issues and themes following discussion of said issues and themes with key players in your teaching life such as other teachers, your mother (also a teacher) and your flat mate (also a teacher) from your first teaching position. You will want to present your dissertation as a novel that interweaves these interviews with literature that you have encountered on your research journey *but* you will be strongly discouraged from doing this by your supervisor, other doctoral students and critical friends because this is seen as being too radical – radical to the point that the chances of receiving your PhD will be in jeopardy. So you compromise. You present your thesis as two volumes. One is the novel about your life as a teacher. You stipulate that this should be read first so that the reader experiences your life as you see it. *Then* the reader is invited to read part 2 – the traditional thesis, including literature review, methodology section and data analysis section. This section draws on excerpts from the novel, the interviews with participants in your life, and relevant literature. This makes the grade. You receive your PhD and go on and publish from this thesis (see de Vries, 2000).

Peter1996:   I do?
Peter2010:   You do. But let's pretend that you are contemplating beginning a PhD in 2010. Where do you go to find out more?

First stop . . .
Stacy Holman Jones's (2005) chapter on autoethnography in *The Sage Handbook of Qualitative Research* provides a solid overview of the autoethnography literature. But more than that, she demonstrates how autoethnography can provide a space not just for understanding the self, but providing a text to 'move writers and readers, subjects and objects, tellers and listeners into this space of dialogue, debate and change' (p. 764).

Then jump in the deep end . . .
Read Carolyn Ellis's (2004) *The Ethnographic I: A Methodological Novel about Autoethnography,* which focuses on a fictional graduate course she teaches. She presents the rich possibilities of autoethnography in terms of moving beyond the academic text to writing a novel – and drawing on the elements of fiction in her writing. Read about the lives of her students as they come to grips with their own autoethnographic research projects. This is a good one to prepare yourself for the dilemmas you might encounter doing autoethnographic research.

Something more structured . . .
Try Heewon Chang's (2008) *Autoethnography as Method.* This is a step-by-step guide to doing autoethnography, although as a text it has had

its critics, including Leon Anderson, whose analytic autoethnography (Anderson, 2006) has clearly influenced the author. The text is worth reading alongside Anderson's review of the book (Anderson, 2010). As a guide to the novice autoethnographer Chang's text is on the opposite end of the spectrum to Ellis's *The Ethnographic I.*

Still not exactly sure if it's autoethnography that you should be doing?
Mary Lynn Hamilton, Laura Smith and Kristen Worthington (2008) can help with this decision as they explore, contrast and compare narrative, autoethnography and self-study. All three share similarities, but there's also differences.

Thinking of using autoethnography with other people?
So it's not all about you – but about other people you might be researching or researching with. Jon Austin and Andrew Hickey (2007) present the work they have done with preservice teachers and current teachers undertaking professional development where the participants use autoethnography to explore their professional identities.

Revisiting the past . . .
For other good overviews of the autoethnography literature and how autoethnography has been enacted in educational settings head to John Quicke's book *Inclusion and Psychological Intervention in Schools: A Critical Autoethnography* (2008), or his subsequent article 'Narrative strategies in educational research: reflections on a critical autoethnography' (2010). The latter is particularly interesting because John revisits those initial autoethnographic stories from the book to examine the process of creating the stories (good for the novice narrative writer) as well as outlining possible criteria for judging these stories.

Peter1996:   But none of these texts are available to me back in 1996!!!
Peter2010:   True. As a research method autoethnography is still relatively new and emerging and there are plenty of critics out there who have pointed out its weaknesses.
Peter1996:   Like what?
Peter2010:   That it's self-indulgent (see Coffey, 1999; Foster, McAllister and O'Brien, 2006) for a start. There is also the danger of other voices other than the writer's voice being marginalized (Trahar, 2009). Holt's (2003) analysis of reviewer feedback to his autoethnographic account of endeavouring to get an autoethnographic manuscript published showed up two issues seen as being weaknesses of the method: use of inadequate verification strategies and self as only data source. And one of the hardest

things to pull off successfully is to bring your private life (the inner) into the public arena (Foster, McAllister and O'Brien, 2006, p. 49); and that is essential because autoethnography is all about drawing on *you* – your thoughts, your feelings, the often intimate detail that sheds light on you. But for the most detailed look at the weaknesses of autoethnography read Sara Delamont's (2009) article 'The only honest thing: autoethnography, reflexivity and small crises in fieldwork'. She argues that autoethnography cannot meet core social science objectives, citing various critics of the genre. It's worth reading this before embarking on autoethnographic research. In particular, concerns about the ethical nature of autoethnographic writing are highlighted in terms of the portrayal of other actors in this kind of writing, in particular the difficulty in disguising the identity of these people in autoethnographic writing.

Peter1996:   And the strengths . . .?

Peter2010:   You're always there! You are the central character in the research so access is not problematic. You can revisit and rethink the data you collect about yourself in an ongoing way. This is data immersion gone wild. But seriously, good autoethnographies draw the audience in. I've found with my own students at university that when I present autoethnographies to them they really listen and respond. This is the power of narrative, of story. The fact that these stories stem from the author's experiences gives them even greater resonance, and as Atkinson (Chapter 38, this volume, p. 518) writes, makes them emotionally high charged. So when I stand up and read from autoethnographic accounts of my teaching this is about the person reading the account out. It provides that forum for readers/listeners to engage with the text. Importantly, though, it's not just about writing about these experiences – it's about *making meaning* of these experiences (Ellis, 1999). This is what gives this particular kind of storying strength. Autoethnography allows the researcher/writer to explore their own lived experience in ways that other research methods don't, fostering 'self-awareness and reflexivity' (Trahar, 2009, para. 19) that can lead to a questioning of dominant discourses and practices. You will find that when you've finished your autoethnography of your lived experience as a music teacher you will question some of your teaching practices, you will question what goes on around you as a teacher in a school, in an education system, in a country like Australia.

Peter1996:   Tell me more.

Peter2010:   I won't, because doing autoethnography is a journey – an exciting journey of self-discovery full of surprises, disappointments and everything in between. And it won't end when the PhD is done either – once you start with autoethnography it's difficult to stop. So enjoy – I know you will.

REFERENCES

Anderson, L. (2006), 'Analytic autoethnography', *Journal of Contemporary Ethnography*, **35** (4), 373–95.

Anderson, L. (2010), 'Book review: Heewon Chang, autoethnography as method', *Qualitative Research*, **10** (4), 493–4.

Austin, J. and Hickey, A. (2007), 'Autoethnography and teacher development', *International Journal of Interdisciplinary Social Sciences*, **2**, available at http://www.SocialSciences-Journal.com (accessed 15 June 2010).

Chang, H. (2008), *Autoethnography as Method*, Walnut Creek, CA: Left Coast Press.

Coffey, A. (1999), *The Ethnographic Self*, London: Sage.

Delamont, S. (2009), 'The only honest thing: autoethnography, reflexivity and small crises in fieldwork', *Ethnography and Education*, **4** (1), 51–63.

de Vries, P. (2000), 'Learning how to be a music teacher', *Music Education Research*, **2** (2), 165–79.

de Vries, P. (2006), 'It's (being an) academic', *Cultural Studies Critical Methodologies*, **6** (3), 330–34.

Duncan, M. (2004), 'Autoethnography: critical appreciation of an emerging art', *International Journal of Qualitative Methods*, **3** (4), Article 3, available at http://www.ualberta.ca/~iiqm/backissues/3_4/pdf/duncan.pdf (accessed 19 June 2010).

Ellis, C. (1999), 'Heartful autoethnography', *Qualitative Health Research*, **9** (5), 669–83.

Ellis, C. (2004), *The Ethnographic I: A Methodological Novel about Autoethnography*, Walnut Creek, CA: AltaMira Press.

Foster, K., McAllister, M. and O'Brien, L. (2006), 'Extending the boundaries: autoethnography as an emergent method in mental health nursing research', *International Journal of Mental Health Nursing*, **15** (1), 44–53.

Hamilton, M.L., Smith, L. and Worthington, K. (2008), 'Fitting the methodology with the research: an exploration of narrative, self-study and auto-ethnography', *Studying Teacher Education*, **4** (1), 17–28.

Holman Jones, S. (2005), 'Autoethnography: making the personal political', in N. Denzin and Y. Lincoln (eds), *The Sage Handbook of Qualitative Research*, 3rd edn, London: Sage, pp. 763–92.

Holt, N. (2003), 'Representation, legitimation, and autoethnography: an autoethnographic writing story', *International Journal of Qualitative Methods*, **2** (1), 18–28, available at http://www.ualberta.ca/~iiqm/backissues/2_1/pdf/holt.pdf (accessed 10 June 2010).

LaBoskey, V. (2004), 'The methodology of self-study and its theoretical underpinnings', in J. Loughran, M. Hamilton, V. LaBoskey and T. Russell (eds), *International Handbook of Self-study of Teaching Practices*, Dordrecht: Kluwer, pp. 817–69.

Leavy, P. (2010), 'A/r/t: a poetic montage', *Qualitative Inquiry*, **16** (4), 240–43.

Lee, K. (2010), 'An autoethnography: music therapy after laser eye surgery', *Qualitative Inquiry*, **16** (4), 244–8.

Quicke, J. (2008), *Inclusion and Psychological Intervention in Schools: A Critical Autoethnography*, Dordrecht: Springer.

Quicke, J. (2010), 'Narrative strategies in educational research: reflections on a critical autoethnography', *Educational Action Research*, **18** (2), 239–54.

Reed-Danahay, D. (ed.) (1997), *Auto/Ethnography. Rewriting the Self and the Social*, Oxford: Berg.

Trahar, S. (2009), 'Beyond the story itself: narrative inquiry and autoethnography in intercultural research in higher education', *Forum: Qualitative Social Research*, **10** (1), available at http://nbn-resolving.de/urn:de:0114-fqs0901308 (accessed 7 July 2010).

26. Interviewing individuals
Martin Forsey*

STARTING WITH THE END IN MIND

Interviews are arguably the most used instrument in qualitative research (Briggs, 1986, p. 11; Alvesson, 2002; Elliot, Chapter 20; Currie, Chapter 29, this volume). Reasons for this are manifold: they offer expedient ways of gathering richer data than a pen and paper survey can offer; they make sense in an 'interview society' (Atkinson and Silverman, 1997); and provide tangible, 'work-withable' data in a field of endeavour that oft times feel abstract, difficult to pin down. More positively, or at least less pragmatically, the research interview provides an opportunity for creating and capturing insights of a depth and level of focus rarely achieved through surveys, observational studies, or the majority of casual conversations held with fellow human beings. We interview in order to find out what we do not and cannot know otherwise. And we record what we hear in order to systematically process the data and better understand and analyse the insights shared through the dialogue.

It is tempting to portray listening as the most significant skill for an interview project (Seidman, 2006, p. 78; Elliott, Chapter 20, this volume). If all we did was talk with people I would not argue with this proposition, but the project requires a wide variety of social, organizational and academic skills. Writing, for instance, is vital. Without 'good enough' research reports, all of the excellent listening that helped produce the data in the first place was for naught. 'Keep the end point in sight' urge Kvale and Brinkmann (2009, p. 111) in their important account of 'learning the craft of qualitative research interviewing'; clarity about the product of the research project is crucial to both outcome and conduct of the project.

Familiarizing ourselves with the published products of interview-based projects is a helpful part of our preparation. For instance, I am intrigued by Miller's recent monograph *The Comfort of Things* (2008). Based originally on 100 interviews exploring how persons living in a particular street in London express themselves through their possessions, the book presents a selection of 30 individual 'portraits' produced as separate chapters. This is not the place to go into the subtleties of argument for and against this particular approach, but I believe it is worth emulating (see Forsey, 2010). In the writing-up of research findings, I believe we should strive to avoid wrenching people out of their social milieu, butchering their often exciting stories 'into atomistic quotes and isolated variables' (Bowe et al., 1994, Kvale & Brinkmann, 2009, p. 269).

We should not rush into this most used of qualitative research instruments. Some argue that interviews alone are notoriously unreliable. Incomplete or faulty memories and particular forms of image management conspire to ensure interviewees offer only what they are prepared to reveal about their subjective perceptions of events and opinions (Walford, 2007, p. 147). For Walford, interviews work best when used as part of a suite of approaches applied to knowledge generation (see Becker and Geer, 1957, Trow, 1957 for an early debate on this topic). Interviewing is not the only, or necessarily the best, method for conducting qualitative research and many a researcher incorporates interviews into a broader, participatory project. That said, this chapter focuses on individual interviewing and proceeds by asking fundamental questions about the circumstances leading researchers to choose the interview as a significant component of her research.

TO INTERVIEW OR NOT TO INTERVIEW, THAT IS THE SECOND QUESTION

The first is what is my research question? It seems an obvious point to make, but before deciding upon how to do the research, it helps to know what is going to be researched. In practice things are rarely clear-cut, so it is useful to acknowledge that various methodological limitations influence the sorts of questions asked. Sometimes it is best to use interviews as part of a suite of techniques used to address particular problems, but as Seidman (2006, p. 6) points out, sometimes the in-depth interview offers the best, or the only way to address certain types of questions. He stops short of telling us what these questions might be, so let me suggest 'school choice' as a useful example, not least because it is one I and many others have pursued. Choosing a school takes place in an instant but is usually the result of some process of discernment. If the questions one wishes to pursue do not lend themself to observable moments, interviews are likely to be the best way to address the research questions (Forsey, 2010). Furthermore, if the questions require comprehension of what particular events, behaviours or phenomena 'mean' to individuals or groups of people, in-depth interviews are probably necessary to the project.

One question any researcher wants to avoid is 'how will I cope with all of this material'? Kvale and Brinkmann (2009) calls this the 1000 page question (TPQ) and make the simple point, never pose the question of how to analyse transcripts *after* you have conducted the interviews (p. 190). There are two questions behind the TPQ – how many do I need to interview? And how should I process the information? Both are related to discussions about how one imagines or conceptualizes the research process.

TYPES AND STYLES OF INTERVIEW

> Interviewing is rather like marriage: everybody knows what it is, an awful lot of people do it, and yet behind each closed front door there is a world of secrets. (Oakley, 1981, p. 31)

Many a secret has been revealed since Oakley's observation, especially by researchers taking a deliberative, reflexive approach to their work. Training and personal predisposition clearly play a part in the research projects pursued and their manner of conduct. Seidman's (2006) insightful description of his 'conversion' from 'scientific' experimenter to phenomenological interviewer helps illuminate the effects of training and personality on the shaping of research approaches. It also sheds light on a continuum brought to our attention by Roulston (2010), who believes a key step for novice interviewers is located in learning to use interviews in ways consonant with the epistemological and theoretical assumptions underlying a study's design. She describes six broad 'conceptions of qualitative interviews' (p. 203), ranging from a positivist neutrality producing 'objective' knowledge, to those conceiving themselves as 'co-constructors of knowledge' striving for collaborative, transformative relationships with research participants (p. 224). While Roulston's typology allows us to break away from overly simplistic dichotomous models of research processes, there is still some conceptual purchase located in some of the dichotomies on offer. Kvale and Brinkmann (2009, pp. 48–50) conceptualize two divergent metaphors of the interviewer:

1. The industrious miner digging for nuggets of objective facts, insights and meanings using methods 'unpolluted by any leading questions'.
2. The intrepid traveller, the interpreter of reality seeking a depth of engagement which allows fellow travellers to tell their own stories.

How one conceptualizes a research approach obviously helps determine the style of interview pursued. Those committed to minimizing researcher bias, and all other forms of 'contamination', in a style described somewhat pejoratively by some as 'neo-positivist' (Alvesson, 2002; Roulston, 2010), are the ones most likely to follow the more formal paths of 'tightly structured survey interviews with preset, standardized, normally closed questions' (Seidman, 2006, p. 15). The phenomenologically oriented traveller is more inclined to follow the less constrained path of open-ended or semi-structured interviews.

Feminist ethics and epistemology is now part of mainstream practice in qualitative research. Stressing the importance of overcoming the negative effects of positivistic and/or exploitative research, many contemporary researchers argue the need for gauging the effects of our research, minimizing its harm to the people who volunteer to share their stories with us and for building reciprocal relationships between researcher and respondent (Bloom, 1997, p. 111; Sinding and Aronson, 2003, p. 96). The self-consciously ethical practice produced by feminist engagement is important, but the shift in focus to the 'effects' of the interview on the research participant has produced its own scrutinizable effects. Sinding and Aronson (2003, p. 95) capture these secondary effects well in discussing claims about what qualitative interviews 'do' to research participants: 'At one extreme interviews allegedly empower, generate self-awareness, or offer a kind of therapeutic release for interviewees; at the other, they draw reproach for feigning intimacy with, and then abandoning, the people they engage.'

It is useful to ask, in light of these insights, why we are doing what we do? I never think of my work as therapy. The interview may be cathartic for some participants, but this is certainly not the reason why I meet with them, or they with me (see Seidman, 2006, pp. 107–9). As with Weiss (1995), I interview in order to access the observations and insights of others. My aim is to better understand the world in which I live and to share this understanding, with all of its limitations, with whoever takes the time to read it. We certainly need to be aware of the potential, and actual, harm caused by social research, but as Bloom (1997) shows in her fascinating discussion of the rejection of reciprocity expressed by one of her research participants, those we interview have their own agenda in meeting with us (Watson, Chapter 34, this volume) and may be using us just as much as we use them. It is a very human encounter.

Brinkmann (2007) reminds us of the links between reciprocal, empathetic research and psychology/psychotherapy. He argues for an 'epistemic' approach to interviewing, moving from the currently dominant 'doxic' state of invoking simply the opinions of those we interview, to a more engaged questioning of their beliefs and values. According to Brinkmann (2007, p. 1136), compared to the long monologues produced from phenomenological and narrative approaches, more readable interview reports are generated from the challenge and confrontation of doxic interview schedules. Whilst cautioning against conceptualizing epistemic interviews as focusing on the opportunities they can bring to the inter-viewee for finding a more authentic 'civic voice' – it may well be a useful side-effect – the call to keep developing a more critically engaged interview process than is currently in evidence suggests a purposeful agenda for future types and styles of interviews.

LOCATING INTERVIEWEES

I'll come to your birthday party and do an interview for a hot dog and a glass of orange juice . . . – Wrestler Chris Jericho. (Figure four Online, 2007)

We probably won't get people to agree to be interviewed quite as easily or readily as the publicity-seeking Chris Jericho, but many people are nonetheless willing to offer their perspective on the world and the ques-tions brought to them by inquisitive social scientists. Not all people of course, so locating a productive, valid number of interviewees can pose some difficulties depending upon the nature of the topic and the target group – (see Clark, 2010 for a useful exploration of motivations for engaging with qualitative research). For example, Head (2009) describes the challenges faced in locating sufficient participants for a study of caring and paid work in the lives of lone mothers. In the end she felt the need to amend her recruitment posters, highlighting that '£10 will be paid for each interview'. In contrast, John Reed, who heads up a US-based social research company, argues that offering incentives for professional and corporate research participants confuses matters, concluding that 'if we are doing something that professionals feel is important and we are doing it in a professional manner, then they will participate' (cited in Patton, 2002, pp. 413–14). This logic, he argues, is transferable to other communities.

There are sound ethical and epistemological reasons to pay something for the services rendered by our research participants (Thompson, 1996; Simmons and Wilmott, 2004; Bagley et al., 2007). However, whilst I believe we all need to exercise a degree of ethical pragmatism when faced with the realities of our work, and perhaps because I have not yet shared Head's frustrations at not being able to locate sufficient research participants, I tend to concur with Reed. I worry about the potential for research incen-tives to degrade the idea of a common good to which research contributes.

A question pursued with much more vigour in the literature than the implications of 'incentivizing' research participants revolves around how many interviewees we need to recruit. Kvale (1996), who trained as a psychologist in the 1960s, describes how when he converted to qualitative research the 'holy trinity' of generalizability, reliability and validity emerged as a means for mainstream researchers to disqualify his work:

> The stimulus 'qualitative research interview' appeared automatically to trigger conditioned responses like: 'The results are not reliable, they are produced by leading interview questions'; 'The interview findings cannot be generalized, there are too few interview subjects'; and 'The results are not valid, they are only based on subjective interpretations.' (p. 230)

Whilst one can hope that qualitative researchers do not encounter such primitive forms of scientism in contemporary departments of education studies, or similar arenas of research activity, quantitative ideals are deeply entrenched in university research regimes (Pérez Huber, Chapter 27; Tierney and Clemens, Chapter 19, this volume; McCracken, 1988; St Pierre and Roulston, 2006; Forsey, 2008). I remember well a review of a research funding proposal I had submitted for a project considering school choice. The main question raised centred on the validity of a study based on three groups of 20 interviews. I appreciated being able to cite Kvale's (1996, p. 102) authoritative work in response in arguing the standard number of interviews in qualitative studies to be 15± 10. It was deeply satisfying to comment that whilst I was clearly going above the standard requirement, it was probably safer to do so for one who was an early career researcher. I did get the grant!

The point is that one interviews as many persons as necessary to find out what one needs to know. This might involve capturing a predetermined number of respondents, which is as dependent upon available resources as much as anything, or we interview until reaching saturation point – when new interviews no longer yield fresh insights (Kvale and Brinkmann, 2009, p. 113). We need to be as clear and secure as possible in knowing that qualitative research is opportunistic, and aims at glimpsing the 'complicated character, organization and logic of culture' rather than locating groups representing a distinct sample of the larger world (McCracken, 1988, p. 17). How we go about locating and analysing this knowledge through the interview process is picked up in the following sections.

SETTING THE SCENE

Questions are never indiscreet. Answers sometimes are. (Oscar Wilde)

An example from an interview I conducted recently helps set the scene for what I wish to discuss here.

> I met Ashley (not her real name) in the foyer of the social club of the university in which I work. She is a student and first heard about the research I was doing via one of my lectures, when I mentioned I was about to head to a town in the north to continue a project started earlier in the year. She came from the town in question and was keen to share her thoughts on her educational experiences there. The club is a good venue for such an interview. It has various spaces to sit, is relatively quiet, and offers an opportunity for me to buy the volunteer participant a drink.
>
> Ashley requested a cup of tea and whilst I ordered this, I invited her to read the project information sheet. Upon returning I handed Ashley a consent form and a pen with which to sign her agreement to (1) be interviewed, (2) to have the interview recorded, and (3) to allow me to use the data generated in conference presentations and future publications. As she prepared to sign, I pointed out that she would be anonymised in any research reports, and, reiterated what the form stated about being able to withdraw from the project at any time without prejudice. Ashley dismissed this comment as irrelevant; she was quite sure there would be no need for that.

Wilde's witty insight in the epigraph opening this section reminds us that interviews can yield never meant to be shared truths (Clark and Sharf, 2007, p. 407). The warm understanding and attention offered by skilful researchers can lead interviewees to reveal intimate details they may come to regret sharing (Kirsch, 1999, p. 29). Obviously, participants should be protected from unwitting vulnerability, embarrassment or loss of reputation (Seidman, 2006, p. 61). Even if no regret is realized by the participant, research interpretations and analyses may pose some problems or dangers to them (see Lieblich, 1996; Sinding and Aronson, 2003; Clark and Sharf, 2007). Because of these realities, it is useful to denaturalize the interview before we begin recording and to ensure that the interviewee is well informed about the consent they are giving. Reminders of the right to withdraw at any point without prejudice and clarifying what is likely to happen to the words captured by the recording instrument are vital pieces of information.

Audio recording is not compulsory of course. Some choose to use pen and paper to record their conversations, and sometimes this is what our participants prefer. My experiences of conducting interviews without using electronic recording equipment indicate that audio recording is less distracting to both parties. If I jot down a note when someone is speaking to me, invariably the person's gaze is drawn to the pen and the paper. My impression is that they are concerned about what I am noting, wondering what they had said to trigger such a response (Elliott, Chapter 20, this volume). Digital equipment is of such quality now and size that one need not worry very much about the recorder being obtrusive, or about how well it will record the sound. External microphones are rarely necessary. One can relax and listen carefully to what one's interlocutor is saying.

I recommend opening interviews by asking people about their origins. Such questions signal an interest in the person and the stories they have to tell, they are usually easy enough for people to answer and usually help warm the interviewee to the topic and the process. Significantly, they also help position individuals and the events of their lives in a broader socio-cultural context (Zaharlick, 1992, p. 117). For example, I opened the interview with Ashley by asking her to tell me her name – for recording purposes – and a little bit about herself, 'where she was born, grew up, what her parents did, that sort of thing'. Ashley expressed mild surprise and then proceeded to tell me that she was born in Melbourne and had spent a good deal of the first few years of her life travelling around the country because her parents worked in the army. Such details help reveal the cultural context of individual lives, the beliefs, the values, the material conditions and structural forces underpinning their socially constructed realities (Forsey, 2008). They can also help make the stories you end up telling from the interview more engaging for the reader.

DOING THE INTERVIEWS

> Treating interviewing as a social encounter in which knowledge is constructed means that the interview is more than a simple information gathering operation; it is a site of, . . . producing knowledge itself. (Holstein and Gubrium, 2003, p. 4)

Regardless of the type of project, research interviews are highly social events. Holstein and Gubrium (1995) argue that in order for research interviews to yield valid, reliable information, they should not be stripped of their interactional, and so-called 'biased' ingredients. Understanding the local scene through the eyes of the informant is vital to asking good questions and interpreting the answers (Briggs, 1986; Holstein and Gubrium, 1995, p. 45). In this spirit, some of the most commonly agreed upon 'hows' of interviewing is that the questions should be open-ended, use everyday language (Elliott, Chapter 20, this volume), and they should be asked naively (Spradley, 1979, p. 59) – inviting the interviewee to share her or his expertise in such a way that any prior knowledge of the interviewer is superfluous. However, regardless of setting, it is always a 'knowing' naivety – or at least it should be. Knowing at least some of the intricacies of local issues and concerns is vital to the asking of good questions and interpreting the answers (Holstein and Gubrium, 1995, p. 45).

At an early stage of the project, it is more than reasonable for the interviewer to refer to a carefully considered interview schedule. It is also more than reasonable to be referring to this schedule – probably amended by experience – during the final interview of the project. For a semi-structured interview, the schedule should guide rather than determine the shape of the interview. I like to keep the opening and closing questions more or less the same, but the conversations proceed in different directions in moving from beginning to end. Much depends upon where the interviewee takes you, but even with very open-ended projects, the research interview will never be a complete free-for-all.

Listening is definitely the primary skill for this part of the project, and it is important to attend to this skill-base before beginning the interviews. Listening to what people have to say to us as researchers is certainly more significant than 'airing our views' on the topic at hand (Spender, 1985). We listen to the eloquence and poetry of our interlocutor, as well as her or his 'halting, hesitant, tentative talk' (Devault, 1990, p. 103) as we grasp for meaning together. Seidman (2006, pp. 78–9) elucidates three levels of active listening: internalizing what participants say; listening for 'inner voice' (after Steiner, 1978); and being attentive to the processual aspects of the interview, such as timekeeping, energy levels, non-verbal cues and so on. Taking our participants' language seriously is a vital component of active listening, encouraging their inner thoughts out into the open. Seidman encourages the interviewer to gauge his or her listening skills by comparing the length of time both interviewer and interviewee speak. 'If the interviewer is listening well, his or her [transcript] paragraphs will be short and relatively infrequently interspersed among the longer paragraphs of the participant's responses' (2006, p. 79).

Lest we fall into the trap of thinking, however, that good interview technique means adopting an empathetic demeanour, with the interviewer developing a Rogerian 'humanistic, nondirective approach, valorizing the respondent's private experiences, narratives, opinions, beliefs, and attitudes' (Brinkmann, 2007, p. 1121), let us remind ourselves that good interviews can also be about 'discourses crossing swords' (Tanggaard, 2007). Good and productive listening can also involve producing knowledge through an engagement exploring societal goals and values and people's positions in relation to these, as much as it is about their private experiences and opinions (Brinkmann, 2007, p. 1118).

CLOSING AND MOVING ON

My interviews are never cold, because I fall in love with the person who is in front of me, even if I hate him or her. An interview is a love story for me. It's a fight. It's a coitus. (Oriana Fallaci, Journalist)

'So how was that for you?' It is probably not the best question with which to close an interview, but it is better than many, including some I have used (see Forsey, 2008). I am not sure how Fallaci would have done it, but it is helpful to find ways of finishing the conversation that enable both interviewer and interviewee to disentangle and move on. Closing off an interview poses some interesting challenges. There is invariably more to say, but at about the 40-minute mark of a good interview energy levels usually begin to flag (Elliott, Chapter 20, this volume).

Returning to the earlier described interview with Ashley, before closing off I made sure that I asked about any other persons she knew of who might be able to contribute to the project. I then asked if there were any other things she would like to comment on, gave her time to respond, and then informed her that the recording will be professionally transcribed. Reiterating the point that I would anonymize her as much as possible in any writing, I also pointed out that sometimes this can be difficult, especially if some of the specific details of her life were instructive to the writing. 'If I wanted to use details that might make you identifiable', I told her, 'then I would endeavour to ensure you have the opportunity to read this before sending it out for publication'. My final words were of thanks, to which she added the customary 'no worries'.

As with the opening of the interview, it is helpful to remind the participant that her words are power-filled, that they will be captured in a transcript and could well be used in future publications. It is also important not to be disingenuous about our own processes and to be aware that simply changing the name of the interviewee does not necessarily protect them from public scrutiny. Space should be left for further questions and comments and it is good practice to remind the interviewee that should she have any further questions that she can contact you using the details on the information sheet handed out at the beginning of the interview.

PROCESSING AND WRITING UP THE DATA

> the single most serious shortcoming related to the use of interviews in the social sciences . . . is the commonsensical, unreflexive manner in which most analyses of interview data are conducted. (Briggs, 1986, p. 102)

Data processing is perhaps the most secret of activities in all of qualitative research. An excellent discussion of transcription processes is there for you to read in this volume so I won't go into details here (Hammersley, Chapter 32, this volume). The production of public documents in the form of reports, papers and monographs should be a major goal of any research project; there seems very little point in doing them otherwise. As we prepare to write up our research it is helpful to acknowledge the creative tension created by the straddling of positivism and interpretivism characterizing contemporary qualitative inquiry, particularly in the field of education (St Pierre and Roulston, 2006, p. 677). As Roulston (2010) reminds us, it is helpful to know where one stands in relation to the debates that swirl around the disciplinary arenas in which we are involved.

For example, I am not a great fan of coding; I resist its fragmenting, decontextualizing tendencies (Nespor and Barylske, 1991, p. 810), preferring instead to translate all transcripts into individual 'portraits' or 'profiles' (Seidman, 2006, pp. 119–25) of the research participants (Tierney and Clemens, Chapter 19, this volume). Aimed at revealing cultural contexts behind the lived experiences of research participants, the portraits capture the beliefs, the values, the material conditions and structural forces underpinning the socially patterned behaviour of the person that emerged in the interview. Key quotes are incorporated into these portraits to provide added texture. In using this technique the researcher is like a gallery curator who in not being able to display all of the available pictures has to select particular pieces and summarize the invisible in exhibition notes (see Forsey, 2008, 2010). I mentioned earlier Miller's *The Comfort of Things,* which offers a particularly compelling example of a 'gallery exhibition' of interviews drawn from a much larger body of work. As Miller (2008, p. 5) says of the approach taken in his book, the 30 portraits selected for the book 'pay respect to whoever these people happen to be and . . . paint a bigger portrait that starts to emerge as an image of the modern world'.

A FINAL NOTE

This chapter aimed at offering a glimpse of the richness one encounters when entering the world of qualitative interview research. It is an arena worth entering, particularly if one is open to exploring the complexities and contradictions of social life in schools and beyond. Entering the arena requires preparation and there are many, many books and articles to read. I want to commend two texts to the new researcher – Kvale and Brinkmann's (2009) 'manual' for learning the craft of qualitative research interviewing and Seidman's (2006) phenomenological guide to interviewing for education and social science researchers. Other combinations will undoubtedly suffice; however, these provide a good starting point. Whilst they do not, and could not, cover all that one needs to know about the conduct of qualitative research interviews, between them they offer informed, well-reasoned and helpful overviews of many of the main methodological, epistemological and ethical issues and concerns surrounding the qualitative research interview. I would want anyone I work with on an interview-based project to be familiar with the arguments raised in both texts. Any postgraduate student combining these with a thorough reading of Roulston's (2010) recent coverage of her six-part typology of approaches to research interviewing would instil confidence that she or he is well prepared for the tasks ahead.

NOTE

* I gratefully acknowledge 'The Media Interview' website for pointing me to a number of the quotes about interviews cited in this chapter (see http://www.themediainterview.com/category/quotes-about-interviews/).

REFERENCES

Alvesson, M. (2002), *Postmodernism and Social Research*, Buckingham: Open University Press.

Atkinson, P. and Silverman, D. (1997), 'Kundera's immortality: the interview society and the invention of the self', *Qualitative Inquiry*, **3**, 304–25.

Bagley, S.J., Reynolds, W.W. and Nelson, R.M. (2007), 'Is a "wage-payment" model for research participation appropriate for children?' *Pediatrics*, **119** (1), 46–51.

Becker, H. and Geer, B. (1957) 'Participant observation and interviewing: a comparison', *Human Organization*, **16** (3), 28–32.

Bloom, L.R. (1997), 'Locked in uneasy sisterhood: reflections on feminist methodology and research relations', *Anthropology and Education Quarterly*, **28** (1), 111–22.

Bowe, R., Gewirtz, S. and Ball, S. (1994), 'Captured by the discourse? Issues and concerns in researching parental choice', *British Journal of Sociology of Education*, **15** (1), 63–78.

Briggs, C. (1986), *Learning How to Ask: A Sociolinguistic Appraisal of the Role of the Interview in Social Science Research*, Cambridge: Cambridge University Press.

Brinkmann, S. (2007) 'Could interviews be epistemic? An alternative to qualitative opinion polling', *Qualitative Inquiry*, **13** (8), 1116–38.

Clark, M.C. and Sharf, B.F. (2007), 'The dark side of truth(s): ethical dilemmas in researching the personal', *Qualitative Inquiry*, **13** (3), 399–416.

Clark, T. (2010) 'On "being researched": why do people engage with qualitative research?', *Qualitative Research*, **10** (4), 399–416.

Devault, M. (1990), 'Talking and listening from women's standpoint: feminist strategies for interviewing and analysis', *Social Problems*, **37** (1), 96–116.

Figure Four Online (2007) 'Chris Jericho on Fight Network Radio', http://www.f4wonline.com/content/view/4374/105 (accessed 2 September 2010).

Forsey, M. (2008), 'Ethnographic interviewing: from conversation to published text', in G. Walford (ed.), *How to do Educational Ethnography*, London: Tufnell Press, pp. 57–75.

Forsey, M. (2010), 'Publicly minded, privately focused: Western Australian teachers and school choice', *Teaching and Teacher Education*, **26** (1), 53–60.

Head, E. (2009), 'The ethics and implications of paying participants in qualitative research', *International Journal of Social Research Methodology*, **12** (4), 335–44.

Holstein, J. and Gubrium, J. (1995), *The Active Interview*, Thousand Oaks, CA: Sage.

Holstein, J. and Gubrium, J. (2003), 'Inside interviewing: new lenses, new concerns' in J. Holstein and J. Gubrium (eds), *Inside Interviewing: New Lenses, New Concerns*, London: Sage, pp. 3–32.

Kirsch, G.E. (1999), *Ethical Dilemmas in Feminist Research*, Albany, NY: State University of New York Press.

Kvale, S. (1996), *InterViews: An Introduction to Qualitative Research Interviewing*, Thousand Oaks, CA: Sage.

Kvale, S. and Brinkmann, S. (2009), *InterViews: Learning the Craft of Qualitative Research Interviewing*, Thousand Oaks, CA: Sage.

Lieblich, A. (1996), 'Some unforeseen outcomes of conducting narrative research with people of one's own culture', in R. Josselson (ed.), *Ethics and Process in the Narrative Study of Lives* (The Narrative Study of Lives), Vol. 4, Thousand Oaks, CA: Sage, pp. 172–84.

McCracken, G. (1988), *The Long Interview*, Newbury Park, CA: Sage.

Miller, D. (2008), *The Comfort of Things*, Cambridge: Polity Press.

Nespor, J. and Barylske, J. (1991), 'Narrative discourse and teacher knowledge', *American Educational Research Journal*, **28** (4), 805–23.

Oakley, A. (1981), 'Interviewing women: a contradiction in terms', in H. Roberts (ed.), *Doing Feminist Research*, New York: Routledge pp. 30–61.

Patton, M.Q. (2002), *Qualitative Research and Evaluation Methods*, 3rd edn, Thousand Oaks, CA: Sage.

Roulston, K. (2010), 'Considering quality in qualitative interviewing', *Qualitative Research*, **10** (2), 199–228.

Seidman, I. (2006), *Interviewing as Qualitative Research: A Guide for Researchers in Education and the Social Sciences*, 3rd edn, New York: Teachers College Press.

Simmons, E. and Wilmot, A. (2004), 'Incentive payments in social surveys – a literature review', Office for National Statistics, Newport, South Wales, available at http://www.ons.gov.uk/about/who-we-are/our-services/data-collection-methodology/reports-and-publications (accessed 15 September 2010).

Sinding, C. and Aronson, J. (2003), 'Exposing failures, unsettling accommodations: tensions in interview practice', *Qualitative Research*, **3** (1), 95–117.

Spender, D. (1985), *Man Made Language*, 2nd edn, London: Routledge Kegan.

Spradley, J. (1979), *The Ethnographic Interview*, New York: Holt, Rinehart and Wilson.

Steiner, G. (1978), 'The distribution of discourse', in G. Steiner (ed.), *On Difficulty and Other Essays*, New York: Oxford University Press, pp. 61–94.

St Pierre, E. and Roulston, K. (2006), 'The state of qualitative inquiry: a contested science', *International Journal of Qualitative Studies in Education*, **19** (6), 673–84.

Tanggaard, L. (2007), 'The research interview as discourses crossing swords: the researcher and apprentice on crossing roads', *Qualitative Inquiry*, **13** (1), 160–76.

Thompson, S. (1996), 'Paying respondents and informants', *Social Research Update, Autumn*, **14**, available at http://sru.soc.surrey.ac.uk/SRU14.html (accessed 24 March 2011).

Trow, M. (1957), 'Comment on "Participant observation and interviewing: a comparison"', *Human Organization*, **16** (3), 33–5.

Walford, G. (2007), 'Classification and framing of interviews in ethnographic interviewing', *Ethnography and Education*, **2** (2), 145–57.

Weiss, R. (1995), *Learning from Strangers: The Art and Method of Qualitative Interview Studies*, New York: The Free Press.

Zaharlick, A. (1992), 'Ethnography in anthropology and its value for education', *Theory into Practice*, **XXXI** (2), 116–25.

27. *Testimonio* as LatCrit methodolgy in education
Lindsay Pérez Huber[1]

INTRODUCTION

Testimonio is grounded in a collective history of resistance. It is used by non-dominant groups to challenge oppression and brings attention to injustice in an effort to transform it. For example, one of the most widely known contemporary *testimonios* is the book, *Me Llamo Rigoberta Menchú y Así Me Nació La Conciencia* that documented the *testimonio* of Rigoberta Menchú, a human rights activist from an indigenous Guatemalan community (Burgos, 1983).[2] Her *testimonio* recounted the violence and death she survived during a horrific civil war, and how she became an active leader in the struggle for indigenous and human rights in her country. The book was translated in multiple languages and brought international attention to the injustices and violence faced by poor indigenous communities in Guatemala.

As *testimonio* has served as a powerful tool by non-dominant groups, it has encountered considerable controversy and debate around 'legitimate' knowledge in academia. American anthropologist David Stoll, for example, went to great lengths in his academic work to discredit Rigoberta Menchú's *testimonio*. In fact, in 1999 Stoll published the book, *Rigoberta Menchú and the story of All Poor Guatemalans* that challenged Menchú's accounts of the guerilla warfare that led to the tragic deaths of her family. The strong opposition to Menchú's *testimonio* by Western scholars is indicative of the power of *testimonio* to disrupt the marginalization and exclusion of non-dominant forms of knowledge in the academy.

Acknowledging the power of *testimonio* to advocate for social justice, scholars are using it as a tool in qualitative research. This chapter discusses how *testimonio* was used in a LatCrit education research study. First, I provide a brief overview of how scholars have described and used *testimonio* in academia. Next, I explain as a case example how I used *testimonio* as a methodological process that utilized Latina/o critical theory (LatCrit) and was situated within a Chicana feminist epistemology in educational research. Finally I discuss further considerations for *testimonio* in educational research. This chapter illustrates how *testimonio* can be used as critical qualitative methodology generally, and in critical case research in particular, joining a range of other critical race methodologies in education (Solorzano and Yosso, 2002; Duncan, 2006; Yosso, 2006; Velez and Solorzano, 2007).

OVERVIEW OF THE STUDY

In the following sections, I refer to a study previously conducted on how racism emerged in the educational trajectories of US born and undocumented immigrant Chicana[3] undergraduate students (Pérez Huber, 2010). Using a LatCrit framework, I examined how the women encountered various forms of racism at the intersections of race, immigration status, gender, and class within and beyond educational institutions. I positioned this study within a Chicana feminist epistemology (CFE) that validated the lived experiences of the women and allowed us to enter the research in a collaborative process. Thus, CFE allowed us to work together to co-construct knowledge and theory. I offer this description as one example of how *testimonio* is used as methodology in educational research. I also acknowledge the many roles *testimonio* can take in developing research processes, pedagogies, and praxis that have explicit anti-racist and social justice agendas (Delgado Bernal et al., 2009).

FOLLOWING A TRADITION OF *TESTIMONIO*

Testimonio emerged from Latin American human rights struggles and has generally been used to document the experiences of oppressed groups and denounce injustices (Booker, 2002; Delgado Bernal et al., 2009). Scholars have identified several important elements of *testimonio* to consider. For example, Yúdice describes *testimonio* as 'authentic narrative, told by a witness who is moved to narrate by the urgency of a situation' (1991, p. 17). Brabeck describes *testimonio* as a 'verbal journey . . . of one's life experiences with attention to injustices one has suffered and the effect these injustices have had on one's life' (2001, p. 3). Cienfuegos and Monelli[4] describe the process of *testimonio*, which 'allows the individual to transform past experience and personal identity, creating a new present and enhancing the future' (1983, p. 46). The Latina Feminist Group (2001) describes the method of *testimonio* as a way to create knowledge and theory through personal experiences, highlighting the significance of the process of *testimonio* in theorizing our own realities as Women of Color. Delgado Bernal and co-authors (2009) have highlighted the representation of the 'collective story' in *testimonio*, and its significance in healing from oppressive experiences.

Through the years, *testimonio* has progressed in important ways. It has moved beyond Latin American human rights struggles and into academic fields such as anthropology, education, ethnic studies, humanities, psychology, and women's studies (Cienfuegos and Monelli, 1983; Angueira, 1988; Benmayor, 1988, 2008; Yúdice, 1991; Zimmerman, 1991; Behar, 1993; Latina Feminist Group, 2001; Brabeck, 2003; Haig-Brown, 2003; Beverley, 2004; Irizarry, 2005; Burciaga and Tavares, 2006; Cruz, 2006; González, 2006; Burciaga, 2007; Gutiérrez, 2008; Delgado Bernal et al., 2009; Diaz Soto et al., 2009; Espino et al., 2010; Flores Carmona, 2010). Scholars in these fields, and in particular Women of Color scholars (as cited above), have found use of *testimonio* to document and/or theorize their own experiences of struggle, survival, and resistance, as well as that of others.[5] These scholars have used *testimonio* in academic research in multiple ways. For example, *testimonio* is often told by a witness,[6] motivated by a social and/or political urgency to voice injustice and raise awareness of oppression. *Testimonios* are usually guided by the will of the narrator to tell events as she sees significant, and is often an expression of a collective experience, rather than the individual.

Similar to Kris Gutiérrez (2008) I use *testimonio* as a 'syncretic' process, acknowledging the contradictions that emerge between the performance of *testimonio* and *testimonio* as written text. Thus, I use *testimonio* in educational research recognizing the 'double-bind' of creating theory and knowledge from People of Color within a research process that has historically functioned as a colonial project (Gutiérrez, 2008). Furthermore, I use *testimonio* acknowledging similar strategies for documenting life experiences such as life histories, autobiographies, documentaries, and counterstories, yet agree with Delgado Bernal and co-authors (2009) that *testimonio* can be used as not only method, but methodology. *Testimonio* as methodology departs from the Eurocentricity of traditional educational research and is guided by an anti-racist and anti-hierarchical agenda. That is, the process of *testimoniando*[7] is to denounce racial and social injustice and allows for the repositioning of power in the traditional roles of researcher–'subject' relationships (Cruz, 2006). In previous work, I have co-theorized with the women participants included in the research study to understand the process of *testimonio* as 'a verbal journey of a witness who speaks to reveal the racial, classed, gendered, and nativist injustices they have suffered as a means of healing, empowerment, and advocacy for a more humane present and future' (Pérez Huber, 2009).[8]

TESTIMONIO AS METHODOLOGY IN LATCRIT RESEARCH

I have used *testimonio* to document and theorize the experiences of 20 Chicana women attending a four-year public research institution in California. Ten of these women were undocumented, meaning they had no 'legalized' status in the US at the time they were interviewed. The other ten Chicana women were US born, initially included in the study as a comparison group that would allow me to examine the similarities and differences in the experiences of undocumented and US born students. However, through the process of *testimoniando* the women showed me that their stories and experiences are powerful as a collective. The following section will describe how I employed *testimonio* as methodology in a LatCrit educational research study.

Aligning *Testimonio* and a LatCrit Framework

Critical race theory (CRT) in education is a framework that draws from the lived experiences of People of Color to understand how systems of power mediate educational trajectories (Solorzano and Yosso, 2001). LatCrit is a branch of CRT that specifically explores the experiences of the Latinas/os (Solorzano and Delgado Bernal, 2001). Daniel Solorzano (2009), a leading CRT scholar in the field of education, suggests that critical race researchers should always be looking for strategies that can inform CRT research, pedagogy, and practice. In researching the ways *testimonio* has been used by scholars across time and disciplines, I saw clear areas of overlap between the elements that constitute a LatCrit framework and those of *testimonio*. Specifically, I saw five areas of alignment as provided below.[9]

1. Revealing injustices caused by oppression: *testimonio* describes the injustices People of Color face as a result of oppression. A LatCrit lens helps expose the structural conditions, which cause oppression in Latina/o communities.
2. Challenging dominant Eurocentric ideologies: implicit in the use of *testimonio* and a LatCrit framework is a direct challenge to the apartheid of knowledge that exists in academia.[10]
3. Validating experiential knowledge: similar to this tenant of LatCrit, the process of *testimonio* builds from the lived experiences of People of Color to document and theorize oppression.
4. Acknowledging the power of human collectivity: *testimonio* and LatCrit acknowledge the emancipatory elements of revealing

oppression through lived experiences, which are rooted in the histories and memories of a larger community.
5. Commitment to racial and social justice: revealing oppression moves People of Color toward dismantling and transforming oppressive conditions to end injustice.

Acknowledging these congruencies, *testimonio* serves as an important strategy to conduct LatCrit research, guided by an anti-racist and social justice agenda. In previous work, I have considered the term 'critical race *testimonio*' to explicitly link *testimonio* with critical race research (Pérez Huber, 2008). However, as my work with *testimonio* has progressed, I realize *testimonio* is a powerful tool that can stand alone, particularly when it is positioned within a critical race-gendered epistemology, such as Chicana feminist epistemologies in education.[11] Thus, I detail these congruencies to build on the work of past scholars who have developed and acknowledged critical race methodologies and critical race-gendered epistemologies to in education, that emerge from the cultural knowledge of Communities of Color (González, 1998, 2001; Trinidad Galván, 2001; Delgado Bernal, 2002). The following section describes how I positioned this work within a Chicana feminist epistemology in education.

Bringing *Testimonio* to 'Life' in Educational Research

Undertaking this study in 2007, I was not consciously positioned within a particular epistemological stance, but was cautious in the methodological design because of several concerns. First was the concern to design a methodology that told the stories of the undocumented and US born Chicana students in this study, without romanticizing their experiences. Second was the concern that traditional methodological approaches would produce findings that did not accurately capture the complexity and power of the women's experiences. Third was the concern in the authoritative positionality of the researcher that this work sought to counter.

As I engaged in the process of *testimonio*, my thinking about the research design continued to develop. During this time, I revisited the work of Rebeca Burciaga (2007) who explained how positioning *testimonio* within a Chicana feminist epistemology 'brings the method of *testimonio* to life' in educational research. In retrospect, I realized that although I had not initially positioned this study within a Chicana feminist epistemological framework, it was from my own 'cultural intuition' that these methodological concerns emerged (Delgado Bernal, 1998). According to Delgado Bernal (1998), there are four sources of cultural intuition Chicana researchers draw upon during the research process – personal, academic, professional, and the analytic process itself. Personal experience includes the researcher's background and personal history that shape the ways she understands, interprets, and makes sense of events, circumstances, and data during the research process. Academic experiences inform how we make sense of related literature on our research topic. Our professional experiences, often within our own communities, provide us with significant insight into the research process. The final source of cultural intuition lies in the analytical research process itself to 'bring meaning' to our data and larger study (Delgado Bernal, 1998).

A Chicana feminist epistemology in education allows Chicana researchers and participants to utilize our multiple sources of knowledge to inform the research process – from the research questions we ask, the theoretical frameworks we use, the methodologies we employ, to how we write about our findings. A Chicana feminist epistemological standpoint not only brings *testimonio* to 'life' in educational research, but changes the process of *testimonio* from method to methodology by allowing for the co-construction of knowledge through collaborative data analysis. While a Chicana feminist epistemological standpoint allows Chicana researchers to engage the research process in these ways, I use a LatCrit framework to examine and understand how structures of oppression mediate the experiences of the women in this study. Using a LatCrit framework is critical to the process of *testimonio* in this context, to expose, understand, and further theorize the role of social and institutional structures in maintaining and perpetuating oppressive conditions.

Data Collection and Analysis

In line with grounded theory analysis strategies, data collection and analysis occurred simultaneously in this study (Glaser and Strauss, 1967; Glaser, 1978; Strauss and Corbin, 1990; Charmaz, 2006). Each of the 20 women participated in a series of two *testimonio* 'interviews' (for a total of 40) that were audio-recorded. Here, the women discussed how forms of oppression at the intersections of race, immigration status, gender, and class emerged in their educational trajectories. I conducted two additional focus groups with the women that were used as collaborative sites of data analysis, which I will discuss shortly.

Data collection and analysis was conducted in a three-phase process that included: (1) preliminary, (2) collaborative, and (3) final data analysis stages. Figure 27.1 provides a visual model of this three-phase approach where each of these stages build from each other in a continuous process, to arrive at a final set of findings. Each of these phases is discussed below.

Figure 27.1   Visual model of three-phase data analysis process

Preliminary data analysis
Following the audio recording of the 40 *testimonios* of the women, transcriptions were created. During this phase of analysis, I reviewed the 40 *testimonios* using a critical race grounded theory approach (Malagón et al., 2009). This approach allowed simultaneous involvement in data analysis and advancing theory development, strategies primarily used in grounded theory (Glaser and Strauss, 1967; Glaser, 1978). However, this approach also allowed me to utilize a LatCrit lens to isolate thematic categories that emerged from the data and explicitly explore subordination due to race, immigration status, gender, and class. Following this initial analysis, I extracted samples of data that represented each of these emergent categories. These representative samples were used in a critical reflection exercise in the collaborative data analysis phase.

Collaborative data analysis
The collaborative data analysis phase took place in a focus group environment. There were two focus groups included in the study, each with six to eight women. The reflections constructed from the preliminary analysis were used to create a 'reflection exercise' where each woman was given a series of reflections to read aloud as a group and had individual time to respond in writing. Following the reflecting, the group engaged in a dialogue around the themes they would use to categorize this data, how and why they would use these themes, and how their own experiences agreed with or refuted the group's findings. Arriving at a group consensus about data analysis was not the goal of this collaborative process. Rather, this process was used as an opportunity to reflect on personal experiences and engage in dialogue that allowed both researcher and participant to 'see' the data in ways that we would not have seen on our own and thus, provide a richer understanding (Krueger and Casey, 2000).

This dialogue allowed us to connect our experiences with that of others, and consider how larger social and institutional structures have shaped those experiences. This process also provided the opportunity to member-check.[12] Engaging in this dialogue allowed us to share lived experiences and theorize possible explanations for the multiple forms of subordination they experienced throughout their educational trajectories. During these meetings, the women also discussed and reflected on the process of *testimonio*, including our data collaboration.

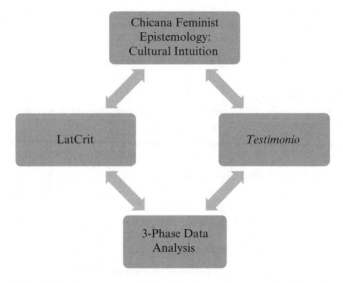

Figure 27.2   Visual representation of testimonio *as methodology in LatCrit research*

Final data analysis
This phase combined the findings of the preliminary and collaborative phases to engage in knowledge production that incorporated participants into the analytic process, and allowed for the development of a collaborative relationship to be built between the participants and myself. To bring the previous stages of data analysis together, I utilized several strategies. Thematic categories were identified and brought to the group through the reflection exercise, where participants were able to reflect, discuss, and engage in dialogue about how we could provide a clearer understanding of the categories that would represent their experiences as told through their *testimonios*. We also discussed how certain indicators of those themes could be used as codes and developed a final coding scheme. At this point in the analysis, I also had an additional source of data, the reflection exercises themselves, used to document their thoughts about a particular category. During this phase, I regularly used concept mapping to explore the relationships between categories, and developed analytic codes that led to identifying larger theoretical connections, advancing the utility of LatCrit to help make sense of these experiences.

Figure 27.2 illustrates the three-phase data analysis process as a critical component of the larger epistemological and methodological design of this study. The figure shows how a Chicana feminist epistemological framework, and in particular cultural intuition, guides a continuous and cyclical process of bridging and building theory (LatCrit), method (*testimonio*), and data analysis. We used our cultural intuition in the process of *testimonio* and developed a methodology that allowed the women to theorize and construct knowledge from their own lived experiences. Thus, I concur with the Latina Feminist Group (2001) who argued that the process of *testimonio* is just as significant as the product of our theorizing.

The process described above has clearly blurred traditional academic research boundaries. It has allowed me to form meaningful relationships with the women in this study and share our most intimate fears and dreams for the future. It also allowed us to openly discuss the reality of being an undocumented and US born Chicana woman navigating through educational institutions that were not created, nor function with us in mind. In this study, *testimonio* was a co-constructed process that emerged as we progressed through the process of *testimoniando*. This is an important point to make, as it is not my intention to speak *for* the women in this study, but to co-construct knowledge about their experiences. In sharing their *testimonios*, the women have demanded the attention of the academy to listen. Cindy Cruz explains, 'What *testimonio* does best is to connect a reader or an audience, positioning a reader or an audience for self-reflection . . . the listener/reader/audience becomes witness' (2006, pp. 31–2). Using *testimonio* in the research process to create new knowledge about experiences that are often untold in the academy connects scholars to the stories of non-dominant communities. This is the power of *testimonio* – to connect human beings in ways that enable us to bear witness to experiences and struggles of those beyond our own realities. Cruz (2006) explains that there is an 'inherent intersubjectivity' in *testimonio*, which positions the listener, reader, and/or audience as witnesses, regardless of the ideologies, beliefs, and perceptions we hold, or positions we come from.

FURTHER CONSIDERATIONS AND CONCLUSIONS

As I conclude this discussion of *testimonio* as methodology, I have several points of further consideration. The first is regarding the issue of authenticity. Earlier in this chapter, I explained how Rigoberta Menchú's *testimonio* is an example of an ongoing debate in academia regarding the authenticity of narratives – whose story is and is not 'authentic.' In fact, Yúdice (1991) uses the concept of authenticity in his definition of *testimonio* described earlier in this chapter. I want to be clear that *testimonio*, as used in this study, does not make a claim for or against authenticity. In fact, I would argue the notion of authenticity is a concept rooted in a

Western perspective where dichotomies dominate logical reasoning and where the question of authenticity directly relates to the contestation of truth. My role is not to determine what is truth in the *testimonios* these women have shared with me, but to understand their realities within a larger context of structural and systematic inequality – within and beyond educational institutions.

The second consideration of *testimonio* as methodology lies in the possible appropriation of *testimonio* by 'non-critical' academics. As Tierney (2000) warns, the use of *testimonio* can become vulnerable to appropriation of anyone telling a story of struggle or conflict, including those in more privileged positions in society. However, we must remember the original purpose of *testimonio* – to center the knowledge and experiences of the oppressed. Thus, when adapted in research and pedagogical practice, it is important to recognize *testimonio* as a tool *for* the oppressed, and not the oppressor. *Testimonio* should not function as a tool for elite academics to 'diversify' their research agendas or document their personal stories.

Testimonio makes important contributions to critical qualitative methodology in general, and to critical race research in education specifically. First, *testimonio* allows for participants to work in collaboration with the researcher, honoring *their* lived experiences and knowledge. As a result, participants play a crucial role in deciding how knowledge about their experiences is produced in the research process. Second, similar to critical race counterstories, *testimonio* recognizes the power in telling one's story that is rooted in traditions of storytelling in Latina/o, African American, and Native American communities (Booker, 2002; Yosso, 2006). Third, locating *testimonio* within a Chicana feminist epistemology provides an explicit method of data analysis, and guides the research strategies used throughout the research process. The similar elements, purposes, and goals of *testimonio* to a LatCrit framework make *testimonio* a powerful tool for critical race research, where the very tenants of LatCrit inform the research process.

Using *testimonio* as methodology located within a Chicana feminist epistemology in LatCrit research deconstructs the Eurocentricity of traditional academic research and disrupts the apartheid of knowledge this Eurocentricity has helped create. Furthermore, this methodological approach acknowledges and draws from foundations of knowledge which exist outside of the academy and within Communities of Color. This allows researchers to engage in a process of knowledge production that draws from the strengths of Communities of Color to provide a rich and multidimensional understanding of the experiences of People of Color.

I have utilized *testimonio* as a methodological process within the context of education, located within a critical race gendered theoretical and epistemological orientation. In this chapter, I shared how I have built on the work of others to develop a methodological process that served the purposes of my research well – to understand, expose, and challenge the many forms of racism Latina/o students encounter in education. My use of *testimonio* as methodology has been specific to Latinas/os in the US. However, I hope that in sharing this methodological approach, other critical qualitative researchers will see the power of *testimonio* as a collective strategy of resistance for People of Color across the globe.

NOTES

1. This chapter is an abbreviated version of the previously published article: Lindsay Pérez Huber 'Disrupting apartheid of knowledge: *testimonio* as methodology in Latina/o critical race research in education' *International Journal of Qualitative Studies in Education*, **22**, 6 (2009), pp. 639–54. Portions are reprinted with the permission of the publisher, Taylor & Francis, Ltd.
2. Elisabeth Burgos (Later Elisabeth Burgos-Debray), a Venezuelan anthropologist, was named author of the original version of this book. However, Burgos was clear that it was dictated by Menchú. The original version as cited here was printed in the Spanish language. Later versions were published in English and titled I, *Rigoberta Menchú: An Indian Woman in Guatemala* (Verso), where Burgos is also named editor and in some versions, Menchú as co-author.
3. I use the term Chicana to describe women of Mexican descent. While other factors may be considered in defining a Chicana identity (that is, commitment to community, opposition to racial and gendered hierarchies), I use a more general definition and asked participants to explain how they define their own identities.
4. Cienfuegos and Monelli are Chilean psychologists who published under these pseudonyms to protect their identities while conducting research on the use of *testimonio* in therapeutic settings to help victims of political repression. Because of the dangerous political situation that took place at the time in their country, they did not use their true names, which are now known as Elizabeth Lira and Eugenia Weinstein (see Booker, 2002).
5. Psychology scholars Angueira (1988), Booker (2002), and Cienfuegos and Monelli (1983) use *testimonio* in a therapeutic environment to treat patients who have experienced traumatic life events such as rape and torture.
6. In this chapter, I use the term 'witness' to describe the person who is providing their *testimonio*.
7. Providing one's *testimonio*, telling of a collective story.
8. For a more detailed description of how I co-theorized with the women to arrive at this understanding of testimonio, see Pérez Huber (2009).
9. See Pérez Huber (2009) for a more thorough explanation of CRT and LatCrit in education.
10. See Delgado Bernal and Villalpando (2001) for their description of the apartheid of knowledge that exists in higher education.
11. Delgado Bernal (2002) describes critical race-gendered epistemologies as systems of knowledge that emerge from the experiences of People of Color at the intersections of racism, sexism, classism, and other forms of oppression.
12. See Maxwell (1996).

REFERENCES

Angueira, K. (1988), 'To make the personal political: the use of testimony as a consciousness-raising tool against sexual aggression in Puerto Rico', *Oral History Review*, **16** (2), 65–93.

Behar, R. (1993), *Translated Woman: Crossing the Border with Esperanza's Story*, Boston, MA: Beacon Press.

Benmayor, R. (1988), 'For every story there is another story which stands before it', *Oral History Review*, **16** (2), 1–13.

Benmayor, R. (2008), 'Digital storytelling as a signature pedagogy for the new humanities', *Arts and Humanities in Higher Education*, **7** (2), 188–204.

Beverley, J. (2004), *Testimonio: On the Politics of Truth*, Minneapolis, MN: University of Minnesota Press.

Booker, M. (2002), 'Stories of violence: use of testimony in a support group for Latin American battered women', in L.H. Collins, M.R. Dunlap and J.C. Chrisler (eds), *Charting a New Course for Feminist Psychology* Westport, CT: Praeger, pp. 307–21.

Brabeck, K. (2001), 'Testimonio: bridging feminist ethics with activist research to create new spaces of collectivity', Paper presented at the Feminisms in Participatory Action Research Conference, Newton, Massachusetts, 22–24 June.

Brabeck, K. (2003), 'Testimonio: a strategy for collective resistance, cultural survival and building solidarity', *Feminism Psychology*, **13** (2), 252–8.

Burciaga, R. (2007), 'Chicana PhD students living nepantla: Educación and aspirations beyond the doctorate' Unpublished Dissertation, University of California, Los Angeles.

Burciaga, R. and Tavares, A. (2006), 'Our pedagogy of sisterhood: a *testimonio*', in D. Delgado Bernal, C.A. Elenes, F. Godinez and S. Villenas (eds), *Chicana/Latina Education in Everyday Life: Feminista Perspectives on Pedagogy and Epistemology*, Albany, NY: State University of New York Press, pp. 133–42.

Burgos, E. (1983), *Me Llamo Rigoberta Menchú y Así Me Nació La Conciencia*, Barcelona: Editorial Argos Vergara.

Burgos-Debray, E. (1984), *I, Rigoberta Menchú: An Indian Woman in Guatemala*, New York: Verso.

Charmaz, K. (2006), *Constructing Grounded Theory: A Practical Guide through Qualitative Analysis*, Thousand Oaks, CA: Sage Publications.

Cienfuegos, A.J. and Monelli, C. (1983), 'The testimony of political repression as a therapeutic instrument', *American Journal of Orthopsychiatry*, **53** (1), 43–51.

Cruz, C. (2006), 'Testimonial narratives of queer street youth: towards an epistemology of a brown body', Unpublished Dissertation, University of California, Los Angeles.

Delgado Bernal, D. (1998), 'Using a Chicana feminist epistemology in educational research', *Harvard Educational Review*, **68** (4), 555–82.

Delgado Bernal, D. (2002), 'Critical race theory, Latino critical theory and critical race-gendered epistemologies: recognizing students of color as holders and creators of knowledge', *Qualitative Inquiry*, **8** (1), 105–26.

Delgado Bernal, D. and Villalpando, O. (2001), 'An apartheid of knowledge in academia: the struggle over the "legitimate" knowledge of faculty of color', *Equity and Excellence in Education*, **35** (2), 169–80.

Delgado Bernal, D., Flores Carmona, J., Alemán, S., Galas, L. and Garza, M. (Latinas Telling Testimonios) (2009), *Unidas We Heal: Testimonios of the Mind/Body/Soul*, Salt Lake City: University of Utah Press.

Diaz Soto, L., Cervantes-Soon, C.G., Villarreal, E. and Campos, E.E. (2009), 'The Xicana sacred space: a communal circle of compromiso for educational researchers', *Harvard Educational Review*, **79** (4), 755–75.

Duncan, G.A. (2006), 'Critical race ethnography in education: narrative, inequality and the problem of epistemology', in C.K. Rousseau and A.D. Dixson (eds), *Critical Race Theory in Education*, New York: Routledge, pp. 191–212.

Espino, M., Muñoz, S.M. and Kiyama, J.M. (2010), 'Transitioning from doctoral study to the academy: theorizing trenzas of identity for Latina sister scholars', *Qualitative Inquiry*, **16**, 804–18.

Flores Carmona, J. (2010), 'Transgenerational educación: Latina mothers' everyday pedagogies of cultural citizenship in Salt Lake City, Utah', Unpublished Dissertation, University of Utah, Salt Lake City.

Glaser, B.G. (1978), *Theoretical Sensitivity: Advances in the Methodology of Grounded Theory*, Mill Valley, CA: The Sociology Press.

Glaser, B.G. and Strauss, A.S. (1967), *Strategies for Qualitative Research*, Hawthorne, NY: Aldine.

González, F.E. (1998), 'The formations of Mexicananess: Trenzas de identidades multiples: growing up Mexicana: braids of multiple identities', *International Journal of Qualitative Studies in Education*, **11**, 81–102.

González, F.E. (2001), 'Haciendo que hacer: cultivating a Mestiza worldview and academic achievement, braiding cultural knowledge into educational research, policy, practice', *International Journal of Qualitative Studies in Education*, **14** (5), 641–56.

González, N. (2006), 'Testimonios of border identities: Una mujer acomedida donde quiera cabe', in D. Delgado Bernal, C.A Elenes, F. Godinez and S. Villenas (eds), *Chicana/Latina Education in Everyday Life: Feminista Perspectives on Pedagogy and Epistemology*, Albany, NY: State University of New York Press, pp. 197–213.

Gutiérrez, K. (2008), 'Developing a sociocritical literacy in the third space', *Reading Research Quarterly*, **43** (2) 148–64.

Haig-Brown, C. (2003), 'Creating spaces: testimonio, impossible knowledge and academe', *International Journal of Qualitative Studies in Education*, **16** (3), 415–33.

Irizarry, Y. (2005), 'The ethics of writing the Carribean: Latina narrative as *testimonio*', *Literature Interpretation Theory*, **16**, 263–84.

Kruger, R.A. and Casey, M.A. (2000), *Focus Groups: A Practical Guide for Applied Research*, 3rd edn, Newberry Park, CA: Sage.

Latina Feminist Group (2001): *Telling to Live: Latina Feminist Testimonios*, Durham, NC: Duke University Press.

Malagón, M., Pérez Huber, L. and Velez, V. (2009), 'Our experiences, our methods: a research note on developing a critical race grounded theory methodology in educational research', *Seattle University Journal for Social Justice*, **8** (1), 253–72.

Maxwell, J.A. (1996), *Quantitative Research Design: An Interactive Approach*, Thousand Oaks, CA: Sage.

Menchú, R. (1984), *I, Rigoberta Menchú: An Indian woman in Guatemala*, ed. E. Burgos-Debray, trans. A. Wright, London: Verso.

Pérez Huber, L. (2008), 'Building critical race methodologies in educational research: a research note on critical race *testimonio*', *Florida International University Law Review*, **4** (1), 159–73.

Pérez Huber, L. (2009), 'Disrupting apartheid of knowledge: *testimonio* as methodology in Latina/o critical race research in education', *International Journal of Qualitative Studies in Education*, **22** (6), 639–54.

Pérez Huber, L. (2010), 'Sueños Indocumentados: using LatCrit to explore the testimonios of undocumented and U.S. born Chicana college students on discourses of racist nativism in education', Unpublished Dissertation, University of California, Los Angeles.

Solorzano, D. (2009), 'Developing critical race methodologies', Presentation in the UCLA Graduate School of Education & Information Studies Research Apprenticeship Course (RAC), Los Angeles, California.

Solorzano, D. and Delgado Bernal, D. (2001), 'Examining transformational resistance through a critical race and LatCrit theory framework: Chicana and Chicano students in an urban context', *Urban Education*, **36** (3), 308–42.

Solorzano, D. and Yosso, T. (2001), 'Critical race and LatCrit theory and method: counter-storytelling Chicana and Chicano graduate school experiences', *International Journal of Qualitative Studies in Education*, **14** (4), 471–95.

Solorzano, D.G. and Yosso, T. (2002), 'A critical race counterstory of race, racism, and affirmative action', *Equity and Excellence in Education*, **35** (2), 155–68.
Stoll, D. (1999), *Rigoberta Menchú and the Story of All Poor Guatemalans*, Boulder, CO: Westview Press.
Strauss, A. and Corbin, J. (1990), *Basics of Qualitiative Research: Grounded Theory Procedures and Techniques*, Newbury Park, CA: Sage.
Tierney, W.G. (2000), 'Beyond translation: truth and Rigoberta Menchú', *International Journal of Qualitative Studies in Education*, **13** (2), 103–13.
Trinidad Galván, R. (2001), 'Portraits of mujeres desjuiciadas: womanist pedagogies of the everyday, the mundane and the ordinary', *International Journal of Qualitative Studies in Education*, **14** (5), 603–21.
Velez, V. and Solorzano, D. (2007), 'A critical race spatial analysis of high schools along the Alameda corridor', Paper presented at the annual meeting of the American Educational Research Association, Chicago, Illinois, April.
Yosso, T.J. (2006), *Critical Race Counterstories Along the Chicana and Chicano Educational Pipeline*, New York: Routledge.
Yúdice, G. (1991), 'Testimonio and postmodernism', *Latin American Perspectives*, **18** (3), 15–30.
Zimmerman, M. (1991), 'Testimonio in Guatemala: Payeras, Rigoberta and beyond', *Latin American Perspective*, **18** (4), 22–47.

28. Using focus groups
Jude Robinson

WHAT ARE FOCUS GROUPS?

Focus groups were first used in the 1920s in market research and subsequently adopted as an academic research method in the 1950s by the sociologist Robert Merton, who developed the 'focussed interview' (Merton et al., 1990). For good potted histories of the rise of the use of focus groups in social science see Morgan (1997), Bloor et al. (2001) and Krueger and Casey (2000). The word 'focus' comes from the direction of the group's discussion to a particular topic or issue (Kitzinger, 1994). However not all group discussions are equal, and there is something 'special' and distinct about focus group discussions (Litoselliti, 2003) compared to group interviews (Currie and Kelly, Chapter 29, this volume). Krueger and Casey (2000, p. 10) have identified five characteristics of focus groups, namely: '(1) the people who (2) possess certain characteristics and (3) provide qualitative data (4) in a focussed discussion (5) to help understand the topic of interest'. There are a number of excellent introductory texts that take researchers through the process of designing and conducting focus groups research step by step, and I will refer to these throughout this chapter as I introduce some key concepts, issues and dilemmas that researchers are likely to encounter before going on to critically assess an example of my own focus group research.

THE INTERACTIVE ELEMENT OF FOCUS GROUPS

In the introduction to the six book series of the Focus Group Kit that he co-edits with Richard Krueger, David Morgan describes focus groups as fundamentally a way of listening to people and learning from them' (Morgan, 1998a). However unlike individual interviews, focus groups are designed to promote and facilitate 'interaction' between participants. One of the best introductions to focus group interaction remains Jenny Kitzinger's article from 1994, where she explains in her discussion of The AIDS Media Research Project that she was not just interested in what people thought, 'but *how* they thought and *why* they thought as they did' (Kitzinger, 1994, p. 104, emphasis in original).

Unlike individual interviews that dislocate the person from their social context, focus group discussions create an important social space for individuals to interact with each other and so generate data and insights that would not otherwise be accessible to the researcher (Kitzinger, 1994; Wilkinson, 1998, 1999; Duggleby, 2005; Morgan, 2010). Wilkinson (1999) argues that as feminist research is all about empowering women, challenging assumptions about the role and position of women within societies, and understanding the person within their social worlds, the group interview is almost uniquely adapted to enabling appropriate data collection (Madriz, 2003; Kamberelis and Dimitriadis, 2005). Jarrett (1993) describes how, by taking an empathetic and reflexive approach, researchers can actively break down any barriers between the researcher and the researched.

Not only is the role of the researcher reduced (Madriz, 2000), but their control over the topic and direction of the discussion, sometimes resulting in what Kitzinger refers to as 'unruly' groups (Fine and Addelson, 1996; Wilkinson, 1998, 1999; Wilkinson and Kitzinger, 2000). This interaction between participants can enable them to challenge each other, effectively revealing more private, 'backstage' behaviours and allowing the discussion to move deeper into a topic area (Hyde et al., 2005; Robinson, 2009). This is not to ignore the problems of focus groups, as the advantages are multiplied, so are the potential disadvantages, such as a loss of control by the researcher and the possibility that the group may collaborate, collude or intimidate other members of the group and/or the researcher, and/or create a silence on a topic (Smithson, 2000).

WHEN TO USE FOCUS GROUPS AND WHY?

Kreuger and Casey (2000) provide a good summary of what focus groups can and can't do, and when and why you may want to use them. Similarly Morgan (1997, 1993, 1998a) considers the differences between the data generated by focus groups as compared to participant observation and individual interviews. There is a common assumption that focus groups are an inappropriate means of talking about sensitive topics, as people will not come forward to participate, and if they do, they will only talk about the topic in a general way which is unlikely to provide a new insight into the topic under research (Farquar and Das, 1999). Yet even a cursory glance at the research literature will tell you that focus groups have been successfully used to discuss sensitive topics, at times with marginalized groups (Morgan and Krueger, 1993; Kitzinger, 1994; Lather and Smithies, 1997; Madriz, 1998; Lehoux et al., 2006; Robinson and Kirkcaldy, 2007a, 2007b).

When I hear focus groups described as 'quick and dirty' I always remind people that unless you have identified an existing group, of an appropriate size, that meets regularly in an appropriate and accessible venue, then getting the right people together at a single time, often for over an hour, can be very time consuming and requires considerable organizational skills (Morgan, 1993; Krueger and Casey, 2000; Barbour, 2007). MacDougall and Fudge (2001) discuss in some detail the issues they believe researchers should consider when planning their recruitment, and following Krueger (1998b) they emphasize the importance of making and maintaining personal contact with gatekeepers and participants to identify and address any issues as early as possible in the process.

ROLE OF THE MODERATOR AND OBSERVER

The moderator, sometimes called the facilitator, is responsible for the smooth running of the group, but more importantly is responsible for enabling the discussion (and interaction) to take place. This is more than simply asking the right questions at the right time and in the right place, but involves engaging with the subject and working with participants to provide a sociable environment within which issues can be discussed (Litoselliti, 2003). This has less to do with the physical environment, as I have conducted some excellent groups in some very spartan settings, but more to do with tone, pace, delivery and the ability to impart to participants just how valuable their contribution is to the research (Kitzinger, 1994; Lehoux, et al., 2006).

Establishing a rapport with participants can be challenging, as there may not have been time to meet with people beforehand and much of the first contact, as with any research project, is concerned with administrative details, such as obtaining informed consent, dealing with travel claims and queries, and the vagaries of particular venues and the people working there (Krueger, 1998c). This is why ground rules and warm-up exercises are a good idea, what Krueger (1998c) calls 'small talk' as however keen you (and some participants) may be to discuss what seems to you to be the heart of the matter, others may not be ready to talk, and their nonparticipation could make all the difference to the success of the group. For a discussion of some group exercises see Kitzinger (1994). As a rule of thumb, the more focus group participants talk, and talk to each other, the better the level of interaction and the closer participants move towards becoming 'co-researchers' (Kitzinger, 1994).

As with all qualitative research, moderating a focus group is more than a data collection exercise, as the moderator must also use their judgement to skip topics, to include new ideas, follow leads, recognize a blind alley, and even close down discussions when appropriate to generate a productive discussion. As issues of judgement are critical, the moderator needs to be immersed in the study, as knowledge of the area, or prior knowledge of the participants and a well-developed schedule is no guarantee of success (Currie and Kelly, Chapter 29, this volume). However Lehoux and colleagues (2006) question the need for moderators to be 'neutral' and cite Crossley's work where she describes acting as a 'stooge' for the group to react to, in order to further understandings as to how health promotion literature is received (Crossley, 2002). The group is therefore more than just a forum for people to air their views, but presents a real chance to enable the discussion of topics, for issues to be reassessed, revalued and revised though the discussion (Lehoux et al., 2006). If the moderator has strong views supported by professional identity and training, it is possible that they may be tempted to steer the issues around accepted orthodoxy. This is not to say that practitioners cannot lead focus group discussions, but their involvement may involve them engaging with additional reflexive practices to make any values and beliefs explicit at an early stage of their research and before they start to collect data using focus groups.

COMPOSITION OF THE FOCUS GROUP

Much attention has been given in the research literature to the ideal composition of a focus group, with good reason (Morgan, 1998b; Bloor et al., 2001). Although the group consists of individuals, the data are produced by the interactive contributions from everyone and this is heavily influenced by the dynamics between participants. It all depends on what you want your groups to do: go into some depth on a particular topic and share views and experiences? In which case, you may try to make the groups homogeneous. Or do you want them to illustrate the wide range of experiences and issues, and any variations and tensions in issues and problems? In which case, you may go for an apparent mix of people, who you believe may hold different, even opposing views. However as Barbour and Kitzinger (1999) point out, the group you get is as much a result of pragmatic considerations as selection and sampling. Generally, you will have to consider age, sex, gender, ethnicity, socio-economic class, education even before you have got on to thinking about the specifics of your research topic.

The ideal number for participants in a focus group is usually around 6–8, with 12 people generally agreed to be the maximum. If four or fewer people attend, I tend to switch roles (and methods) to convert the schedule to a topic guide, and become an interviewer, as group interviews can be conducted successfully with two or more people (Currie and Kelly, Chapter 29, this volume). Although it can be tempting to go for high numbers if people come forward, and I have been asked if I could run a focus group with an entire class of 32 children, I would always caution against it. Not only would it be impossible to let everyone have their say, or to explore any complexity or ambiguity in the responses, and probably difficult to moderate and keep to the schedule and to time, it would no longer be a focus group. So smaller groups of around 6–8 people are far more useful as they provide a more intimate and supportive group and allow more active and meaningful participation and discussion.

ETHICS, GROUND RULES AND GROUP MANAGEMENT

Any group discussion should be mindful of confidentiality and the issue explicitly raised and discussed within groups as an underlying principle for the session. However discussions around confidentiality, tacitly or explicitly, serve as a warning to participants about over-disclosure, as rules about confidentiality are not enforceable in any way. So unless participants are prepared to have what they have said repeated outside the room, then they will need to consider whether this is the appropriate time and place to disclose their views or experiences. As it is impossible to predict what will actually happen once your groups get going, you as moderator will have to rely on your skills and understandings of situated field ethics, which are the judgements researchers make about the conduct of their research throughout the research process.

Following the practice of market research companies and some medical research, particularly research sponsored by pharmaceutical companies, you may decide to pay respondents for taking part in the group. However it is important to make it clear that this, or any claim for expenses, is not performance related, so participants do not feel that they have to respond to all questions or to over disclose to receive the payment, whether cash, vouchers or expenses. A number of the introductory texts have a good discussion of ethics (Litoselliti, 2003), the payment of incentives and ground rules (Bloor et al., 2001), so it is worth spending time and developing any protocols to make sure you consider at least some of the issues that may arise and how to handle them (Morgan, 1998b).

One way to make sure people do not have to disclose personal information during the group discussion is to develop a mini-questionnaire that you can administer at the start of the group to capture anything from demographic information, such as age, sex or someone's first language, to more sensitive data, such as how many units of alcohol they drink, or what drugs they have taken or their specific diagnosis for mental health problems (Krueger, 1998c; Bloor et al., 2001). To reassure participants and encourage them to respond I prefer to keep such documents anonymous, only identifiable by the group number or date, so these questionnaires are kept separately from signed consent sheets. Whether these questionnaires are completed at the beginning or the end of the focus group discussion is up to you and after a brief straw poll of colleagues I believe that essentially this a matter of judgement. Some people feel completing questionnaires before the main discussion fails to set the right tone for the group and can prevent engagement with the issues, and so leave them until the end. People who prefer to leave them until the end also believe that the participants have 'warmed up' and are more likely to engage with some of the questions and answer 'truthfully'. However other researchers who prefer to complete any questionnaires as people are joining the group say that they like to engage participants in a 'task' early on, and as participants will have already filled in consent sheets, the questionnaire follows on nicely. Furthermore, they cite their concerns that if they leave it until the end of the discussion, participants will be mentally exhausted and will not properly engage with the task, and of course leaving them until the end may mean that you miss people who leave early.

TIMING, VENUE AND REFRESHMENTS

As I have mentioned, providing an appropriate venue for discussion can affect the quality of the encounter between the moderator and participants, and therefore the quality of the data you co-produce. As researchers consistently note, there is no point going to all the trouble of recruiting your sample only to have people arriving late to an inaccessible venue, or cramming people into a broom cupboard, or have them whispering self-consciously in a corner of a hall or auditorium (Morgan, 1998b; Bloor et al., 2001; Barbour, 2007). This does not mean an expensive venue, but one that is accessible, with a room with enough comfortable seating, good access to WCs, appropriate lighting (and shading), not too hot or cold, where you can easily serve refreshments when they arrive or after the group has finished. Unlike group interviews, focus group discussions do not necessarily try to recreate the 'natural setting' of the group (Currie and Kelly, Chapter 29, this volume) so unless you are researching an existing group, it is unlikely that any single setting will be previously known to all your participants. Indeed, in focus groups with mothers of young children

I believed that it was necessary to bring the women together outside their homes, and away from the immediate vicinity of their babies and young children, to enable the discussion to take place at all (Robinson and Kirkcaldy, 2007a, 2007b).

However difficult it is to predict how long people want to talk, the discussion should not run over 90 minutes, although I have tried in the past to bring the discussion to a close after this time and people have been unwilling to stop. I have also run successful groups that lasted less than an hour, so researchers should not feel the need to generate long lists of questions to try and fill a predetermined timeframe. Allocate timings to topics and try to stick to them, and have other material to hand, such as other questions, or photos, posters and even video clips, as depending on the group, you may race through the topics and be short of things to say rather than short of time.

DEVELOPING YOUR TOPIC GUIDE

The development of your topic guide will take time and energy and will depend on your overall approach to the research, your personal style, the nature of the topic and the time and composition of your group. A particularly thoughtful guide is provided by Morgan in *Planning Focus Groups* (1998b) and also by Krueger in *Developing Questions for Focus Groups* (1998a). However all the texts cited in this chapter give an overview and deal with some of the complexity of developing questions, so it is worth reading more widely. Yet in my own experience, it is never possible to anticipate exactly how a question or a line of questioning will be received by a group, or more importantly, what new information, concepts and ideas a focus group discussion may generate. So despite the need to present ethical committees or review boards with data collection instruments in advance of the study taking place, I always make it clear that the focus group schedule I present at this early stage is likely to be developed and refined throughout the data collection process.

RECORDING THE DISCUSSION

Most researchers choose to audio-record their discussions (Krueger, 1998c; Hammersley, Chapter 32, this volume) and I also like to include an observer if possible, to make a note of any non-verbal actions and interactions during the session. However the moderator can also make retrospective notes if it is not possible to include an observer. Others have used video equipment to record their sessions, so that they could make some additional observations of interaction and also correctly assign each contribution to a particular participant (Krueger, 1998b). However the introduction of expensive and intrusive equipment into a group discussion is not always possible or desirable, and it is generally accepted within focus group data, it is less important to know just who is speaking, but enough to separate individual contributions so that the collective and interactive nature of the data can be studied (Barbour, 2007). It is also important, as Bloor emphasizes, to ensure that all of the recorded speech is transcribed, including when people interject as they talk over one another (Bloor et al. 2001 and see a more detailed discussion of issues concerned with transcription in Hammersley, Chapter 32, this volume).

ANALYSIS

The analysis of focus group data is usefully described in various texts, and most authors describe a process related to the principles of good thematic analysis (Krueger, 1998b; Barbour, 2007). However there is also the dimension of interaction to be discovered, and in the past researchers have been criticized for abstracting text from a single speaker and presenting it in isolation, in effect replicating how we present data from individual interview studies. While it is permissible to do this in some instances, particularly if the quotation is a lengthy one, the presentation of the findings from the research should involve a detailed consideration of the interaction between all participants, including the moderator, which has produced the data. Hollander (2004) identifies four key social contexts that can facilitate or inhibit the quality of social interaction: the associational; status; conversational; and relational. Hydén and Bülow (2003) track the process of interaction by exploring how participants can establish a 'common communicative ground' and how they can add their 'contribution to the common ground'. Kitzinger (1994) identifies two possible forms of interaction within groups: complementary and argumentative. In complementary interaction the participants appear to have shared ideas about issues, and group members demonstrate this by supporting one another's statements and contribute additional comments that demonstrate their understanding and agreement as to what is being said. In argumentative groups, participants display differences through misunderstandings, hostility, opposition and argument. Different forms of interaction can give valuable and informative data and crucially, give an insight into how people construct their views in relation to others.

In addition to the non-verbal interaction that should be noted from the group discussions there are also the non-spoken yet audible dimensions such as laughter (Wilkinson et al., 2007; Robinson, 2009). The presence of 'jokes' has been noted as being an indicator of the 'naturalness' of the encounter (Kitzinger, 1994), but could equally indicate 'unnaturalness' or discomfort (Billig, 2005). Silences on particular topics and participants can be harder to analyse, but should be noted as part of the analysis. Therefore there is a need to develop an analytical approach that incorporates spoken, other verbal communication, and observations of the non-verbal dimension of data.

MY OWN RESEARCH ON YOUNG PEOPLE'S ACCESS TO CIGARETTES

In 2009, a colleague from the University of Edinburgh, Amanda Amos, and I were commissioned by the Central England Trading Standards Association (CEnTSA) to find out from young people how they were able to access cigarettes after the rise of the age of sale from 16 to 18 in October 2007 (Robinson and Amos, 2010). CEnTSA is a regional arm of the UK government's Trading Standards Institute, set up to ensure compliance with consumer legislation. We had both successfully explored sensitive issues around smoking using focus groups (Amos et al., 2004; Robinson and Kirkcaldy, 2007a, 2007b) and we decided to recruit young people aged 12–15 years to discuss cigarettes and smoking within pre-existing structures, namely members of the same year or class, and people belonging to groups within community centres. From previous research, we were aware that smoking is a gendered issue, and so we decided to hold only single sex groups.

As the local Trading Standards office had a schools liaison officer, who was already working with secondary schools in the area, we asked them to contact 13 secondary schools in disadvantaged areas in Birmingham, and any responses were forwarded to us. Four schools were able to take part within the study timeframe: two girls' schools (four groups), one mixed school (two groups) and one school mainly for boys (four groups). To include young people from outside a school environment, we approached the youth leaders from two community youth clubs (four groups).

As we did not want to identify young people as 'smokers' within a school or a community environment, or to focus on a particular age group, we asked for schools to ask for volunteers who were smokers or had some sustained contact with smoking, such as having smoking friends or living in a home with smoker(s). One week before the research was due to take place at a given site, teachers and youth workers distributed an information sheet to potential participants who were asked to give a further information sheet to their parents/carers giving the contact details for a named member of school staff and the research team for them to talk to in case they had any concerns or questions about the research.

Eighty-five young people were recruited, 47 females and 38 males, from a range of ethnic backgrounds. Twenty-six young people reported that they were current smokers in their written responses to a brief questionnaire completed at the start of the group, but several others later revealed that they smoked, and other 'non-smokers' described smoking occasional cigarettes with friends, suggesting that over half of the participants were currently smoking some cigarettes. Furthermore, other young people discussed how they had tried smoking in the past, and many were friends of current smokers, and so the majority of participants were able to talk first-hand about how to access cigarettes.

The groups involved 2–12 participants, with nine groups having 5–8 participants. A topic guide was developed which covered: a general discussion about the area, their leisure time activities, local cultures around smoking, how under-18s obtained cigarettes, main sources including the black market, impact of the increase in age of sale, issues around preventing underage sales and this topic guide was developed throughout the data collection period. Discussions lasted from 30 to 60 minutes and participants were given a £15 store voucher as a 'thank you' for taking part. These vouchers were given out at the start of the group so young people would not feel that they had to 'over disclose' to get their voucher.

WHAT DID WE FIND?

We found that while young people did use social sources to access cigarettes, most obtained cigarettes from smaller local shops (Robinson and Amos, 2010). Smoking and non-smoking participants knew which shops sold to underage children and what strategies to employ, suggesting a widespread acceptance of underage sales in some communities. Some young people bought directly from retailers, reporting that the retailers did not ask for ID. Other young people waited outside shops and asked strangers to buy them cigarettes (proxy sales). Individual cigarettes were available for purchase in schools and smoking took place on some school grounds. They expressed cynicism about some shopkeepers' motives, who they believed knew that they were selling to under-18s, but did not care as long as they made a profit. We concluded that while past UK studies had found that young people tended to get their cigarettes via family and friends, our findings highlight the importance of proxy sales for some young people.

CRITICAL REVIEW OF OUR APPROACH

Overall, the young people who spoke to us were candid, and we believe that we created an environment where they could talk, establish trust and where we managed conflict and any disagreements, leading to the generation of new knowledge. Using the key contacts we had in the local Trading Standards office to contact schools meant that we rapidly accessed a group of education professionals who were concerned about teenage smoking. As it is impossible to approach young people at school without formally asking the school's permission, we accepted this as a necessary step and the teacher's (the 'gatekeeper's') enthusiasm for the discussions to take place made this a very positive experience for us. However it also meant that we did not contact all schools in the geographical areas we were covering, and so may have missed some key groups and experiences. Our approach, informed by the literature, meant that we approached schools in socially and economically disadvantaged areas, where rates of smoking are known to be high. However we know that young people from different social and economic backgrounds smoke, so again, we limited the possible breadth of the study and so limited our understanding of the issues. As we wanted to talk to young people outside their school environment, we were put in touch with community leaders and those who ran outreach youth groups. Again, a very positive experience for us, but this limited our recruitment to those young people who were more or less engaged with the youth initiatives, knowing that many more were not.

When we were discussing the research, we were concerned that young people would not be willing to talk to us about sources of cigarettes and share their knowledge of smoking. However most of the young people seemed very happy to talk about smoking and sources of cigarettes at great length, and the discussions were punctuated by laughter and were generally lively. However there were some participants who remained very quiet in the discussions and who, despite gentle prompting and the creation of space for them to contribute, preferred not to talk. As this was likely to be due to pre-existing dynamics between participants, we did not press them to talk. Despite the establishment of ground rules, and a clear brief that the discussion was to be general, with no names or places mentioned, most young people gave names, dates, places, relationships, and referred to their own (non-) smoking status. While any such over-disclosures were managed, and did not appear in any reports and so on this could have presented a difficult issue for us as a research team had we been required to pass on any information to the authorities. Other issues included an over-large group of 12 people where, if I am honest, it was more an exercise in crowd control than a meaningful discussion, and despite giving some useful data, was not repeated. Two of the male groups requested that the discussion was not audio-recorded, and so some data may have been lost despite my frantic scribbling of notes after the discussion.

CONCLUDING REMARKS

Focus group data are qualitatively different data than interview data, even from group interview data, as focus group data are co-produced by the dynamic interaction between the researcher (moderator) and the participants, and between the participants themselves, and therefore offer the opportunity for greater breadth. In the studies where I have chosen to use focus groups I believe that some of the issues simply would not have been raised in individual interviews, as the interaction acts as a catalyst on the topic as people contribute in new and unexpected ways (even to themselves).

REFERENCES

Amos, A., Wiltshire, S., Bostock, Y., Haw, S. and McNeill, A. (2004), '"You can't go without a fag . . . you need it for your hash" – a qualitative exploration of smoking, cannabis and young people', *Addiction*, **99** (1), 77–81.

Barbour, R.S. (2007), *Doing Focus Groups*, London: Sage.

Barbour, R.S. and Kitzinger, J. (eds) (1999), *Developing Focus Group Research: Politics, Theory and Practice*, London: Sage.

Billig, M. (2005), *Laughter and Ridicule: Towards a Social Critique of Humour, Theory, Culture & Society*, London: Sage.

Bloor, M., Frankland, J., Thomas, M. and Robson, K. (2001), *Focus Groups in Social Research*, London: Sage.

Crossley, M. (2002), '"Could you please pass one of those health leaflets along?" Exploring health, morality and resistance through focus groups', *Social Science & Medicine*, **55** (8), 1471–83.

Duggleby, W. (2005), 'What about focus group interaction data?', *Qualitative Health Research*, **15** (6), 832–40.

Farquar, C. and Das, R. (1999), 'Are focus groups suitable for "sensitive" topics?', in R. Barbour and J. Kitzinger (eds), *Developing Focus Group Research: Politics, Theory and Practice*, London: Sage, pp. 47–63.

Fine, M. and Addelson, J. (1996), 'Containing questions of gender and power: the discursive limits of "sameness and difference"', in S. Wilkinson (eds), *Feminist Social Psychologies: International Perspectives*, Buckingham: Open University Press, pp. 66–86.

Hollander, J.A. (2004), 'The social contexts of focus groups', *Journal of Contemporary Ethnography*, **33** (5), 602–37.

Hyde, A., Howlett, E., Brady, D. and Drennan, J. (2005), 'The focus group method: insights from focus group interviews on sexual health with adolescents', *Social Science & Medicine*, **61** (12), 2588–99.

Hydén, L.-C. and Bülow, P.H. (2003), 'Who's talking: drawing conclusions from focus groups – some methodological considerations', *International Journal of Social Research Methodology*, **6** (4), 305–21.

Jarrett, R.L. (1993), 'Interviewing with low-income minority populations', in D. Morgan (ed.), *Successful Focus Groups: Advancing the State of the Art*, London: Sage, pp. 184–201.

Kamberelis, G. and Dimitriadis, G. (2005), 'Focus groups: strategic articulations of pedagogy, politics and inquiry' in N. Denzin and Y. Lincoln (eds), *Handbook of Qualitative Inquiry*, 3rd edn, London Sage, pp. 887–913.

Kitzinger, J. (1994), 'The methodology of focus groups – the importance of interaction between research participants', *Sociology of Health & Illness*, **16** (1), 103–21.

Kreuger, R.A. (1998a), *Developing Questions for Focus Groups, Focus Group Kit 3*, London: Sage.

Krueger, R.A. (1998b), *Analyzing and Reporting Focus Group Results, Focus Group Kit 6*, London: Sage.

Krueger, R.A. (1998c), *Moderating Focus Groups, Focus Group Kit 4*, London: Sage.

Krueger, R.A. and Casey, M.A. (2000), *Focus Groups: A Practical Guide for Applied Research*, London: Sage.

Lather, P. and Smithies, C. (1997), *Troubling the Angels: Women Living with HIV/AIDS*, Boulder, CO: Westview Press.

Lehoux, P., Poland, B. and Daudelin, G. (2006), 'Focus group research and "the patient's view"', *Social Science & Medicine*, **63** (8), 2091–104.

Litoselliti, L. (2003), *Using Focus Groups in Research Continuum Research Methods*, London: Continuum.

MacDougall, C. and Fudge, E. (2001), 'Planning and recruiting the sample for focus groups and in-depth interviews, *Qualitative Health Research*, **11** (1), 117–26.

Madriz, El. (1998), 'Using focus groups with lower socioeconomic status Latina women', *Qualitative Inquiry* **4** (1), 114–28.

Madriz, El. (2000), 'Focus groups in feminist research', in N. Denzin and Y. Lincoln (eds), *Handbook of Qualitative Research*, 2nd edn, London: Sage, pp. 835–50.

Madriz, El. (2003), 'Focus groups in feminist research', in N. Denzin and Y. Lincoln (eds), *Collecting and Interpreting Qualitative Materials*, Thousand Oaks, CA: Sage, pp. 363–88.

Merton, R.K., Lowenthal, M.F. and Kendall, P.K. (1990), *The Focussed Interview: A Manual of Problems and Procedures*, New York: The Free Press.

Morgan, D.L. (ed.) (1993), *Successful Focus Groups*, London: Sage.

Morgan, D.L. (1997), *Focus Groups as Qualitative Research, Qualitative Methods Series 16*, London: Sage.

Morgan, D.L. (1998a), *The Focus Group Guidebook, Focus Group Kit 1*, London: Sage.

Morgan, D.L. (1998b), *Planning Focus Groups, the Focus Group Kit 2*, London: Sage.

Morgan, D.L. (2010), 'Reconsidering the role of interaction in analyzing and reporting focus groups', *Qualitative Health Research*, **20** (5), 718–22.

Morgan, D.L. and Krueger, R.A. (1993), 'When to use focus groups and why', in D. Morgan (ed.), *Successful Focus Groups: Advancing the State of the Art*, London: Sage, pp. 3–19.

Robinson, J. (2009), 'Laughter and forgetting: using focus groups to discuss smoking and motherhood in low-income areas in the UK', *International Journal of Qualitative Studies in Education*, **22** (3), 263–78.

Robinson, J. and Amos, A. (2010), 'A qualitative study of young people's sources of cigarettes and attempts to circumvent underage sales laws', *Addiction*, **105** 1835–43.

Robinson, J. and Kirkcaldy, A.J. (2007a), 'Disadvantaged mothers, young children and smoking in the home: mothers' use of space within their homes', *Health & Place*, **13** (4), 894–903.

Robinson, J. and Kirkcaldy, A.J. (2007b), '"You think that I'm smoking and they're not": why mothers still smoke in the home', *Social Science & Medicine*, **65** (4), 641–52.

Smithson, J. (2000), 'Using and analysing focus groups: limitations and possibilities', *International Journal of Social Research Methodology*, **3** (2), 103–19.

Wilkinson, C., Rees, C. and Knight, L. (2007), '"From the heart of my bottom": negotiating humor in focus group discussions', *Qualitative Health Research*, **17** (3), 411–22.

Wilkinson, S. (1998), 'Focus groups in feminist research: power, interaction, and the co-construction of meaning', *Womens Studies International Forum*, **21** (1), 111–25.

Wilkinson, S. (1999), 'Focus groups – a feminist method', *Psychology of Women Quarterly*, **23** (2), 221–44.

Wilkinson, S. and Kitzinger, C. (2000), 'Thinking differently about thinking positive', *Social Science & Medicine*, **50**, 797–811.

29. Group interviews: understanding shared meaning and meaning-making
Dawn H. Currie and Deirdre M. Kelly

Talking with people is probably the most common way that qualitative researchers generate data. As we have seen in previous chapters, this talk can take many different forms. In this chapter we explore group interviews.

Little consensus exists on exactly what constitutes a 'group interview'. This may be surprising in light of their distinguished history. Bogardus is credited with pioneering group interviews to test his social distance scale in 1926. Since then, Thompson and Demerath (1952) used group interviews to identify management issues in the military, and Zuckerman (1972) to interview Nobel Laureates. More recently, Green and Hart (1999) used group interviews in their research on accidents involving children in order to understand how children define 'risk', and Kitzinger (1994) to access the ways people construct social knowledge through peer interaction. Frey and Fontana (1991) suggest that group interviews likely have been used extensively in ethnographic research, but not reported as such. An example might be William Whyte's (1943) classic study, *Street Corner Society*.

Robert Merton (1986) sheds light on the situation, reporting that 'focus interviews with groups' were employed by sociologists throughout the 1940s and 1950s. Due to the cost effectiveness of talking with more than one participant at a time, the technique was popularized by marketing researchers during the 1960s and transformed into 'focus group discussions' (FGDs, see Chapter 28). One result is the continued conflation of group interviews with FGDs. When used by marketers, FGDs solicit 'opinions' from participants with diverse backgrounds. FGDs are held in formal, prearranged settings and follow a flexible, but set agenda of questions focused on a predetermined topic. When used by social scientists, FGDs can involve a less structured process where the interviewer becomes a facilitator or moderator of discussion (O'Leary, 2004, p. 165). Given that qualitative researchers favour the latter approach, it is not surprising that group interviews continue to be mistaken for FGDs (see Brewer and Miller, 2003; Jackson, 2003; Babbie, 2008).

Despite their similarity to FGDs, in this chapter we treat group interviews as a distinct method of data generation (also see Maykut and Morehouse, 1994; Krathwohl, 1998; Denzin and Lincoln, 2005; Wellington and Szcerbinski, 2007). There are considerable differences between FGDs and group interviews in terms of recruiting participants and the amount of flexibility that is desirable. When used to access the co-construction of a 'reality', for example, the participants in group interviews exercise relatively more control than the interviewer over the direction of the talk. Moreover, naturally occurring groups are desired so that interviewing often occurs in a field setting, such as a classroom (Bamberg, 2004) or where skydivers gather (Lyng and Snow, 1986).

Reviewing how group interviews are used in sociology, Denzin and Lincoln (1998) offer a typology, based on purposes for the interview and the role for the interviewer. While such classification schemas are useful for identifying the unique characteristics of group interviews (p. 55), or comparing group interviews to other forms of interviews (see Krathwohl, 1998, p. 378–80), Frey and Fontana (1991) warn that typologies carry the risk of reifying methodological techniques while ignoring how interviewing actually takes place (p. 176). Heeding this warning, below we discuss purposes served by group interviews before considering the logistics of group interviews. Within this context we review the advantages and challenges of this method of data generation (also see Watts and Ebbutt, 1987). We conclude by moving from 'textbook' discussion to an example of how group interviews can be used to explore the co-construction of context-specific meanings.

CHOOSING GROUP INTERVIEWS

Frey and Fontana (1991) identify four distinct purposes for group interviews: exploratory, pre-testing, triangulation and phenomenological research. Group interviews are frequently used in the initial or exploratory stages of a project where the researcher needs to map unfamiliar terrain. The group interview can sensitize the researcher to nuances of the social context, including specificities of a social grouping's language or use of cultural symbols that might otherwise remain unacknowledged. An extension of the exploratory purpose is piloting questionnaire items or using group interviews to generate hypotheses. In the latter case, the interview will be loosely structured, allowing the interviewer to 'float ideas or thoughts . . . to spontaneous groups that form in a natural field setting' (Frey and Fontana, 1991, p. 178). Group interviews thus may be a source of grounded theory.

On the other hand, group interviews can be used to complement other methods of data generation in the same study. For example, they can 'lend methodological rigor to the one-on-one interpretive nature of field interviews and ethnographic reports' (p. 178). Finally, the dynamics of group interviews renders them effective in phenomenological research, to help the researcher gain a 'feel' for participants' experiences or understand how talk works to co-construct a shared reality. Thus group interviews provide an excellent way to establish what Alfred Shutz (1967) calls 'inter-subjectivity'.

Given these diverse purposes, the logistics of group interviews also vary. Because of the importance of group dynamics, both the size and composition of the group have a significant impact on the quality of data generated. In the final analysis, there are no guidelines in terms of size of the group; researchers variously report groups as small as 'more than one' (O'Leary, 2004, p. 165), others with four to 12 participants (Maykut and Morehouse, 1994), while Schafer, McClurg, Morehouse and Maykut (1991) recruited groups of 13 to 23 veterans in their study of service during the first Gulf War ('Operation Desert Storm') (cited in Maykut and Morehouse, 1994, p. 87).

Larger groups may benefit from having two interviewers, in order to avoid researcher fatigue and to better attend to group dynamics, although Watts and Ebbutt (1987, p. 28) warn that this strategy may damage group dynamics. As for all interviewing, thought must be given to background characteristics of the interviewer(s). It would be a mistake, however, to assume that 'insider status' will necessarily improve the quality of the data generated. Regardless of group size or composition, talking with more than one participant requires higher quality recording equipment than individual interviews. Fontana and Frey (2005, p. 704) claim that group interviews also require higher quality training and interviewing skills.

Exactly who should be recruited into the 'group' also depends on the specific purpose of the interview. Here 'group' is an ambiguous term that could refer to a dyad as well as a large assembly of respondents (Frey and Fontana, 1991, p. 176). As argued above, group interviews are favoured when research concerns naturally occurring social groups or 'communities'. As a result, group interviews are likely to recruit participants who are homogeneous on specific characteristics or experiences. In many studies, recruitment is based on friendships or a network of peers, enabling the researcher to assess how people arrive at social knowledge through interaction. In the final analysis, both the size of the group and the composition of participants is a judgement call on the part of the researcher, rather than a methodological prescription.

ADVANTAGES AND CHALLENGES OF GROUP INTERVIEWS

One of the most important advantages of group interviews is their ability to generate rich data through participant interaction. In our research with girls, for example, the flexibility of group interviews led us to issues that we did not anticipate. This is because group dynamics can stimulate participants, increasing their recall of specific events and encouraging elaboration beyond what the interviewer may have intended and what would have emerged in one-on-one interviews. In our research, data were enhanced by interviewing friendship pairs and trios together. Girls often interrupted or freely disagreed with one another, correcting each other's accounts of what 'really' happened. This is not to make claims that we generated 'naturalistic' or more 'valid' data; as for all research, the co-construction of data through interviews is a context-specific activity. Recognition of the constructed nature of the data brings unique challenges for the interviewer and, as we discuss below, for the subsequent analysis of data.

As for all qualitative interviews, in a group setting the interviewer must be flexible and empathic. In addition, they must be an active listener because interviews can take unexpected twists and turns; the skilled interviewer will treat these unexpected moments thoughtfully and tactfully. Fontana and Frey (2005, p. 704) argue that because the interviewer is less able to direct the interview, they must 'simultaneously worry about the script of questions and be sensitive to evolving patterns of group interaction'. An emergent group culture may interfere with individual expression so that a single, outspoken participant can dominate the interview. In this case, some commentators (see Krathwohl, 1998) maintain that it is the interviewer's responsibility to ensure that everyone has an opportunity to respond to the interviewer. On the other hand, group dynamics may themselves constitute research findings. An example would be research exploring how meaning is constructed through peer interaction. Here analysis of interviews must attend to the group dynamics in order to identify the speaker's intended audience – are responses to the interviewer's questions intended for the researcher, or for other participants? In their research with young women, for example, Frith and Kitzinger (1998) concluded that the other women being interviewed, and not the interviewer, were being addressed. For this reason, as acknowledged by Denzin and Lincoln (1998, p. 55), exactly how directive the interviewer needs to be depends upon the purpose of the research. Whatever the case, detailed field notes about group dynamics are mandatory and should be constructed as soon as possible after the interview ends, to be used when considering what actually transpired. Given the importance of group dynamics in data analysis, video-taping group interviews is ideal (but not always practical).

As in the case of FGDs, a further challenge for group interviews concerns the need for anonymity and confidentiality (see Chapter 28). Can the researcher ensure that all members of a group interview will honour the ethical standards held by the researcher? In group interviews, the role of 'trust' is somewhat reversed: while research participants are typically asked to trust that their identity will be protected, for example, in a group situation the interviewer is required to trust that interview participants will hold themselves to the ethical standards asked of them. In this case age plays an important role, as children and young people are less likely to comprehend fully what is at stake. For this reason, the researcher must carefully consider what types of topics are ethical for group settings and who should be targeted for recruitment.

Given their dynamic nature, group interviews present unique challenges when it comes to transcription. When the talk is spontaneous, 'People tend to "talk over" each other, or make asides as others speak; voices are often unattributable, and much of the interpersonal communication is lost in non-verbal interaction' (Watts and Ebbutt, 1987, p. 30; also see Chapter 32). As for most interviews, group interviews need to be audio-recorded or, ideally, video-taped. While it is common practice in recorded group settings (such as FGDs) to ask speakers to identify themselves by name, a productive group interview is one that results in spontaneous and often chaotic dialogue. While offering rich data, transcribing such an interview requires an astute transcriber. This is especially true for groups of three participants or more. While video-taping groups enhances the accuracy of transcription, this strategy is not always feasible; an experienced transcriber is required for such data and careful auditing of transcriptions by the interviewer is a must.

One final challenge, not often discussed in research textbooks, concerns analysis of group interview data. As noted above, research 'findings' are influenced not only by dynamics between the interviewer and research participants, but also by the dynamics among participants and the context of the interview (see Kitzinger, 1994; Green and Hart, 1999). Unlike FGDs, where participants may not know each other (see Krueger, 1994), group interviews are more likely to recruit intimate partners, friends or peers. Especially in the latter case, peer culture is an important context for what is said, as well as what may not be said (also see Krathwohl, 1998, p. 380). For this reason, data analysis concerns the 'process' of meaning-making as well as meaning itself. In this case the 'discourse community' rather than the individual is the unit of analysis.

In summary, interviewing several participants together is not simply a cost-saving measure as some commentators claim; group interviews offer a unique research tool. While used in various ways, they are especially valuable when the researcher is interested in understanding local communities of shared meaning. Given the growing interest, especially among qualitative researchers, in the 'process' rather than 'content' of social knowledge, we expect them to become more important in the future.

As Green and Hart (1999, p. 21) note, most of our knowledge about the efficacy of group interviews comes through personal experience rather than systematic investigation. In the next section we illustrate the potential, as well as the challenges, of group interviews through a discussion of our own research that explores the identity practices of girls at school.

FROM THE FIELD: TALKING WITH GIRLS

Titled 'Girl Power', our research was initiated amidst academic as well as popular debate over the status of contemporary girlhood (see Currie, Kelly and Pomerantz 2009). Because we are interested in girls' agency, we asked how girls themselves, rather than adult observers of girls, actively re/define girlhood. We directed attention to discourses that make possible and sustain their redefinitions.

A total of 71 girls participated in our research. The study employed both individual and group interviews. Some girls were interviewed more than once – alone and with friends. Our interview schedule was semi-structured and included open-ended questions about girls' social life at school. We were interested in 'what it means to be a girl' and how this meaning plays itself out in youth cultures at school. We were particularly sensitive to the ways in which research relations – in this case between an adult and girls aged 12 to 16 – can construct context-specific patterns of talk. Most of the interviews were conducted by a 'youthful' doctoral student, Shauna Pomerantz, hired because of her passion for girl culture and skill as an interviewer.

In the following interview, two enthusiastic 12-year-old friends, GG and Vicki (self-chosen pseudonyms), describe themselves to Shauna:

GG: With the guys, you just have to show that you are tough and not the little sissy that they think you are. A lot of guys, like they think you are like this little innocent girl. They're wrapped around you, like 'I will protect you.' All macho man. . . . But that's not what we're all about. I mean, we can defend ourselves!
Vicki: You have to be like one of those outgoing controlling people who like, knows what to do in every situation.

GG: Or everyone is going to treat you like some sissy who needs to be defended all the time, which is not so true. Girls can defend themselves.

This excerpt caught our attention because the girls draw upon the popular discourse of 'girl power'. This discourse enabled GG and Vikki to construct two mutually exclusive identities for girls: the 'little innocent girl' who needs male protection versus the girl who can 'defend herself' and who can control any situation. At first GG ridicules the innocent girl by describing her as a *little* girl' and by calling her a 'sissy'. GG and Vikki reject this identity category and align themselves instead with 'girls who can defend themselves'. It therefore is interesting to listen to the continuation of this exchange:

Shauna: And we're talking not physical, we're talking –
GG: Oh no. Even verbally or mentally or emotionally. Like we can defend ourselves in all of those categories. We don't need some macho man to stand up for us. I mean, it's so cool when a guy does, but . . . I like it when a guy – I think it's so cool when a guy is like 'Don't mess with my girl' sort of thing. . . . You know that the guy cares for you, obviously. Right? And when he stands up to one of his buddies and says 'Hey. Don't mess with my girl' like that's pretty good. Like he is actually going against one of his really good friends for you and that's gotta mean a lot.

Neither GG nor Vikki saw this subsequent discourse as contradicting their claims to be girls 'in control' who 'can defend themselves'. In order to understand their reasoning, Shauna asked GG whether or not it has ever happened to her, that a guy 'stood up' for her. At this point GG confessed, 'No. Only in the movies'. What are we to make of their talk?

At first glance, it may be tempting to (simply) decide that these young participants are attempting to please Shauna whom they have identified as a 'powerful woman', giving her at first a response that she might expect, before revealing their 'true' feelings. However appealing this common sense explanation, such an interpretation is problematic: it expects to find and looks for an 'authentic' identity for the speaker. It also locates contradiction within the individual speaker. Against this view, contradictory 'reasoning' was not limited to GG and Vikki; we heard it in other interviews. For us, it signalled the way in which girls have available to them various competing discourses about what it means to be a 'girl'. We thus set as our task an understanding of how participants were able to construct and sustain coherent and stable identities throughout and across interviews.

Some commentators, especially poststructuralists, have claimed that contradictory moments in interview data testify to the instability, hence impossibility, of a stable coherent subject (see Scheurich, 1995, for example). While we are sensitive to the ways in which identities are unstable co-constructions, interviews are only possible because those involved are able to negotiate shared meaning. Thus, group interviews were analytically productive because they helped us see how participants co-assemble the discursive elements at their disposal in ways that smooth over contradiction or matter-of-factly dismiss inconsistencies. In the example above, dismissal occurred when GG invoked the discourse of 'romantic love'. The way this discourse wins out is both theoretically and politically important. The spectre of a boy protecting 'his' girl does not simply undermine GG's construction of herself as a girl who can 'defend herself'; it engages GG in a discourse that historically has offered cultural support for male violence. So this mundane example is not innocuous. In GG's talk, the discourse of 'romantic love' helps reconstitute the world of male entitlement to girls'/women's sexuality, an issue that although 'not named' by the girls in our study, gave rise to many of their stories about the 'difficulties' of life at school (for a fuller account, see Currie, et al., 2009). Because the discourse of romantic love trumps a discourse of girl power, we refer to (heterosexual) romance as an example of a 'trump discourse'.

A trump discourse is the discourse that overrides competing discourses that invite contradiction in meaning-making. It is analytically significant because it imparts context-specific coherence to a speaker's statements, no matter how contradictory her statements may seem to the researcher. Because it operates as 'common sense' to the speaker, it is more often than not 'latent' in girls' talk; that is, a trump discourse remains unspoken because it is shared by members of a social group. The social character of group interviews helped to bring trump discourses to our attention; they thus helped us see how power works through (but not as) discourse. In short, group interviews helped us study the discursive agency that brings a particular social reality into existence.

CONCLUSION

Group interviews offer a unique research tool. They have been used in various ways – to familiarize the interviewer to the research context, to pilot ideas or questionnaires, or to sensitize the researcher to the lived experiences of study participants. They can be used alone, or to complement other data generation strategies. Given the flexibility that they allow, group interviews are useful in exploring how social meaning is constructed. When used in this way, analytical attention shifts from what was said (although this of course remains important) to how shared meaning is possible. What we heard in our research were ways the girls co-constructed context-specific meaning, shared by interview partners but not necessarily the interviewer: language-use emerged that would not likely be used in personal interviews designed to solicit 'answers'; group interviews solicit discussion in ways that allow the analyst to study language-in-use. Given the growing interest in 'discourse analysis' among qualitative researchers, group interviews are likely to become more common in the near future.

FURTHER READING

On Group interviews

Denzin, N. and Lincoln, Y.S. (eds) (2005), *The Sage Handbook of Qualitative Research*, Thousand Oaks, CA: Sage.
Frey, J.H. and Fontana, A. (1991), 'The group interview in social research', *Social Science Journal*, **28** (2), 175–88.
Watts, M. and Ebbutt, D. (1987), 'More than the sum of the parts: research methods in group interviewing', *British Educational Research Journal*, **13** (1), 25–34.
Wellington, J. and Szcerbinski, M. (2007), *Research Methods for the Social Sciences*, London: Continuum International Publishing.

Examples of the Use of Group Interviews

Bamberg, M. (2004), '"I know it may sound mean to say this, but we couldn't really care less about her anyway": form and functions of "slut bashing" in male identity constructions in 15-year-olds', *Human Development*, **47**, 331–53.
Currie, D.H., Kelly, D.M. and Pomerantz, S. (2007), 'Listening to girls: discursive positioning and the construction of self', *International Journal of Qualitative Studies in Education*, **20** (4), 377–400.
Frith, H. and Kitzinger, C. (1998) '"Emotion work" as a participant resource: a feminist analysis of young women's talk-in-interaction', *Sociology*, **32** (2), 299–320.
Lyng, S.G. and Snow, D.A. (1986), 'Vocabularies of motive and high-risk behavior: the case of skydiving', *Advances in Group Processes*, **3**, 157–79.
Smart, C. (2007), 'Same sex couples and marriage: negotiating relational landscapes with families and friends', *The Sociological Review*, **55** (4), 671–86.

REFERENCES

Babbie, E. (2008), *The Basics of Social Research*, Belmont CA: Thompson Wadsworth.
Bamberg, M. (2004), '"I know it may sound mean to say this, but we couldn't really care less about her anyway": form and functions of "slut bashing" in male identity constructions in 15-year-olds', *Human Development*, **47**, 331–53.
Bogardus, E.S. (1926), 'The group interview', *Journal of Applied Sociology*, **10**, 372–82.
Brewer, J.D. and Miller, R.L. (2003), *The A-Z of Social Research*, London: Sage.

Currie, D.H., Kelly, D.M. and Pomerantz, S. (2009), *'Girl Power': Girls Reinventing Girlhood*, New York: Peter Lang.

Denzin, N.K. and Lincoln, Y.S. (1998), *Collecting and Interpreting Qualitative Materials*, Thousand Oaks, CA: Sage.

Denzin, N. and Lincoln, Y.S. (eds) (2005), *The Sage Handbook of Qualitative Research*, Thousand Oaks, CA: Sage.

Fontana, A. and Frey, J.H. (2005), 'The interview: from neutral stance to political involvement', in N. Denzin and Y.S. Lincoln (eds), *The Sage Handbook of Qualitative Research*, Thousand Oaks, CA: Sage, pp. 695–722.

Frey, J.H. and Fontana, A. (1991), 'The group interview in social research', *Social Science Journal*, **28** (2), 175–88.

Frith, H. and Kitzinger, C. (1998), '"Emotion work" as a participant resource: a feminist analysis of young women's talk-in-interaction', *Sociology*, **32** (2), 299–320.

Green, J. and Hart, L. (1999), 'The impact of context on data', in R.S. Barbour and J. Kitzinger (eds), *Developing Focus Group Research*, London: Sage, pp. 21–35.

Jackson, W. (2003), *Methods: Doing Social Research*, Toronto: Pearson Education.

Kitzinger, J. (1994), 'The methodology of focus groups: the importance of interaction between research participants', *Sociology of Health & Illness*, **16** (1), 103–21.

Krathwohl, D.R. (1998), *Methods of Educational and Social Science Research: An Integrated Approach*, New York: Longman.

Krueger, R.A. (1994), *Focus Groups: A Practical Guide for Applied Research*, 2nd edn, Thousand Oaks, CA: Sage.

Lyng, S.G. and Snow, D.A. (1986), 'Vocabularies of motive and high-risk behavior: the case of skydiving', *Advances in Group Processes*, **3**, 157–79.

Maykut, P. and Morehouse, R. (1994), *Beginning Qualitative Research: A Philosophical and Practical Guide*, London: The Falmer Press.

Merton, R. (1986), 'The focussed interview and focus groups: continuities and discontinuities', *Public Opinion Quarterly*, **51** (4), 550–66.

O'Leary, Z. (2004), *The Essential Guide to Doing Research*, London: Sage.

Schafer, R., McClurg, K., Morehouse, R.M. and Maykut, P.S. (1991), 'Exploring the experience of coming home from Desert Storm', Unpublished research materials.

Scheurich, J.J. (1995), 'A postmodernist critique of research interviewing', *Qualitative Studies in Education*, **8** (3), 293–52.

Shutz, A. (1967), *The Phenomenology of the Social World*, Evanston, IL: Northwestern University Press.

Thompson, J.D. and Demerath, N.J. (1952), 'Some experiences with the group interview', *Social Forces*, **31** (2), 148–54.

Watts, M. and Ebbutt, D. (1987), 'More than the sum of the parts: research methods in group interviewing', *British Educational Research Journal*, **13** (1), 25–34.

Wellington, J. and Szcerbinski, M. (2007), *Research Methods for the Social Sciences*, London: Continuum International Publishing.

Whyte, W.F. (1943), *Street Corner Society*, Chicago, IL: University of Chicago Press.

Zuckerman, H. (1972), 'Interviewing an ultra-elite', *Public Opinion*, **36** (2), 159–75.

30. Using pictures to analyse and construct knowledge
Paul Reader

A LENS ON VISUAL RESEARCH

Visual research in education poses significant questions about what it means to 'analyse'. When and where should analysis be embedded in or replaced by holistic methods of construction? The underlying premise of this chapter is that there are different forms of knowledge, not all of which are reducible to linear written texts in any economical way. The ubiquity of visual communication in online social networking has challenged education and research institutions, and the acceptance of verbal reasoning as the prime form of academic communication (Krier and Woodman, 2008). Not all cultures know and understand life in so verbal a way as in the academic culture of the last few hundred years, so it is timely to begin a closer look at how pictures can be better used in educational research.

Working with pictures, still images, painting, drawing or image sequences such as video, can result in discovery or construction of different kinds of knowledge, including qualitative research outputs evident in the photo methods discussed by Allen (Chapter 17, this volume) and in the mixed methodology of including participant visual constructions as written text, with interview techniques explored by Thomson and Holland (Chapter 22, this volume). Depending on the research method, working with the pictures will involve juxtapositioning (seeing what occurs when placing images next to each other), building and integrating of visual material, as often as it involves overt analysis as verbal reasoning and decision-making. The visual process is often iterative, and recursive, working through multiple channels of information and multiple knowledges. That people may know something for which there is no verbal expression in the first instance can provide a central motive for using visual methods. Under such circumstances, analytical processes may be embodied deep within the act of picture-making or drawing, where they lay devoid of names or formal description. Over the course of this chapter, I hope to provide some examples of how construction and analysis are related, and to explore related issues involved in researching with pictures.

Preconceptions about what it means to do research impact strongly on analysis in visual arts-based education research. The historical roots of education research practice lay in the social and ultimately natural science research traditions. Artists and educators, who predominantly research through pictures, regularly find a need to unpick assumptions about "scientific" research methods which influence the idea of research in these professions. In contrast, visual research perspectives can be found in various contemporary academic disciplines; in art as research (Sturken and Cartwright, 2001; Sullivan, 2005; MacLeod and Holdridge, 2006), as arts-based research in education (Willis et al., 2000; Knowles, 2008; Hoggan et al., 2009), in arts therapy (McNiff, 1998) and as visual ethnography and anthropology (Prosser, 1998; Banks, 1999; Pink et al., 2004; Pink, 2007). Cross-disciplinary approaches between the social sciences, art education and art have also been advanced from time to time (Lawrence-Lightfoot and Hoffman-Davis, 1997; Reader, 2008). Ironically the use of pictures and visual representation is sometimes more common in the natural sciences than in education and the humanities (Elkins, 2007). In recent years, the development of computer generated imagery (CGI), geographic information systems (GIS) and multi-dimensional computer modelling (3D and C4D) which enable spatial analysis and construction of time-based data sequences have extended picture-making capacity.

In developing research proposals it can be difficult to describe the visual research method in linear terms that can be easily understood by funding agencies, partners and decision-makers, and this in turn may have impacts on how analysis is framed within the research. Educational, political and ethical constraints also constrain visual research design as Allen has identified (Chapter 17, this volume). Elkins (2006) questions the role of intuition in research, but intuition and insight are critical to holistic studies and constructive approaches to knowledge. Reductive research approaches lead to limited concepts of 'analysis' that may be too restrictive when researching with pictures. Making a distinction between reductive, inductive and constructive approaches to research is critical in determining how and when researchers analyse. The problem is not limited to educational and visual research and it is helpful to take James Lovelock's example from the physical sciences and biological sciences:

> Science is broadly divided between rational Cartesian thinking of Earth and life scientists and holistic thinking physiologists, engineers and physicists. The holistic scientists speak in mathematical languages and are all too often incomprehensible to the rationalists. Rational scientists dislike insights; they much prefer step-by-step explanations based on reliable and orderly data. Insight they see as the child of intuition, something irrational drawn from a mess of

apparently conflicting data. Dislike it they may, but large steps in science come as often from insight as from rational analysis and synthesis. (2009, p. 127)

The same distinction between linear reductive processes and the messy business of working with pictures and complex data sets is relevant when framing educational research. It is easy to inadvertently slip between rational and holistic research paradigms when approaching visual data. Working with mess (Law, 2004), and the visual metaphor of the perspective grid (Latour, 1999, 2005) are central to actor network theory, an approach to tracing complex relationships. The role of both analysis and construction may be reformed as a research project evolves. Under such circumstances analysis will begin to act recursively, occurring in a distributed way throughout the research process and not limited to activity which immediately follows data collection. In designing a visual research project the chosen method should release the true power of working visually and avoid using imagery rhetorically to enhance a simple reasoned argument.

HOW DO WE COME TO KNOW?

What it may mean to analyse pictures is conditioned by what we accept as meaningful knowledge and definitions that research is the orderly process of discovering or constructing knowledge. Order can be simple or complex, so complex that we may have difficulty discussing it in any efficient way. Knowledge takes different forms, regardless of any convergence of art and science suggested above. Habermas (2001), citing Cassirer (1954), sees logic and reason completely separated from art and religion. When researchers talk about analysing pictures do they mean they are going to deploy logic and reason to analyse pictures, or are they going to work in a visual form to reveal knowledge directly in a form that may be pictorial? Sometimes they do both by providing visual works and exegesis or arguments. It is the separation of these forms, logic and reason, art and religion, and the tendency to privilege the former (as I am doing here) that can lead to abstract research products being less effective than direct representations of mediated experiences.

Biological references of heart, head and eye are distinctions commonly given to different forms of knowledge, although historically, feelings along with direct visual knowing have been discounted in research, despite their importance in conditioning learning. Instead of producing a concentrated, distilled view from analysis, holistic construction builds or arrives at representations of the "bigger pictures", including experiences of body language and the ineffable. What is less important when abstracting can become very important in 'holising'(if I am permitted to introduce a new term to counter the power of the word 'analyse'). Thomson and Holland (Chapter 22, this volume) recount how participant constructed "memory books" became important to both the researchers' construction of in-depth case studies and the participants' construction of self, providing an example of just how knowledge can be constructed in advance of verbal conceptualization.

THE DIKW HIERARCHY

Pictures are often discussed as being 'data' or 'information' or 'representations', depending on their setting within a research project. Sometimes data and information are terms used interchangeably, however, in information science a precise hierarchy is offered; from data to information, knowledge and wisdom – the DIKW hierarchy. In this view data is the raw material of information; when referring to pictures as data or information it is necessary to consider the context. Image data could just be pixels, or it could be a single image in a video sequence, or it could be a whole sequence among many, depending on the informational context being considered. In a quantitative research survey, data might be answers to yes or no questions. The data elements of an image compose information; a snow leopard eating a sheep. The quantitative research equivalent might be the information that 22 out of 1000 participants returned the answer 'no' to the question. Knowledge is derived as meaning made out of information. We know there is still a snow leopard in the vicinity, and there is one less sheep; we know only a small proportion of people answered 'no' to the survey question. On the basis of this knowledge it would be wise for villagers to guard their sheep. If the survey happened to be of villagers' beliefs about the existence of snow leopards in their vicinity, then it might be wise to engage in an education campaign, perhaps using the image of the snow leopard eating a sheep. Despite its obvious constraints, researchers could find the DIKW hierarchy useful when considering, discussing and evaluating how image data is to be used to construct information and how the research will create knowledge.

In the simplistic reductionist form, researchers or scholars analyse information and in doing so create higher order ideas that become knowledge. The analytical processes are typically located between DI and KW, as DI are analysed to produce KW. A picture is taken as information, or a sequence or mosaic of images are taken as data, to make a composite whole picture, which is further analysed in a rational way to arrive at a written form of knowledge, such as a critique or exegesis of the image. This process sits comfortably within a reductive research genre, but it is not the only way to learn or come to know a wide range of subjects, feelings and experiences through research.

In the holistic genre, messy research, analysis and construction have no fixed site, they can be recursive and multi-linear. The researcher may have a hundred pictures or a video sequence as data from which to extract information, or to build informative scenes and reveal knowledges, including some which are unspeakable, which do not result in reductive analysis, but instead, directly inform changes in education practice.

Research methods in this genre are predicated on human ability to know something in advance of thinking about it, or give expression in words – inaccurately theorized as tacit knowledge (see Reader, 2008). Researchers seeking to develop a visual method are likely to draw upon a visual methodology that will require experimentation or exploration in the use of visual and technical media in advance of or alongside data collection and theoretical development. Painters present good examples of practitioners who work in this way (Reader, 2007). Image capture devices (phone cameras and so on.) are now so common that data and information are often collected before a project proposal is even framed (see White, Chapter 23, this volume for a fuller discussion of technologies). Data capture has become almost second nature to record social events, accidents and as a deterrent to law-breaking. Environmental disasters invite research activity where video data capture appears well in advance of formal research design (McCutcheon, 2009).

Working with large complex data inputs such as video, multiple linear visual sources or other rich imagery encourages the researcher to choose techniques and stances that facilitate sensory random access to data, maximizing the opportunity for insight. The painter's studio, littered with stimulating finds, or the incident rooms of TV crime shows provide useful metaphors. In these work-spaces, working drawings, newspaper clippings, photos, mind maps and other forms of data can be distributed across the floor or pinned to the wall, enabling non-linear access to the data. As a working technique all the data is positioned to trigger intuition and insight, raising questions like 'what is it about this image, face or expression that bugs me?'.

This posting up of images can also be applied to pages of written text. Draft chapters of doctoral dissertations can litter the floor or be adhered to walls all in aid of facilitating random access to all parts of the work in progress simultaneously.

The power of the visual inquiry into feelings and the ineffable underpins art therapy and art practice more generally. Foucault describes an episteme as 'the 'apparatus' which makes possible the separation, not of the true from the false, but of what may from what may not be characterized as scientific' (1980, p. 197). The senses' capacity to break through epistemic constraints on thinking can reveal what is present but unthinkable. Depending on how we analyse pictures we can either reconfirm such constraints or transform the way we think, talk and write. Powerful analytical questions posed by pictures are: what is happening in the picture? What do I feel when I look at a picture, and why is it so? How do, or might, others respond to this image? How am I or others likely to be changed by viewing this image, or the process of having constructed it?

ANALYSING OR HOLISING?

The desire to see 'whole pictures' of education contexts, of student actions and learning in progress, or recognition for the social determinants of learning, all lend themselves as subjects for investigation through pictures. To illustrate how analysis and construction are related in holistic research, examples of animated film production, including one conveniently described by Pixar Animation studios (2010, online), can prove illustrative. While arguably not pure research, the methods and processes do expose the complexity of working in visual construction on large projects, in ways which share a commonality with visual research projects, where the features may be less obvious. Pixar's method does not lead to an abstraction, but to the building of a complete picture that begins with a few ideas as 'a pitch'. The research question or aim is to create a popular film rich in emotion, the reverse of analytical research. They start with a loose abstract idea and end up with the holistic experience of cinema. An 'idea' proceeds through the various stages and channels, building as it goes. The inputs are non-linear, 'many treatments of the same idea will be developed in order to find the right balance between solid ideas and open possibilities, which will be filled in later by development and storyboard artists'. Storyboard drawing is the part of the development stage informed by scripts and 'beat outlines', 'map[s] of the characters' emotional changes that need to be seen through actions'. Storyboards become sequences that are pitched back to the director. Pixar's web pages continue to describe the various channels and departments that are working in iterative cycles, discursively informing each other as the project advances on its time line. Informational drawing and sculpture proceed into 3D computer modelling, where 'They are given "avars," or hinges, which the animator will use to make the object or character move.' Eventually the channels converge under the director's supervision, when the shots are laid out before the virtual camera. Again at this stage, 'multiple versions of the shots are created to provide the editorial department with choices for cutting the scene for maximum storytelling effect'. Shots are then animated. Pixar describes its animators as 'like actors or puppeteers' manipulating the animation software. 'The computer then creates the "in-between" frames, which the animator can then adjust as necessary.' Finally all the channels of 'information' are rendered into a consolidated product where any additional sound effects and editorial alterations can still be made before the final production.

The multiple channels of decision-making, refinements and multiple generations of possibilities are common to the visual creative culture. As a research activity, researchers find their way, constructing, bringing together approved stages and representations. Analysis and decision-making form small periodic episodes, distributed throughout the channels and stages of development. At particular points, such as the articulation of avars, human emotions may be seen for the first time on an anthropomorphized animal or machine which acts as the vector of emotional content.

In Bagdasarian Productions live action/CGI film *Squeakuel* (2009) the viewer is presented with a range of emotions displayed through anthropomorphized male and female chipmunks. The emotions do not need to be named, we (humans) can recognize human body language even when transferred to animated chipmunks. Body language is not axiomatic, it is open to interpretation and refinement by nuance. Analysis does not help us. Are we witnessing love? Flirtatious behaviour ? Mixed feelings? Teenage bewilderment? As a viewer, I tend to accept the range of possibilities that may become clearer through later reflection or reviewing. Similar "range" possibilities can confront the researcher viewing visual information in the search for knowledge. Each stage of the research opens up more possibilities than it closes off, until decisions are made to deliberately close off avenues or versions of a theme.

In CGI and modelling system software some layers of analysis are entirely automated, provided as part of the software tools. The same is true for drawing and painting; people, including children, construct knowledge without verbal reasoning (Brooks, 2002; Adams, 2004, 2009). By juxtaposition, trial and error, and a good deal of prior learning the animation companies give their projects and characters action and substance to convey a holistic understanding. Pixar's claims demonstrate their business is to develop and sell emotion, it is a key ingredient of their products. In doing so they research and explore the same cultural norms so often the interest of education research.

Pixar's movie-making is orderly but complex, its methods bring representations together, by comparing and contrasting possibilities, juxtaposing views, all edited and amended in a multi-linear and a frequently recursive, growing construction, with relatively free progression between building, analysis and back to building.

Many educational research questions lend themselves to this kind of inquisitorial construction (see Thomson and Holland, Chapter 22, this volume). If we want to learn how to live a more exciting life while consuming less energy, then the research has to discover a route to this new life, much as the film production company has to find its way to the next compelling movie. I am not suggesting that life is like a movie, although there are arguments that we are in an age where life is interpreted that way (Krug, 2005). I am stressing that many of the problems researched with pictures are not problems reducible by simple reasoning, but are problems of integrating aesthetic, spiritual dimensions of life which can sometimes be understood through mediated construction (Reader, 2011).

OTHER DIMENSIONS OF WORKING WITH VISUAL DATA

Questions also arise as to what is not included in a picture, and the significance and meaning of "negative spaces" within a picture. Omissions may be incidental or deliberate, created on the part of an author or participant, or by the researcher advancing the picture to a final representation. False data can be created. Images of politicians kissing babies could be false if it is implied that the politician is emotionally warm and sensitive when on most days they are not. The same data could be true when being used to create a representation of how politicians act during election campaigns. Banks (1999) draws attention to the ambiguity of truth in early ethnographic film of reconstruction tribal ceremony. The tendency to misrepresent or overstate by editing is compelling. One of the most celebrated misuses of visual material by a government was when the Australian government in 2001 released images of asylum seekers allegedly throwing their children overboard from a boat attempting to enter Australian waters. Later the Australian Senate (2002) discovered no children were thrown overboard. Photographs released to the media of children thrown overboard on 7 October were actually pictures taken the following day, while the boat was sinking.

Education researchers need to be alert to the reliability of data sources and any claims made about images. It may be that the researcher has to critique the circumstances under which the images are presented, and this may draw the researcher deeper into the epistemic underpinning of the whole research enterprise.

Negative space may be important in other ways than simply omission;

sometimes it is a condition of the recorded data itself. What is missing in an image can be as important as what is contained. The absence of the suspect on CCTV footage at the scene of the crime may really mean they were somewhere else. In the case of the maritime incident above, the uncropped image later revealed another vessel and it was this extended data that positively confirmed the date of the image as false.

PAINTING, MANIPULATING OR WRITING?

Advising on doctoral studies, Kambler and Thomson say: 'We write to work out what we think. It's not that we do the research and then know. It's that we write our way to understanding through analysis' (2006, p. 4). This kind of writing has a parallel when working with visual data and information to produce knowledge and insight. Painting or manipulating images are analogous to writing as researching (Reader, 2007). It is possible to paint or draw ourselves into new space, new identity or new form of understanding. We can juxtapose images or video sequences, and in manipulating these juxtapositions, repositioning, we can also come to new understandings. Kambler and Thomson go on to say that; 'Writing is physical, emotional and aesthetic labour' (2006, p. 4). The same is true for working with pictures, although these aspects are often as much the content of the research as the process of production.

It is important to remain mindful that analytical processes can occur in episodes throughout research projects, and while some research conventions designate analytical stages, when it comes to working with images, analysis can be intuitive, automated and so often inscribed in larger integrating and constructing processes which together create new knowledge and understanding.

Postscript: It seems paradoxical to write a chapter on the power of images and analysing pictures without modelling a single process. Some of the authors cited above explore particular methods in detail, other links to web-media are included in the references. These point to more appropriate places to experience visual research in full.

REFERENCES

Adams, E. (2004), *Power Drawing Notebooks,* London: Central Books.
Adams, E. (2009), *Power Drawing Active Learning,* London: Central Books.
Australian Senate (2002), 'The report of children overboard: dissemination and early doubts',

A Certain Maritime: Incident, Chapter 4, 23 October, Commonwealth of Australia, Canberra, available at http://www.aph.gov.au/Senate/committee/maritime_incident_ctto/ report/ (accessed 9 December 2010)

Banks, M. (1999), *Rethinking Visual Anthropology*, New Haven, CT: Yale University Press.

Brooks, M. (2002), 'Drawing to learn', PhD Thesis, University of Alberta, Canada, available at http://www.une.edu.au/Drawing/main.html (accessed 30 April 2005).

Cassirer, E. (1954), 'Die Begriffsform in mythischen Denken', in *Wesen and Wirkung des Symbolbegriffs*, WBG, Darmstadt, p. 7.

Elkins, J. (2006), 'Afterword: on beyond research and new knowledge', in K. Macleod and L. Holdridge (eds), *Thinking through Art: Reflections on Art as Research*, Abingdon: Routledge, pp. 241–47.

Elkins, J. (2007), *Visual Practices Across the University*, München: Wilhelm Fink Verlag.

Foucault, M. (1980), *Power/Knowledge,* Brighton: The Harvester Press.

Habermas, J. (2001), *The Liberating Power of Symbols*, Cambridge: Polity Press.

Hoggan, C., Simpson, S. and Stuckey, H. (eds) (2009), *Creative Expression in Transformative Learning: Tools and Techniques for Educators of Adults*, Malabar, FL: Kreiger Publishing.

Kambler, B. and Thomson, P. (2006), *Helping Doctoral Students Write, Pedagogies for Supervision*, New York and London: Routledge.

Knowles, G. (2008), *Handbook of the Arts in Qualitative Research*, Thousand Oaks, CA. Sage.

Krier, D. and Woodman, W. (2008), 'An unblinking eye: steps for replacing traditional with visual scholarship', in *Proceedings of World Conference on Educational Multimedia, Hypermedia and Telecommunications*, Chesapeake, VA: AACE, pp. 3965–70.

Krug, G. (2005), *Communication, Technology and Cultural Change*, Thousand Oaks, CA: Sage.

Latour, B. (1999), *Pandora's Hope: Essays on the Reality of Science Studies*, Cambridge, MA: Harvard University Press.

Latour, B. (2005), *Reassembling the Social: An Introduction to Actor-Network Theory*, Oxford: Oxford University Press.

Law, J. (2004), *After Method: Mess in Social Science Research*, Abingdon: Routledge.

Lawrence-Lightfoot, S. and Hoffman-Davis, J. (1997), *The Art and Science of Portraiture*, San Francisco, CA: Jossey-Bass.

Lovelock, J. (2009), *The Vanishing Face of Gaia: The Final Warning*, Camberwell, Victoria, Australia: Penguin Books.

MacLeod, K. and Holdridge, L. (eds) (2006), *Thinking Through Art Reflections on Art as Research* (Innovations in Art and Design), London and New York: Routledge.

McCutcheon, P. (2009), 'Oil spill damage could last for years', 7.30 Report, Australian Broadcasting Corporation, available at http://www.abc.net.au/7.30/content/2009/ s2517725.htm (accessed 16 March 2009).

McNiff, S. (1998), *Arts-based Research,* London and Philadelphia, PA: Jessica Kingsley Publishers.

Pink, S. (2007), *Doing Visual Ethnography: Images, Media and Representation in Research*, London: Sage.

Pink, S., Kürti, L. and Afonso, A.I. (eds) (2004), *Working Images, Visual Research and Representation in Ethnography*, London and New York: Routledge.

Pixar Animation Studios (2010), 'How we do it', http://www.pixar.com/howwedoit/index. html (accessed 10 December 2010).

Prosser, J. (ed.) (1998), *Image-based Research: A Sourcebook for Qualitative Researchers*, London: Falmer Press.

Reader, P. (2007), 'Painterly methodology: painting and digital inquiry in adult learning', Doctoral Thesis, University of New England, excerpts available at http://www.artlearn. net/origin/current.html (accessed 20 February 2011).

Reader, P. (2008), 'A painterly methodology for learning and research,' *International Journal of Qualitative Studies in Education*, 21 (3), 297–311.

Reader, P. (2011), 'Could ecological self-portraiture be useful in reframing learning priorities for a post-carbon world?', Ecological and Community Justice, 2011 Conference of the American Educational Research Association, New Orleans, 8–12 April.

Sturken, M. and Cartwright, L. (2001), *Practices of Looking: An Introduction to Visual Culture*, Oxford and New York: Oxford University Press.

Sullivan, G. (2005), *Art Practice as Research: Inquiry in the Visual Arts*, Thousand Oaks, CA, London and New Delhi: Sage.

Willis, P., Smith, R. and Collins, E. (eds) (2000), *Being, Seeking, Telling: Expressive Approaches to Qualitative Adult Education Research*, Flaxton, Queensland: Post Pressed.

31. The role of documents in social research
Lindsay Prior

In her history of research methods in America, Platt (1996) outlined the different ways in which the conduct of social research was heavily dependent on the collection and analysis of documentary data during the first half of the twentieth century. And as a measure of their importance she pointed out how the role of documents and records in empirical inquiry was appraised and assessed on a number of occasions under the auspices of the (US) Social Science Research Council. The authors of those appraisals – Allport (1942), Blumer (1939) and Gottschalk et al. (1945) – are probably unfamiliar to modern readers, yet in their day they exerted considerable influence on the development of various fields of social science; ranging from anthropology and criminology to politics, sociology and social psychology. The materials that they reviewed covered such items as family letters written by members of Chicago's Polish community during the 1910s, the personal diaries of immigrants and criminals, life histories of delinquent boys and jack-rollers, Navaho Indians and Chicago gang members – Angrosino (1989) and Plummer (2001) have provided excellent and more recent assessments of the work involved in many of the relevant studies. In addition, of course, mid-century social scientists were also aware of the importance to the design and support of empirical social research projects of various public and administrative documents such as the census, as well as court, crime, educational, financial, newspaper, and other kinds of record. Indeed, it was often the role of the public and administrative record in social research that was underlined and highlighted in the textbooks of the age.

Unfortunately and despite the diversity of sources that were available as data, the general approach to the study of documents and records was rather uniform; namely a focus on content. Indeed, the primary method of document analysis that was recommended from the 1940s onward was content analysis – see, for example, Berelson (1952), Festinger and Katz (1953) and Goode and Hatt (1952) – and as I shall indicate below, the marked preference for analysis of content persists today. Nevertheless, it was and is quite clear that the 'diary', the 'letter', the 'life-history' as well as many other types of document – such as the field-note, the research memo and the questionnaire – not only have content, but also fulfil certain kinds of function (Chapter 22). Indeed, it is evident that documents 'do' things as well as contain things. Despite this, studies that emphasize the dynamic role of documentation in social affairs are rare, and it comes as little surprise to note that the use of documents in social research is most commonly associated with 'unobtrusive' methods (Lee, 2000). This dominance of content over function has important implications for questions of research design in general, and for matters of data collection and data analysis in particular. In the following sections it is my intention to pinpoint some of those implications.

FOUR APPROACHES TO THE STUDY OF DOCUMENTS AND RECORDS

One of the problems that arise from an undue focus on what is 'in' documents is that it encourages us to think of writing and documentation as peripheral to action and interaction – a secondary feature, if you like, of the 'real' action that is to be found in the talk and behaviour of human beings. It is certainly a view that is widespread in contemporary textbook and *vade-mecum* discussions of documents in social research, and commonly associated with the idea that documents and humans, text and action, exist in entirely separate realms. Thus Bryman, for example, in his chapter on documents in his *Social Research Methods* (2008, p. 515) states, 'the objects that are the focus of this chapter are simply "out there" waiting to be assembled and analysed': that is, they are non-reactive. And across the decades and across all levels of research expertise one can see these claims echoed repeatedly – see, for example, Blaxter et al. (2006, p. 168), Festinger and Katz (1953, p. 300), Hodder (2000, p. 703), May (1997, pp. 157–8) and Scott (1990). They are, of course, claims that need to be challenged, and I have previously proposed (Prior, 2008) that in contemporary social research we can see at least four very distinct ways of approaching the study of documents and documentation. I classified the approaches as follows (Table 31.1).

In the sections that follow I will expand upon how the classification in Table 31.1 relates to the use of documents in social and educational research by making reference to a range of published studies. What is being offered here, however, is not intended to serve as a definitive overview of all relevant studies but as a set of pointers to work that can be associated with each of the relevant approaches. Indeed, my aim is not to map the entire field but, in the words of Wittgenstein (2009, p. 154), to show the reader 'how to go on'.

Table 31.1   Four approaches to the study of documents

Focus of Research Approach	Document as Resource	Document as Topic
Content	1. Approaches that focus almost entirely on what is 'in' the document.	2. 'Archaeological' approaches that focus on how document content comes into being.
Use & Function	3. Approaches that focus on how documents are used as a resource by human actors for purposeful ends.	4. Approaches that focus on how documents function in, and impact on schemes of social interaction, and social organization.

Source: Prior (2008).

THE STUDY OF DOCUMENT CONTENT

Work associated with box 1 in Table 31.1 reflects a vision of documentary data as 'informant', that is, as a somewhat inert and more pliable version of the sociologists' interviewee. This is, for example, exactly the position adopted towards documents by Glaser and Strauss (1967, p. 163) in their *Discovery of Grounded Theory*. Other writers associated with this tradition are Platt (1981) and Scott (1990).

The views of such authors were no doubt influenced by the fact that during most of the twentieth century documents (especially 'documents of life') were collected and analysed precisely for their content – as stories, diaries and so forth. One type of document that was much favoured was the personal letter, and the collection and analysis of such letters came to influence a wide field of studies – particularly studies on immigration to the USA, the most famous of which is that of Thomas and Znaniecki (1958). Gerber (1997) provides an excellent overview of the importance of the personal letter to twentieth-century American scholarship in a variety of fields, and Middleton also draws on personal letters as a source of data in Chapter 21 of this volume.

Naturally, the handwritten letter is only one of many kinds of 'documents of life' that can figure as a data source. The 'confession' and the 'true story' (Simonds, 1988), as well as the personal diary, stand as alternative genres. Plummer (2001) regards the diary as the document of life par excellence. In a contemporary context Alaszewski (2006) also indicates the contribution that can be made to research by the use of the unsolicited or 'naturally occurring' diary. Thomson and Holland (Chapter 22, this volume) make reference to the use of memory books in this kind of research. One might of course consider ID papers, birth certificates and the like as the most fundamental examples of documents of life – see Rule et al. (1983). Yet, despite the growing significance of identification and its counterpart 'identity theft' across the globe there are surprisingly few academic papers on the role of documentation in underpinning and establishing 'identity' as a social phenomenon – a relatively rare example is provided by Navaro-Yashin (2007) though her focus is more on identity than on documentation.

In the frame of looking at what is in documents and records, other potentially useful studies include discussion of the business Memo (Yates, 1989) as a data source; news media (Kollmeyer, 2004; Pollack and Kubrin, 2007); and graffiti (Klofas and Cutshall, 1985; Carrington, 2009). In the twenty-first century of course one has to put electronic text in to the frame. Indeed, in a paper published in 2001 Geisler et al. referred to the new genres of writing as 'IText', and the authors indicated how rhetorical theory, activity theory, genre theory and associated approaches can be brought to bear on the study of the ways in which electronic text is called upon and used in the modern world. However, that degree of theoretical complexity encourages one to move into discourse analysis rather than content analysis (Krippendorf, 2004) and thereby to a view of documentation as something more than inert matter.

THE ARCHAEOLOGY OF DOCUMENTATION

In a paper published in 1974, Dorothy Smith (see Middleton, Chapter 21, this volume) spoke of 'documentary reality'. By using that term she sought to draw attention to the way in which much of our knowledge about the physical, ideational, social and economic features of the world is mediated via reports in documents (statistical tables, graphs and images, written descriptions and so forth). The 'facts' contained in this reality, she observed, are necessarily social productions, yet the manner of their production is more often than not hidden from everyday view behind complex organizational processes that operationalize both a system of categorization and particular technical procedures by means of which the things that are categorized are grouped and counted. And it is these behind-the-scenes processes of fact production that Smith suggests we ought to focus upon.

Smith's claims belong to a distinct phase in sociological thinking – a phase that was heavily influenced by the work of the ethnomethodologists during the 1960s and 1970s. Some early interests of the latter are well represented in a paper by Kitsuse and Cicourel (1963) on the production of official statistics. It's a paper that holds important lessons for social researchers even today, and especially for anyone interested in how facts about crime, the economy, health or education are actually produced. In terms of the production of crime statistics, of course, there are numerous examples as to how the approach can be used and what can be gained from studying documents in this way. Thus Meehan (2000), for example, demonstrates the key issues in relation to the production of gang statistics in 'Bigcity' and 'Plantville', and he reports on what he calls the 'organizational career' of a gang statistic – ranging from the deployment of a 'gang' categorization in a 911 call to the police from the public, to the recording of a 'gang' incident in a police log. His general claim (2000, 364) that 'social science research must focus on those interactional and record-keeping processes that constitute the careers of organizational statistics rather than treat statistics as standing in a correspondence relationship to the incidents they purport to represent' can be very easily extended to the study of procedures involving the production of educational, financial, health or any other form of descriptive statistics. Indeed, I have previously used the approach myself (Prior, 1985) to study how cause-of-death and social class data held by the office of the Registrars General get woven into global reports on mortality from accidents, heart disease, cancers and the like. And it is a style of investigation that can prove to be just as fruitful in the study of qualitative as well as of quantitative reports. Thus, Margolin (1992), for example, looked at ways in which social work records have been deployed to 'prove' that someone was guilty of child sexual abuse, and how labelling of people as 'abusers' can be usefully viewed as a bureaucratic accomplishment every bit as much as a reflection of complex interpersonal interactions in the 'real world'. Whilst Langer et al. (2008) provide an excellent example as to how this kind of approach can be applied to coroners' records.

Collating reports naturally depends on acts of classification and categorization and in that context it can be often be useful to ask questions about how we put things in order (see Bowker and Star, 1999) and to look at schemes of taxonomy per se. This is a tradition spurred on by the work of Michel Foucault (1970) who was very much concerned with the 'order of things' – the underlying structure of knowledge systems in terms of which phenomena are set and sorted. One might also say that he was concerned with the 'archaeology of documentation'; the act of digging into the classificatory foundations that underpin our knowledge of the world. In this mould some of the most interesting studies have been undertaken on the nosologies by means of which we come to understand the distribution of disease, disability and death in contemporary society. Thus detailed studies of the *Diagnostic and Statistical Manual of Mental Disorders* (or DSM) by the likes of McCarthy and Gerring (1994), for example, or that of Bowker (1998) on the International Classification of Diseases (ICD) serve to illustrate how our images and representations of pathology depend more on the ideologies and interests of specific professional groupings than on the existence and delineation of 'natural kinds'.

On another level, the concept of representation is itself worthy of consideration. For example, Michael Roth and others have argued that there is much more to be gained from thinking in terms of the Latourian concept of 'inscription' than the Moscovician notion of representation. Thus in a paper on representing as social practice Roth and McGinn (1998) explored the role of graphical inscription in educational practice and demonstrated how craftwork connected to inscription in the classroom is used to render previously invisible facts about the physical composition of the world, visible – to produce the physical world as it were. In so doing they emphasized that it is not so much a question of mental images (representations) being at the heart of the image generating process – but of social practices of classroom production. In this vein, it is clear that some of the most striking examples as to how the world is and can be made through inscription (rather than merely 'represented') are those that focus on cartographic practice, and there are numerous fascinating studies on the latter of which Brian Harley's (1992) exploration of the construction of (European) maps of the Columbian encounter is just one.

DOCUMENTS IN USE

In his *Philosophical Investigations*, Wittgenstein placed considerable emphasis on how people used things – especially words. Indeed, at one point he suggested that the meaning of a word is its use in the language (2009, p. 43). Of more relevance is the fact that his strategy towards words can be very easily extended to a consideration of text, and in that light it is clear that it can often be far more profitable to explore how people use text (and documentation) in episodes of interaction than to ask questions about the content or meaning of the text. For anyone who doubts this proposition we need move no further than studies of divination and in particular studies of text-based (or book-based) divination.

Turner's (1975) study of basket divination among the Ndembu provides a first class example of the relevant processes, wherein he indicates how divination enables diviners to 'read' into the same objects a multitude of meanings. Victor Turner's divination was not of course text-based (for examples of the latter see Zeitlyn, 2001), but what his work does is to emphasize that issues of 'meaning' and 'interpretation' have little to do with either the objects in question or the internal cognitive capacities of the readers. Indeed, the objects that are interpreted in divination rituals have a meaning only in terms of the situated and contingent practices of the ritual. This notion of 'reading' as social rather than as cognitive practice has also been taken up by Roth et al. (2002) in their study of the ways in which graphs and graphical data are used and interpreted in educational settings and in which they conjecture that graphs are components of (scientific) language games. The latter, of course, is also a term used by Wittgenstein and it is suggestive of the idea that our focus ought to be on the social practices that are associated with the ways things are used to organize everyday life rather than with the subjective meaning of text and other forms of inscription.

The study of ways in which documents are used does not of course have to be restricted to reading. Indeed there are numerous examples of the use of documents *in situ* (what we might call ethnographies of documentation). The latter range from studies of documentation in laboratories (Lynch, 2002), to studies in clinics (Berg, 1997; Prior et al., 2002), classrooms (Schryer, 1993), courtrooms (Ulmer and Kramer, 1998) and engineering workshops (Henderson, 1995). Middleton's chapter in this volume also touches on some of these issues (Chapter 21). All of these studies demonstrate that human actors call upon and use documents and records in ways that are often far removed from issues relating to document content. For example, one of the key messages that is to be drawn from such studies is that inscription devices often function as conscription devices in organizational settings. That is to say, it is often the 'reading' of print-outs, visual images, graphs and drawings that constitute an occasion for members of workgroups to assemble as a unit and it is often the circulation of such documents in the workplace that serve to 'glue' spatially separated members of an organization together.

It is in such ways that we can begin to frame and explore the study of documents and records in organizational affairs, and my use of the term 'ethnography' is chosen to suggest a range of appropriate methods for collecting and for analysing the relevant data (further examples are given in Prior, 2004). However, there are many occasions when people not only use documents but are, in turn, driven by them: rather like the broom and the apprentice of Goethe's (or if you prefer, Walt Disney's) *Sorcerer's Apprentice*. How that might be done is the focus for the next section.

DOCUMENTS AS ACTORS

The notion of documents and records as actors may seem absurd to many. Yet it is an idea that can be approached from a variety of very sensible directions. Cooren (2004), for example, draws on ideas of John Searle (1979) concerning 'speech acts' to argue that there are various ways in which documents can be said to 'do' things – and to do things in a way that directly structures human action. Thus, suggests Cooren, texts can function as 'assertives' – that is, they can certify, prophesy, attest, remind, proclaim, denounce and refute. They can also function as 'commissives' in so far as they can promise, guarantee, vouch, assure and threaten. They can function as 'directives' in so far as they advise, incite, notify and summon; and as 'declarations' in so far as they declare, dismiss, ratify, bless, condemn, reprieve and endorse.

Others (Bazerman, 1997; Winsor, 1997) draw on what is sometimes referred to as Vygotskyan activity theory to suggest ways in which documents can act back upon rather than be merely acted upon by humans. Thus Bazerman (1997), for example, cites the deployment of a pilot's check-list to emphasize the ways in which the list enacts (regulations), controls the action of the pilot and the co-pilot, structures communication between the cockpit and the ground crew and so forth. Vygotsky, of course, was in turn influenced by Engels in these matters; especially in so far as the latter was interested in how 'tools' shape their users.

Finally, it is possible to draw on Actor-Network-Theory or ANT. The idea of conceptualizing things (non-human agents) as actors or 'actants' was, to my knowledge, first proposed by adherents of ANT (see, for example, Callon, 1986). And a key assertion within ANT is that the traditional distinction – indeed, the asymmetry – between material objects and human beings be not just problematized, but overturned. In the same way, it is argued that the traditional distinction between subject and object be dispensed with. So, for example, non-human 'things' are not to be regarded as mere (passive) resources that merit consideration only when activated by human actors, but are to be viewed and understood as playing a vital role in economic, technological, scientific and all other forms of organizational life in their own right. That is to say, 'things' can be seen to instigate and direct as well as be directed. This is not the place in which to explore these arguments (Cooren's 2004 paper provides a sound set of published references on ANT), but it is appropriate to emphasize that ANT can provide a serious theoretical basis for reorientating our understanding of the place of text and documentation in everyday life. In all of these cases, of course, the focus of the analysis is on the role of documents as actors rather than as carriers of content.

CONCLUSION

I have argued then that there is far more in heaven and earth than document content. Indeed, by embracing the concepts of function and use we are able to considerably extend our vision of the range of documentary data that can be collected by social and educational researchers to say nothing of the methods used to amass and to analyse the attendant data. Nevertheless, in the above sections I have done little more than sketch out what the various approaches can look like and what they might entail. For those interested in discovering further examples of such approaches, or for exploring more detailed issues relating to the study of documents I refer them to Prior (2003, 2011), both of which contain more complex discussion of the issues raised in the paragraphs above.

REFERENCES

Alaszewski, A. (2006), 'Diaries as a source of suffering narratives: a critical commentary', *Health, Risk and Society*, **8** (1), 43–58.
Allport, G.W. (1942), *The Use of Personal Documents in Psychological Science*, New York: Social Science Research Council.
Angrosino, M.V. (1989), *Documents of Interaction. Biography, Autobiography, and Life History in Social Science Perspective*, Gainsville: FL: University of Florida Press.
Bazerman, C. (1997), 'Discursively structured activities', *Mind, Culture, and Activity*, **4** (4), 296–308.
Berelson, B. (1952), *Content Analysis in Communication Research*, Glencoe: IL: Free Press.
Berg, M. (1997), 'Of forms, containers, and the electronic medical record: some tools for a sociology of the formal', *Science Technology and Human Values*, **22** (4), 403–33.
Blaxter, L., Hughes, C. and Tight, M. (2006), *How to Research*, Milton Keynes: Open University Press.
Blumer, H. (1939), *An Appraisal of Thomas and Znaniecki's 'The Polish Peasant in Europe and America'*, New York: Social Science Research Council.
Bowker, G.C. (1998), 'The kindness of strangers. Kinds and politics in classification systems', *Library Trends*, **47**, 255–92.
Bowker, G.C. and Star, S.L. (1999), *Sorting Things Out. Classification and its Consequences*, Cambridge, MA: MIT Press.
Bryman, A. (2008), *Social Research Methods*, 3rd edn, Oxford: Oxford University Press.
Callon, M. (1986), 'Some elements of a sociology of translation: domestication of the scallops and the fishermen of Saint Brieuc Bay', in J. Law (ed.), *Power, Action and Belief: A New Sociology of Knowledge?*, The Sociological Review Monograph, Vol. 32, London: Routledge and Kegan Paul, pp. 196–233.
Carrington, V. (2009), 'I write, therefore I am. Texts in the city', *Visual Communication*, **8**, 409–25.
Cooren, F. (2004), 'Textual agency: how texts do things in organizational settings', *Organization*, **11** (3), 373–93.
Festinger, L. and Katz, D. (1953), *Research Methods in the Behavioral Sciences*, New York: Holt, Rinehart and Winston.
Foucault, M. (1970), *The Order of Things. An Archaeology of the Human Sciences*, London: Tavistock.
Geisler, C., Bazerman., C., Doheny-Farina, S. et al. (2001), 'IText. Future directions for

research on the relationship between information technology and writing', *Journal of Business and Technical Communication*, **15** (3), 269–308.

Gerber, D.A. (1997), 'The immigrant letter between positivism and populism: the uses of immigrant personal correspondence in twentieth-century American scholarship', *Journal of American Ethnic History*, **16** (4), 3–34.

Glaser, B.G. and Strauss, A.L. (1967), *The Discovery of Grounded Theory. Strategies for Qualitative Research*, New York: Aldine De Gruyter.

Goode, W.J. and Hatt, P.K. (1952), *Methods in Social Research*, New York: McGraw-Hill.

Gottschalk, L. Kluckhohn, C. and Angell, R. (1945), *The Use of Personal Documents in History, Anthropology, and Sociology*, New York: Social Science Research Council.

Harley, J.B. (1992), 'Rereading the maps of the Columbian encounter', *Annals of the Association of American Geographers*, **82** (3), 522–36.

Henderson, K. (1995), 'The political career of a prototype. Visual representation in design engineering', *Social Problems*, **42** (2), 274–99.

Hodder, I. (2000), 'The interpretation of documents and material culture', in N.K. Denzin and Y.S. Lincoln (eds), *Handbook of Qualitative Research*, 2nd edn, London: Sage, pp. 703–16.

Kitsuse, J.I. and Cicourel, A. (1963), 'A note on the use of official statistics', *Social Problems*, **11** (2), 131–9.

Klofas, J.M. and Cutshall, C.R. (1985), 'The social archaeology of a juvenile facility. Unobtrusive measures in the study of institutional cultures', *Qualitative Sociology*, **8** (4), 368–87.

Kollmeyer, C.J. (2004), 'Corporate interests. How the news media portray the economy', *Social Problems*, **51**, 3432–52.

Krippendorf, K. (2004), *Content Analysis. An Introduction to its Methodology*, 2nd edn, London: Sage.

Langer, S., Scourfield, J. and Fincham, B. (2008), 'Documenting the quick and the dead: a study of suicide case files in a coroner's office', *The Sociological Review*, **56** (2), 293–308.

Lee, R.M. (2000), *Unobtrusive Methods in Social Research*, Buckingham: Open University Press.

Lynch, M. (2002), 'Protocols, practices and the reproduction of technique in molecular biology', *British Journal of Sociology*, **53** (2), 202–20.

Margolin, L. (1992), 'Deviance on record: techniques for labeling child abusers in official documents', *Social Problems*, **39** (1), 58–70.

May, T. (1997), *Social Research. Issues, Methods and Process*, Buckingham: Open University Press.

McCarthy, L.P. and Gerring, J.P. (1994), 'Revising psychiatry's charter document: DSM-IV', *Written Communication*, **11**, 147–92.

Meehan, A.J. (2000), 'The organizational career of gang statistics: the politics of policing gangs', *The Sociological Quarterly*, **41** (3), 337–70.

Navaro-Yashin, Y. (2007), 'Make-believe papers, legal forms and the counterfeit. Affective interactions between documents and people in Britain and Cyprus', *Anthropological Theory*, **7** (1), 79–98.

Platt, J. (1981), 'Evidence and proof in documentary research I. Some specific problems of documentary research', *The Sociological Review*, **29** (1), 31–52.

Platt, J. (1996), *A History of Sociological Research Methods in America, 1920–1960*, Cambridge: Cambridge University Press.

Plummer, K. (2001), *Documents of Life 2. An invitation to Critical Humanism*, London: Sage.

Pollack, J.M. and Kubrin, C.E. (2007), 'Crime in the news. How crimes, offenders and victims are portrayed in the media', *Journal of Criminal Justice and Popular Culture*, **14** (1), 59–83.

Prior, L. (1985), 'Making sense of mortality', *Sociology of Health & Illness*, **7** (2), 167–90.

Prior, L. (2003), *Using Documents in Social Research*, London: Sage.

Prior, L. (2004), 'Documents', in C. Seale, G. Gobo, J.F. Gubrium and D. Silverman (eds), *Qualitative Research Practice*, London: Sage, pp. 375–90.

Prior, L. (2008), 'Repositioning documents in social research', *Sociology*, Special Issue on Research Methods, **42**, 821–36.

Prior, L. (2011), *Using Documents and Records in Social Research*, four vols, London: Sage.

Prior, L., Wood, F., Gray, J., Pill, R. and Hughes, D. (2002), 'Making risk visible: the role of images in the assessment of (cancer) genetic risk', *Health Risk and Society*, **4** (3), 241–58.

Roth, W.-M. and McGinn, M.K. (1998), 'Inscriptions: toward a theory of representing as social practice', *Review of Educational Research*, **68** (1), 35–59.

Roth, W.-M., Bowen, G.M. and Masciotra, D. (2002), 'From thing to sign and "Natural Object": toward a genetic phenomenology of graph interpretation', *Science Technology and Human Values*, **27** (3), 327–56.

Rule, J.B., McAdam, D., Stearns, L. and Uglow, D. (1983), 'Documentary identification and mass surveillance in the United States', *Social Problems*, **31** (2), 222–34.

Schryer, C.F. (1993), 'Records as genre', *Written Communication*, **10**, 200–234.

Scott, J. (1990), *A Matter of Record. Documentary Sources in Social Research*, Cambridge: Cambridge University Press.

Searle, J.R. (1979), *Expression and Meaning*, Cambridge: Cambridge University Press.

Simonds, S. (1988), 'Confessions of loss. Maternal grief in true story 1920–1985', *Gender and Society*, **2** (2), 149–71.

Smith, D.E. (1974), 'The social construction of documentary reality', *Sociological Inquiry*, **44** (4), 257–68.

Thomas, W.I. and Znaniecki, F. (1958), *The Polish Peasant in Europe and America*, 2nd edn, New York: Dover Publications.

Turner, V. (1975), *Revelation and Divination in Ndembu Ritual*, Ithaca, NY: Cornell University Press.

Ulmer, J.T. and Kramer, J.H. (1998), 'The use and transformation of formal decision-making criteria: sentencing guidelines, organizational contexts, and case processing strategies', *Social Problems*, **45** (2), 248–67.

Winsor, D.A. (1997), 'Genre and activity systems: the role of documentation in maintaining and changing engineering activity systems', *Written Communication*, **16** (2), 200–224.

Wittgenstein, L. (2009), *Philosophical Investigations*, Revised 4th edn by P.M.S. Hacker and J. Schulte, Chichester: Wiley-Blackwell.

Yates, J. (1989), 'The emergence of the memo as a managerial genre', *Management Communication Quarterly*, **2** (4), 485–510.

Zeitlyn, D. (2001), 'Finding meaning in the text: the process of interpretation in text-based divination', *Journal of the Royal Anthropological Institute*, **7** (2), 225–40.

PART 4

ANALYSIS AND REPRESENTATION

32. Transcription of speech
*Martyn Hammersley**

Since the 1960s, many qualitative researchers have used audio- and/or video-recordings – and transcriptions of these – as data.[1] This applies across most data collection methods, but especially those involving interviews or collective discussion (See in this volume Currie and Kelly, Chapter 29; Elliott, Chapter 20; Forsey, Chapter 26; Robinson, Chapter 28; Tierney and Clemens, Chapter 19). Indeed, in many quarters, reliance upon electronic recording and transcription has come to be so taken-for-granted over the past few decades that fieldnotes are now treated by some as a second-class form of data, if their use is not ruled out completely. A few researchers have seen reliance upon electronic recordings and transcription as finally enabling human social interaction to be studied scientifically, since 'the data' are preserved and can be reproduced: this means that they are open to repeated analysis, and furthermore can be made available to readers of research reports so that analyses can be checked (and, in effect, replicated) by others. This is a view that can be found among conversation analysts (see Peräkylä, 1997, 2011; ten Have, 2002, p. 2; Housley, Chapter 33, this volume). And there has been a long tradition of reliance upon detailed transcriptions among linguists (Green and Stewart, Chapter 5, this volume). However, most qualitative researchers probably treat electronic recordings and transcripts simply as a convenient alternative to fieldnote writing, one that provides enhanced detail and accuracy.[2]

There is now a substantial literature on issues surrounding transcription of audio- and video-recordings, though this literature does not seem always to have been given the attention it deserves by practising educational researchers.[3] Much of it has been produced by those engaged in sociolinguistic research, though there are also discussions that relate to qualitative research more generally. A dominant theme in this literature is that transcription is a process of 'construction' rather than simply a matter of writing down what was said (see, for example, Mishler, 1991). In part, what is meant by the constructional character of transcription is that a whole variety of decisions are involved, and that there cannot be a single correct transcription of any stretch of audio- or video-recording. For this reason, neither transcripts nor electronic recordings should be treated as data that are simply given, in an unmediated fashion.

MULTIPLE DECISIONS

The fact that a variety of decisions have to be made in the course of transcription is highlighted by the rather different kinds of transcript used by people working within different research traditions. One sharp contrast here is between the very detailed transcripts used by some sociolinguists and conversation analysts (see, for example, the influential transcription system developed by Gail Jefferson, 2004), and the much less detailed ones employed by other sorts of qualitative researcher.

The decisions involved in transcription include the following:

1. Whether to transcribe any particular audio- or video-recording, and if so how much of it to transcribe. Even conversation analysts do not always transcribe all of the recordings they make (Peräkylä, 1997, p. 206). Other qualitative researchers may be even more selective, though they usually write summaries of what is contained on those parts of a recording not transcribed.

2. How to represent the recorded talk. Here, there is variation according to whether the emphasis is on capturing the actual sounds made or on identifying the words used and presenting these via traditional orthography. More specifically, there are decisions about whether to try to represent such features as intonation, pitch, amplitude, and pace of talk. Associated with this is the issue of whether to aim at capturing distinctive forms of language use, such as dialects. And, if pronunciation is to be represented, there is then the question of how to do this: whether through deviant spelling within traditional orthography (for example, 'Whaaaat's this?', 'having a larf', etc.) or via a phonetic transcription system (see Atkinson, 1992, chapter 4).

3. In multi-party talk, there is the issue of whether there should be an indication of to whom the speaker is primarily addressing the talk, where this is not indicated explicitly in what is said. While people sometimes address their speech to the whole company present, they do not always do this; sometimes they will pick out a sub-set of the group, even though other people will overhear what they say. And, occasionally, comments are exchanged between two or more members of a group in such a way as to try to avoid these being overheard by others, and this fact may be significant in understanding what is said. Some researchers using video-recording have sought to document to whom speech is directed by monitoring direction of gaze.

4. There is also the question of whether to include non-word elements: such as back-channel noises (for instance, 'uhuh'), laughs and other sounds that may be expressive. Also at issue is whether to report

in-breaths and out-breaths, coughs and other noises that may be regarded as non-expressive but still significant in some way. What noises are and are not intended to be communicative is not always clear; and, as Goffman (1959) pointed out long ago, information 'given off' can be as important as what is intentionally communicated.

5. Should silences and pauses be included in the transcript, should they be timed, and if so how? There are difficulties here about what counts as a silence or a pause, and about whether in timing them what is important is their actual length in seconds or alternatively whether they are likely to be perceived by speakers as long or short, significant or insignificant. In one sense we might treat silence as simply the absence of talk, but there is a difference between this and notable silences or significant pauses. We also need to ask: significant or notable for whom?

6. Should we try to include relevant gestures and fine or gross physical movement, including, for example, what Peräkylä refers to amusingly as 'ambulatory events' (Peräkylä 1997, p. 204), in other words, walking about? Detailed information about these may be available via fieldnotes or where the events have been video-recorded.

7. There is also the issue of how to lay out talk on the page in transcripts. While it is most common to use a playscript format of some kind, there are alternatives to this (see Ochs, 1979). Moreover, even within the playscript format there are further decisions to be made. One concerns whether to treat all of what one person says, before another speaks, as a single continuous utterance; or to split and place on separate lines what might be interpreted as consecutive, distinct utterances by the same speaker, especially if these are separated by lengthy or significant pauses or silences. There is also the question of whether, and how, to indicate overlapping talk. It is important to note that overlapping talk is a distinct category from, albeit one that overlaps with, interruption.

8. There are alternative options in how to label the speakers. One possibility, rarely used, would be simply to number each utterance without indicating when the same person is speaking. In some ways, this might be in line with a postmodernist conception of identity as multiple and occasioned. More usually, labels are employed to indicate different speakers so that we can identify which utterances came from 'the same' source. However, it is important to remember here that speakership is not a straightforward matter, since people may speak on behalf of others or to a script written by others (Goffman, 1981), and because all talk continually draws on other voices (Bakhtin, 1981). Furthermore, any labels we give to speakers, beyond numbers

or letters, may convey information about them, and this raises questions about what information should and should not be included. For example, names can be taken to indicate gender (and inferences here can be false as well as true), and giving gendered names could imply that gender is the most significant factor in the interaction, which it may or may not be. Similarly, using role labels in transcripts, such as Teacher/Student, gives information and implies that all of a person's utterances were 'in role', and perhaps also that these roles are the most important consideration in understanding what was going on.

9.   When it comes to providing extracts from transcripts in research reports, there are further questions: where to begin and end the extract (for example, in the case of interview data, should the interviewer's questions be included? See Rapley, 2001); whether to use the same transcript conventions as were used in the process of analysis, or ones tailored to the particular point being being made in the text and/or to the audience; how many extracts to use in support of any point; what background information to provide about the speakers and the situation; and so on.

While the fact that decisions about these matters must be taken indicates that transcriptions are in an important sense constructed, it is equally important to remember that the aim of transcription is to produce an accurate record of what was said, 'in the words used'. Emphasis on the constructed character of transcripts sometimes degenerates into the idea that the data are 'created' by the transcriber rather than representing more or less adequately 'what occurred'. *In extremis*, this leads to a radical epistemological scepticism that is self-undermining (see Hammersley, 2010a, p. 7).

PRACTICAL CONCLUSIONS

A first practical conclusion to be drawn from all this is that great care is needed in transcription: it is easy for errors to creep in (Poland, 1995, 2002; Kitzinger, 1998) and these can lead to false inferences. We need to try to ensure that we are identifying the words, and/or phonetic characteristics, accurately. At the same time, in the process of analysis we must not treat transcripts as sacred and infallible texts. Careful transcription of the words spoken does not, in itself, tell us what someone was meaning to say or what they were doing. We have to 'interpret' the words, and in doing so we will and should draw on our experience of observing the events concerned (where available), fieldnote descriptions of them, video components of recordings, general background knowledge, and so on. So, while we must be careful not to over-interpret what people say – in the sense of engaging in highly speculative ascription of intentions and motives, social functions, and so on – what words they literally pronounce does not in itself tell us what they were intending to communicate or do.

A related issue concerns who should do the transcription: the researcher who carried out the observation or interview and made the recording, or, say, a trained transcriber? There are conflicting views here. It is often argued that it is essential for the researcher to do her or his own transcription, but some deny this, or even argue that it is not desirable (McCracken, 1988, pp. 41–2; Forsey, 2008; see also Tilley, 2003). My own view is that it is usually a good idea to employ a trained audio-typist to produce the first drafts of transcriptions but that the researcher should always listen to the recordings to check and correct the transcriptions. In fact, the recording will almost always need to be reviewed several times before adequacy is achieved, this varying with the level of detail required.

As noted earlier, different sorts of transcript may be required depending upon the purpose being pursued. Most obviously, what should be included in a transcript, and how this should be represented, will vary according to the nature of the investigation. For example, it will be different if we are seeking to analyse turn-taking in conversations from if we are using data for the purposes of understanding social strategies employed by parents to control their children. However, it is also important to recognize that what is the best form of transcription may well vary over the course of any single inquiry. At the beginning, the researcher may be unclear about what would and would not be relevant to include in transcripts for the purpose of facilitating the analysis. And it is very important here not to allow some single transcription scheme to determine this. The focus must be on producing relevant and accurate descriptive material with which to try to answer one's research questions. Transcripts are only tools to be used in this work, they never exhaust the potential data; nor, for that matter, do the audio- or video-recordings. Towards the end of a research project what is and is not relevant may be much clearer, and a rather different sort of transcript may be most useful in facilitating the analysis. This parallels the situation in quantitative research, where it may be necessary to produce different sorts of numerical table at different stages of inquiry.

It is also important to consider how extracts from the transcribed data should be presented in research reports. There are conflicting considerations here. On the one hand, we need to make the nature of the evidence we are using clear to our audience. One implication of this might be that long, complex and detailed transcripts will not serve us very well, since for many audiences they will be unreadable – this is true of the sorts of detailed transcripts produced both by conversation analysts and by some linguists. On the other hand, we ought to provide readers with sufficient data and evidence in a form that allows them to at least consider whether alternative interpretations from those we have put forward would be plausible. And this may require that we include lengthy and detailed extracts from transcripts. Of course, there is no possibility of including in a transcript everything that 'could' possibly be relevant. While the researcher should identify and assess plausible alternative interpretations, and provide transcripts that allow these to be assessed, he or she will not be able to anticipate all alternatives. And, as already indicated, too much detail may obscure relevant data and how it relates to the knowledge claims being made. There is a challenging dilemma here. (Of course, it may be possible to make detailed transcripts, and even the recordings themselves, available via appendices or archives, though this is not entirely straightforward for ethical and other reasons. On the issues surrounding archiving and reworking qualitative data see Heaton (2004) and the Qualidata website: http://www.esds.ac.uk/qualidata/about/introduction.asp.)

In this area, as in many other aspects of research method, careful reflection and judgement, and some trade-off between alternatives, are required. There are no simple rules to be followed.

NOTES

*   This chapter includes extracts from Hammersley (2010a).
1   For useful practical guidance about the basics of recording and transcription, see Burke et al., 2010 and Swann, 2001.
2   Of course, it is not always feasible even to audio-record the processes of interaction in which one is interested, and the requirement to do so may exert undesirable constraints on what can be studied, where data collection can be carried out, and perhaps also on the length of the data collection period, given the sheer amount of data likely to be generated through electronic recording. It is important to recognize these restrictions.
3   Bird (2005) reviews some of this literature, and provides insight into how a novice researcher came to recognize the significance of the process of transcription. For a bibliography on transcription in social research, see Hammersley (2010b).

REFERENCES

Atkinson, P. (1992), *Understanding Ethnographic Texts*, Thousand Oaks, CA: Sage.
Bakhtin, M.M. (1981), *The Dialogic Imagination: Four essays*, ed. M. Holquist, Austin, TX: University of Texas Press.
Bird, C. (2005), 'How I stopped dreading and learned to love transcription', *Qualitative Inquiry*, **11** (2), 226–48
Burke, H., Jenkins, L. and Higham, V. (2010), 'Transcribing your own data', *Realities Toolkit No. 8*, available at http://www.socialsciences.manchester.ac.uk/realities/resources/

toolkits/transcribing-your-data/08-toolkit-transcribing-your-qual-data.pdf (accessed 9 June 2010).

Forsey, M. (2008), 'Ethnographic interviewing: from conversation to published text', in G. Walford (ed.), *How to do Educational Ethnography*, London Tufnell Press pp. 57–75.

Goffman, E. (1959), *The Presentation of Self in Everyday Life*, Harmondsworth Penguin.

Goffman, E. (1981), *Forms of Talk*, Oxford: Blackwell.

Hammersley, M. (2010a), 'Reproducing or constructing? Some questions about transcription in social research', *Qualitative Research*, **10** (5), 1–17.

Hammersley, M. (2010b), 'A selective and partially annotated bibliography of the literature on transcription', available at http://oro.open.ac.uk/21674/ (accessed 2 August 2010).

ten Have, P. (2002), 'Reflections on transcription', *Cahiers de Praxematique*, **39**, 21–43, available at http://www.paultenhave.nl/Transcription-rv2.pdf (accessed 27 August 2008).

Heaton, J. (2004), *Reworking Qualitative Data*, London: Sage.

Jefferson, G. (2004), 'Glossary of transcript symbols with an introduction', in G.H. Lerner (ed.), *Conversation Analysis: Studies from the First Generation*, Amsterdam: Benjamins, pp. 13–23.

Kitzinger, C. (1998), 'Inaccuracies in quoting from data transcripts: or inaccuracy in quotations from data transcripts', *Discourse and Society*, **9**, 136–43.

McCracken, G. (1988), *The Long Interview*, Newbury Park, CA: Sage.

Mishler, E.G. (1991), 'Representing discourse: the rhetoric of transcription', *Journal of Narrative and Life History*, **1** (4), 225–80.

Ochs, E. (1979), 'Transcription as theory', in E. Ochs and B.B. Schieffelin (eds), *Developmental Pragmatics*, London: Academic Press, pp. 43–72.

Peräkylä, A. (1997), 'Validity and reliability in research based on tapes and transcripts', in D. Silverman (ed.), *Qualitative Analysis: Issues of Theory and Method*, London: Sage, pp. 201–20.

Peräkylä, A. (2011), 'Validity and reliability in research based on tapes and transcripts', in D. Silverman (ed.), *Qualitative Analysis: Issues of Theory and Method*, 3rd edn, London: Sage, pp. 365–82.

Poland, B.D. (1995), 'Transcription quality as an aspect of rigor in qualitative research', *Qualitative Inquiry*, **1** (3), 290–310.

Poland, B. (2002), 'Transcription quality', in J.F. Gubrium and J.A. Holstein (eds), *Handbook of Interview Research*, Thousand Oaks, CA: Sage. Reprinted in Holstein, J.A. and Gubrium, J.F. (eds) (2003), *Inside Interviewing: New Lenses, New Concerns*, Thousand Oaks, CA: Sage, pp. 267–87.

Rapley, T. (2001), 'The art(fulness) of open-ended interviewing: some considerations on analysing interviews', *Qualitative Research*, **1** (3), 303–23.

Swann, J. (2001), 'Recording and transcribing talk in educational settings', in C. Candlin and N. Mercer (eds), *English Language Teaching in its Social Context*, London: Routledge, pp. 163–76.

Tilley, S.A. (2003), 'Transcription work: learning through coparticipation in research practices', *International Journal of Qualitative Studies in Education*, **16**, (6), 835–51.

33. Ethnomethodology, conversation analysis and educational settings
William Housley

Ethnomethodological and conversation analytic research of educational settings is now well established and has produced a significant corpus of studies that inform the social scientific understanding of the situated social organization of educational processes and practices. It has also provided a cumulative set of empirical studies which serve to inform contemporary and ongoing educational research. Traditionally the 'School' has provided an important institutional context within which interactionist and phenomenological conceptualization of labelling and social types have found fertile empirical ground (Hargreaves et al., 1975). Complementary work began to examine the interaction order of educational settings by focusing on practical action, discourse and talk-in-interaction often through an examination of naturally occurring data as well as detailed ethnographic observation (Hammersley, 1977). This type of work has been heavily influenced by ethnomethodological conceptualizations of social action and organization. In order to appreciate how this approach has influenced educational research it is necessary to outline some of the basic ideas associated with this approach.

THE ETHNOMETHODOLOGICAL PROGRAMME

Ethnomethodology is a heterogeneous sociological programme. According to sociological orthodoxy ethnomethodology began with the publication of Harold Garfinkel's *Studies in Ethnomethodology* (1967). Garfinkel had been a student of the famous structural functionalist Talcott Parsons. He was influenced by the phenomenological work of Alfred Schutz with whom Parsons maintained a troublesome correspondence. Some of Garfinkel's early work involved the use of 'breaching experiments' with which Garfinkel illustrated the normative grounding of social order via the explication of common sense methods which people followed and displayed in the business of constituting social activities. For Garfinkel, Parsons's notion of the social system obscured the very phenomena that constituted the essence of the social and more specifically the very phenomena of 'social order' that Parsons has sought to examine. For Garfinkel, the normative grounding of social order was a member's achievement and he began to focus on the routine methods by which members reflexively constituted social activity. Furthermore, Garfinkel viewed social activity as demonstrable of social order and as a local, praxiological achievement of members in any given interactional context. According to Lena Jayussi (1991, p. 235), Garfinkel's 'study policy' is characterized by the:

> redirection of the way the problem of 'social order' is possible . . . [it] is a question which in Garfinkel's work can be seen to be reconstituted via (i) a focus on the produced detail that is a proper answer to the puzzle of the how, and (ii) a deconstruction of the generic notion of 'social order' into the notion of particular 'orders' of various occasioned settings in everyday life. It is these 'orders' which, when examined, turn out to be the generative constituents of the 'macro' social order, as it is encountered and oriented to by both actors and investigators.

The analytical concerns of ethnomethodological inquiry can be summarized into five main themes. These include practice and accomplishment, indexicality, reflexivity, accountability and the ethnomethodological notion of membership. A brief consideration of each of these themes will now be provided.

PRACTICE AND ACCOMPLISHMENT

Ethnomethodological inquiry is concerned with the commonsensical procedures and methods that members use in achieving a sense of orderliness. Furthermore, the distinction between topic and resource (Button, 1991) in sociological endeavour is of central importance to the ethnomethodological approach. Traditional sociology takes standard concepts such as norms and values, rules and structures and assumes that they have an epistemological connection with a transcendent reality independent of their interactional context and production. As such, 'topics' of social enquiry become 'unexplicated resources' for describing an assumed illustration of the world. As Lynch notes, paraphrasing Garfinkel, traditional sociological enquiry 'fetishizes the sign' (Lynch, 1991). That is to say, the social world is contingent upon the everyday actions of members and it is these methods of social accomplishment that should be investigated in attempting to explain and illuminate how society is possible. A concern with the practical accomplishment of social organization (for example, classroom order, teacher–pupil interaction, educational psychological counselling, staff meetings, marking and grading) is central to the business of ethnomethodological inquiry and informs the starting point from which situated action can be located, described and recovered for analytic inspection.

INDEXICALITY

For Garfinkel, social life is very much realized through linguistic dimensions of interaction. That is to say, much of the local work involved in carrying out practical everyday accomplishments is realized through the situated, contextually sensitive natural use of language. For Garfinkel one of the major aspects of language was the prevalence of what English language philosophy has described as 'deitic terms'. Deixis can be understood to relate to the way in which the meaning of certain words or phrases is realized through the identification and interpretation of contextual information. From an ethnomethodological point of view this linguistic phenomenon can be understood to manifest itself through the indexical properties of language. Furthermore, indexicality, meaning and context are routine practical problems for members that are remedied through a variety of methods in everyday interaction.

Harvey Sacks in his *Lectures in Conversation* (1992a, 1992b) describes the prevalence of 'indexical expressions' within natural conversation. In particular, he draws our attention to indexical pronouns such as 'I' and 'We' that are articulated and understood in terms of the context of their occurrence. Indexical expressions draw our attention to the way in which language and terms within language derive their meaning from their 'index' within a given linguistic contextual arrangement. For Garfinkel this meaning-in-context was not an arbitrary process but a dynamic interactional process grounded in the commonsensical methods of members. Furthermore, for Garfinkel language as an interactive medium is irremediably indexical. Thus, indexicality is not merely a philosopher's problem but a practical matter for members.

For ethnomethodology, the prevalence of indexicality throughout language draws our attention to the way in which meaning is contextually, interactionally and socially produced within local *in situ* instances of practical action. For Garfinkel, the 'objective expressions' of traditional sociological inquiry are themselves rooted in an attempt to deal with the indexicality of describing the 'social'. The formations of language games that deal in 'objective expressions' are themselves subject to the irrepairability of indexicality. As Lynch (1993, p. 19) notes:

> Whenever logicians or philosophers try to affix truth values to particular formal statements or to give stable definitions to terms, they invariably must contend

with the fact that when a statement contains indexical expressions, its relevance, referential sense, appropriateness, and correctness will vary whenever it is used by different speakers, on different occasions, and in different texts. In order to remedy this problem, philosophers attempted in various ways to replace indexicals with spatiotemporal references, proper names, technical terms and notations, and 'objective expressions'.

Consequently, the ways, strategies and methods for repairing indexicality are grounded in practices and orientations common both to the philosopher, sociologist and ordinary member. While the methods employed may vary and the complexities of language games differ, the fundamental orientation to repairing indexicality remains an inexorable feature of social interaction.

REFLEXIVITY

The notion of reflexivity, in an analytical sense, draws our attention to the way in which the 'subject' and 'object' of philosophical discourse are mutually constituted. Furthermore, in a member's sense, reflexivity refers to the way in which members constitute the activities to which they are oriented. The concept of reflexivity has been used by sociologists pursuing different strands of sociological thought to explain a number of interrelated phenomena. For example, in postmodernist theory it is invoked as a means of drawing our attention to the way in which the reflexive constitution of narratives proceed to a circularity of signification within which language can be seen to exhibit 'infinite play' (Derrida, 1981). However, for Garfinkel reflexivity provides a central concept for appreciating how members achieve a sense of local order. For members, Garfinkel argues, reflexivity refers to those praxiological, occasioned instances, which describe and constitute the social at one and the same time. Reflexivity can, for example, manifest itself through members' descriptive work that according to Garfinkel (1967) is a constituent feature of the setting that such descriptions seek to describe. This is not problematic but central to understanding and documenting how action-in-order is realized in and through interaction.

ACCOUNTABILITY

Accountability (or accountable action) is a concept that seeks to illustrate how members make their actions praxiologically and reflexively recognizable and understandable. One of the most famous studies that included a description and explanation of the whole process of 'accountability' can be found in Garfinkel's study of Agnes. Garfinkel (1967) had interviewed Agnes, a transsexual, who had chosen to become a 'woman'. Garfinkel's research suggested that in order to 'pass as a woman' Agnes had to learn continually and routinely to display the accountable features of her chosen gender. Whilst through reification and the natural attitude members may 'forget' the orderly business of making such features available during interaction, for Agnes, this had to be 'learnt' through sustained observation to an extent that it became routinized. In contemporary terms the social constitution of gender comes as no surprise. However, it is the methods through which the social interactional work of identity is done which caught Garfinkel's attention. Thus, accountability can be seen to be a constitutive feature of interaction, members 'inform' and 'display' certain categories of identity and orientation as a means of structuring and achieving a local sense of order.

THE NOTION OF MEMBERSHIP

The final concept identified by Coulon (1995) is the notion of 'member' and 'membership'. As Coulon notes, the notion of member is not a 'social category' per se but refers to a relationship with language, namely natural language competence. The notion of 'member' is an analytical device in many respects. Furthermore, it is a term that highlights the indexical and reflexive concerns of ethnomethodological inquiry. Through reference to interlocutors as members of a given interactive and linguistic 'activity', the occasioned and situated character of interactional work is emphasized. Membership of that interactive activity reflexively constitutes the parameters and features of membership within the context of its articulation and realization. In many respects it pre-empts the postmodernist notion of decentring the subject, in that membership is not a transcendental subjective state which provides for epistemological certainty. Rather it is a socially achieved and negotiated set of parameters which is reflexively and indexically embedded within social interaction on a 'no time out basis' in order to get the day's work done.

ETHNOMETHODOLOGY AND THE ANALYSIS OF LANGUAGE

Ethnomethodology is not exclusively concerned with language and society. However, much of the early ethnomethodological work and the contribution of Harvey Sacks ensured that language became an important area of study. In many respects the concern with practical action and the emergence of language as a major area within which members' methods were observable pre-empted the linguistic turn within mainstream sociology. However, this development emerged some ten to twenty years after the publication of Garfinkel's *Studies in Ethnomethodology* (1967) and Sacks's lectures at UCLA. Furthermore, the interactive quality of language and language use was a natural area for investigation into how practical reasoning and locally produced senses of order were achieved through observable strategies and methods by members. Many of these members' methods were essentially conversational and the ethnomethodological concerns with members' 'talk' became established relatively quickly. The work of Harvey Sacks has been well documented by those working within the field of ethnomethodology and conversation analysis. Sacks's work (1992a, 1992b) encompasses interests in the sequential and descriptive dimensions of language use. From an ethnomethodological reading, Sacks was documenting the social organization of language and is remembered particularly for the attention he gave to the sequential aspects of language and language use. Conversation analysis perhaps starts from the observation that language as a social process is sequentially organized into recognizable procedures and units. For example, topic organization, topic changing, turn taking, pauses and adjacency as discussed by Sacks (1992a, 1992b), are seen to form the primal soup from which the sequential analysis of conversation emerged. A key concern here is the conversational practice of recipient design. For Sacks, recipient design is a feature of conversational interaction. For example, with turn taking, second speakers design their utterances in terms of the recognizable features of the categories displayed in the previous speaker's utterance. Furthermore, the second part of a turn taking unit is recipiently designed, sequentially. For example, an answer follows a question and is coherent in terms of the previous sequential order displayed in the first speaker's question. This can be best illustrated through Sacks's related concept of the adjacency pair that has become an important aspect of the sequential analysis of conversation. Examples of these forms of sequential (and recipiently designed) structures include question\answer sequences, greeting pairs and the Initiation–Response– Evaluation pedagogic turn taking structure identified by McHoul (1978) within the classroom setting. As may be inferred from the reference to formal systems of turn taking in classrooms a key application of early conversation analysis and ethnomethodology can be found in the study of pedagogic and formal educational settings. It is to a consideration of these applications that we now turn.

ETHNOMETHODOLOGY AND THE ANALYSIS OF EDUCATIONAL SETTINGS AND PRACTICE

An early edited collection by Payne and Cuff (1982) gives a flavour of the distinctive character of the approach that centred around the concept of 'doing teaching' within formalized educational settings. This collection sought to identify taken for granted practices that were fundamental to the understanding of the social organization of everyday teaching practice. As Payne and Cuff (1982, p. 2) state:

> This approach to understanding the social world has direct relevance for a study of teaching. Doing teaching, like doing being ordinary, requires work yet it is overwhelmingly accomplished effortlessly. Now before all teachers rise up in anger, or stop reading at this point, let us immediately explain further what we mean. Clearly, we are not saying that teaching is not demanding; we know that it requires planning and organization, physical and mental efforts, and a deal of emotional involvement. What we are saying, however, is that some aspects of teaching activities become so much a part of the ordinary day's work that they can often be accomplished, albeit expertly and efficiently, without great anxieties, without too much trouble, sometimes without thinking about them. Additionally, and perhaps more importantly than is usually recognised, there are a multitude of ordinary routine day-to-day activities engaged in by teachers in such a taken for granted manner that they go unnoticed. Dealing with late-comers, starting lessons, telling stories, hearing children read, sending them out to play – these are all activities which are seen, but go unnoticed as anything special.

These early studies have been influential on classroom ethnography, conversation analysis, the institutional talk programme and more recent 'discursive psychological' approaches to adult–child interaction. Hester and Francis (2000) in their excellent book identify six strands that characterize early proto-ethnomethodological work that prefigured and shaped some of the conversation analytic and related work in these types of setting.

The first strand is exemplified by the *The Educational Decision Makers* (Cicourel and Kitsuse, 1963) that examined the mundane work of the school counsellor in relation to the accomplishment of students' career choices. This approach relied on Schutzian phenomenology through which an examination of different educational types, categories and sense making practices were identified within this aspect of schooling. This included an examination of how educational professionals involve themselves in routine decision making that involves 'allocating, assessing, testing, sorting, referring and so forth' (Hester and Francis, 2000, p. 8). Further studies in this area developed the examination of the embedded nature of common sense practices in educational decision making practices (for example, Leiter, 1974; Mackay, 1974; Mehan et al., 1986).

A second aspect of this work involves the examination of formal educational assessment and standardized testing (for example, Mackay, 1974; Roth, 1974; Leiter, 1976; Mehan, 1976; Heap, 1980, 1983). This body of work examined how formal strategies of assessment relied on taken for granted understandings and knowledge. Thus the use of reading tests were shown not to have a direct relationship to the measurement of reading skills due to the interpretive and interactional variability between what was being elicited (as a resource) in relation to categories of measurement (frame).

The third dimension involves the examination of classroom management which has been identified as the most prolific area for both earlier and later studies (Hester and Francis, 2000, p. 9). This dimension produced studies that, on the one hand, examined issues concerning situated social control, classroom interaction and the categorization of behaviour or practices as 'deviant' (for example, Hargreaves et al., 1975; Payne and Hustler, 1980) and, on the other, those that began to 'drill down' towards the sequential organization of teacher–pupil interaction (for example, Mehan, 1979). Mehan's study of the I–R–E (Initiation–Response–Evaluation) formal classroom speech exchange system drew educational researcher's attention to the highly organized ways in which classroom talk was organized. This was complemented by McHoul's work that began to draw on the groundbreaking conversation analytic work of Sacks et al. (1974). These developments demonstrated the grounding of pedagogic work in sequential methods of conversational organization that lent themselves to systematic scrutiny.

A fourth and related dimension involves the consideration of classroom activities (for example, the use of storytelling, Hester and Francis, 1995) and the social organization of 'the lesson' (for example, Payne, 1976).

A fifth aspect of the situated study of educational practice has involved an examination of the social organization and practical accomplishment of academic knowledge (for example, Heap, 1983; Livingston, 1986; Lynch and Macbeth, 1998). One of the most celebrated of these studies can be found in McHoul and Watson's (1982) analysis of the situated use of formal and informal geographic knowledge within pedagogic practice. The study demonstrates how the formal axis of geographic knowledge within the classroom setting is underpinned by mundane cultural resources and everyday geographical sense making practices.

Finally, the examination of children's cultural worlds, practical action and adult–child interaction has formed the sixth dimension of ethnomethodological related studies within educational and related settings (for example, Speier, 1976, 1982; Baker, 1982; Goodwin, 1985, 1995; Maynard, 1985; Payne and Ridge, 1985; Goode, 1986; Baker and Freebody, 1987). These studies have sought to examine the child as 'oractical actor' who draws from specific cultural materials that are often distinct from adult culture in making sense of their world and accomplishing tasks. This has contributed to a reconsideration of educational testing in terms of children's culture, the examination of restricted speech rights and assymetrical turn taking between adults and children in interaction and the distinctive character of children's sense making activities.

LOCAL EDUCATIONAL ORDER? RESPECIFYING EDUCATIONAL PHENOMENA

Hester and Francis's collection on ethnomethodology and *Local Educational Order* (2000) include contributions that build on these early themes and studies and in itself is an interesting point of comparison with Payne and Cuff's (1982) earlier collection given that it includes a number of scholars associated with the development of this field of educational inquiry. Of critical significance here is Macbeth's analysis of classrooms as installations where strategies for discovering and knowing the 'world' are routinely assembled. This involves 'building knowledge-in-place' (Macbeth, 2000, p. 60) as the primary means for 'identifying tasks and distinguishing achievements of classroom teaching in the early grades' (Macbeth, 2000, p. 60). Further contributions include James Heap's examination of writing in a classroom where situated interactional events contribute to the accomplishment of writing as an act of multiple agents as opposed to isolated subjects. Danby and Baker examine the interactional management and organization of disputes, deviance and resolution between students whilst Freebody and Frieberg the moral organization of accountable action as an accomplished aspect of situated everyday classroom management. Of further note is Armour's investigation of the use of colour in relation to artistic pedagogic practice. Drawing from ethnomethodology and Wittgensteinian philosophy Armour (2000) demonstrates the occasioned nature of colour in relation to artistic practice and as an aspect of practically undertaking and achieving artistic endeavour. Armour (2000, p. 185) states:

> As ethnomethodological phenomena the dynamics of colour consists in and only in an assemblage of techniques and materials for producing colour behaviour/dynamics in situ and whatever the techniques and materials are they are nothing more nor less than the techniques and materials by which such dynamics are constructed, presented and used. As a practical accomplishment the dynamics of colour is an embedded and embodied activity identified with circumstantially contingent material arrangements and rearrangements such contingencies being found in and as a course of locally situated work.

As outlined earlier ethnomethodological and conversation analytic work has paid significant attention to educational practices and processes beyond the classroom. One of the most significant dimensions of these types of studies has involved the examination of teachers' and related professions' (for example, educational psychologists) work in the constitution and description of deviance and related forms of categorization. Hester (1991, 1992, 1998) has provided a series of studies that has examined how membership categorization practices form a central component for securing descriptions associated with 'special educational needs' by relevant professionals. Of critical relevance here is the social organization of accounts and categorization practices in referral meetings that provide the routine grounds for the accomplishment of the 'individualistic' categorization of students outside the collective life and interactional intricacies of educational settings.

The significance of the studies outlined above is found in the move to respecify educational phenomena in terms of local educational order. For Lynch and Bogen (1997, p. 273) respecification can be characterized in terms of the following procedures:

(1.) Take a 'methodological problem' distinction, problem, or concept (for instance the difference between fact and opinion, the distinction between intended action and unintended behaviour, the relationship between what someone says and what they 'really mean', the question of whether professed reasons should be accepted as adequate explanation).
(2.) Treat the 'problem' as a matter of routine, local relevance for a particular kind of practical enquiry (such as juror deliberations).
(3.) Describe the way members make use of the distinction or concept, and how they handle any problems associated with its use, and show how this use is embedded in routine courses of action (jury deliberations and their outcomes, coroner's investigations into the causes of death, suicide prevention center personnel's methods for discerning the difference between a serious and a crank caller, etc.).

For Lynch, Bogen and other ethnomethodologists such an approach provides for a means of fleshing out and describing the methods through which such concepts are oriented to and dealt with by members. The advantage of such an approach is to situate such conceptual 'problems' around the way members repair, cope or deal with such issues in everyday contexts. For Lynch, this provides a rich and differentiated account of how such phenomena are used and negotiated as a member's practical concern rather than treating them as 'concepts on holiday' (Lynch and Bogen, 1997, p. 273). In terms of the studies discussed in this section this represents an orientation to the examination of educational practices and organization as phenomena in their own right as opposed to signatures of some predefined social scientific process or problematic (Hester and Francis, 2000, p. 12). For some educational researchers this may well be problematic or viewed as digressive from the core tasks of social scientifically inspired educational research. However, what it does allow for is an orientation to analysing educational practices that keep first order phenomena in view in ways that provide empirically grounded descriptions and analyses of the social life and organization of educational and related worlds.

BEYOND THE CLASSROOM?

As stated earlier, ethnomethodological and related work's concern with pedagogic practice extends beyond the classroom. A significant study in this regard can be found in Carolyn Baker's (1984) study on the 'search for adultness' and interview talk. Baker's study identifies the routine operation of stage of life devices (Sacks, 1992a, 1992b) and their management in relation to adolescent interview participants. The identification of category-bound activities, through interview questions, that relate to different stage of life devices serves to demonstrate its ubiquitous operation and moral force where failure to clearly identify with a particular stage of life device (for example, adult) necessitates explanation, remediation and repair. In the following example, gathered from an interview where the interviewer is construed as the adult whilst the interviewee is construed as the adolescent (they being high school students), P = Pam and I = Interviewer.

1.I: Are there any ways in which you consider yourself to
2.   still be partly a child?
3.P: Well, I like to watch TV and, uh,
4.I: Well, adults do that
5.P: Yeah, I still read the comics ((laugh))
6.I   Adults do that
7.P: That's about, only thing I can think of (Baker, 1984, p. 316)

In this exchange Baker notes how adult/child overlap constitutes an improper description; although it may arise where liminality is a possibility (for example, adolescence). This helps to demonstrate how the descriptive cultural apparatus does not allow for the simultaneous categorization of a member of a given population as both adult and child.

Interest in stage of life devices in relation to everyday interaction and membership categorization has informed the examination of settings outside the professional work of the school and the classroom. This has included after school clubs (Butler, 2008), family mealtimes (Butler and Fitzgerald, 2010) and sibling interaction. Whilst these represent settings for interaction outside formal educational parameters they also serve to identify general pedagogic strategies, methods of situated regulation and control, the practical management of children's social realities and the social organization of children's activities. Butler and Fitzgerald (2010) identify the situated operationalization of membership categories that relate to family, setting and wider senses of human organization (for example, adult and child) within the local and routine setting of the family meal. Of significance and interest is ways in which different activities are bound up in contextually generated identities, on the one hand, and wider human or structural, identities, on the other. In this way activities such as encouraging 'good manners', sharing a joke or enacting discipline can be indexed to different forms of categorization and thence cultural work in fairly regular ways. The paper also examines visual data and the work of gesture and gaze in relation to adult–child interaction during family mealtimes.

In some respects these studies represent a realization that ethnomethodology, conversation analysis and related forms of analysis can inform new theories of human development through an understanding of practical interactional competencies as opposed to cognitive affordances and properties that are often hidden from view. If this sounds like a form of behaviourism then analysts would respond by emphasizing the empirical appreciation of the artful and situated character of children's interaction that is in contrast to explanations based solely on conditioned responses or indeed genetic predisposition.

REFERENCES

Armour, L. (2000), 'Socio-logic and the use of colour', in S. Hester and D. Francis (eds), *Local Educational Order*, Amsterdam: John Benjamins, pp. 163–96.

Baker, C. (1982), 'Adolescent-adult talk as a practical interpretive problem', in G. Payne and E.C. Cuff (eds), *Doing Teaching*, London: Batsford.

Baker, C. (1984), 'The "search for adultness": membership work in adolescent-adult talk', *Human Studies*, 7 (3–4), 301–23.

Baker, C.D. and Freebody, P. (1987), '"Constituting the child" in beginning school readers', *British Journal of Sociology Education*, 8, 55–76.

Butler, C.W. (2008), *Talk and Social Interaction in the Playground*, Ashgate: Aldershot.

Butler, C. and Fitzgerald, R. (2010), 'Membership-in-action: operative identities in a family meal', *Journal of Pragmatics*, 42 (9), 2462–74.

Button, G. (ed.) (1991), *Ethnomethodology and the Human Sciences*, Cambridge: Cambridge University Press.

Cicourel, A. and Kitsuse, J. (1963), *The Educational Decision Makers*, New York: Bobbs-Merril.

Coulon, A. (1995), *Ethnomethodology*, London: Sage Publications.

Derrida, J. (1981), *Positions*, trans. A. Bass, Chicago, IL: University of Chicago Press.

Garfinkel, H. (1967), *Studies in Ethnomethodology*, Cambridge: Polity Press.

Goode, D.A. (1986), 'Kids, culture and innocents', *Human Studies*, **9**, 83–106.

Goodwin, M.H. (1985), 'The serious side of jump rope: conversational practices and social organisation in the frame of play', *Journal of American Folklore*, **98**, 315–30.

Goodwin, M.H. (1995), 'Co-construction in girls' hopscotch', *Research on Language and Social Interaction*, **28** (3), 261–81.

Hammersley, M. (1977), 'School learning: the cultural resources required by pupils to answer a teacher's question', in P. Woods and M. Hammersley (eds), *School Experience: Explorations in the Sociology of Education*, London: Croom Helm, pp. 57–86.

Hargreaves, D.H., Hester, S.K. and Mellor, F.J. (1975), *Deviance in Classrooms*, London: Routledge and Kegan Paul.

Heap, J.L. (1980), 'What counts as reading: limits to certainty in assessment', *Curriculum Inquiry*, **10**, 265–92.

Heap, J.L. (1983), 'Frames and knowledge in a science lesson', *Curriculum Inquiry*, **13**, 397–417.

Hester, S.K. (1991), 'The social facts of deviance in school: a study of mundane reason, *British Journal of Sociology*, **42**, 443–63.

Hester, S.K. (1992), 'Recognising references to deviance in referral', in G. Watson and R. Sieler (eds), *Text in Context: Contributions to Ethnomethodology*, Newbury Park: Sage.

Hester, S.K. (1998), 'Describing deviance in schools: recognizably educational psychological problems', in C. Antaki and S. Widdecombe (eds), *Identities in Talk*, London: Sage, pp. 133–50.

Hester, S. and Francis, D. (1995), 'Words and pictures: collaborative storytelling in a primary classroom', *Research in Education*, **53**, 65–88.

Hester, S. and Francis, D. (eds) (2000), *Local Educational Order*, Amsterdam: John Benjamins.

Jayussi, L. (1991), 'Values and moral judgement', in G. Button (ed.), *Ethnomethodology and the Human Sciences*, Cambridge: Cambridge University Press, pp. 227–51.

Leiter, K. (1974), 'Ad hocing in the schools: a study of placement practices in the kindergarten of two schools', in A.V. Cicourel, K. Jennings, S. Jennings, K. Leiter, R.Mackay, H. Mehan and D. Roth (eds), *Language Use and School Performance*, New York: Academic Press, pp. 17–75.

Leiter, K. (1976), 'Teachers' user of background knowledge to interpret test scores', *Sociology of Education*, **49**, 59–65.

Livingston, E. (1986), *The Ethnomethodological Foundations of Mathematics*, London: Routledge and Kegan Paul.

Lynch, M. (1991), 'Method: measurement – ordinary and scientific measurement as ethnomethodological phenomena', in G. Button (ed.), *Ethnomethodology and the Human Sciences*, Cambridge: Cambridge University Press, pp. 227–51.

Lynch, M. (1993), *Scientific Practice and Ordinary Action: Ethnomethodolgy and the Social Studies of Science*, New York: Cambridge University Press.

Lynch, M. and Bogen, D. (1997), *The Spectacle of History: Speech, Text, and Memory at the Iran-Contra Hearings*, Durham, NC and London: Duke University Press.

Lynch, M. and Macbeth, D. (1998), 'Demonstrating physics lessons', in J. Greeno, and S. Goldman (eds), *Thinking Practices: Mathematics and Science Learning*, Palo Alto, CA and Mahwah, NJ: Institute for Research on Learning and Lawrence Erlbaum Associates, pp. 269–98.

Macbeth, D. (2000), 'Classrooms as installations: direct instruction in the early grades', in S. Hester and D. Francis (eds), *Local Educational Order*, Amsterdam: John Benjamins, pp. 21–72.

Mackay, R.W. (1974), 'Conceptions of children and models of socialization', in R. Turner (ed.), *Ethnomethodology*, London: Penguin, pp. 180–93.

Maynard, D.W. (1985), 'On the functions of social conflict among children', *American Sociological Review*, **50**, 207–23.

McHoul, A. (1978), 'The organizations of turns at formal talk in the classroom', *Language in Society*, **7**, 183–213.

McHoul, A. and Watson, D.R. (1982), 'Two axes for the analysis of "commonsense" and "formal" geographical knowledge in the classroom', *British Journal of the Sociology of Education*, **5**, 281–302.

Mehan, H. (1976), 'Assessing children's school performance', in M. Hammersley and P. Woods (eds), *The Process of Schooling*, London: Routledge and Kegan Paul.

Mehan, H. (1979), *Learning Lessons: Social Organization in the Classroom*, Cambridge, MA: Harvard University Press.

Mehan, H., Hetwick, A. and Meihls, J.L. (1986), *Handicapping the Handicapped: Decision Making in Student's Educational Careers*, Stanford, CA: Stanford University Press.

Payne, G. (1976), 'Making a lesson happen', in M. Hammersley and P. Woods (eds), *The Process of Schooling*, London: Routledge and Kegan Paul.

Payne, G.C.F. and Cuff, E.C. (1982), *Doing Teaching: The Practical Management of Classrooms*, London: Batsford Academic.

Payne, G. and Hustler, D. (1980), 'Teaching the class: practical management of a cohort', *British Journal of Sociology of Education*, **1**, 49–66.

Payne, G. and Ridge, E. (1985), 'Let them talk – an alternative approach to language development in the infant school', in E.C. Cuff and G.C.F. Payne (eds), *Crisis in the Curriculum*, London: Croom Helm, pp. 11–32.

Roth, D.R. (1974), 'Intelligence testing as a social activity', in A. Cicourel et al. (eds), *Language Use and School Performance*, New York: Academic Press.

Sacks, H. (1992a), *Lectures on Conversation*, Vol. I. ed. G. Jefferson with introduction by E.A. Shegloff, Oxford: Basil Blackwell.

Sacks, H. (1992b), *Lectures on Conversation*, Vol II, ed. G. Jefferson with introduction by E.A. Shegloff, Oxford: Basil Blackwell.

Sacks, H., Schegloff, E.A. and Jefferson, G. (1974), 'A simplest systematics for the organization of turn-taking for conversation', *Language*, **50**, 696–735.

Speier, M. (1976), 'The child as conversationalist: some culture contact features of conversational interactions between adults and children', in M. Hammersley and P. Woods (eds), *The Process of Schooling*, London: Routledge and Kegan Paul, pp. 98–103.

Speier, M. (1982), 'The everyday world of child', in C. Jenks (ed.), *The Sociology of Childhood: Essential Readings*, Aldershot: Gregg Revivals, pp. 188–218.

34. Analysing narratives: the narrative construction of identity
Cate Watson

The rise of narrative in social and educational research has been led by a widespread recognition of the fundamental importance of narrative to the organization of human experience and our understanding of how lives are lived. Narrative integrates ways of knowing and being and is therefore intimately linked with questions of identity, currently the focus of much interest in social and educational research. The idea that identity is constructed through narrative is widely held. As Hinchman and Hinchman (2001, p. xviii) succinctly put it, 'identity is that which emerges in and through narratives'. Indeed, to the extent that all narratives of personal experience involve the positioning of self in relation to the other, all may be said to be concerned with identity. The aim of this chapter, therefore, is to explore forms of narrative analysis that explicitly relate to the construction and performance of personal and professional identities considered as a narrative endeavour. However, while there may be broad consensus that identity is narratively constructed, there is perhaps less agreement about how this is accomplished or how it should be conceptualized. Tensions around the narrative analysis of identity therefore arise both from contrasting perspectives as to what counts as a narrative and the nature of identity, a concept which has undergone a radical shift in recent years from a unitary and enduring attribute of selfhood, to notions of identities as constructed, multiple and in flux (see Jenkins, 2008). Approaches to analysis turn on both these issues, and are further complicated by different philosophical positions adopted by researchers (for a useful discussion of this, see Smith and Sparkes, 2008a).

WHAT IS A PERSONAL NARRATIVE?

What counts as a personal narrative for analytical purposes? In an influential piece of work Labov and Waletzky (1967[1997]) (see Cortazzi and Jin, Chapter 35, this volume, for an elaboration of this) defined fully formed oral narratives as consisting of:

- an abstract (a summary of what the story is about);
- orientation (setting the scene);
- complicating action (the narrative core – what happened);
- evaluation (the significance of the story to the narrator);
- resolution (how the situation pans out);
- coda (how the narrator moves out of the story-world and back into the here and now).

Narratives of personal experience do not necessarily show all these features. Rather, they occupy a number of what Ochs and Capps (2001) refer to as 'narrative dimensions and possibilities' related to tellership, tellability, embeddedness, linearity and moral stance. The 'default narrative', Ochs and Capps say, tends to 'exhibit a cluster of characteristics that fall at one end of these continua: one active teller, highly tellable account, relatively detached from surrounding talk and activity, linear temporal and causal organization and certain, constant moral stance' (p. 20). Yet not all personal narratives can be characterized in this manner. Ochs and Capps (2001, p. 54) suggest that 'narratives of personal experience cover a range of discourse formats, running from virtuoso verbal performances to more prosaic social exchanges . . . [personal narrative] resists delineation in terms of a set of fixed, generic defining features'. Perhaps a useful starting point is provided by Gubrium and Holstein (1997, p.146) who consider narratives of personal experience to be:

> accounts that offer some scheme, either implicitly or explicitly for organizing and understanding the relation of objects and events described. Narratives need not be full-blown stories with requisite internal structures, but may be short accounts that emerge within or across turns at ordinary conversation, in interviews or interrogations, in public documents, or in organizational records.

While some might argue that such a broad definition of narrative carries the danger of rendering the term meaningless, it could equally be argued that for the social sciences an expansive definition of what counts as narrative confers significant advantages, opening up for analysis a range of verbal utterances and interactions and allowing analytics developed within other disciplines to be brought to bear to generate new insights.

ANALYSIS OF NARRATIVES OR NARRATIVE ANALYSIS?

Polkinghorne (1995) distinguishes between analysis of narratives and narrative analysis each of which, he argues (following Bruner, 1991), depends on different forms of cognition. Analysis of narrative involves 'paradigmatic reasoning' which results in 'descriptions or themes that hold across stories or in taxonomies of types of stories, characters or settings' (Polkinghorne, 1995, p.12). Analysis of narratives therefore starts with narratives and breaks them down into non-narrative form. Conversely, in narrative analysis 'researchers collect descriptions of events and happenings and synthesize or configure them by means of a plot into a story or stories (for example, a history, case study or biographic episode)' (Polkinghorne, 1995, p. 12) (see Tierney and Clemens, Chapter 19, this volume). More recently, Smith and Sparkes (2008b) have produced a typology 'intended to tease and untangle some of the analytical threads and coils that make up the web of narrative analysis' (p. 20) which distinguishes between 'story analysts' and 'storytellers'. Story analysts employ 'analytical procedures, strategies and techniques in order to abstractly scrutinise, explain and think about its certain features'. Story analysts then report these findings as a 'realist tale' in the form of a research paper. For storytellers, on the other hand, 'analysis is the story'. Storytellers use 'creative analytic practices' (Richardson and St Pierre, 2005), which might include fictional forms of writing, ethnodrama, autoethnography, poetry and so on to analyse and represent the findings of their research. In practice, there may be considerable blurring between what story analysts and storytellers do. Perhaps the key aspect that separates Polkinghorne from Smith and Sparkes is the acknowledgement by the latter that in both the analysis of narratives and narrative analysis what is produced is another narrative – and this highlights one of the complicating aspects of narrative research in that narrative is both the phenomenon or process being studied and the methodological approach adopted for analysis (and furthermore the means of representation of the research findings) – to paraphrase a well-known expression, it's narratives all the way down.

EXPLORING THE NARRATIVE CONSTRUCTION OF IDENTITY

From all this it will be readily appreciated that analysing narratives is a complex practice for which no definitive guidance can be given. This freedom can be discomfiting, and not just for the beginning researcher. When first confronted with, for example, a lengthy recording or transcript of an interview it is a fairly common experience to wonder what on earth to actually do with it. A first reading may not reveal anything of interest – you begin to wonder if it can be analysed as narrative at all. Gradually, as you become immersed in the data meanings emerge, an analytical approach suggests itself and takes you forward. But this is not to say that a narrative contains one meaning or can be subject to a 'correct' reading. Narrative analysis is about interpretation – as much about the construction of a persuasive narrative for your readers as the one you set out to analyse. When approaching narrative data then what is required is not slavish adherence to a rubric but an open, yet attentive approach, sensitive to nuance, which is nonetheless informed by a number of principles. First and foremost of these perhaps is the key point that narratives should not be regarded as providing unmediated access to 'reality'. Narratives are artful constructions and analysis must be concerned with both the content of the narrative and the form of its construction. For the narrative scholar, Riessman and Quinney (2005, p. 393) write, there must be

> attention to how the facts got assembled that way. For whom was this story constructed, how was it made, and for what purpose? What cultural resources does it draw on – take for granted? What does it accomplish? Are there gaps and inconsistencies that might suggest alternative counter-narratives?

This focus on the form and function of narrative is a key factor separating narrative research from other forms of qualitative inquiry such as grounded theory. Analysing narratives is not about decontextualizing data but about treating the narrative as a (more or less) coherent whole.

Riessman (1997, p.157) talks about the 'tyranny' of narrative arguing that 'the term has come to mean anything and everything'. But there is another sense in which we can talk about the tyranny of narrative. In some quarters, narrative has become almost revered as an empowering practice that can be used by the weak against the strong (the genre of narrative writing known as 'testimonio' is predicated on this idea, for example, see Beverley, 2005). While there is no doubt that narratives do have the power to subvert social norms, there is another side to narrative. A darker side. Narrative can equally be viewed as a form of violence done to experience, 'by constructing narratives we not only ultimately erase part of our lived experience but also impose a particular way of thinking about experience' (Hendry, 2007, p. 491). In this view narration is an ideological process, and this is so both for the research participant, whose narratives of personal experience we are keen to exploit, but also for the research narratives that we construct in response. As Currie (1998) says, we learn to narrate from the outside. Narratives teach us how to conceive of ourselves and it is important to remain reflexively alert to this while conducting analyses in order to be aware of the socio-cultural constraints within which narration occurs.

Neither should we assume that in eliciting narratives from our research participants, for example, in the narrative research interview, that we are going to arrive at shared understandings. Scheurich (1995, p. 243) warns that:

> Interview interactions do not have some essential, teleological tendency toward an ideal of 'joint construction of meaning' . . . Instead, interactions and meanings are a shifting carnival of ambiguous complexity, a moving feast of differences interrupting differences.

Easy assumptions of empathy with our research participants are equally to be avoided as both complacent in research terms and, in the lack of acknowledgement of difference between ourselves and our research participants, unethical in practice (Watson, 2009a). Indeed, it is often in the acknowledgement of difference, the gap between ourselves and our participants, that analysis gains a purchase. We may be engaged in 'co-construction' of the narrative, but this does not necessarily imply shared meanings.

THREE APPROACHES TO ANALYSING NARRATIVES OF IDENTITY

To give an idea of the range of possible approaches to analysis I now give three examples illustrating the different ways in which narratives can be elicited and what can be done with them. Space precludes a lengthy discussion of the decisions regarding transcription, though it must be understood that this stage is a vital part of the analysis. Edward Mishler's (1991) paper remains a classic in this regard and Lapadat (2000) and Riessman (2008) also present useful discussions.

Teachers' Professional Identities: A 'Big' Story

My first example is drawn from a semi-structured interview, lasting some three hours, with an experienced teacher, who I referred to as Dan, the purpose of which was to elicit narratives of practice in order to analyse dimensions of personal and professional identity (Watson, 2006a). The overarching question the research aimed to answer was: who am I as a teacher and how did I get that way? The analysis focused on sections of the transcript which, though they did not necessarily conform entirely to 'fully formed' stories as defined by Labov and Waletzky (1967[1997]), were nonetheless bounded and 'story-like', that is, told of something that happened and made a point in relation to Dan's practice. The analysis was concerned both with the content of the stories and their construction in order to show how they contributed to Dan's 'identity work'. They were not analysed therefore as representing some 'reality' in the sense that they necessarily tell what 'really happened' (this has been an enduring, though misguided, criticism of narrative research considered from a positivist viewpoint). Rather they have to be analysed as narratives that Dan draws on to position himself, other staff and his pupils, within a framework of institutional and wider educational and social discourses.

While transcribing the interview I listened to Dan's voice, over and over until I could hear his voice in my head when I read the transcript. Developing this level of familiarity with the data is for me an essential part of this kind of analysis, though it is undeniably time-consuming. I also sent him the transcript, though this raises some important methodological and ethical issues. For example, if you do this, do you 'clean up' the transcript removing the ums, ers and 'dialect respellings' that can seem patronising and offend the interviewee? (Preston (1985) refers to this as 'Li'l Abner syndrome'.) You need also to be clear about your attitude to changes – do you allow the participant to go beyond checking for accuracy of transcription? Your answers to these kinds of questions will depend on a number of factors including the aim of your research, your relationship with the participant/s, their role in the research and so on. (Gready (2008) discusses the methodological and ethical issues associated with 'ownership' of narratives.)

One theme that emerged very strongly from the interview with Dan was how he positioned himself as different to the other teachers. In the biographical information he provided (and which formed the basis for another paper, see Watson, 2009b), it seemed clear that he grounded these claims of difference in his early childhood experiences of school failure which he narratively constructed as providing a motive for becoming a teacher, that is, to give his pupils a better experience than he had himself. This is an example of the way in which we learn, to read time backwards, rewriting our narratives to make sense of the present (Ricœur, 1981).

A number of the stories I identified in the transcript related to this positioning of self as different and as subversive within the system. For example,

Orientation:	Aye then, unorthodox methods of discipline
Abstract:	A boy at the door
	(the one that I was telling you about
	that was involved with this attempted murder)
	and he's a bit of a hard nut y'know
Complicating action:	and he's at the door, blethering to someone else
	and not going into the classroom
	and blocking the room

	and I **do** things that I'm not supposed to,
	and I said 'Sit down or I'll kiss you'
	You've never seen a pupil head for his seat . . .
Evaluation:	It was funny, y'know.

This is the form in which the story is presented in the paper. It conforms quite well to the fully formed story of Labov and Waletzky (I have indicated the constituent parts here, though others may not agree with the designations I have given). The transcription was intended to be quite naturalistic, bringing out the rhythm of the story by emphasizing the repetition but looking back, I wonder at some of the decisions I came to. I drew on this story in another paper and transcribed it rather differently, presenting it as a poem of three stanzas (Watson, 2006b).

As I wrote in the paper, this story shows the construction and performance of identity in the material practices of teacher and taught. It deals with the management and control of clearly, a very deviant pupil (itself a defining aspect of teacher professional identity) and indicates the 'unorthodox' methods through which Dan positions himself as subversive. Overall, the stories analysed gave an insight into how Dan constructed himself as a teacher in and through his narratives of practice.

What is presented in this paper can be considered, in Bamberg's terms, to be the analysis of a 'big story'.

> 'Big Stories' are typically stories that are elicited in interview situations, either for the purpose to create research data or to do therapy – stories in which speakers are asked to retrospect on particular life-determining episodes or on their lives as a whole, and tie together events into episodes and episodes into a life story, so that something like 'a life' can come 'to existence'. (Bamberg, 2006, p. 64)

The formal interview situation encouraged a retrospective reflection on Dan's teaching career, and although in places there are clear moments of co-construction of dialogue in the interview, it seems reasonable to assume that many of the 'stories' have been rehearsed and polished – the 'unorthodox methods of discipline' story has probably been told many times. In addition, the autobiographical elements conform to certain cultural storylines – the storying of self as 'wanting to give pupils a better experience' is a fairly common one among teachers. It is a variant of the 'redemption narrative' in which, through suffering something better emerges, and through which something is given back to society, a potent narrative in Western culture (McAdams, 2005).

To a certain extent, the traditional semi-structured interview encourages this kind of response. There are few other social situations when people get to tell long stories without interruption. A completely different kind of narrative emerges from a more conversational interaction, as my second example indicates.

Developing Professional Competence – A 'Small Story'   DBStories?

This analysis draws on what might be termed a vicarious interview between two student teachers – who I called Andrea and Jim – about their recent school experience placement (see Watson, 2007). This was part of a study of the development of professional identities in beginning teachers. These two students were part of a larger cohort I recruited and interviewed as a group several times over the course of their one-year teaching diploma. However, on this particular occasion only Andrea and Jim were able to come along – and due to another engagement I couldn't be there either. They agreed to have a conversation around a few starter questions I gave them and to record it. (Although I wasn't present, it would be a mistake to assume that the participants were unaware of my vicarious presence and the likely influence this had – see Currie and Kelly, Chapter 29, this volume, and the 'speaker's intended audience'). The analysis centres on what Bamberg (2006, p. 71) refers to as a 'small story'. Small stories are

> most often about very mundane things and everyday occurrences, often even not particularly interesting or tellable; stories that seem to pop up, not necessarily even recognized as stories, and quickly forgotten; nothing permanent or of particular importance – so it seems.

In this example, the story is told by Andrea about a teacher at the school in which she had completed her second placement. Andrea refers to this teacher as 'a youngster' and the focus of the story is this teacher's inability to control his classes, even the 'Higher' class (in Scotland 'Highers' are the most advanced exams taken in secondary schools).

Part of the transcript is reproduced here to indicate what I mean by a 'small story' and to show the co-construction of the narrative (in this transcription I have removed a lot of the ums and erms and added conventional punctuation to render the transcript more readable):

A: . . .There was also a youngster who I imagine he'd done a maths degree but I imagine he'd gone into teaching straight after, but he
J: or like a lot of people on our course where they've done one or two years
A: doing something
J: doing [A: yeah] little things.
A: Well trouble is, well trouble is, he had got himself into a right state. He only lasted two weeks after I got there. I was taking his Higher class

but he was very, very tired all the time, and he left after those two weeks, got himself signed off two weeks, got himself signed off for another two weeks and now he's signed off for another eight weeks. His Higher class [laughing] are of the opinion that he's having a nervous breakdown and I think probably, y'know could well be the case.

J: Is he newly qualified or what?

A: I wasn't, well I dunno, I think this was his first Higher class so he's maybe been teaching a couple of years [J: uh huh] but I mean he's a young-ster, but he was just very, very stressed about everything even taking the Higher class and the Higher class were a nice group of kids y'know

J: If you can get the maths sorted in your head then teaching a Higher class is

A: is no bother, I mean I didn't have any problems with them and I

J: it's not like teaching 5th year Intermediate 2

A: [part of transcript deleted] and they never really gave me any prob-lems whatsoever. If I asked them y'know to be quiet they generally were, y'know no nonsense whatsoever, but y'know he was very frenetic and I think some of the problem is some of the bottom sets are horrendous to have to deal with. It's quite aggressive in the classroom, y'know I met his 4th year and they were dire y'know [part of transcript deleted]

Bamberg (for example, Bamberg, 2003, 2004a, 2004b; Bamberg and Georgakopoulou, 2008) has developed 'positioning analysis' as a means to analyse these small stories produced through talk-in-interaction. The approach draws on Davies and Harré's (1990) notion of 'positioning' which they define as 'the discursive process whereby selves are located in conversations as observably and subjectively coherent participants in jointly produced story-lines' (Davies and Harré, 1990, p. 48).

Positioning analysis operates at three levels, which move progres-sively from the localized context of the talk to broader socio-cultural levels of discourse, to analyse the identity claims made by participants in conversation. Briefly, Level 1 positioning analyses how the characters are established within the story and answers the questions: 'What is this story about?' and 'Who are the characters and why are they positioned this way?' Level 2 examines the question of what the narrator is trying to accomplish with the story, the narrative strategies and the interactional effects: 'Why is it told this way?' 'Why here and why now?' While Level 3 draws together the analysis to provide an answer to the question: 'Who am I vis-à-vis what society says I should be?' A claim which can transcend the current local context. By doing this, Bamberg (2004b, p. 367) argues, 'we are better situated to make assumptions about the ideological master narratives within which the speakers are positioning a sense of self', that is, the approach assumes an agentive positioning of self within discourse, while recognizing that such agency arises within the discursive framework in which subjects are positioned.

My analysis looked at the way Andrea, as narrator, used the story about 'the youngster' to make claims for her own developing professional identity. In effect, Andrea constructs and performs her own identity through this 'small story', an ephemeral, conversational story produced jointly with Jim. Through this story Andrea and Jim are able to make claims for their own developing competence as teachers in three areas key to a teacher's professional identity: pedagogical expertise, subject expertise and discipline. The transcript can be analysed as Jim and Andrea 'doing' identity, constructing themselves as competent teachers through their interactional talk. In addition, the language used by them can be analysed in terms of how they are enculturated into the profession, for example, in the language that equates ability with niceness ('the Higher class were a nice group of kids') and lack of ability with deviance ('bottom sets are horrendous to have to deal with'). Ability therefore becomes an issue of morality in schools. Positioning analysis can therefore link talk-in-interaction with wider socio-cultural discourses.

Positioning analysis has been criticized for placing too much emphasis on these ephemeral narratives, in effect making them do too much in terms of identity. Thorne (2004) and Hall (2004) both question the relevance to identity of jointly produced small storylines. While to some extent Bamberg and his critics seem to approach the question of significance in relation to identity from two distinct theoretical groundings which may render the meanings they attach to these ideas incommensurable, nonetheless, it is pertinent to question not only the significance of these locally produced identities, but within the context of an ephemeral and jointly constructed narrative, the salience for whom. In response to this Bell (2009) has introduced the concept of the 'middle story' operating between the autobiographical account and the conversational remark which focuses on the recent past and acts as a bridge, drawing together meanings taken from small stories and starting a process of reflective synthesis. My own analysis, though it focused on a single story co-constructed by Jim and Andrea, was informed by interviews conducted over the course of a year and I was therefore in a better position to judge the salience of the identities produced in this single exchange.

Being a Storyteller – Developing Fictional Narratives

My final example is, in Smith and Sparkes's (2008b) terms, in storyteller mode. The research concerned the construction and performance of professional identities of teachers and members of staff of an agency offering therapeutic support services located within schools (Watson, 2012). The aim of the research was to examine interagency/interprofessional working in schools through a narrative analysis of identities mobilized by staff within the two organizations. Unlike the previous examples, in this instance the analysis was presented as a fictionalized 'case study' of interprofessional working in a school. For this, I drew very closely on the dialogue actually spoken by the interviewees (though in some cases this was altered to provide greater anonymity), but their words were condensed and juxtaposed so as to highlight particular aspects of the performance of identity and the 'individuals' presented were all fictional characters, amalgamations of the actual interviewees. This approach did not aim at the transparent representation of data (itself a fiction) but at its re-presentation in such a way as to create 'narrative truths'. Clough (2002), defending such fictionalizations in educational research says, 'as a means of educational report, stories can provide a means by which those truths, which cannot be otherwise told, are uncovered' (p. 8). Fictionalizations confer anonymity as well as offering researchers 'the opportunity to import fragments of data from various real events in order to speak to the heart of social consciousness' (p. 8). In this paper however a key aim of the representation was to construct a satirical narrative as a means to highlight the ways in which, within the ambiguous embrace of the organization, teachers, other professionals and their respective managers construct and mobilize their identities.

What emerged very clearly from the interviews was how members of both organizations positioned themselves in relation to the other. Thus, while ostensibly praising the work carried out by the therapeutic support agency, the teachers signalled their own professional commitment by highlighting the 'part-time' nature of the support workers, as in this extract:

Interviewer: So how helpful have you found the support being offered?
Teacher 1: It's great. Having the support workers here has just become part of the whole structure of the day, well, not the day exactly, because they are not here every day.

Similarly, the support workers constructed their own concerns with the 'whole child' by positioning the teachers as only interested in the child's behaviour and academic achievement:

Support Worker 1: One of the challenges is working in a therapeutic way within an educational setting because there are two obviously really different aims going on. And it needn't be a conflict, I mean because in these schools they are very kind of open to us and they are really kind of welcoming about it but nevertheless we have got a completely different goal. It's not about good behaviour you know and then going back to the classroom where it's very much about being good and doing things right and achieving. So there is a real conflict.

What also emerged from the interviews was the way in which the tensions and frustrations of the teachers and support workers were smoothed over by senior management, and how the systems and structures imposed by the organizations contributed to the difficulties experienced by both groups of staff. The fictional narrative aimed to represent this state of affairs and to bring it out by means of satire. The 'case study' presented *was* the analysis, with no further interpretation added. Sparkes (1997, p. 33) says, of such fictional narratives, 'The end result is a powerful story that has the potential to provoke multiple interpretations and responses from readers who differ in their positioning to the story provided.'

For some, fictionalization of research data is a step too far raising difficult questions around notions of validity (see, for example, Bridges, 2003). However, Barone (2007, p. 466) defends the practice arguing that 'our aim as researcher-storytellers is not to seek certainty about correct perspectives on educational phenomena but to raise significant questions about prevailing policy and practice that enrich an ongoing conversation'. Eisner (1997) too argues that such alternative forms of representation serve as a means to 'enlarge understanding' and that this is a legitimate aim of research. (See Watson (2011) for a discussion of the use of fiction in social and educational research.)

CONCLUSION

The three analyses presented in this chapter draw on narrative in very different ways. In the first two examples my role was as a 'story analyst', in the first case looking at an individual's account of their practice; in the second examining the conversational talk between two beginning teachers. In the final example I adopt the 'storyteller' stance, crafting a narrative from interview data.

What I have presented is by no means intended to be exhaustive, rather I have tried to indicate the possibilities provided by narrative in research on identities. While each is very different a common thread emerges. Notable across the three stories I tell is the positioning of self in relation to the other. In effect, we narratively construct the other and through this construction we establish claims for our own identities. We do this whether we draw on events from the distant past or more recently, and whether we are being asked to reflect on our lives as a whole or whether we are 'doing identity' in our mundane and everyday conversations.

By presenting these different analyses I hope to have opened up a dialogue around the possibilities presented by narrative as a means to research identities. It has often been said that we are as a species '*Homo fabulans*', the teller of stories, it is part of our cognitive repertoire. But we are not just the tellers of narratives, rather we are, as Currie (1998, p. 2) says, 'interpreters' of narrative too, looking for meanings and endlessly generating our own research narratives in response to those told us by our participants. In conclusion, the turn to narrative provides us with a rich and creative resource which has transformed, and will continue to transform, the research landscape.

REFERENCES

Bamberg, M. (2003), 'Positioning with Davie Hogan. Stories, tellings and identities', in C. Daiute (ed.), *Narrative analysis: Studying the Development of Individuals in Society*, London: Sage, pp. 135–57.
Bamberg, M. (2004a), 'Narrative, discourse and identities', in J.C. Meister (ed.), *Narratology Beyond Literary Criticism*, Berlin and New York: Walter de Gruyter, pp. 213–37.
Bamberg, M. (2004b), 'We are young, responsible and male. Form and function of "slut-bashing" in the identity constructions in 15-year-old males', *Human Development*, **47** (6), 331–53.
Bamberg, M. (2006), 'Biographic-narrative research, *quo vadis*. A critical review of "big stories" from the perspective of "small stories"', in K. Milnes, C. Horrocks, N. Kelly, B. Roberts and D. Robinson (eds), *Narrative, Memory and Knowledge: Representations, Aesthetics and Contexts,* Huddersfield: University of Huddersfield Press, pp. 63–79.
Bamberg, M. and Georgakopoulou, A. (2008), 'Small stories as a new perspective in narrative and identity analysis', *Text and Talk*, **28** (3), 377–96.
Barone, T. (2007), 'A return to the gold standard? Questioning the future of narrative construction as educational research', *Qualitative Inquiry*, **13** (4), 454–70.
Bell, N.J. (2009), 'Making connections: considering the dynamics of narrative stability from a relational approach', *Narrative Inquiry*, **19** (2), 280–305.
Beverley, J. (2005), 'Testimonio, subalternity, and narrative authority', in N. Denzin and Y. Lincoln (eds), *Handbook of Qualitative Research*, 3rd edn, London: Sage, pp. 547–58.
Bridges, D. (2003), *Fiction Written Under Oath?: Essays in Philosophy and Educational Research*, Dordrecht: Springer.
Bruner, J. (1991), 'The narrative construction of reality', *Critical Inquiry*, **18** (1), 1–21.
Clough, P. (2002), *Narratives and Fictions in Educational Research*, Milton Keynes: Open University Press.
Currie, M. (1998), *Postmodern Narrative Theory*, London: Macmillan Press.
Davies, B. and Harré, R. (1990), 'Positioning: the discursive production of selves', *Journal for the Theory of Social Behaviour*, **20** (1), 43–63.
Eisner, E.W. (1997), 'The promise and perils of alternative forms of data representation', *Educational Researcher*, **26**(6), 4–10.
Gready, P. (2008), 'The public life of narratives: ethics, politics, methods', in M. Andrews, C. Squires and M. Tamboukou (eds), *Doing Narrative Research*, London: Sage, pp. 137–50.
Gubrium, J.F. and Holstein, J.A. (1997), *The New Language of Qualitative Method*, Oxford: Oxford University Press.
Hall, R. (2004), 'Attaching self and others to social categories as an interactional and historical achievement', *Human Development*, **47** (6), 354–60.
Hendry, P.M. (2007), 'The future of narrative', *Qualitative Inquiry*, **13** (4), 487–98.

Hinchman, L. and Hinchman, S. (eds) (2001), *Memory, Identity, Community. The Idea of Narrativity in the Human Sciences*, New York: New York University Press.

Jenkins, R. (2008), *Social Identity*, Abingdon: Taylor & Francis.

Labov, W. and Waletzky, J. ([1967]1997), 'Narrative analysis: oral versions of personal experience', *Journal of Narrative and Life History*, **7** (1–4), 3–38.

Lapadat, J.C. (2000), 'Problematizing transcription: purpose, paradigm and quality', *International Journal of Social Research Methodology*, **3** (3), 203–19.

McAdams, D.P. (2005), *Redemptive Self: Stories Americans Live By*, Oxford: Oxford University Press.

Mishler, E. (1991), 'Representing discourse: the rhetoric of transcription', *Journal of Narrative and Life History*, **1** (4), 255–80.

Ochs, E. and Capps, L. (2001), *Living Narrative*, Cambridge, MA: Harvard University Press.

Polkinghorne, D.E. (1995), 'Narrative configuration in qualitative analysis', in J.A. Hatch (ed.), *Life History and Narrative*, London: Falmer Press, pp. 5–23.

Preston, D.R. (1985), 'The Li'l Abner syndrome: written representations of speech', *American Speech*, **60** (4), 328–36.

Richardson, B. (2000), 'Recent concepts of narrative and narratives of narrative theory', *Style,* **34** (2), 168–75.

Richardson, L. and St Pierre, E. (2005), 'Writing: a method of inquiry', in N.K. Denzin (ed.), *Handbook of Qualitative Research*, 3rd edn, London: Sage pp. 959–78.

Ricœur, P. (1981), 'Narrative time', in W.J.T. Mitchell (ed.), *On Narrative*, Chicago, IL: University of Chicago Press, pp. 165–86.

Riessman, C. (1997), 'A short story about long stories', *Journal of Narrative and Life History*, **7** (1–4), 155–58.

Riessman, C. (2008), *Narrative Methods for the Human Sciences*, London: Sage.

Riessman, C.K. and Quinney, L. (2005), 'Narrative in social work: a critical review', *Qualitative Social Work*, **4** (4), 391–412.

Scheurich, J. (1995), 'A postmodernist critique of research interviewing', *Qualitative Studies in Education*, **8** (3), 239–52.

Smith, B. and Sparkes, A.C. (2008a), 'Contrasting perspectives on narrating selves and identities: an invitation to dialogue', *Qualitative Research*, **8** (1), 5–35.

Smith, B. and Sparkes, A.C. (2008b), 'Narrative and its potential contribution to disability studies', *Disability & Society*, **23** (1), 17–28.

Sparkes, A.C. (1997), 'Ethnographic fiction and representing the absent other', *Sport, Education and Society*, **2** (1), 25–40.

Thorne, A. (2004), 'Putting the person into social identity', *Human Development*, **47** (6), 361–65.

Watson, C. (2006a), 'Narratives of practice and the construction of identity in teaching', *Teachers and Teaching. Theory and Practice*, **12** (5), 509–26.

Watson, C. (2006b), 'Encounters and directions in research. Pages from a Simulacrum journal', *Qualitative Inquiry* **12** (5), 865–85.

Watson, C. (2007), '"Small stories", positioning analysis, and the doing of professional identities in learning to teach', *Narrative Inquiry*, **17** (2), 371–89.

Watson, C. (2009a), '"The impossible vanity": uses and abuses of empathy in qualitative inquiry', *Qualitative Research*, **9** (1), 105–17.

Watson, C. (2009b), '"Teachers are meant to be orthodox": narrative and counter narrative in the discursive construction of "identity" in teaching', *International Journal of Qualitative Studies in Education*, **22** (4), 469–83.

Watson, C. (2011), 'Staking a small claim for fictional narratives in social and educational research', *Qualitative Research,* **11** (4), 395–408.

Watson, C. (2012), 'The pretty story of joined-up working. Questioning interagency partnership', in J. Forbes and C. Watson (eds), *The Transformation of Children's Services. Examining and Debating the Complexities of Inter/professional Working*, London: Routledge.

35. Approaching narrative analysis with 19 questions
Martin Cortazzi and Lixian Jin

Qualitative researchers have research questions which are developing as their research proceeds: this is also true as we proceed through phases in applying methods. Two simple, but often profound and recurrent questions for analysing narratives are: What is the nature of the data? What is the nature of this kind of research? Behind these, a researcher immersed in data analysis can keep some equilibrium by holding other questions continually in mind: What questions are you asking? Why are they worthwhile? What answers do you have? Why are these worthwhile?

This chapter is organized around 19 narrative questions, particularly questions about stories, recounts and accounts in education given as oral versions of personal experience, shared by teachers and students in relation to learning. This focus on particular ways of learning in education could be termed 'narrative learning' (Cortazzi et al., 2001; Trahar, 2006; Goodson et al., 2010). Questions 1–4 relate to the context of narrating, questions 5–12 focus on narratives themselves and analysis, and questions 13–19 focus on wider evaluations in narrative-based research. The point about these questions is to go beyond a content analysis. Similar questions should apply to other varieties of educational narratives: stories of institutional or curriculum development, of management or professionalism, and to narrative texts such as written entries in journals and learning diaries, or multimodal and visual narratives in the form of drawings, photos or film (Kalaja et al., 2008) or to children's narrative (McCabe and Peterson, 1991; Bamberg, 1997a; Minami, 2002). Parallel questions relate to the surprisingly large range of models of narrative analysis available (Cortazzi, 1993; Mishler, 1995) and to wider approaches of narrative inquiry (Clandinin, 2007) and can complement other chapters here (notably Chapters 19, 20, 21 and 34, and also Chapter 22 and 31).

 There is no single method of narrative analysis: some focus on the meaning, others on the structure and yet others on social interaction and the context, but we can combine elements of any of these or choose a method that suits our own particular research purposes, the kind of narratives in hand and a preferred style of qualitative research. Working through questions such as these is one way to generalize in the attempt to overcome a dilemma. This dilemma is that narrative data in educational research are so often specific to participants, contexts, institutions and occasions – and with an investment of the person and the humane, which is why they are narratives rather than reports or descriptions of events – that the relevance of a particular analysis to another kind of narrative may not be apparent. However, questions can generally frame other narrative research. Questioning is transferable, adaptable, a long-lasting skill, which is why many research supervisors ask newer researchers questions in supervisory discussions: novices expect answers, while the veteran knows that research is all about asking the right kinds of questions, the answers to which often yield further questions.

QUESTIONS ABOUT THE SOCIAL, INTERACTIVE AND CONTEXTUAL FRAMING OF NARRATIVES

For instance, an oral story shared in a research interview might be taken, in analysis, as evidence of what is being investigated and it might be treated as a fixed or frozen piece of content; however, in working with the transcription on page or screen it is worth recalling that for the teller the interview was an event, perhaps a welcome (or annoying) interruption of teaching and learning, that the story was probably part of an answer to a question; the fashioning of that answer was probably steered by previous questions-and-answers and by what the respondent thought the purpose of the interview was – the stated purpose may not be what the respondent came to feel was the underlying purpose. The events and meanings of the story would almost certainly be differently selected and expressed in other speech events like a casual conversation or a piece of gossip, as part of a formal lecture presentation or part of a classroom task or staff development activity, a snatched discussion at a parents' evening, or a segment of family conversation about school.

All this suggests an immense variability in the verbal packaging of narrative data and sometimes their transience as presented accounts. We need to ask:

1.   What is the occasion of the narrative?

We need to know what sort of speech event it is for the speaker to tell this story at the time (formal, casual, unfamiliar or routine?) and how important or meaningful it is. Different tellers give different kinds of narratives, not just in content but in manner, style, genre and presentation, so an analyst needs to ask:

2.   *Who is the teller?*

This could refer to obvious features, such as age, gender, ethnicity, rank, status and role. It could also refer to less easily specifiable aspects, like identity and self-image, which will be presented, and over time constructed, through narrative (see Watson, Chapter 34, this volume). It is worth noticing that some stories have more than one teller when an account is jointly constructed between people who shared an experience and recall it together (say, as a collective memory, celebration or commiseration). In such cases, parts of the story are spread across speakers who collaboratively tell it, often correcting or expanding what earlier speakers said (Ochs and Capps, 2001).This can happen in social gatherings, staffrooms and teachers' offices, among groups of children and students, and in focus groups (see Chapter 29, this volume). A researcher can inadvertently find that this is happening in a series of interviews, when different respondents give narratives about the same event from different points of view – this becomes useful confirmation and validation, but it may be problematic to sort out the differing perspectives.

3.   *Who is the audience?*

Are listeners seen by tellers as strangers, colleagues, friends, peers, children, senior adults or 'researchers'? Any oral story of personal experience is likely to be told differently to another audience, which raises another question:

4.   *What is the relationship between the teller and audience?*

This is not necessarily straightforward: it may change because the very act of telling a particular story adds to whatever relation already exists and is then part of an ongoing context and a developing interaction. Oral narratives are constituted in talk and social contexts, but once told they contribute to, and help to construct, subsequent interaction. Second, or later, stories are different from earlier ones for this reason. A later story on the same topic is often intended to surpass or 'cap' the previous one and elicit greater audience reaction.

For interviewers, while we are listening to a narrative being told it is worth observing how audience eye contact, facial expressions and body language, brief feedback remarks of interest, and markers of emotion (surprise reactions, exclamations and expressions of empathy) shape the length and manner of telling: in this way an active audience is part of the telling. Some narratives are jointly negotiated with interviewers; participants ask for feedback ('Is this the kind of thing you want?' or 'Is that any use?') as interviewees pay close attention to audience responses to glean clues for how to tell forthcoming stories. This can matter for analysis when a researcher hearing a recording suddenly realizes how an interviewer has built on these incidental contributions – the story is actually a joint construction and should probably be analysed as such (see Chapter 20).

A more complex context-related related question is:

5.   *What is the function of the story?*

To answer this in relation to particular narrative data we need to examine the story closely but we also need to pay close attention to what was going on in preceding and subsequent talk. Inspection of preceding talk may indicate how a particular story is intended as an illustration, some evidence, a demonstration of professional competence, a critical event or a landmark in identity formation, a positive piece of projected self-imagery or perhaps as an implied criticism or counter-argument. This function might be lost if the analyst extracts the story from the surrounding linguistic context. The analyst needs to consider that many teachers' and learners' stories have more than one function and, thus, a range of meanings which may include cognitive, affective, socio-cultural and personal symbolic meanings besides moral or allegorical overtones, and these can vary across cultures.

Interactively, stories control talk since once begun they are difficult to interrupt without seeming impolite or aggressive. As longer turns in talk, stories help speakers to hold the floor. They give temporary conversational power: this can be seen in committee and staff meetings. Many stories in education, irrespective of content, have entertainment and dramatic functions of highlighting learning events to show personal involvement and the human interest of relationships, the enthusiasm and struggle, the sense of frustration or tragedy, the humour and fun of teaching and learning. This means that educational narratives in the telling are often performed – a point lost in a basic content analysis. Teachers, especially, show the drama of their work in the way they share narratives as well as in the substance of stories. They readily imitate children's, student's or colleague's voices as they re-enact conversations with key quotes, mimetic gestures, whispers and mock voices using juvenile ranges of pitch and intonation patterns (Cortazzi, 1991, 1993). Analytically, entertainment and performance functions overlap with other representations of classroom reality.

Further key questions are:

6.   *Why did the teller tell this narrative just then?*

7.   *What is the relationship between the teller and the story?*

Is the teller a 'neutral' or partial observer (as in a third person narrative, grammatically featuring 'he', 'she' 'they'), a protagonist (as in a first
person narrative, 'I' or 'we'), a relayer or animator of a known story, a
ventriloquist speaking with another's voice (like taking roles in drama), a
representative of others' voices (a spokesperson speaking on their behalf,
with a team or community voice) or a combination of these? For some
narrative analysts, a main reason for their research is to allow space for
voices which might otherwise be peripheral (Hymes, 1996; Cortazzi, 2001)
(see Chapter 20). This implies another question:

8.   *What is the point of view in the narrative?*

INSIDE THE NARRATIVE

A prime question when we examine a narrative must be:

9.   *What does the story mean?*

A good entry point is to start with the kind of narrative structure exemplified by Labov and others, which pays special attention to the evaluation
– or rhetorical underlining of the meaning – by the speaker (Labov and
Waletsky, 1967; Labov, 1972; Bamberg, 1997b; Schegloff, 2003). In this
model there are five main structures, each of which has functions which
can generally be identified by asking questions (Table 35.1).

This model, particularly the ideas about evaluation, has been systematically applied to primary teachers' narratives in Britain (Cortazzi,
1991) and, with other models, to narratives in different cultural and international contexts of education (Trahar, 2006). The evaluation can be
shown linguistically in many ways. These ways include evaluation 'in' the
narrative (within the internal structure, as above), 'of' the narrative (when
a speaker explicates narrative meaning separately after the story itself is
finished) or 'through' the narrative (when the story itself is supposed to
lead the hearer to implied meanings held between or beyond the lines)
(Cortazzi and Jin, 2000). Evaluation is realized differently across cultures
and might well be missed by outsiders but may be brought out by a stanza
analysis of narratives (Scollon and Scollon, 1981; Hymes, 1996; Gee, 2005)
in which the story is laid out in tone units of intonation to preserve speech
rhythms, and these units are grouped in sets of lines (stanzas) devoted to a
single topic, event or image.

Table 35.1   Narrative structural elements, their functions and identifying questions

Narrative Structural Elements	Narrative Content	Identifying Questions
Abstract	This summarizes a story in advance and is an optional element which states a general proposition or point which the following story will illustrate. In a longer story this may indicate the meaning.	*What was this about?*
Orientation	It gives details of the time, persons, place or situation of the characters. Such background information may come at different points in the story, especially if there are changes of location or character.	*Who? When? What? Where?*
Complication	This gives the main event sequence and shows a crisis, problem or turning point, which later parts of the story will remedy or change. It suggests tension in a plot.	*Then what happened?*
Evaluation	This section may be dispersed here and there in a story and may overlay other sections. It shows listeners or readers how to understand the meaning; it reveals the teller's attitude by emphasizing parts of the story. Arguably this is the most interesting part and most important part for researchers. Evaluation can be signalled by the voice (by a different pitch, intonation, pausing and tone of voice) or grammar (with different syntax, repetition or exclamations for emphasis).	*So, what is the point?* Or, simply: *So what?*
Resolution/Result	This shows the resolution to the complication, but it may be followed by another complication which in turn leads to another resolution in a cycle.	*What finally happened?* Or *How did it all turn out?*
Coda	A short optional section which simply brings listeners to the end and returns conversation to normal talk.	

EXAMPLES OF ANALYSING NARRATIVES

Some examples show how this kind of analysis may work, using a coding A, O, C, R, E, Coda. It should be noted that these categories generally occur in more complex sequences and cycles (Complications and Resolutions often form mini-cycles and Evaluations can overlap other parts in layers), but that an analyst who has understood the basis of how they work can usually find the structure and the teller's point using a method that others can follow and reproduce. Identifying narrative episodes or cycles can help analysts to answer further important questions:

10.   *How can chronology, causation and explanation be analysed in stories?*

Example 1: Learning Different Ways of Learning

Here, a Malaysian parent/teacher talks about her son's experience in British and Malaysian primary schools; the narrating implicates the teller's identity and that of her child, whose identity is challenged.

> Malaysian students do not ask questions in class. [A]
> It's probably because they respect the teacher, the teacher as a guru,
> but they do ask after the class,
> you know, by going up to the teacher after the lesson.
> My son [aged eight at the time] was in Scotland for nine months [O]
> and during that time he learned to speak up in class, ask questions and all that,
> but when we came home to Malaysia there was a real problem for about six months. [C]
> He wanted to talk a lot in class,
> ask lots of questions.
> He would volunteer to go up to the front and write on the board
> but all the other children, you know, called him 'matsalleh' [an insulting reference in Malay to a white person]
> and he was disturbed and unhappy. [E]
> It's better now. [R/E]
> He has quietened down and doesn't ask questions any more, [E]
> just sits there like everyone else.

This narrative was shared in Malaysia (authors' data). It portrays homecoming as a reverse culture shock in which British verbal interaction patterns for classroom learning, into which the child had been successfully acculturated, became a source of racial insults to the Malay child in the Malaysian classroom. The Abstract establishes the background ideas and a cultural point, headlining 'not asking questions' as the topic. The Orientation presents the character, time, place and setting. The 'real problem' is the Complication, elaborated with details and the outcome of the insults (this part is arguably an Outcome or Result), resolved [R] by the child learning to be silent. The interviewer here, one of us, elicited further details which emerged in non-narrative form but are clearly part of the whole event: the parent elaborated that the problem of the child's disturbance was severe enough to warrant calling in a clinical psychologist. The teller's understanding of the British ways of learning – as a teacher herself she had visited British primary schools – sharpens the contrast in reported patterns of questioning. The tone of the final comment is important, and it is this tone which confirms its evaluative function [E]: it was given with irony but not sadness, and a mocking glance upwards to heaven, implying a cultural adaptability to and fro between educational interaction systems, which emerged later in interview as part of the teller's own professional identity. There is an issue here of how the story as such relates to the whole interview – it cannot be analysed without reference to later talk which was interspersed over some minutes and is not easily represented here. This suggests another question:

11.   How far is the meaning of the story implicated in non-narrative talk?

Example 2: Breakthroughs in Learning with Young Children

Here, a British primary teacher talks about boys learning basic maths.

> One boy that I've had a lot of trouble with . . . [O1]
> His reading is not good
> But his number work [maths] was appalling [C1]
> He couldn't count
> He couldn't recognize any numbers
> And then all of a sudden [R1]
> In the space of about two or three weeks
> It seemed to click [E1]
> And I could see him beginning to go
> He's now beginning to understand it
> It suddenly came on [R1/E1]
> And then another boy who just did not understand addition at all [O2/C2]
> You name, I tried it, [C2]
> And then all of a sudden he just came in one day [R2]
> and [the teller clicks his fingers] it seemed to click [E2]
> and I could really see the breakthrough

These two narratives (authors' data) are somewhat truncated but the categories seem clear: 'appalling' and 'just did not understand' signal the problems in the Complications [C1 and C2]. The Resolution or Result is 'sudden'; exactly how this happened (which must be of interest) is unexplained. The Evaluation is underlined by the metaphor of the verb 'click': 'it clicked' means that everything came together in a sudden illumination,

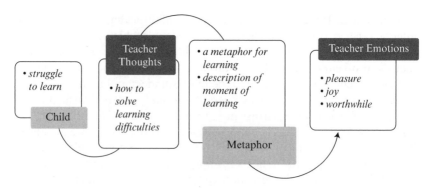

Figure 35.1   Teachers' versions of breakthroughs in learning with primary children

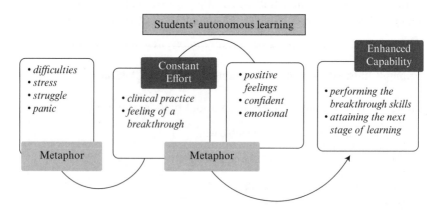

Figure 35.2   Medical and health students' versions of breakthroughs in autonomous learning

like switching on a light. Three metaphors emerged commonly from an analysis of 97 stories of breakthroughs in primary children's learning told by British teachers (Cortazzi, 1991): the moment of learning is 'a click', 'light', or 'movement'. This emerges from the narrative analysis through close attention to the Evaluations. Metaphors of light and movement are seen in extracts from narrative Evaluations from another teacher, with accompanying feelings: 'her achievements went up in leaps and bounds . . . she has suddenly taken off in her reading . . . you can see the light dawn on their face . . . that to me is worth – well, you can't put a worth on it in financial terms. . . .. suddenly it dawns on you that the child is improving, suddenly the reading is coming on. It's a most exciting moment.'

This suggests the question:

12. How can the outcomes of a narrative analysis be presented?

A model or schema (Figure 35.1) can show the common order of giving this kind of narrative. This is one way to get beyond particular examples to try to generalize across tens or hundreds of stories. It shows the teachers' perspectives, expressions of thoughts and feelings for breakthroughs.

This can be compared to an independently derived model (Figure 35.2) obtained by analysing 33 breakthrough stories from adult students of medicine and health care about their learning in clinical contexts (Cortazzi et al., 2001). Teachers or mentors are rarely mentioned since these students are telling stories about hospital wards and clinics in relation to patients and clients.

The emerging awareness of the crucial importance of metaphors for learning has led to the development of a qualitative method of metaphor analysis in educational research (Cortazzi and Jin, 1999, 2009; Jin and Cortazzi, 2008, 2011; Cortazzi et al., 2009).

NARRATIVE NETWORKS AND LEARNING NETWORKS

In analysing the narrative context about stories of learning, we notice chains of learning transmission among health professionals in training (Cortazzi et al., 2001). In these chains, a student shares first-hand experience of a learning event in a clinical placement with a peer, who in turn narrates the story to a third student, who tells another and so on, so that vicarious learning is progressively shared through stories by a chain of participants.

Extracts from stories of student midwives (authors' data) show such a chain in action among a group of students:

> 'We phone each other up . . . when I had my waterbirth [assisting as a student midwife], the next day I had to phone up most of the group and tell them, because I was all excited. I was the only one in the group who had had one.'
>
> 'Some stories have gone the rounds when different things have happened, like one of the girls saw a waterbirth so we all talked about that and that all got shared around, and if something bad happens, something really serious, that all gets shared around.'

A second-year student nurse's comment shows how stories are embedded in peer learning across student cohorts, from Year Three to Two to One:

> *'I've picked up most of the things from other nursing students further on in the course. More senior students seem able to teach me more. I think it's because they*

realize what I haven't done . . . and then we've got the first years . . . and I've found
myself relaying it back to her [a first-year student] *as well . . .'*

A researcher who hears only one story and is unaware of the learning network would miss the narrative chain and thus ignore significant informal learning. Such collaborative narrative learning can be mapped with grids or diagrams. We should ask:

13.   How does a set of stories function in communities of learning?

Investigating narrative learning in educational contexts is an approach to research which restores the value of the voice of individual and group learning experience. Stories of learning show the personal influence of teachers, the value of learner relationships, and often reveal human qualities, such as determination, dedication, patience, imagination, sociability and a sense of enthusiasm and enjoyment This re-establishes a humane dimension in research activity – itself an unfolding story.

NARRATIVES OF RESEARCH AND META-NARRATIVES

This suggests a need for reflexivity. A narrative researcher needs to engage in self-critical reflection on possible biases, preferences and presuppositions, and to critically inspect the whole research process. Researchers should subject their own work to the kinds of narrative questions asked here. Much qualitative research writing is reported and presented as a story, with a constructed plot with a rhetorical design aimed at persuading readers of the interest and the truth of the research. Ethnographic studies are often written up as quests of discovery and interpretation, as a research journey from outsider to insider understanding. The researcher constructs a meta-narrative while relaying and interpreting the accounts of informants (Van Maanen, 1988; Atkinson, 1990; Golden-Biddle and Locke, 1997; Wolcott, 2001, see also Chapter 34).

An instructive example which can be tracked in publications, video recordings and media events is the Mead-Freeman controversy. The seminal 1920s research of Margaret Mead (Mead, 1928 [1948]) into adolescence on a Pacific island of Samoa was reinterpreted by Freeman (1983, 1999) in light of later narrative and other evidence. Mead's fieldwork included living as a 23-year-old in a Samoan household as 'one of the girls' and she had suggested that young Samoan girls did not seem to experience the tensions that American adolescents suffer. She concluded that this was because of the kind of social arrangements in Samoa which made an easy transition from adolescence to adulthood – a crucial point for North American education and the nature-nurture debate with considerations of cultural relativism at the time. Mead's findings were widely read in her best-selling *Coming of Age in Samoa* (1928 [1948]), which was intended to arouse public interest and was not written as a research report (unlike Mead, 1930). Nevertheless, the book was studied as a staple text and was transmitted in academic narrative over several generations from teachers to students in social science learning communities. The book – and Mead – had become iconic in the American academy. Fifty-five years later, Derek Freeman (1999) claimed that one of Mead's main informants (then aged 86; 61 years earlier she had given Mead narrative accounts of local sexual practices) told him that with other girls at the time she had been teasing Mead with joking reports about sex, because they were embarrassed by Mead's questions. Freeman concluded that Mead had been misinformed and misled by what other anthropologists called 'recreational lies', and that her results were systematically distorted. Both Freeman and Mead had to consider that Samoans, like others, 'operate in a world of multiple truths' where different versions are narrated, depending on the situation (Shankman, 2009, p. 143). Whether the informant's first narrative (to Mead) or the second narrative (to Freeman) was basically 'correct', either may have been influenced by her and others' perception of what the researcher wanted to know or what was appropriate to say. Either may have been shaped by political and religious views in Samoa on the research topic (Freeman took the informant's account as valid because she was willing to swear on the Bible that it was true 'as a confession'). Such views are part of the changing layers of the context of telling. Samoa has modernized and Samoan culture has changed. Some current Samoans, from a Christian perspective of modesty and sexual restraint, would rather not be seen in the liberal or permissive image which was apparently disseminated in North America and thus repudiate both the stories given to Mead and her 1928 book. This changing historical context involved the memory of the key informant over 60 years, possibly shaped by distortions of time, by rationalizations from present perspectives and by changes in the teller's sense of identity (in this case overlaid by the postcolonial transition). With regard to narratives as entertainment and performance and the status of their validity as truth or recalled experience, we can ask:

14. *What is the personal and cultural stance of the teller on what is narrated?*

Freeman (1999) had claimed that Mead crucially relied on a single evening's narratives from two informants who were fooling her, but Shankman (2009) shows how Mead's narrative data were consistent with her other detailed data and that she did not at all rely on just two people's stories; rather, if anything, Freeman was relying on one of the informant's later accounts and there is no compelling evidence that Mead was hoaxed. We should ask:

15.   How does a narrative analysis fit other data and other research in the context?

Many Samoans repudiated Mead's portrayal. Few read her book or report, but many resented not knowing about them and not having the opportunity to approve of their content. Later, many Samoans, but not the 86-year-old narrative informant, realized that Freeman was making films and writing books about the controversy and that he claimed to speak for them. We should ask:

16.   What images of participants are presented in narrative analysis and how do they feel about such images?

The context of this example further involves the relationships between the research protagonists of the controversy as portrayed by the media: Mead, a respected authority, widely recognized as one of America's outstanding academic women, and a New Zealand-born challenger who waited until Mead's death in 1978 before publicizing any evidence. In fact, Mead had known of Freeman's views. He had spent far more time than Mead in Samoa and talked with older people, chiefs and modern Samoans who disagreed with both Mead and with her adolescent inform-ants: but these are different sets of narrators in terms of age, gender, social rank and generation. These are two sets of insiders with different viewpoints. While Mead moved away from narrative data to express her personal views about adolescence, Freeman had ignored Mead's more impartial 1930 technical report but focused almost entirely on the popular 1928 book as 'a hoax'.
    We should ask:

17.   What is the personal stance of the researcher in interpreting narrative data?

The above considers a range of perspectives on this controversy, but there are also aspects of simplification, overstatement, selectivity of evi-dence, accuracy in reporting and relationships with the media involved (Shankman, 2009). Generally, we need to employ narrative sensibilities about our own narrative research as we ask:

18.   How do we tell the story of narrative research?

and further:

19.   What are the standards or criteria to judge narrative analyses?

Answers to this question include: coherence, trustworthiness, plausibility, persuasiveness, generalizabilty, verisimilitude, reflexiveness, harmonization with results from other data sources and member validation. Since the narrative researcher needs to gain participants' trust and confidence to get narrative data and access to valid knowledge of their meanings, the researcher can hardly be impartial – this needs to be allowed for in interpretation.

In the Mead-Freeman narrative, it is notable how the criteria for research are seen differently by media reporters, the general public and by different scholars, the researchers themselves and by the narrative participants. Noticeably, some evaluation criteria for the conduct of research have developed over the chronology of this story. To conclude, we need combinations of the above questions to evaluate narrative research. Evaluating a story of research like this with 19 questions also depends on perceptions of the function, aim and audience of the research report, which brings us full circle back to those initial questions. Research results in more questions: there is no final question.

REFERENCES

Atkinson, P. (1990), *The Ethnographic Imagination, Textual Constructions of Reality,* London: Routledge.

Bamberg, M. (ed.) (1997a), *Narrative Development: Six Approaches,* Mahwah, NJ: Lawrence Erlbaum.

Bamberg, M. (ed.) (1997b), 'Oral versions of personal experience: three decades of narrative analysis', Special Issue, *Journal of Narrative and Life History,* **7** (1–4).

Clandinin, D.J. (ed.) (2007), *Handbook of Narrative Inquiry,* Thousand Oaks, CA: Sage.

Cortazzi, M. (1991), *Primary Teaching, How it is: A Narrative Account,* London: David Fulton Publishers.

Cortazzi, M. (1993), *Narrative Analysis,* London: Falmer Press.

Cortazzi, M. (2001), 'Narrative analysis in ethnography', in P. Atkinson, A. Coffey, S. Delamont, L. Lofland and J. Lofland (eds), *Handbook of Ethnography,* London: Sage, pp. 384–94.

Cortazzi, M. and Jin, L. (1999), 'Bridges to learning: metaphors of teaching, learning and language', in L. Cameron and G. Low (eds), *Researching and Applying Metaphor,* Cambridge: Cambridge University Press, pp. 149–76.

Cortazzi, M. and Jin, L. (2000), 'Evaluating evaluation in narrative', in S. Hunston and G. Thompson (eds), *Evaluation in Text,* Oxford: Oxford University Press, pp. 102–20.

Cortazzi, M., Jin, L. and Wang, Z. (2009), 'Cultivators, cows and computers: Chinese learners' metaphors of teachers', in T. Coverdale-Jones and P. Rastall (eds), *Internationalizing the University, the Chinese Context,* London: Palgrave Macmillan, pp. 107–29.

Cortazzi, M., Jin, L., Wall, D. and Cavendish, S. (2001), *Narrative Learning through Clinical Experience,* Final project report, Leicester: Trent Regional Education & Development Group.

Freeman, D. (1983), *Margaret Mead and Samoa: The Making and Unmasking of an Anthropological Myth,* Cambridge, MA: Harvard University Press.

Freeman, D. (1999), *The Fateful Hoaxing of Margaret Mead: A Historical Analysis of Her Samoan Research,* Boulder, CO: Westview Press.

Gee, J. (2005), *An Introduction to Discourse Analysis, Theory and Method,* New York: Routledge.

Golden-Biddle, K. and Locke, K.D. (1997) *Composing Qualitative Research,* Thousand Oaks, CA: Sage.

Goodson, I., Biesta, G., Tedder, M. and Adair, N. (2010), *Narrative Learning,* London: Routledge.

Hymes, D. (1996), *Ethnography, Linguistics, Narrative Inequality, Towards an Understanding of Voice,* London: Taylor & Francis.

Jin, L. and Cortazzi, M. (2008), 'Images of teachers, learning and questioning in Chinese cultures of learning', in E. Berendt (ed.), *Metaphors We Learn By,* London: Continuum, pp. 177–202.

Jin, L. and Cortazzi, M. (2011), 'More than a journey: 'learning' in the metaphors of Chinese students and teachers', in L. Jin and M. Cortazzi (eds), *Researching Chinese Learners, Skills, Perceptions, Adaptations,* London: Palgrave Macmillan, pp. 67–92.

Kalaja, P., Menezes, V. and Barcelos, A.M.F. (eds) (2008), *Narratives of Learning and Teaching EFL,* Houndmills: Palgrave Macmillan.

Labov, W. (1972), 'The transformation of experience in narrative syntax', in W. Labov, *Language in the Inner City,* Philadelphia, PA: University of Pennsylvania Press, pp. 352–96.

Labov, W. and Waletsky, J. (1967), 'Narrative analysis: oral versions of personal experience', in C.B. Paulston and G.R. Tucker, (eds) (2003), *Sociolinguistics, the Essential Readings,* Oxford: Blackwell Publishing, pp. 74–104.

McCabe, A. and Peterson, C. (1991), *Developing Narrative Structure,* Hillsdale, NJ: Lawrence Erlbaum.

Mead, M. ([1928] 1948), *Coming of Age in Samoa,* Harmondsworth: Penguin Books.

Mead, M. (1930), *Social Organization of Manu'a,* Bulletin 76, Honolulu: Bernice P. Bishop Museum.

Minami, M. (2002), *Culture-specific Language Styles: The Development of Oral Narrative and Literacy,* Clevedon: Multilingual Matters.

Mishler, E.G. (1995), 'Models of narrative analysis: a typology', *Journal of Narrative and Life History,* **5** (2), 87–123.

Ochs, E. and Capps, L. (2001), *Living Narrative, Creating Lives in Everyday Storytelling,* Cambridge, MA: Harvard University Press.

Schegloff, E.A. (2003), '"Narrative analysis" thirty years later', in C.B. Paulston and G.R. Tucker (eds), *Sociolinguistics, the Essential Readings,* Oxford: Blackwell Publishing, pp. 105–13.

Scollon, R. and Scollon, S.W. (1981), *Narrative, Literacy and Face in Interethnic Communication,* Norwood, NJ: Ablex.

Shankman, P. (2009), *The Trashing of Margaret Mead, Anatomy of an Anthropological Controversy,* Madison, WI: University of Wisconsin Press.

Trahar, S. (ed.) (2006), *Narrative Research on Learning,* Oxford: Symposium Books.

Van Maanen, J. (1988), *Tales of the Field, on Writing Ethnography,* Chicago, IL: University of Chicago Press.

Wolcott, H. (2001), *Writing Up Qualitative Research,* Thousand Oaks, CA: Sage.

36. Analysing fieldnotes: a practical guide
Zoë B. Corwin and Randall F. Clemens

Fieldnotes are a critical yet often underemphasized component of the research and writing process. In qualitative research, fieldnotes have long held a significant role in data collection and analysis. Seldom, however, are fieldnotes the focus of research methods sections or 'how to' guides. Perhaps this is because researchers view fieldnotes as of minor importance compared to the overall research methodology or methods (Shank, 2006). Lederman (1990), highlighting the difficulty of categorizing fieldnotes, writes, 'It is no wonder that fieldnotes are hard to think and write about: they are a bizarre genre. Simultaneously part of the "doing" of fieldwork and of the "writing" of ethnography, fieldnotes are shaped by two movements: a turning away from academic discourse to join conversations in unfamiliar settings, and a turning back again' (p. 72). Fieldnotes at the same time represent the research process and product. And yet, despite the use of fieldnotes as an essential part of qualitative research, few texts exist in which the authors fully explore the role and mechanics of fieldnotes, specifically within the field of education research. Notable exceptions include Emerson et al.'s (1995) comprehensive overview *Writing Ethnographic Fieldnotes* and Sanjek's (1990) edited volume *Fieldnotes: The Making of Anthropology.*

In this chapter, we present a synthesis of pertinent literature regarding fieldnotes and then offer a detailed description of how to analyse fieldnotes. The first section summarizes the philosophical and theoretical underpinnings of fieldnotes in qualitative research and is intended to highlight the interrelated nuances of collecting and analysing fieldnotes. The second section shares concrete examples from a large-scale qualitative research project to illustrate the mechanics of analysing fieldnotes during and after data collection. The ultimate goal of the chapter is to illustrate that analysing fieldnotes is a process that begins from the moment one conceptualizes a study.

DEFINING FIELDNOTES

Much of qualitative research requires keen, detailed, and reflective observations of social settings. Emerson et al. (1995) describe ethnographic field research as involving two components: 'First, the ethnographer enters into a social setting and gets to know the people involved in it . . . second, the ethnographer writes down in regular, systematic ways what she observes and learns while participating in the daily rounds of life of others' (p. 1). To record what they observe in the field, qualitative researchers rely on fieldnotes, or 'detailed, nonjudgmental (as much as possible), concrete descriptions of what has been observed' (Marshall and Rossman, 2011, p. 139). Most often, fieldnotes chronicle settings, people, and activities (Merriam, 1988). High quality and carefully constructed fieldnotes provide 'thick description' in which a researcher not only describes behavior but the context as well, thereby focusing on how people make meaning of their social worlds (Geertz, 1973). Fieldnotes can provide a portal from the reader to the research setting. For a discussion about the anthropological approach to ethnographic work, including collecting fieldnotes through extended fieldwork see Mills (Chapter 3, this volume).

Writing fieldnotes is a selective and active process. Accordingly, 'the first stage of conventional, textual representation is the construction of fieldnotes' (Atkinson, 2001, p. 89). As a researcher observes a social phenomenon or location, she determines what to include in the fieldnotes; this process affects how she constructs and describes the social world. Stated in another way, fieldnotes are 'authored representations of ongoing social life' (Emerson, 2001, p. 132).

Content and style of fieldnotes vary among researchers and projects. The content of fieldnotes are determined by a myriad of factors, including research questions, site selection, participants, and length and time of study. Fieldnotes might be collected for a project with solely one researcher or for a project involving a team of researchers from the same or different institutions. Some researchers include charts, diagrams, and pictures in their notes; others write minute details of social interactions or settings they have observed; and still others opt for using uniform observational protocols that can be shared among researchers. Some researchers choose to limit their fieldnotes to recording observations of setting and activities while others include more personal notations in the margins or in an additional column. Researchers may choose to integrate their own reactions and perceptions into the core of their fieldnote writing. 'Jottings' taken down in the field serve to remind researchers of significant actions or possible connections to larger themes (see Emerson et al., 1995, Saldana, 2009). In some instances, researchers indicate reflections through the notation 'OC' (observer's comments) that incorporate 'researcher's feelings, reactions, hunches, initial interpretations, and working hypothesis' (Merriam, 1988, p. 98). Some researchers maintain records solely through handwritten notes while others rely on much more systematic and clearly typed up notes. For an interesting discussion of what to include in fieldnotes see de Vries (Chapter 25, this volume).

The nature of the data collection site, composition of research team, and topic of query influence when and how notes are recorded and written. While there is no prescribed format for fieldnotes, 'effective' fieldnotes do involve an awareness of how data are being collected and recorded, including acknowledging the role of the researcher in that process. Take, for example, a study analysing the social networks of drug dependent teenagers. Even after they have given consent to participate in the study, might a researcher and notepad significantly affect the types of behaviors and conversations in which the informants engage? How does the personal background of the researcher (for example, age, race, gender) potentially affect data? Will research informants change their behavior because of the note taking process? Many aspects of data collection have significant implications for the ultimate trustworthiness of study findings. Analysing fieldnotes begins with an awareness of how research design and methods can influence data collection and analysis. In the next section, we draw a connection between the theoretical underpinnings of qualitative research and their influence on fieldnotes.

UNDERSTANDING FIELDNOTES

Acknowledging the underlying paradigmatic assumptions that affect the way a researcher approaches each step of qualitative research is as important as understanding the mechanics of collecting fieldnotes. The purpose of acknowledging the foundational concepts in qualitative inquiry is not to devolve into an overly theoretical discussion removed from practical considerations. Instead, we attempt to highlight the importance of understanding one's own perspective and positionality and the related implications for the research process.

Every researcher either knowingly or unknowingly adopts the conventions of one or multiple paradigms. Put simply, a paradigm is a worldview.[1] Paradigms range from positivist to constructivist, from believing an absolute, knowable reality exists to believing in a restricted, socially constructed reality. Each worldview contains its own set of ontological questions – how is reality defined, and what does existence mean – and epistemological questions – what is knowledge, and what is the relationship between the knower and the known. Other key questions relate to methodology and axiology. For instance, what phenomena does a researcher investigate and how, and what criteria does she use to judge their inquiry? Based on one's own beliefs, the answers to these questions may vary drastically.

The researcher's own paradigmatic associations have important implications for the way she approaches research in general and fieldnotes in particular. For instance, an individual who situates himself or herself within a positivist epistemological framework believes in fieldnotes as a method to obtain truth (Kvale, 2007). A postmodernist, in contrast, believes fieldnotes to be constructions or, using Clifford Geertz's (1973) language, 'fictions,' because they are recreations of authentic acts. Similarly, a positivist may seek input from subjects about the content of fieldnotes in order to ensure the validity of data whereas a critical theorist may use fieldnotes as a venue to facilitate an evolving dialogue between researcher and participant.

USING FIELDNOTES TO IMPROVE TRUSTWORTHINESS

The caliber of fieldnotes has significant implications for data analysis and presentation. In the previous section, we discussed paradigms and the basic categories that define them, including ontological, epistemological, and methodological. Trustworthiness answers an axiological question by providing criteria to judge qualitative research.[2] Considering the process and product of research, fieldnotes can improve the trustworthiness of data (Guba, 1981; Lincoln and Guba, 1985; Sanjek, 1990) and limit misunderstanding from the text (Wolcott, 1990). Member checks and triangulation are two strategies that the researcher can use to improve the rigor of research. Ethnographic fieldnotes provide a helpful tool for member checks. By sharing fieldnotes and seeking input from informants about how data collected represents their experiences, fieldnotes can ensure more accurate data collection and analysis by the researcher (LeCompte and Goetz, 1982). Fieldnotes also allow for triangulation with alternative data sources, like interviews and document analysis, in order to reduce researcher bias and improve credibility (Guba, 1981). In relation to creating a useful archive of data – what Lincoln and Guba (1985) refer to as a research audit – fieldnotes fulfill a vital role, along with research diaries, memorandums, and interview transcripts. Lastly, descriptive fieldnotes minimize the chances that readers will misinterpret the text (Wolcott, 1990) and maximize the transferability – analogous to the quantitative concept of generalizability – of the research (Guba, 1981). Fieldnotes, whether quoted or summarized in the final product, allow for thick description (Geertz, 1973) in a text and permit the reader to vicariously experience the research setting. By presenting rich data, the researcher enables the reader to make an informed decision about whether or not the research may be applied to her own studies, a key concern of transferability.

Questions to consider prior to entering the field (with implications for analysis):

- How will I record my observations?
- What tools/supplies do I need (for example, paper, pencil, tape recorder, camera)?
- How often will I take fieldnotes?
- Where and when will I write down fieldnotes?
  - Will the act of jotting down cause people in the social setting to act differently?
- When will I begin to code data, and how might that coding process affect subsequent observations?
- How does my own positionality affect what I might choose to write down?

ANALYSING FIELDNOTES

Data analysis entails a process of translation and negotiation when data collection and analysis often occur concurrently. Multiple techniques exist to analyse data, including content analysis, discourse analysis, grounded theory, and narrative analysis (Kvale, 2007). We acknowledge the value of each of these lenses to analyse data. For the purposes of clarity in this chapter, however, we adopt a grounded theory approach that emphasizes theory generation as a product of data collection (Glaser and Strauss, 1967; Charmaz, 2001, 2006).

The mainstay of most qualitative analysis involves coding data. Like fieldnotes, coding purposes and strategies vary across methods, projects, and researchers. Nevertheless, the overarching goal of coding is to move from 'unstructured and messy data to ideas about what is going on in the data' (Richards and Morse, 2007, p. 133). Codes enable researchers to describe data, categorize data by topic, draw connections, and, consequently, develop theoretical concepts and identify themes (Richards and Morse, 2007).[3]

Once a researcher collects fieldnotes, she then codes data based on discrete categories (as illustrated below in the 'Examining Fieldnotes' section). Gibbs (2007) offers a helpful list of items that may be coded:[4]

1. Specific acts, behaviors
2. Events

3. Activities
4. Strategies, practices, or tactics
5. States
6. Meanings (including concepts, significance, symbols)
7. Participation
8. Relationships or interactions
9. Conditions or constraints
10. Consequences
11. Settings
12. Reflections on researcher's role in the research process.

Items coded are guided by the research question(s) and increasingly focused inquiry. While the researcher may start with a broad range of observable data, the categories should decrease as data collection proceeds.

When a research project involves multiple researchers, coding involves a more lengthy process of identifying codes and discussing themes together. A group-based analytic process creates an opportunity for colleagues to clarify, make connections, and think through concepts with the support, critique, and insight of other informed researchers. Due to the varying perspectives participating in the analysis of data, multi-researcher analysis has the potential to enhance the trustworthiness of findings in contrast to a lone researcher who runs the risk of missing key themes when working in isolation. For researchers analysing data alone, robust literature reviews and member checking (Lincoln and Guba, 1985) can mitigate the potential to overlook key codes and themes.

EXAMINING FIELDNOTES

To illustrate one possible way to analyse data, we provide a step-by-step review of how a team of researchers analysed fieldnotes for a large-scale qualitative project. In doing so, we aim to illustrate how analysis is not just a culminating step in the life-course of a study, but rather plays an integral role in the entire research process. It is imperative to note that while we present the steps below in a linear format, steps often occur in a simultaneous, recursive process and various phases of the research process inform each other.

Background

In 2005, researchers from the Center for Higher Education Policy Analysis at the University of Southern California conducted a qualitative study funded by the US Department of Education to determine the key characteristics of effective college preparation programs. Six researchers, split among sites in California, collected data at 12 high schools during the course of three school years. Researchers used a case study approach (Stake, 1995) to examine differences and similarities in program implementation and effectiveness. Data collection entailed observations of a wide variety of school events and extracurricular activities as well as interviews and focus groups with students, teachers, administrators, and family members. Data collection was extensive, spanning multiple sites, informants, and researchers. Researchers relied heavily on fieldnotes to record observations, share data, and discuss emerging findings with the research team. Findings were summarized for academic, practitioner, and policymaker audiences. Using an inductive approach to hypothesis generation, grounded theory guided the overall approach to the study (Glaser and Strauss, 1967; Charmaz, 2001, 2006).

Steps Guiding Data Collection and Analysis

In what follows, we outline the key components of the research process for the college access study and highlight how each phase influenced the analysis of fieldnotes.

Step one: Research questions
The first step related to analysis involved reviewing literature related to the topic in order to inform the study's research questions. Our goal was to identify major topics highlighted in discussions of college access in order to provide a focus for our observations. Major topics of interest included academic preparation, guidance, peers, family, mentors, culture, extracurricular activities, the timing of interventions, and the cost-effectiveness of programs. There were two initial overarching research questions: first, what role do students' social support networks play in college preparation? And second, what elements in a college preparation program facilitate college preparedness?

Step two: Site selection
Before we started collecting data, we had to identify sites that would provide rich sources of data. This step entailed researching and analysing the demographics at each site and developing relationships with administrators in order to secure access. These two steps were critical to ensuring that the case study sites would allow for the collection and analysis of robust data and therefore contribute to the trustworthiness of data.

Step three: Initial data collection

For the initial phase of data collection, researchers took notes about the activities and social interactions that transpired during the site visits. Fieldnotes across researchers lacked uniformity when initially written in notebooks. In most cases, one researcher would not be able to read the notations of the others. After researchers typed up their notes, we were able to share what we had written.

Due to the benign nature of the study, we opted to clarify our presence in the classroom, explaining to students in general terms why we spent time with them. Consequently, students were at ease when researchers took notes. Researchers dressed in attire that was appropriate for the school environment, that is, clothes a teacher would wear as opposed to business attire, and usually positioned themselves in the back of the room, thereby minimizing the distraction of additional adults in the classroom. Perhaps most relevant to implications for the trustworthiness of the study, the longitudinal nature of the study meant that students became familiar and at ease with the researchers' presence in the classroom.

Step four: Generation of fieldnotes

A considerably time intensive facet of the research process, and one critical to data analysis, involved typing up fieldnotes. Typing up fieldnotes was initially essential so that researchers could read each other's notes and so that notes could be entered into a qualitative data analysis program (described below).

At this stage, researchers also started to tease out significant themes and reflected on their observations. Saldana (2009) describes a process of 'preliminary jottings' when researchers begin the coding process as they write up fieldnotes. In preliminary jottings, researchers start to write potential codes in the margins of notes or transcripts or in separate analytic memos to return to later. These notes assist researchers to develop codes in later stages of analysis. Saldana (2009) cautions researchers to 'be wary of relying on your memory for future writing. Get your thoughts, however fleeting, documented in some way' (p.17). For the college access project, researchers kept a list of preliminary codes that were later shared with the research team in group meetings. Preliminary codes informed the first phase of data analysis.

Step five: Initial data analysis

After fieldnotes were typed up and shared, researchers embarked on the process of identifying and defining initial codes. We used a data-driven approach for the first phase of analysis during which we attempted to let

Table 36.1   Excerpt from fieldnotes with open codes

Observations	Data-driven Codes	Observer Comments
Students were given a problem set of SAT-type questions to work on. One student didn't begin for a while because he didn't have a pencil.	• ACTIVITY • SUPPLIES • PARTICIPATION	• Was the student unprepared? Or could he not afford the necessary supplies?
The advisor suggested that students "shouldn't need help" and that they should work by themselves.	• ADVISOR/ LEADERSHIP STYLE	• What if students did need help?
A prize was offered to the first person to turn in their answers.	• INCENTIVES	• Why was the incentive necessary? What type of message does this send to students?
Advisor asked the whereabouts of specific students. The other students present knew where most students were.	• PEERS	• The students appear to be a tight-knit group.
Throughout the meeting, 8 students filtered in late. Most stayed the whole (25 min.) session. A small group came and the end of the session, signed in and then left.	• EXPECTATIONS • PARTICIPATION	• Useful to track attendance and punctuality over time.

the data illustrate what was happening as opposed to imposing an existing theory on the data (Glaser and Strauss, 1967). This process is also known as open or emic coding (Gough and Scott, 2000; Gibbs, 2007; Bernard and Ryan, 2010). At this point in data analysis, researchers coded fieldnote data by hand. We developed a code list and identified nine major themes that we wanted to highlight during subsequent data collection (Table 36.1).

Step six: Additional data collection
Due to the complex nature of data collection (multi-researcher, multi-site), we opted to use an observational protocol across observations

for the secondary phase of data collection. Subsections of the protocol included:

- Background/setting
- People in attendance
- Agenda/Points discussed/Activities observed
- Evidence of themes
- Insights/themes/policy implications
- Questions to follow up.

Under 'evidence of themes,' researchers recorded notes on the major themes identified during the literature review and initial coding: academic preparation, extracurricular activities, guidance, peers, family, mentors, and culture. The observational protocol facilitated analysis of data because it focused the researchers' observations on specific themes and simplified cross-site analysis because researchers collected robust data on similar themes.

Step seven: Detailed coding
After subsequent stages of collecting data and writing up fieldnotes over the course of several months, we started to enter fieldnote write-ups into Atlas. ti, a qualitative software analysis tool. The tool allowed the research team to code large amounts of data in a systematic way. With an advanced literature review complete (see Tierney, et al., 2005) and considerable amount of data collected, the research team shifted our analysis approach to a primarily concept-driven approach, also known as etic coding (Gough and Scott, 2000). By organizing data according to concepts from the literature, we were able to narrow our analysis and make it applicable to the literature. Gibbs (2007) points out that data-driven and concept-driven coding are not mutually exclusive, 'most researchers move backwards and forwards between both sources of inspiration during their analysis' (p. 46) (Table 36.2).

Step eight: Identification of themes
After a close reading of the fieldnotes and transcripts and engaging in line by line coding, the research team turned to expanding connections and identifying themes. Atlas.ti proved helpful in these conversations because we were able to print out reports according to codes. We could, for example, print out all excerpts from the text that pertained to 'peers.' Seeing all data related to a particular theme was helpful to analysis. While Atlas.ti (and software analysis tools MAXQDA, NVivo, and Hyperresearch) offers functions to map out connections between themes, the research team opted to explore and expand upon themes in verbal discussions.

Table 36.2   Excerpt from fieldnotes with concept-driven codes

Observations	Data-driven Codes	Observer Comments
When we arrived, the counseling coordinator announced that she was available to meet with students one-on-one to work on their college essays.	• COUNSELOR AS INSTITUTIONAL AGENT • COLLEGE SUPPORT	
One student followed up with her.	• PARTICIPATION	• Why did only one student follow up? Preparedness or lack of comfort?
When asked, one senior knew that the college application deadline was Friday.	• INSTITUTIONAL DEADLINES • LOW COLLEGE KNOWLEDGE	
The advisor told students they need to turn everything in online. He told students that sometimes the computer system crashes on the deadline day, suggesting that students could turn in materials a day late.	• TECHNOLOGY • MISINFORMATION • DETRIMENTAL ADVICE • ADULT AS GATEKEEPER	• Follow up to see when students turned in applications.

Step nine: Trustworthiness

In order to make sure that study findings were trustworthy, researchers shared excerpts from fieldnotes and emerging findings with research participants. Participants were asked if fieldnotes and findings reflected their experiences accurately. In addition, researchers triangulated data by conducting observations, interviews, and focus groups with various stakeholder groups, for example, students, teachers, administrators, counselors, and family members. This was a critical step as themes that emerged through triangulated data and feedback from participants affected follow-up data collection and analysis.

Step ten: Presentation of findings

Writing up findings entailed a different focus of analysis. We first had to determine the audience for study results and then the best way to communicate findings to that audience. While the themes identified as salient did not change across audiences, presentation of data varied depending on whether a publication was intended for academic, practitioner, or policymaker audiences. Federal reports summarized findings and incorporated charts and tables; academic articles included rich data with thick descriptions and quotes from study informants; and practitioner monographs presented data in concise ways that included illustrative quotes. To see how the research team incorporated data from fieldnotes and analysis in narrative form, see *Urban High School Students and the Challenge of Access: Many Routes, Difficult Paths* (Tierney and Colyar, 2009).

CONCLUSION

Presentation of data follows the culmination of hours of diligent and methodical data collection and analysis. As with the research process, no one correct way exists to present data. The manner in which fieldnotes are presented, however, has significant implications for the analysis of data from the reader's perspective. Consider how the reader interprets data when she reads direct excerpts from fieldnotes versus summaries of observations. While both examples are textual representations, readers react differently to data depending on its presentation. Bourgois and Schonberg's (2009) recent photoethnography, *Righteous Dopefiend,* for instance, offers a compelling example of fieldnotes in a text. The reader learns by reading actual fieldnotes and examining photographs interspersed between the authors' analysis about the lives of heroin addicts living on the streets of San Francisco. The book invokes lively classroom discussions when we have pushed students to consider how the text might be different without the inclusion of their rich, detailed fieldnotes.

Presentation of data depends on multiple factors, including the intent of the author, data available, audience, and publication type. In concluding this text, we want to highlight the potential of fieldnotes to elevate the imaginative possibilities of data presentation. Focusing attention to the collection, analysis, and presentation of fieldnotes heightens the potential of researchers to fulfill key purposes of qualitative inquiry – to illuminate and provoke, to address social issues and provide alternative solutions. The creative, thoughtful, and purposeful treatment of fieldnotes increases the likelihood that the researcher will connect the reader to researched in meaningful ways.

NOTES

1. For a more in-depth treatment of paradigms, see Kuhn (1970) and, for a description of qualitative paradigms, see Eisner (1990), Smith, (1990), and Guba and Lincoln (2005).
2. Trustworthiness (Guba, 1981; Lincoln and Guba, 1985) establishes criteria for rigorous research. The four criteria are credibility, transferability, dependability, and confirmability. They are qualitative responses to criteria for quantitative research – internal validity, external validity, internal reliability, and external reliability. If the reader is interested in reading further about ongoing discussions about criteria for qualitative research, we suggest beginning with Eisenhart and Howe (1992), Lincoln (2001), and Tierney and Clemens (2011).
3. See Richards and Morse (2007) for a discussion of the different types of codes, how to use them, and how to manage codes.
4. See Gibbs (2007) for a more comprehensive description of coding that includes examples.

REFERENCES

Atkinson, P. (2001), 'Ethnography and the representation of reality', in R.M. Emerson (ed.), *Contemporary Field Research*, 2nd edn, Long Grove, IL: Waveland Press, pp. 89–101.
Bernard, H.R., and Ryan, G.W. (2010), *Analyzing Qualitative Research: Systematic Approaches*, Thousand Oaks, CA: Sage.
Bourgois, P., and Schonberg, J. (2009), *Righteous Dopefiend*, Berkeley, CA: University of California Press.
Charmaz, K. (2001), 'Grounded theory', in R.M. Emerson (ed.), *Contemporary Field Research*, 2nd edn, Long Grove, IL: Waveland Press, pp. 335–52.
Charmaz, K. (2006), *Constructing Grounded Theory: A Practical Guide through Qualitative Analysis*, Thousand Oaks, CA: Sage.
Eisenhart, M.A. and Howe, K.R. (1992), 'Validity in educational research', in M.D. LeCompte, W.L. Millroy and J. Preissle (eds), *The Handbook of Qualitative Research in Education*, San Diego, CA: Academic Press, pp. 642–80.
Eisner, E.W. (1990), 'The meaning of alternative paradigms for practice', in E.G. Guba (ed.), *The Paradigm Dialog*, Newbury Park, CA: Sage, pp. 88–104.
Emerson, R.M. (2001), 'Fieldwork practice: issues in participant observation', in R.M. Emerson (ed.), *Contemporary Field Research*, 2nd edn, Long Grove, IL: Waveland Press, pp. 113–52.
Emerson, R.M., Fretz, R.I. and Shaw, L.L. (1995), *Writing Ethnographic Fieldnotes*, Chicago, IL: University of Chicago Press.
Geertz, C. (1973), 'Thick description: toward an interpretive theory of culture', in *The Interpretation of Cultures: Selected Essays*, New York: Basic Books.
Gibbs, G.R. (2007), *Analyzing Qualitative Data*, Los Angeles, CA: Sage.
Glaser, B.G. and Strauss, A.L. (1967), *The Discovery of Grounded Theory: Strategies for Qualitative Research*, Chicago, IL: Aldine.
Gough, S. and Scott, W. (2000), 'Exploring the purposes of qualitative data coding in educational enquiry: insights from recent research', *Educational Studies*, **26**, 339–54.
Guba, E.G. (1981), 'Criteria for assessing the trustworthiness of naturalistic inquiries', *Educational Communication and Technology*, **29** (2), 75–91.
Guba, E.G. and Lincoln, Y.S. (2005), 'Paradigmatic controversies, contradictions, and emerging confluences', in N.K. Denzin and Y.S. Lincoln (eds), *Handbook of Qualitative Research*, 3rd edn, Thousand Oaks, CA: Sage, pp. 191–215.
Kuhn, T.S. (1970), *The Structure of Scientific Revolutions*, 2nd edn, Chicago, IL: University of Chicago Press.
Kvale, S. (2007), *Doing Interviews*, Thousand Oaks, CA: Sage.

LeCompte, M.D. and Goetz, J.P. (1982), 'Problems of reliability and validity in ethnographic research', *Review of Educational Research*, **52** (1), 31–60.

Lederman, R. (1990), 'Pretexts for ethnography: on reading fieldnotes', in R. Sanjek (ed.), *Fieldnotes: The Making of Anthropology*, Ithaca, NY: Cornell University Press, pp. 71–91.

Lincoln, Y.S. (2001), 'Varieties of validity: quality in qualitative research', in J. Smart and W.G. Tierney (eds), *Higher Education: Handbook of Theory and Research*, New York: Agathon Press, pp. 25–72.

Lincoln, Y.S. and Guba, E.G. (1985), *Naturalistic Inquiry*, Beverly Hills, CA: Sage.

Marshall, C. and Rossman, G.B. (2011), *Designing Qualitative Research*, 5th edn, Los Angeles, CA: Sage.

Merriam, S.B. (1988), *Case Study Research in Education: A Qualitative Approach*, San Francisco, CA: Jossey-Bass Publishers.

Richards, L. and Morse, J.M. (2007), *Readme First for a User's Guide to Qualitative Methods*, 2nd edn, Thousand Oaks, CA: Sage.

Saldana, J. (2009), *The Coding Manual for Qualitative Researchers*, Thousand Oaks, CA: Sage.

Sanjek, R. (1990), 'On ethnographic validity', in R. Sanjek (ed.), *Fieldnotes: The Making of Anthropology*, Ithaca, NY: Cornell University Press, pp. 385–418.

Shank, G.D. (2006), 'Observing', *Qualitative Research: A Personal Skills Approach*, 2nd edn, Upper Saddle River, NJ: Pearson, pp. 21–37.

Smith, J.K. (1990), 'Alternative research paradigms and the problem of criteria', in E.G. Guba (ed.), *The Paradigm Dialog*, Newbury Park, CA: Sage, pp. 167–97.

Stake, R.E. (1995), *The Art of Case Study Research*, Thousand Oaks, CA: Sage.

Tierney, W.G. and Clemens, R.F. (2011), 'Qualitative research and public policy: the challenges of relevance and trustworthiness', in J. Smart and M.B. Paulsen (eds), *Higher Education: Handbook of Theory and Research*, Vol. 26, New York: Springer, pp. 57–83.

Tierney, W.G. and Colyar, J.E. (2009), *Urban High School Students and the Challenges of Access: Many Routes, Difficult Paths*, New York: Peter Lang.

Tierney, W.G., Corwin, Z.B. and Colyar, J.E. (eds) (2005), *Preparing for College: Nine Elements of Effective Outreach*, Albany, NY: State University of New York Press.

Wolcott, H.F. (1990), 'On seeking – and rejecting – validity in qualitative research', in E. Eisner and A. Peshkin (eds), *Qualitative Inquiry in Education: The Continuing Debate*, New York: Teachers College Press, pp. 121–52.

37. Considering CAQDAS: using and choosing software
Kate Stewart

INTRODUCTION

A now widely used part of the researcher's toolkit and an ever popular topic for research training courses, Computer Assisted Qualitative Data Analysis Software packages (CAQDAS) refer to 'a wide range of packages . . . concerned with taking a qualitative approach to qualitative data' (Lewins and Silver, 2009, p. 3). This chapter introduces some of the issues researchers should consider when both deciding whether to use a CAQDAS package in their research project, and then if necessary in deciding between the available packages. Much of this advice is informed by my experiences providing support and training to researchers over the past 15 years, as well as the available literature.

Computer analysis tools for qualitative methods developed somewhat behind the development of quantitative analysis packages, which had emerged in the 1960s and 1970s with fully featured statistical packages being available on microcomputers from the 1980s. Rudimentary qualitative mainframe programs performing simple tasks such as word frequency counts and experiments using qualitative data on the new quantitative packages were used in a small number of projects in the mid 1980s and it was towards the end of that decade that the first versions of dedicated qualitative packages such as Ethnograph, Qualpro and TAP appeared, with a rapid growth in the number of available packages following. As important as the technological developments during this time was the growing social acceptance of software options that were originally met with suspicion (Fielding and Lee, 1998).

Contemporary packages are, like the computers we use them with, almost unrecognizable from these early versions. Now packages can be used at practically every stage of the research process, from literature reviews, to listening to and transcribing audio, coding data, developing theories, generating graphical representations of the data, and even writing up. Now software is so feature rich and flexible that the limitations on the analysis tasks you can achieve using them are more likely to be determined by the limitations of your PC hardware than a lack of software functionality (Bringer et al., 2006).

Over the past decade two 'industry leaders' have emerged in the University sector: ATLAS.ti and NVivo, with numerous other packages including DRS, HyperRESEARCH, MaxQDA and Qualrus also available, as well as the Ethnograph, first released in 1984 and a once dominant package, and now in its sixth version. These packages are updated regularly, and a comparison of the functionality of all of them is beyond the scope of this chapter, as any such comparison will become obsolete relatively rapidly. Instead the focus here will be on more enduring considerations regarding whether, when and for what tasks a researcher might consider using a CAQDAS package.[1]

CHOOSING BETWEEN MANUAL ANALYSIS AND USING CAQDAS

Descriptions of the appeals of using CAQDAS often include references to them enhancing the speed, efficiency, rigour and consistency of the analysis process: surely attributes no researcher would reject? Beyond the appealing hyperbole it is still important to question if and why any of these packages will be beneficial to a project's research strategy. The main advantages of using CAQDAS are largely unchanged from when the first dedicated packages appeared: in making the management of data easier, allowing researchers to explore their data in ways very difficult or impossible without the software, and to save time and increase efficiency. The software ameliorates the technical and clerical tasks while the researcher is, and must still be, in charge of thinking about the data (Tesch, 1990). As Bringer et al. (2006) remind us, focussing on the CAQDAS versus manual decision may suggest the tool is the main determinant of the research outcome, rather than the methodology. Just because the features are available in packages, you do not have to use them all: your analysis must be driven by your methodology. Furthermore, being seduced to use software features because they are there is all too easy and some of the features CAQDAS offer, such as finer grain coding, can distract from the original focus of the research and slow things down rather than speed them up (Froggatt, 2001). The introduction and proliferation of CAQDAS packages may sometimes be seen as having transformed the time consuming and laborious to the rapid and rigorous, but this notion may be illusory (Rambaree, 2007). There is a danger that using CAQDAS without a clear rationale for doing so will in fact lead to a prolonged, inefficient and unfocussed analysis process. CAQDAS packages do not perform, suggest or guide analysis for you: while some researchers still view packages with the suspicion that their early incarnations received, it is now more likely researchers face an expectation that they will use the packages, as if they act as some sort of byword for having done the analysis 'properly'. It remains contested as to whether using CAQDAS distances researchers from data too much, or whether it encourages too much granularity over generalization (King, 2010). Limiting use to basic code and retrieve functions can risk a loss of context, and an over fragmentation of data (Coffey and Atkinson, 1996). To help guard against such concerns it is important to have a clear strategy for data management and analysis independently of whether software is used or not (Schiellerup, 2008).

One of the significant attractions and main advantages of using CAQDAS is the ease with which large datasets can be organized and data retrieved from them in comparison with working with all data in hard copy (Coffey and Atkinson, 1996). Early software development was driven by this very issue of addressing the problems associated with managing large volumes of physical records (Richards and Richards, 1994). With moderate to large quantities of data, the organization and retrieval of records may be much easier with the use of a CAQDAS package, but in small projects it may not be too difficult to manage paper records. The easier portability of datasets in digitized formats means vast quantities of research materials can be transported, shared and archived with relative ease.

These are essentially data management issues with implications for the analysis process, and raise the related observation that the 'analysis' in the term 'computer assisted qualitative data analysis software' points to only part of the story: these packages now offer functionality in practically every stage of the research process including literature reviewing, storing raw data (such as audio files or fieldwork diaries, Corwin and Clemens, Chapter 36), transcription, then the various eponymous analysis tasks, and even writing up. Indeed there is even the possibility that these packages may be of use to you even if you reject the more conventional analysis functionality: for example, this chapter has been written entirely in NVivo 8, for storing and organizing relevant literature, making notes, planning an outline and drafting the text.

The easy management of volume described above also applies to the management of coding: it is not only large amounts of data that are more easily managed using CAQDAS, large numbers of coding categories plus related relevant information such as definitions and notes on the development and refinement of ideas are also more easily managed and stored, making perhaps otherwise unmanageable coding strategies possible (Tesch, 1990). In addition to these features relating to managing volume of codes, the flexibility of managing and merging codes in CAQDAS packages means inter- and intra-coder reliability can be more easily facilitated, and likewise features allowing the writing of memos and annotations to record information as the analysis proceeds can help strengthen reliability and validity (Rambaree, 2007). These functions can, when used effectively and appropriately, contribute to the rigour and consistency of the analysis process, although again without a clear analysis approach by no means guarantees it.

Lewins and Silver (2009) identify researchers' preferred working styles as a key consideration in the choice of CAQDAS package, and this is as important in the decision whether to use a package at all as it is in any decision as to which package to use. Many researchers need to 'feel the paper', and feel less able to think productively about their data in the computerized medium. It is important to accept that this is not an either-or choice: many researchers will combine working with hard copy and working with a CAQDAS package, perhaps printing out paper versions of transcripts and scribbling notes in the margins before organizing these more creative thoughts using the software. By employing a software package, researchers are not committing themselves to a rejection of manual analysis, or the completion of all the tasks the software facilitates. The vast majority of researchers using CAQDAS appear to work most effectively combining both manual and digitized analysis.

The ability to execute your analysis plan profitably using CAQDAS does still somewhat depend on the type of analysis you are undertaking, despite recent developments in the flexibility and functionality of these packages. CAQDAS packages have traditionally been used less in projects involving conversation analysis, as the software features of many of the packages facilitate this kind of analysis less well than other forms of analysis, and manual coding remains preferable for many (King, 2010), while the packages have been particularly popular with researchers using a grounded theory approach (Bringer et al., 2006) (see Clarke, 2005; Charmaz, 2006; Bryant and Charmaz, 2010 for material on the grounded theory approach).

Finally, learning to use any analysis software requires energy and attention. For smaller projects with challenging timetables and straightforward analysis tasks, the time a researcher needs to choose between software packages and then train to use one may render any potential benefits to the research project minimal (Lewins and Silver, 2009; Schiellerup, 2008).

CHOOSING BETWEEN CAQDAS PACKAGES

When a decision to use a CAQDAS package is made, the decision as to which package to use should be informed by the research needs of the project, while simultaneously ensuring that early management of materials, including transcription, can be informed by package-specific functionality (King, 2010). Early awareness of issues such as whether line numbers can be inserted into transcripts using the software, and how automated functions use headings and paragraph styles will help the preparation of research materials in a way that best exploits the functions of the software. Despite trialling two available packages before making her choice, Schiellerup (2008) felt that a better grasp of the analytical process she would undertake would have helped her choice greatly.

Despite the sophisticated functionality in many contemporary packages, relatively simple code and retrieve tasks remain their most used features, rather than theory building or writing functions they offer (Schiellerup, 2008): so while the sophisticated features of high profile expensive packages may be impressive and alluring, some of the simpler and less expensive packages such as QDA Miner or The Ethnograph may meet your software needs perfectly adequately.

While the increasing feature-richness of leading CAQDAS packages offer a flexibility of approach that makes them useful to most research designs, some researchers find certain features less well suited to their projects. These determinants are far less rigid as they once were as the functionality and flexibility of packages has improved. Schiellerup (2008) felt that the hierarchical structures in coding in NVivo were unsuitable for her grounded theory approach, and settled on ATLAS.ti as a more suitable package for her research needs, although Bringer et al. (2006) found NVivo to be a useful tool for the grounded theory approach in their project. While it is less rigid than in earlier versions, the 'coding tree' structure remains at the heart of NVivo's coding functionality, and from my experiences providing training in both NVivo and ATLAS.ti, a like or dislike of this is often the crucial difference that leans novices one way or the other in choosing a package. Traditionally, ATLAS.ti has also been the more popular package for researchers requiring theory building functions (Rambaree, 2007). However, there have been major changes in software versions released in recent years and both ATLAS.ti and NVivo are both very flexible, feature-rich tools, and in terms of functionality there is now little difference between them as far as the research needs of most users are concerned.

Consequently considerations other than functionality are becoming increasingly persuasive in researchers' choices between packages. The issues of preferred working style and whether using software helps or hinders your ability to think analytically about your data applies to choices between packages: neither Schiellerup nor Bringer were right or wrong in terms of which package is 'best' for grounded theory approaches, rather they identified which package enabled them to execute their research design most effectively. Issues as apparently benign as the appearance of the user interface can be as important a factor in choosing between packages as more objective criteria relating to functionality.

Wider technological developments in recent decades have resulted in not only the digitization of the analysis process but also of data collection tasks, and also in the production of digitized audio, video, photographic and mapping data (Reader, Chapter 30, this volume) all of which can be managed directly within some packages alongside more traditional text data (Froggatt, 2001). If your analysis needs require the continued handling of such data beyond transcription or text-based descriptions, then packages that handle multimedia data are a great asset to analysis. A few years ago, NVivo (and its previous incarnation NUD*IST) were seen as being less suitable for handling multimedia data compared to ATLAS. ti, but versions 8 and 9 have reversed this for many who now see NVivo as the stronger multimedia equipped package. But the margins are slight, and each new version or service pack changes things slightly again. Either way, both of these packages now handle a variety of digitized data types excellently, but if you won't need these features, investing in purchasing and learning these multimedia enabled packages isn't necessary and may be harmful to your project.

Technological and software developments have impacted both the way in which as researchers we observe and interpret the worlds that we study and also on the worlds that we study themselves, and the use of CAQDAS has developed accordingly. Using hypertext and hypermedia to work with and present qualitative data offers multiple non-linear ways for both researchers and readers to navigate mixed media data, following authored links, fostering more of a cross-referencing approach rather than the indexing offered by conventional CAQDAS packages (Dicks and Mason, 1998). Packages such as ATLAS.ti, HyperRESEARCH and latterly newer versions of NVivo have incorporated hypertext functionality, to expand the range of analysis approaches possible with CAQDAS.

If you will be conducting analysis as part of a team, there are some issues to bear in mind regarding the choice of package. Firstly, if you find yourself in part of a team who are established users of a specific package and the analysis will be shared, the time that needs investing in training means you are more likely to have to adopt their preferred package unless you can make a very strong case for a whole group or researchers to have to retrain. If you will have sole or primary responsibility for the analysis tasks, the preferences and expertise of team members with other software may be less of an issue. Secondly, different packages manage multiple users in different ways, and understanding how a package supports team-work and what your team-working needs will be must be clear to make the most suitable choice between packages. Some packages allow multiple users to log in to a single shared file, while others facilitate a system of duplicating a master file for each team member and then merging them back into one file as the work progresses. All the packages retain records of which researcher performed which task and when, and offer features to compare and measure inter-coder agreement.

In considering your software options you should, perhaps rather incongruously, consider any non-qualitative needs you may have in the project, which you often may not need until the later stages of analysis. Most CAQDAS packages offer a range of options for outputting data in formats suitable for further analysis in statistical packages such as SPSS, and NVivo 9 even offers database functionality within the software, and these can be useful for the management of demographic or descriptive items of information coded within the CAQDAS package. There is a lack of consensus regarding demonstrating the trustworthiness of qualitative research findings, and there is a variety of approaches in how this is claimed including the use of multiple researchers (Freeman et al., 2007). One way of evidencing this claim to trustworthiness is using the inter-coder comparison features in CAQDAS packages, which can report on the levels of agreement and disagreement between coders.

Finally, on a pragmatic level, the choice of package may be influenced by what is available at your institution if it has a site licence for a particular package, which covers use for everyone across the institution. This consideration is not only financial, although that is an important factor if you are not in a position to budget for your preferred software in a research funding application. As importantly as the financial consideration of institutional availability is the likelihood that you will be more able to benefit from the support and advice of other users if a package is supported by your institution.

CONCLUSIONS

The following questions briefly summarize the issues discussed here which might help inform the decision to use a CAQDAS package at all:

1.   Whether using a CAQDAS package will help with the management of data and coding materials.
2.   Whether any other functionality of available software packages will be useful to the research.

3. Whether using software will help or hinder your ability to think analytically about your data.
4. Whether the time invested in being trained to use software is worthwhile to other project needs.

And similarly, if deciding between packages, questions may address:

1. What are you intending to use the software for, and how well suited are the different packages to achieving these?
2. Does the user interface of a particular package facilitate your ability to think analytically about your data?
3. Do you have any multimedia needs in your research?
4. What team-working issues impact on your choice?
5. How well do the packages meet any non-qualitative output needs such as outputting to statistical packages or inter-coder comparison?
6. What is available to you, either through an institutional licence or to purchase from available budgets?

This chapter has reviewed some of the main considerations when deciding whether to use a CAQDAS package, and if so, which. While the issues covered here will help inform the decision, they are most useful when combined with hands on experience of the packages. Even if the decision is all but made, it can still be enormously useful to have some direct experience of more than that package, either through introductory training courses, or through the independent use of the software. If you cannot access the full versions of software you wish to try, most packages offer free trial periods, with either slightly limited functionality or a time limited licence. Extensive online support materials are available for all main packages to allow you to identify and get a feel for the practicalities of using the features you plan to use in your research. Guidance documents and training are enormously helpful resources in making choices about CAQDAS, but there are few universal answers, and ultimately deciding which package to use, if any, needs to be informed above all else by a clear understanding of your research and analysis strategy.

NOTE

1. At the time of writing, online resources reviewing the features of specific packages are provided by the CAQDAS Networking Project at the University of Surrey and the Online QDA project at the University of Huddersfield.

REFERENCES

Bringer J., Halley Johnson, L. and Brackenridge, C. (2006), 'Using computer-assisted qualitative analysis software to develop a grounded theory project', *Field Methods*, **18** (3), 245–66.

Bryant, A. and Charmaz, K. (eds) (2010), *The Sage Handbook of Grounded Theory*, London: Sage.

Charmaz, K. (2006), *Constructing Grounded Theory: A Practical Guide through Qualitative Analysis*, London: Sage.

Clarke, A.E. (2005) *Situational Analysis: Grounded Theory After the Postmodern Turn*, Thousand Oaks, CA: Sage.

Coffey, A. and Atkinson, P. (1996), *Making Sense of Qualitative Data*, London: Sage.

Dicks, B. and Mason, B. (1998), 'Hypermedia and ethnography: reflections on the construction of a research approach', *Sociological Research Online*, **3** (3), http://www.socresonline.org.uk/3/3/3.html (accessed 15 April 2011).

Fielding, N. and Lee, R. (1998), *Computer Analysis and Qualitative Research*, London: Sage.

Freeman, M., deMarrais, K., Preissle, J., Roulston, K. and St and Pierre, E. (2007), 'Standards of evidence in qualitative research: an incitement to discourse', *Educational Researcher*, **36** (1), 25–32.

Froggatt, K. (2001) 'The analysis of qualitative data: processes and pitfalls', *Palliative Medicine*, **15**, 433–8.

King, A. (2010), '"Membership matters": applying Membership Categorisation Analysis (MCA) to qualitative data using Computer-Assisted Qualitative Data Analysis (CAQDAS) software', *International Journal of Social Research Methodology*, **13** (1), 1–16.

Lewins, A. and Silver, C. (2009), '*Choosing a CAQDAS package*', 6th edn, available at http://eprints.ncrm.ac.uk/791/1/2009ChoosingaCAQDASPackage.pdf (accessed 24 February 2011).

Rambaree, K. (2007), 'Bringing rigour in qualitative social research: the use of a CAQDAS', *University of Mauritius Research Journal*, Special Issue, **13A**, 1–15.

Richards, T. and Richards, L. (1994), 'Using computers in qualitative research', in N. Denzin and Y. Lincoln (eds), *Handbook of Qualitative Research*, London: Sage, pp. 445–62.

Schiellerup, P. (2008), 'Stop making sense: the trials and tribulations of qualitative data analysis', *Area*, **40** (2), 163–71.

Tesch, R., (1990), *Qualitative Research: Analysis Types and Software Tools*, Bristol, PA: Falmer.

Wickham, M. and Woods, M. (2005), 'Reflecting on the strategic use of CAQDAS to manage and report on the qualitative research process', *The Qualitative Report*, **10** (4), 687–702.

38. The literary and rhetorical turn
Paul Atkinson

How we write makes a difference. We produce texts that reconstruct particular social worlds, institutions and groups. We create accounts of local cultures, mundane practices and specialized actions. Written language is not a neutral medium through which we can convey equally neutral 'findings' about the social world. Language, spoken and written, is a 'thick' medium. It has its own conventions that impinge directly on what we can and what we cannot convey by way of written texts. This, of course, is not confined to social or educational research. It applies to any and every form of writing. Our academic disciplinary cultures are characterized by the textual conventions that they display, as well as by many other methodological commitments. For instance, the 'standard' scientific journal paper reflects just one restricted set of textual conventions. It is not, as it were, just a 'natural' way of representing scientific work. Although it does not strike us as being an especially 'literary' mode of representation, even the journal paper is a distinctive kind of textual genre. When it comes to more obviously discursive forms of writing – such as the production of an ethnography – then it is more obvious that we ought to pay attention to issues of authorship. In this context it is worth noting the convergence of method and textual product in the term 'ethnography' itself.

The 1970s and 1980s witnessed a flurry of interest in the rhetoric of social science texts – anthropological, sociological and other. This in turn reflected a yet wider scholarly interest in the 'rhetoric of inquiry'. Sociologists commented on the rhetorical and textual character of their own discipline. Brown (1977) argued that an understanding of sociological argumentation rests on an analysis of its rhetorical forms. He examined the characteristic use of figures of speech and metaphors. The use of root metaphors, for instance, pervades sociological texts. Key examples include the use of sociological irony, whereby :'Unexpected similarities are revealed, as are unnoticed differences; opposites are seen to require each other or even to converge; sincerity is seen as bad faith, therapy as manipulation, law as opposed to order, evil as containing hidden good' (Brown, 1977, p. 185). Edmondson (1984) also applied a rhetorical analysis to sociologists' textual forms. Based on a close reading of several major sociological texts – not all of them ethnographic – Edmondson displays a number of recurrent rhetorical devices. Of particular relevance to ethnographic representation is her account of 'rhetorical induction'. By that she means the deployment of examples and instances from which the reader can interpret generic aspects of social situations. One way of accomplishing this, Edmondson suggests, is through the use of the 'actual type'. Unlike the sociological device of the ideal type, actual types are reports of concrete events, spoken utterances and so on that are characteristic (not necessarily representative in the statistical sense) of a broader analytic category. Both Brown and Edmondson made important contributions to our understanding of how sociological texts are constructed, and how they are interpreted. They emphasized that there is no fundamental distinction between explicit theory and the implicit theorization that is inscribed in rhetorical features and devices.

Atkinson (1983, 1990, 1992, 1996) specifically addressed the textual conventions of sociological ethnography, particularly – but not exclusively – urban and organizational ethnography. Pointing out, in common with Carey, the mutual influences of ethnographic research and the interactionist tradition, Atkinson (1983) focused on the irony that although interactionism was founded on a recognition of how 'language' is constitutive of social reality, interactionists seemed to pay insufficient attention to their own written language. There seemed to be a disjuncture between the sensitivities of ethnographic fieldwork and the relative insensitivity of interactionist writing. While the influences of literary and other genres were apparent, they were implicit.

Van Maanen (1988) authored an incisive analysis of the different genres of ethnographic writing. He identified, amongst other things, the contrast between conventional, realist ethnographic texts and the 'confessional' mode of autobiographical narrative. In the classic genres of urban ethnography, these two modes of writing were normally kept separate. The confessional, autobiographical mode of writing was normally confined to a somewhat marginal position: it was to be found in the methodological appendix to the monograph, or in collections of autobiographical essays by field researchers (which could safely be read in a more light-hearted way than the research papers and monographs that reported the research). The difference created a kind of textual cordon sanitaire between the personal and the scholarly. As we shall see, this is a distinction that has become increasingly blurred. Van Maanen also identified a third ethnographic genre, which was couched in more impressionistic or evocative written styles. In recent years, such writing has become more prominent. At the same time, the genres that he identified have – in the hands of many authors – become more blurred. We shall outline these developments later in this chapter.

Atkinson (1990, 1992) examined the textual conventions whereby classic sociological ethnographies are constructed. He demonstrated some of the literary devices and conventions that are deployed by ethnographic authors in order to construct plausible and persuasive reconstructions of social settings, actions and actors. Whereas Brown and Edmondson drew their analytic insights primarily from the world of rhetoric, Atkinson's treatment of the subject was more overtly formed by an engagement with aspects of literary critical theory. Atkinson's analyses were intended to convey the extent to which ethnographic texts – mostly monographs – deploy textual conventions to create recognizable and plausible social worlds, while sociological arguments are carried at an implicit level through those textual or rhetorical resources. Atkinson extended that form of argument to an examination of the style of Erving Goffman (Atkinson, 1989). Goffman's work is a clear case, though by no means unique, of a sociological vision that is sustained through a distinctive written style.

Cultural anthropologists were exposed to a parallel set of arguments concerning the textual conventions of ethnographic monographs. In many ways, anthropology as a discipline was more troubled by the textual or rhetorical turn than was sociology. There were two closely related possibilities for that. First, virtually all practising anthropologists were authors of at least one ethnographic monograph themselves, and so the entire discipline was implicated in any epistemological or methodological critique. Secondly, anthropological debate and theoretical disagreement had, to that point, been based on a corpus of texts that were themselves taken for granted. The classic texts of anthropology were exemplars of the discipline, and anything that appeared to undermine their credibility and legitimacy thus struck at the roots of the discipline itself.

The key text in this epistemological 'crisis' was an edited collection of essays (Clifford and Marcus, 1986). *Writing Culture* precipitated considerable controversy among anthropologists, and in some quarters was felt to amount to a radical critique of the discipline. As we have said, it threatened some of the discipline's foundations more deeply – some believed – than any theoretical disputes (such as the divide between structuralism and functionalism, or the contrasts between American cultural anthropology and British social anthropology, or the debates engendered by Marxist critiques of the discipline). In many ways the impact of *Writing Culture* was more symbolic than based on the specific contents of the various chapters. Overall, the collected essays conveyed the general argument that ethnographic monographs classically inscribed a very particular sort of world-view. The social world under scrutiny was presented in terms of a single, dominant perspective – that of the epistemologically privileged author-anthropologist. There was a direct continuity between this mode of perception and its textual realization, and the imperialist heritage of pre-anthropological writing. It was portrayed as an essentially hegemonic mode – in itself inimical to anthropology's stated embrace of cultural relativism and cultural egalitarianism. In other words, implicit textual conventions ran counter to the discipline's explicit motivations. Among other things, the critique of anthropological writing led to an endorsement of more 'messy' texts and more polyvocalic modes of representation. Not all anthropologists, of course, were equally moved by these and similar arguments: for a cool and sceptical view see Spencer (1989, 2001).

Clifford and Marcus are male American anthropologists, and although their influential collection was not by an all-male authorship, it contained only one chapter by a woman, and focused only on the texts of male anthropologists. The first major responses came from women in American anthropology: Behar and Gordon (1995) redressed the gender balance by using women authors to write about women anthropologists such as Elsie Clews Parsons and Zora Neale Hurston. Central to their book was the argument that many women anthropologists had rejected the canonical textual styles of their contemporaries and experimented with 'other' literary forms. A collection of responses from men and women in British social anthropology was edited by James, Hockey and Dawson (1997).

All three edited collections revolved around the textual nature of ethnographic work. The authors questioned some of the taken-for-granted practices of anthropologists as authors. They threw into critical relief many of the background assumptions of anthropological writing, especially the style and structure of the ethnographic monograph. In particular, the debates centred on the relationship between authority and authorship. The conventional, traditional ethnographic monograph tended to be written in a particular style, in which the authority or legitimacy of anthropological reconstruction was represented through the authorial voice of an omniscient observer/narrator. The surface of the ethnographic text presented a unified portrayal of the culture in question, all observed and reported from a single viewpoint. Parallels with colonialist writing were highlighted. An appeal to more 'messy' texts, with varying perspectives was called for, with multiple voices, rather than the single and dominant voice of the ethnographer-as-author. These ideas readily found echoes and parallels elsewhere, and sparked off lively debates within anthropology and beyond. The anthropologist's text became as much an object of scrutiny as the culture reported in it. The ethnographic monograph could no longer be viewed (if it ever had been) as a relatively innocent and transparent medium of reportage: it had epistemological and ideological implications in its own right. It was necessary to recognize that textual forms and conventions themselves played an active part in forming the anthropological analysis. From within American cultural anthropology, Clifford Geertz also devoted attention to the stylistic and rhetorical features of anthropological writing (Geertz, 1988). His own reflections on textual practice in many ways reflected Geertz's commitment to an interpretive anthropology. He was, therefore, especially sensitive to the analytic work performed by textual conventions, and conscious of the close relationships between textual conventions and styles of anthropological thought. Boon's earlier accounts of the textual representation of anthropological analysis in many ways set the tone for these later reflections (Boon, 1982).

Partly as a result of these critiques of traditional forms of reportage, a significant number of scholars have in recent years turned to the production of 'alternative' literary forms. Recognizing that – as we have seen – writing is itself a form of analysis, and that literary constructions are reconstructions of the social world – sociologists and anthropologists have explicitly and deliberately experimented with written genres. These have included various overtly 'literary' styles as ethnographic fiction, autobiographical writing, poetry and drama. Many of these styles have their origins in texts originally conceived as performance pieces. As a consequence, we now have a number of commitments to styles of writing that, in various ways and to different degrees, depart from the previously taken-for-granted literary forms. There are, in other words, multiple genres in the field (see Somerville, Chapter 40, this volume). They include a commitment to literary styles that celebrate polyvocality, such that the authorial voice of the social scientist author is disrupted, and different 'voices' are rendered audible or visible (see Gitlin, Chapter 39, this volume). The 'alternative' genres include a far greater emphasis on 'personal' writing that places emphasis on the introspective experience of the researcher herself or himself. These textual forms include, therefore, 'autoethnography', in which the author is simultaneously the subject and the object of the ethnographic gaze (see Delamont, Chapter 41, this volume). Textual forms have also been extended to include writing that is explicitly 'fictional'. Here the author attempts to evoke social settings and social actors through a fictionalized reconstruction, rather than a literally factual one. The author is thus able to explore the full range of fictional styles in the act of textual production (see Sikes, Chapter 43, this volume). In a similar vein, researchers have even explored forms of representation and reconstruction that are not dependent on conventional written forms at all. These include performance genres such as dance (see Bagley and Castro-Salazar, Chapter 44, this volume). These and other forms of representation thus add up to a highly variegated field of texts, performances and voices. Of course, this does not mean that more conventional textual forms have been abandoned. Social science is still preponderantly published in traditional forms. Ironically, anthropologists themselves seem to have lost interest in textual commentary, as if it could be treated as a passing fad. On the other hand, scholars in communication studies and some varieties of sociology continue to generate a multiplicity of textual types.

Some early ventures into ethno-poetry took informants' original words and rearranged them into verse-like forms, in order to bring out aspects of the ethnopoetics of the original discourse. The personal and emotional dynamics of informants' original accounts were thus foregrounded in such an act of editorial engagement with their original words. More recently, it is clear that authors are seeking licence to create their own verses, developing more personal, writerly texts. These often no longer convey any implicit claim to enhance the ethnopoetics of indigenous spoken accounts, but are more appropriately seen as the creations of the authors themselves.

The adoption of a poetic voice is but one way in which novel genres can be used. Another is 'ethnodrama' (Mienczakowski, 2001). Here the essential feature is that selected aspects of everyday life are reconstructed not through a conventional realist ethnographic text, but are represented in dramatic form. The methods and compositional techniques for such exercises can vary. The ethnographer may undertake more-or-less traditional field research and draw on those data – observations, interviews, transcribed talk – and choose to write the results in a dramatic form. Such dramas may be therefore constructed in such a way as to reflect the dramaturgical character of everyday life and social interaction. On the other hand, the author may use a more 'impressionistic' approach, more distinctly removed from field data, constructing what is essentially a new dramatic enactment on the basis of her or her understanding of a given setting. Different again is the form of ethnodrama that is not simply 'authored' by the ethnographer-observer, but is a collective project, produced collaboratively with chosen social actors. In other words, the ethnodrama is a form of social activity in its own right. It may be a way of mobilizing a particular group, so as to give them voices that might otherwise go unheard. Here the dramatic reconstruction is a form of action research in its own right. There is a potential criticism of any or all ethnodrama that parallels a potential criticism of ethno-poetry. There is no doubt that everyday life is intensely performative. The work of major authors like Erving Goffman has repeatedly shown forms of social life that are intrinsically dramaturgical. Arguably, it is the task of the social analyst to 'examine' those dramaturgical forms, rather than imposing extrinsic dramatic reconstructions.

Such experimental writing will serve a number of purposes. It subverts the smooth surface of the text in order to disrupt the monologic style in which the ethnographer-observer occupies the sole vantage point, and from whose standpoint the entire account is provided. The kaleidoscopic presentation of different textual styles and fragments thus allows the writer and the reader to shift from one perspective to another. Couched in such innovative ways, the ethnographer may well be seeking to 'evoke' a social setting and social action. The writing may, therefore, be impressionistic in character. Moreover, the evocative text is evaluated in terms of its connotative or affective quality as much as, or more than, its denotative precision.

There have been several book-length works of fiction by ethnographers. Pfohl, for instance, conducted conventional sociological research, including work on the practical reasoning that psychiatrists undertake in order to predict 'dangerousness'. His *Death at the Parasite Café* is a very different exercise, mingling fictional texts in an exercise in political commentary (Pfohl, 1992). Carolyn Ellis, who has championed many of the recent developments in new genres of ethnographic text has also composed an 'ethnographic novel', *The Ethnographic I* (Ellis, 2004). This particular work takes ethnographic reflexivity to a particular extreme, through the construction of a fictionalized account of the conduct of ethnographic and autoethnographic work. Unlike some other fictional writing in this genre, it retains an explicitly pedagogic function, as well as taking ethnographic pedagogy as its subject-matter. (See also Banks and Banks, 1998.)

The development of writerly texts, and a renewed emphasis on the author, has led to the expansion of 'autoethnography' as a genre (Ellis and Bochner, 1996; Bochner and Ellis, 2002). Reflexivity and first-person narratives lead directly to the possibilities of autoethnography. The term itself has several connotations. Here we shall focus briefly on analyses that are based substantially or even exclusively on the writer's personal experiences, memories and actions. This, therefore, moves the personal from the marginal notes of the confessional tale to occupy the central place of sociological or anthropological analysis. Autoethnography and autobiography can be virtually indistinguishable. The resulting accounts can be highly charged emotionally for the author and reader alike (for example, Tillman-Healy, 1996). Reed-Danahay's (1997) collection, and her overview (2001) showcase these developments. In these autoethnographic exercises, the ethnographer treats herself or himself as the primary object of scrutiny, or at least a major part of it. Here, as in other forms of 'experimental' writing, the textual character of interpretation is granted prominence. The textual wheel has turned almost full circle since the days of the classic ethnographic monograph. In the older texts, the authorial gaze was an impersonal scrutiny of 'the other'; now we have a personal gaze on the 'self'.

This does not imply, however, that all ethnographic writing has become 'writerly', or that the field is entirely dominated by performance pieces, fictions, poems or autoethnographies. The anthropological and sociological journals continue to publish papers that are not couched in experimental forms. Publishers produce large numbers of monographs that do not depart significantly from traditional forms and styles. Talk of 'crises' and epistemological 'turns' inevitably exaggerates the nature and impact of novelty. On the other hand, whatever styles and genres of representation may be adopted, we can no longer – individually or collectively – claim innocence. We know that there is no neutral medium of representation and communication. We know that what we write and how we write are mutually implicated. A commitment to methodological reflexivity must always take account of the forms though which our social reconstructions are achieved.

At the present time, then, we have a variegated intellectual scene. Many authors continue to write in 'traditional' ways that reflect little if any of the past decades of debate and commentary. At the opposite end of the textual spectrum there are those who have embraced the literary turn enthusiastically, committing themselves to forms of fiction, drama and poetry. The former continue to reflect long-standing criteria of rigour and excellence in their written work; the latter emphasize aesthetic and evocative criteria for their work. Between two extremes, many authors are today willing to write themselves into the texts of their research, adopting more varied styles of reportage, while avoiding a primarily aesthetic approach to their written work. The sheer variety of perspectives and practices, as well as the recent history of representational reflection and experimentation may be judged from the contents of the four-volume set edited by Atkinson and Delamont (2008). This chapter is a much abbreviated version based on the extended introductory essay for that anthology.

REFERENCES

Atkinson, P.A. (1983), 'Writing ethnography', in H.J. Helle (ed.), *Kultur und Institution*, Berlin: Duncker und Humblot.

Atkinson, P. (1989), 'Goffman's poetics', *Human Studies*, **12**, 59–76. Reprinted in G.A. Fine and G.W.H. Smith (eds), *Erving Goffman*, four vols, London: Sage.

Atkinson, P.A. (1990), *The Ethnographic Imagination: Textual Constructions of Reality*, London: Routledge.

Atkinson, P.A. (1992), *Understanding Ethnographic Texts*, Thousand Oaks, CA: Sage.

Atkinson, P.A. (1996), *Sociological Readings and Re-Readings*, Aldershot: Avebury.

Atkinson, P.A. and Delamont, S. (2006), 'In the roiling smoke: qualitative inquiry and contested fields', *International Journal of Qualitative Studies in Education*, **19** (6), 747–55.

Atkinson, P.A. and Delamont, S. (eds) (2008), *Representing Ethnography*, four vols, London: Sage.

Banks, A. and Banks, S. (1998), *Fiction and Social Research: By Ice or Fire*, Walnut Creek, CA: AltaMira.

Behar, R. and Gordon, D. (eds) (1995), *Women Writing Culture*, Berkeley, CA: University of California Press.

Bochner, A. and Ellis, C. (eds) (2002), *Ethnographically Speaking: Autoethnography, Literature and Aesthetics*, Walnut Creek, CA: AltaMira.

Boon, J.A. (1982), *Other Tribes, Other Scribes: Symbolic Anthropology in the Comparative Study of Cultures, Histories, Religions, and Texts*, Cambridge: Cambridge University Press.

Brown, R.H. (1977), *A Poetic for Sociology*, Cambridge: Cambridge University Press.

Clifford, J. and Marcus, G.E (eds) (1986), *Writing Culture*, Berkeley, CA: University of California Press.

Edmondson, R. (1984), *Rhetoric in Sociology*, London: Macmillan.

Ellis, C. (2004), *The Ethnographic I: A Methodological Novel About Autoethnography*, Walnut Creek, CA: AltaMira.

Ellis, C. and Bochner, A. (eds) (1996), *Composing Ethnography: Alternative Forms of Qualitative Writing*, Walnut Creek, CA: AltaMira.

Geertz, C. (1988), *Works and Lives: The Anthropologist as Author*, Cambridge: Polity.

James, A., Hockey, J. and Dawson, A. (eds) (1997), *After Writing Culture*, London: Routledge.

Mienczakowski, J. (2001), 'Ethnodrama: performed research – limitations and potential', in P. Atkinson, A. Coffey, S. Delamont, J. Lofland and L. Lofland (eds), *Handbook of Ethnography*, London: Sage, pp. 468–76.

Pfohl, J. (1992), *Death at the Parasite Café: Social Science (Fictions) and the Postmodern*, London: Macmillan.

Reed-Danahay, D. (ed.) (1997), *Auto/Ethnography: Rewriting the Self and the Social*, Oxford: Berg.

Reed-Danahay, D. (2001), 'Autobiography, intimacy and ethnography', in P. Atkinson, A. Coffey, S. Delamont, J. Lofland and L. Lofland (eds), *Handbook of Ethnography*, London: Sage, pp. 407–25.

Spencer, J. (1989), 'Anthropology as a kind of writing', *Man*, **24** (1), 145–64.

Spencer, J. (2001), 'Ethnography after postmodernism', in P. Atkinson, A. Coffey, S. Delamont, J. Lofland and L. Lofland (eds), *Handbook of Ethnography*, London: Sage, pp. 443–52.

Tillman-Healy, L.M. (1996), 'A secret life in a culture of thinness', in C. Ellis and A.P. Bochner (eds), *Composing Ethnography*, Walnut Creek, CA: AltaMira, pp. 76–108.

Van Maanen, J. (1988), *Tales of the Field*, Chicago, IL: University of Chicago Press.

39. From voice: exploring the possibilities of experimental art
Andrew Gitlin

Voice, in subtle, and not so subtle ways, has played an important role in many progressive educational methodologies (that is, those methodologies that in one way or the other attempt to correct long-standing cultural hierarchies and inequities). One such methodology, for example, is Critical Race Theory (CRT). The underlying foundation of this methodology is the sense that only dominant stories have been told, thereby reproducing the legitimacy of these dominant positions and the institutions, rules, and contexts that support those positions (Ladson-Billings and Tate, 1995). Calmore (1995), for example, suggests that CRT tends:

> toward a very personal expression that allows our experiences and lessons, learned as people of color, to convey the knowledge we possess in a way that is empowering to us, and it is hoped, ultimately empowering to those on whose behalf we act. (p. 321)

CRT is about voice – the significance of the experiences of cultural actors of color (Dixson and Rousseau, 2005). Voice is used as a marker to differentiate those who have an opportunity to speak and are listened to, and those whose voices have been muted and excluded from public discourse. By making this differentiation voice becomes a way to provide a balance, a social justice of sorts, for those who have been denied an opportunity to make history as opposed to being only an object of that history.

In much the same vein, narrativists use a methodology based on telling stories of those who have been silenced and/or not heard (McLaughlin and Tierney, 1993). Weis and Fine (1993), in their introduction to *Beyond Silenced Voices*, talk about the relation between silence and voice:

> From within the very centers of structured silence can be heard the most critical and powerful, if excluded, voices of teachers and students in public education. Further, we soon recognized that our volume would need to move 'beyond silencing' not only by listening to those who had been institutionally banished from the center to the margins, but by deconstructing those policies and practices that have historically encoded power privilege, and marginality in our public schools. (p. 1)

Challenging silence is one way narrativists, storytellers, try to achieve their progressive aims. In this way voice is used to provide a counterpoint to the dominance of certain stories over others. This dominance is problematic because those excluded or at least marginalized have been limited in shaping public discourse. While narrativists are less overtly political than CRT scholars, in a general sense voice is used in a similar way – to provide opportunities for those people and stories that have not been given the opportunity to contribute to public discourse, especially the discourse that has been dominant in a particular context and time.

Voice is also an underlying foundation for the progressive methodology of critical pedagogy (Freire, 1970). These critical scholars use voice or the limitations of voice as a link to oppression of many kinds – race, class, and gender specifically. In particular, these critical pedagogical scholars are activists trying to upend long standing inequities. Given this purpose, it is central to their project that the means of change do not contradict the ends of change. It is at this intersection that voice comes in. Voice is a way to equalize and show solidarity with others – for example, teachers and students, academics and union workers, African-Americans and Caucasians. No group should have their voices rule over another group and so voice becomes a central conceptual bridge to equality.

Ironically, some clarity on voice comes from a critic of critical pedagogy. In an article that helped launch postmodernism in the USA, Ellsworth's (1989) critique of critical pedagogy begins with the claim that student voices are partial–partial in the sense that they project certain group interests over others (p. 305). She is suggesting that the way critical pedagogy utilizes and actualizes student (and teacher) voice prioritizes certain inequities and overlooks others. For example, heterosexuality, at times, is overlooked in analyses associated with Marx, critical theory, and class.

Voice is also problematic, according to Ellsworth, because critical pedagogues do not consider the imbalances of power between 'empowerer' and student, the ways to change this imbalance, and the institutional context that supports that imbalance (p. 306). Put differently, critical pedagogues, according to Ellsworth, give us little instruction on how to work within institutional contexts like schools to set up the type of relationships between teacher and student that would lead to the forms of social justice desired.

Within these critiques, Ellsworth is not questioning voice itself but rather the specific way voice tends to be used within many forms of critical pedagogy. In a reverse type of logic, her critique of critical pedagogy leaves the notion of voice, although a different conceptualization, in place. Even critics of critical pedagogy see voice as a central aspect of this progressive methodology as long as voice is more open to all sorts of cultural inequities and addresses imbalances of power found in many educational institutions.

Given this reverse logic, a claim can be made that voice has informed critical pedagogy narrativists and CRT. This is not to say that voice is generally accepted. As was true of Ellsworth, most criticisms of voice have to do with making it better. These criticisms are informative for what they emphasize and what they leave out. By chronicling some of these critiques, I intend to set the stage for how the progressive methodologies articulated in this chapter try to make voice better rather than seeing its connection to an underlying epistemology, that of subjective science, which stands in contrast to the ambitions of these progressive methodologists.

CRITICAL RESPONSES TO VOICE

One such critique of voice is articulated by Schneider (2003). Schneider builds on Ellsworth in thinking about the limits of voice. Using a postmodern perspective, Schneider suggests Lacan's psychoanalytic semiotics can overcome many of the limits found in CRT and its use of voice. According to Schneider, Lacan's analysis focuses on the connections between the subject (marginalized) and discourse (voice as storytelling) and in this way postmodernism captures the complexities of subjects and provides a way to better understand complex social systems (pp. 94–6). As Schneider states, 'contrary to some internal critique levied by CRT, postmodernism can successfully contribute to a more informed analysis of race, class, and gender by aiding the further development of insights in how stories are communicated and constructed' (p.101).

Schneider, as is true of Ellsworth, is trying to develop a better view of voice or storytelling. Both Ellsworth and Schneider are critical of the way progressive methodologists use rationalistic meta-theories to look at race, class, and gender and other forms of oppression. The solution, according to this perspective, is to move to a postmodern theory that allows for the local discourses to be considered, thereby paving the way for a more inclusive view of oppression, and a more practical contextual account that captures the complexity of everyday living. In both these cases, and many related critiques of a postmodern type, what is included is a more sophisticated and nuanced view of voice. What is left out is the possibility that voice is limited given its reliance on a dominant epistemology – subjective science.

Postmodernism has been a constant critic of voice. This line of criticism, however, is not singular and not limited to the types of arguments made by Ellsworth and Schneider. Other scholars under the broad umbrella of postmodernism/post-structuralism have ventured into other directions in their critique of voice. One of the most powerful positions is laid out by Dennis Carlson (1998) in 'Finding voice, and losing our way'. Let me briefly describe his position.

Carlson begins his argument by stating that 'we hear much talk these days about voice' (p. 541). Some who see their identity as radical according to Carlson have lost their way because they do not consider the truth games – the norms that determine who can speak and what one can speak about nor the rhetorical style in which to speak or write that helps shape notions of voice. The truth game Carlson focuses on is reflected in a text by Ladwig (1996) who argues for a type of science that makes radicals expert witnesses not preachers (p. 547). The problem with this truth game according to Carlson is that 'we are beginning to realize there is no easy way to separate out the preacher from the expert witness' (p. 548). According to Carlson, this push for evidence-based science cannot satisfy a true radical or progressive politic.

Instead of moving toward this evidence-based science, Carlson suggests that voice might benefit from allowing at least two rhetorical styles to exist simultaneously (he does mention a third but it takes us too far from the main point). According to Carlson, Plato's logos and mythos (p. 550) is suggestive in this regard. Logos is a focus on reason, logic, and evidence, while mythos is the seductive language of poetry, metaphor, fiction, and mythology. For Carlson, logos and mythos should direct the academic educational left so that they embrace 'storytelling and the subjective' (p.550). He concludes his discussion of voice by saying that 'storytelling, autobiography, the use of literary references, and other expressions of mythos, has enriched progressive discourse' (p. 553).

Notice at least one important move that Carlson has accomplished – mythos as poetry and fiction has been expanded to include storytelling, autobiography, and the use of literary references including poetry and fiction. Yet, as I have suggested, Carlson is trying to make voice better by including the stories of those left out and articulating the autobiographies of the oppressed and others who can express their voices more clearly through the writing process. While Carlson does begin to express a move beyond a singular notion of voice, his reliance on methodologies such as autobiography, or storytelling (a narrative perspective) more generally, suggests that making voice better is still part of his primary motivation. Put differently, according to Carlson, voice is improved if it includes the insight of Plato's logos and mythos. Making voice better is accomplished by avoiding objective science (an evidence-based science) and embracing the subjective as seen in storytelling, autobiography, and literature.

In sum, the many critics of voice often stop short of looking at voice as having epistemological assumptions. The section that follows tries to consider some commonly held assumptions of voice – namely those associated with a subjective science. To see these assumptions and their limits, it is essential to say more about the nature of subjective science before moving forward.

RIGOR, DISCIPLINARY NORMS AND LANGUAGE

Most forms of what is referred to as normal science is based on notions of rigor, community discipline, and language use (Rorty, 1982). Because progressive methodologies tend to be subjective, they do not follow the exact codes that normal science does. However, at the core their use of rigor, community discipline, and dominant language enable progressive methodologies to achieve legitimacy and bolster claims of authority and expertise. So when I make the claim that progressive methodologies embrace science, I mean that they employ forms of rigor, they discipline those who go beyond the codes of rigor and employ dominant language, thereby overlooking the relation between the development of new languages and a progressive politic.

The progressive methodologies mentioned, CRT, narrative texts, and critical pedagogy, utilize three forms of rigor: the need to make a clear a priori political statement concerning inequities; the importance of using disciplines like anthropology, sociology, and history to enhance the authority of the methodologies used; and the need to be at the site of practice including interviews with actors, observing relations in schools, and so on. The limit of the a priori political statement is that the problem is defined before the fact – this means the problem is not visionary or innovative but rather based on historical assumptions. The limitation of using other disciplines is that their codes may be ill suited to the progressive ambitions and are typically developed to provide a sense of legitimacy for those disciplines. Again progressives, in particular, need methodological codes in line with progressive ambitions. And finally, the focus on what is happening in practice, while not applicable to all progressive methodologies surely is at the forefront of progressive methodologies using voice. Critical pedagogy is about redefining student-teacher relations and narrativists and CRT want stories that speak to practices and relations that have been accepted in part because the counter stories have not been heard. Again, the focus is on the past injustices not the innovative visionary future which lies at the core of a progressive methodology – a new and better future.

Community discipline is another aspect of science that is found among progressive methodologists using voice. This discipline is established through historical struggles with winners and losers. The winners get a greater say in the codes that disciplines utilize to make the claim of having authority other others (Apple, 1979). Authority over others, and a focus on history/present is skewed to the status quo because authority over others runs directly in contrast to the democratic and egalitarian aims of progressive methodologies.[1] And clearly a perspective that reflects the status quo stands in contrast to the political ambitions of these methodologists.

Finally, the use of established languages and categories is also part of what might be referred to as normal science used by progressive methodologists. In particular, the voice methodologies noted embody a conservative perspective because the language and categories come out of the past and not just any past but a past made by those who contribute most centrally to the making and meaning of language and the categories widely accepted (Dewey in Sleeper, 2001, Danto, 2005). As such, those who endorse voice and subjective science use language and categories that in part reflects oppressive formations as it fights for justice. This is an unholy war to say the least. This does not mean that moving beyond voice requires the total rejection of subjective science. Rather, I will suggest we work the borderlands between subjective science and experimental art.

EXPERIMENTAL ART

To articulate what working the borderlands between subjective science and experimental art means, two questions need to be asked: What is experimental art? And what is meant by working the borderlands between subjective science and experimental art?

A Notion of Experimental Art

Experimental art is a title that has been used to name a variety of perspectives on art that represent radically innovative challenges to traditional community boundaries including painting dance music, and so on. For example, Jonathan Cage (in Danto, 1981) would be an experimental artist because his music included an assault on the traditional boundaries of what is music. Specifically, Cage worked on a piece of music called '4 minutes and 33 seconds'. This piece was performed outside in a beautiful natural setting in up-state New York. The pianist who was playing the piece came before the hushed crowd, sat at the piano and when the crowd settled never moved his fingers to the keys, only up and down to indicate differing stanzas. After 4 minutes and 33 seconds the pianist rose and went off 'stage.' The crowd, as expected, was very upset. It was assumed by many that this was a bad joke or worse a type of charade aimed at fooling the audience. Yet a few people, very few, did see something in the work. They were able to see that what Cage was doing was introducing us to an expanded view of music, one coming from the natural environment. What the audience could hear if they listened was the sounds of an impending thunderstorm, the birds heading for shelter, the wind whistling in the trees. And clearly, for a few, this was some of the most beautiful non-music music they had heard. Cage was doing experimental art.

When Joan Miro (in Umland, 2008), decided that he had to leave painting because he was trapped in the boundaries of what makes a successful painter, he invented collage. He spoke in a new language with new ambitions and purposes, paying close attention to the way success and I would add community discipline can trap up and make us think we are innovating even though we are actually working toward authority, expertise, and success within a particular genre community and wider context. Miro, in this sense, was an experimental artist.

When Duchamps signed his ready-mades on the back, he was not only challenging the notion of authority–authorship, but also the boundaries of art (Cros, 2006). Was is possible to take what is already made and put in an alternative context with alternative purposes and by doing so create art? Duchamps did this work against violent responses from most in the art world. With Cage and Miro, he was challenging the community discipline authority and the notion that art was only about techniques. Duchamps was an experimental artist with his 'ready-mades.' And of course, there is Warhol (1975) and his famous work with the Campbell soup can. Was this a commodity you would find in the supermarket or type of art that conflated the relation between art commodity and popular culture? Again, Warhol was asking a question about the boundaries of a community, the status of a community, and the need to rethink and expand our vision of what is art. A new language was developed to speak to an expanded boundary of what counts as art. Warhol was an experimental artist.

In case you are thinking that all experimental art has come and gone and I have some romantic fantasy about the past, let's move to a recent article about dance that might take some of you by surprise. The article begins with this quote. 'When two performers barely move while starring into each other's eyes for nearly 90 minutes . . . conventional notions of dance dissipate like phantoms (Kourlas, 2010, p. 7). What is produced according to Kourlas is an experimental form of dance that confuses what counts as dance, in spite of grants that try to reel the artist toward the center. As he notes, 'crossing the line dismisses labels by rendering them meaningless' (p. 7). Further, this series of dance builds context around art and the world in which it is created which allows dance and world to be seen in relation to each other as both are challenged and reconfigured. The purposes are explicitly political dealing with questions of what is normal. In part, these experimental artists are taking dance out of dance 'homes' and making the relation more intimate. These experimental artists are redefining dance, redefining the context of dance, and ultimately developing a more intimate language that shakes the foundations of a disciplined community at its core. Surely, they are experimental artists.

Working the Borderlands

Working the borderlands between experimental art and subjective science is a metaphor that speaks to the importance, of the need, to escape the powerful normative push of community discipline. It really doesn't matter what community one is referring to. Over time the community discipline gets stronger, more normative, and pays continuous homage to the glory of the status quo. Those interested in change and even transformation must not only be aware of this force, they must act directly to quiet its intentions and directive. Working the borderlands is a way of saying we need to escape the teeth of the status quo and the role of community discipline in feeding this bottomless pit. Even the most avant-garde of artists, in short measure, will come into conflict with their political ambitions when subjected to such discipline. One of the few counter proposals to this seduction is to be both in a community and outside the community such that what has become commonplace and common sense no longer is just that. For example, as I have mentioned, the subjective scientists who utilize voice have based much of their inquiry and knowledge on the importance of history. History surely has its possibilities and potentialities but often overlooked is the way history seduces us to support the status quo. This seduction occurs because history focuses on the past and its connections to the present. We often say we must learn from the past to remake the future. I would say we must be very cautious about the past, because it is our perception that allows for new realities, not so-called facts and truths anchored in historical thinking and contexts. Given that there is no need to have an alternative perception to be a good historian, only the ability to present a realist history – the real story of a particular history – can have the influence of linking the future to the past as either alternative (in other words, a negation) to, or in line with, the perceptions, events, and institutions that have made it what it is. Compare this to Cage and his piece '4 minutes and 33 seconds.' There is no history in his piece of music. There is no attempt to discipline or satisfy what has come before.

The only attempt is visionary, a new world, a new perspective, a new sense of the relation between silence, sound, and music. In short hand, one could say that experimental art errors to the future and subjective science errors to the past. Working the borderlands is being aware of both disciplinary codes and the way they force us back to the status quo. And also seeing the way our perspectives, forms of common sense, normative inklings, can stand in contrast to the freedom that is required for new worlds to emerge from our dream-like visions not found solely in the past (Rorty, 1982).

My claim is we need both subjective science and experimental art. We need to pay attention to the illusion of history because it has become a form of community discipline. But we can't be seduced by this history. Instead, we also need Cage, an experimental art orientation. We need a vision that works outside of established categories, develops a new language and importantly an alternative perspective that goes beyond the power relations already established. History held at a distance with vision is at the core of what is meant by working the borderlands between subjective science and experimental art.

TURNING POINT

What can be made of working the borderlands between subjective science and experimental art? Or what are some of the constructs that change if we leave voice to the side and instead focus our attention on the borderlands between subjective science and experimental art?

One of the first constructs that comes to mind is that an alternative view of the relation between change/transformation and knowledge begins to emerge. For example, one of the major perspectives on change and knowledge comes from Thomas Kuhn (1962). Within his view paradigms develop and over time some gain authority and legitimacy based on confirming knowledge. In the background are alternatives to this view. Once counter perspectives are developed within the dominant paradigms, these perspectives can start to gain authority. And at points of change an alternative becomes the 'new' dominant, the new paradigm. Again, I am not suggesting that this view is inherently wrong or misguided. I do think is it one view as opposed to *the* view of normal science and change. And surely this view has its limits especially for those using methodologies based on transformation or even significant change proposals. Why? Because Kuhnian views of change accept community discipline as a good, as a natural part of change and knowledge development. In contrast, working the borderlands between subjective science and experimental art confronts the traditional view of community discipline. It views community discipline as a process that stands as a road block for change. It is a road block to a type of change that focuses attention on a visionary view in lieu of the authoritative view. This authoritative view may work well for knowledge forms associated with the status quo but actually is a limit for transformative views like CRT, narrativists, and critical pedagogues. What working the borderlands between experimental art and subjective science does is replace discipline and the construction of authority with a continuous process of innovation that is never subsumed by the authority of dominant paradigms.

The work of the 'voice' methodologies has not only implicitly endorsed discipline and dominant notions of change, such as community discipline, within their own communities; they have also been too ready to accept history as one of the significant keys in looking at and understanding schooling and its relation to societal inequities. History is one of the most overlooked assumptions of the progressive methodologies mentioned. Sadly, this focus when utilized in its totality minimizes a future that is not so tied to the past; it is defined by the past and the notions of dominance associated with that time.

In contrast, working the borderlands between subjective science and experimental art looks to the past and balances this with an illusionary-visionary future. Further, because the realism of history is balanced with the surrealism of experimental art, transformation can be based on a balance between the past and a future not seen in the present – on the unknown future. And it is this unknown future that is at the heart of experimental art and significant notions of transformation. For example, getting the health bill correct in the USA is not only a matter of funding or providing health care for all, it is also a matter of redefining what is health care. And it is this last part that is missing from many policies and proposals that are intended to be transformative and one of the strengths of experimental art.

Working the borderlands between experimental art and subjective science also allows transformation to go hand in hand with categories and language more generally that are in line with the purposes and ambitions of the progressive 'voice' methodologists. One such limit is the utilization of the categories and language that are dominant within this community and society as well. The categories of race, class, and gender, for example, are indicative of this type of limit. What is limiting about these categories is that they are seen as realist. Put differently, they assume that using race, class, and gender, and others, in some combination, reflect how relations are formed in practice. But these three categories and others are not sufficient to capture reality. In fact, trying to capture reality is a problem in itself. Adding more and finding new ways to combine them may be a step in the right direction, but will never be real, because the category is historic while the reality is changing ever faster toward an unknown future. It is also the case that these categories are closed. They don't change as change takes place in society. Now working the borderlands between experimental art and subjective science doesn't throw out these categories but balances their closed realist nature with the fluidity and openness of surrealism emerging from experimental art. For example, almost all the experimental artists developed new and transitory notions of art, music, and even dance. As such, category development and traditional categories are both involved in the production of new knowledge.

Finally, working the borderlands between subjective science and experimental art allows the dominant epistemological debate – objectivity and subjectivity – to move beyond this narrow focus to consider the question of transformation and illusion or the unknown. The debate between objectivity and subjectivity has informed the 'voice' methodologies in powerful ways. Subjectivity has been endorsed as a way to study culture, and combine moral, political, and ethical issues with the technical aims to improve schools. This has been a major step forward. However, this debate has allowed the relation between knowledge and transformation to be at least only a second thought. Regardless of whether a methodology is subjective or objective, it can be in line with transformation or not. What seems lacking is an epistemology that moves fluidly back and forth from understandings coming out of subjective science to visions that challenge the construction of dominance and speak to the unknown. The known and the unknown are balanced, vision and understanding, work together to inform and be informed by an activist agenda aimed at transformation.

NOTE

1. Some of you may respond to my claim about experiential knowledge by saying we are already doing experiential knowledge in our qualitative, ethnographic work and in auto-biography and action research. In a way this is true as all these groups use experiential knowledge. But I would claim it is also experiential knowledge that gives authority to the author, an author likely to be an academic if for no other reason than it is written over and retold through a writing academic lens. By doing so, the knowledge no longer is the expression of an actor about experience, it is an expression of experience by someone who has observed or rewritten that experience and therefore has changed its meaning and even more foundationally the story itself. The democratic potential is minimized if not lost. When combined with the closed categories and language of the academic, the conservative nature of this type of work becomes clear. As opposed to looking back to the center to gain authority, expertise, and the claim of superiority, progressives writing experiential stories of others might simply foster the collection of everyday stories of people who consistently reflect on their life as they live their experiences.

REFERENCES

Apple, M. (1979), *Ideology and Curriculum*, New York: Routledge and Kegan Paul.

Calmore, J.(1995), 'Critical race, theory, Archie Shepp and fire music: securing an authentic intellectual life in a multicultural world', in K. Crenshaw, N. Gotanda, G. Peller and K. Thomas (eds), *Critical Race Theory: The Key Writings that Formed the Movement*, New York: The New Press, pp. 315–29.

Carlson, D. (1998), 'Finding voice and losing our way', *Educational Theory*, **48** (4), 541–53.

Cros, C. (2006), *Marcel Duchamps*, London: Reaktion Books.

Danto, A. (1981), *The Transfiguration of the Commonplace*, Boston, MA: Harvard University Press.

Danto, A. (2005), *Unnatural Wonders: Essays From the Gap Between Art and Life*, New York: Columbia University Press.

Dixson, A. and Rousseau, C. (2005), 'And we are still not saved: critical race theory in education ten years later', *Race, Ethnicity, and Education*, **8** (1), 7–27.

Ellsworth, E. (1989), 'Why doesn't this feel empowering? Working through the repressive myths of critical pedagogy', *Harvard Educational Review*, **59** (3), 297–323.

Freire, P. (1970), *Pedagogy of the Oppressed*, New York: Continuum Publishing.

Kourlas, T. (2010), 'Beyond modern dance', *New York Times*, 30 May, 7–9.

Kuhn, T. (1962), *The Structure of Scientific Revolutions*, 2nd edn, Chicago, IL: University of Chicago Press.

Ladson-Billings, G. and Tate, W. (1995), 'Toward a critical race theory of education', *Teachers College Record*, **97** (1), 47–68.

Ladwig, J. (1996), *Academic Distinctions: Theory and Methodology in the Sociology of School Knowledge*, New York: Routledge.

McLaughlin, D. and Tierney, B. (1993), *Naming Silenced Lives: Personal Narratives and the Processes of Educational Change*, New York: Routledge.

Rorty, R. (1982), *The Consequences of Pragmatism*, Minneapolis, MN: University of Minnesota Press.

Schneider, C. (2003), 'Integrating critical race theory and postmodernism: implications of race, class and gender', *Critical Criminology*, **12** (1), 87–103.

Sleeper, R. (2001), *The Necessity of Pragmatism: John Dewey's Conception of Philosophy*, Chicago, IL: University of Chicago Press.

Umland, A. (2008), *Joan Miro: Painting-Anti-Painting*, New York: MOMA Publishing.

Warhol, A. (1975), *The Philosophy of Andy Warhol*, San Diego, CA: Hart Brace and Company.

Weis, L. and Fine, M. (1993), *Beyond Silenced Voices; Class, Race and Gender in United States Schools*, New York: State University New York Press.

40. Textual genres and the question of representation
Margaret J. Somerville

> We now can embrace sophisticated theoretical stances on critical and qualitative race and ethnic perspectives, border voices, queer, feminist, indigenous and other non-Western lenses and epistemologies. Previous generations of inquirers could distinguish themselves simply as qualitative researchers; we know now that the field and its practitioners are neither unitary nor united, except in their critical and/or interpretive stances. (Denzin et al., 2006, p. 778)

For over thirty years qualitative research has proliferated and flourished. During the past ten years there have been a number of attempts to characterize and defend the nature of the field and the various paradigms within it (for example, Atkinson and Delamont, 2006; St Pierre and Roulston, 2006; Cairns, 2010). In this chapter I take the approach that the strength of the field of qualitative research is that it is based on 'difference'. A proliferation of methods of data collection and analysis has generated ongoing and rigorous debate. The debates concern the relationship between the subjects of our investigations – the people, including ourselves, whose lives we investigate – and the ways that we undertake the investigations. This includes an essential relationship to the means through which we represent the knowledge produced through our research in public and scholarly dissemination.

While there have been varying responses to the pressures from national governments to reduce the breadth and complexity of the field (Denzin et al., 2006), qualitative research continues to grow in strength, coming of age in a new openness to examination as a tradition of research that continues to interrogate the relationship between knowledge claims and the actions on which those claims are based. Difficult and intransigent social problems, big and small, local and global, and ethical responsibilities to the people on whose lives our labours impact, are addressed. It could be argued that qualitative research as a field of scholarship and intellectual endeavour is predicated on a study of difference.

A reflexive concern with the 'crisis of representation' is appropriate in a field concerned with difference. Originating in social anthropology as a fundamental critique of the possibility of representing 'the other', the crisis of representation precipitated concerns about the 'death of ethnography'.

Ethnography is at the heart of qualitative research as method. Derived from the Greek *ethnos*, meaning people, and *grapho* meaning to write, it fundamentally evokes the relationship between the study of peoples and the ways we write about them. Anthropology as a disciplinary field of study, however, emerged from the colonization of large numbers of peoples of the world. By the mid 1980s critiques were mounting about the colonizing nature of anthropological knowledge, and the impossibility of the colonizer to represent the lives of the colonized other. Similar critiques emerged from the perspective of gender (Behar, 1995), class (Walkerdine, 1997), race (Smith, 1999), from the global south (Connell, 2007), and other disciplines in the human sciences, notably sociology, education and health. These critiques have strengthened and enhanced the growing field of qualitative research.

Ethnographic researchers, and qualitative research more generally, have responded to these critiques with a serious engagement with issues of representation. Researcher reflexivity, the acknowledged presence of the researcher within the text reflecting on the processes of knowledge production, is a key response. The tradition of auto/ethnography sprang from this response and produced wide ranging texts of self experience (for further elaboration see Ellis and Bochner, 2002; Ellis, 2004). However, the reflexive 'I' is possibly one of the most challenging forms of academic writing and knowledge production. The challenges of the writing 'I' of ethnography in educational research are highlighted in the reflexive and disruptive writings of St Pierre (1997), Lather (2000) and Richardson (1997).

Both St Pierre and Lather offer examples of poststructural deconstructive texts that reflect on iterative processes of representation and writing. St Pierre takes up the metaphor of 'the field' to open up a space for a Deleuzian deterritorialization by the nomadic ethnographer. For St Pierre, the 'smooth spaces of the field' produce its corollary, the aside, a transgressive space, where meaning is constantly under erasure. Lather thinks through her metaphor of angels in writing about women living with HIV-Aids to articulate an epistemology of the in-between and generate new forms of writing: 'My investment is, rather, to work towards innovations leading to new forms . . . the angels mark the incomplete rupture with philosophies of the subject and consciousness that undergird the continued dream of doing history's work' (Lather, 2000, p. 307). For both the disruptive stance is an essential quality of the production of knowledge through qualitative inquiry.

In a landmark article 'Writing: a method of inquiry' Richardson (1994) claimed writing itself as the means of coming to knowledge. Most powerfully explicated in her construction of the Laura Mae transcript as poetry (Richardson, 1997), this idea is demonstrated in her practice over the next two decades in writing research as drama, responsive readings, narrative poetry, pagan ritual, lyric poetry, prose poems and autobiography (Richardson, 1997, 2001; Richardson and St Pierre, 2005). For Richardson, each time research data is represented in a new form of writing, new insights emerge. The aim of these transgressive forms is to open up taken-for-granted ways of interpreting the world and to reflexively reveal the nature of knowledge in its processes of generation: 'Casting sociology into evocative forms reveals the underlying labour of sociological production and its rhetoric, as well as its potential as a human endeavour' (Richardson, 1994, p. 521).

Following Richardson, textual genres continue to proliferate in a different sense than earlier exemplary representations of ethnographic research in creative forms (see, for example, Gannon, 2004; Connelly, 2010), because of the inclusion of a necessary reflexivity on the part of the researcher. An enduring question, then, for ethnographic reflexivity is: 'Where am I in this research? How do my actions as a researcher shape the knowledge made possible through this research and its representations?

My own engagement as a female, Antipodean, third generation Scottish immigrant researching in the context of the relations between Indigenous and non-Indigenous knowledge systems in Australia has pushed these questions of representation beyond writing as a method of inquiry. I have become interested in the limits of language, particularly, but not only, in relation to the hegemony of western knowledge systems. My research involves place, collaborations and partnerships, a contact zone of cultural difference, and the necessity to work across disciplinary boundaries and research paradigms.

Here I digress briefly into the realm of the natural sciences. There are two images that I will draw on here to develop a particular idea. The first is one that I always think of when I am poking in and out of the rock holes and infinite curves and shapes of the shoreline. Mandlebrot asks the question: How long is the British coastline? His response is that it stretches to infinity; it is through the movement from embodied knowledge of place, to its representation on a map, that the British coastline becomes measurable and knowable. The second is Latour's image of science in the savanna – the precise moment when the soil is removed from the swaying fields of grass and placed in coded test tubes. In observing the passage of soil from savanna to test tube, Latour is seeking to understand how one brings the world into words, how one makes 'reference' – how to understand whether 'the referent' (the thing in the world) 'is what I point to with my finger outside of discourse or . . . what I bring back inside' (Latour, 1993, p. 32). Under what he terms the 'old settlement', science, nature and society are separate. Latour, however, advances a very different and 'unsettling' idea:

a webwork of persons/text/things, fundamentally connecting the natural and human sciences. This is the space of representation. It is a space where difference is both constituted and violated.

In educational research, Green (2009) traces the translations of teaching and learning as a relational, pedagogical act into its representation in written curriculum. Drawing on Biesta (2004, cited in Green, 2009) Green argues that attention needs to be given to the relationality of teacher and learner, to their relation, literal and symbolic, and to the 'difference-relation' that enfolds them. The gap between teacher and learner is crucial for education and so too is the 'gap' between knowledge and identity, arguably so central to curriculum. 'The practical implication here', he writes, 'is the value of lingering in the in-between, learning as a form of indwelling' (Green, 2009, p. 11).

In what follows I inhabit the passage through which knowledge was produced in my collaborative research with Aboriginal partner researcher Chrissiejoy Marshall. For Marshall, even though her doctoral study was about developing a conflict resolution package, in order to think anything at all, she had to 'think through country'. The methodology of thinking through country evolved directly from her relationship to her birth country, and was developed in visual, oral and written forms. She produced a painting and an accompanying oral story that structured and informed each cluster of meanings, or chapters, based on her knowledge frameworks of country. She produced a CD of visual images and oral stories to accompany the written document. By moving between the paintings, the oral storytelling and the writing, and consciously reflecting on the development of a radical alternative methodology, Marshall was able to articulate meanings that would otherwise be inaccessible in the written word.

In the CD of her recorded oral performance Marshall presented a series of computer-generated digital images of her paintings and explained how the stories of the paintings articulated elements of her research:

> There is no one word in any Aboriginal language that I can find for the term 'art', which is lucky for me, who, not for one moment considers myself an artist. That these paintings may be seen as *unremarkable art* by Anglicised standards, is of no consequence, it is far more important that the paintings actually describe to the viewer the information that I am telling. What anthropologists and others have described as crude and unsophisticated art, was actually Aboriginal pictorial reflections simply for the passing on of knowledge, so that the listener or learner could visually grasp the concept or subject matter being given. Similarly, that which is now described as dance, song and ceremony was (simplistically put) much more a way of passing on information including history, lore and laws, than the recreational pursuits that are presently ascribed. The symbols and drawings described by those anthropologists and historians actually constitute a

complex code of interaction that continually reflects on Aboriginal cosmology, philosophies, spirituality, history and laws that have been used for thousands and thousands of years. (Marshall, 2008, emphasis in original)

Marshall is self-reflexively aware that she is generating knowledge in the context of a western academic institution, in the English language, and using mainly western iconography in her images. Her paintings and stories are constituted in the contact zone between these two knowledge traditions. They are an example of new knowledge emerging rather than old knowledge being re-told. She creates a carefully orchestrated performance of emergence in conversation with her non-Indigenous audience using her paintings, oral storytelling, Yuwalarayi language and the self-conscious act of translation. Each of these elements creates meaning in relation to each other part of the performance. Meaning, and indeed difference, is created from the space between the different elements of her performance, of the different representations that are assembled for the purpose.

I have observed other students in Australia, and in other parts of the world, for whom the same challenges exist at the limit-edge of writing. They operate in a wide range of registers and emphasize different sensory modalities. Their research is characterized by multiple acts of translation – always on the borderline between different forms of representation. In these multiple acts of translation they take Richardson's 'writing as a method of inquiry' (Richardson, 1994; Richardson and St Pierre, 2005) to a new dimension, through their engagement with other forms such as oral storytelling, painting, dance and conversation. They are deeply skeptical of standard forms of academic writing; some are skeptical of all writing, especially in the English language. They bend the forms of academic writing and use different genres of writing side by side to generate intertextual meanings. A recurring theme is the absences and silences, the things that cannot be spoken, the in-between spaces that have no name or are too difficult to name, the private and the shameful.

In attempting to articulate the nature of these innovative processes of representation in qualitative research I developed a Special Edition of the *International Journal of Qualitative Studies in Education* to explore this work (Somerville, 2008). In analysing the researchers' pieces, I identified a particular metaphor or image that carried the meaning of the ontological and epistemological project in their papers. Marlene Atleo, for example, began her paper with an ontological question expressed through her cell phone voice message: 'Hi, this is Mar(e), Marlene, or Marilyn'. This provided an entrée to exploring her multiple selves and their relation to an unfolding methodology. The very terms by which we give an account of ourselves, by which we make ourselves intelligible to ourselves, and to others, are not of our making. They are social in character, they establish social norms, a domain of unfreedom and substitutability within which our singular stories are told (Butler, 2005, p. 20).

As a young German immigrant to Canada, Atleo had married a First Nations leader. Her exploration of the simple everyday message on the cell phone allowed her to examine the complex self–other relationships in her research study of Nuu-chah-nulth health programmes. It allowed her to explore the implications of '?eh-?eh-naa-too-kwiss', the self she 'does not have and have not the heart to capture her in the technospace of her voice-mail box'. '?eh-?eh-naa-too-kwiss' is her Nuu-chah-nulth First Nations traditional name as the *hakum* (chief's female partner) in the *haoothee* (system of spiritual, moral, social, political and economic rights and obligations) of the Nuu-chah-nulth chiefdomships. Through the device of the mode of address and naming, she can write about the complex relationships of cultures, languages and thought that are central to her research and to her unfolding methodology.

For de Carteret the metaphor was of the spaces or holes that produce the patterns in lace, drawn from an old family tradition of lacemaking. Through attending to 'the uncertainties and knowledge spectres – hauntings, consonant with the inquiry itself' she could work through the silenced and shameful in the production of classed subjectivities. Her focus on the absences in her own and her participant's storytelling opened her research to 'the opacity of the subject' and the limits of knowability. This led to a methodology that evolved through conversations where the absences were as significant to meaning-making as the spoken words as collective, relational selves come into being. The words, and the silences, are made visible as spaces on the arrangement of scanned transcript lines.

Martin Mantle took up the challenge of his own 'blurred vision' to better understand his topic of the image of the blind man in literature. His intention in his paper was to explore 'the absences and interstices in academic writing as sources of knowledge', using the poetry that he was unable to include in his dissertation. His paper beautifully juxtaposes poetry, personal writing, academic theory and narrative text. As with Marshall's work, meanings are generated intertextually with an emphasis on 'the embodiment of absence', the importance of the spaces between textual genres in meaning-making. At the simplest level this is realized in the spatiality of lines of poetry on a white page. At a deeper level poetic writing evokes deeper layers of meaning extending the limits of rational academic writing, the semiotic of Kristeva's 'madness, holiness and poetry'.

Nancy Toncy reflected on iterative acts of representation through different sensory modalities in her research. As a Muslim woman living in New York, Toncy speaks both Arabic and English and returned to

Egypt to conduct her research on Muslim women. She chose neither English nor Arabic as the vehicle for her research, however, recognizing that 'movement has always been the form in which I expressed myself'. Her methodology evolved as a creative response to the difficulties experienced at each stage of her research. Movement, like dance, became the method of her data collection, analysis, interpretation and representation as a subtly nuanced way to research the meaning of Egyptian Muslim women's lives. She choreographed a dance in response to each woman's individual story, danced the dance back to the woman and then refined her dance-as-analysis. The elements of each pause in this iterative process of representation and reflection – the audio recording of the woman's story, the dance, and the video of the dance, the refinement of the dance as analysis, are then available for further assemblages of representational forms. The process culminated in the choreography of a final dance piece to represent the collective meanings gained through the research process.

In thinking through the evolving processes of these and other doctoral students, I came to realize two things. The first was that these qualitative researchers had no choice but to work in this way. Their struggles with methodology and representation were not about an attempt to better present the results of their qualitative research in some authentic way. For them the development of new forms was an essential precondition of the generation of knowledge from working the boundaries of the in-between. The second was the recognition of the need for a new understanding of representation itself.

This new understanding of representation embraces multiple modes of expression, such as story, song, dance and visual images, as well as interviews, academic prose and so on. The focus is on creation of meaning from the relationship between the parts. These multiple creations are naïve in the sense that, although they may be subject to the erasure of deconstruction, they are produced and valued in and of the moment. Each is a pause in an iterative process of representation, engagement and reflexivity. These naïve forms are the means by which we display and engage with the ongoing products of our research. A tape-recorded interview, for example, can be regarded as such a pause, a relational artefact of the interaction between researcher and researched, a recorded oral performance. This recorded oral performance retains its own integrity of form and meaning in the pause, but it can also be transcribed and reinterpreted at any time by its inclusion in an assemblage of other representations. Digital technologies have made all this more possible and may even be integral to this new way of working as qualitative researchers.

The production of these forms of representation enables researchers and participants to engage with the research and to present it to others outside the research act. Meaning, however, is dynamic and is constituted intertextually between the various elements of each performance or representation. These evolving genres of representation do not reject academic writing but strain at the very limits of what writing can mean. They inhabit the passage between the real of the world, the difference of the infinite folds and curves of the shoreline, and the meanings we generate with lines on a page.

ACKNOWLEDGEMENTS

I would like to acknowledge the collaboration with my partner researcher Chrissiejoy Marshall and her permission to quote from the CD prepared for our collaborative research 'Bubbles on the Surface: a place pedagogy of the Narran Lakes' funded by the Australian Research Council 2006–09. I would also like to acknowledge the collaboration with the newly completed doctoral candidates who contributed to the Special Edition of the International Journal of Qualitative Studies in Education as referenced in the chapter.

REFERENCES

Atkinson, P. and Delamont, S. (2006), 'In the roiling smoke: qualitative inquiry and contested fields', *International Journal of Qualitative Studies in Education*, **19** (6), 747–55.
Behar, R. (1995), 'Introduction: out of exile', in R. Behar and D.A. Gordon (eds), *Women: Writing Culture*, Berkley, CA: University of California Press, pp. 1–32.
Butler, J. (2005), *Giving an Account of Oneself*, New York: Fordham University Press.
Cairns, K. (2010), 'The methodological dilemma: creative, critical and collaborative approaches to qualitative research', *International Journal of Qualitative Studies in Education*, **23** (6), 755–8.
Connell, R.W. (2007), *Southern Theory: The Global Dynamics of Knowledge in Social Science*, Cambridge: Polity.
Connelly, K. (2010), 'What body part do I need to sell? Poetic re-presentations of experiences of poverty and fear from low-income Australians receiving welfare benefits', *Creative Approaches to Research*, **3** (1), 16–42.
Denzin, N.K., Lincoln, Y.S. and Giardina, M.D. (2006), 'Disciplining qualitative research', *International Journal of Qualitative Studies in Education*, **19** (6), 769–78.
Ellis, C. (2004), *The Ethnographic I: A Methodological Novel about Autoethnography*, Lanham, MD: Rowman Altamita.
Ellis, C. and Bochner, A. (2002), *Ethnographically Speaking: Autoethnography, Literature, and Aesthetics*, Walnut Creek, CA: AltaMira Press.
Gannon, S. (2004), 'Out/performing in the academy: writing "The Breast Project"', *International Journal of Qualitative Studies in Education*, **17** (1), 66–84.

Green, B. (2009), 'From communication studies to curriculum inquiry', *Curriculum Perspectives*, **29** (3), 14–23.

Lather, P. (2000), 'Drawing the line at angels: working the ruins of feminist ethnography', in E.A. Pierre and W.S. Pillow (eds), *Working the Ruins: Feminist Poststructural Theory and Methods in Education*, London and New York: Routledge, pp. 284–311.

Latour, B. (1993), *We Have Never Been Modern*, trans. C. Porter, Cambridge, MA: Harvard University Press.

Marshall, C.J. (2008), Script for DVD 'Thinking through country', Bubbles on the surface exhibition, Switchback Gallery, Monash University, Gippsland.

Richardson, L. (1994), 'Writing: a method of inquiry', in N. Denzin and Y. Lincoln (eds), *Handbook of Qualitative Research*, Thousand Oaks, CA: Sage.

Richardson, L. (1997), *Fields of Play: Constructing an Academic Life*, New Brunswick, NJ: Rutgers University Press.

Richardson, L. (2001), 'Getting personal writing stories', *International Journal of Qualitative Research in Education*, **14** (1), 33–8.

Richardson, L. and St Pierre, E.A. (2005), 'Writing: a method of inquiry', in N.K. Denzin and Y.S. Lincoln (eds), *The Sage Handbook of Qualitative Research*, Thousand Oaks, CA: Sage, pp. 959–78.

Smith, L.T. (1999), *Decolonizing Methodologies: Research and Indigenous Peoples*, London: Zed Books.

Somerville, M. (2008), 'Emergent methodologies', Special Edition, *International Journal of Qualitative Studies in Education*, **21** (3).

St Pierre, E. (1997), 'Methodology in the told and the irruption of transgressive data', *International Journal of Qualitative Studies in Education*, **10** (2), 175–89.

St Pierre, E.A. (2007), 'Book review', *International Journal of Qualitative Studies in Education*, **20** (3), 371–4.

St Pierre, E.A. and Roulston, K. (2006), 'The state of qualitative inquiry: a contested science', *International Journal of Qualitative Studies in Education*, **19** (6), 673–84.

Walkerdine, V. (1997), *Daddy's Girl: Young Girls and Popular Culture*, Cambridge, MA: Harvard University Press.

41. Autobiography: tales of the writing self
Sara Delamont

The autobiographies discussed in this chapter are those published by academic qualitative social science researchers, focused on how their careers and scholarly ideas have evolved, and on their recollections about specific research projects. So the types of publication discussed are Leach's (1984) account of his life in British social anthropology, Bernard's (1990) and Greeley's (1990) intellectual autobiographies written as distinguished American sociologists for a volume edited by Berger (1990) and Behar's (2007) reflections on her family background and research among the Jewish community in Cuba. These are scholars who have done qualitative research, and have written about how that data collection, analysis and textual production fitted into their lives, changed them and led to their success. Those who fail to complete their doctorates, fail to get lectureships and fail to publish are not asked to publish their autobiographies.

These texts are sometimes called 'confessionals', but that has rather negative connotations: it implies that the scholar has done unethical, immoral or shameful things in the past. It is ironic that successful researchers who publish autobiographical pieces, or weave autobiographical ideas into their books, frequently choose to present themselves as cultural incompetents in their own society and in that of their informants; as people who are unable to maintain their personal relationships; and as lacking in skills such as choosing appropriate clothes (Hobbs, 1988, p. 6), knowing when people are telling them tall stories (Foltz and Griffin, 1996) or when not to have a sexual relationship (Wolcott, 2002).

Behar is a case in point. Behar (2007) was born in Cuba, but left as a child. Her Jewish grandparents had left Europe in the 1920s to join a small community that had settled there after 1989. Many of the European Jews were hoping to use Cuba as a way station to the USA. One grandfather, a Russian, was trying to get to Argentina. Her parents married in Cuba in 1956 and left after the revolution of 1959 along with nearly the whole Jewish population of around 16 500 people. Behar writes that she always wanted to revisit the island, and as a doctoral student in anthropology she hoped to do her thesis research there. That was not politically possible, although she did visit in 1979. She did research in Spain and Mexico, and only returned to Cuba in the 1990s. Behar uses this text to choose to reveal herself as hopelessly vulnerable, self-obsessed, perpetually terrified of life, and as someone driven by others rather than controlling her own life. The reader is told, for example,

> I have a terrible sense of direction. I can't read a map and I am capable of getting lost a few blocks from my house in Michigan. (p. 249)

Earlier she had told her audience that she had 'panic attacks', 'Fidelphobia' (p. 16) and that she 'no longer knew how to be Jew anywhere in the world' (p. 15).

Academic autobiography needs to be distinguished from Autoethnography (de Vries, Chapter 25, this volume), in which the researcher studies 'herself': her life and experiences are the research topic. The growth of autoethnographic publications in social science is associated with Ellis and Bochner (1996). Anderson (2006a, 2006b) provides an introduction to autoethnography in general, and other useful overviews are Atkinson (2006) and Delamont (2009).

This chapter appears in the part of the volume on representation: on the rhetorical or literary turn (Clifford and Marcus, 1986; Behar and Gordon, 1995), on genre, on reflexivity about reading, writing, publication and their interface(s). It makes four points: first, it stresses the ways in which autobiographical writing is a variety of narrative (Elliott, Chapter 20, Tierney and Clemens, Chapter 19, Pérez Huber, Chapter 27, Watson, Chapter 34, Cortazzi and Jin, Chapter 35, this volume), and the texts need to be analysed. Then it offers one analytic frame within which such accounts can be analysed. The benefits of reading the autobiographical accounts of educational ethnographers are summarized, and finally, the risks for the author are outlined.

AUTOBIOGRAPHY AS A NARRATIVE GENRE

The scholars who write autobiographical narratives are self-consciously producing an account of their lives that they intend to be entertaining, informative and self-affirming. Most are produced as essays, invited by the editors of year books as Leach (1984) was, or edited collections (the Berger, 1990 volume) or special issues of journals (for example, *The Waikato Journal of Education*, 2005 vol. 11, no. 1). It is an 'honour' to be asked, a mark of success. They are produced by experienced authors, and need to be understood as crafted, not spontaneous, produced for an audience according to cultural conventions; such autobiographies should not be read as simple accounts of the 'facts' or as uniquely insightful, revelatory, 'true confessions'. Until the publication of Clifford and Marcus

(1986), the autobiographical genre was normally kept well away from the main academic publications: segregated into appendices or separate volumes, and not appearing at all in the high status journals (Brown, 1977; Edmonson, 1984; Wolf, 1992; James, Hockey and Dawson, 1997). Autobiographical narratives may have a superficial resemblance to, but are not autoethnographies. The growth of the autoethnography, in which a person does not do any research on anyone but themselves, is a more recent development in qualitative research, which is highly problematic for reasons spelt out elsewhere (Delamont, 2009).

There have been autobiographical writings about the processes of field-work for many years. Some of the early ones were fictionalized and published under pseudonyms, such as Laura Bohannan's *Return to Laughter* published 'officially' by Elenore Smith Bowen (1954). In sociology the collection edited by Hammond (1964) was a landmark, and there was a flurry of such volumes in the 1980s, such as Bell and Newby (1977), Bell and Encel (1978), Bell and Roberts (1984), especially in education (for example, Burgess, 1984, 1985a, 1985b, 1985c, 1989; Walford, 1987, 1991, 1994, 1998). Among the many more recent collections are De Marrais (1998), Lareau and Shultz (1996), Generett and Jeffries (2003), Spindler and Hammond (2006), McLean and Leiberg (2007), Puddephatt, Shaffir and Kleinknecht (2009), Faubion and Marcus (2009) and Young and Goulet (1994). The key point is that these texts are narratives, produced in an era that celebrates narrative as a social science method (Atkinson, 1982, 1989; Atkinson and Silverman, 1997; Atkinson and Delamont, 2006).

THE NATURE OF NARRATIVE

Most social sciences, and most empirical areas, have been enriched by narrative research done in the past 20 years (Atkinson and Delamont, 2006). However there are some distinctly unscholarly, and frankly naïve, writings on narrative around. The boom in illness narratives is one case in point (Atkinson, 1997). Collecting a narrative does not provide a window through which we can see, feel and hear 'the truth' about any social phenomenon. Narratives are produced by social actors, they are performative, they are speech acts, and they can only be useful to social science if that is recognized. (Of course a narrative can be entertaining or frightening or have a pedagogic purpose or be a great basis for poetry or drama or fiction . . . but those are not the proper concerns of social science.) Along with a naïve belief that a narrative is a transparent, 'neutral' window through which we can see social action, there is also a retreat from analysis in favour of presenting the words of the informant 'untouched' by the social scientist in the name of 'authenticity' or 'democracy'. That is equally an abrogation of the social scientists' duty, to analyse data.

These two basic precepts apply equally to the life histories of miners' wives in the Rhondda, or Maori elders in New Zealand, or retired chemistry teachers, or gravity wave physicists, as they do to published autobiographical accounts of social scientists about their research projects or liberal arts undergraduates at the University of Kansas. Narratives are performances, are accounts, must be analysed, and not just celebrated naïvely as 'authentic' or 'true' (Atkinson and Delamont, 2006). The arguments about the interview, rehearsed in Atkinson (1997) and Atkinson and Silverman (1997) apply just as strongly to academics' autobiographies, confessional accounts and autoethnographies (Delamont, 2003).

One analytic strategy useful for the study of academic autobiographies was demonstrated by Atkinson (1996) who produced an analysis of six published autobiographical accounts of ethnographic fieldwork in urban America, including Whyte's (1981) *Street Corner Society* and Liebow's (1967) *Tally's Corner*. He used the structuralist approach (pioneered by Propp to analyse the Russian folk tale), treating the corpus of ethnographers' autobiographical accounts as a genre of narrative, that were, for analytic purposes, parallel to folk tales. The typical story concerns a journey (a quest) for the Hero to find or retrieve a desired object (the grail, the princess, the treasure, the bluebird of happiness) being held by The Enemy (Smaug, The Wicked Witch of the West). The Hero has, in many stories, been born with a head start (the seventh child of the seventh child). The Hero faces setbacks, meets and is betrayed by a false friend, encounters and is helped by a true friend who often provides a magical object (seven league boots, a cloak of invisibility, Excalibur) that facilitates success. Eventually the Hero overcomes the enemy (Sauron, Smaug the Dragon, The Snow Queen, The Wicked Witch of the West), obtains or retrieves the desired object, and lives happily ever after. The six American urban ethnographers had, it transpired, all chosen that 'quest' structure to describe their fieldwork.

So, too, had the eight feminist ethnographers of neopagan witchcraft whose autobiographical accounts I analysed (Delamont, 2010). Using the eight women's accounts I showed that the reflexive autobiographical text *is* a type of narrative; and that it should be analysed, not just enjoyed, or celebrated, or read naïvely. These accounts share formal structural properties, being constructed as three layered quest narratives: (1) a typical quest for good ethnographic data; (2) a quest to find ways to write a scholarly, rational, technical account of studying an unscholarly, irrational, anti-technical phenomenon (magic); and (3) a quest to enter one or more 'other' worlds via initiation and 'otherworldly' experiences. The writing about the third quest, in particular, blurred the boundary between the long established, even traditional, autobiographical narrative about social research and the newer genre of research and writing, the autoethnography. Any scholar planning to write an autobiography should probably plan to do so as a quest narrative, as that has become the normative narrative structure.

THE BENEFITS FOR THE READER

Autobiographical writings about how a particular project was carried out are enormously useful for readers who are themselves trying to do qualitative research, especially novices. Anyone thinking of studying a school would learn a great deal about how to do fieldwork from Linda Valli (1986). She carefully explains how she recorded her data: the observations and the interviews; and how she filed them. Her foreshadowed problems are carefully specified, as are the issues that arose with her key informant, Mrs Lewis. Perhaps most useful for a novice are her admissions of the four abandoned analytic frameworks she tried on her data before she felt satisfied with her analytic strategy. Generally any prospective school researcher would learn more from Valli's autobiographical account than from a textbook, because she focuses on issues like what to record, and how to do the analysis, that are easier to understand in one concrete case than in the abstract. Similarly, Blanche Geer's (1964) classic account of her initial encounters with student culture at Kansas State University in the early 1960s is a wonderful insight into how foreshadowed problems are created and abandoned; and how one's own biography can help, and hinder, fieldwork.

Whether or not the actual, conventional autobiographies written by distinguished scholars are useful or entertaining for future generations of investigators is an unresearched question. The collections of autobiographical papers by American sociologists (Riley, 1988; Berger, 1990) and the three volumes of autobiographical pieces by women (Orlans and Wallace, 1994; Goetting and Fenstermaker, 1995; Laslett and Thorne, 1997) that I analysed (Delamont, 2003) provide glimpses of lost worlds of American universities that only admitted a small quota of Jews, and refused to consider women for tenure. It is hard to see them helping anyone, male or female, plan a career in 2012, but they do give insights into the history of the discipline. It is striking, for example, that in 1980 Goffman (1992) described his friendships in academic life and his intellectual world as 'entirely male' between 1950 and 1980. It is not clear whether Goffman intended to portray the Chicago sociology department as a women-free zone (it was not), or that only the male sociologists' ideas mattered, or that he had no women in his friendship or intellectual circles. However de facto that is what he (and most of his contemporaries) did. The care that the author needs to take when publishing autobiography is the focus of the last section – using a pseudonym is a much wiser course.

THE RISKS FOR THE AUTHOR

The main risks for the author of an autobiographical piece are twofold. First, admissions of incompetence may be read not as contributions to a genre, in which it is a cultural requirement to describe oneself as an accident prone mistake maker, but as a literal, true account. Second, friends, family and former colleagues may be distressed, offended or angry about the account. When Bell (1977) wrote about the restudy of Banbury (a town in England), he offended and distressed the surviving members of the research team. One was dead, and the two survivors were angry about how they, and the dead colleague, were portrayed in the essay. What Bell probably meant as a self-deprecating account of how he had been a brash young man who had not appreciated his colleagues' strengths, nor had empathy for their personal circumstances, came over as an offensive attack on their (in)competencies compared to his skills as a researcher.

Family members, friends and people who were fellow graduate students or colleagues may not wish to appear as characters in the author's story. Revealing high levels of alcohol consumption (Hobbs, 1988) or drug use (Jackson, 2004) may harm employment prospects, or be used to prevent visas being issued. While it may be very satisfactory to write confessional texts, publishing them may not be sensible. Writing fiction is safer, especially if it is clearly labelled fiction. There is a strong genre of campus novels (Carter, 1990) and contributing to that, especially using a pseudonym, is a much wiser course.

REFERENCES

Anderson, L. (2006a), 'Analytic autoethnography', *Journal of Contemporary Ethnography*, **35** (4), 373–95.
Anderson, L. (2006b), 'On apples, oranges, and autopsies', *Journal of Contemporary Ethnography*, **35** (4), 450–65.
Atkinson, P.A. (1982), 'Writing ethnography', in H.J. Helle (ed.), *Kultur und Institution*, Duncker and Humblot: Berlin, pp. 77–105. Reprinted in P. Atkinson and S. Delamont (2008) (eds), *Representing Ethnography*, London: Sage, pp. 218–47.
Atkinson, P.A. (1989), 'Goffman's poetics', *Human Studies*, **12**, 59–76.
Atkinson, P.A. (1996), *Sociological Readings and Rereadings*, Aldershot: Ashgate.

Atkinson, P.A. (1997), 'Narrative turn or blind alley', *Qualitative Health Research*, **7** (4), 325–44.

Atkinson, P.A. (2006), 'Rescuing autoethnography', *Journal of Contemporary Ethnography*, **35** (4), 400–404.

Atkinson, P.A. and Delamont, S. (eds) (2006), *Narrative Analysis*, London: Sage.

Atkinson, P.A. and Delamont, S. (eds) (2008), *Representing Ethnography*, London: Sage.

Atkinson, P.A. and Silverman, D. (1997), 'Kundera's *Immortality*: the interview society and the invention of the self', *Qualitative Inquiry*, **3** (4), 304–25.

Behar, R. (2007), *An Island Called Home*, New Brunswick, NJ: Rutgers University Press.

Behar, R. and Gordon, D.A. (eds) (1995), *Women Writing Culture*, Berkeley, CA: University of California Press.

Bell, C. (1977), 'Reflections on the Banbury restudy', in C. Bell and H. Newby (eds), *Doing Sociological Research*, London: Allen and Unwin, pp. 47–62.

Bell, C. and Encel, S. (eds) (1978), *Inside the Whale*, Rushcutters Bay: Pergamon.

Bell, C. and Newby, H. (eds) (1977), *Doing Sociological Research*, London: Allen and Unwin.

Bell, C. and Roberts, H. (1984), *Social Researching*, London: Routledge.

Berger, B. (ed.) (1990), *Authors of their Own Lives*, Berkeley, CA: University of California Press.

Bernard, J. (1990), 'Jessie Bernard', in B. Berger (ed.) *Authors of their Own Lives*, Berkeley, CA: University of California Press, pp. 193–216.

Bohannan, L. (1954) See entry for Bowen (below).

Bowen, E.S. (1954), *Return to Laughter*, London: Gollancz.

Brown, R.H. (1977), *A Poetic for Sociology*, Cambridge: Cambridge University Press.

Burgess, R.G. (ed.) (1984), *The Research Process in Educational Settings*, London: Falmer Press.

Burgess, R.G. (ed.) (1985a), *Field Methods in the Study of Education*, London: Falmer Press.

Burgess, R.G. (ed.) (1985b), *Strategies of Educational Research*, London: Falmer Press.

Burgess, R.G. (ed.) (1985c), *Issues in Educational Research*, London: Falmer Press.

Burgess, R.G. (ed.) (1989), *The Ethics of Educational Research*, London: Falmer Press.

Carter, I. (1990), *Ancient Cultures of Conceit*, London: Routledge and Kegan Paul.

Clifford, J. and Marcus, G.E. (eds) (1986), *Writing Culture*, Berkeley, CA: University of California Press.

De Marrais, K.B. (ed.) (1998), *Inside Stories*, Mahwah, NJ: Erlbaum.

Delamont, S. (2003), *Feminist Sociology*, London: Sage.

Delamont, S. (2009), 'The only honest thing', *Ethnography and Education*, **4** (1), 51–64.

Delamont, S. (2010), 'Neopagan narratives', *Sociological Research On-Line*, **14** (5), 15pp., http://www.socresonline.org.uk/14/5/18.html

Edmonson, R. (1984), *Rhetoric in Sociology*, London: Macmillan.

Ellis, C. and Bochner, A. (eds) (1996), *Composing Ethnography*, Walnut Creek, CA: Alta Mira Press.

Ezzey, D. (2004), 'Religious ethnography', in J. Blain, D. Ezzy and G. Harvey (eds), *Researching Paganisms*, Walnut Creek, CA: Alta Mira Press, pp. 113–28.

Faubion, J.D. and Marcus, G.E. (eds) (2009), *Fieldwork is Not What it Used to Be*, Ithaca, NY: Cornell University Press.

Foltz, T.G. and Griffin, W. (1996), '"She changes everything she touches"; ethnographic journeys of self discovery', in C. Ellis and A.P. Bochner (eds), *Composing Ethnography*, Walnut Creek, CA: Alta Mira Press, pp. 301–29.

Geer, B. (1964), 'First days in the field', in P. Hammond (ed.), *Sociologists at Work*, New York: Basic Books, pp. 372–98.

Generett, G.G. and Jeffries, R.B. (eds) (2003), *Black Women in the Field*, Cresskill, NJ: Hampton Press.

Goetting, A. and Fenstermaker, S. (eds) (1995), *Individual Voices, Collective Visions*, Philadelphia, PA: Temple University Press.

Goffman, E. (1992), 'An interview with Erving Goffman, 1980', *Research on Language and Social Interaction*, **26** (3), 317–48.

Greeley, A. (1990), ' The crooked lines of God', in B. Berger (ed.), *Authors of their Own Lives*, Berkeley, CA: University of California Press, pp. 133–51.

Hammond, P.E. (ed.) (1964), *Sociologists at Work*, New York: Basic Books.

Hobbs, D. (1988), *Doing the Business*, Oxford: Clarendon Press.

Jackson, P. (2004), *Inside Clubbing*, Oxford: Berg.

James, A., Hockey, J. and Dawson, A. (eds) (1997), *After Writing Culture*, London: Routledge.

Lareau, A. and Shultz, J. (eds) (1996), *Journeys through Ethnography*, Boulder, CO: Westview Press.

Laslett, B. and Thorne, B. (eds) (1997), *Feminist Sociology: Life Histories of a Movement*, New Brunswick, NJ: Rutgers University Press.

Lather, P. (2000), 'Drawing the line angels: working the ruins of feminist ethnography', in E.A. Pierre and W.S. Pillow (eds), *Working the Ruins: Feminist Poststructural Theory and Methods in Education*, London and New York: Routledge, pp. 284–31.

Leach, E.R. (1984), 'Glimpses of the unmentionable in the history of British social anthropology', *Annual Review of Anthropology*, **13**, pp. 1–23.

Liebow, E. (1967), *Tally's Corner*, London: Routledge.

McLean, A. and Leiberg, A. (eds) (2007), *The Shadow Side of Fieldwork*, Oxford: Blackwell.

Orlans, K.P.M. and Wallace, R. (eds) (1994), *Gender and the Academic Experience*, Lincoln, NE: University of Nebraska Press.

Puddephatt, A.J., Shaffir, W. and Kleinknecht, S.W. (eds) (2009), *Ethnographies Revisited*, London: Routledge.

Riley, M. (ed.) (1988), *Sociological Lives*, Newbury Park, CA: Sage.

Spindler, G. and Hammond, L. (eds) (2006), *Innovations in Educational Ethnography*, Mahwah, NJ: Erlbaum.

Valli, L. (1986), *Becoming Clerical Workers*, London: Routledge.

Walford, G. (ed.) (1987), *Doing Sociology of Education*, London: Falmer Press.

Walford, G. (ed.) (1991), *Doing Educational Research*, London: Routledge.

Walford, G. (1994), *Researching the Powerful in Education*, London: UCL Press.

Walford, G. (1998), *Doing Research about Education*, London: Falmer Press.

Whyte, W. (1981), *Street Corner Society*, 3rd edn, Chicago, IL: University of Chicago Press.

Wolcott, H.F. (2002), *Sneaky Kid and its Aftermath*, Walnut Creek, CA: Alta Mira.

Wolf, M. (1992), *The Thrice Told Tale*, Stanford, CA: Stanford University Press.

Young, D.E. and Goulet, J.-G. (eds) (1994), *Being Changed by Cross-cultural Encounters*, Ontario: Broadview Press.

42. Performing findings: tales of the theatrical self
Rachel Holmes

INTRODUCTION

This chapter offers a brief overview of aspects of critical, performance and surrealist ethnography as ways to represent research findings. It evokes performances amongst the written-ness of (con)text and the challenges of classroom encounters as they each become entangled together as expressions of findings. It puts moments of 'data' to work as I try to interrupt my more familiar classroom performances of 'self', by turning to data in the form of narratives to provoke 'ontological stammering' (Lather, 1998, p. 495). Using and writing through a story of a classroom encounter as an integral component of reflexive ethnography, attempts are made to perform some of my growing uncomfortable-ness as a teacher within this higher education landscape.

CRITICAL, PERFORMANCE AND SURREALIST ETHNOGRAPHY

According to Haseman (2006, p. 299), 'the stark and abiding difference between quantitative and qualitative research lies in the way that research findings are expressed. Quantitative research is 'the activity or operation of expressing something as a quantity or amount – for example, in numbers, graphs or formulas' (Schwandt, 2001, p. 215). However, qualitative research, with its concern to capture the observed, interpreted and nuanced properties of behaviours, responses and things refers to 'all forms of social inquiry that rely primarily on . . . nonnumeric data in the form of words' (Schwandt, 2001, p. 213). However, even within the qualitative genre, there is increasing variation and innovation in the ways research findings are expressed. Hayano (1979) argues that as anthropologists moved out of the colonial era of ethnography (Atkinson, Chapter 38, this volume), they would begin to study the social worlds and subcultures of which they were a part: 'Self-reflexivity . . . in the ethnographic process, alongside the crisis in ethnography and the "linguistic" and "cultural turn" in socio-cultural theory has led to demands for experimentation in the representation of ethnographic data' (O'Neill, 2002, p. 71).

The increasingly prevalent body of ethnographic educational research including, for example, Devine (1996), Fine (1994), Paley (1992) and Ayers (1997) continues to explore alternative 'readings' of the social world, as 'methodologically speaking, the construction and reproduction of ethnographic print-based texts has in the main conformed to a particular set of traditional conventions' (O'Neill, 2002, p. 70). Due to its traditional conformity, Quantz (1992) believes there is some sense of the field being in a state of creative disarray. Denzin and Lincoln (2000) describe a growing crisis of representation illustrated through seven historical 'moments' where qualitative researchers have begun to imagine and produce new forms of their work. The current (seventh) moment in the twenty-first century is 'the methodologically contested present' (Denzin and Lincoln, 2005, p. 1116), a time of tension between quantitative and qualitative researchers, and more specifically, a time when qualitative researchers are exploring varied methodologies, paradigms and perspectives for their inquiries. Denzin (1997) and Atkinson and Coffey (1995) propose that this crisis of representation in anthropology is paralleled by an increasing debate and scrutiny of ethnographic texts questioning their intellectual status within sociology and the ways in which they claim to represent cultural phenomena. Quantz (1992) suggests that ethnography should continue to participate in a larger 'critical' dialogue rather than exclusively follow any particular set of methods or research techniques and Genet writes, 'Nothing will prevent me, neither close attention nor the desire to be exact, from writing words that sing' (1993, p. 59), which suggests the need to embrace, rather than deny ever-more inclusive, creative and eclectic approaches to ethnography. Haseman (2006) insists that research outputs and claims to knowing must be made through the symbolic language and forms of their practice, suggesting that 'data works performatively. It not only expresses the research, but in that expression becomes the research itself' (p. 101).

This move towards creativity and innovation in relation to representation and the need to recognize findings that emerge from a diversity of research contexts and practices proposes that in undertaking critical ethnography, researchers aim 'to move people to see themselves and their relation to a particular set of circumstances differently' (Pignatelli, 1998, p. 416). One way of doing this is to assemble and juxtaposition texts that emanate from diverse genres of writing and other modes of representation, drawing on Clifford's exploration of ethnography and surrealism to examine the play between the familiar and the strange,

> that moment in which the possibility of comparison exists in unmediated
> tension with sheer incongruity . . . the cuts and sutures of the research process
> are left visible: there is no smoothing over or bending of the work's raw 'data'
> into a homogeneous representation . . . as well as . . . data not fully integrated
> within the work's governing interpretation. . . . (Clifford, 1981, p. 563)

This incongruity, unexpectedness and juxtapositioning of the familiar
with the strange, or the familiar finding some way to become strange to,
and in itself, is suggestive that there may be opportunities for the 'roughly
textured, choppy . . . less seamless narration . . .' (Pignatelli, 1998, p. 419)
within the ethnographic 'text(s)' to argue with itself. Referring to Derrida,
Cornell takes up the themes of attacking the familiar, of interruption and
the unexpected in discussing ways to represent the Other in the ethnographic text, 'The auratic gaze defies the organization of looking as a form
of mastery . . . The Other is allowed to be in her distance precisely so that
she can look back' (Cornell, 1992, p. 77).

A method of ethnography drawing on juxtapositioning of (con)texts
and growing out of cross-disciplinary work in sociology, anthropology,
communication studies, performance arts and cultural studies is performance (auto)ethnography, often understood to lie within the field of
qualitative research. According to Denzin (2003), performance (auto)
ethnography is a genre within critical, postmodern ethnography, a variation on what Paget (1990) calls ethnoperformance, what Mienczakowski
(1995) calls ethnodrama or ethnotheatre, what Glass (2001) makes reference to as critical performance pedagogy, what Giroux (2000) discusses
amongst performative cultural politics, what Fine cited in Denzin and
Lincoln, 2003 calls participatory performance action inquiry and what
Turner (1982) calls reflexive anthropology. According to Charmaz (2006),
early performance ethnography began to integrate autobiography with
ethnography, self-observation in ethnographic research that necessarily
attended to the worlds in which ethnographers were participating. In other
words, attending to the all-too-familiar in an attempt to render strange.
Smith and Gallo (2007) discuss an interesting historical version of the
development of 'performance' in art history, sociology and anthropology,
drawing on the work of Turner (1982), Geertz (1995) and Goffman (1974).
They then take these early theories of performance and combine them with
ethnographic research, drawing on the work of contemporary social scientists such as Conquergood (2002), Denzin (1997, 2003), Madison (1998)
and Madison and Hamera (2006). Smith and Gallo suggest that often performance ethnography is presented as a performance text that one or more
people write and read for an audience. The material on which the text is
based can be autobiographical stories, ethnographic field notes, reflexive
journal entries or specific memories of a life event (Smith and Gallo, 2007,

p. 521). The purpose of the text is to engage the audience fully, so that performer and listener meet in the liminal (or threshold) space that lies between them p. 522).

Returning to Denzin and Lincoln (2005), the driving force of the current qualitative focus is towards more feminist, ethical, communitarian, democratic, engaged, performative and social justice-oriented research. Pollock (2006) writes, 'the object of ethnography has . . . shifted the relationship of the researcher and the ostensibly "researched" (the field and field subjects), reconfiguring longstanding subject-object relations as co-performative' (p. 326). There are numerous literal responses to ethnographic 'texts' being re-presented through performance. For example O'Neill (2002) discusses a project that uses video and live art performance as a response to transcripts of interviews with women working as prostitutes and fuses dance, text, sound and video. She reflects on how the re-presentation of ethnographic data in artistic form can access 'a richer understanding of the complexities of lived experiences . . . and reach beyond academic communities (p. 70).

With the idea of 'lived experiences' in mind, Clifford (2002) discusses the notion of ethnographic surrealism, whereby an approach 'cuts across retrospectively established definitions . . . to recapture . . . a situation in which ethnography is again something unfamiliar and surrealism not yet a bounded province of modern art or literature . . . genres do not remain firmly anchored' (pp. 117–18). He suggests that 'ethnographic surrealism is a statement about past and future possibilities for cultural analysis' (p. 119). Similarly within critical and performance ethnography, de-stabilized approaches to ways 'lived experiences' are being re-presented are recognized. This chapter will draw eclectically from developments within these fields in an effort to mobilize ideas around fragmentation, juxtapositioning and incompleteness as the complexities of lived experiences in the classroom as a teacher-researcher are explored.

My interest here lies in the potential of the university classroom as (con)text and the students as active audience or co-subjects that enable pedagogical performances where reflexive ethnography finds itself being negotiated, 'a pedagogical borderland, in the spaces where rhetoric, politics, parody, pastiche, performance, ethnography and critical cultural studies come together' (Conquergood, 1992, p. 80). I would argue for the university classroom as an act of immersive ethnography in which,

> contrary to the hidden 'I' of allegedly objective recording; or the deferential 'I' apparently standing fixed . . . the self-subject of the researcher is immersed in the co-subject, entangled with, even ravished by the co-creative process such that the subjectivity of the researcher is diffused within, even to the point of disappearing into, the field's body. Accordingly, we no longer see the scholar

'I' at work but we certainly feel her passion, his grace. . . . (Pollock, 2006, p. 326)

The university classroom seems to be an interesting context for co-subjects (teacher and students) to become entangled in the unfolding pedagogy of performance. I turn now to the university teacher as a writer of that performative (con)text.

TEACHER AS A WRITER, WRITER AS A TEACHER: THE CLASSROOM ENCOUNTER

Within the diverse context of the university classroom, I 'find' myself becoming increasingly uncomfortable as a teacher, contributing to the mistaken stability of the cultural and structural relationships that characterize a particular version of western-style education. This is particularly pertinent for me as I work with students on undergraduate degrees in childhood studies who will themselves go on to work with children. I believe that in their 'preparation' for work with children, students need to be challenged to engage with complex constructions of the child, become mindful of the ways in which political systems affect these constructions and how they impact upon the work they will go on to do in different early years' contexts. For students, this requires them to think and talk critically about the process of education and schooling and to go on to act on ideas that disrupt the re-production of legitimized and privileged forms of knowledge. However, this poses particular tensions for me as a white, female teacher, constructed as part of a system that seems to legitimize and privilege certain forms of knowledge. These mistakenly stable notions of 'knowledge' lie amongst unstable and always shifting and diverse cultural, racial and religious classroom 'realities' within which as a teacher, I aspire to foster students' criticality. To unpack some of these tensions, I intend to reflect upon one of the many narratives I have written during my (life) time as a teacher that probe the intricacies of teacher-student encounters. This narrative will be used to explore how, as a teacher-researcher, I am able to disturb my understandings of 'performances' within a classroom encounter, by moving towards writing an 'incomplete frame' (Stronach, 1996, p. 365) that otherwise might 'enclose' particular understandings of myself as a teacher, and of students.

The session I am about to reflect upon was part of a series of units called 'Explorations', which provide an integrating mechanism at each level of the degree programme for studying the different ways in which children and their families have been and continue to be understood.

The aim within these units is to explore ways to deconstruct narratives and visually symbolic representations of the child and to facilitate the students' reframing of deeply embedded concepts and understandings. In Explorations sessions, I often use film, photographs and documentary so that previously 'known' texts are disturbed and students might engage in discussions that question the ways they 'know' these texts. I introduced this particular classroom session by talking to students about my uneasiness with being a white female teacher, about to discuss and 'teach' aspects of race, culture and religion to a mixed racial and cultural group of undergraduate students.

> The classroom, Tuesday morning. I asked the students to consider why they thought the Asian community was 'absented' in this documentary (Last white kids, Thompson, 2003) and in response, a white student suggested that the Asian voice was not represented because 'most Asian women would stay at home' and would not have 'good enough command of the English language' to talk to the documentary-makers. A British-Kashmiri student immediately responded, suggesting this was a 'ridiculous stereotype' and an 'offensive misunderstanding' of Asian families and particularly Asian women. She seemed agitated and angry towards the white student, who seemed to respond in what I perceived as a defensive way. At this point, I began to feel uncomfortable, conscious that I wanted all students to be able to express themselves, but mindful that the emotionality swirling between students seemed to be moving them towards a confrontation. A further comment came from the British-Kashmiri student who suggested that, as a white teacher I should not allow the 'Asian' community to be constructed as an all-encompassing homogeneity, but rather as differentiated Pakistani, Bangladeshi and Indian families within the community. I felt 'interrupted'. This interruption to my habitual performance as 'teacher' rendered me feeling vulnerable in the classroom, a place where I do not usually feel inadequate. (Journal extract, 2005)

My intention here is to develop an ever more complex story of 'performing findings' as a 'theatre of the self' (Cavarero, 2000, p. 34), interrupted and problematized by co-subjects that enables pedagogical performances where reflexive ethnography finds itself being negotiated. The literature that opened this chapter establishes an ever-changing theoretical and methodological context, put to work here as a documented series of interwoven texts. Shifting between author, spectator, reader and editor of these texts, I become a storyteller, telling a story about other stories and reader, reading myself as a storyteller. Latterly, I have introduced the classroom encounter (that in and of itself draws from a plethora of other labyrinthine autobiographical stories), lying within a broader and intricate methodological story that is 'Chapter 42 Performing findings: tales of the theatrical self'. The classroom encounter becomes a context for self-interrogation where I attempt to evoke co-subjects in a co-performance of findings.

Different characters become 'the necessary others' (Cavarero, 2000, p. 88), portrayed as storytellers themselves. I want to consider what I can learn about myself (as a teacher) in relationship with those 'necessary others' as I engage in telling stories about those storytellers.

What strikes me about this classroom story is the infestation of barely written, barely formed and dimly glimpsed sensations (MacLure et al., 2010, p. 2) that nevertheless constitute an overwhelming odour of emotional discomfort. Documenting the students as necessary others, I sense an attack on the familiar, of interruption and the unexpected, where jolts and emotional ruptures rendered me (mis)recognized, appearing to myself by way of 'the gaze of others' (Arendt, 1958 [1977], cited in Brightman, 1995, p. 294). Perhaps this sense of (mis)recognition could be reconceptualized as 'mimicry', which 'must continually produce its slippage . . . Mimicry is at once resemblance and menace' (Bhabha, 1994, p. 86). Were these moments of me, the classroom, the students, the teaching/learning encounter being familiar but made strange? Despite opening this session with a confessional introduction to my own vulnerabilities, limits to my interpretations, understandings, trying to summon autobiographical data that would help students (and myself) situate my own racial struggles, I still seem to have be striving to remain camouflaged (familiar) as a woman, as a teacher, yet menaced (made strange) by the ruptures, the emotional slippages that seemed to infest the classroom encounter.

DEMOCRATIC DIALOGUES(?)

The student who made reference to me as a 'white teacher' presents a particular moment of recognition. As the 'teacher' (resemblance), the student seemed to express her expectations of me to confront the emotional and racially motivated struggles within the classroom. However, as 'white' (menace), perhaps she was not surprised, but nevertheless troubled that I did not disturb homogenizing tendencies and reductive critiques embedded within the classroom discussions. In this example, despite my introductory proclamations that I saw myself as white, something menacing around my 'practices' of being a 'white' teacher ruptured the classroom discourse. Drawing on media studies, literary theory and the work of psychoanalytical feminism, Ellsworth describes 'coming up against stuck place after stuck place' (1997, p. xi) as a way to keep moving with 'the impossibility of teaching' (p. 9), perhaps Lather's 'ontological stammering' (1998, p. 495), a critical performance pedagogy, where we learn from ruptures, failures, breaks and refusals. With the students as co-subjects, audience, actors and storytellers in the classroom encounter and me as teacher-researcher-performer, I can begin to think about this narrative as stuck place after stuck place, a stammering rupture to my usual 'stylized repetition of [classroom] acts' (Butler, 1990, p. 40).

In order to re-consider ways I might look upon my emotionality as entangled within my stammering 'performances as teacher' in the classroom encounter, I turn to Lorde (1984, p. 63) who links the conceptual and political work of confronting racism with the capacity to be angry and to tolerate and use anger. Perhaps this potentially provocative relationship between my own ontological stammer(ing), the sharp jolts of classroom emotions amongst discussions of culture and race are usually tamed, 'some forms of multiculturalism are closely bound up with efforts to . . . cultivate a particular sort of civility' (Mayo, 2001, p. 78). Mayo suggests that the discourse of civility asserts that teachers and students ought to be respectful and tolerant of everyone, which serves to neglect aspects of emotionality that appear to be in and of themselves uncivil or distasteful. This suggests there is a 'civil' discussion to be had, one in which everyone in their tolerance wants to know and be known, wants to understand and to be understood. Gillborn is similarly concerned about exclusionary practices that 'operate beneath a veneer of professed tolerance and diversity' (2006, p. 11), whereby de-politicized language 'is evacuated of all critical content' (p. 16). McIntyre finds difficulty 'understanding the chasm that exists between their [educators] antiracist ideals and their tendency to appropriate long-standing strategies for teaching that benefit the dominant group' (1997, p. 132). Gillborn and McIntyre's uses of terms such as 'chasm' and 'veneer' lead me back to Clifford's notions of scissions and sutures (1981), here the procurement of procedures that divide, then work hard to restore, always incapable of disguising the invasive praxis of restoration. I wonder how my usual classroom practices become all-too-familiar and accomplished processes of cutting into the student group with a 'white hegemonic gaze' and subverting anti-racist ideals to disguise the workings of colonial restoration, subversive conformity and imperial cultural workings? Such a 'civil' discussion is also suggestive of what Berlak (2005, p. 143) describes as a 'democratic dialogue' which could be understood to foster a form of repetition that stabilizes the common wisdom. However, it might also function to suppress strong emotions and confrontation in the classroom. According to bell hooks (1994), dialogue is often confined to the standards of acceptable bourgeois decorum, which operates to undermine constructive forms of confrontation and conflict that emerge from intense, and often aversive, responses.

My worries around these issues are that this democratic tolerance and respectfulness is tainted by what Jones (cited in Lather, 1998) claims is a cannibal desire to know the other through being fed by her. Lather (1998) suggests that there is a voyeuristic refusal at work, one which refuses to know that the Other may not want to be known. This classroom encounter has pushed me to contemplate Lather's ideas, but also contemplate that the Other may not have a choice, but may find herself assuming to be known in particular and reductive ways.

In the classroom story by constituting something of my white, western identity as a teacher, was I denying the presence of voices who might disrupt the comfort of certain absences? Given my own cultural practices and the discursive discourses that swirl amongst dominant white narratives of race, did I police what I thought was appropriate for the classroom and by doing so, collude with the white student, failing to interrupt her constructions of all non-white families as 'Asian'? The British-Kashmiri student took the opportunity to disrupt my habitual 'performances' as teacher in her challenges to the ways I was 'performing' being white and being unemotional around what could be described as emotive issues of race.

FOOTNOTES

This chapter has begun to disturb ways I understand particular 'performances' of myself as teacher and of 'findings' within reflexive inquiry, where stories of emotionality and race were juxtaposed with an assumed professional competence that classroom encounters are based on straight-forward liberal-humanist practices embodied by the teacher-self. It has shifted any sense of comfortable-ness around the teacher (actor)–student (audience), as well as student–student relationships. The idea of students as co-subjects becomes an opportunity to embrace ideas around a 'fertile space . . . producing bafflement' (Lather, 2004, p. 2), but also becomes a much more dangerous space as I interrogate 'performances of self' alongside difficult issues, de-stabilizing and politicizing taken-for-granted 'knowledges' about self and other. If I recognize that dominant regimes of truth (Foucault, 1977) cannot be left undisturbed, and that a move to 'democratic dialogue' can serve to reinscribe particular absences, then how uncomfortable or 'uncivil' should it become in the classroom? How could I perceive and regulate the boundaries around acceptable and unacceptable emotionality in different, less 'enclosed' ways without constraining emotional engagement and expression? Minha-ha Trinh (1989) suggests that we need to 'practice ways of reading and writing, speaking and listening, in which one's authority comes from one's ability to confront one's own privileges rather than to merely confront the privileges of others' (p. 193). If I perceive my 'whiteness' as a privilege, then I must consider the painful and lingering work of exposure, together with the difficult notion of declaration as the 'admission', which 'itself becomes seen as good practice' (Ahmed, 2004, p. 71). I would want to encourage students and myself to be challenged by our mutually critical, albeit stammering gazes that obstruct and resist our comfortableness as these moments could provoke both students and myself to re-think our assumptions about ourselves and each other.

With reference to performing findings within teacher research, reflecting upon a classroom narrative as particular 'performance of findings' enabled me to find my 'self' juxtaposed with students as the 'necessary others' (Caverero, 2000, p. 8). This shifting process of self- and other-representation seems to have dislocated my understandings of myself from 'enclosed' conceptual positionings and I now find myself entangled amongst Derrida's 'folding back' process (1981, p. 104), using writing as a process of 'dis-covering' (p. 154), where the text becomes a tissue, a web or a tapestry. I find possibilities within what Derrida (1981, p. 83) describes as 'the same tissue, within the same texts, we will draw on other filial filaments, pull the same strings once more, and witness the weaving or unraveling of other designs'. This chapter has allowed me space to speak within particular discursive practices about things not generally spoken of, or only spoken of in particular ways before. For example, I feel that my teacher-researcher role has begun to be re-imagined as I re-consider the emotional character of the deeply interwoven teaching and research processes where 'emotional matters belong to the researcher at least as much as the researched' (Burman, 1998, p. 14).

REFERENCES

Ahmed, S. (2004), 'Declarations of whiteness: the non-performativity of anti-racism', *Borderlands E-Journal* 3 (2), 69–84.

Arendt, H. ([1958]1977), *The Human Condition*, Chicago, IL: University of Chicago Press.

Atkinson, P. and Coffey, A. (1995), 'Realism and its discontents: on the crisis of cultural representation in ethnographic texts', in B. Adam and S. Allan (eds), *Theorizing Culture. An Interdisciplinary Critique After Postmodernism*, London: UCL Press.

Ayers, W. (1997), *A Kind and Just Parent: The Children of Juvenile Court*, Boston, MA: Beacon Press.

Berlak, A.C. (2005), 'Confrontation and pedagogy: cultural secrets, trauma, and emotion in antioppressive pedagogies', in M. Boler (ed.), *Democratic Dialogue in Education: Troubling Speech, Disturbing Silence*, New York: Peter Lang, pp. 123–44.

Bhabha, H. (1994), *The Location of Culture*, New York: Routledge.

Brightman, C. (1995), *Between Friends: The Correspondence of Hannah Arendt and Mary McCarthy 1949–1975*, New York: Harcourt Brace.

Burman, E. (1998), 'Engendering developments', Professorial inaugural lecture paper presented in Manchester Metropolitan University, 8 October.

Butler, J. (1990), *Gender Trouble: Feminism and the Subversion of Identity*, New York: Routledge.

Cavarero, A. (2000), *Relating Narratives: Storytelling and Selfhood*, London: Routledge.
Charmaz, K. (2006), 'The power of names', *Journal of Contemporary Ethnography*, **35** (4), 396–9.
Clifford, J. (1981), 'On ethnographic surrealism', *Comparative Studies in Society and History*, **23**, 539–64.
Clifford, J. (2002) *The Predicament of Culture: Twentieth-century Ethnography, Literature, and Art*, Cambridge, MA: Harvard University Press.
Conquergood, D. (1992), 'Ethnography, rhetoric and performance', *Quarterly Journal of Speech*, **78**, 80–97.
Conquergood, D. (2002), 'Performance studies: interventions and radical research' *The Drama Review*, **46**, 145–53.
Cornell, D. (1992), *The Philosophy of the Limit*, New York: Routledge.
Denzin, N. (1997), *Interpretive Ethnography: Ethnographic Practices for the 21st Century*, London: Sage.
Denzin, N.K. (2003), 'Performing [Auto] ethnography politically', *Review of Education, Pedagogy, and Cultural Studies*, **25** (3), 257–78.
Denzin, N.K. and Lincoln, Y.S. (eds) (2000), *Handbook of Qualitative Research*, 2nd edn, London: Sage.
Denzin, N.K. and Lincoln, Y.S. (eds) (2003), *The Landscape of Qualitative Research*, London: Sage.
Denzin, N.K. and Lincoln, Y.S. (eds) (2005), *The Sage Handbook of Qualitative Research*, 3rd edn, London: Sage.
Derrida, J. (1981), *Dissemination*, trans. B. Johnson, Chicago, IL: University of Chicago Press.
Devine, J. (1996), *Maximum Security: The Culture of Violence in Inner-city Schools*, Chicago, IL: University of Chicago Press.
Ellsworth, E. (1997), *Teaching Positions: Difference, Pedagogy and the Power of Address*, New York: Teachers College Press.
Fine, M. (1994), 'Working the hyphens: reinventing self and other in qualitative research', in N.K. Denzin and Y.S. Lincoln (eds), *Handbook of Qualitative Research*, Thousand Oaks, CA: Sage, pp. 70–82.
Foucault, M. (1977), *Discipline and Punish*, London: Penguin.
Geertz, C. (1995), *After the Fact: Two Countries, Four Decades, One Anthropologist*, Cambridge, MA: Harvard University Press.
Genet, J. (1993), 'Miracle of the rose' in E. White (ed.), *The Selected Writings of Jean Genet*, Hopewell, NJ: The Ecco Press, pp. 52–68.
Gillborn, D. (2006), 'Critical race theory and education: racism and anti-racism in educational theory and praxis', *Discourse*, **27** (1), 11–32.
Giroux, H. (2000), *Impure Acts: The Practical Politics of Cultural Studies*, New York: Routledge.
Glass, R.D. (2001), 'On Paulo Freire's philosophy of praxis and the foundations of liberation education', *Educational Reseacher*, **30**, 15–25.
Goffman, E. (1974), *Frame Analysis*, Harmondsworth: Penguin Books.
Haseman, B. (2006), 'A manifesto for performative research', *Media International Australia Incorporating Culture and Policy*, **118**, 98–106.
Hayano, D. (1979), 'Auto-ethnography: paradigms, problems, and prospects', *Human Organization*, **38**, 99–104.
hooks, b. (1994), 'Confronting class in the classroom', In b. hooks (ed.), *Teaching to Transgress*, New York: Routledge, pp. 77–92.
Lather, P. (1997), 'Drawing the line at angels: working the ruins of feminist ethnography', *International Journal of Qualitative Studies in Education*, **10** (3), 285–304.
Lather, P. (1998), 'Critical pedagogy and its complicities: a praxis of stuck places', *Educational Theory*, **48** (4), 487–97.
Lather, P. (2004), 'Getting lost: feminist efforts toward a double(d) science', Paper presented at the AREA, San Diego, California, 12–16, April, available at http://www.petajwhite.

net/Uni/910/Legit%20and%20Representation/Representation%20Precis/lather%20Getting
%20lost.pdf (accessed 18 March 2011).
Lorde, A. (1984), *Sister Outsider: Essays and Speeches*, The Crossing Press feminist series,
Trumansburg, NY: Crossing Press.
MacLure, M., Holmes, R., MacRae, C. and Jones, L. (2010), 'Animating classroom ethnog-
raphy: overcoming video-fear', *International Journal of Qualitative Studies in Education*.
First published on 29 April 2010 (iFirst).
Madison, D.S. (1998), 'Performances, personal narratives, and the politics of possibility',
in Sheron J. Dailey (ed.), *The Future of Performance Studies: Visions and Revisions*,
Annadale, VA: National Communication Association, pp. 276–86.
Madison, D.S. and Hamera, J. (eds) (2006), *The Sage Handbook of Performance Studies*,
Thousand Oaks, CA: Sage.
Mayo, C. (2001), 'Civility and its discontents: sexuality, race, and the lure of beautiful
manners', *Philosophy of Education 2001*, 78–87.
McIntyre, A. (1997), *Making Meaning of Whiteness: Exploring Racial Identity with White
Teachers*, New York: State University of New York Press.
McIntyre, A. (2002) 'Exploring whiteness and multicultural education with prospective
teachers', *Curriculum Inquiry*, **32** (1), 31–49.
Mienczakowski, J. (1995), 'The theater of ethnography: the reconstruction of ethnography
into theater with emancipatory potential', *Qualitative Enquiry*, **1** (3), 360–75.
Minha-ha Trinh, T. (1989), *Woman, Native, Other: Writing Postcoloniality and Feminism*,
Bloomington, IN: Indiana University Press.
O'Neill, M. (2002), 'Renewed methodologies for social research: ethno-mimesis as perform-
ance praxis', *The Sociological Review*, **50** (1), 69–88.
Paget, M. (1990), 'Performing the text', *Journal of Contemporary Ethnography*, **19**, 136–55.
Paley, V.G. (1992), *You Can't Say You Can't Play*, Cambridge, MA: Harvard University
Press.
Pignatelli, F. (1998), 'Critical ethnography/poststructuralist concerns: Foucault and the play
of memory', *Interchange*, **294**, 403–23.
Pollock, D. (2006), 'Marking new directions in performance ethnography', *Text and
Performance Quarterly*, **26** (4), 325–9.
Quantz, R.A. (1992), 'On critical ethnography (with some postmodern considerations)', in
M.D. LeCompte, W.L. Milroy and J. Preissle (eds), *The Handbook of Qualitative Research
in Education*, San Diego, CA: Academic Press, pp. 447–506.
Schwandt, T.A. (2001), *Dictionary of Qualitative Research*, Thousand Oaks, CA: Sage.
Smith, C.A.M. and Gallo, A.M. (2007), 'Applications of performance ethnography in
nursing', *Qualitative Health Research*, **17** (4), 521–8.
Stronach, I. (1996), 'Fashioning post-modernism: tales from the fitting room', *British
Education Research Journal*, **22** (3), 359–75.
Thompson, S. (2003), *Cutting Edge: The Last White Kids*, Channel Four, 30 October.
Turner, V. (1982), 'Performing ethnography', *The Drama Review*, **26**, (2), 33–50.

43. The literary turn: fictions and poetry
Pat Sikes

INTRODUCTION

My relationship with educational research writing began on Monday, 23 September 1974 when I was handed a *Required and Recommended Research Reading List* at the start of a Certificate of Education course at Doncaster College of Education. As is the case for most people, I was a consumer before I became a producer and, inevitably, what I have read over the years since I received that list has influenced and had implications for my own writing. Today, as I begin work on this chapter, it's 2 September 2010. As I try to order my thoughts, or more precisely, as I start exploring and articulating my understandings via a writing process which is consciously and explicitly also a method of inquiry (Richardson, 1994), I reflect on how different research reporting/re-presenting/writing can be now compared with how it usually was even as relatively recently as 20 years ago, let alone back in 1974. Indeed, as a supervisor and examiner of doctoral and masters students I have to confess to a degree of jealousy with regard to the variety of forms of social science writing and re-presentation that are permissible and accepted as legitimate these days (see Richardson, 1997a, 1998; Denzin and Lincoln, 2005). It certainly seems that there are so many options available which potentially, at least, offer greater possibilities for more closely capturing, describing and evoking the social experiences and phenomena that are the focus of our research. In this chapter, however, I want to narrow the field and concentrate on considering literary, specifically fictional and poetic, approaches to re-presenting educational research.

Obviously and inevitably, what I have to say here is my own personal view. I am not presenting this chapter as containing **the** definitive account. In saying this I feel that it is important to begin by explaining that when I talk about social science research generally and educational research particularly, I understand 'research', as did Lawrence Stenhouse, to refer to 'systematic inquiry made public' (1975). Here is not the place for a critical discussion of what constitutes 'systematic' but the reason for offering this definition is to make it clear that within this chapter research is conceived of as an activity which involves the collection of 'data' according to certain, albeit maybe idiosyncratic, specified and justified criteria. I put 'data' in inverted commas to indicate that researchers define what constitutes data in any particular research project. So, and on this view, data could be: personal feelings, thoughts or interpretations of events as would be the case in autoethnography; or observational fieldnotes, photographs, films, interview transcripts and examples of children's work adding to a case study; or documentary evidence used in historical or policy research; or texts reviewed and critiqued in the course of scholarly endeavour and so on. Thus, when I talk about fictional or poetic approaches to research re-presentation I am referring to accounts which use these literary forms for writing about and communicating – in Stenhouse's terms, making public – the constituent parts of the inquiry in question. I am not talking about random musings or 'think pieces' or writings of any kind which have no basis in activity which could be described as research. In setting down this qualification I am conscious of the artificiality of such boundaries and of how weak they seem once one begins to consider what fits into which category. However, here, in this chapter, it is the claim made by an author that a particular piece of writing re-presents 'research' that is being taken to be the defining characteristic.

Following on from this I also want to emphasize that my concern here is not with accounts which are entirely invented and imaginary – although when talking about and describing social life it is hard to conceive of anything happening or being amenable to description or comprehension which does not have some foundation in life as variously lived. As Virginia Woolf put it when discussing the ingredients of successful fiction writing,

> the writer must get into touch with his *(sic)* reader by putting before him something which he recognises, which, therefore, stimulates his imagination, and makes him willing to co-operate in the far more difficult business of intimacy. And it is of the highest importance that this common meeting place should be reached easily, almost instinctively, in the dark, with one's eyes shut. (1992, p. x)

Woolf is referring here to the relationship between writer and reader, invoking particularly the need for this to be based on trust. This need is, I would suggest, especially urgent when it comes to research writing for, as Laurel Richardson points out,

> claiming to write 'fiction' is different from claiming to write 'science' in terms of the audience one seeks, the impact one might have on different publics, and how one expects 'truth claims' to be evaluated. These differences should not be overlooked or minimized. (2000, p. 926)

Certainly they should not and nor, in my opinion, is it ethical for social scientists who use literary approaches to fail to make it crystal clear when they are writing fictions; to omit to explain/justify why they are doing so; or, to abdicate all responsibility for interpretation and analysis. Writing/ re-presenting 'like all intentional behaviour . . . is a site of moral responsibility' (Richardson, 1990, p. 131). Consequently it carries a heavy ethical burden and therefore demands authorial honesty (Sikes, 2010a). I will be returning to some of these points later but for now I want to move on and consider briefly: the antecedents of contemporary usages of fiction and poetry to report/re-present educational research; the reasons why researchers/writers chose to use these approaches; and what writers/ researchers need to consider when using them. As is always the case, these subheadings are there for presentational purposes, to provide a framework for comprehension of a complex, messy and interrelated range of issues and considerations.

ANTECEDENTS

I started this chapter by suggesting that researchers in the twenty-first century had more options than did their predecessors when it came to forms of re-presentation. There is no doubt that, from the 1960s onwards and stemming from the thinking of French structuralists, it is possible to begin to track an explicitly conscious narrative and literary turn within anthropology, literary studies, historiography, philosophy, the humanities and law as well as within the social sciences generally (Rorty, 1979; Plummer, 2001; Hyvarinen, 2007; Chapters 38 and 42 in this volume). Education has not been exempt from the trend. This obvious shift to storying as the vehicle for 'scientifically' interpreting and explaining social life is not surprising given that human beings are storying beings. Storying is what we do and how we function: 'there does not exist, and has never existed, a people without narratives' (Barthes, 1966, p. 14). Having said this in the context of this chapter a distinction is being made between narrative and fiction which hinges on whether or not an account seeks to report specific, historical and 'real' situations, experiences, perceptions – for instance, what was observed happening in a maths lesson in an actual classroom and how the particular teacher and children involved claim to have perceived and experienced it – or if it describes an imaginary school and made-up characters. I make this differentiation because I share Donald Polkinghorne's understanding that essentially, 'narrative meaning is created by noting that something is a "part" of a whole, and that something is a "cause" of something else' (Polkinghorne, 1988, p. 6). On this view, and like Laurel Richardson, I am of the opinion that because social communication takes place through narrative,

narrative is quintessential to the understanding and communication of the sociological. All social science writing depends upon narrative structure and narrative devices, although a 'scientific' frame frequently masks that structure and
those devices, which is, itself a metanarrative (cf Lyotard, 1979). The issue is
not whether sociologists *(or I would add, psychologists, historians, philosophers,
educational researchers etc)* should use the narrative, but which narratives will
be provided to the reader. (1997b, p. 27, emphasis added)

Indeed, and as Patricia Clough has pointed out, 'all factual representations
of reality, even statistical representations, are narratively constructed'
(1992, p. 2) (see also Chapter 38, this volume).

Here, however, I am not going into any more detail around the nature
and definition of narrative and narrative inquiry since these are contested
areas which have provoked considerable discussion and debate that interested readers can pursue elsewhere (see, for example, Barthes, 1966, 1977;
Bruner, 1986; Polkinghorne, 1988; Van Maanen, 1988; Riessman, 1993,
2008; Porter Abbott, 2002, 2005; Chase, 2005; Rudrum, 2005; Stanley and
Temple, 2008). For the most part that discussion is consequent upon an
understanding and recognition that writing/language is not neutral and
innocent in nature, form or content, but is, rather, culturally situated and
laden with meaning beyond the words, constructions and literary structures
that are used in any specific instance. Usually this notion is linked with
postmodernism and poststructuralism (see also Chapter 38, this volume).

Norman Denzin and Yvonna Lincoln (2005) argue that the development of qualitative research, its conceptualization, conduct and representation has to be considered through an historical gaze which can
trace the influence of dominant modes of thought. Taking this approach
it would definitely seem to be the case that one outcome of poststructuralism and postmodernism and the so-called 'crisis of representation' (p. 3)
they provoked and which, from the mid 1980s onward, can be seen to have
influenced 'a new generation of qualitative researchers who are attached
to poststructural and/or postmodern sensibilities' (p. 11), has been greater
use and acceptance of literary forms of research re-presentation (see also
Richardson, 1995; Richardson and Lockridge, 2004; Richardson and St
Pierre, 2005). And yet, consider this:

If one is to show the school as it really is, it is not enough to be unprejudiced.
It is necessary to achieve some sort of literary realism . . . To be realistic, I
believe, is simply to be concrete. To be concrete is to present materials in such
a way that characters do not lose the qualities of persons, nor situations their
intrinsic human reality . . . The purpose of [*this*] book, however it is used, is to
give insight into concrete situations typical of the typical school. I have hewed
to this line, and to no other. Whatever seemed likely to give insight has been
included, and all else, however worthwhile in other respects, has been excluded.

> A certain amount of fictional material has been included. This must be judged
> as fiction; it is good fiction, and it is relevant to our point, if it is based upon
> good insight. (Waller, 1932, Preface)

Writing in the early 1930s in a classic work on teachers' lives and careers, Willard Waller explains how and why he has used fiction. Somewhat confusingly (although drawing on the discourses of the period) he talks about what he has done in terms of aiming to achieve concrete, literary realism. In other words, he states that he was seeking to re-present 'reality'. Today, writers/researchers are unlikely to make such a claim as it is generally acknowledged that there are no techniques for totally, accurately and truthfully capturing and relating aspects of life – or indeed, any observations or hypotheses about the natural and physical world. All attempts, whether they come in words or numbers or visual images, can only be re-presentations, and, hence, interpretations. However, the salient points are that Waller obviously regards his use of fiction as appropriate, if not even as essential, and even more pertinently, that he is upfront, honest and unapologetic about employing it.

Waller was a student in the 1920s at the University of Chicago's School of Sociology and his work is clearly within the tradition of qualitative, ethnographic and auto/biographical social science research and writing for which that School became famous in the first three decades of the twentieth century (see Bulmer, 1984). Within anthropology there were also early exponents of literary approaches. Zora Neal Huston, for instance, published literary anthropological studies in the 1930s (Huston, 1935[1991], 1938; also see Chapter 38, this volume). The development and growing acceptance of statistical methods in the 1940s led to the sidelining of qualitative approaches but it is important to note that there were and continued to be those like Waller who explicitly and for a variety of reasons employed creative and fictional approaches in their research writing. (It seems highly likely that there were others who did it covertly too and those using quantitative approaches are not exempt from this observation either.) Leading on from this, John Van Maanen (1988) has identified the various forms that ethnographers' 'tales from the field' take, acknowledging that creativity, imagination and invention are always involved in research writing.

Whilst the use of fictional narrative may not actually be that novel a phenomenon within the social sciences I would suggest that use of poetry is a much more recent development. Once again though anthropologists were in the van with the ethnopoetic works of Jerome Rothenberg (1968) and Denis Tedlock (1972) appearing in the 1960s and 1970s but surprisingly perhaps and as Val Thompson (2009) points out, even within the natural and physical sciences, poetic re-presentation of research is not an entirely new concept either (see Harris, 2002; King-Hele, 2003). Thompson cites Erasmus Darwin's late eighteenth and early Nineteenth-century epic poems dealing with plant classification, the origins of life and evolution to support her claim. Nevertheless it is not until the 1990s that a literature discussing and using poetry within social science begins to appear. Ian Brady's (1991) *Anthropological Poetics,* and Laurel Richardson's (1992) 'the poetic representation of lives: writing a postmodern sociology' are amongst the first examples. By 2002, the uptake of the approach within the range of social science fields prompted Zali Gurevitch (2002) to contend that 'the poetic moment' has been reached (p. 403). This timing does directly coincide with and relate to postmodernism and the growing legitimacy of 'alternative' forms of re-presentation. It is entirely possible to pass fictional narrative off as factual and objective writing. However, poetry, whether its content be direct reportage of, for instance, an interview transcript (for example, Richardson, 1992), an imaginative attribution of perceptions (for example, Saunders, 2003) or poetry 'found' within other texts (for example, Sullivan, 2002), clearly looks very different from traditional scientific writing and is, therefore, likely to elicit a different response.

WHY RESEARCHERS/WRITERS CHOOSE TO USE FICTIONAL AND POETIC APPROACHES

Undoubtedly there are as many reasons why researchers choose to use fictional and poetic approaches as there are researchers using them. Brett Smith, for instance, suggests that fictional re-presentation of research can

> evoke emotions; broaden audiences; illuminate the complexity of body self relationships; include 'researcher', 'participant' and 'reader' in dialogue; help us to think with stories; and . . . invite the reader-as-witness to morally breathe and share a life within the storytelling relation . . . *they* are a powerful means of conveying complexity and ambiguity without prompting a single, closed, convergent reading . . . The genre becomes an opportunity and a space where one may relinquish the role of the declarative author persuader and attempt to write as, and be represented by, an artfully persuasive storyteller. (Smith, 2002, pp. 113–14)

With regard to poetry Lesley Saunders says that it seeks to

- present rather than argue;
- offer insights rather than build theory;
- add to the sense of the world's variety rather than negotiate and refine a consensus;

- play (with ideas) rather than work towards a closure;
- 'make new' rather than seek to replicate or systematically build on what has gone before;
- proceed by association and image rather than evidence and logical consequence;
- engage, surprise, attract, shock, delight, connect the unconnected, stir the memory and fertilise the unconscious;
- communicate something ultimately unsayable (the paradox of poetry) because uniquely arising from the poet's personal vision and interpretation. (Saunders, 2003, p. 176)

In a later paper Saunders writes,

> I see the relationship between poetry and research as fractured and ambiguous and multiple; also infinitely interesting and generative. For me, what is essential about poetry as distinct from research is that it is something, a thing, an aesthetic object, made in language. It is not a representation of something other than itself (*Ceci n'est pas une pipe*). So I feel, as I admitted in the later paper, an unease about the possibility of poetry being pressed into serving some purpose other than its own passage from silence into language and back into an (altered) silence, to paraphrase Abbs (2006). I have expressed a notion that poetry needs to be 'gratuitous' as well as 'necessary' and in the earlier paper I had groped towards a definition of these terms like this:
>
> > one could say that a poem's gratuitousness resides in how much it surprises us, moves us, invites our imagination to take wing. Its necessity lies in its capacity to convince us that the poem in question is the only form this thought or feeling could have had, and indeed, that the thought or feeling itself, expressed in this way, is of paramount importance to our sense of the world. (Saunders, 2003, p. 178). (Saunders, 2007, p. 34)

It would seem to be of paramount importance that a poetical or fictional approach should be the best, if not the only, way to do whatever it is that we are seeking to do. Decisions to use particular methodologies or methods should be made on grounds of necessity rather than to serve what Saunders describes as 'some other purpose'. It was on this basis that Heather Piper and I adopted a composite fictional approach to re-present our research which investigated the perceptions and experiences of teachers (and those of members of their families, their friends and colleagues) who had been accused of sexual abuse of pupils which they said they had not committed and of which they were eventually cleared (Sikes and Piper, 2010).

The primary consideration influencing our decision was concern to protect our informants from exposure and the sort of negative media attention that anyone suspected of paedophilia is liable to attract in the current climate of moral panic pertaining around child protection and abuse (Bauman, 2006; Sikes, 2008, 2010b). However as do other advocates of fictional approaches (for example, Banks and Banks, 1998; Clough, 2002; Pelias, 2004; Sparkes, 2007), we wanted to capitalize on the ways in which fictionalizing can conjure up a sense of feel and place (Sikes, 2005), evoke the richness and complexity of life and invite readers to identify and empathize with the experiences and perspectives described.

In various places (Piper and Sikes, 2010a, 2010b; Sikes and Piper, 2010) we have described how we went about crafting the composite stories through which we attempted to depict various experiences stemming from a false accusation of sexual abuse. Ours was one approach, others do it differently (see, for instance, Richardson and Lockridge, 1998, 2004; Clough, 2002; Selbie and Clough, 2005) but essentially what we did was interview a number of accused teachers and family members and colleagues of those so accused. Having made transcripts of what was said we sat down with the accounts given by people in the group whose particular story we wanted to tell (be that accused teachers, family members or colleagues) and read each account over and over looking for similarities and patterns. We then constructed a cast and a storyline which enabled us to include all of the perceptions and experiences we wanted to re-present. So, for example, in telling the story about what it can be like for the spouse and children of an accused teacher

> we chose to have a family with four youngsters of different ages rather than a childless couple because the latter wouldn't have allowed us to make use of the data that we had about the effect of accusation upon teachers' own children. Strained relationships between husband and wife were common to all of the stories that we were told by wives but only one woman spoke openly about sexual matters. Nevertheless we chose to incorporate her account into the story because others had also alluded to difficulties in this area. (Sikes and Piper, 2010, p. 52)

We told this family story through the wife's voice and similarly used the first person to tell the individual accused teachers' stories because we wanted to evoke the immediacy of personal experience. However, when we were seeking to portray the effect that a false accusation can have on the various members and the life of a school community, we used a variation of the third person omniscient because we felt this offered more scope.

Our aim was also to provoke what Andrew Sparkes (2003) terms 'active readership' which involves and implicates readers in interpretation and meaning making and which can 'lead to praxis, empowerment and social change' (Denzin, 2003, p. 133). However, we agree with Richardson that 'if ethnography claims *only* to be "fiction" then it loses any claims it might have for groundedness and policy implications' (1997c, p. 108). Our approach that explicitly combined fiction and ethnographic data aimed to 'bring the written product of social research closer to the richness and complexity of lived experience' (Bochner and Ellis, 1998, p. 7) taking the view that evocation of what being in a particular situation feels like can help to

> invoke (if not kick start) the sociological imagination, linking personal to public (Mills, 1959[1970]) thereby improving the chances of influencing policy. And indeed, that we were invited, on the basis of our work, to make a submission to a (House of Commons) Children, Schools and Families Select Committee Inquiry into *Allegations Against School Staff* (CSF, 2009) does support this contention (Piper and Sikes, 2010b, p. 568)

Having said this it is clear that my view is that fictional and poetic re-presentations of research have socially transformative potential. Use of these and other 'alternative' approaches acknowledges diversity by challenging traditional, dominant and hegemonic forms of interpreting and re-presenting the world, which can be not only personally liberating and transformative (Richardson, 1997d) but can also make them attractive to those seeking to advance critical and decolonizing agendas (see Tuhiwai Smith, 1999; various contributors to Denzin, et al., 2008; and Chapter 39, this volume). As was suggested at the start of this section, reasons for adopting fictional and poetic approaches are diverse as are motivations for undertaking research in the first place. Nevertheless as it seems difficult, if not impossible, to justify research which does not in some way contribute to the good, so it feels equally hard to support the use of approaches which do not play a similar role. Using fiction or poetry purely for reasons of self-indulgence and personal gratification or because it is currently fashionable (Flyvbjerg, 2001) are, it is argued, not good enough cause.

WHAT WRITERS/RESEARCHERS NEED TO CONSIDER WHEN USING FICTIONAL AND POETIC APPROACHES

In the editorial that launched a new online journal dedicated to *Creative Approaches to Research* and under the subheading of 'What do creative approaches to research mean for researchers?' one of the executive editors wrote,

> challenging the shape and appearance of research opens the door to issues of authority, legitimacy, responsibility and power, which go to the core of how we view the world and what we value. This raises many complexities for researchers. Here are three of the tensions that creative researchers need to learn to work with:

- Knowing the rules AND challenging assumptions
- Being creative AND maintaining rigour
- Honouring content AND exploring form.

These sets of paired ideas are not dualities. They can be true simultaneously. Many questions emerge from the interplay of these ideas. (Brearley, 2008, p. 4)

These tensions and the sorts of questions they generate do need to be given serious consideration by those contemplating the use of fiction or poetry. The key questions that I generally put to students who say they are thinking about using them relate to: honesty and ethics; the skills and abilities of the researcher/writer; the need to take responsibility as a social scientist; and personal career implications. I address each, and very briefly, in turn.

Honesty and Ethics

I have already stated that in my view it is necessary for researcher/writers to be absolutely explicit when they are using fiction. I share both Mike Angrosino's view that 'a story doesn't have to be factual in order to be true' (1998, p. 34) and Margaret Attwood's contention that 'a thing can be true, but not true, but true nonetheless' (2008). However and like Laurel Richardson, quoted earlier, I think that readers picking up something which makes claims to be social science should be told exactly what they are reading, whether that be fiction, mixed genre work or writing which aims to provide objective, realist reporting. Failure to make this declaration or to show the processes of analysis and how writings have been constructed on the basis of the data, is, to my mind, unethical and disrespectful of readers. Furthermore the scandals/controversies which erupt when doubt is cast on the veracity of particular writings (a key example being whether or not Carlos Casteneda really was apprenticed to don Juan Matus and did become a Nagual with super/supra natural powers) do a serious disservice to the social sciences.

Obviously those who use fiction and poetry are as subject to the need to be ethical as any other researchers. In their depictions and descriptions they need to ensure that they do all that they can to protect the people involved in their research – and they need to remember that simply saying that an account is fictional is not an excuse to thinly disguise individuals, places or events. In my experience, even when characters or settings are entirely fictionalized readers will often claim to know who is being referred to, so if the fictionalizing is 'weak' the risk of identification (if that is required) is the greater.

The Skills and Abilities of the Researcher/Writer

Social scientists are not necessarily good writers of fiction or poetry. Deciding to use these approaches actually introduces another criterion – that of aesthetic quality – into the list of those against which the quality of any piece might be judged. Jane Piirto (2002), Laurel Richardson (2000, 2002) and Carolyn Ellis (2004), for example, all recommend that those who decide to use creative approaches should take classes and/or join writers' groups or poetry circles in order to develop their skills. Bad fiction and poetry do no service to their author or to the acceptance of them as legitimate forms of social science re-presentation.

The Need to Take Responsibility as a Social Scientist

Social scientists do have a responsibility to make an interpretation, an analysis of the data they collect and then re-present (Delamont, 2007). Saying this does not prescribe the form that analysis should take and it could be that the analysis is manifest in the way a poem is set out, for instance, or in the choice of words, narrative structure, characterization and so on, of a fictional story. Once again the issue centres on the claims an author makes. For example, Charles Dickens's *Oliver Twist* and Charles Kingsley's *The Waterbabies* were presented as fictions. Both of these works can be attributed with making a contribution to social reform and that end, no doubt, was one of the aims behind their respective creation. This is an aim that many social scientists would subscribe to. However, the extent to which *Oliver Twist* and *The Waterbabies* were the outcome of 'systematic inquiry made public' (Stenhouse, 1975) is not made explicit and, at the present time in the UK at least, this would debar them from being given a research rating in the Research Excellence Framework exercise (other countries have their equivalents that would similarly disqualify them). Whilst this may not be an entirely sound reason for dismissing their sociological significance it does lead neatly into considerations around . . .

Personal Career Implications

Using non-traditional approaches to research and re-presentation can have implications for academic career development (Sikes, 2006). Nowadays there is, as has been claimed throughout this chapter, far greater acceptance of creative approaches of all kinds and it is the case that people who have used them are obtaining masters and doctoral degrees and gaining employment as academics. Funding from research councils and other bodies, however, does still seem to tend to favour those proposing traditional methodologies, methods and forms of re-presentation and anecdotal evidence suggests that promotion is more easily obtained by people who can demonstrate command of these. Pointing this out is not to say do not use fiction and poetry but rather be aware of possible consequences of so doing.

FINALLY

In this chapter I have tried to give an overview of some of the issues and considerations around fiction and poetry as approaches to research re-presentation. I have talked about how things have changed during my own academic career and I have no doubt that change will continue. To go back to where I began: when I started reading the works on that *Required and Recommended Research Reading List* I quickly realized that, for the most part but not entirely, they were boring, hard to follow, made much use of jargon and inaccessible language, adopted obfuscatory and archaic style and were simply not engaging. Of course there is no excuse for bad social science writing as people like Howard Becker (1986) and Peter Woods (2006) make clear. It does seem that the literary and narrative turn has led to greater consideration of, and attention to, form and style generally, although there is still bad writing of all kinds in abundance. Good fiction and poetry do have much to offer social science. I look forward to seeing more in the years to come.

REFERENCES

Angrosino, M. (1998), *Opportunity House: Ethnographic Studies of Mental Retardation*, Walnut Creek, CA: AltaMira Press.

Attwood, M. (2008), 'Close to home: a celebration of Margaret Attwood', *Guardian Review*, 11 October, 2–4.

Banks, A. and Banks S. (eds) (1998), *Fiction and Social Research: By Ice or Fire*, Walnut Creek, CA: AltaMira.

Barthes, R. (1966), 'Introduction to the structural analysis of narratives', in S. Sontag (ed.), (1982), *A Barthes Reader*, New York: Hill and Wang.

Barthes, R. (1977), 'The death of the author', in *Image-Music-Text*, Glasgow: Fontana/Collins (Originally published in French, 1968).

Bauman, Z. (2006), *Liquid Fear*, Cambridge: Polity.

Becker, H. (1986), *Writing For Social Scientists*, Chicago, IL: University of Chicago Press.

Bochner, A. and Ellis, C. (1998), 'Series editors' Preface', in A. Banks and S. Banks (eds), *Fiction and Social Research: By Ice or Fire*, Walnut Creek, CA: AltaMira, pp. 7–8.

Brady, I. (ed.) (1991), *Anthropological Poetics*, Savage, MD: Rowman and Littlefield.

Brearley, L. (2008), 'Introduction to creative approaches to research', *Creative Approaches to Research*, **1** (1), 3–12, available at http://search.informit.com.au/browsePublication;py=2008;vol=1;res=IELHSS;issn=1835-9434;iss=1 (accessed 9 September 2010).

Bruner, J. (1986), *Actual Minds, Possible Worlds*, Cambridge, MA: Harvard University Press.

Bulmer, M. (1984), *The Chicago School of Sociology: Institutionalization, Diversity and the Rise of Sociological Research*, Chicago, IL: University of Chicago Press.

Chase, S. (2005), 'Narrative inquiry: multiple lenses, approaches, voices', in N. Denzin and Y. Lincoln (eds), *The Handbook of Qualitative Research*, 3rd edn, Thousand Oaks, CA: Sage, pp. 651–79.

Clough, P. (1992), *The Ends of Ethnography*, London: Sage.

Clough, P. (2002), *Narratives and Fictions in Educational Research*, Maidenhead: Open University Press.

CSF (2009), *Allegations Against School Staff*, London: The Stationery Office.

Delamont, S. (2007), 'Arguments against autoethnography', *Qualitative Researcher*, **4** February, 2–4, available at http://www.cardiff.ac.uk/socsi/qualiti/QualitativeResearcher/QR_Issue4_Feb07.pdf (accessed 7 September 2011).

Denzin, N. (2003), *Performance Ethnography, Critical Pedagogy and the Cultural Politics of Change*, Thousand Oaks, CA: Sage.

Denzin, N. and Lincoln, Y. (2005), 'Introduction: the discipline and practice of qualitative research', in N. Denzin and Y. Lincoln (eds), *The Sage Handbook of Qualitative Research*, 3rd edn, Thousand Oaks, CA: Sage, pp. 1–32.

Denzin, N., Lincoln, Y. and Tuhiwai Smith, L. (eds) (2008), *Handbook of Critical and Indigenous Methodologies*, Thousand Oaks, CA: Sage.

Ellis, C. (2004), *The Ethnographic I: A Methodological Novel About Autoethnography*, Walnut Creek, CA: AltaMira.

Flyvbjerg, B. (2001), *Making Social Science Matter: Why Social Inquiry Fails and How It Can Succeed Again*, Cambridge: Cambridge University Press.

Gurevitch, Z. (2002), 'Writing through: the poetics of transfiguration', *Cultural Studies Critical Methodologies*, **2** (3), 403–13.

Harris, S. (ed.) (2002), *Cosmologia*, Chichester: RPM Reprographics.

Huston, Z. ([1935]1991), *Mules and Men*, London: HarperCollins.

Huston, Z. ([1938]1991), *Tell My Horse*, London: HarperCollins.

Hyvarinen, M. (2007), 'Revisiting the narrative turns', Paper presented at the ESRC Seminar Narrative Turn: Revisioning Theory, University of Edinburgh, 23 March 2008.

King-Hele, D. (2003), 'Introductory note', in E. Darwin ([1803]2003), *The Temple of Nature*, King's Lynn: Biddles Short Run Books.

Mills, C.W. ([1959]1970), *The Sociological Imagination*, Penguin: Harmondsworth.

Pelias, R. (2004), *A Methodology of the Heart*, Walnut Creek, CA: AltaMira.

Piirto, J. (2002), 'The question of quality and qualifications: writing inferior poems as qualitative research', *Qualitative Inquiry*, **15** (4), 431–46.

Piper, H. and Sikes, P. (2010a), '"All teachers are vulnerable, but especially gay teachers": using composite fictions to protect research participants in pupil-teacher sex related research', *Qualitative Inquiry*, **16** (7), 566–74.

Piper, H. and Sikes, P. (2010b), '"Parenting" in loco parentis and cultural change', *Sociological Research Online*, **15** (4), http://www.socresonline.org.uk/15/4/5.html, 10.5153/sro.2194

Plummer, K. (2001), *Documents of Life 2: An Invitation to a Critical Humanism*, London: Sage.

Polkinghorne, D.E. (1988), *Narrative Knowing and the Human Sciences*, Albany, NY: State University New York Press.

Porter Abbot, H. (2002), *The Cambridge Introduction to Narrative*, Cambridge: Cambridge University Press.

Porter Abbot, H. (2005), *The Cambridge Introduction to Narrative*, 2nd edn, Cambridge: Cambridge University Press.

Richardson, L. (1990), 'Narrative and sociology', *Journal of Contemporary Ethnography*, **19** (1), 116–35.

Richardson, L. (1992), 'The poetic representation of lives: writing a postmodern sociology', *Studies in Symbolic Interaction*, **13**, 77–82.

Richardson, L. (1994), 'Writing: a method of inquiry', in N. Denzin and Y. Lincoln (eds), *Handbook of Qualitative Research,* Thousand Oaks, CA: Sage, 516–29.

Richardson, L. (1995), 'Writing stories: co-authoring "The Sea Monster", a writing-story', *Qualitative Inquiry,* **1** (2), 189–203.

Richardson, L. (1997a), *Fields of Play: Constructing an Academic Life,* New Brunswick, NJ: Rutgers University Press.

Richardson, L. (1997b), 'Narrative knowing and sociological telling', in L. Richardson, *Fields of Play: Constructing an Academic Life,* New Brunswick, NJ: Rutgers University Press, pp. 26–35.

Richardson, L. (1997c), 'Trash on the corner: ethics and ethnography', in L. Richardson, *Fields of Play: Constructing an Academic Life,* New Brunswick, NJ: Rutgers University Press, pp. 102–11.

Richardson, L. (1997d), 'Consequences of poetic representation', in L. Richardson *Fields of Play: Constructing an Academic Life,* New Brunswick, NJ: Rutgers University Press, pp. 147–153.

Richardson, L. (1998), 'The politics of location: where am I now?', *Qualitative Inquiry,* **4** (1), 41–8.

Richardson, L. (2000), 'Writing: a method of inquiry', in N. Denzin and Y. Lincoln (eds), *The Handbook of Qualitative Research,* 2nd edn, Thousand Oaks, CA: Sage, pp. 923–48.

Richardson, L. (2002), 'Poetic representation of interviews', in J.F. Gubrium, and J.A. Holstein (eds), *Handbook of Interview Research Context and Method,* Thousand Oaks, CA: Sage, pp. 877–92.

Richardson, L. and Lockridge, E. (1998), 'Fiction and ethnography: a conversation', *Qualitative Inquiry,* **4** (3), 328–36.

Richardson, L. and Lockridge, E. (2004), *Travels With Ernest: Crossing the Literary: Sociological Divide,* Walnut Creek, CA: AltaMira.

Richardson, L. and St Pierre, E. (2005), 'Writing: a method of inquiry', in N. Denzin and Y. Lincoln (eds), *The Handbook of Qualitative Research,* 3rd edn, Thousand Oaks, CA: Sage, pp. 959–78.

Riessman, C. (1993), *Narrative Analysis,* London: Sage.

Riessman, C. (2008), *Narrative Methods for the Human Sciences,* Los Angeles, CA: Sage.

Rorty, R. (1979), *Philosophy and the Mirror of Nature,* Oxford: Blackwell.

Rothenberg, J. (1968), *Technicians of the Sacred,* Berkeley, CA: University of California Press.

Rudrum, D. (2005), 'From narrative representation to narrative use: towards the limits of definition', *Narrative,* **13** (2), 195–204.

Saunders, L. (2003), 'On flying, writing poetry and doing educational research', *British Educational Research Journal,* **29** (2), 175–87.

Saunders, L. (2007), 'An alternative way of responding to powerful ideas: notes to accompany the poem entitled Five Principles of Quality in Narratives of Action Research', *Educational Action Research,* **15** (1), 33–40.

Selbie, P. and Clough, P. (2005), 'Talking early childhood education: fictional enquiry with historical figures', *Journal of Early Childhood Education,* **3** (2), 115–26.

Sikes, P. (2005), 'Storying schools: issues around attempts to create a sense of feel and place in narrative research writing', *Qualitative Research,* **5** (1), 79–94.

Sikes, P. (2006), 'On dodgy ground? Problematics and ethics in educational research?', *International Journal of Research & Method in Education,* **29** (1), 105–17.

Sikes, P. (2008), 'At the eye of the storm: an academic(s) experience of moral panic', *Qualitative Inquiry,* **14** (2), 235–53.

Sikes, P. (2010a), 'The ethics of writing life histories and narratives in educational research', in A. Bathmaker and P. Harnett (eds), *Exploring Learning, Identity and Power Through Life History and Narrative Research,* London: Routledge/Falmer, pp. 11–24.

Sikes, P. (2010b), 'Researching teacher-student sexual relations: key risks and ethical issues', *Ethnography and Education,* **5** (2), 143–57.

Sikes, P. and Piper, H. (2010), *Researching Sex and Lies in the Classroom: Allegations of Sexual Misconduct in Schools,* London: Routledge/Falmer.

Smith, B. (2002), 'The (in)visible wound: body stories and concentric circles of witness', *Auto/Biography*, **10** (1),131–21.

Sparkes, A. (2003), 'Men, sport, spinal cord injury and narrative time', *Qualitative Research*, **3** (3), 295–20.

Sparkes, A. (2007), 'Embodiment, academics and the audit culture', *Qualitative Research*, **7** (4), 521–50.

Stanley, L. and Temple, B. (2008), 'Narrative methodologies', *Qualitative Research*, **8** (3), 275–81.

Stenhouse, L. (1975), *An Introduction to Curriculum Development and Research*, London: Heinemann.

Sullivan, A. (2002), 'The necessity of art: three found poems from John Dewey's "Art As Experience"', *International Journal of Qualitative Studies in Education*, **13** (3), 325–7.

Tedlock, D. (1972), *Finding the Center: Narrative Poetics of the Zuni Storyteller*, New York: Dial Press.

Thompson, V. (2009), 'A taste of higher education: exploring a culinary arts degree through arts-based approaches', Unpublished PhD Thesis, University of Sheffield.

Tuhiwai Smith, L. (1999), *Decolonizing Methodologies: Research and Indigenous Peoples*, London: Zed Books.

Van Maanen, J. (1988), *Tales of the Field*, Chicago, IL: University of Chicago Press.

Waller, W. (1932), 'Preface', in *The Sociology of the Teacher*, New York: John Wiley.

Woods, P. (2006), *Successful Writing For Qualitative Researchers 2nd edn*, London: Routledge.

Woolf, V. (1992), 'Mr Bennett and Mrs Brown', in V. Woolf and R. Bowlby (eds), *A Woman's Essays*, London: Penguin.

44. Dance: making movement meaningful
Carl Bagley and Ricardo Castro-Salazar

INTRODUCTION

In recent years the academy has witnessed an increasing number of qualitative researchers across a range of academic disciplines including education, reflecting on the use of the arts to inform practice; notable edited collections on this theme include Cahnmann-Taylor and Siegesmund (2008), Knowles and Cole (2008), Leavy (2009) and Liamputtong and Rumbold (2008). Arguably, these publications are indicative of increasing efforts by a number of researchers to define and position arts-based or arts-informed research as an important and emergent genre within the qualitative paradigm. While in this sense a 'performative sensibility' (Denzin, 2001, p. 25) could be claimed to be awakening, it should be noted that such stirrings are still relatively limited (especially when set against the plethora of other qualitative research endeavours), are far more marked in North America than in the UK or Europe, and from certain academic quarters face severe criticism (see, for example, Walford, 2009).

In terms of those researchers embracing arts-based practices, work has tended to be of a literary nature, encompassing the use of short story (Kilbourne, 1998), creative fiction (Angrosino, 1998) and poetry (Richardson, 2002), or represented/staged in dramatic form (Goldstein, 2001; Mienczakowski, 2001; Saldana, 2005) or utilized in the visual arts (Knowles et al., 2007). Significantly, much less in evidence in the literature, and thus a relatively small performative fish in a relatively small academic qualitative pool, is the use of dance and movement. Indeed, it could be argued that the place and voice of dance within social and educational research generally remains one of the least heard, situated and documented. Undoubtedly, dance, as an ephemeral performance-based art form, raises particular questions concerning its adoption and application in educational research. The social research literature, in which dance does feature, tends to do so in one of several ways: firstly, as the research subject; secondly, as a metaphorical or actual means of data generation and analysis; and thirdly, as a means of data dissemination and representation.

In this chapter, we reflect on these social research manifestations, with the ultimate aim – through case study portrayal – of revealing dance and movement, as literally and evocatively a 'moving' form, which can be used to 'create empathetic connection, raise awareness' and help 'promote social justice' (Snowber, 2009, pp. 178–80).

DANCE AS THE RESEARCH SUBJECT

In the first half of the twentieth century the initial research focus was on the anthropological connotations of dance (sometimes fused with other artistic forms such as music and theatre) with individuals, described by Stinson and Dils (2008) as 'Western dance ethnographers' (p. 183). For example, de Zoete and Spies (1938) observed and wrote about 'dance practices within cultures other than their own' (Stinson and Dils, 2008, p.183) in countries such as Bali and India. Other notable dance ethnographers include Boas (1942) whose research on the Kwakiutl in British Columbia, contributed to the anthropology of dance through observing the culture and practices of native peoples within North America; a tradition which continued into the twentieth century with, for example, the work of dance scholars such as Kealiinohomoku (1985[1993]) writing on the music and dance of the Hawaiian and Hopi peoples. Indeed, Stinson and Dils (2008) cite a particular seminal work of Kealiinohomoku (1997) entitled 'An anthropologist looks at ballet as a form of ethnic dance', as helping to progress the field from a more historical standpoint, grounded in 'chronologies of Western dance and biographies of great artists' (p. 183), to a more 'hybrid, interdisciplinary "dance studies" approach' (p. 183). Accompanying this interdisciplinary move, dance educators came to focus not simply on the dance practices of 'other' cultures, but dance culture in Western dance classes, clubs and communities (Stinson and Dils, 2008).

Snowber (2009) notes how not simply within the academic dance community but within anthropology generally there are a continuing, if not increasing, interest amongst anthropologists on dance and movement as a source of cultural information. She cites as an example the special issue of the *Australian Journal of Anthropology* published in 2000 on the anthropology of dance. The introduction to which states:

> We theorise dance practices as domains of lived experience and position movement as a performative moment of social interchange that is not merely reflective of prior political, personal and social and cosmological relations but also constitutive of the relationships of them . . . Attention to the ways in which movement is able to infuse space with socio-religious and socio-political meaning requires that dance practices be viewed as historically embodied, contextual, discursive and interconnected domains of lived experience. (Henry, 2000, cited in Snowber, 2009, p. 181)

In the main all the above studies be they undertaken by dance scholars or non-dance educated anthropologists, tended to draw on the traditional lexicon of qualitative methods such as participant observation, interviews and documentary analysis. It was not until relatively recently that dance itself was used as a methodological tool in the conduct and dissemination of social research.

DANCE AS A METHOD OF DATA GENERATION AND ANALYSIS

One of the qualitative utilizations of dance to inform the research process has been as metaphor (see, for example, Stinson, 1995; Janesick, 1998). Janesick (1998) in her book, *'Stretching' Exercises for Qualitative Researchers*, discusses the systematic processes that a dancer must go through before a performance. She contends that in the same way in which a dancer engages in warming-up, stretching, improvising, having bodily experiences and making aesthetic decisions, so 'metaphorically' does the qualitative researcher.

Similarly, Silveira et al. (2002) in a paper entitled 'Dance of discovery' present the methodology they used for collecting data developed through the metaphor of dance. They write:

> dance is an interpretative form of art and the design of qualitative research is as interpretative as dance. For us, well . . . the research, as carried out by us, looks like dance for other reasons too: the rehearsals; the soundtrack which drives us; the uncertainty of knowing whether we will set up suitable choreographies; the inventiveness and flexibility to wait for our, literally, partners/participants' steps; the doubt if our performance will please those who evaluate us; and, finally, the risk of 'slipping up' if something goes wrong. (Silveira et al., 2002, pp. 2–3)

Aside from any debate around the veracity of dance as metaphor to inform qualitative practice, for those engaged in research which encompasses dance there is a debate as to whether a specific methodological approach intrinsic to dance should be developed (Stinson and Dils, 2008). One method which does specifically relate to movement and which has been adopted by some researchers to study dance in cultural contexts is Laban Movement Analysis (LMA) (see, for example, Freedman, 1991).

LMA, pioneered by Rudolf von Laban (see Maletic, 1987 for a detailed exposition of the method), is a research method applied to contexts in which movement is a significant factor and which conceptually perceives movement as configured around three defined components:

body, effort and space, each of which may be analysed separately or together depending on the nature of the investigation. The body component relates to 'what' movement is undertaken, for example, a particular gesture; the effort component concerns 'how' the movement is made and might include flow and weighting; the space component relates to 'where' the movement is conducted and the configuration of spatial harmony. Consequently in dance research LMA might be used to critically view, describe and appraise a specific dance technique, dancer's performance or a choreographic approach. As Stinson and Dils (2008) note however:

> As with all analysis systems, these parameters cannot be applied across cultures and reveal only certain kinds of information; researchers create new ways of attending to bodily sensations and the rhythmic and visual organization of movement to meet the needs of individual research projects. (Stinson and Dils, 2008, p.183)

Notwithstanding the above observation of Stinson and Dils (2008), it is the case, certainly over the last 20 years, that dance and movement has been increasingly perceived not only as a subject nor simply a metaphorical device, but rather a methodological tool for generating and analysing data; the use of the dancer-researcher's bodily movement and awareness used in developing a relationship with data and to build theory. In essence dance and movement teaches a person to internalize their use of the body as a source of knowledge and focal point of understanding (Stinson, 2004). In this way scholars informed through dance may perceive a concept somatically before having the words to express it (Stinson and Dils, 2008), the body functioning as a multi-sensory repository and conduit 'through which social actors have relations to an object and through which they give and receive information' (Grosz, 1994, cited in Snowber, 2009, p. 183).

Fraleigh (1987), working from an existential phenomenological perspective, developed a descriptive aesthetic in her work *Dance and the Lived Body*, to explore self as instrument within the research process. As a dancer-researcher, she seeks to integrate her multiple selves into her knowing. In a similar way, Snowber's (2002) interdisciplinary work combines dance, poetry and spirituality to understand the researcher-dancer as the instrument of discovery within the research process. Her work uses 'body data' to create 'body narratives'. She writes,

> Largely using the art of improvisation, I repeatedly dance the narratives of my own life and the questions and responses from my students as a way of accessing, developing, chiseling, editing, and creating material. (Snowber, 2002, p. 23)

In a further auto-ethnographic vein McNiff (2007), as an artist and art therapist, considers the ways in which movement can enhance his relationship with his art through crafting a number of paintings which he subsequently interprets through 'spontaneous body movement' in order to gain new insights, and become more intimately connected to the painting,

For Blumenfeld-Jones (2008, p. 175) the contribution a qualitative dancer-researcher is able to make to social science research relates to their inside/r understanding and somatic engagement with the meaning of human movement as a phenomenological experience within social settings; the dancer-researcher, not only analysing bodily action, but placing that analysis into action with her or his own body through motion, organizing motion into choreography and performing the choreography possibly for others. In this way a dancer-research may 'gain new insights on the meanings in the social scene under investigation, insights available as a direct outcome of having thought through motion' (p. 175). Similarly, in Cancienne and Bagley (2008), Cancienne provides two vignettes on the way in which she uses dance and movement as part of a qualitative research process. In the first vignette she explores and evaluates the use of dance in relation to practical work on and with the professional development of teachers, in particular the notion of team building and developing a sense of community. It shows how teacher engagement with movement even at a very elementary level can engender a wider appreciation of the art form. In the second vignette Cancienne outlines a movement-based action research study in which teachers were asked to 'walk' through and observe a local community, and subsequently explores the use of improvisational dance as an analytical method for making sense of data the 'walk' generated. Cancienne sums up the process in the following way:

> Using improvisational dance as a method of analysis, I connected to the teachers in an empathetic, emotional way. One of the choreographer's most important tools is the body/mind that connects emotionally with the participants through kinesthetic awareness. The choreographer who has access to embodied techniques can tap into the participants' feelings. Many people ask me why I dance as a way of making sense of data. I tell them that when I dance I find something important to say. (Cancienne and Bagley, 2008, p. 177)

As Stinson (1995, p. 53) observes, dance and movement 'allow us to perceive more clearly, and understand more deeply the embodied others who are subjects if not participants in educational research'. Arguably, as we discuss in the final section, it also provides an evocative genre through which to (re)present qualitatively generated research data to an audience.

DANCE AS A METHOD OF DATA REPRESENTATION

In turning to the use of dance and movement in the representation of qualitative research, this has been achieved either by trained dancers who are also researchers performing their own data (see, for example, Blumenfeld-Jones, 1995; Snowber, 2002) or involved non-dance trained researchers working with dancers to choreograph and stage their work (see, for example, Bagley and Cancienne, 2001; Bagley, 2008). Here we provide a case example of the latter. The reason why in this section we focus in detail on the facilitation of a collaborative performance-based approach is twofold. Firstly, we would contend that as a medium for data representation, dance and movement is particularly well suited. Secondly, it reveals the opportunity for qualitative researchers not trained in dance to still embrace the medium.

In the case example we present, unlike the previous work of Bagley (2008), there is a clear political imperative underpinning both the research and the dance performance.

In a social scientific sense the notion of taking qualitative data and utilizing it for the purpose of dance performance may be situated within a revised interpretive interactionist and sociologically informed research approach termed performance ethnography (Denzin, 2003). Performance ethnography takes as its guiding principle that artistic (re)presentations of ethnographically derived findings from interviews, documentary analysis and participant observation provide an aesthetic-ally grounded and multi-layered textual rendering of cultural others. The data's evocation through artistic (re)presentation such as dance propagating a discernment of multiple meanings, interpretations and voices which evocatively engage the reader/viewer in recognition of lived diversity and complexity.

In our case the performance – in which dance featured – was derived from a Critical Race Theory (CRT)-informed (Ladson-Billings, 1998), life history-based research project, on the educational experiences of undocumented American students of Mexican origin residing without 'official' legal status in the Southwestern United States. The grounding CRT-informed premise of our work is that this group are one of the most vulnerable, victimized, and subjugated (Chávez, 2005; Massey, 2005) in the United States; subject to economic exploitation, and cultural mar-ginalization (Cacho, 2000; Sarther, 2006; Ramos Cardoso, 2007), and largely excluded from public services such as education (De Genova, 2004; Barclay, 2005; Massey, 2005; Archibold, 2006) (for a more detailed account see Castro-Salazar and Bagley, 2010).

Moreover, we believe the dominant ideology, in dehistoricizing race and racism has attempted 'to close down any space in which to question racism and the structures that produce and sustain it' (Macedo and Gounari, 2004, p. 3). As Nabokov (1967) states:

> The ordinary man, whose existence is far removed from centers of power, is rarely prompted to recall his days. While men of renown have always documented their experiences, or storytellers have done it for them, only recently have representatives of a culture been asked to relate the rhythms of their lives. (Nabokov, 1967 p. xi, cited in Wolcott, 1999, p. 159)

It was thus our methodological intent to give voice to the experiences of undocumented Americans of Mexican origin, and to relate through the powerful and synergetic lenses of CRT, counter life history and ultimately live performance, the cultural 'rhythms of their lives' (Nabokov, 1967, p. xi, cited in Wolcott, 1999, p. 159). For the purposes of this chapter we concentrate on revealing the process by which these undocumented lives came to be evocatively expressed through the performative rhythm of dance (for a more detailed discussion of the whole performance see Bagley and Castro-Salazar, 2011).

In order to recover the life history narratives, which were to form the basis for the development of a performance-based text, a study of six individuals was undertaken, focusing on the characteristics, conditions and complexity of their lives. In line with CRT, the counter life history narratives were explored in their multifaceted contexts and dimensions, not simply as individual productions, but also as the product of cultural and ideological contexts (Delgado and Stefancic, 2001; Bell, 2003). The narratives were elicited by prolonged unstructured in-depth interviews with each participant, culminating in the grounded analysis (Glaser and Strauss, 1967) of 30 hours of taped transcript. These transcripts, along with other contextual data on the background to the project, were shared with artists of Mexican origin. One of whom was a choreographer/dancer, who was asked to read and interpret the data in order to create a dance performance to be staged as part of a live performance.

While dancer-researcher Blumenfeld-Jones (2008) acknowledges that the gap between dancer and choreographer can at times be difficult to distinguish, he contends that the research potential of dance resides not so much in the dancing but in the choreography. He states:

> The fact is that dancers re-present a choreographer's ideas to the choreographer but it is the choreographer who composes, either creating movement to be performed or shaping movement s/he elicits from the dancers . . . in making real the choreographer's movements that were previously in the mind or were worked out on the choreographer's body, the choreographer sees what is

> actually possible as opposed to what is only, originally, conceptually possible. Only through this actualization does knowledge emerge; form and knowledge are inseparable. (Blumenfeld-Jones, 2008, p. 177)

In the case of our research the choreographer-dancer Yvonne Montoya described her approach to the choreographic process in the following terms:

> I really believe to portray something so profound, dramatic and emotional I think that the dancer needs to feel it. I think the dancer needs to have a spiritual connection to the work and the way to evoke that is to have the dancers involved in the choreographic process.

In order to achieve this connection Yvonne initially read through the life history transcripts and highlighted the direct quotes she thought were the most powerful and 'represented the authentic student voice'. She then worked in a dance studio with two other dancers using improvisation. Yvonne would read one of the quotes she had identified from the life histories and get the dancers to do a free write, in which they wrote down all their feelings, emotions and thoughts evoked by the selected quotes. The dancers then read out what they wrote, and were asked by Yvonne to pick three words from their text in order to create subtle gestures such as the tucking of hair behind the ears or the placing of a hand to the face. These gestures were repeated with the dancers asked to 'play' with the intensity and sequence of movement. Randomly selected taped music was then played, with the dancers allowed to become more expressive in their movement but only permitted to dance within the context of the three gestures. Finally, the dancers were asked to say the words they associated with the gestures. For example, one of the dancers would dance and at a point in the sequence say the word suicide. In this way an improvisational intertextual layering of words and movement was created.

For Yvonne – artistically influenced by dance theatre – the mix of words and music was important. She believed this would help to ground the piece more, especially for audience members not familiar with viewing a dance performance. Moreover, in linking the dance with words spoken in both English and Spanish, the piece sought to engage with the bilingualism and multiple identities of the voices coming through the transcripts.

The improvisational dance sessions lasted approximately three hours and three were held prior to the final rehearsal and performance. Yvonne video taped all the improvisations, which she viewed after each session to reflect further and move the choreographic process forward. Interestingly, one of the main artistic catalysts initially came neither from the improvisations nor the video reflections, but an event in Yvonne's life which occurred at the time she was working on the choreography and which spoke directly to the US immigrant experience. She described it in the following terms:

> We were on the way to the interview for my husband's *green card* and I suddenly became very aware of all the forms we had had to complete from US Department of Homeland Security, and in particular that each of these forms had been assigned letters and numbers, and it was a kind of eureka moment. I could see how these anonymous numbers could help shape a dance narrative around the quest for citizenship, and the clandestine emotive implications of being undocumented. Hence, I came to the name clandestina for the dance performance.

Clandestina[1]

The dance sequence was subsequently performed as a vignette within a larger artistic performance, at a small traditionally configured theatre in downtown Tucson, Arizona. The audience was predominantly of Mexican origin including undocumented individuals, community activists, representatives of the Mexican Consulate, and students and academics of Mexican origin. Importantly, in terms of engendering a wider breadth of support, the audience also included a significant minority of non-Mexican individuals and groups sympathetic to the political cause of undocumented peoples.

For the dance performance a table was placed centre stage with three dancers on stage. One stands on the table with her head bowed, a second has her back to the audience and stands in the shadows at the rear stage, while a third dancer sits stage left of the table. The dancer on the table speaks, simultaneously stating (in English) and physically signalling with arm and leg movement, text derived from actual Homeland Security forms (Figure 44.1):

> Form I 425A Application to register for permanent residence or adjust status
> I 864 I 765 AR 11 I 797 C
> Notice of Action I-130 Biometrics Processing data
> I 485 Dept of Homeland Secrutiy (With armed behind her back and chest out in a quasi-military pose)
> You are hereby notified to appear for the interview as scheduled below:
> Number A 047 0847912
> Application denied. Failure to establish legitimacy based on 8CFR 247A 12C

The stage goes dark and when the lights are raised a dancer is sat on the floor next to a table staring out towards the audience, eyes wide open and looking scared. This time the sequence of words spoken is in Spanish, interspersed with a series of powerful movements of the head, upper torso and

Figure 44.1   Clandestina

arms. A second dancer stands in the shadows at the rear of the stage, simultaneously twisting and turning in series of physical balletic movements.

> *Clandestina, Clandestina* (clandestine, clandestine)
> *Reprimida* (repressed)
> *Por qué nací yo de lado equivocado* (why was I born on the wrong side)
> *Por qué te adelantaste, adelantada* (why do you deny us, are you embarrassed of us?)
> *Escondida* (hidden)
> *Clandestina I remain*

The stage goes black.

Following the performance interviews were conducted with audience members, the response to the dance piece encapsulated in the following quote:

> The dance performance really hit home. I have many family members who are undocumented and when she moved and said clandestina I really felt it. I know what it is like to have all these feelings and experiences, to be afraid, to be

exploited, to have hopes and dreams fall down . . . to be on my knees. Watching this I had tears in my eyes. But I was also inspired by the performance, inspired to carry on. (Audience member)

As the quote above suggests, and as Denzin (2003, p. 13) contends, 'performance authorizes itself . . . through its ability to evoke and invoke shared emotional experience and understanding between performer and audience'.

The dance performance as a means of representing the so often hidden, frequently contested and occasionally inspirational rhythms of 'undocumented' lives arguably touched the audience in a manner no written text-based rendering ever could. The kinaesthetic energy of the dance performance, providing the research with a lifelike dimension, elevating and celebrating the embodied sensory feelings, experiences and voices contained within the data, in a way only dance and movement can.

CONCLUDING COMMENT . . .

Constas (1999, pp. 36–7) offers a 'three-dimensional model' that elucidates the key aspects and 'unifying elements' which signify 'the discourses of educational inquiry as it moves towards a post modern perspective'. In terms of the methodological, it relates to the ways in which data are generated and analysed with a movement away from normative approaches and concerns with prescribed guidelines, to more individualised, idiosyncratic and stylized approaches, emphasizing the significance of the researcher's relationship to the study. The representational dimension concerns the forms and ways in which data are reported and presented and a move away from 'depersonalized, distanced and objective' writing styles often in the third person, which he refers to as discursively 'highly bounded' and exclusive, to alternative 'unbounded' representational styles such as dance (Constas, 1999, pp. 38–9).

In the same way as the theoretical model of Constas (1999) heuristically delineates educational research according to methodological and representational variants in line with their postmodern materialization, so in this chapter we have shown how in recent years the role of dance in qualitative research has moved away from functioning simply as research subject, to be concerned with the methodological process of data generation and analysis, and ultimately an unbounded format in which data resulting from research may be (re)presented.

We would contend that critically informed debate around the use of dance in these ways can help to re-evaluate the meaning of qualitative research, the ways in which it should be undertaken and represented, and its epistemological value. To this end we situate dance within a wider call for methodological renewal, in which research approaches are able to engage with and (re)present the sensory, emotional and kinaesthetic realities of social and cultural phenomena in the twenty-first century to greater effect (Law and Urry, 2004).

At the time of writing the academic authorization for the use of arts-based mediums in qualitative research and particularly the use of dance as one of those artistic forms remains undoubtedly contested and certainly embryonic. In so far as critics might perceive those academics championing such approaches as living in Alice in Wonderland, we feel it befitting to end with the following quote from Lewis Carroll:

> Will you, won't you, will you, won't you, will you join the dance?
> Will you, won't you, will you, won't you, won't you join the dance?
> (Lewis Carroll, 1994, p. 120)

NOTE

1. A DVD showing an abridged version of the performance including the dance sequence can be viewed at http://www.tinyurl.com/bagley-salazar/performancemedium.wmv.

REFERENCES

Angrosino, M. (1998), *Opportunity House*, London: Altamira Press.

Archibold, R.C. (2006), 'Democratic victory raises spirits of those favoring citizenship for illegal aliens', *New York Times*, Section A, 27.

Bagley, C. (2008), 'Educational ethnography as performance art: towards a sensuous feeling and knowing', *Qualitative Research*, **8** (1), 53–72.

Bagley, C. and Cancienne, M.B. (2001), 'Educational research and intertextual forms of (re)presentation: the case for dancing the data', *Qualitative Inquiry*, **7** (2), 221–37.

Bagley, C. and Castro-Salazar, R. (2011), 'Critical arts-based research in education: performing undocumented historias', *British Educational Research Journal*, ifirst, 1–22.

Barclay, E. (2005), 'Mexican migrant communities may be on verge of HIV/AIDS epidemic', Population Reference Bureau, http://www.prb.org (accessed August 20 2006).

Bell, L.A. (2003), 'Telling tales: what stories can teach us about racism', *Race, Ethnicity and Education*, **6** (1), 3–28.

Blumenfeld-Jones. D. (1995), 'Dance as a mode of research representation', *Qualitative Inquiry*, **1** (4), 391–401.

Blumenfeld-Jones, D. (2008), 'Dance, choreography, and social science research', in J.G. Knowles and A.L. Cole (eds), *Handbook of the Arts in Qualitative Research: Perspectives, Methodologies, Examples, and Issues*, Thousand Oaks, CA: Sage, pp. 175–85.

Boas, F. (1942), *The Function of Dance in Human Society. Seminar on Primitive Society*, New York: The Boas School.

Cacho, L.M. (2000), 'The people of California are suffering: the ideology of white injury in discourses of immigration', *Cultural Values*, **4** (4), 389–418.

Cahnmann-Taylor, M. and Siegesmund, R. (eds) (2008), *Arts-based Research in Education: Foundations for Practice*, New York: Routledge.
Cancienne, M.B. and Bagley, C. (2008), 'Dance as method. The process and product of movement in educational research', in P. Liamputtomg, and R. Rumbold (eds), *Knowing Differently. Arts-based and Collaborative Research Methods*, New York: Nova Science Publishers, pp. 169–86.
Carroll, L. (1994), *Alice's Adventures in Wonderland*, London: Penguin.
Castro-Salazar, R. and Bagley, C. (2010), '"Ni de aqui in from there" Navigating between contexts: counter narratives of undocumented Mexican students in the United States', *Race, Ethnicity and Education*, **13** (1), 23–40.
Chávez, L. (2005), 'Immigration: the real world. The quiet assimilation of the undocumented', *Los Angeles Times*, 20 December, Part B, p. 15.
Constas, M.A. (1999), 'Deciphering postmodern educational research', *Educational Researcher*, **27** (9), 36–41.
De Genova, N. (2004), 'The legal production of Mexican/migrant "Illegality"', *Latino Studies*, **2** (2), 160.
de Zoete B. and Spies W. (1938), *Dance and Drama in Bali*, London: Faber and Faber.
Delgado, R. and Stefancic, J. (2001), *Critical Race Theory*, New York: State University of New York Press.
Denzin, N.K. (2001), 'The reflective interview and a performative social science', *Qualitative Research*, **1** (1), 23–46.
Denzin, N.K. (2003), *Performance Ethnography. Critical Pedagogy and the Politics of Culture*, Thousand Oaks, CA: Sage.
Fraleigh, S.H. (1987), *Dance and the Lived Body: A Descriptive Aesthetics*, Pittsburg, PA: University of Pittsburg Press.
Freedman, D.C (1991), 'Gender signs: an effort/shape analysis of Romanian couple dances', *Studia Musicologica Academiae Scientiarum Hungaricae*, **33** (1), 335–45.
Glaser, B.G. and Strauss, A.C. (1967), *The Discovery of Grounded Theory: Strategies for Qualitative Research*, New York: Aldine.
Goldstein, T. (2001), 'Hong Kong, Canada', *Qualitative Inquiry*, **7** (3), 279–303.
Grosz, E. (1994), *Volatile Bodies. Toward a Corporeal Feminism*, Bloomington, IN: Indiana University Press.
Henry, R. (2000), 'Introduction – anthropology of dance', *Australian Journal of Anthropology*, **11** (3), 253–60.
Janesick, V.J. (1998), *'Stretching' Exercises for Qualitative Researchers*, Thousand Oaks, CA: Sage.
Kealiinohomoku ([1985]1993), 'Music and dance of the Hawaiian and Hopi peoples', in R.L. Anderson and K.L. Field (eds), *Art in Small Scale Societies: Contemporary Readings*, Englewood Cliffs, NJ: Prentice-Hall, pp. 334–48.
Kealiinohomoku (1997), 'An anthropologist looks at ballet as a form of ethnic dance', in D. Williams (ed.), *Anthropology and Human Movement: the Study of Dances*, Vol. 1, Lanham, MD and London: Scarecrow Press pp. 15–36 (Reprint of 1969–70 article in *Impulse Magazine*).
Kilbourne, B. (1998), *For the Love of Teaching*, London: Althouse Press.
Knowles, J.G. and Cole, A.L. (eds) (2008), *Handbook of the Arts in Qualitative Research Perspectives, Methodologies, Examples, and Issues*, Thousand Oaks, CA: Sage.
Knowles, J.G., Luciani, T., Cole, A.L. and Neilsen, L. (eds) (2007), *The Art of Visual Inquiry*, Vol. 3, Arts-informed Inquiry Series, Halifax, Nova Scotia and Toronto, Ontario: Backalong Books and Centre for Arts-informed Research.
Ladson-Billings, G. (1998), 'Just what is critical race theory and what's it doing in a nice field like education?', *International Journal of Qualitative Studies in Education*, **11** (1), 7–24.
Law, J. and Urry, J. (2004), 'Enacting the social', *Economy and Society*, **33** (3) 390–410.
Leavy, P. (2009), *Method Meets Art: Arts-based Research Practice*, New York: The Guilford Press.

Liamputtong, P. and Rumbold, J. (eds) (2008), *Knowing Differently: Arts-based and Collaborative Research Methods*, New York: Nova Science Publishers.

Macedo, D. and Gounari, P. (2004), 'Globalization and the unleashing of new racism: an introduction', in D. Macedo and P. Gounari (eds), *The Globalization of Racism*, Boulder, CO: Paradigm Publishers, pp. 3–35.

Maletic, V. (1987), *Body, Space, Expression: The Development of Rudolf Laban's Movement and Dance Concepts*, New York: Mouton de Gruyter.

Massey, D.S. (2005), 'Five myths about immigration: common misconceptions underlying U.S. border-enforcement policy', *Immigration Policy in Focus*, **4** (6), 1–11, Washington, DC: Immigration Policy Center (A division of the American Immigration Law Foundation).

McNiff, S. (2007), 'Art-based research', in J.G. Knowles and A.L. Cole (eds) (2008), *Handbook of the Arts in Qualitative Research: Perspectives, Methodologies, Examples, and Issues*, Thousand Oaks, CA: Sage, pp. 29–40.

Mienczakowski, J. (2001), 'Ethnodrama', in P. Atkinson, A. Coffey, S. Delamont, J. Lofland and L. Lofland (eds), *Handbook of Ethnography*, London: Sage, pp. 468–76.

Nabokov, P. (1967) (ed.) *Two Leggings: The Making of a Crow Warrior*, New York: Thomas Crowell.

Ramos Cardoso, A. (2007), 'Monitoreo de Iniciativas Anti-immigrantes en Arizona', Presentation for Fundación México by the Mexican Consul for Media and Political Analysis, Tucson, Amzona, 27 October.

Richardson, L. (2002), 'Poetic representations of interviews', in J. Gubrium and J. Holstein (eds), *Handbook of Interview Research*, London: Sage, pp. 877–91.

Saldana, J. (2005), *Ethnodrama: An Anthology of Reality Theatre*, Walnut Creek, CA: AltaMira Press.

Sarther, D.P. (2006), 'An exploratory study of the experiences of Mexican American women attending community college', Unpublished doctoral dissertation, Northern Illinois University.

Silveira M.F.A., Gualda, D.H.R., Sobral, V. and Garcia, A.M.G.S. (2002), 'Dance of discovery', *International Journal of Qualitative Methods*, **1** (1), Winter, 2–3.

Snowber, C. (2002), 'Bodydance: enfleshing soulful inquiry through improvisation', in C. Bagley and M.B. Cancienne (eds), *Dancing the Data*, New York: Peter Lang, pp. 20–33.

Snowber C. (2009), 'Dance and movement', in P. Leavy (ed.), *Method Meets Art: Arts-based Research Practice*, New York: The Guilford Press, pp. 179–97.

Stinson, S.W (1995), 'Body of knowledge', *Educational Theory*, **45** (1), 43–54.

Stinson, S.W (2004), 'My body/myself: lessons from dance education', in L. Bresler (ed.), *Knowing Bodies, Moving Minds Toward Embodied Teaching and Learning*, London: Kluwer Academic, pp. 153–68.

Stinson, S.W. and Dils, A. (2008), 'Dance in qualitative research', *The Sage Encyclopedia of Qualitative Research Methods*, Thousand Oaks, CA: Sage, available at http://www.sage-ereference.com/research/Article_n92.html (accessed 16 May 2011).

Walford, G. (2009), 'For ethnography', *Ethnography and Education*, **4** (3), 271–82.

Wolcott, H. (1999), *Ethnography: A Way of Seeing*, Oxford: AltaMira Press.

Index